CRITICAL THINKING AND AMERICAN GOVERNMENT

2nd Edition

Kent M. Brudney
Cuesta College

John H. Culver
California Polytechnic State University

Mark E. Weber
Cuesta College

Australia • Canada • Mexico • Singapore • Spain
United Kingdom • United States

THOMSON
WADSWORTH

Executive Editor: David Tatom
Editorial Assistant: Dianna Long
Technology Project Manager: Mindy Newfarmer
Marketing Manager: Caroline Croley
Project Manager: Belinda Krohmer
Print/Media Buyer: Judy Inouye
Permissions Editor: Bob Kauser

Production Service: Kristi Arnold, G&S Typesetters, Inc.
Copy Editor: Barbara Bell
Cover Designer: Jeanette Barber
Cover Image: Getty Images
Cover Printer: Edwards Brothers
Compositor: G&S Typesetters, Inc.
Printer: Edwards Brothers

Printed in the United States of America

1 2 3 4 5 6 7 06 05 04 03 02

For more information about our products, contact us at:
Thomson Learning Academic Resource Center
1-800-423-0563
For permission to use material from this text, contact us by:
Phone: 1-800-730-2214 **Fax:** 1-800-730-2215
Web: http://www.thomsonrights.com

Library of Congress Control Number: 2002105845

ISBN 0-155-05848-7

Wadsworth/Thomson Learning
10 Davis Drive
Belmont, CA 94002-3098
USA

Asia
Thomson Learning
60 Albert Street, #15-01
Albert Complex
Singapore 189969

Australia
Nelson Thomson Learning
102 Dodds Street
South Melbourne, Victoria 3205
Australia

Canada
Nelson Thomson Learning
1120 Birchmount Road
Toronto, Ontario M1K 5G4
Canada

Europe/Middle East/Africa
Thomson Learning
Berkshire House
168-173 High Holborn
London WC1V 7AA
United Kingdom

Latin America
Thomson Learning
Seneca, 53
Colonia Polanco
11560 Mexico D.F.
Mexico

Spain
Paraninfo Thomson Learning
Calle/Magallanes, 25
28015 Madrid, Spain

TABLE OF CONTENTS

PREFACE

Most of the students in our classes are bright and eager to learn about politics. Yet discussions with colleagues confirm our experience that far too many students lack critical thinking skills. This is a special problem in the information age. Absent the ability to analyze and use the wealth of information available to them, students are simply overwhelmed. In this book we address the problem by giving students both the tools for developing a number of critical thinking skills within the context of American politics and practice using them.

The exercises focus on the analysis and interpretation of data: the discovery of basic relationships among variables; and the ability to read critically, to summarize information concisely, to formulate generalizations and hypotheses, and to draw logical inferences.[1] The exercises also hone expository writing skills and reinforce and deepen students' understanding of the material covered in most American government courses.

The material is divided into chapters that correspond to the major topics in virtually all American government texts in use today. Most of the exercises are designed to stand alone—that is, students should not need to refer to other sources. But throughout the book are exercises that require students to utilize resources available on the Internet. All of the exercises are flexible: Students can complete them individually, or they can be used for in-class group work or for class discussion. Furthermore, many exercises are structured to allow instructors to assign selected components of them.

The exercises ask students to think critically about data and readings from a wide variety of sources, including the Constitution, Supreme Court opinions, the *Federalist Papers,* public opinion surveys, exit polls, and government regulations and reports. In addition, several exercises examine controversial issues—abortion, homosexuality, affirmative action, racial and gender inequality, terrorism, American–Cuban relations, and government regulation of genetic technology—that should get students thinking and talking.

We have made several key changes in this new edition of *Critical Thinking and American Government.* The most important is the addition of a third author, Mark Weber, who has contributed new exercises and has reshaped many others to make them more challenging or to place them more clearly in the context of American political history. We've also updated the copy, inserting material on a number of important political events that have occurred in the five years since the first edition was published. There are new exercises, for example, that focus on the pardons President Bill Clinton granted in his last days in office, the plight of Elian Gonzalez, the controversy over the 2000 presidential election, and America's response to the terrorist attacks on September 11, 2001.

We are indebted to many faculty members and students for the new approaches, exercises, and topics they suggested for this edition. We thank them, too, for pointing out inconsistencies in the first edition, allowing us to clarify and amend where necessary. Of course any remaining sins of omission or

---

[1] See Appendix 1 for the basics of data analysis.

commission are ours alone. The staff of the Kennedy Library at Cal Poly and Mary Carpenter of Cuesta College's Computer Services Department were most helpful. So were the professionals at Wadsworth: Our editor, David Tatom, could not have been more encouraging; while Dianna Long, Kristi Arnold, and Barbara Bell ensured smooth production at their end. Lastly, thanks to Shelby Jameson, Eric Levine, Katrina Culp Ladopoulus, and Michael MacDonald for their help with the Instructor's Manual.

INTRODUCTION

The goal of the exercises in this workbook is to encourage you to think systematically about political relationships and behaviors so that you can more easily understand the reality of American government. The goal of this introduction is to explain in general terms what it means to think critically about things political, to reason, and to interpret information.[1]

An example of the scientific method at work in the real world comes from Farley Mowat's engaging book, *Never Cry Wolf.*[2] Not long after receiving a degree in biology, Mowat landed a job with the Canadian Wildlife Service. The service had received a large number of complaints about the declining caribou population. (Most of us know the caribou as reindeer.) Although Mowat's predecessor suggested hunters were responsible, Mowat's bosses believed that wolves were killing large numbers of caribou, and they assigned him the task of documenting that. In short order, Mowat was dropped off at a base camp in the tundra on the western side of Hudson Bay in early spring. Among his provisions and scientific instruments were a government pamphlet describing wolves as powerful, savage killers, and several firearms to protect him from the wolves.

Mowat located a wolf den near his base camp and began observing the two wolves and several pups that lived in the den. Among other things, he discovered that the wolves were not aggressive toward him. In fact, they were curious about him. After several encounters with the animals, Mowat concluded that many preconceptions about wolves—including the government's—were wrong. Once he realized that his observations contradicted prevailing thinking about wolves, Mowat made a decision: "From this hour onward, I would go open-minded into the lupine world and learn to see and know the wolves, not for what they were supposed to be, but for what they actually were" (p. 77).

Mindful of his work assignment, Mowat turned his attention to the wolves' food. What were they eating? What were they feeding their pups? Then Mowat saw one of the adult wolves regurgitate mice for the pups. The warm spring weather had thawed the ice-covered tundra, and the soggy turf was an ideal breeding ground for mice—a situation the wolves turned to their advantage.

But Mowat was skeptical about the nutritional value of mice. Could an animal as large and active as a wolf actually survive on a diet of mice alone? To find out, Mowat experimented on himself. His hypothesis (the assumption underlying the experiment): Wolves can sustain themselves on a diet of mice. For a period he ate only boiled mice; then he returned to his usual rations, canned meat and fresh fish. At the end of each interval, he ran physiological tests on himself to determine the effects of the two diets. After eating just mice, Mowat began to crave fats. That, he realized, was because of the way he prepared the mice, removing their skin and the contents of their abdominal cavities before cooking them. The wolves, of course, ate mice whole, including the skin and the contents of the abdominal cavities, where fats are stored. In a second trial, Mowat ate the mice whole, discarding only the skin. His finding: The mouse diet did have enough nutritional value to keep him going, lending support to his hypothesis that wolves can sustain themselves on a diet of mice.

[1] An explanation of analytical tools can be found in Appendix 1.

[2] The book was published by Little, Brown, in Boston, in 1963. A movie was released in 1983.

Mowat was told by some Eskimo hunters that wolves also eat fish, squirrels, and caribou, but the last only on a selective basis. Wolves follow migrating herds of caribou and kill the weak. According to Eskimo folklore, by eating the weak, the wolves keep the caribou herds strong and healthy. Mowat confirmed the wolves' diet by examined their scat (droppings). He discovered that about half of their fecal matter contained the remains of small rodents; the rest came from caribou, ducks, and small birds.

Apparently the wolves were not decimating the caribou. Then who or what was? Mike, one of the Eskimos Mowat befriended, supplied one theory. Mike was a trapper who used a dog sled for transportation. By his own admission, he killed two or three caribou each week to feed his dogs. According to Mike, that was common practice among trappers. Other theories came from Mowat's own observations. At the end of his study, Mowat saw that hunters in light planes were killing both caribou and wolves for trophies and, in the case of the wolves, for bounty (the government paid a bounty for each dead wolf the hunters brought in). In his report to the Canadian Wildlife Service, Mowat held people, not wolves, responsible for the fall-off in the caribou population.

In his study of wolf behavior, Mowat applied the scientific method, "a very rigorous method, allowing confrontation of hunches and suspicions with evidence and facts from the real world." He followed a logical sequence of steps to conduct a value-free inquiry, to test "ideas about what actually exists, and why."[3] Mowat began with the theory set forth by the wildlife service, that wolves were killing large numbers of caribou. But he soon found that that theory was contradicted by his own observations, by evidence he collected, and by experiments he performed. He eventually determined that wolves did indeed kill caribou, but not in large enough numbers to account for the decline in the caribou population.

Mowat's story shows the danger of operating on the basis of preconceptions. Preconceptions, however, are an important jumping-off point in a scientific investigation. Casual observation of daily happenings can lead to assumptions about how and why things happen, assumptions that may or may not prove accurate. All scientific investigation begins with the recognition that those assumptions are not tested and may need to be modified as information is gathered, analyzed, and tested. The scientific method is a continual search for alternative explanations.

An example: Suppose you're studying party identification among voters in the United States. Table 1 shows party identification in selected years between 1937 and 1999. You've been asked to write one paragraph describing the trends illustrated by the data in Table 1 and to depict the data in a different configuration, so that the trends are more apparent. You think about the assignment for a bit and then decide that the easiest way to begin is by reconfiguring the data. That's part of the assignment anyway, and it should help you identify trends. Of course, before you can start, you have to look at the data. Do you want to use all of the numbers or just some of them? Notice that for the years 1979 to 1995, the data are presented annually; the remaining data are presented for selected years only. In reconfiguring the data, instead of including each year since 1979, you decide to show the data at four-year intervals. Your reasons are twofold: First, you want to reduce the amount of data so that trends can be tracked easily. Second, there's a logic to linking the data to presidential elections, times when citizen awareness of political party identification is highest. The data are here for the elections from 1960 through 1992. For earlier and later years, you simply use the limited information you have.

Two alternative ways of displaying the data are shown in Figure 1. Both allow you to compare changes in political party identification over time more clearly than the simple list of data in Table 1.

Before you write a paragraph about trends in party identification, you should examine the data. What stands out in the figures? For example, what were the highest and lowest levels of identification with each group? In what year was identification with each group highest? Lowest? Were there years when party identification levels were close? You want to note those periods when party identification was rising, falling, or staying about the same. The key in assessing trends is to watch for change. Rarely do political attitudes and the corresponding party identification of citizens remain constant over time.

Among the trends you might write about in your paragraph are the following:

- More people consistently identify with the Democratic Party than with the Republican Party or with those who identify themselves as independents, although independents had surpassed both Republicans and Democrats by 1999.

[3] Leonard Champney, *Introduction to Quantitative Political Science* (New York: HarperCollins, 1995), p. 42.

TABLE 1 POLITICAL PARTY IDENTIFICATION, 1937–1999

YEAR	REPUBLICAN	DEMOCRAT	INDEPENDENT*
1937	34	50	16
1946	40	39	21
1950	33	45	22
1954	34	46	20
1960	30	47	23
1964	25	53	22
1968	27	46	27
1972	28	43	29
1975	22	45	33
1976	23	47	30
1979	22	45	33
1980	24	46	30
1981	28	42	30
1982	26	45	29
1983	25	44	31
1984	31	40	29
1985	33	38	29
1986	32	39	29
1987	30	41	29
1988	30	42	28
1989	33	40	27
1990	32	40	28
1991	30	39	31
1992	28	39	33
1993	26	40	34
1994	28	39	33
1995	29	38	33
1999	28	34	38

* There is no Independent political party. The Gallup Organization uses the classification to identify citizens who are not aligned with either the Democrat or the Republican party.

SOURCES: The Gallup Poll #359 (August, 1995), p. 45 and Gallup Poll Analyses, April 9, 1999.

- Since 1964, the percentage of people who identify themselves as Republicans and as independents has been quite close. In two periods (1972–1980 and 1992–1999), more citizens identified themselves as independents than Republicans.
- Identification with the Democratic Party generally has fallen since 1976. Republican Party identification has fallen since 1984. And, again, there has been an increase in those who identify themselves as independents.

Thinking critically about politics requires analyzing political information in a reasoned, logical, systematic way. The exercises in the following chapters encourage you not only to acquire information but also to *interpret* it.

FIGURE 1

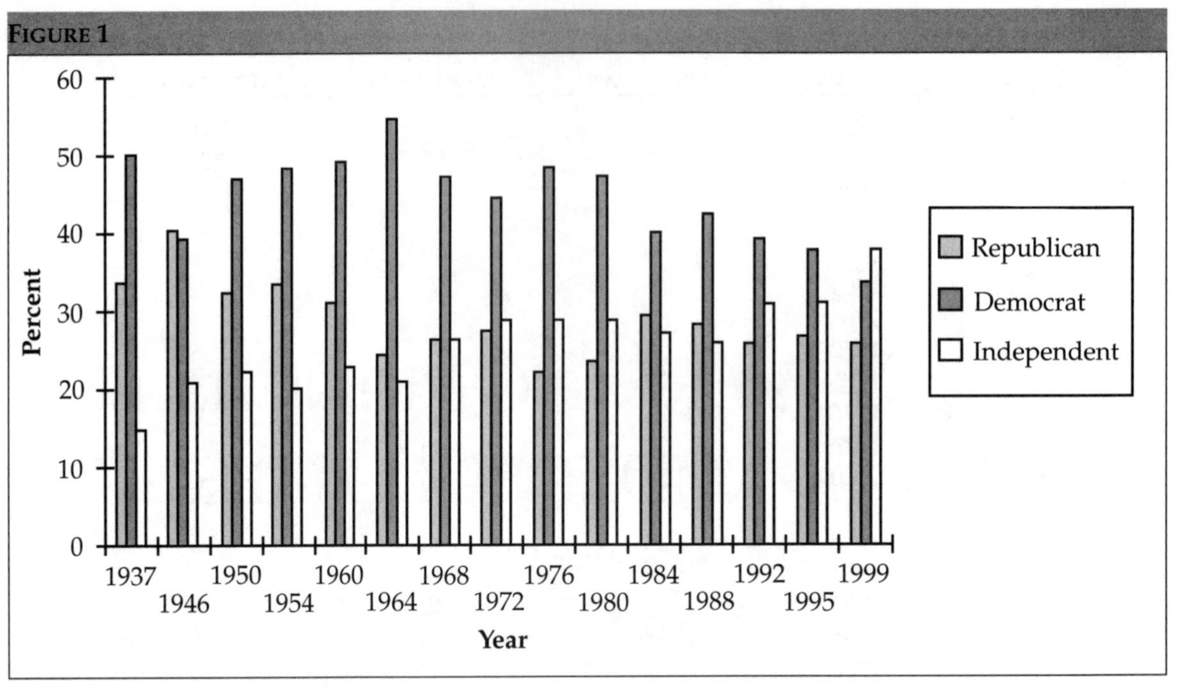

60
50
40
30
20
10
0
Percent
1937
1946
1950
1954
1960
1964
1968
1972
1976
1980
1984
1988
1992
1995
1999
Year
Republican
Democrat
Independent

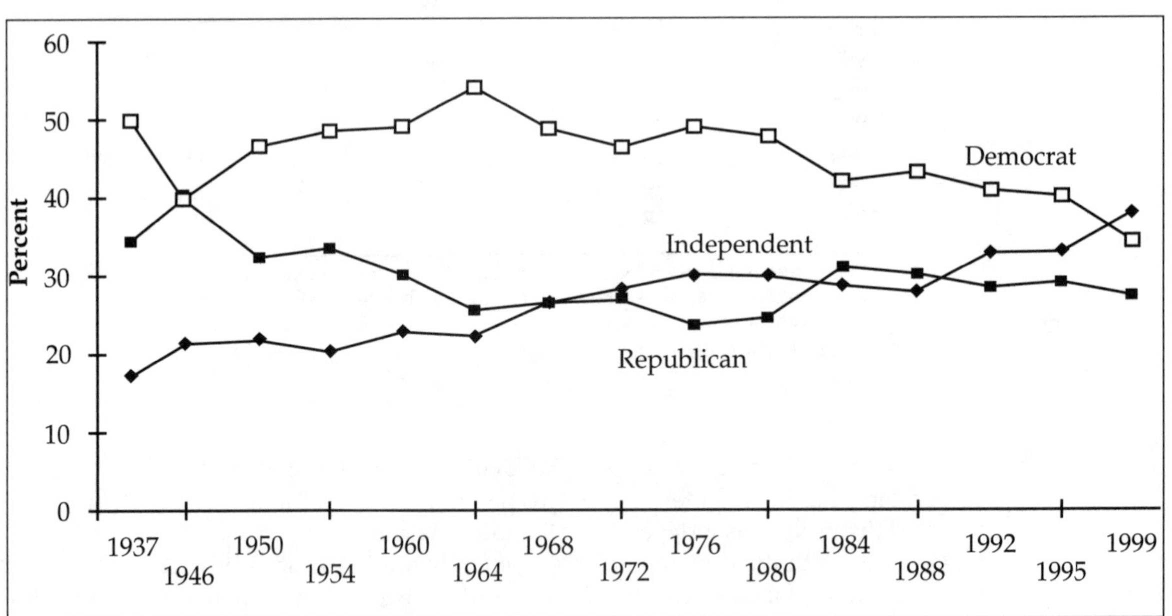

60
50
40
30
20
10
0
Percent
Democrat
Independent
Republican
1937
1946
1950
1954
1960
1964
1968
1972
1976
1980
1984
1988
1992
1995
1999

GOVERNING PRINCIPLES AND IDEOLOGIES

EXERCISE 1.1 READING THE CONSTITUTION

BACKGROUND

The U.S. Constitution establishes the fundamental principles, processes, and structures of the American political system. Among them are representative government, republicanism, popular sovereignty, and individual rights; the process of checks and balances; and the structures of separation of power and federalism. The Constitution grants power to government institutions, to officeholders, and to citizens, and constrains all of them in their exercise of power. Under the Constitution, sovereignty is divided among the people, the state governments, and the national government, preventing a concentration of power that could endanger the liberties of citizens.

That the Constitution has endured for more than two centuries is a function of four extraordinary innovations in the theory and practice of republican government. First, American constitutions were written. This innovation was employed in creating state constitutions and later in the Articles of Confederation and the Constitution of 1787. Written constitutions were a significant departure from the British model, a vague body of law and precedent, some written and some not. During the colonial and revolutionary periods, Americans had found that an informal constitution was a weak and unreliable guarantor of citizens' liberties. So they insisted that their constitutions be written.

Second, the American constitutions were separate from and superior to the government they sought to restrain. This too was a departure from the British model. In England, citizens customarily looked to Parliament to protect their liberties from the abuse of power by the king. But Americans learned from their experience with state governments between 1776 and 1787 that duly elected legislatures and even citizens themselves might abuse power and had to be restrained by a higher authority. Their written constitutions would be that separate and paramount authority.

The third innovation was a process for creating and then amending the documents. A constitution separate from and superior to the government could not be created or altered by the government it was meant to control. So Americans located the power to create and alter the Constitution of 1787 in special conventions of citizens that were separate from the national and state governments in existence at the time.

Article V of the Constitution of 1787 divides the amendment power between the national and state governments, on the one hand, and popular conventions of citizens on the other. Popular conventions have been employed only once since the adoption of the Constitution, when the Twenty-First Amendment, which repealed Prohibition, was ratified by popularly elected conventions in the states in 1933. But their inclusion in the Constitution illustrates the Americans' conviction that fundamental law must be separate from the institutions of government.

The fourth innovation was *judicial review,* the power of judges to say what a constitution means and to strike down government actions that conflict with the authority of the Constitution. Judicial review was rooted in the belief that the nation's fundamental law is both separate from and superior to the government: Clearly, government officials cannot evaluate their own performance against the standards set forth in the Constitution. The framers, or authors, of the Constitution could have made the people the instrument for assessing the government's compliance with the Constitution. But they, like many Americans at the time, held a dim view of democracy and feared the consequences of locating power in the citizenry.

Actually, judicial review is nowhere mentioned in the Constitution of 1787. But the concept of a fundamental law that binds the government pointed to the need for interpretation by some impartial body. Judges at the state government level were the first to exercise judicial review. In 1803, the U.S. Supreme Court asserted the power for the first time, striking down a law passed by Congress. In *Marbury v. Madison,* Chief Justice John Marshall claimed for the Supreme Court the power to interpret the Constitution: "A law repugnant to the Constitution is void." The exercise of judicial review confirmed that Americans had elevated the fundamental law above their government and had found a practical way to maintain that separation.

The framers intended the Constitution to be the foundation for "A New Order of the Ages," yet it is a surprisingly brief and often ambiguous document. Both its brevity and ambiguity suggest the wisdom of its authors: They did not want the document to be so detailed that it would constrain policymakers in future generations, tying them to the interests and issues of the founding period. The framers knew that a free people facing ongoing political change would cast off any document that could not be adapted to new circumstances. The spareness of the Constitution has helped it endure as the fundamental law in the United States for over two hundred years.[1]

Some of the matters on which the Constitution is ambiguous are important. The interests of those at the Constitutional Convention were often too diverse to reconcile through bargaining and compromise. Ambiguous language allowed the parties to agree on issues that if dealt with specifically would have deadlocked the convention. Since 1787, ambiguities in the Constitution have been sorted out in the practice of American political life and through interpretation by the federal courts. Still the meaning of certain phrases—"necessary and proper" (Article I, Section 8) and "equal protection" (Fourteenth Amendment), for example—are likely always to be contested.

On a number of important matters the Constitution is silent. The framers did not explicitly confer the right to vote on anyone. Until the Fifteenth Amendment was ratified in 1870, state governments alone determined who could vote. Subsequent amendments granted the right to vote to women and citizens age 18 or older. The framers did not set out the role political parties should play in the political system or a process for canceling treaties. Over the years, state legislatures and Congress have defined in law the functions and responsibilities of parties in the electoral arena. And it wasn't until the late 1970s that the treaty issue was resolved. In 1978, President Jimmy Carter abrogated (canceled) a mutual defense treaty with Taiwan without securing the approval of the Senate. A group of senators challenged the president's action in court. In *Goldwater v. Carter* (1979), the Supreme Court ruled that the case involved a political question and refused to decide the matter. With both the Constitution and the Supreme Court silent on the authority to abrogate treaties, it seems that authority is now the president's by virtue of a president's having claimed it and successfully exercised it.

The Constitution offers neither law nor much guidance on certain difficult social issues. It was the Supreme Court that legalized abortion in *Roe v. Wade* (1973). And the courts are just now beginning to

[1] By contrast, many state constitutions suffer from excessive detail. They often run on for hundreds of pages, arcane specifications further confused by scores of amendments. They are commonly documents that only legislators, lawyers, and judges can make sense of.

examine and rule on laws governing the right to die. Judges will have to look deeply into the Constitution and their own notions of truth and justice to confirm or strike down those laws.

ASSIGNMENT, PART A: THE CONSTITUTION'S BASIC PROVISIONS

The following questions should familiarize you with the organization of the Constitution and several of its provisions. Consult the Constitution in Appendix 2 at the back of this textbook. In your answers, always cite the number of the relevant article or amendment. Preview the questions before you read the Constitution so that you know what to be looking for as you read the document.

1. Read each article of the Constitution. In just one sentence, state the general purpose or subject of each article.

Article I: ______________________________

____

Article II: ______________________________

____

Article III: ______________________________

____

Article IV: ______________________________

____

Article V: ______________________________

____

Article VI: ______________________________

____

Article VII: ______________________________

____

2. a. In the Constitution of 1787—the unamended document—how many times do the words *slave* or *slavery* appear?

____

b. How many times do the words *woman* or *women* appear?

____

3. The powers the Constitution specifically grants to the branches of government or to officeholders are called *enumerated powers*.

a. Identify two enumerated powers of the president.

____

____

b. Identify two enumerated powers of the vice president.

____

____

c. Identify two enumerated powers of Congress.

____

____

4. a. How were U.S. senators chosen before the Seventeenth Amendment was ratified in 1913?

b. How have U.S. senators been chosen since 1913?

5. a. Identify two powers the Constitution prohibits to Congress.

b. Identify two powers the Constitution prohibits to the states.

6. a. What eligibility requirements does the Constitution establish for members of the House and Senate?

b. What eligibility requirements does the Constitution establish for the president?

7. According to the principle of checks and balances, each branch of the government must have some degree of scrutiny and control over the other branches. The Constitution accomplishes that in large part by giving each branch one or more roles in the affairs of the others. Looking at the first three articles of the Constitution, identify one of each of the following types of checks and balances:

a. A power that the executive branch holds over the legislative branch

b. A power that the executive branch holds over the judicial branch

c. A power that the legislative branch holds over the executive branch

d. A power that the legislative branch holds over the judicial branch

e. A power that the judicial branch holds over the executive branch

f. A power that the judicial branch holds over the legislative branch

8. The *court of original jurisdiction* is the first court that hears a case. *Appellate courts* hear cases on appeal from lower courts. Although the Supreme Court functions primarily as an appellate court, it is the court of original jurisdiction in certain kinds of cases. What are those cases?

9. The Constitution has comparatively little to say about the structure and composition of the Supreme Court. Identify two aspects of the Court's structure and composition that the Constitution does not specify. (The Constitution does specify these two basic aspects of structure and composition for the other branches.)

____

____

10. In your own words, explain the supremacy clause (see Article VI).

____

____

____

11. a. What are the two ways that amendments to the Constitution can be proposed?

____

____

____

b. What are the two ways that amendments to the Constitution can be ratified?

____

____

____

12. Article V of the Constitution of 1787 singles out two matters that are beyond the reach of the amendment process. What are they?

____

____

____

13. Identify by number two amendments that

a. extended individual rights.

____

b. extended civil rights (including voting rights).

____

c. prohibited certain practices by the states.

____

d. changed specific language in the Constitution.

____

14. The Twenty-Fifth Amendment describes the sequence of events that would install the vice president as acting president against the will of the president. Outline that sequence of events.

____

____

____

____

____

15. Identify two terms in the Constitution that you do not understand. Look up the meanings of the terms, and define them here. (A good resource for reference books is the Web site www.Bartleby.com.)

ASSIGNMENT, PART B: MAJORITY AND SUPERMAJORITY

Essential to the functioning of government and to balancing the relative powers of its three branches are the numeric requirements the Constitution sets forth for overriding a presidential veto, ratifying treaties, and carrying out other tasks and procedures. The three numeric requirements specified in the Constitution are the simple majority and two supermajority levels, two-thirds and three-fourths. The simple majority and two-thirds margins apply to the number of House and Senate members actually casting votes, not to the total number of votes residing in each body. For example, the requirement for passing legislation in the House is a simple majority, or 50 percent plus 1 of the number of votes cast. There are 435 members in the House. A simple majority of 435 is 218. But 218 votes are needed to pass a bill only if all 435 members vote. If only 400 members vote on a bill, then just 201 votes would satisfy the simple-majority requirement.

The Constitution makes an additional stipulation that can affect the minimum number of votes required to pass a bill: The House and the Senate are required to have a majority of their members present to conduct legislative business.

1. a. What bodies have the power to override a presidential veto?

b. What margin is required to override a presidential veto?

2. a. What body has the power to ratify treaties?

b. What margin is required to ratify treaties?

3. *To impeach* means "to bring charges against" or "to indict."

a. What body has the power to impeach the president?

b. What margin is required to impeach a president?

4. a. What body has the power to convict the president of charges brought against him in the impeachment process and thereby remove him from the presidency?

b. What margin is required to convict and remove a president?

5. a. What body has the power to accept or to reject a president's nominations to the Supreme Court?

____

b. What margin is required to elevate a president's nominee to a seat on the Court?

____

6. a. If no candidate for the presidency wins a simple majority of the total number of electoral votes, what body has the power to choose the president?

____

b. What margin is required to choose the president?

____

7. If the House can muster only the minimum requirement for a quorum, what number of votes would be needed to pass a bill?

____

8. The Constitution specifies a three-fourths majority for just one process. What is it?

____

EXERCISE 1.2 THE AMENDMENT PROCESS

BACKGROUND

The Constitution has evolved over time and through case law. It also has evolved through the amendment process. The framers recognized that an amendment process was necessary to make the Constitution both flexible and enduring. Government processes and the allocation of political power would have to be adjusted as the nation evolved and faced new challenges. The threat of tyranny—the abuse of power—surely would arise from quarters and situations the framers had not anticipated, and the Constitution would have to be able to meet that threat.

The problem, of course, was where to locate the immense power to alter the nation's fundamental law. To vest the power of amendment exclusively in government officials would be foolish: A primary objective of the Constitution is to restrain those very officials. To vest the power of amendment directly in the citizens would raise the threat of majority tyranny and was likely to result in transitory popular interests being incorporated into the law. In the end, to guard against abuse of the amendment power, the framers divided it more extensively than any other power and subjected it to a supermajority requirement found nowhere else in the Constitution. James Madison claimed in "Federalist No. 53" that the amendment mechanism guarded "equally against that extreme facility, which would render the Constitution too mutable, and that extreme difficulty, which might perpetuate its discovered faults."

The amendment process established by Article V consists of two distinct phases: proposal and ratification. Changes to the Constitution do not take effect until the requirements of both phases have been satisfied. There are two ways to satisfy the requirements of each phase. Amendments to the Constitution can be *proposed* by a two-thirds vote in the House and Senate or by a constitutional convention called by Congress at the request of two-thirds of the states. All twenty-seven amendments to the Constitution have been proposed by Congress. The *ratification* phase of the amendment process requires approval by three-fourths of the state legislatures or by special ratifying conventions in three-fourths of the states. Congress decides which path a proposed amendment will follow in the ratification phase.

The three-fourths requirement for ratification is extraordinary: It is the most stringent margin in the Constitution. It makes changing the nation's fundamental law a very difficult task, one that can be accomplished only with the widespread support of the states. It also increases the probability that changes to the Constitution will prove enduring, that transitory beliefs are unlikely to become law. And for the most part, that has been the case. Only the Eighteenth Amendment has been repealed. Of course the supermajority requirement also can block important change: It took women well more than a century to obtain the right to vote through the Nineteenth Amendment (1920).

One authority estimates that over 11,000 amendments have been introduced in Congress.[2] Recent amendments that were not approved by Congress include one to allow devotional Bible reading in public schools and one to prohibit burning the American flag as a form of protest. Only thirty-three amendments have completed the proposal phase of the amendment process. Of those, only twenty-seven have been ratified. The first ten amendments—the Bill of Rights—were proposed by the First Congress as a gesture of conciliation to the remaining opponents of the new government. They were ratified by the state legislatures in 1791. The seventeen subsequent amendments were adopted between 1795 and 1992.

The states have never achieved the two-thirds requirement (thirty-four states) necessary for Congress to call a second constitutional convention. They came close when opposition developed to the Supreme Court's decision in *Reynolds v. Sims* (1964), which requires the reapportionment of state legislatures on the basis of population (see Exercise 7.5). By 1967, thirty-three state legislatures had petitioned Congress to call a constitutional convention. Their objective: to use the amendment process to reverse the ruling in *Reynolds*. But a thirty-fourth state legislature never gave its assent.

All but one amendment have been ratified by the state legislatures. The Twenty-First Amendment (1933), which repealed the Eighteenth, was routed by Congress through and then approved by special ratifying conventions in three-fourths of the states. Members of Congress believed that supporters of Prohibition (the "drys") controlled too many state legislatures, and that repeal would be more likely if

[2] J. W. Peltason, *Understanding the Constitution* (New York: Harcourt, 1997), p. 188.

the matter was decided in special ratifying conventions. Delegates to the ratifying conventions ran on "wet" or "dry" slates, so the conventions reflected the voters' will in each state.

The amendment process is a testament to the framers' conviction that the only good power is one that has been divided. No other process in the Constitution is so complex; no other procedure requires the assent of so many at so many levels of government. And in no other process do the states play so prominent and powerful a role, giving citizens a voice in the process that is independent of their elected representatives in Washington, D.C. Of course if the amendment process amplifies the power of the states and their citizens, it restricts the role of the national government. Congress cannot effect constitutional change by itself; and the executive and judicial branches play no formal role in either phase of the amendment process.

Great power can be achieved by amending the Constitution, but proponents of constitutional change often have found their victories less than complete. In the case of Prohibition, the amendment was repealed. Advocates of women's suffrage were disappointed following the ratification of the Nineteenth Amendment in 1920 that the voting rate for women remained below that for men until the 1950s. The Supreme Court narrowed the scope of the Fourteenth Amendment (1868) so severely in the late nineteenth century that racial discrimination remained a legal reality in the South until the 1960s. The Fifteenth Amendment (1870), which guarantees the voting rights of blacks, was not implemented across the nation for nearly one hundred years after its ratification. What these examples show is that constitutional change is effective only in the presence of political and social change.

Congress has charged the National Archives and Records Administration (NARA) with managing the ratification process. NARA's Web site (www.nara.gov/fedreg/amdhome.html) offers information that should help you understand the amendment process. The Web site also has links to the Treasures of Congress exhibit, which offers additional information on the Bill of Rights and the Thirteenth, Seventeenth, and Nineteenth Amendments.

ASSIGNMENT

The Constitution stipulates two-thirds and three-fourths majorities for the proposal and ratification phases of the amendment process. We might assume, then, that changing the Constitution requires the support of a very large number of the nation's citizens. Questions 1 through 4 test that assumption.

Consider an amendment to the Constitution that would change the basis of representation in the House. Under this amendment, the bargain struck at the Constitutional Convention between the large and small states would be nullified. The amendment would revise Article I, Section 2, making representation in the House equal for every state by increasing the size of the House to 500 members and awarding 10 seats to each state.

1. The proponents of the amendment introduce it in the House and Senate hoping to marshal the required two-thirds support. Table 1.2 lists the population of each state and its representation in the House based on the 2000 census.

a. Use the data in the table to determine the number of votes cast in the House and Senate for and against proposing the amendment. Assume that the members of Congress vote solely on the basis of the effect of the amendment on their state's voting power in the House, that they do not consider other issues raised by the amendment. Virginia, for example, would vote against the amendment because its delegation in the House would be reduced by one member. Assume that Massachusetts, the only state with ten representatives in the House—and so nothing to gain or lose—votes in favor of the amendment.

Vote in the House: ______________________

Vote in the Senate: ______________________

b. Are the margins in the House and Senate sufficient to approve the proposed amendment and forward it to the states? Explain your answer.

____

____

____

____

TABLE 1.2 POPULATION AND REPRESENTATION IN THE HOUSE BY STATE, 2000 CENSUS DATA

STATE	POPULATION	NUMBER OF REPRESENTATIVES IN THE HOUSE
Alabama	4,461,130	7
Alaska	628,933	1
Arizona	5,140,683	8
Arkansas	2,679,733	4
California	33,930,798	53
Colorado	4,311,882	7
Connecticut	3,409,535	5
Delaware	785,068	1
Florida	16,028,890	25
Georgia	8,206,975	13
Hawaii	1,216,642	2
Idaho	1,297,274	2
Illinois	12,439,042	19
Indiana	6,090,782	9
Iowa	2,931,923	5
Kansas	2,693,824	4
Kentucky	4,049,431	6
Louisiana	4,480,271	7
Maine	1,277,731	2
Maryland	5,307,886	8
Massachusetts	6,355,568	10
Michigan	9,955,829	15
Minnesota	4,925,670	8
Mississippi	2,852,927	4
Missouri	5,606,260	9
Montana	905,316	1
Nebraska	1,715,369	3
Nevada	2,002,032	3
New Hampshire	1,238,415	2
New Jersey	8,424,354	13
New Mexico	1,823,821	3
New York	19,004,973	29
North Carolina	8,067,673	13
North Dakota	643,756	1
Ohio	11,374,540	18
Oklahoma	3,458,819	5
Oregon	3,428,543	5
Pennsylvania	12,300,670	19
Rhode Island	1,049,662	2
South Carolina	4,025,061	6
South Dakota	756,874	1
Tennessee	5,700,037	9
Texas	20,903,994	32
Utah	2,236,714	3
Vermont	609,890	1
Virginia	7,100,702	11
Washington	5,908,684	9
West Virginia	1,813,077	3
Wisconsin	5,371,210	8
Wyoming	495,304	1
Total	281,424,177*	435

*This is the total apportionment population. The populations of the District of Columbia, Puerto Rico, and the U.S. Island Areas are excluded from the apportionment population because they do not have voting seats in the U.S. House of Representatives.

2. Determine the fate of the reapportionment amendment in the ratification phase. Assume that each state legislature votes solely on the basis of the effect the amendment would have on the state's voting power in the House.

a. How many state legislatures would vote to ratify the amendment?

---

b. Is the number of state legislatures in favor of the amendment sufficient to change the Constitution?

---

3. a. Using the data in Table 1.2, calculate the approximate population of the twelve largest states.

---

b. Calculate the approximate population of the thirty-eight smallest states.

---

c. What percentage of the nation's population lives in the twelve most populous states?

---

d. What percentage of the nation's population lives in the thirty-eight smallest states?

---

e. What do your calculations indicate about the extent of popular support for this constitutional amendment?

---

4. Why does the reapportionment amendment meet a different fate in the proposal and ratification phases of the amendment process?

---

5. a. Design an alternative to the Constitution's amendment process that gives a less prominent role to the states and that is more consistent with the principles of representative democracy.

---

b. Make an argument in support of your alternative amendment process.

---

c. Make an argument against your alternative amendment process.

EXERCISE 1.3 THE FRAMERS OF THE CONSTITUTION AND REPUBLICANISM

BACKGROUND

The U.S. Constitution establishes a republic. The framers chose the republican form of government over all other forms, including monarchy, aristocracy, and democracy.

Americans often differed over what constituted republican government. But they agreed in large part on the fundamental principles and elements of republican government:

- *Republican government is limited.* The powers of government are circumscribed to diminish the possibility of tyranny. In the Constitution, the framers set broad limits on the powers exercised by the national government over the states and over individuals.
- *Republican government is representational.* The exercise of power by government over citizens is legitimate only when citizens are represented in government by the elected members of legislative assemblies. The framers admired the representative institutions of the Roman Republic. They even named the U.S. Senate for the Roman Senate. But they did not decide—and Republicanism offered no standard position on—the extent of representation (how many representatives for how many people), the responsibility of legislators (to their constituents, to their own conscience, or to the public interest), or who would elect the representatives (the Constitution of 1787 left this issue to the states).

  On the issue of direct versus indirect representation, the framers were divided. The Constitution always has provided for the direct election of members of the House; but initially U.S. senators were elected indirectly, chosen by members of their state legislature. Remember that the framers didn't think too highly of the public's character or of its ability to handle political power wisely. So the framers chose not to expand the right to vote beyond what the individual states had established. Later, a series of constitutional amendments, Supreme Court decisions, and popular movements would democratize representation and expand the eligible electorate.
- *In republican government, the people are sovereign.* Republicans believe that the people at large create, authorize, and empower government, and that government must be accountable to the people. A government rooted in the people cannot act without the consent of the people. The word *republic* comes from the Latin *res publica* ("the public thing"), which means that government is a common enterprise, originating from and belonging to the people. Thomas Jefferson made this principle clear in the Declaration of Independence: "Governments are instituted among Men, deriving their just powers from the consent of the governed. . . . Whenever any Form of Government becomes destructive of these ends, it is the Right of the People to alter or to abolish it, and to institute new Government."

ASSIGNMENT

Several of the following questions require a close look at the Constitution. Consult the Constitution in Appendix 2 at the back of this textbook.

1. Identify three significant elements of the Constitution (including amendments) that embody the republican principle of limited government. Explain and support your answers.

___

___

___

___

___

___

___

2. a. Identify three significant elements of the Constitution of 1787 that embody the framers' commitment to representation.

b. What type of representation did you identify? Direct versus indirect, state representation versus popular representation, or legislative representation versus executive representation? Explain and support your answer.

3. Identify three amendments to the Constitution that expanded democratic representation, and explain what each amendment has accomplished.

4. Identify one passage in the Constitution that expresses the republican principle of popular sovereignty.

EXERCISE 1.4 CONTEMPORARY POLITICAL IDEOLOGIES

BACKGROUND

Over time, the terms *liberal, left wing, conservative,* and *right wing* have come both to describe political thought and to influence it. Their negative connotations can make these words political weapons. For example, in 1988, Republican presidential candidate George Bush Sr. accused his opponent, Democrat Michael Dukakis, of being the "*L* word," of being *liberal*. Bush was able to make the label stick, and it likely cost Dukakis the election.

Although ideological labels are widely used and often shape people's perceptions of politics, many Americans do not know what they mean. A *political ideology* is a set of coherent and deeply felt political beliefs through which individuals interpret political events and decide what is politically right and wrong. Despite the utility of the labels in making sense of political issues and actors, most Americans are not ideologues: They may hold ideological positions on particular issues, but they do not think of themselves in terms of a political ideology. Most Americans are pragmatists—positioned in the middle of the political spectrum—and are unlikely to judge issues or candidates by a set of rigid political beliefs. Indeed, Americans historically have rejected both movements and candidates with rigid ideologies. Several cases in point: In 1964 the staunchly conservative Republican presidential candidate, Barry Goldwater, was defeated by a landslide, as was liberal Democrat George McGovern in 1972. And in 1996, American voters rejected the conservative agenda of House Republicans, the Contract with America.

Still, ideological labels do help voters sort out a bewildering array of political arguments; and to some extent they do reflect political positions, especially among political elites, which tend to be more ideological than other Americans. But the task of identifying ideological positions has become more difficult in recent decades as the relatively simple divisions of the New Deal era—based largely on the economy and the role of government in the economy—have fragmented into ever-more diverse and complex thinking about the economy; moral, religious, and social issues; and foreign policy . . . especially in the wake of the Vietnam War and the end of the cold war.

What follow are definitions of seven ideological positions that are prominent on the American political landscape today. Recognize that the descriptions below have been simplified. The political views of individuals and movements are often too complex, even contradictory, to be captured completely by any political label.

Liberalism Liberals generally support the government's intervention in a broad array of contemporary issues, from economic policy to civil rights. But liberals are likely to oppose that intervention when they believe it threatens civil liberties—the freedom of speech, for example, or the individual's right to privacy. Liberals believe that government must play an active role in creating equal opportunity, through antidiscrimination laws, through affirmative-action programs, and through grants to and subsidies for disadvantaged individuals, organizations, and municipalities. Their commitment to government activism often focuses on the national government because it has both the financial resources and the potential to promote equal treatment for Americans in all states. For many liberals, taxes are not so much a means of distributing wealth equally as they are a means of redistributing wealth downward. Liberals believe that all levels of government are responsible for preventing and punishing market practices that hurt consumers and threaten the environment. In foreign and defense policy, liberals want less dependence on military and unilateral action and more dependence on negotiations and multilateralism, especially through the United Nations.

Neoliberalism Neoliberalism emerged in the 1970s as an effort to pull liberals back toward the political center. Neoliberals believe that rigid adherence to the tenets of traditional liberalism is not likely to address the nation's social and economic problems, nor is it likely to command broad public support. Like traditional liberals, neoliberals believe the national government is responsible for the nation's social and economic welfare, but they are less likely to support new government programs and expanded government regulation. According to neoliberals, the way to solve social and economic problems is to combine direct government action with incentives for the private sector—through tax policies and public subsidies, for example. Neoliberals also believe that the cooperation of state and local governments with national objectives is better than the national government's encroachment on state and local affairs.

The Left Wing From the 1930s to the 1960s, the earmarks of the American Left were its support for socialist, or Marxist, economics (public ownership of the means of production and the redistribution of wealth to foster economic equality); its opposition to American "imperialistic" foreign policy; and its efforts to eradicate racism in America. In the decades since, with the increasingly conservative trend in American politics and the end of the cold war, the left has splintered into a number of movements, each with its own passionate criticism of American society. Among those movements are radical feminism (speaking out against patriarchal relationships), radical environmentalism (speaking out against the ethos of acquisitiveness and the rape of nature), and radical multiculturalism (speaking out against the dominant European worldview that marginalizes people of color).

Conservatism Conservatives want to reduce the role of government in the nation's social and economic affairs. For conservatives, the role of government is limited to defending the people from foreign aggressors, maintaining law and order, and protecting the people from immediate threats to their health and safety. (Picture a night watchman.) Not surprisingly, conservatives want government funds spent on defense, not on social programs. Although many conservatives have made peace with the main components of the welfare state—social security and medicare—they don't want to see those programs grow, and some would like to see the programs scaled down.

Conservatives believe that the economy functions best with less government regulation and management. And, in recent decades, they have worked to privatize government functions that they believe are better left to the private sector, to deregulate the economy, and to return responsibility for social programs to state governments.

Conservatives today are split on economic policy. Supply-siders advocate across-the-board tax cuts—even a flat tax—which they believe will stimulate economic growth. Fiscal conservatives, on the other hand, worry more about budget deficits: They are reluctant to cut government revenues; instead they want to see existing programs downsized.

Although most conservatives now support antidiscrimination laws and regulations, many are reluctant to embrace broader efforts to promote civil rights. They are afraid that affirmative action and other measures create special rights for minority groups, in the process interfering with the rights of businesses and individuals. Most conservatives believe that individual liberties must be balanced against the government's responsibilities to maintain law and order and to defend core American values (for example, the flag) or Judeo-Christian values (for example, voluntary prayer in public schools).

Conservatives support a foreign policy that vigorously advances Americans interests abroad and protects American prestige—unilaterally if necessary. In the post–cold war world, conservatives worry that multilateral organizations like the United Nations may undermine U.S. sovereignty and constrain America's freedom to act on the world stage. But conservatives are reluctant to intervene abroad in places like Somalia solely to relieve famine or to subdue fighting in civil wars.

Neoconservatism Neoconservatism, like neoliberalism, is in part an effort to stake out middle ground between traditional liberals and traditional conservatives. Neoconservatives are less enamored of the free market than are traditional conservatives and are more supportive of government activism. Still, neoconservatives oppose many welfare programs, alleging that they undermine the individual initiative of recipients and foster dependence on government. Neoconservatives call for a renewed commitment to the virtues of individual responsibility and community obligation that they believe have been eroded by liberal policies. They advocate for the cultural and moral traditions of Western civilization—freedom, democracy, and capitalism, for example—and urge the strong defense of those traditions particularly in the government's defense and foreign policies.

Religious Conservatism (Christian Conservatism or the Religious Right) Economically, religious conservatives are not very different from other conservatives. What distinguishes them are their efforts to promote morality and defend Judeo-Christian values against a perceived assault by secular society, particularly by liberalism. Religious conservatives believe that America was founded on and owes its greatness to Judeo-Christian principles. They argue that the family has been besieged by the liberal worldview in education and in the media. A key issue for religious conservatives is abortion, and their focus on that issue has put them at odds with other conservatives, who remain more concerned about the economy and defense.

The Right Wing The right wing includes a number of groups united by their fear of modern industrial society and the increasing scope of government authority, and the belief that both society and government have undermined individualism, constitutionalism, private property rights, Christianity, or the white race's "rightful" status. The right wing believes that the national government has established a tyranny over the individual and that American sovereignty has been destroyed by affiliation with the United Nations and other alliances. Some right-wing groups are based on an ideology of racial supremacy; others are anti-Semitic. In recent years, several right-wing groups have come to believe that armed resistance to perceived sources of oppression is necessary.

ASSIGNMENT

1. Identify at least one public figure (living or dead) and one organization (active or inactive) that you associate with each of the ideologies in the chart below.

Political ideology	Public figure	Organization
Liberalism		
Neoliberalism		
Left wing		
Conservatism		
Neoconservatism		
Religious conservatism		
Right wing		

2. Listed below are eight hypothetical statements. Following each statement, identify the ideology it reflects and briefly explain your choice.

a. "Government is part of the problem, not part of the solution."

____

____

b. "We must end welfare."

____

____

c. "We must end welfare as we know it."

____

____

d. "The college core curriculum should teach our shared Western cultural heritage."

____

____

e. "If elected, I will get government off your backs and release the great energy of the American people."

____

____

f. "So long as I am president, no American shall go to bed hungry, no American shall suffer the burden of discrimination, and no American shall fall ill without the benefit of medical help."

____

____

g. "Abortion is the modern equivalent of the Nazi holocaust."

____

____

h. "Workers of the world, unite; you have nothing to lose but your chains."

____

____

3. In the space below describe your political ideology and why you support it. If your ideology reflects one or more of those described above, include the labels in your description.

____

____

____

____

____

____

____

____

4. Go to the Directory of U.S. Political Parties at www.politics1.com/parties.htm. The site briefly describes the ideologies of the two major political parties in the United States, Democratic and Republican, and more than thirty minor parties, and offers a link to each party's Web site. Read through the descriptions, and identify a political party that embodies each of the political ideologies we've examined. Briefly explain why you think the party you selected is a good example of the ideology.

Liberalism: ____

____

Neoliberalism: ____

____

The left wing: ____

____

Conservatism: ____

____

Neoconservatism: ____

____

Religious conservatism: ____

____

The right wing: ____

____

EXERCISE 1.5 DIRECT DEMOCRACY: ELECTRONICALLY

BACKGROUND

In a direct democracy, all citizens over a certain age exercise political power directly by making the laws that govern them. Direct democracy was practiced in ancient Athens, although women, slaves, and the foreign born were not eligible for citizenship and so were excluded from the process. The Athenian statesman Pericles (ca. 495–429 B.C.) said, "We do not say that a man who takes no interest in politics minds his own business; we say that he has no business here at all."[3] The major theoretical defense of direct democracy was made by philosopher Jean-Jacques Rousseau (1712–1788), who argued in *The Social Contract* that the moment citizens surrender their will to a representative, they become slaves.

The framers of the Constitution were vehemently opposed to direct democracy. In "Federalist No. 10," Madison wrote that "such democracies have ever been spectacles of turbulence and contention; have ever been found incompatible with personal security and the rights of property; and have in general been as short in their lives as they have been violent in their deaths." Not surprisingly, then, there are no examples of direct democracy in the U.S. Constitution in its original or amended form.

Direct democracy is practiced in the United States today under the provisions of some state constitutions and under local option. Many state constitutions provide for the *initiative,* which allows citizens to vote yes or no to enacting laws, and the *referendum,* which allows voters to approve or repeal laws. Neither practice conforms precisely to the Athenian understanding of direct democracy because the citizens do not assemble to debate and discuss the legislation. In fact, many citizens are woefully ill informed about ballot measures. Moreover, measures that do pass are subject to modification or even nullification in the courts. Still, towns in certain states, mainly in New England, do conduct some or all of their public business in town meetings, at which citizens assemble to vote on everything from budget allocations to local ordinances.

ASSIGNMENT

Traditionally, direct democracy limited the size of the political community to that of a city-state.[4] Three factors were at work: First, the logistics—too many people would have made assemblies impossible. Second, the smaller the community, the greater the relevance of public affairs to the citizens. Third, smaller communities facilitated the establishment of trust and friendship among citizens, bonds that were important in the exercise of direct political power. The size and complexity of the modern nation-state would seem to prohibit the practice of direct democracy today. Not so, say the supporters of direct democracy, who point to the possibility of using electronic technology to simulate assemblies.

Reading 1.5 presents one vision of electronic direct democracy. Study the model and then answer the questions that follow it.

READING 1.5 A MODEL OF ELECTRONIC DIRECT DEMOCRACY

The national government, at public expense, would provide all eligible voters with an electronic voting machine for use in the privacy of their homes. The electronic voting machines would allow voters to choose yes, no, or abstain. The machines would be tied into a series of regional government computers. Public voting stations would be established for the homeless or for people who are away from home on election day. To prevent voter fraud, access to voting machines would be allowed only through a thumbprint scanner, and access would be cut off after the individual has voted.

Legislative initiatives could be placed on the electronic ballot by an act of Congress, by executive order of the president, or by citizens' petitions. The petition route would require a number of verified signatures equal to 5 percent of the eligible voters. All legislative initiatives would be phrased in simple

[3] Quoted in Thucydides, *The Peloponnesian War* (Baltimore: Penguin Books, 1954), p. 119.

[4] Athens at its most populous had about 100,000 residents, some 20,000 of whom were citizens.

language and would require a simple yes or no vote. For example, the voters might be asked "Should all Americans be guaranteed insurance that covers 80 percent of their health-care costs annually?" or, perhaps, "Should the United States send troops to Bosnia to guarantee truce agreements and a subsequent peace agreement?" The results of the electronic vote would be binding on the nation's citizens.

The system of direct democracy would require some modification of the existing structure of government. First, the courts would be stripped of the power to strike down the will of the people. Second, although citizens would continue to elect members to the House and Senate—to write legislation and to appropriate funds—the actions of Congress would be subject to a nationwide electronic referendum. And third, although the executive branch still would be required to enforce the law, the actions of the president or executive-branch agencies could be challenged in a nationwide electronic referendum.

Campaigns for and against electronic ballot measures would be allowed. In addition, a bipartisan commission, appointed by the president with the consent of Congress, would be responsible for arranging televised debates about each legislative initiative or referendum during the three weeks preceding the vote. Participants in each debate would include a spokesperson for each position and an independent analyst who would provide an expert opinion on the consequences and costs of the measure. This model of electronic direct democracy would be implemented by the passage of the necessary constitutional amendments, according to Article V of the Constitution.

---

1. Do you support or oppose the idea of electronic direct democracy? Explain and defend your position.

2. Assume you're an opponent of electronic direct democracy. Which two features of the model described in Reading 1.5 would you oppose most strongly? Explain and defend your position.

3. Assume you're an advocate of electronic direct democracy. Which two features of the model described in Reading 1.5 would you support most strongly? Explain and defend your position.

FEDERALISM

EXERCISE 2.1 BALANCING THE RESPONSIBILITIES OF NATIONAL AND STATE GOVERNMENTS

BACKGROUND

In 1781, American forces defeated the British at Yorktown. A year later Great Britain agreed to recognize the independence of the United States; and in 1783, it signed the Treaty of Paris. The war over, Americans were able to give their full attention to this question: What form of government would be most suitable for the newly independent republic?

In 1777 the colonies joined together to fashion America's first national government under the provisions of the Articles of Confederation. Americans were in no mood in 1777 to create a strong central government that might abuse power and suppress the liberties of citizens as the British government had done. A central feature of the new government was specified in Article II: "Each State retains its sovereignty, freedom and independence, and every power, jurisdiction, and right, which is not by this confederation expressly delegated to the United States in Congress assembled." The colonies were stingy in their grants of power to the new government, denying to it powers that Americans today take for granted. That first national government, for example, had no executive or judicial branch: All power was vested in Congress, but a weak Congress, without the power to tax or to regulate foreign or domestic commerce. According to one historian, the Congress of the Confederation "could ask for money but not compel payment; it could enter into treaties but not enforce their stipulations; it could provide for raising of armies but not fill the ranks; it could borrow money but take no proper measures for repayment; it could advise and recommend but not command."[1]

By 1787 many Americans recognized the folly of their experiment with a central government too weak to maintain order, conduct foreign relations, or provide for the citizens of the Republic. That year, proponents of a stronger central government gathered in Philadelphia to consider revising the Articles. Instead, the delegates to the constitutional convention went considerably further: They produced a new

---

[1] Quoted in George Brown Tindall, *America: A Narrative History* (New York: Norton, 1984), p. 246.

constitution that vested in the national government many of the powers denied to it under the Articles of Confederation.

Proponents of the new government faced the formidable task of persuading citizens in the thirteen states to ratify the new constitution. Those proponents, who would have been described most accurately as nationalists, instead called themselves *federalists.* They wanted to emphasize that state governments would retain considerable powers under the new constitution. Federalists also emphasized that the new national government would be limited and restrained by the separation of powers and checks and balances. Opponents of the new constitution, called *antifederalists,* objected, insisting that the document proposed to empower the new national government largely at the expense of state governments. For example, under the Articles of Confederation the states reserved exclusively to themselves the power to tax. Under the new constitution—for the first time—the national government would have the power to tax citizens directly. Antifederalists favored decentralized government and the preservation of the powers and prerogatives of the states.

A debate raged in the new nation over the transfer of power to the national government as well as over many other features of the new constitution. As historian Benjamin Fletcher Wright noted:

> In spite of the prevalence and the bitterness of the opposition to the Constitution because of the greatly increased powers of the central government, Publius makes no concession, so far as concerns the essential principle of adequate powers to achieve the ends to be attained. The argument is rather that if the government is properly constituted . . . the powers delegated may safely be entrusted to it.[2]

Publius represented the collaborative efforts of Alexander Hamilton, John Jay, and James Madison to defend and promote the Constitution. Eighty-five of their Publius articles were reprinted as *The Federalist* in 1788, a collection usually referred to as *The Federalist Papers.* The degree to which the arguments advanced in *The Federalist* persuaded the public of the time is debatable, but today the collection remains an essential explanation of the structure and functions of the government established by the Constitution.

ASSIGNMENT

"Federalist No. 45," written by James Madison, appeared in the *New York Packet* on January 29, 1788. In the article, Madison sought to dispel the fear that the new constitution would undermine the powers and prerogatives of the state governments. Refer to Reading 2.1, which contains excerpts from "Federalist No. 45," to answer the questions that follow it.

READING 2.1 JAMES MADISON, "FEDERALIST NO. 45"

To the People of the State of New York:

Having shown that no one of the powers transferred to the federal government is unnecessary or improper, the next question to be considered is, whether the whole mass of them will be dangerous to the portion of authority left in the several States.

The adversaries to the plan of the convention, instead of considering in the first place what degree of power was absolutely necessary for the purposes of the federal government, have exhausted themselves in a secondary inquiry into the possible consequences of the proposed degree of power to the governments of the particular States. But if the Union, as has been shown, be essential to the security of the people of America against foreign danger; if it be essential to their security against contentions and wars among the different States; if it be essential to guard them against those violent and oppressive factions which embitter the blessings of liberty, and against those military establishments which must gradually poison its very fountain; if, in a word, the Union be essential to the happiness of the people

---

[2] Alexander Hamilton, James Madison, and John Jay, *The Federalist,* ed. Benjamin Fletcher Wright (Cambridge, Mass.: Belknap Press, 1961), p. 45.

of America, is it not preposterous, to urge as an objection to a government, without which the objects of the Union cannot be attained, that such a government may derogate from the importance of the governments of the individual States? Was, then, the American Revolution effected, was the American Confederacy formed, was the precious blood of thousands spilt, and the hard-earned substance of millions lavished, not that the people of American should enjoy peace, liberty, and safety, but that the government of the individual States, that particular municipal establishments, might enjoy a certain extent of power, and be arrayed with certain dignities and attributes of sovereignty? . . .

Several important considerations have been touched in the course of these papers, which discountenance the supposition that the operation of the federal government will by degrees prove fatal to the State governments. The more I resolve the subject, the more fully I am persuaded that the balance is much more likely to be disturbed by the preponderancy of the last than of the first scale.

We have seen, in all the examples of ancient and modern confederacies, the strongest tendency continually betraying itself in the members, to despoil the general government of its authorities, with a very ineffectual capacity in the latter to defend itself against the encroachments. Although, in most of these examples, the system has been so dissimilar from that under consideration as greatly to weaken any inference concerning the latter from the fate of the former, yet, as the States will retain, under the proposed Constitution, a very extensive portion of active sovereignty, the inference ought not to be wholly disregarded. . . .

The State governments will have the advantage of the Federal government, whether we compare them in respect to the immediate dependence of the one on the other; to the weight of personal influence which each side will possess; to the powers respectively vested in them; to the predilection and probable support of the people; to the dispositions and faculty of resisting and frustrating the measures of each other.

The State governments may be regarded as constituent and essential parts of the federal government; whilst the latter is nowise essential to the operation or organization of the former. Without the intervention of the State legislatures, the President of the United States cannot be elected at all. They must in all cases have a great share in his appointment, and will, perhaps in most cases, of themselves determine it. The Senate will be elected absolutely and exclusively by the State legislatures.* Even the House of Representatives, though drawn immediately from the people, will be chosen very much under the influence of that class of men, whose influence over the people obtains for themselves an election into the State legislatures. Thus, each of the principal branches of the federal government will owe its existence more or less to the favor of the State governments, and must consequently feel a dependence, which is much more likely to begat a disposition too obsequious than too overbearing towards them. . . .

The number of individuals employed under the Constitution of the United States will be much smaller than the number employed under the particular States. There will consequently be less of personal influence on the side of the former than the latter. . . .

The powers delegated by the proposed Constitution to the federal government are few and defined. Those which are to remain in the State governments are numerous and indefinite. The former will be exercised principally on external objects, as war, peace, negotiation, and foreign commerce; with which last the power of taxation will, for the most part, be connected. The powers reserved to the several States will extend to all the objects which, in the ordinary course of affairs, concern the lives, liberties, and properties of the people, and the internal order, improvement, and prosperity of the State.

The operations of the federal government will be most extensive and important in times of war and danger; those of the State governments in times of peace and security. As the former periods will probably bear a small proportion to the latter, the State governments will here enjoy another advantage over the federal government. The more adequate, indeed, the federal powers may be rendered to the national defence, the less frequent will be those scenes of danger which might favor their ascendancy over the governments of the particular States.

If the new Constitution be examined with accuracy and candor, it will be found that the change which it proposes consists much less in the addition of NEW POWERS to the Union, than in the invigoration of its ORIGINAL POWERS. The regulation of commerce, it is true, is a new power; but that seems to be an addition which few oppose, and from which no apprehensions are entertained. The

---

* The Twelfth Amendment (1804) provided for the election of the president by electors chosen by the public, and the Seventeenth Amendment (1913) provided for the direct election of U.S. senators.

powers relating to war and peace, armies and fleets, treaties and finance, with the other more considerable powers, are all vested in the existing Congress by the articles of Confederation. The proposed change does not enlarge these powers; it only substitutes a more effectual mode of administering them. . . . Had the States complied punctually with the articles of Confederation, or could their compliance have been enforced by as peaceable means as may be used with success towards single persons, our past experience is very far from countenancing an opinion, that the State governments would have lost their constitutional powers, and have gradually undergone an entire consolidation. To maintain that such an event would have ensued, would be to say at once, that the existence of the State governments is incompatible with any system whatever that accomplished the essential purposes of the Union.

Publius

---

1. Identify six arguments made by Publius to support his contention that the Constitution is not a threat to the powers and prerogatives of the state governments.

____

____

____

____

____

____

2. In two sentences, using your own words, summarize the last paragraph in "Federalist No. 45."

____

____

____

____

____

3. The distribution of power between the national and state governments in the United States today is governed by several key passages in the Constitution, the Supreme Court's interpretation of those passages, and legislation enacted by Congress and the state legislatures. Two clauses in the Constitution are particularly important. Study Article I, Section 8. Pay close attention to the last clause, which gives Congress the power "to make all Laws which shall be necessary and proper for carrying into Execution the foregoing Powers, and all other Powers vested by this Constitution in the Government of the United States, or in any Department or Officer thereof." Look next at the Tenth Amendment: "The powers not delegated to the United States by the Constitution, nor prohibited by it to the States, are reserved to the States respectively, or to the people." Compare these provisions with Article II in the Articles of Confederation: "Each State retains its sovereignty, freedom and independence, and every power, jurisdiction, and right, which is not by this confederation expressly delegated to the United States in Congress assembled."

a. In your own words, explain how the two methods for dividing power between the national and state governments differ.

____

____

____

____

____

b. What is the effect of including the word *expressly* in Article II of the Articles of Confederation? Why didn't the authors of the Tenth Amendment to the Constitution include the word *expressly?*

c. In Article I, Section 8, of the Constitution, what possibility is created by the use of the phrase *necessary and proper?*

EXERCISE 2.2 THE EVOLUTION OF FEDERALISM

BACKGROUND

A system of dual federalism maintained the balance between the federal and state governments from 1791 to the late 1920s. The national government managed foreign affairs, national defense, and interstate relations; and the states focused on policies that affected their citizens and on intrastate economic matters. Textbooks often describe dual federalism as *layer-cake federalism,* comparing the government to a cake made up of two separate layers. Although the national government had begun to increase its power following the Civil War, until the late 1920s, the states were the top layer: They dominated politics in the United States.

The situation changed dramatically with the Great Depression. The New Deal policies of the Roosevelt administration were designed to alleviate the economic consequences of the depression by expanding the role of the national government in matters previously left to the states. Quite simply, the states could not respond to the economic collapse on their own. Congressional enactment of the Social Security Act (1935), unemployment insurance, and public assistance programs extended the influence of the national government to legislative matters that were once reserved for the states. Massive public works projects—dams, highways, and public buildings—were undertaken under the auspices of the national government to hasten economic recovery. The role of the national government continued to expand as a result of World War II and the emergence of the United States as a global military and economic power in the postwar era. The structure of government in this period often is referred to as *cooperative,* or *marble-cake, federalism.* The analogy is to a two-layer cake in which some of the ingredients of the top layer are found in various spots in the bottom layer. The primary concept of cooperative federalism is shared responsibility for various programs.

A new period of creative federalism began with the Johnson administration's War on Poverty in the 1960s. That program was a comprehensive effort on the part of the national government to eradicate the root causes of poverty in the states. To that end, the national government made an increasing number of grants to the states. Although most of the programs established under the War on Poverty have been discontinued, some survive, including Head Start, which continues to prepare preschoolers from impoverished backgrounds for elementary school.

Over the past several decades, the national government has experimented with ways to entice the states to carry out national objectives. Usually inducement comes in the form of *grants-in-aid,* offers to pay a large percentage of the costs of cleaning up toxic wastes, building highways, making buildings accessible to those with physical handicaps, or enacting educational programs. In fact, some states receive more federal funds for programs than those states send to Washington in the form of taxes.[3] This is especially true of the poorer states.

Grants-in-aid fall into two categories. The first is *categorical grants,* grants for specific projects. These funds come with strings attached, giving the national government greater control. The second is *block grants,* which give state and local officials more leeway over how the money is spent. For example, a state might receive a block grant to improve education, with means and methods left to local officials.

Opposition to the growth of the national government was evident in 1980, in the election of Ronald Reagan to the presidency. Voters were responding to high taxes, new regulations, and an expanded bureaucracy in Washington, D.C.—to the loss of rights and responsibilities that had traditionally been the states'. Reagan and his successor, George Bush Sr., both Republicans, worked to return responsibilities for public assistance and other programs to the states. And faced with the election of a Republican Congress in 1994, Democrat Bill Clinton continued in that vein—a departure from the Democrats' traditional commitment to the poor. Not surprisingly, Republican George W. Bush has pledged to transfer more power from Washington to the states.

The vote is still out on how successful the states have been at taking over the national government's responsibilities. One prominent political scientist believes decentralization is encouraging *competitive federalism* among the states, a battle to offer the best services at the lowest costs.[4] Even with decentral-

[3] See Russell L. Hanson, "Intergovernmental Relations," in *Politics in the American States,* 6th ed., ed. Virginia Gray and Herbert Jacob (Washington, D.C.: CQ Press, 1996).

[4] Thomas Dye, *American Federalism* (Lexington, Mass.: Lexington Books, 1990), p. xvi.

TABLE 2.2 FEDERAL GRANTS-IN-AID TO STATE AND LOCAL GOVERNMENTS BY FUNCTION, SELECTED FISCAL YEARS 1965–1994 (IN MILLIONS)

	FISCAL YEAR			
FUNCTION	1965	1975	1985	1994
Health	$ 624	$ 8,810	$ 24,451	$ 91,524
Income security	3,512	9,352	27,153	52,234
Education, training, employment, and social services	1,050	12,133	17,817	34,429
Transportation	4,100	5,864	17,055	23,049
Community and regional development	643	2,842	5,221	6,300
Natural resources and environment	183	2,437	4,069	4,192
General government	226	7,072	6,838	2,370
Agriculture	517	404	2,420	1,041
Administration of justice	—	725	95	1,253
Energy	9	43	529	464
Veterans' benefits and services	8	32	91	226
National defense	33	74	157	175
All other	4	2	2	8
Total	$10,910	$49,791	$105,897	$217,265

SOURCE: Adapted from U.S. Advisory Commission on Intergovernmental Relations, *Significant Features of Fiscal Federalism*, vol. 1 (Washington, D.C., December 1994), p. 31.

ization, the two basic issues of federalism continue to stir controversy. First, should government in general become involved in addressing a particular problem? Second, which level of government should take responsibility for the matter?

ASSIGNMENT

Data on federal grants-in-aid to the states from 1965 to 1994 are shown in Table 2.2. Use those data to answer the following questions.

1. From 1965 to 1994, what was the percentage increase in total grants-in-aid to state and local governments?

____

2. The pie chart on the following page shows the percentage breakdown by function of grants-in-aid in 1965. Use the empty circles to create similar pie charts for 1985 and 1994. Be sure to label the percentages.

3. Which function experienced the largest percentage decrease in federal grants-in-aid from 1985 to 1994?

____

4. The national government wants to help the states meet the educational needs of public school students. Should the national government give all states a specific amount of money per pupil to help meet national educational goals (the categorical-grant approach)? Or should the government in Washington, D.C., simply give the states money for education and tell them to meet whatever educational goals they establish for their students (the block-grant approach)? Explain and support your answer.

____

____

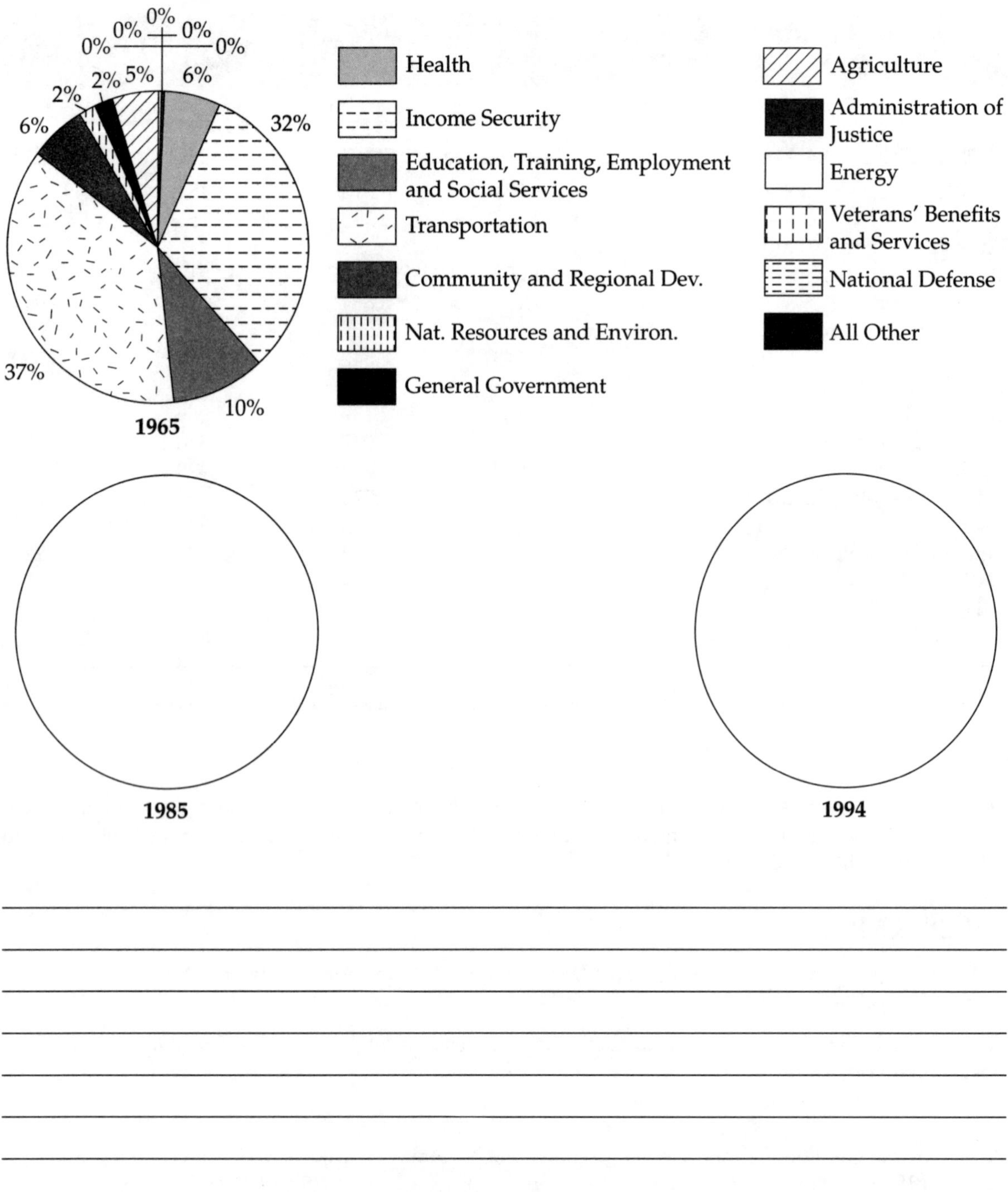
0%
0%
0%
0%
0%
2%
5%
6%
2%
6%
32%
37%
10%
1965
Health
Income Security
Education, Training, Employment and Social Services
Transportation
Community and Regional Dev.
Nat. Resources and Environ.
General Government
Agriculture
Administration of Justice
Energy
Veterans' Benefits and Services
National Defense
All Other
1985
1994

EXERCISE 2.3 GOVERNMENT ACCOUNTABILITY

BACKGROUND

People commonly complain that government at all levels has become too bureaucratic—too cumbersome, too ineffective, and too resistant to change. And there is validity to their argument: For example, most American government textbooks offer examples of bipartisan reform efforts that have failed to streamline the bureaucracy.[5]

In early 1993, President Clinton announced the creation of the National Performance Review, a project whose goal, the president said, was "to make the entire federal government less expensive and more efficient, and to change the culture of our national bureaucracy away from complacency and entitlement toward initiative and empowerment." The president assigned Vice President Al Gore to lead the effort and to give him a progress report within six months. Gore's report on proposals to make government "work better and cost less" took on a life of its own and evolved into the National Partnership for Reinventing Government (NPR). It was the eleventh attempt at reforming the national government in the twentieth century.

By the time the Clinton–Gore administration left office in early 2001, some twelve hundred specific proposals to make government more efficient and less costly had been set forth, and almost two-thirds had been implemented. At one point in the mid-1990s, Vice President Gore appeared on the *Late Show with David Letterman,* where he shattered a glass ashtray to demonstrate the excesses of certain government regulations. As the vice president explained, there were more than ten written regulations on the requirements for ashtrays in federal buildings.

Among the more notable accomplishments of the NPR were the reduction of the federal civilian workforce by more than 400,000 positions, the elimination of some 640,000 pages of agency rules, and the creation of annual performance reports to demonstrate the government's success in meeting stated goals.

Part of the NPR's work was to address federal–state–community relations with the goal of achieving better coordination among different government agencies. For example, all three levels of government usually respond to damages resulting from hurricanes, floods, earthquakes, fires, and other natural disasters. The importance of their agencies' working together became that much more significant after the September 11, 2001, terrorist actions in New York City and Washington, D.C. NPR recommended that the Advisory Commission on Intergovernmental Relations "develop appropriate benchmarks and performance measures" to clarify policy choices, to shift the focus of policies to the public, and to allow the public to gauge the performance of government agencies.

ASSIGNMENT

Oregon developed a number of benchmarks for public works, measures that gauge performance, identify problems, and establish goals. Questions 1 through 6 below are based on Table 2.3, which lists both historical and target benchmarks in Oregon from 1980 through 2010.

1. Assume Oregon met its 2000 target for water quality (benchmark 110) in state rivers and streams. By what percentage would water quality have improved over the 1990 standard?

____

2. a. Why do you think air transportation (benchmark 151) is included?

____

____

____

[5] See, for example, Steffan W. Schmidt, Mack C. Shelley, and Barbara A. Bardes, *American Government and Politics Today* (Stamford, Conn.: Wadsworth, 2001), chap. 11; and Thomas E. Patterson, *The American Democracy* (New York: McGraw Hill, 2001), chap. 16.

TABLE 2.3 BENCHMARKS FOR PUBLIC WORKS, OREGON, 1980–2010

BENCHMARKS FOR PEOPLE	HISTORICAL							TARGETS		
GROUND TRANSPORTATION	1980	1989	1990	1991	1992	1993	1994	1995	2000	2010
67. Percentage of adults who use vehicle safety restraints consistently		41	48	75	76			80	90	95
BENCHMARKS FOR QUALITY OF LIFE										
WATER										
110. Miles of assessed Oregon rivers and streams not meeting state and federal government in-stream water quality standards*			1,100		1,100			723	75	0
131. Number of Oregonians (in thousands) with drinking water that does not meet EPA safe drinking water standards										
a. 1974 standards	133	67	63	20	17	0	0	0	0	0
b. 1986 standards (Phase I VOCS)		22	3	0	0	0	0	0	0	0
c. 1986 standards (surface water treatment)				129	124	70	65	<1994	<1995	<2000
d. 1986 standards (coliform)				11	0	1	0	0	0	0
e. 1986 standards (lead/copper)					523	818	842	<1994	<1995	<2000
f. 1986 standards (Phase 2)					5	0	0	0	0	0
WASTE WATER										
132. Number of Oregonians (in thousands) with sewage disposal that does not meet government standards		200		143		82		134	67	0
GROUND TRANSPORTATION										
108. Percentage of Oregonians living where the air meets government ambient air quality standards*†	30	90	54	51	58	100		100	100	100
109. Carbon dioxide emissions as a percentage of 1990 emissions			100	106	108			100	100	100
128. Percentage of new residential development, as measured in housing units with the Portland Urban Growth Boundary, where occupants are within ¼ mile of										
a. commercial services							48			
b. parks							39			
c. schools							20			
d. existing public transport							56			
e. all of the above							7			

TABLE 2.3 (CONTINUED)

BENCHMARKS FOR QUALITY OF LIFE	HISTORICAL							TARGETS		
GROUND TRANSPORTATION	1980	1989	1990	1991	1992	1993	1994	1995	2000	2010
129. Percentage of existing residential development, as measured in housing units within the Portland Urban Growth Boundary, where occupants are within ¼ mile of										
a. commercial services							78			
b. parks							51			
c. schools							28			
d. existing public transit							80			
e. all of the above							14			
136. Percentage of Oregonians who commute to work (one way) within 30 minutes			88		88		84	88	88	88
137. Percentage of miles of limited-access highways in Oregon metropolitan areas that are not heavily congested during peak hours	81‡	52	57	44	42			60	60	60
138. Access to alternative transportation modes:										
a. Transit hours per capita per year in Oregon metropolitan areas	1.03		0.95	0.96	0.962	0.97	.99	1.3	1.5	1.7
b. Percentage of arterial and collector street miles in urban areas that have adequate pedestrian and bicycle facilities										
139. Percentage of Oregonians who commute to and from work during peak hours by means other than a single-occupancy vehicle					24		25	29	33	38
140. Vehicle miles traveled per capita in Oregon metropolitan areas (per year)	5,782	7,738	7,733	7,824	7,710	7,727		7,864	7,942	7,443
149. Percentage of Access Oregon Highways built to handle traffic at a steady 55 mile-per-hour rate							82	82	83	85
150. Percentage of Oregonians living in communities with daily scheduled inter-city passenger bus, van, or rail service			92		92	99		99	99	99
AIR TRANSPORTATION										
151. Percentage of Oregonians living within 50 miles of an airport with daily scheduled air passenger service			90					90	92	95

SOURCE: Adapted from U.S. Advisory Commission on Intergovernmental Relations, *Intergovernmental Accountability* (Washington, D.C., May 1996), pp. 108–109.

*Benchmarks that need to be addressed immediately.

†Core benchmarks, benchmarks that define the qualities Oregonians seek in life.

‡Data from 1983.

b. Looking at benchmark 151, what assumption can you make about access to air transportation in Oregon? Explain your answer.

____

____

____

____

3. Benchmark 128 focuses on the distance between residents' homes and commercial services, parks, schools, and existing public transportation. What does this benchmark tell us about how residents in Portland access services? Explain your answer.

____

____

____

____

4. Below, draw a new planned residential development that meets the benchmarks in 128. Locate 128's a-b-c-d factors within the boundary of the development. (Note: your boundary for the residential development can be a square, circle, or other reasonable configuration that would enable one to see how the a-b-c-d factors fit in your plan).

5. The historical and target percentages noted in benchmark 136 are quite consistent. In one sentence, describe what these data tell us beside the fact that the vast majority of Oregonians commute 30 minutes or less to work?

6. Identify three different methods that the government in Oregon can employ to meet the targets in benchmark 67.

7. You are charged with writing a benchmark to measure the extent of recycling in your community.

a. What do recycling data tell us about the quality of life in a community?

b. Why is recycling something that should concern local, state, and national governments?

8. a. List an agency at each level of government that is involved in efforts to reduce air pollution in the states.

Local: ______

State: ______

National: ______

b. Would it be better to simply assign responsibility for reducing air pollution to one level of government? Explain your answer.

EXERCISE 2.4 WHO'S IN CHARGE? THE ONGOING DISPUTE OVER POLICYMAKING BETWEEN NATIONAL AND STATE GOVERNMENTS

BACKGROUND

The Constitution delegates certain powers to the national government and others to the states. For example, the national government has the power to coin money, to make treaties, to conduct foreign relations, and to declare and wage war. State governments are responsible for regulating trade within their borders, establishing local governments, and ensuring their citizens' health and safety. And the Constitution gives to both levels of government certain concurrent powers: the right to tax, to establish courts, and to borrow money.

Some areas of responsibility are clearly specified in the Constitution: Article I, Section 8, for example, clearly enumerates the powers that belong to Congress and hence to the national government. Other responsibilities are not as clear. The Tenth Amendment (1791) states: "The powers not delegated to the United States by the Constitution, nor prohibited by it to the States, are reserved to the States respectively, or to the people." American political history is replete with disputes centering on the distribution of those powers.

The Supreme Court is the final arbiter in those disputes. But because the political landscape constantly is changing in response to international and domestic events, the Court has not always been consistent in its interpretation of the respective powers of the national and state governments. Still, from the mid-1930s to the mid-1990s, the Court tended to find for the national government. At times it would cite implied powers to support federal claims to power over the states. According to the Court, *implied powers* are those that Congress rightfully infers as its own from the necessary and proper clause of the Constitution (see Exercise 7.1). For example, the Court has held it proper for Congress to pass legislation prohibiting racial discrimination in hotels, motels, and restaurants.[6] That authority is implied by the Constitution, which grants Congress the authority to regulate interstate commerce. The Court reasoned that because travelers make use of public accommodations as they go from one state to another, the businesses are engaged in interstate commerce and therefore are subject to federal regulation.

Over the past several years, the Court increasingly has found for the states in federal–state disputes.[7] For example, in *United States v. Lopez* (1995), the Court held that a federal law prohibiting the possession of a gun within 1,000 feet of a school was unconstitutional because it was not within the meaning of commerce that can be regulated by Congress. In 1997, in *Printz v. United States,* the Court struck down a provision of the Brady Bill, a federal law that required local law enforcement officers to do background checks on prospective gun buyers. In 2000, in *Kimel v. Florida Board of Regents,* the Court found that state governments do not have to comply with federal laws that prohibit discrimination against older workers. And in *Solid Waste Agency v. U.S. Army Corps of Engineers* (2001), the Court ruled that the Clean Water Act could not be used to protect migratory waterfowl because, as Chief Justice William Rehnquist wrote, enforcement of the federal law "would result in a significant impingement of the State's traditional and primary power over land and water use." Still, in the most controversial case in recent years, *Bush v. Gore* (2000), the Court held that the state of Florida could not recount ballots cast in the 2000 presidential election because a recount would violate the equal protection clause of the Fourteenth Amendment.

In the 1980s, the national government used highway funds to restrict the sale of alcoholic beverages across the country. At issue: the minimum drinking age. Although most states set the minimum age at 21, several allowed the consumption of some types of alcoholic beverages at ages from 18 to 21. The national government eventually adopted the argument of Mothers Against Drunk Driving, that an under-21 drinking age creates an incentive for young people to drive from surrounding states to purchase and consume alcoholic beverages and then to return to their home states. Actuarial tables showed that arrests for driving under the influence and drunk-driving accidents among 18- to 21-year-old drivers increased in states that bordered a state with a low minimum drinking age. So Congress enacted the National Minimum Drinking Age Amendment of 1984. That statute directed the secretary of trans-

[6] See *Atlanta Motel v. United States* (1964); and *Katzenbach v. McClung* (1964).

[7] Republican appointees on the Court—the majority—often vote as a bloc to limit federal power and expand state power.

portation to withhold 5 percent of otherwise allocable federal highway funds from states where those under 21 could legally purchase or consume alcoholic beverages.[8]

South Dakota, which allowed those 19 years or older to purchase and consume 3.2 percent beer, filed suit in federal court seeking a declaratory judgment that the amendment was an invalid exercise of the spending clause in Article I, Section 8, of the U.S. Constitution, and that it also violated the Twenty-First Amendment, which gives the states the power to impose restrictions on the sale of liquor. The federal court rejected South Dakota's claim and was upheld by the U.S. court of appeals. South Dakota then appealed to the Supreme Court. South Dakota was the plaintiff; the respondent was Elizabeth Dole, then the secretary of transportation. In a 7–2 vote, the justices rejected South Dakota's claim.

ASSIGNMENT

Excerpts from the majority and minority opinions in *South Dakota v. Dole* (1987) are reprinted in Reading 2.4. Refer to the reading to answer the questions that follow it.

READING 2.4 South Dakota v. Dole, 483 U.S. 203 (1987)

Mr. Chief Justice Rehnquist delivered the opinion of the Court.

In this Court, the parties direct most of their efforts to defining the proper scope of the Twenty-first Amendment. . . . South Dakota asserts that the setting of minimum drinking ages is clearly within the "core powers" reserved to the States under §2 of the Amendment. . . . The Secretary in response asserts that the Twenty-first Amendment is simply not implicated by §158 [the National Minimum Drinking Age Amendment]; the plain language of §2 [of the Twenty-First Amendment] confirms the States' broad power to impose restrictions on the sale and distribution of alcoholic beverages but does not confer on them any power to *permit* sales that Congress seeks to *prohibit.* That Amendment, under this reasoning would not prevent Congress from affirmatively enacting a national minimum drinking age more restrictive than that provided by the various state laws; and it would follow a fortiori that the indirect inducement involved here is compatible with the Twenty-first Amendment.

These arguments present questions of the meaning of the Twenty-first Amendment, the bounds of which have escaped precise definition. . . . Despite the extended treatment of the question by the parties, however, we need not decide in this case whether that Amendment would prohibit an attempt by Congress to legislate directly a national minimum drinking age. Here, Congress has acted indirectly under its spending power to encourage uniformity in the States' drinking ages. As we explain below, we find this legislative effort within constitutional bounds even if Congress may not regulate drinking ages directly.

The Constitution empowers Congress to "lay and collect Taxes, Duties, Imposts, and Excises, to pay the Debts and provide for the common Defence and general Welfare of the United States." Art. I, §8, Cl. 1. Incident to this power, Congress may attach conditions on the receipt of federal funds, and has repeatedly employed the power "to further broad policy objectives by conditioning receipt of federal moneys upon compliance by the recipient with federal statutory and administrative directives." . . . The breadth of this power was made clear in *United States v. Butler* . . . where the Court, resolving a long-standing debate over the scope of the Spending Clause, determined that "the power of Congress to authorize expenditure of public moneys for public purposes is not limited by the direct grants of legislative power found in the Constitution." Thus, objectives not thought to be within Article I's "enumerated legislative

[8] Apparently there is some flexibility with the minimum-age law. The International Center for Alcohol Policies reports that alcohol can be consumed by those under 21 in nineteen states under certain circumstances. Exceptions include consumption for medical or religious reasons, in private clubs or establishments, and in the company of a spouse, parent, or guardian. See www.icap.org/publications/report4.html.

fields," . . . may nevertheless be attained through the use of the spending power and the conditional grant of federal funds.

The spending power is of course not unlimited . . . but is instead subject to several general restrictions articulated in our cases. The first of these limitations is derived from the language of the Constitution itself: the exercise of the spending power must be in pursuit of "the general welfare." . . . In considering whether a particular expenditure is intended to serve general public purposes, courts should defer substantially to the judgment of Congress. . . . Second, we have required that if Congress desires to condition the States' receipt of federal funds, it "must do so unambiguously . . . , enabl[ing] the States to exercise their choice knowingly, cognizant of the consequences of their participation." . . . Third, our cases have suggested (without significant elaboration) that conditions on federal grants might be illegitimate if they are unrelated "to the federal interest in particular national projects or programs." . . .

South Dakota does not seriously claim that §158 is inconsistent with any of the first three restrictions mentioned above. We can readily conclude that the provision is designed to serve the general welfare, especially in light of the fact that "the concept of welfare or the opposite is shaped by Congress. . . ." Congress found that the differing drinking ages in the States created particular incentives for young persons to combine their desire to drink with their ability to drive, and that this interstate problem required a national solution. The means it chose to address this dangerous situation were reasonably calculated to advance the general welfare. The conditions upon which States receive the funds, moreover, could not be more clearly stated by Congress. . . . And the State itself, rather than challenging the germaneness of the condition to federal purposes, admits that it "has never contended that the congressional action was . . . unrelated to a national concern in the absence of the Twenty-first Amendment." . . . Indeed, the condition imposed by Congress is directly related to one of the main purposes for which highway funds are expended—safe interstate travel.

This goal of the interstate highway system had been frustrated by varying drinking ages among the States. A Presidential commission appointed to study alcohol-related accidents and fatalities on the Nation's highways concluded that the lack of uniformity in the States' drinking ages created "an incentive to drink and drive" because "young persons commut[e] to border States where the drinking age is lower." . . . By enacting §158, Congress conditioned the receipt of federal funds in a way reasonably calculated to address this particular impediment to a purpose for which the funds are expended.

The remaining question about the validity of §158—and the basic point of disagreement between the parties—is whether the Twenty-first Amendment constitutes an "independent constitutional bar" to the conditional grant of federal funds. . . . Petitioner, relying on its view that the Twenty-first Amendment prohibits direct regulation of drinking ages by Congress, asserts that "Congress may not use the spending power to regulate that which it is prohibited from regulating directly under the Twenty-first Amendment." . . . But our cases show that this "independent constitutional bar" limitation on the spending power is not of the kind petitioner suggests. *United States v. Butler* . . . , for example, established that the constitutional limitations on Congress when exercising its spending power are less exacting than those on its authority to regulate directly.

We have also held that a perceived Tenth Amendment limitation on congressional regulation of state affairs did not concomitantly limit the range of conditions legitimately placed on federal grants.

These cases. . . establish that the "independent constitutional bar" limitation on the spending power is not, as petitioner suggests, a prohibition on the indirect achievement of objectives which Congress is not empowered to achieve directly. Instead, we think that the language in our earlier opinions stands for the unexceptionable proposition that the power may not be used to induce the States to engage in activities that would themselves be unconstitutional. Thus, for example, a grant of federal funds conditioned on invidiously discriminatory state action or the infliction of cruel and unusual punishment would be an illegitimate exercise of the Congress's broad spending power. But no such claim can be or is made here. Were South Dakota to succumb to the blandishments offered by Congress and raise its drinking age to 21, the State's action in so doing would not violate the constitutional rights of anyone.

Even if Congress might lack the power to impose a national minimum drinking age directly, we conclude that encouragement to state action found in §158 is a valid use of the spending power. Accordingly, the judgment of the Court of Appeals is affirmed.

Justice O'Connor dissenting.

The Court today upholds the National Minimum Drinking Age Amendments. . . as a valid exercise of the spending power conferred by Article 1, §8. But, §158 is not a condition on spending reasonably related to the expenditure of federal funds and cannot be justified on that ground. Rather, it is an attempt to regulate the sale of liquor, an attempt that lies outside Congress' power to regulate commerce because it falls within the ambit of §2 of the Twenty-first Amendment.

My disagreement with the Court is relatively narrow on the spending power issue: it is a disagreement about the application of a principle rather than a disagreement on the principle itself.

The Court reasons that Congress wishes that the roads it builds may be used safely, that drunken drivers threaten highway safety, and that young people are more likely to drive while under the influence of alcohol under existing law than would be the case if there were a uniform national drinking age of 21. It hardly needs saying, however, that if the purpose of §158 is to deter drunken driving, it is far too over- and under-inclusive. It is over-inclusive because it stops teenagers from drinking even when they are not about to drive on interstate highways. It is under-inclusive because teenagers pose only a small part of the drunken driving problem in this Nation.

When Congress appropriates money to build a highway, it is entitled to insist that the highway be a safe one. But it is not entitled to insist as a condition of the use of highway funds that the State impose or change regulations in other areas of the State's social and economic life because of an attenuated or tangential relationship to highway use or safety. Indeed, if the rule were otherwise, the Congress could effectively regulate almost any area of a State's social, political, or economic life on the theory that use of the interstate transportation system is somehow enhanced. . . .

As discussed above, a condition that a State will raise its drinking age to 21 cannot fairly be said to be reasonably related to the expenditure of funds for highway construction. The only possible connection, highway safety, has nothing to do with how the funds Congress has appropriated are expended. Rather than a condition determining how federal highway money shall be expended, it is a regulation determining who shall be able to drink liquor. As such it is not justified by the spending power.

The immense size and power of the Government of the United States ought not obscure its fundamental character. It remains a Government of enumerated powers. . . . Because 23 USC 158 . . . cannot be justified as an exercise of any power delegated to the Congress, it is not authorized by the Constitution. The Court errs in holding it to be the law of the land, and I respectfully dissent.

---

1. What are the three restrictions on the spending power identified in the majority opinion?

____

____

____

2. According to the majority opinion, the Twenty-First Amendment does not constitute an "independent constitutional bar" to the conditional grant of federal funds. What is the rationale supporting this finding?

____

____

____

____

3. In her dissent, Justice Sandra Day O'Connor says that the National Minimum Drinking Age Amendment is not "reasonably related to the purpose for which the funds are expended." How does she justify her position?

4. Do you find the Court's decision in this case a reasonable one? Should the national government have the authority to pressure states to raise their drinking age to 21 despite the specific language of the Twenty-First Amendment?

EXERCISE 2.5 RECONFIGURING STATE BOUNDARIES

BACKGROUND

The distribution of power and responsibility between the national and the state governments has been debated throughout American history. In the past decade, the debate has become particularly intense as the Supreme Court has leaned toward locating more power and responsibility in the states.

Clearly the Court has the authority to assign power to state governments. Another way to increase the power of the states in relation to that of the national government is through the reconfiguration of state boundaries. If the fifty states were consolidated into some smaller number of states, the resulting states would wield more power and influence in their relationship with the national government by virtue of commanding larger geographic, economic, and population bases. A consolidation of states would fundamentally alter American federalism and change the terms of the debate over the division of power and responsibility between the national and state governments.

It may seem farfetched to propose the consolidation of states, but three arguments support the idea. First, all but five of the fifty states were admitted to the Union before 1900—the most recent additions, Alaska and Hawaii, in 1959.[9] Current state boundaries were set at the time of each state's admission to the Union: They do not reflect the fundamental political, social, and economic changes that have transformed the United States since. Second, many state boundaries do not accord with the nation's geography. Rarely do state boundaries conform with rivers or mountain ranges, and often they divide landforms arbitrarily, based on little more than the imperatives of surveying. Figure 2.5 shows the linear thinking that defines many state boundaries. Third, reconfiguring state boundaries could bring together people with shared cultural and economic experiences. For instance, many residents of Northern California identify more strongly with and have more in common with residents of the states of Oregon and Nevada than with residents of the central and southern regions of California.

If you think the idea of redrawing state boundaries is whimsical, take a look at journalist Joel Garreau's book and rationale for reconfiguring North America as nine nations.[10] You also might consider the case of Canada, which is larger geographically than the United States yet divided into only ten provinces and two territories.

ASSIGNMENT

1. Read Article IV of the Constitution. In your own words, state the requirements that must be met to reduce the number of states.

---

2. Consolidate the fifty states into ten, grouping together states that share common geographic characteristics. For example, you might consolidate ten existing states on the Great Plains into one. If you prefer, you can use criteria other than or in addition to geography. Those other criteria might include economic similarities or cultural compatibility in demographic characteristics, historical development, or religious affiliation. On the map in Figure 2.5, show the boundaries of your ten states; then briefly explain the criteria you employed. The boundary lines of your new states must follow the boundary lines of an existing state.

---

[9] The other three are Oklahoma (1907), New Mexico (1912), and Arizona (1912).

[10] *The Nine Nations of North America* (Boston: Houghton Mifflin, 1981).

FIGURE 2.5 THE CONTINENTAL UNITED STATES

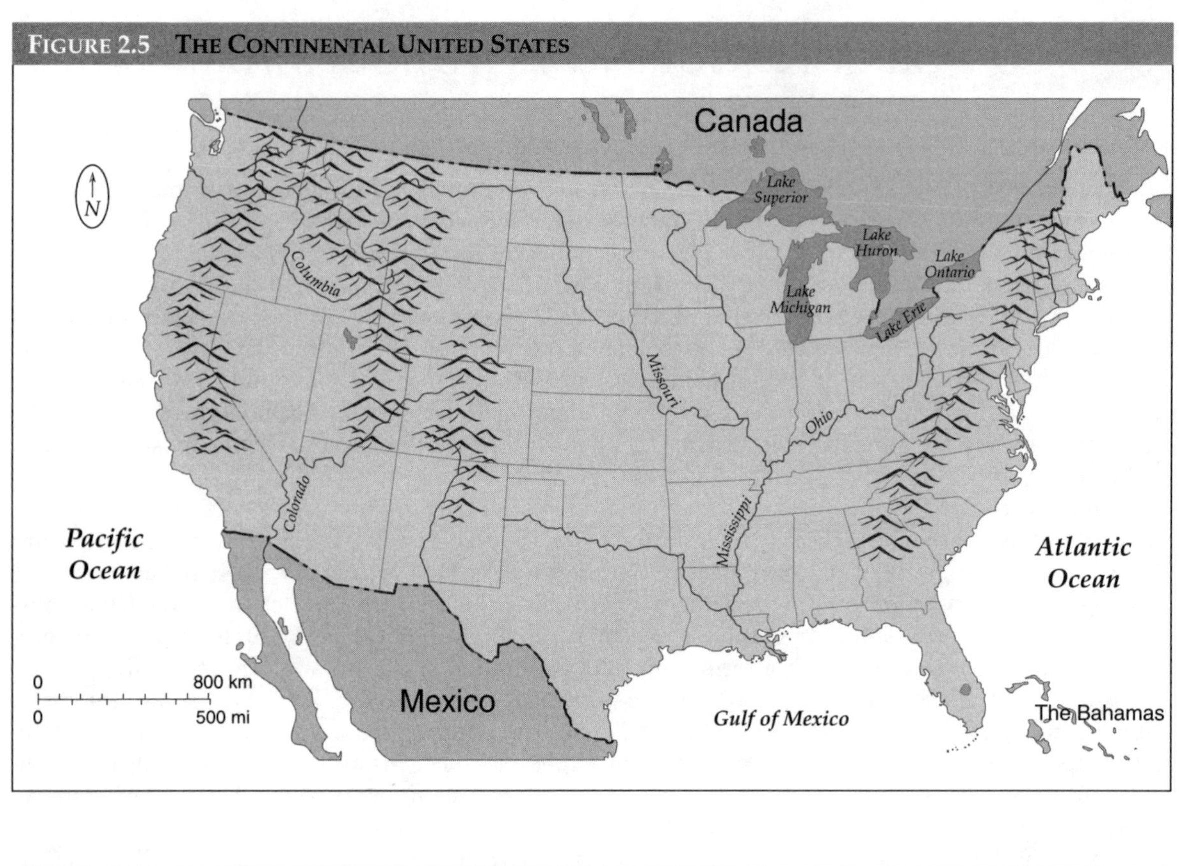

---

3. Would the legislatures in the fifty states likely vote to accept consolidation into ten states? Why or why not?

---

4. Article I, Section 3, of the Constitution requires that every state have two U.S. senators.

a. If the fifty states were consolidated into ten, what change in the size of the U.S. Senate would be required?

---

b. Would the Senate likely vote to consolidate the fifty states into ten? Why or why not?

---

5. What change to the Constitution's requirement that every state have two senators might increase the likelihood of Senate support for consolidating the fifty states into ten?

6. Assume that under any consolidation plan the size of the House remains at 435 members and that House districts continue to contain about 650,000 people.

a. Explain how consolidating the fifty states into ten would affect the political power and prestige of individual members of the House.

b. Would the House likely vote to consolidate the fifty states into ten? Why or why not?

7. a. Choose one of the new states you've created, and calculate its approximate population based on the data in Table 2.5.

b. Assuming that the House stays at 435 members, how many seats in the House would this new state control?

8. Study the amendment process defined in Article V of the Constitution.

a. How many states are needed today to ratify an amendment to the Constitution?

b. What number of states would be needed to ratify an amendment under your consolidation plan? Explain your answer.

TABLE 2.5 POPULATION OF THE STATES, 2000 CENSUS DATA

STATE	POPULATION	STATE	POPULATION
Alabama	4,461,130	Montana	905,316
Alaska	628,933	Nebraska	1,715,369
Arizona	5,140,683	Nevada	2,002,032
Arkansas	2,679,733	New Hampshire	1,238,415
California	33,930,798	New Jersey	8,424,354
Colorado	4,311,882	New Mexico	1,823,821
Connecticut	3,409,535	New York	19,004,973
Delaware	785,068	North Carolina	8,067,673
Florida	16,028,890	North Dakota	643,756
Georgia	8,206,975	Ohio	11,374,540
Hawaii	1,216,642	Oklahoma	3,458,819
Idaho	1,297,274	Oregon	3,428,543
Illinois	12,439,042	Pennsylvania	12,300,670
Indiana	6,090,782	Rhode Island	1,049,662
Iowa	2,931,923	South Carolina	4,025,061
Kansas	2,693,824	South Dakota	756,874
Kentucky	4,049,431	Tennessee	5,700,037
Louisiana	4,480,271	Texas	20,903,994
Maine	1,277,731	Utah	2,236,714
Maryland	5,307,886	Vermont	609,890
Massachusetts	6,355,568	Virginia	7,100,702
Michigan	9,955,829	Washington	5,908,684
Minnesota	4,925,670	West Virginia	1,813,077
Mississippi	2,852,927	Wisconsin	5,371,210
Missouri	5,606,260	Wyoming	495,304
Total	281,424,177*		

*This is the total apportionment population. The populations of the District of Columbia, Puerto Rico, and the U.S. Island Areas are excluded from the apportionment population because they do not have voting seats in the U.S. House of Representatives.

READING 3.4 Elian Gonzalez: A Chronology

November 25, 1999: Elian Gonzalez rescued off the coast of Florida; hospitalized but released the following day to the custody of Lazaro and Angela Gonzalez, Elian's father's uncle and aunt.

November 27: Juan Gonzalez, Elian's father, demands his son be returned to him in Cuba.

December 10: Lazaro Gonzalez applies to the INS for asylum for Elian.

January 5, 2000: An INS commissioner rules that Elian belongs with his father and should be returned to him by January 14 and that the boy does not have the right to an asylum hearing; the Miami relatives ask the INS to reconsider.

January 10: In response to the Miami family's petition for custody, family court judge Rosa Rodriquez grants them emergency custody of Elian.

January 12: Attorney General Janet Reno publicly supports the INS ruling that Elian be returned to his father and states that the Miami court lacks jurisdiction in the matter.

January 19: Lazaro Gonzalez files a lawsuit in federal court challenging the INS ruling.

February 22: A hearing is set to hear the relatives' challenge to the INS ruling that Elian does not have a right to an asylum hearing.

March 21: A U.S. district judge rejects the lawsuit challenging the INS ruling.

April 12: Attorney General Reno meets with the Florida relatives and orders them to turn Elian over to federal officials.

April 22: Federal agents seize Elian from his relatives' home in Miami.

April 27: A circuit court of appeals rejects an emergency motion filed by Elian's Miami relatives claiming that the child has a right to an independent advocate to represent him in judicial appeals.

June 1: A federal appeals court unanimously turns down the relatives' request for an emergency asylum hearing.

June 26: The Miami relatives ask the U.S. Supreme Court to order the government to give Elian a political asylum hearing and to prevent his departure for Cuba.

June 27: The Supreme Court rejects the relatives' appeal.

June 28: Elian flies back to Cuba with his father.

---

1. In the space below, draw a line graph depicting the changes in public opinion indicated by polling question 1 in Table 3.4.

a. List the polling dates on the horizontal (x) axis.

b. List the three possible responses on the vertical (y) axis.

c. Look at the events noted in the chronology for January 5 and March 21. Then, starting on the x axis, draw a vertical line up from each of those dates. Use a broken line.

d. Do either or both of the events appear to have had an impact on the public's opinion about Elian's future?

TABLE 3.4 PUBLIC OPINION: ELIAN GONZALEZ

1. Question: "Do you think it would be in the best interests of the boy to remain in the U.S. to live with relatives who have requested he stay here or for him to live with his father in Cuba, as his father has requested?"

POLL DATE	STAY IN U.S.	LIVE WITH FATHER IN CUBA	OTHER/NO OPINION
12/17/99	45%	45%	10%
1/10/00	36	56	8
1/28/00	33	60	7
4/11/00	31	60	9

2. Question: "How closely have you followed the news about this story?

POLL DATE	VERY CLOSELY	SOMEWHAT CLOSELY	NOT TOO CLOSELY	NOT AT ALL
12/17/99	23%	45%	18%	13%
1/26/00	34	44	17	4
4/4/00	32	46	16	6

3. Question: "As you may know, bills have been introduced in Congress that would grant Elian Gonzalez U.S. citizenship, or give him permanent resident status. Would you favor or oppose passage of such a law by Congress?"

POLL DATE	FAVOR	OPPOSE	NO OPINION
1/26/00	37%	54%	9%
4/2/00	39	51	10

4. Question (April 2, 2000): "Based on what you know and have seen in the news, how sympathetic are you towards each of the following people involved in the Elian Gonzalez situation?"

	VERY SYMPATHETIC	SOMEWHAT SYMPATHETIC	SOMEWHAT UNSYMPATHETIC	VERY UNSYMPATHETIC	NO OPINION
a. Elian Gonzalez	73%	19%	3%	2%	3%
b. Elian's father in Cuba	39	38	10	8	5
c. Elian's relatives in Miami	22	44	15	14	5

5. Question (April 2, 2000): "Do you think the Clinton Administration and Justice Department are making their decisions in this case mostly on the basis of what they feel is in the best interests of Elian Gonzalez or what they feel is in the best interests of U.S. relations with Cuba?"

BEST INTERESTS OF ELIAN	U.S. RELATIONS WITH CUBA	BOTH EQUALLY	NEITHER/ OTHER	NO OPINION
26%	54%	4%	9%	7%

Note: Percentages may not sum to 100 because of rounding.

SOURCE: Questions are from the following polls conducted by the Gallup Organization: December 17, 1999; January 12, 2000; January 28, 2000; April 4, 2000; and April 11, 2000.

2. Taking into account all of the responses in Table 3.4, how consistent was public opinion on what should be done with Elian?

3. What do the responses to question 4 in Table 3.4 suggest about the evenhandedness of the news media in their coverage of the story?

4. a. Which of the polling questions in Table 3.4 seem ambiguous to you?

b. For each question you've identified, describe and explain the source of the ambiguity.

c. Rewrite the question(s) you identified as ambiguous to make them clear.

5. Which polling question in Table 3.4 solicits an opinion on a matter that most Americans probably do not have enough information about to render a thoughtful response? Explain and support your answer.

EXERCISE 3.5 POLITICAL SOCIALIZATION AND UNIVERSITY STUDENTS

BACKGROUND

The study of political socialization investigates how people's attitudes about politics are formed, how those attitudes change over time, and the factors responsible for that change. Parents, educators, religious leaders, and peers are among the primary agents of political socialization because of their power to shape political views, particularly those of young adults. Other likely agents of political socialization include coworkers and the media.

College students have been an intriguing target of political socialization studies. Most college students are ready to question their parents' political views. After all, questioning authority is part of growing up. It also comes of being exposed to new ideas and political viewpoints in classes and elsewhere on campus. In fact, college students are more likely than other groups in the general population to be formulating the political views and attitudes that will guide their political behavior well beyond their college years.

ASSIGNMENT

Reading 3.5 is a condensed report on several studies of the factors that influence the political beliefs of college students. Questions 1 through 3 are based on the reading.

READING 3.5 MEDIA, FACULTY, AND STUDENT SOCIALIZATION

According to the early literature on political socialization, the political attitudes and values of college students are linked directly to their college experience. Moreover, that experience was thought to have a more potent influence on the students than did their background and initial political orientation.

One of the classic studies in the literature of political socialization is the Bennington study.* A major finding that emerged from that study was that peer groups and professors are able to influence students' attitudes in a very different way from their parents. For the most part, the women attending Bennington came from wealthy, conservative families from the northeastern United States. By contrast, the Bennington faculty was decidedly liberal, even leftist, in its political orientation. What social scientist Theodore Newcomb found in his initial 1943 study was that a politically conservative group of female students had changed their political beliefs—had become more liberal—an orientation that was consistent with the rather homogeneous political atmosphere that existed at Bennington during the 1930s. Interestingly, Newcomb and his colleagues interviewed the original sample of five hundred in two follow-up studies: one in 1959–1960 and the second in the mid-1980s. Both of the later studies suggest that the liberal politics adopted by the female students in the 1930s persisted for about five decades.

Following the implications of Newcomb's findings, we undertook a comparative institutional analysis designed to assess the effects of higher education on the political socialization process in the 1990s. The purpose of the study was to investigate several agents of political socialization that are thought to influence the political thinking of college students attending two different state universities.† *Political socialization* is defined as an ongoing process in which the individual is repeatedly exposed to the acceptable political norms through a mixture of indoctrination and learning. A variety of political socialization agents are thought to influence the thinking and behavior of the individual. Among the most important are the family, the media, and especially television, school, and peer-group influence.

READING SOURCE: Adapted from a paper presented by David L. George, Jerry Medler, John Tullius, and David Waguespack at the 1994 meeting of the Western Political Science Association (Albuquerque, New Mexico). The raw data and most of the footnotes in the original essay have been omitted.

* Theodore M. Newcomb, *Personality and Social Change: Attitude Formation in a Student Community* (New York: Dryden Press, 1943).

† Each of these public universities enrolls about 16,000. One is located in Oregon and has a liberal arts focus; the other is in California and has a predominately applied orientation.

In sharp contrast to the 1930s of Newcomb's Bennington study, the 1990s often are described as a media age in which all aspects of society, including politics, have been profoundly affected by the ever-more-intrusive mass media, especially television. Therefore, we included the mass media in the design of this study in an attempt to assess the effects of this agent of political socialization on students of higher education in the 1990s.

Our data are unequivocal. There is no evidence to support the notion that higher education is the source of a new socialization process that replaces previous lessons or values. Although our students tend to be more liberal than their parents, they are not following the lead of their professors. When the similarities between ratings are compared by simple correlations, it is clear that students are most like their parents. In fact, there is virtually no similarity between students and faculty members.

Our data also indicate that the mass media may be greatly overrated as an influence on young adults. Their effect commonly is minimal at best. Interestingly, entertainment programming and music have no effect whatsoever in shaping the political attitudes of young adults.

There were major differences between the Bennington study and the study presented in this paper: The first has to do with markedly different eras. The students Newcomb studied did not have access to the wide array of technological devices that are available to today's students. Second, there are major differences between a small all-women private college and the two public universities that were utilized in the recent study. There is, of course, the issue of size. In addition, both the student body and faculty at Bennington appeared to be far more homogeneous than the student bodies and faculties at the two state universities. The student bodies of both universities are very heterogeneous in terms of socioeconomic status, ethnicity, and political attitudes. Moreover, the faculty at both state universities is far more diverse ideologically than the Bennington faculty.

---

1. What are the independent and dependent variables in the recent state-university study described in Reading 3.5? (For an explanation of independent and dependent variables, see the essay on the tools of political analysis in Appendix 1.)

Independent variable: ____________________

Dependent variable: ____________________

2. In your own words, compare the conclusions of the Bennington study and the state-university study.

____

____

____

____

____

____

3. How do the authors explain the different conclusions of the two studies?

____

____

____

____

____

4. a. Identify the agents of political socialization that have shaped your own political views and attitudes while you've been in college.

____

____

____

b. Rank them below, with number 1 being the most important.

c. Do you think your ranking would apply to most students at your college? Explain your answer.

THE MASS MEDIA

EXERCISE 4.1 THE IMPORTANCE OF DIFFERENT SOURCES OF INFORMATION

BACKGROUND

The importance of free media in a democracy cannot be overstated. One of the characteristics of dictatorships is government control of the media, the means by which those in power regulate the information that is available to the people in print and on the air. By contrast, a hallmark of an open society is public access to an almost unlimited supply of information, even material that is critical of those in power and the policies they advocate.

The significance of a free press in the United States is put clearly in an often-cited passage from a letter written by Thomas Jefferson in 1787: "Were it left to me to decide whether we should have a government without newspapers, or newspapers without a government, I should not hesitate a moment to prefer the latter." The next sentence Jefferson wrote, however, often is overlooked: "But I should mean that every man should receive those papers and be capable of reading them." The essential point Jefferson makes is that a democratic system depends on informed citizens, and that informed citizens have access to different views on public matters.

Throughout the 1800s, the major newspapers in this country were characterized by their adherence to a party line. By the early 1900s, however, most had shed their overt partisan identity—at least in reporting the news. Editorial pages have long been reserved as places where owners and editors can voice their particular views.

Technological advances have changed the way the public learns about local, national, and international affairs from the media. The first radio transmission in 1920 ushered in a period when citizens could get "current" news. By the late 1950s, television was prominent. As the mass media—print and electronic—have matured, the industry has become more professional and more sophisticated. Today the mass media are made up of sixteen hundred daily newspapers, almost eight thousand weekly newspapers, twelve hundred television stations, ten thousand radio stations, and some eleven thousand periodicals.[1]

---

[1] Stephen Hess, "Media Mavens," *Society* 33 (March/April 1996): 75.

Obviously there are many ways by which Americans can obtain competing points of view on public issues. But legitimate questions are being raised about the quality of the media today. For example, some are concerned about the growing trend for big businesses to buy up news outlets: They are afraid that in the near future, those outlets are going to be managed by a few large corporations. And even assuming that the media are able to publish and broadcast without restraint, there's the question of whether citizens will avail themselves of the opportunity to be more informed about public life. Few of us have the time to read several daily newspapers, watch network news regularly, and monitor significant events around the world. Instead, we consume news selectively: We follow the news sources that fit into our schedules and to which we've grown accustomed.

ASSIGNMENT

The data in Table 4.1.1 come from 1995 and 1998 polls on Americans' sources of news. Table 4.1.2 is from a 1998 Gallup Poll on public trust in the media (comparable poll data from 1995 were not available). The questions below rely on information in the tables.

1. From the data for 1995–1998, what conclusions can you draw about the importance of national newspapers as a source of news compared with nightly network news programs?

____

____

____

____

2. Changes in polling data from one period to another reflect changes in the public's attitudes and behaviors. Looking at the data in Table 4.1.1, what conclusions can you draw about where people are most likely to get news on international affairs?

____

____

____

3. Is there a relationship between where people get their news most often and the trust they have in those sources? Explain your answer.

____

____

____

____

4. Give two reasons why you think people trust their local newspapers and television news programs more than they trust major newspapers and network news programs.

____

____

____

____

5. What do the figures in both tables tell us, if anything, about how well informed people are about international, national, and local news?

____

____

____

____

6. What is the relationship between listening to talk radio for news and listeners' perceptions of the accuracy of the information on talk-radio shows?

____

____

____

TABLE 4.1.1 SOURCES OF NEWS AND INFORMATION, 1995 AND 1998

SOURCE	YEAR	EVERY DAY	SEVERAL TIMES A WEEK	OCCASIONALLY	NEVER
Newspapers	1995	52%	17%	27%	4%
	1998	50	13	27	10
Local newspapers	1995	50	12	26	11
	1998	53	15	22	10
Nightly network news programs (ABC, CBS, NBC)	1995	62	20	15	3
	1998	55	19	19	7
Morning news and interview programs on the national TV networks	1995	23	13	34	30
	1998	25	13	27	35
CNN news/ CNN Headline News	1995	23	20	36	21
	1998	21	16	33	29
Local news from television stations in your area	1995	55	18	20	7
	1998	57	15	19	9
National Public Radio	1995	18	11	36	—
	1998	15	12	25	47
Radio talk shows	1995	12	5	21	48
	1998	12	9	21	58
Television talk shows	1995	12	12	47	29
	1998	11	10	40	39
Discussions with friends or family	1995	27	26	42	5
	1998	27	26	41	6

Note: No Opinion not shown.

— = no data.

SOURCE: "Media Use and Evaluation," *Gallup Poll Topics*. 1998 (http://www.gallup.com/poll/indicators/indmedia2.asp).

Table 4.1.2 Trust and the Media (1998)

Source	Yes, Can Trust Accuracy	No, Can't Trust Accuracy	Mixed
Local newspapers	65%	18	15
Nightly network news programs	66	16	2
CNN News/Headline News	66	13	10
Local television/news	73	12	11
National Public Radio	51	20	7
Radio talk shows	23	48	10
Discussions with friends or family	66	16	15

Note: No Opinion not shown.

SOURCE: "Media Use and Evaluation," *Gallup Poll Topics*, 1998 (http://www.gallup.com/poll/indicators/indmedia3.asp)

EXERCISE 4.2 WHAT'S NEWS?

BACKGROUND

Both the electronic and the print media have particular strengths and weaknesses in reporting the news. The major advantage of television news coverage is the ability to bring film footage—and often live coverage of events—to the viewer. In its coverage of wars, fires, killings, and environmental catastrophes, television news delivers an impact that newspapers simply can't. That strength, however, is also a weakness: The breakneck speed of the electronic media, along with the competition to be first with a story, can lead to sensationalistic stories more than reflective reporting. Another weakness plaguing television news is the lack of time for in-depth coverage of national and international events. Most television news shows are formatted for thirty-minute time slots, seven minutes of which are earmarked for commercials. That leaves just twenty-three minutes for actual news reporting. On average, only about ten minutes of that time is devoted to hard news, major events and issues; the rest of the time is spent on human-interest stories and coverage tailored to the age and income of the viewing audience.

To counter public criticism that television news emphasizes negative aspects of society, the major networks and local affiliates increasingly end their news segments with an uplifting story, something designed to reassure viewers that all is not chaos in the nation and the world. You might see firefighters rescuing a puppy stuck in a sewer pipe, learn about a shopkeeper who funds college scholarships for seniors graduating from a ghetto high school, or watch a segment on inner-city kids volunteering to clean up yards and paint houses for their elderly neighbors.

Newspapers, by contrast, are able to provide much broader and deeper coverage. Moreover, newspapers are likely to continue covering stories that have long since disappeared from the evening news broadcasts. The printed word, however, does not capture the attention of people who lack the time or inclination to read a lengthy article on a complicated issue—for example, the state of health care in the United States and the policy options being considered by political leaders. And what with the pace, visual interest, and personalized format of television news, viewers may not even realize that they're not getting the information they need to be informed.

On any given day an astonishing variety of events occurs in the almost two hundred countries around the world. Leaders are selected, overthrown, and assassinated; people take to the streets in protest or rebellion; natural disasters kill thousands and leave many more homeless and hopeless. Newspaper editors and television news producers must decide which stories to cover. Their power to control the flow of news means that editors and producers help determine which issues the public perceives as sufficiently important to require a response from political leaders. In effect, then, editors and producers play a significant role in setting the nation's political agenda.

ASSIGNMENT

Table 4.2 lists the headlines of forty-three stories that appeared one day recently in several major newspapers. In a few cases, the city or state where the story originated is noted. The titles are listed in no particular order. Use the table to answer the following questions.

1. Assume you're the editor of the *New York Times*, a paper that's committed to in-depth, rigorous coverage of the most important national and international events. A large percentage of the *Times*'s subscribers live outside New York City, even outside the United States.

a. Using the numbers in Table 4.2 to identify the stories, choose the twenty stories you would feature. Know that your first five selections would receive front-page coverage; and the second five would appear on inside pages of the first section. The rest of the stories would be relegated to the second section of the paper.

Front page	Inside first section	Second section	
1.	6.	11.	16.
2.	7.	12.	17.
3.	8.	13.	18.
4.	9.	14.	19.
5.	10.	15.	20.

TABLE 4.2 NEWS STORIES

1. Cult Leader in Tokyo Deaths Goes on Trial
2. Medicare Surplus Could Run Dry in 5 Years, Study Warns
3. Small Town Cop, Once a Hero, Pleads Guilty to Stealing-Selling Drugs (Calif.)
4. Sophisticated Techniques Used to Track Global Financial Criminals
5. Discovery of Pottery Vessel, 5400 BC, That Once Held Wine
6. Mad Cow Disease Worries Europeans
7. 2 Americans Still Held Hostage by Muslims in India Since 1990
8. Major Wildfires Go Unchecked in Alaskan Wilderness
9. Lawmaker Alleges Improper Use of FBI by White House
10. Failure of Health Reform Legislation
11. 13-Year-Old Girl Recants Court Molestation Testimony (Wash.)
12. 2 Ohio Men Arrested in Bank Parking Lot with ATM in Their Car
13. L.A. Bus Driver, Vegetarian, Fired for Refusing to Hand Out Free Hamburger Coupons
14. 16th-Century French Fort Found in South Carolina
15. New N.Y. Law to Deal With Physicians Accused of Serious Misconduct
16. Organization of American States Criticizes U.S. for Cuba Embargo
17. Bahrain Coup Suspects Say They Trained in Iran
18. Attempts to Get China to Sign Nuclear Test Ban Treaty
19. Air Pollution in National Parks Worse
20. Rural Health Care Experiment in Mexico a Success
21. HIV Virus Spreading Rapidly in Africa, UN Says
22. Arizona Governor Declares Bankruptcy
23. Can States Ban Same-Sex Marriages?
24. FDA Approves New Drug to Fight Glaucoma
25. War Crimes Trial of Bosnia Serbs in Croatia
26. Promising Program to Curb Teen Crime Unveiled
27. Death of Pol Pot Reported, Ruthless Leader in Kampuchea in 1970s & '80s
28. Earthquake in Columbia Kills 16 in Rural Villages
29. Ex-Rock Group Drummer Dead, Drug Overdose
30. A Profile of Militia Group Supporters in Idaho
31. 5 Marines Die in Helicopter Training Exercise (Tex.)
32. Orphan Bear Cub Found by Hunters, Nursed by Wildlife Officials (Pa.)
33. Pres. Visits Black Church Torched by Arsonists
34. Bulls Win Playoffs
35. Remembering First Woman Judge in Georgia
36. Dispute at Wedding, Minister Shot (N.M.)
37. Chinese Gangs Rule Parts of NYC
38. Burglar Stuck in Chimney (Boston, Mass.)
39. 7 Abused Horses in Care of Animal Shelter (Reno, Nev.)
40. A Look at Forced Youth Labor in Indonesia
41. Gas Prices to Increase Before Decreasing
42. Agric. Price Supports to Drop Over 7 Years
43. New Concerns Voiced About Quality of Urban Water Nationwide

b. Why do you think your top five stories warrant front-page billing?

2. Assume you are the editor of a newspaper in a midwestern community of 67,000 (86,000 within a 25-mile radius). The paper's daily circulation is 45,000; the overwhelming majority of subscribers live in the region. The paper's objective: to provide limited coverage of national and international events and more in-depth attention to local and regional concerns.

a. By story number from Table 4.2, list the twenty stories you would feature in the paper's first and second sections. Again, your first five selections would appear on page 1; and the second five would appear on the inside pages of the first section. The rest of the stories would be relegated to the second section of the paper.

FRONT PAGE	INSIDE FIRST SECTION	SECOND SECTION	
1.	6.	11.	16.
2.	7.	12.	17.
3.	8.	13.	18.
4.	9.	14.	19.
5.	10.	15.	20.

b. Why do you think your top five stories warrant front-page billing?

3. Assume you are a television news producer for a major network. You can run just twelve stories on tonight's evening news. The first one, the lead story, will take up three minutes of airtime, the most devoted to any story. Also assume that you have good film footage to support your lead story.

a. Using the story numbers in Table 4.2, identify and prioritize the top five stories you would choose to run.

1. 2. 3. 4. 5.

b. Explain why you would lead off with the story you chose as number 1 instead of one of the other four you listed.

c. What is your ratio of international to national news coverage?

____

4. Assume you are a television news producer for a local station in central Ohio. You can run just twelve stories on tonight's evening news, and the lead story will take up three minutes of airtime, the most devoted to any story. Also assume that you have good film footage to support your lead story. Using the story numbers in Table 4.2, identify and prioritize the top five stories you would choose to run.

1. 2. 3. 4. 5.

5. Go to the Web sites of the *New York Times* (www.nytimes.com), the *NBC Nightly News* (www.nbcnews.com), a local newspaper, and a local television news broadcast. Does their coverage confirm your choice and ranking of stories for each medium? Explain your answer.

New York Times:

____

____

NBC Nightly News:

____

____

Local newspaper:

____

____

Local television news:

____

____

EXERCISE 4.3 BIAS, ACCURACY, AND THE MEDIA

BACKGROUND

The print and electronic media perform several important functions in contemporary American politics. First, they *inform* the public what elected leaders and government agencies are doing. Second, like watchdogs, they *report* on political wrongdoing and incompetence. Third, they *set the political agenda* by deciding which stories to publish or broadcast and the depth of any coverage. Fourth, the media *frame issues* for consumers of the news by determining the angle a story takes. For example, consider the tax cut President Bush pressed for and Congress enacted in 2001. Some of the media chose to focus on how the wealthiest Americans will benefit the most from the lower tax rates; others chose to focus on how almost all taxpayers will get some sort of tax break. The facts support both angles; but clearly each is more or less supportive of the administration.

The most obvious role of the electronic media in politics is evident every two years, in the weeks leading up to election day. For the past four decades, the public has received most of its information about candidates and their stand on the issues from television—in campaign coverage and paid political advertising. Election-day coverage raises its own issues. In the rush to report results, the electronic media usually predict winners based on exit polls, polls that are conducted well before all the ballots are counted. The accuracy of those polls is one concern: In the 2000 presidential election, the major networks predicted Al Gore would carry the pivotal state of Florida; then they backtracked and said George Bush would take the state's electoral vote; finally, they declared the contest a tossup. Another concern is the impact those surveys have in western states, where exit polls from the East might well influence voter turnout.

The public's reliance on the news for political information has increased over the years; its criticism of the media has increased as well. The nonpartisan Pew Research Center for the People and the Press studied public perceptions of the media in 1985 and 1999. What it found was a 300 percent increase between 1985 and 1999 in people who thought the media was "not professional." In 1999, 38 percent of those surveyed felt the media "hurt democracy"; and 66 percent thought the media tried to cover up their own errors—up 11 percent from 1985. Moreover, 56 percent believed the media were politically biased—an increase of 11 percentage points from 1985.[2]

A word of caution: Just because some segments of the public are critical of the media does not mean that their criticism is always valid. Moreover, there is a tendency for the public to lump the print and electronic media together, blurring the distinctions between them. Still, it's clear the public in 1999 had a less favorable view of the media than it did in the mid-1980s.

One prominent criticism of the media is its perceived emphasis on negative news. Many citizens think critical or negative news stories are evidence of bias. A study of the 2000 presidential campaign looked at both the print and the electronic media's reports on the Bush–Gore contest. It did find that the coverage of the two candidates included more negative than positive references. Interestingly, though, neither candidate was critical of how he was covered in the race.[3]

The public has every right to expect the media to report on politics factually and professionally. Although it isn't necessary for news writers to acknowledge their own biases in their stories, they should make every effort to control for those biases. They also must be alert to the biases of their sources: They should not simply accept the assertions of politicians and government officials about controversial matters without probing for different perspectives. Although most stories are edited to avoid the appearance of bias, that does not mean that the end result is a neutral account of a political campaign, a proposed law, or the actions of a government agency.

A relatively simple way to look for bias in a political news account is to do a content analysis of the story. A *content analysis* is a critical examination of a news story or political document to determine its basic message and concepts. The process involves counting the number of positive and negative references to the subject and the amount of space (or time) given to a particular story. Additionally, one can

---

[2] The Pew survey, "Big Doubts About News Media's Values" is available at www.people-press.org. Click on "Data Archives" and scroll down to the February 25, 1999, survey.

[3] Jeff Leeds, "Study Finds Negative Media Political Coverage—Especially for Gore," *Los Angeles Times,* November 1, 2000, p. A17.

determine the angle of, or approach to, the story and the frequency with which certain adjectives or phrases are used in the story. For example, does a candidate *sail through* or *stumble in* a debate? Is the audience's response to a candidate *enthusiastic* or *cool*? The pictures that accompany the story also can project a positive, neutral, or negative image. A picture from a debate that shows one candidate gesturing to make a point while the other is checking her watch is "saying" that the first candidate is engaged in the contest and that the second candidate is bored by it.

ASSIGNMENT

Two stories appear in Reading 4.3. Both describe President George W. Bush's first trip to Europe after he took office in 2001. Although both stories are fictitious, the events, people, and issues mentioned in them are real. Answer the questions that follow the readings.

READING 4.3 President Bush's First Trip to Europe: Two Accounts

Account 1: The President Introduces Himself to Europe with Mixed Results

George W. Bush and a small entourage of advisers, notably Secretary of State Colin Powell and National Security Adviser Condoleezza Rice, embarked on a whirlwind tour of Europe in the president's first overseas venture since taking office last January. Although the trip was not billed as a summit meeting in which important matters would be discussed, the five-day swing through five countries did allow Mr. Bush to meet with some 20 foreign leaders. As the president said, "I felt it was time I introduce myself to some of America's friends overseas and for some of our allies to hear where we're going on some issues." The trip included stops for brief meetings with leaders in Spain, Belgium, Sweden, Poland, and Slovenia.

By most accounts, European leaders responded warmly to Mr. Bush. He seemed quite at ease in chatting with the officials despite some lapses, such as mispronouncing the last name of Jose Maria Aznar, Spain's president, and his reference to Africa as a nation. He greeted England's Tony Blair as "Landslide," in a good-natured acknowledgment of the prime minister's recent reelection, in which the opposition was crushed.

If the U.S. president was short on substantive remarks, his manner was favorably received. As Italy's Prime Minister Silvio Berlusconi noted, "I'm very pleased to see the human qualities of President Bush," sentiments that were echoed by other officials.

The European press was openly skeptical of the president; and newspaper editorials in France and Spain referred to him as the "toxic Texan," a reference to his refusal to embrace international environmental reforms and to his advocacy of a missile defense system. This is hardly surprising: The European press for the past 25 years has expressed reservations about every U.S. president, including Jimmy Carter, who was called "a peanut farmer," and Ronald Reagan, the "movie star." An estimated 25,000 protesters—largely students—demonstrated during the president's public appearances in Spain, Belgium, and Sweden. Most of the signs they wielded referred to the environment or the fear of a new arms race. Although a few unruly protesters were arrested for throwing eggs and attempting to block a motorcade, most were peaceful. President Bush was warmly received by some 700 students in a speech at Poland's Warsaw University, where he repeated President Clinton's invitation in 1994 for the former Soviet satellite countries to consider joining NATO as a means to "advance the cause of freedom."

The president appeared pleased with the results of the trip. He made it clear that he wanted to maintain the strong ties, political and economic, that had been forged between the United States and Europe in the postwar period. At the same time, Mr. Bush was adamant that his administration would press ahead with the missile defense system and that he would not apologize for his rejection of the Kyoto Protocol, an international policy reached in 1999 to reduce the emissions that are strongly linked to global warming. President Clinton embraced the protocol, but that was in the waning days of his last year in office. Virtually all European leaders oppose the missile defense system, which they believe would lead to a new arms race, and support the Kyoto policy. However, no European country has yet ratified that agreement. The image of a Europe united in the forefront of the effort to protect the environment is not matched by government actions. Still, a reminder that European leaders regard both issues seriously was evident in the open criticism of Mr. Bush by the French president, the German chancellor, and the prime minister of the Netherlands. Usually top officials refrain from openly criticizing their counterparts in friendly countries.

If there was a comment by the president that caused some conservatives in the United States to flinch, it was Mr. Bush's praise for Russian president Vladimir Putin, whom he described as "trustworthy." Mr. Putin, a former agent of the KGB, has been criticized for his harsh crackdown on rebels in Chechnya and his opposition to a free press in Russia. One official in the Bush tour dismissed the remark as a "rookie mistake."

President Bush seemed to establish the rapport he was seeking with the leaders he met. But his future trips, including the forthcoming G-8 meeting in Italy with leaders of the world's largest industrialized nations later this year, will require that he dispel the belief that he is going to lead the United States in a different direction on critical issues without much concern for the opposition of our European allies.

Account 2: Bush Goes Overseas and . . . They Like Him

President Bush enjoyed his fast-paced, "if this is Tuesday, it must be Belgium," five-day swing through five European counties, including Slovenia, a former Soviet republic that was part of Yugoslavia. Previous meetings between U.S. allies and Mr. Bush were confined to one border gathering with Mexico's new president and an overnight trip to Montreal to chat with Canada's prime minister.

The Bush manner—use of colloquial expressions, informality, and a teasing style—was a welcome antidote to the usual pomp and formality that characterize meetings between heads of state. One Dutch diplomat said that President Bush had done his homework but then went on to say that the president seemed to "talk funny." The president enjoyed mugging for the cameras, asking television cameramen about their clothes, and showing off his favorite pair of Texas dress boots.

The meeting, a first, between Mr. Bush and Russia president Vladimir Putin went well. Although Mr. Putin is opposed to a U.S. missile defense system, apparently the topic did not come up; nor did Mr. Bush remind the Russian leader of U.S. concerns about lax Russian control of its extensive nuclear arsenal.

One of the highlights of the trip was President Bush's talk to students at a university in Poland. At one point, Mr. Bush called for an expanded NATO, to include some of the former Soviet satellite countries that are now independent. Mr. Bush spoke in a reassuring manner as he invited other countries to enjoy the freedoms available in western European countries. NATO was created in the early days of the cold war to serve as a political and military buffer against Soviet expansion. But Mr. Bush stated clearly that NATO is not an enemy of Russia today.

President Bush was able to avoid most protesters at the meetings. On several occasions, unkempt young people yelled what sounded to be obscenities at the president. But overall, it was Bush's bon-vivant style that foreign leaders will likely remember most from the visit. President Clinton forged strong personal friendships with several of the leaders while he was in office; and it is only a matter of time before Mr. Bush's frontier openness enables him to do the same. If nothing else, Mr. Bush's image improved. Some European officials initially were concerned that the president lacked legitimacy given the election controversy.

The president did not make any blunders; he was able to answer tough questions without resorting to notes or whispered conversations with advisers; and he seemed quite comfortable in the public sessions and private meetings.

Mr. Bush says he is looking forward to the next round of meetings, which will occur later this year in Italy and elsewhere, as the leaders of the industrialized nations gather to discuss global economic conditions. Mrs. Bush, at her husband's side in Europe this week, will undoubtedly travel abroad with the president in the future. Mrs. Bush and some of the wives of the other dignitaries used their time to visit schools and to shop between brief walks through a number of museums. Although Mrs. Bush is more reserved than her husband, her personality, like his, is sure to win new friends.

1. a. Which press account is more favorable to President Bush?

b. Which words or phrases support your position?

2. Why is the other account more balanced than the one you noted in question 1? What words or phrases support your choice?

3. a. What is the difference in how the student protesters are described in the two accounts?

b. How might that difference affect readers' perceptions of the protesters?

4. Identify three words in each account that could indicate a reporter's bias or coloring of the president's visit.

Account 1: ____________________

Account 2: ____________________

EXERCISE 4.4 HOW DO YOU WANT YOUR NEWS: HARD OR SOFT?

BACKGROUND

Newspeople make a distinction between hard and soft news. *Hard news* is news about public issues or events that are vital to the nation's well-being. *Soft news* refers to human-interest stories and stories about sports celebrities and Hollywood stars.

Because it's a three-dimensional medium (sound, sight, and movement), television is much better equipped to deliver entertainment news than either newspapers or magazines. The upshot? Network television's coverage of the news is increasingly diluted—some would say contaminated—by matters that are hardly newsworthy. That dilution was addressed at a forum of the Committee of Concerned Journalists in 1997. Although entertainment has long been a part of news shows, many are concerned that news broadcasters are surrendering their traditional role—reporter of facts—to peddle entertainment. That transformation has increased the profits of the companies that own the network stations, something that all-news and hard-news formats failed to accomplish. As one journalist cum professor put it: "We must still have a bit of cachet left with the public, because [the parent corporations] haven't had the guts yet to rename [the nightly news shows] 'The Westinghouse Evening News,' 'the GE Nightly News,' or 'Disney World News.' Not yet."[4] Westinghouse owned CBS until 1999, when communications giant Viacom bought the network; NBC is owned by General Electric; the Walt Disney Company owns ABC; and CNN is owned by AOL Time Warner.

A by-product of the increase of soft news on network broadcasts is a blurring of the lines between hard and soft news; another is soft news pretending to be hard news. An example: the extensive coverage the national broadcasts gave to a missing student intern in Washington, D.C., who had been linked with a U.S. representative. As the story of Chandra Levy and California Congressman Gary Condit unfolded in mid-2001, there was no evidence that Levy was a victim of foul play; yet her disappearance without a word to family or friends led many to conclude that she had been abducted and likely killed. The District of Columbia police made it clear that Condit was not a suspect. But the fact that he initially denied a relationship with Levy only to admit a "very close" relationship later fueled speculation that his involvement was greater than he acknowledged. The terrorist attacks on the World Trade Center and the Pentagon on September 11, 2001, sidelined the Levy–Condit story. (It surfaced again, briefly, in March 2002, when Condit lost his primary bid to run for an eighth term in Congress.) But skeptics had been asking well before the terrorist strikes why Levy warranted so much more coverage than that given to other young women who had disappeared recently in the nation's capital. The blunt and obvious answer: The public loves sexual scandal, especially when the participants are a young woman and a prominent older man.

Newspapers also mix entertainment with hard news, though not with the dexterity of television news programs. In 1998, for instance, many newspapers posted a boxed section on their front pages to document the progress of baseball players Mark McGwire and Sammy Sosa toward breaking the home-run record set in the early 1960s by Roger Maris and Mickey Mantle. (As it turned out, McGwire broke the record first, Sosa tied it, and then McGwire extended Maris's 61 home runs in a season to 70; McGwire's record was broken in 2001, when Barry Bonds hit 73 home runs.) One critic wondered if this sports story was significant enough to merit front-page coverage. His answer: Newspaper editors knew that a high percentage of their readers was following the record-setting story.[5]

Actually, newspapers began cutting back their coverage of international news after the Vietnam War ended, in 1975. More reductions were made in overseas bureaus following the dissolution of the Soviet Union in 1991. Overall, coverage of international news stories dropped by as much as 80 percent in a twenty-year period.[6] That trend appears to have reversed itself as a result of the terrorist attacks on the World Trade Center and the Pentagon. CNN Chairman Walter Isaacson said the attacks would help

[4] Richard Reeves, "News of Entertainment/Entertainment as News," Committee of Concerned Journalists, 1997 (www.journalism.org/ccj/resources/USCreports.htm)

[5] J. Polumbaum, "News for the Culture: Why Editors Put Strong Men Hitting Baseballs on Page One," *Newspaper Research Journal*, Spring 2000, pp. 23–39.

[6] David Shaw, "Foreign News Shrinks in Era of Globalization," *Los Angeles Times*, September 27, 2001, p. A20.

b. Are there differences in those groups between CNN and the other networks? Explain and support your answer.

____

____

____

____

5. a. Go to the library and find the topic of the cover story in *Time, Newsweek,* and *U.S. News & World Report* for the current week and the past three weeks. Enter the topics in the table below.

MAGAZINE	ISSUE			
	THIS WEEK'S	FROM LAST WEEK	FROM TWO WEEKS AGO	FROM THREE WEEKS AGO
Time				
Newsweek				
U.S. News & World Report				

b. Write a paragraph in which you compare hard versus soft news as reflected in the cover stories of the three weekly news magazines. (Did the magazines all run the same cover story in any given week? Looking at the cover stories, can you find differences in national or international emphasis, culture, sports, celebrity focus, or the like?)

____

____

____

____

____

____

____

EXERCISE 4.5 TELEVISION'S INFLUENCE ON U.S. FOREIGN POLICY

BACKGROUND

Public opinion, news coverage, and U.S. foreign policy have been intertwined since the beginning of the Republic. George Washington, for example, faced a public energized by the partisan newspapers of the day and divided over whether the United States should tilt in its foreign policies toward Britain or France. In 1898, the popular press whipped up public enthusiasm for war with Spain, and the clamor eventually forced President William McKinley's hand. Television and newspaper coverage of the Vietnam War was pivotal in turning public opinion against the war and in forcing Presidents Lyndon Johnson and Richard Nixon to abandon their hopes for victory over the forces of North Vietnam.

No medium can match the potency of television in shaping public opinion on foreign policy. The immediacy of the images delivered by television resonates deeply with viewers, who respond by asking for action. Political leaders, sometimes oversensitive to public opinion, can find it difficult to resist public pressure to act. The upshot? A rush to action and poorly conceived American initiatives abroad.

In 1994, the House of Representatives Committee on Foreign Affairs convened a hearing to examine the impact of television on U.S. foreign policy. The committee chairman, Lee Hamilton (D–Ind.), opened the hearing by noting that technological advances—from satellites to cellular phones—bring "vivid images of conflict and deprivation" from strife-torn areas around the world into Americans' homes. According to Hamilton, these

> televised images quickly become a central part of the foreign policy debate. They affect which crises we decide to pay attention to or which we ignore. They affect how we think about those crises, and I have little doubt these televised pictures ultimately affect what we do about these problems.

Hamilton also called attention to television's impact on the nation's political leaders, stating that television coverage of events and crises abroad "encourages policymakers to react quickly, perhaps too quickly, to a crisis. It allows the media to set the agenda."[8]

During the hearing, panelists and committee members cited American actions in Somalia as an example of television's influence on U.S. foreign policy. In 1992, network news programs began to carry scenes of starvation in Somalia, a nation wracked for years by civil war and drought. Many American viewers were horrified, and they demanded that the U.S. government act to relieve the suffering. Later that year, the United States announced its support for a multinational humanitarian relief effort in Somalia. The role of the United States expanded months later when efforts to disarm Somali warlords began. After Bill Clinton inherited the operation, U.S. soldiers were ambushed in Mogadishu, and television news broadcast pictures of a dead American soldier being dragged through the streets of the Somalian capital. Public support for the relief effort plummeted, and U.S. troops were withdrawn early in 1994.

That same year, television coverage of events in Haiti captured the public's attention. Jean-Bertrand Aristide had been elected president of Haiti in 1990 but was prevented from taking office by the military and his political enemies. Thousands of Haitians attempted to flee the turmoil, heading for Florida in crude boats and makeshift rafts. Television coverage aroused public concern, which in turn put pressure on President Clinton to stabilize the situation. Clinton dispatched several thousand American troops to Haiti to install Aristide as the rightful president and restore order on the island. The president intervened not only to bring order to a chaotic situation but also to uphold U.S. commitments to the United Nations and U.S. promises to support democracy abroad.

Television coverage of the crises in Somalia and Haiti heightened public concern and generated pressure for presidential action. In both cases, Congress was less than enthusiastic about the interventions, and public support for them—never very strong—quickly eroded.

---

[8] U.S. House Committee on Foreign Affairs, *Hearings on Impact of Television on U.S. Foreign Policy*, 103d Cong., 2d sess., April 26, 1994.

ASSIGNMENT

Reading 4.5 is a condensed version of the statement read by Ted Koppel at the hearing conducted by the Committee on Foreign Affairs on the impact of television on U.S. foreign policy. Koppel, a thirty-year veteran of the broadcast industry, hosts ABC's *Nightline,* a public-affairs program that began in 1980 following the seizure of American embassy personnel in Iran. Refer to the reading to answer the questions that follow it.

READING 4.5 STATEMENT OF TED KOPPEL, ANCHOR, ABC NEWS NIGHTLINE

Thank you, Mr. Chairman.

You have invited us here today to respond to a number of thoughtful questions, some of which are easier to answer than others. For instance, the perception that U.S. foreign policy sometimes shifts in direct response to television coverage—you suggest Somalia and Bosnia as examples—and you ask: "Is that a correct perception?"

The easy answer is: "Of course." Indeed, I am inclined to believe that you intended the question to be all but rhetorical. We would not be here this morning if you and the other members of this committee did not think that television has, in certain instances, had an impact on the government's conduct of foreign policy.

Beyond that, I think there is a reasonable inference to be drawn that you do not think it to be a good idea. Well, neither do I.

It is not, however, a new phenomenon; indeed, it predates the invention of television. When British newspapers reported on the problems of "Chinese Gordon" in Khartoum, public response was such in London that the British government felt obligated to dispatch a relief force under the command of General Kitchener.

Outside factors tend to influence the formation of foreign policy, to a greater or lesser degree, in almost direct proportion to the amount of credible information and policy direction that a government otherwise makes available.

To the degree, in other words, that U.S. foreign policy in a given region has been clearly stated, and adequate, accurate information has been provided, the influence of television coverage diminishes proportionately.

To state that premise in reverse, television's influence increases in regions where an administration has (a) failed to enunciate a clear policy and/or (b) has done little or nothing to inform the American public on the dangers of intervention or failing to intervene. . . .

Prior to the appearance of the first television pictures from Somalia, for example, the Bush administration had done little or nothing to marshal public support for any kind of massive aid operation. It is probably fair to say that the relief operation came together when it did, in part because U.N. Secretary General Boutros-Ghali had been pushing for it for months, in part because President Bush saw an opportunity to perform a great humanitarian act between the time of his November defeat and the inauguration of President-elect Clinton, and in large measure because of intense public reaction to the horrific television pictures of starvation and total anarchy in Somalia that were being shown in this country.

In fairness, the Bush administration did clearly state the mission and the terms. It tried, though, to finesse the issue of how it would deal with the warlords and their huge arsenals; and that, of course, ultimately led to the disorienting image of a retired U.S. admiral, who was heading the United Nations mission, directing a manhunt for General Aideed in a manner that may have reflected U.S. policy at the time. Certainly it no longer reflected U.S. policy once we began seeing television pictures of a dead U.S. Ranger being dragged through the streets of Mogadishu.

Neither the Bush nor the Clinton administration had clearly addressed the issue of what Washington would do in the event of U.S. casualties. Nor had it laid the groundwork for explaining to the American public why such a price might be necessary. . . .

READING SOURCE: "Impact of Television on U.S. Foreign Policy," Hearing, Committee on Foreign Affairs, House, 103rd Congress, 2nd Session, April 26, 1994.

The point, Mr. Chairman, and it is equally applicable to Haiti and Bosnia . . . is that when an administration fails to set forth a clear agenda of its own, it will become the prisoner of somebody else's. For example, I have nothing but admiration for the courage, commitment, and dedication of Randall Robinson, who is now beginning the second week of a hunger strike to protest America's policies in Haiti. But if U.S. policy toward Haiti is right, it should not be changed because of Mr. Robinson's hunger strike. And if that policy is wrong, then changing it now will amount to doing the right thing for the wrong reason. . . .

The absence of a clearly formulated and enunciated policy is like a vacuum. It will be filled by whatever is available, Congressmen having themselves publicly arrested in response to the leadership of a committed activist, voices from the loyal opposition, or, for that matter, television reports, which often contradict reality as presented by administration spokespeople.

In a vibrant democracy like ours, each of these factors will always have some influence; but when a policy and its consequences have not been adequately explained, an informational vacuum will have been created that gives an even greater resonance to those who bear no real responsibility for carrying out U.S. foreign policy.

You ask whether television executives consider the impact of their reporting on foreign policy? Rarely. Should they? In my opinion, almost never.

I realize that still sounds like a revolutionary concept, even though its foundations were laid nearly two hundred years before the advent of television. But we, who report on events, should not be policymakers. We have a responsibility to be fair, accurate, and even-handed; but only in the areas of instances when lives, for example, are clearly and unambiguously at risk should we be expected to take the consequences of our reporting into account.

Should we, for example, have refrained from showing pictures of starving Somalis because it might lead to U.S. intervention and because that intervention could then lead to the death of American personnel? What if we had not shown those pictures? Should we be prepared then to take the responsibility for losing the hundreds of thousands of lives that were reportedly saved by the operation? Should we refrain from showing the American public what is happening now in Rwanda because that might lead to U.S. or U.N. intervention? Or is the argument the very reverse? Should we not have shown that Ranger's body being dragged through the streets of Mogadishu, because now we are disinclined to intervene when perhaps we should?

With all respect, Mr. Chairman, it is our function to inform, it is your function to consider, debate, advise, consent, fund or not fund; and it is the function of the executive branch to make decisions and carry out foreign policy.

No doubt, the seed of satellite communication and the acquired sophistication of both friends and adversaries in using that technology to their own best advantage require a great deal of further attention. Ultimately, though, it boils down to the same thing: If an administration has thought its own foreign policy through, and is prepared and able to argue the merits and defend the consequences of that policy, television and all its new technologies can be dealt with. If, on the other hand, the foreign policy is ill conceived and poorly explained, then it does not much matter whether the news arrives by satellite or clipper ship . . . eventually, the policy will fail.

---

1. a. According to Koppel's testimony, under what conditions is U.S. foreign policy most likely to be influenced by television coverage?

____

____

____

b. Under what conditions is it least likely to be influenced?

____

____

____

2. What arguments does Koppel make to support his position that television executives should rarely if ever consider the impact of their network's reporting on foreign policy?

____

____

____

____

____

____

3. Challenge Koppel's position by making at least one argument that television executives should consider the impact of their network's reporting on foreign policy.

____

____

____

____

____

4. a. Identify one reason why U.S. policymakers should consider American public opinion in the formulation of U.S. foreign policy.

____

____

____

b. Identify one reason why policymakers should minimize the role of public opinion in the formulation of U.S. foreign policy.

____

____

____

5. In his statement, Koppel refers to the "television pictures of a dead U.S. Ranger being dragged through the streets of Mogadishu." In your judgment, are network executives acting responsibly by showing this type of footage on television? Explain and support your answer.

____

____

____

____

____

6. Koppel's testimony should be evaluated within the larger context of congressional hearings. Congressional hearings are used to investigate problems or issues of concern to Congress; they often indicate that Congress is considering corrective action on those problems or issues. The hearings generally are held before a congressional committee, and the testimony for and against legislative action is given by individuals and representatives of interest groups.

a. Although in his testimony Koppel does not address the possibility of corrective legislative action, what would his position on the issue be?

b. What indications do you find in Koppel's testimony that he wants to protect the interests of major television networks?

CHAPTER

5

POLITICAL PARTIES AND ELECTIONS

EXERCISE 5.1 RETROSPECTIVE VOTING IN THE PRESIDENTIAL ELECTION OF 2000: WHY WASN'T IT THE ECONOMY?

BACKGROUND

The sign in Bill Clinton's campaign headquarters read "It's the economy, stupid." Clinton's advisers used the message to keep the candidate focused on the economic recession of 1990–1992—an issue that worked for Clinton and against his opponent, George Bush Sr. Clinton's advisers knew what pollsters, political pros, and political scientists believe to be true: The candidate of the incumbent president's party wins when the economy is good and loses when the economy is bad. Right or wrong, the American people tend to credit the president's party for economic prosperity and blame the president's party for economic hard times. That is especially so when an incumbent president is running for reelection. Witness Jimmy Carter's loss in 1980, Ronald Reagan's victory in 1984, Bush Sr.'s defeat in 1992, and Clinton's win in 1996.

Political scientists remind us that a large percentage of voters, primarily those without strong party ties and without strong ideologies, tends to swing back and forth between the two major parties' presidential candidates according to the voters' assessment of the economy. In what political scientists call *retrospective voting,* swing voters ask themselves the question Reagan posed to voters in 1980: "Are you better off now than you were four years ago?"

Well before the 2000 election, political scientists had concluded that Vice President Al Gore would beat George W. Bush handily, with an average margin of victory of 6 percent of the two-party vote (that is, excluding the vote for minor-party candidates). Those political scientists insisted that both objective and subjective indicators of economic performance favored Gore, the candidate of the incumbent president's party, especially given his position as vice president during the previous six years of economic expansion. They clung to that conventional wisdom even in the face of tracking polls that showed the race was extremely close.

The political scientists were proved wrong in November. Although Gore did eke out a statistically insignificant popular-vote victory over Bush (50.2 percent of the two-party vote), Gore's margin fell well below predictions, and the electoral vote landed Bush in the White House (see Exercise 8.1). Political scientists had a number of explanations for the failure of their predictive models.[1] Among the most common were the following:

- Gore, in trying to distance himself from Clinton, failed to run on the administration's economic record, thereby allowing Bush to showcase his own agenda. Gore's error in judgment may have leveled the playing field.
- By the late summer of 2000, the media were giving attention to signs of an economic downturn. Economic statistics and consumer-confidence polls showed no indication of an economic downturn, but increasingly negative stories about the economy may have helped Bush.
- An incumbent president running for reelection in a period of economic prosperity benefits to some extent because voters perceive that he has been in charge of the economy. Voters may be less inclined to give the same credit to the incumbent's vice president, who seems linked to economic conditions only indirectly.
- The Clinton scandals deprived Gore of at least a number of politically moderate but culturally conservative voters who had supported either H. Ross Perot or Clinton in 1992 and 1996.

ASSIGNMENT

This exercise asks you to explore exit-poll data and maps of the electoral vote in the presidential elections of 1996 and 2000. Questions 1 through 3 are based on Table 5.1.1, a comparison of the presidential races in 1996 and 2000. Questions 4 through 6 are based on Table 5.1.2, selected exit-poll data from the Gore–Bush race of 2000.

1. In presidential elections, candidates win by appealing to moderate and independent voters, the voters in the middle of the political spectrum. The reasons are threefold. First, a plurality of American voters identify themselves as moderate (approximately 40 percent in most surveys), and a majority identify themselves as neither strongly liberal nor strongly conservative (approximately 60 percent in most surveys). Second, the number of independents—those who vote on the basis of individual candidates' qualities instead of their party affiliation—is increasing, running as high as 40 percent in some surveys. Third, moderate and independent voters are most likely to swing back and forth from election to election between the two major-party candidates; liberals routinely vote Democratic, and conservatives consistently vote Republican. The common wisdom is that presidential candidates who run a middle-of-the-road campaign are more likely to win than those who appeal to the parties' liberal and conservative core voters, people who vote for the party's candidate no matter what. Do the comparative data in Table 5.1.1 support the common wisdom? Explain your answer.

2. Since the 1980s, political pundits have talked and written about a gender gap at the polls—women are more likely to support Democratic candidates and men are more likely to support Republican candidates. To what extent was a gender gap evident in 1996 and in 2000?

[1] See "Al Gore and George Bush's Not-So-Excellent Adventure," *PS*, March 2001, pp. 7–58.

TABLE 5.1.1 PRESIDENTIAL VOTE, 1996 AND 2000

VOTERS' TRAITS/ PERCEPTIONS	1996 VOTERS (PERCENT)	CLINTON VS. DOLE (PERCENT)	2000 VOTERS (PERCENT)	GORE VS. BUSH (PERCENT)
Male	48	43 vs. 44	48	42 vs. 53
$50,000–$75,000 annual income	21	47 vs. 45	25	46 vs. 51
Republican	35	13 vs. 80	35	8 vs. 90
Independent	26	43 vs. 35	26	44 vs. 45
Moderate	47	57 vs. 33	50	53 vs. 43
Conservative	33	20 vs. 71	30	16 vs. 82
Most important issue:				
Education	12	78 vs. 16	14	51 vs. 44
Medicare	15	67 vs. 26	7	58 vs. 40
Most important quality:				
Cares about us	9	72 vs. 17	12	63 vs. 30
Family better off than 4 years ago?				
Same	45	46 vs. 45	38	34 vs. 60
Better	33	66 vs. 26	50	61 vs. 34
Voted for Perot in 1996			6	29 vs. 58

SOURCE: All exit-poll data are from MSNBC (www.msnbc.com/m/d2k/g/polllaunch.asp).

3. One test of retrospective voting is the question "Is your family better off (or the same or worse off) than it was four years ago?" What do the data in Table 5.1.1 suggest about retrospective voting in 1996 versus 2000?

4. From Table 5.1.2, what evidence do you find suggesting that a Clinton factor worked against Gore?

5. Again, looking at Table 5.1.2, what evidence do you find that the economy did not work as well for Gore as political scientists predicted it would?

TABLE 5.1.2 PRESIDENTIAL VOTE, 2000

		VOTED FOR	
VOTERS' TRAITS/PERCEPTIONS	VOTERS (PERCENT)	GORE (PERCENT)	BUSH (PERCENT)
White	82	42	53
Black	10	90	8
Hispanic/Latino	6	62	33
Married	66	44	52
Unmarried	34	56	37
Voted for Clinton in 1996	46	81	14
Voted for Dole in 1996	32	8	90
Most important issue:			
Economy/jobs	19	62	34
Taxes	13	15	80
World affairs/defense	12	42	50
Social security	13	58	39
Most important quality:			
Understands complex issues	13	75	18
Honest	24	16	78
Strong leader	13	35	63
Caring about people	12	63	30
Which is more important to you: issues or personal qualities?			
Issues	62	55	40
Leadership/personal qualities	35	35	61
Both can serve effectively as president (Is Bush competent?)	30	29	68
Is Gore too liberal?	43	8	90
Is Bush too conservative?	34	84	10
Condition of economy:			
Excellent	20	71	25
Good	66	45	51
Not so good	11	30	64
Poor	2	30	58
Clinton as a person?			
Favorable	36	82	13
Unfavorable	60	26	69
Vote today:			
To express support for Clinton	10	93	5
To express opposition to Clinton	18	5	90
Clinton not a factor	70	54	41

Note: Gore–Bush percentages do not sum to 100 because votes for minor-party candidates are not shown.

SOURCE: All exit-poll data are from MSNBC (www.msnbc.com/m/d2k/g/polllaunch.asp).

6. Some political scientists fault Gore for positioning himself too far left of center on the political spectrum, abandoning the middle ground that Clinton had claimed in 1992 and 1996. Does the evidence support that contention? Why or why not?

___

___

___

7. Find the state-by-state results of the Clinton–Dole race in 1996 and the Gore–Bush race in 2000. (A good source for the results is the National Archives and Records Administration's electoral college Web site, www.nara.gov/fedreg/elctcoll/index.html#top. On the maps on the following page, shade the states Clinton won in 1996 and Gore won in 2000; leave the states Dole took in 1996 and Bush took in 2000 blank.

8. a. Which states did Gore lose in 2000 that Clinton won in 1996?

b. Which states did Gore win in 2000 that Clinton lost in 1996?

c. Do you find a pattern in, or see anything in common among, the states that Clinton won but Gore failed to capture?

9. a. Which states did the Republican candidates (Dole and Bush) win in both 1996 and 2000?

b. What characteristics are shared by the states (region, size of electoral vote, and the like) most likely to support Republican candidates?

c. If you were the Republican Party chair, would you be confident about Republican prospects in future presidential elections? Why or why not?

CLINTON–DOLE 1996

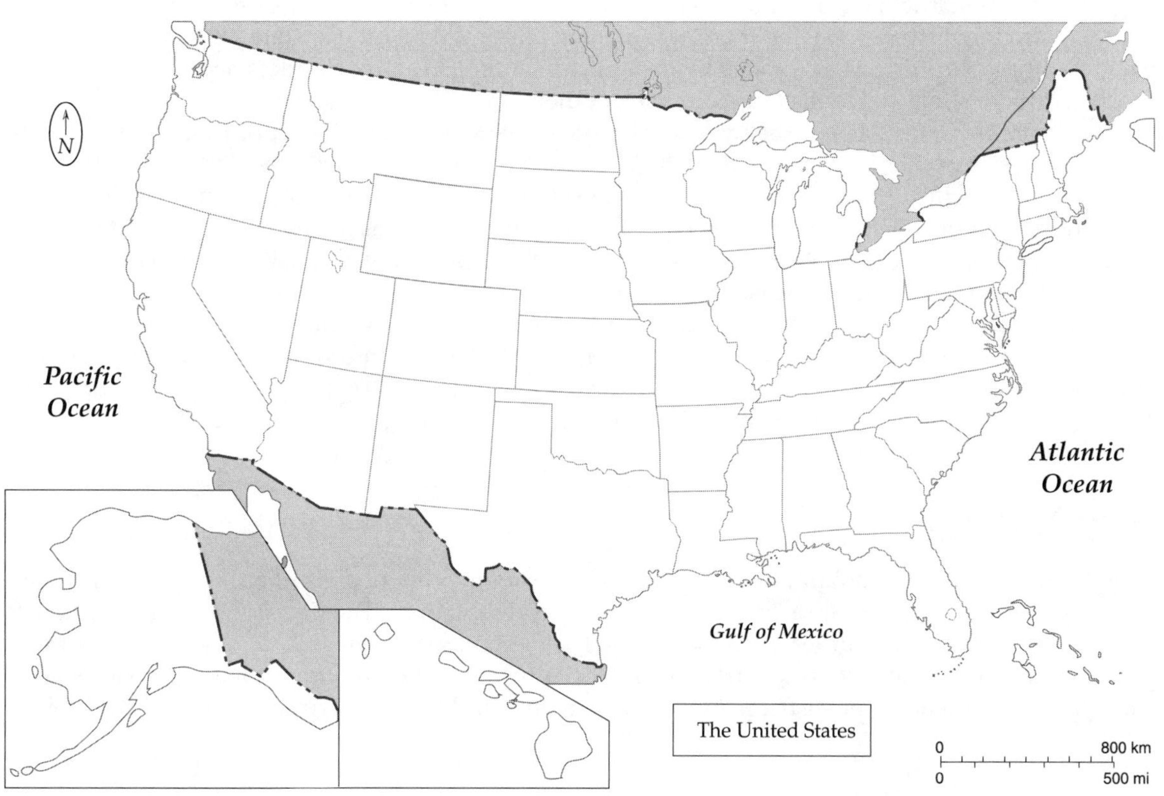

GORE–BUSH 2000

EXERCISE 5.2 GERRYMANDERING

BACKGROUND

Legislative districts come in many shapes, from the compact and ordinary to the distended and bizarre. Describing a legislative district forged in the shape of a salamander, the editor of the *Boston Centinel* in 1811 coined the term *gerrymander*. The governor of Massachusetts who approved the salamander-shaped district was Elbridge Gerry. Since then, Gerry's name has been used to describe the drawing of exotically shaped legislative districts designed to yield political advantage for parties, interests, or incumbents.

Representation in the House is population based: States are awarded seats in the House proportionate to their population. The framers of the Constitution recognized that the population of the new nation would increase and would shift geographically. To ensure that representation in the House reflects changes in the population, Article I, Section 2 of the Constitution requires that a census be taken every ten years to determine the reapportionment (or reallocation) of seats in the House among the states.

The addition or subtraction of one or more of a state's seats in the House usually requires redrawing the boundaries of many—if not all—of the House districts in the state. The task of redistricting is carried out by the state's legislature, which also redraws the boundaries of state legislative districts when necessary. If a state's legislators and governor cannot agree on a redistricting plan, the task reverts to the courts or to an impartial commission. In 1964, the Supreme Court ruled in *Wesberry v. Sanders* and *Reynolds v. Sims* that the equal protection clause of the Fourteenth Amendment requires that legislative districts be roughly equal in population.

State legislators are keenly aware that redistricting is inherently a political process, easily turned to the advantage of a particular political party or interest, or to incumbents generally. In drawing new legislative districts, geographic coherence, demographic similarity, and fairness often are subordinated to political objectives. Those who argue that gerrymandering smacks of politics and self-interest should recognize that redistricting is as much about politics as is a vote on the floor of the House. Although some redistricting schemes may be more egregiously political than others, state legislators are aware that awarding political power to voters by grouping them in legislative districts necessarily works to the advantage of some and to the disadvantage of others.

The Supreme Court has been reluctant to become entangled in the thicket of redistricting, ruling that the matter is political and best left to the citizens and their representatives. In *Davis v. Bandemer* (1986), the Court ruled that a partisan gerrymander might violate the equal protection clause of the Constitution, but that the particular gerrymander before the Court was not extreme enough to require action. No gerrymander has yet been struck down by the Court solely on the grounds that it gives an advantage to one party at the expense of another.

Gerrymandering has been used to dilute the political power of racial minorities, a practice the Supreme Court ruled against in *Gomillion v. Lightfoot* (1960). More recently, racial criteria have been employed to create legislative districts with voting majorities of ethnic or racial groups. The Supreme Court has ruled by narrow majorities in recent years that race cannot be the deciding factor in redistricting.

ASSIGNMENT

To better understand the politics of gerrymandering, examine the model in Figure 5.2.1. This hypothetical state is entitled to four seats in the House of Representatives. The figure shows one method of dividing the state into its four legislative districts. The method seems *nonpartisan,* undertaken without regard for the interest of a political party. The state has been divided into four quadrants, each square and equal in population. The districts appear to be neutral and impartial, drawn solely on the basis of simple geometry.

FIGURE 5.2.1

	D	D	R	R	R	R	R	D	R	D	
	D	D	R	R	R	R	R	R	D	D	
A	D	D	R	R	R	R	R	D	D	D	B
	D	D	R	R	R	R	R	D	R	R	
	R	D	R	R	R	D	R	D	R	R	
	R	D	D	D	D	D	D	D	D	R	
	R	R	D	D	D	D	D	R	D	R	
C	R	R	R	R	D	R	D	D	R	D	D
	R	D	R	D	D	R	D	R	R	D	
	R	R	D	R	D	D	R	R	R	R	

In answering the questions below, assume that Republicans and Democrats vote by party affiliation, that they never cross party lines, and that they never vote for minor-party candidates. Voting behavior in the real world, of course, is much less certain and much more complicated. But this simple model of voting behavior should make the politics of gerrymandering easier to grasp.

1. a. Under the districting plan in Figure 5.2.1, what percentage of the state's seats in the House does the Republican Party command?

b. What percentage of seats does the Democratic Party command?

2. Under the districting plan in Figure 5.2.1, how does each party's share of the state's seats in the House compare to the percentage of Republican and Democratic voters in the state?

3. Under the districting plan in Figure 5.2.1, which party's hold on its seats is more secure? Explain your answer.

4. Under the districting plan in Figure 5.2.1, in which district(s) is the incumbent most secure? Explain your answer.

5. a. The figure on the following page shows the same distribution of voters shown in Figure 5.2.1. Gerrymander the state to give a greater margin of protection to the two Republican and two Democratic incumbents who hold the seats under the districting plan in Figure 5.2.1. In other words, alter the district boundaries so that the Republican incumbents in Districts A and B and the Democratic incumbents in Districts C and D can count on a greater margin of victory on election day. In drawing the boundaries of the new legislative districts, be sure that each district contains 25 voters and that each district is continuous (unbroken) in shape.

D D R R R R R D R D
D D R R R R R R D D
D D R R R R R D D D
D D R R R R R D R R
R D R R R D R D R R
R D D D D D D D D R
R R D D D D D R D R
R R R R D R D D R D
R D R D D R D R R D
R R D R D D R R R R

b. Fill in the table below with the former margin of victory and the new margin of victory for each incumbent.

INCUMBENT (DISTRICT)	FORMER MARGIN OF VICTORY	NEW MARGIN OF VICTORY
A		
B		
C		
D		

6. a. The figure below shows the same distribution of voters shown in Figure 5.2.1. Gerrymander the state to give the Republican Party the maximum possible number of the state's four seats in the House. In drawing the boundaries of the new legislative districts, be sure that each district contains 25 voters and that each district is continuous (unbroken) in shape.

D D R R R R R D R D
D D R R R R R R D D
D D R R R R R D D D
D D R R R R R D R R
R D R R R D R D R R
R D D D D D D D D R
R R D D D D D R D R
R R R R D R D D R D
R D R D D R D R R D
R R D R D D R R R R

describe themselves either as independents (unaffiliated with a party) or as only nominally committed to a political party.

ASSIGNMENT

The three readings below provide different views on political parties and their role in the American political system. Questions 1 through 4 are based on the readings.

READING 5.4.1 JAMES MADISON, "FEDERALIST NO. 10" (1787)

Complaints are everywhere heard from our most considerate and virtuous citizens, equally the friends of public and private faith, and of public and personal liberty, that our governments are too unstable; that the public good is disregarded into conflicts of rival parties; and that measures are too often decided not according to the rules of justice and the rights of the minor party, but by the superior force of an interested and overbearing majority. However anxiously we may wish that these complaints had no foundation, the evidence of known facts will not permit us to deny that they are in some degree true. It will be found, indeed, on a candid review of our situation, that some of the distresses under which we labor have been erroneously charged on the operation of our governments; but it will be found, at the same time, that other causes will not alone account for many or our heaviest misfortunes; and, particularly, for that prevailing and increasing distrust of public engagements, and alarm for private rights, which are echoed from one end of the continent to the other. These must be chiefly, if not wholly, effects of the unsteadiness and injustice with which a factious spirit has tainted our public administrations.

By a faction, I understand a number of citizens, whether amounting to a majority or minority of the whole, who are united by some common impulse of passion, or of interest, adverse to the right of other citizens, or to the permanent and aggregate interest of the community. . . .

The latent causes of faction are thus sown in the nature of man; and we see them everywhere brought into different degrees of activity, according to the different circumstances of civil society. A zeal for different opinions concerning religion, concerning government, and many other points, as well of speculation as of practice; an attachment to different leaders ambitiously contending for pre-eminence and power; or to persons of other descriptions whose fortunes have been interesting to the human passions, have, in turn, divided mankind into parties, inflamed them with mutual animosity, and rendered them much more disposed to vex and oppress each other than to cooperate for their common good.

READING 5.4.2 ALEXIS DE TOCQUEVILLE, "POLITICAL PARTIES" (1835)

Tocqueville, a Frenchman who traveled in the United States from May 1831 to February 1832, offers a classic analysis of public, civic, and private life in the vibrant young democracy.

In the United States, the majority governs in the name of the people, as is the case in all countries in which the people are supreme. This majority is principally composed of peaceable citizens, who, either by inclination or by interest, sincerely wish the welfare of their country. But they are surrounded by the incessant agitation of parties, who attempt to gain their cooperation and support. . . .

The deeper we penetrate into the inmost thought of these parties the more do we perceive that the object of the one is to limit, and that of the other to extend, the authority of the people. I do not assert that the ostensible purpose, or even that the secret aims, of American parties is to promote the rule of aristocracy or democracy in the country; but I affirm that aristocratic or democratic passions may easily be detected at the bottom of all parties, and that, although they escape a superficial observation, they are the main point and soul of every faction in the United States. . . .

READING 5.4.2 SOURCE: From Richard D. Heffner, ed., *Democracy in America* (New York: New American Library, Mentor Books, 1956), pp. 87–91.

It sometimes happens, in a people amongst whom various opinions prevail, that the balance of parties is lost, and one of them obtains an irresistible preponderance, overpowers all obstacles, annihilates its opponents, and appropriates all resources of society to its own use. . . .

This is what occurred in America; when the democratic party [under Andrew Jackson] got the upper hand, it took exclusive possession of the conduct of affairs, and from that time, the laws and the customs of society have been adapted to its caprices. At the present day, the more affluent classes of society have no influence in political affairs. . . .

It is easy to perceive that the rich have a hearty dislike of the democratic institutions of their country. The people form a power which they at once fear and despise.

READING 5.4.3 WILLIAM CROTTY, "A CONCLUDING NOTE ON POLITICAL PARTIES AND THE FUTURE" (1984)

The number of voters participating in elections continues to decline to levels low enough for us to begin to question the relevance, and should the trend continue, the stability and representativeness of American political institutions. The picture is bleak. The electorate has become polarized between the higher socioeconomic-status adults who remain in the 30 to 50 percent of the eligible population that continues to participate in elections and the lower socioeconomic-status groups who have dropped out. . . .

The weakening of party ties has led to a volatile electorate, one capable of swinging from overwhelming majorities in favor of one party to, in the space of one election to the next, competitive outcomes or equally decisive margins in favor of the other party. . . .

To make matters worse, the voters' perceptions of the political parties and of the government continue to be negative. . . .

Lower socioeconomic groups face enormous difficulties in reincorporating themselves into the electorate without the political parties to encourage, organize, and guide their efforts. One of the strengths of the two-party system has been its ability to include large elements of the less well-off in their coalitions. . . .

The campaign functions of the parties have been seriously undercut. Parties are no longer the principal funders of campaigns. [Political action committees] are. Television has replaced the party as the dominant communicator of political information . . . . As the campaign functions of parties have decreased, the role of money—and hence of those who can supply it—has increased dramatically. The new politics is an expensive one.

---

1. One political scientist has said that "the political parties created democracy and . . . modern democracy is unthinkable save in terms of the parties."[4]

a. Which of the three authors would agree with that statement? Explain your answer.

____

____

____

____

b. Which author would most strongly disagree with the statement? Explain your answer.

____

____

READING SOURCE: William Crotty, *American Parties in Decline* (Boston: Little, Brown, 1984), pp. 275–283.

[4] E. E. Schattschneider quoted in William Crotty, *American Parties in Decline* (Boston: Little, Brown, 1984), p. 283.

2. Write a one-sentence thesis statement for each of the three readings. (A *thesis statement* describes the major proposition or argument put forth by an author or speaker.)

James Madison, "Federalist No. 10": ____________________

Alexis de Tocqueville, "Political Parties": ____________________

William Crotty, "A Concluding Note on Political Parties and the Future": ____________________

. All three authors agree that differences among political parties often reflect social and eco- omic differences among groups in society, particularly differences in income, wealth, education, and cial status. *Class* is a term used to describe divisions in society according to those differences. Go to Directory of U.S. Political Parties at www.politics1.com/parties.htm. Search the directory to locate olitical party that clearly is class based, that is organized around social and economic differences l has as its purpose promoting the interests of a particular class over those of other classes. Explore t party's Web site to confirm its class orientation. Then, in the space below, name the party and ex- p n why you identified it as class based.

4. se the Directory of U.S. Political Parties (www.politics1.com/parties.htm) to locate a party that c rly is not organized around class and does not promote the interests of a particular class over those ther classes. Go to and explore that party's Web site. Then, in the space below, name the party l explain why it is not class based.

5. Usi the Directory of U.S. Political Parties (www.politics1.com/parties.htm), estimate the number of litical parties in the United States today. Then explain why there are so many parties at a time when st voters are reluctant to strongly embrace a political party.

EXERCISE 5.5 SOFT MONEY AND CAMPAIGN FINANCE REFORM

BACKGROUND

In the wake of the Watergate scandal, Congress amended the Federal Election Campaign Reform Act. Reacting to the discovery of vast amounts of illegal money in the Nixon reelection campaign of 1972, Congress created a system of federal matching funds for candidates in presidential primaries who limit themselves to contributions of $250 or less. Those contributions are matched dollar for dollar from the Presidential Election Campaign Fund. Congress also created a system of public funding for the major-party candidates in presidential elections: Candidates who accept public funds cannot raise other money. The decision to accept federal matching funds (primary) and public funds (general election) is voluntary. For example, in the Republican primary campaign of 2000, candidate George W. Bush refused matching funds because he already had raised $60 million on his own. The rationale for the presidential campaign reforms: The less candidates have to rely on soliciting funds from rich donors and special interests, the more responsive and accountable they are to the American people. Congress also placed limits on the amount an individual, an organization, and a political party can contribute directly to candidates in a congressional campaign. The purpose here was to limit undue influence by wealthy donors and by special interest groups.

No legislative reform is perfect. The federal election reforms of 1974 adversely affected the interests of many individuals and organizations. They responded by contesting the provisions of the new law and searching for loopholes in the language of the legislation. In 1976, in *Buckley v. Valeo,* the U.S. Supreme Court handed opponents of the new legislation a partial victory by ruling that political campaign contributions in some cases are protected speech under the First Amendment to the Constitution. That decision led to the proliferation of *independent spending campaigns,* in which individuals or political action committees (PACs) raise money independently, advocating on behalf of candidates for federal office. That money remains unregulated, beyond the scope of campaign finance restrictions, so long as there is no collaboration between the candidates' campaigns and the independent spending campaigns. Consequently, many campaign ads, especially attack ads, in federal campaigns actually are funded by interest groups—the National Rifle Association, for example—not by the candidates' campaign treasuries.

The legislation in 1974 also created the Federal Election Commission (FEC), which was charged with enforcing the reforms. Rulings by the FEC in combination with ambiguous language in the bill opened a major loophole in the system of regulating campaign finance. Candidates, parties, individuals, and interest groups have been able to circumvent restrictions on campaign finance by hiding under the cover of soft money. Understanding the difference between hard-money and soft-money campaign contributions is critical to understanding why the controls Congress thought it had established in 1974 have broken down.

Hard-money contributions are made directly to the campaign of a candidate running for federal office and are limited by the reforms of 1974. The limitations depend on who's giving (an individual, a PAC, or the Presidential Election Campaign Fund) and on who's receiving (a congressional candidate, a presidential candidate, or a political party). For example, the law limits hard-money contributions by PACs to congressional candidates to $5,000 per candidate per election.

Soft-money contributions are not limited in any way. These funds flow from donors to the national party organizations and are spent by the parties on activities that benefit each party's candidates. For example, soft money can be used to pay for *issue ads,* ads designed to rally support for or opposition to a particular candidate but that do not specifically tell voters how to cast their ballots. An example: "Congressman X has voted consistently against environmental protection. Call Congressman X and tell him that the environment needs protection." Soft money also can be funneled to state party organizations, which were not covered by the 1974 reforms, and then spent by those organizations on behalf of the party's national candidates.

The upshot? Presidential candidates can have their cake and eat it too: They agree to limit themselves to the hard money from the federal treasury, but they supplement that hefty sum with soft money raised and spent by the political parties on their behalf. Public funding of presidential campaigns was meant to free presidential candidates from the rigors of fundraising so that they could take their cases directly to the people; instead, presidential candidates now spend much of their time raising soft money for their party organizations. This is the loophole that gained notoriety in Clinton's White House, where soft-money donations were raised in exchange for Lincoln Bedroom sleepovers and Oval Office coffee klatches.

After the 1996 campaign, which had witnessed ever more sophisticated attempts to circumvent the intent of the 1974 campaign reforms (see Reading 5.5.1), voices of reform began to be heard. Chief among them was that of Senator John McCain (R-Ariz.), who made campaign finance reform the center of his battle for the Republican presidential nomination against the eventual winner, George W. Bush. On April 2, 2001, McCain's Bipartisan Campaign Reform Act, cosponsored with Senator Russ Feingold (D-Wis.), the so-called McCain–Feingold bill, was passed by the Senate, to the surprise of many and to the consternation of President Bush. The bill appeared dead when opponents in the House of Representatives used procedural obstacles to prevent a vote. But outrage over the collapse of Enron revived the bill, and it finally passed the House by a narrow margin. On March 27, 2002, a reluctant President Bush signed into law the first major campaign finance reform since 1974. The president then flew off to raise funds for the 2002 congressional elections before new limits on fundraising were scheduled to take effect (in November 2002). In the meantime, several lawsuits were filed in federal courts challenging the constitutionality of the law.

ASSIGNMENT

Reading 5.5.1 offers perspective on the extraordinary growth in the amount and use of soft money in the Clinton campaign of 1996. Clinton and the Democrats did not invent soft money, but they were remarkably inventive in finding new ways to raise it. Questions 1 through 3 are based on Reading 5.5.1.

READING 5.5.1 Anthony Corrado, "The Origins and Growth of Party Soft Money Finance"

In 1996, the importance of soft money in the financing of federal elections became even more important as parties changed their strategies and began to place great emphasis on the use of candidate-specific issue ads. This type of advertising provided parties with a way of using soft money to pay for broadcast advertisements that featured specific federal candidates. The parties claimed that such ads are not federal campaign expenditures and thus may be paid for with a combination of hard and soft money funds. In 1996, the use of such ads, which was spurred by the efforts of the Democratic Party to bolster President Clinton's prospects for reelection, was a bold innovation. It represented an aggressive effort to push the limits of the FECA restrictions and circumvent the contribution and spending limits established by the law. In the intervening four years, this innovation has become the standard practice, the new norm for how party committees conduct their federal election campaigns, and a major factor in the continued growth in soft money fundraising.

While the national party organizations had engaged in issue advocacy advertising before the 1996 election cycle (most notably during the debate over Clinton's health care proposal in 1993 and 1994), they had never before used such advertising in a significant way to promote a presidential candidate in an election year. But the Democrats quickly recognized the potential benefits of this tactic. The ads could be used to deliver the President's basic message, policy proposals, and accomplishments, and criticize Dole's views and record. As long as they avoided the "magic words" [*vote for* or *vote against*] that would trigger the definition of express advocacy, none of the monies spent in this way would be considered "campaign spending" under the law. It was a loophole in the federal regulatory scheme that the Democrats aggressively exploited.

For a year, July 1995 to June 1996, the Democratic National Committee (DNC) and state Democratic party organizations spent millions of dollars on ads designed to promote Clinton's reelection. These spots were mostly aired in smaller media markets where broadcast time is less expensive. The party avoided states where Clinton had won by large margins in 1992, and also stayed away from those states

READING SOURCE: Quoted in the *Congressional Record*, April 2, 2001, pp. 3252–3255.

where they felt Clinton had no chance—Texas, the Great Plains states, and Southern Republican strongholds like South Carolina and Virginia. In the fall of 1995, the Democrats ran ads attacking the Republican budget that covered 30 percent of the media markets in the country. By the end of December, they had run ads presenting Clinton as a leader seeking tax cuts, welfare reform, a balanced budget, and protection for Medicare and education programs. In all, the Democrats had aired pro-Clinton ads in 42 percent of the nation's media markets by January 1, 1996, at a cost of $18 million, none of which was drawn from Clinton's campaign committee accounts. . . .

The DNC's spending and Clinton's financial advantage entering the final months of the campaign encouraged the Republican National Committee (RNC) to adopt a similar strategy as soon as its presidential nominee was determined. In May, one day after Dole decided to resign from the Senate to devote himself to full-time campaigning, RNC Chair Haley Barbour announced a $20 million issue advocacy advertising campaign that would be conducted during the period leading up to the Republican national convention in August. The purpose of this campaign, said the chairman, would be "to show the differences between Dole and Clinton and between Republicans and Democrats on the issues facing our country, so we can engage full-time in one of the most consequential elections in our history." In essence, the campaign was designed to assist Dole, who had basically reached the public funding spending limit, by providing the additional resources needed to match Clinton's anticipated spending in the remaining months before the nominating conventions. . . .

This innovative form of party spending essentially rendered the contribution and spending limits of the FECA [Federal Election Campaign Act], at least as far as the party nominees were concerned, meaningless. So long as the party committees did not coordinate their efforts with the candidate or his staff, and did not use any of the "magic words" that would cause their spending to qualify as candidate support, they were free to spend as much as they wanted from monies received from unlimited sources on activities essentially geared towards influencing the outcome of the presidential race. Given the availability of polling data and other sources of political information, it was simple for the parties to develop ads that reflected their respective candidates' major themes and positions or presented the most effective attacks against the opponent.

Moreover, this use of soft money gave the party organizations a strong incentive to solicit greater and greater amounts of soft money. Instead of spending one dollar in hard money for a dollar in advertising done as a coordinated expenditure, a national party committee could spend one dollar in hard money to trigger, on average, an additional two dollars in soft money spending. So they were able to get more advertising out of their hard money by relying more heavily on soft money. The tactic thus placed a premium on soft money fundraising. A party could spend as much soft money as it could raise because these funds could be used for television advertising that featured the candidate and essentially advocated his election. . . .

By the election of 2000, national party soft money [is] being used to finance every aspect of a party's campaign efforts in connection with federal contests. It is being used to produce candidate-specific ads and broadcast them on television and radio. It is being used to produce campaign materials such as posters and slate cards that feature federal candidates. It is being used to register, identify, and mobilize voters who support federal candidates. It is therefore not surprising that the party committees have made soft money fundraising a major component of their financial efforts. In every election cycle since its advent, the majority of soft money has been allocated to finance activities that are primarily designed to influence the outcome of federal elections.

---

1. What major innovation in the use of political advertisements did Clinton and the Democrats employ? That is, how did they manage to skirt the law without breaking it?

____

____

____

____

2. a. How does the author support his contention that the Federal Election Campaign Act (FECA) reforms have been rendered meaningless?

____

____

____

b. Do you agree with the author's assertion? Explain and support your answer.

____

____

____

____

3. a. Does the article support the widely held perception that federal regulatory bodies, the FEC among them, are overzealous? Explain your answer.

____

____

____

b. Does it support the widely held view that problems in campaign finance could be corrected by vigorous enforcement of existing law? Explain your answer.

____

____

____

____

4. Reading 5.5.2 consists of selected provisions of the McCain–Feingold bill. Assume you're a writer for the evening news program on one of the major television networks. You are told by the producer to write a summary of the bill for a two-minute piece on the Senate's passage of the bill. You figure you need to limit the summary to a paragraph, about 150 words. Your key points: how the bill abolishes soft money and how it places limitations on the use of issue ads. Write your summary in the space on page 105.

READING 5.5.2 Soft Money Provisions in the Bipartisan Campaign Reform Act of 2000 (S 27) (McCain–Feingold)

TITLE I—REDUCTION OF SPECIAL INTEREST INFLUENCE

SEC. 101. SOFT MONEY OF POLITICAL PARTIES.

(a) IN GENERAL—Title III of the Federal Election Campaign Act of 1971 (2 U.S.C. 431 et seq.) is amended by adding at the end the following:

SEC. 323. SOFT MONEY OF POLITICAL PARTIES.

(a) NATIONAL COMMITTEES—

(1) IN GENERAL—A national committee of a political party (including a national congressional campaign committee of a political party) may not solicit, receive, or direct to another person a contribution, donation, or transfer of funds or any other thing of value, or spend any funds, that are not subject to the limitations, prohibitions, and reporting requirements of this Act.

(2) APPLICABILITY—The prohibition established by paragraph (1) applies to any such national committee, any officer or agent of such a national committee, and any entity that is directly or indirectly established, financed, maintained, or controlled by such a national committee.

both legal and political means. The public is understandably concerned not only about the outcome but also about how it is achieved.

Whoever takes office in January will, regrettably and not deservedly, enter office with widespread partisan questions about his legitimacy. I believe the next president has earned and should be accorded the respect of all Americans, and a fair chance to lead this great nation. I am confident that we will determine who won Florida, and that he won it fairly. But many aggrieved partisans who supported the losing candidate will not, I fear, be quick to share my confidence. That is the new fact of our political life produced by the incredibly narrow margin of victory in this election, and by the resulting confusion and hard feelings in Florida.

The harsh partisanship of recent years that has contributed to the American people's diminished esteem for public officials could grow worse, causing people's faith in government's ability to serve their needs to decline correspondingly. The next president will have to embark immediately on a series of confidence-building measures that might encourage Congress to help him find bipartisan solutions to difficult national problems, allay the suspicions of half the electorate and give hope to all Americans that, just maybe, those of us privileged to govern America are capable under trying circumstances of putting the nation's interests before our own.

Patriots of both parties have offered sensible suggestions toward that end, from the new president's choosing respected members of the other party to serve in his Cabinet to reconciling, with fair compromises, some of the policy priorities of both parties. But let me offer one measure that I think would greatly enhance the prospects for bipartisan progress on the nation's business, help the new president confound expectations of ineffectiveness and begin restoring Americans' faith in the credibility of their leaders.

When all the money that washed through this election cycle is counted, $4 billion or more will have been spent on federal and state campaigns, half again as much as was spent on all races in 1996. Voter turnout, up slightly from 1996, was still only a little more than half of all eligible voters. Most discouraging was the abysmally low turnout among voters age 18 to 29—just 38 percent.

Clearly, the rushing stream of cash, coming in the form of huge, unlimited contributions known as soft money, has done precious little to encourage participation in our democratic processes. On the contrary, it has increased public indifference and cynicism by, among other things, underwriting much of the negative advertising that is intended to drive down voter turnout.

More troubling than the public's widespread neglect of its most fundamental civic responsibility—voting—is its deeply rooted perception, to the point that it has become part of American folklore, that we elected officials of both parties are so narrowly self-interested that we are incapable of reforming the practices and institutions of our democracy to meet the challenges of our times. Public expectations for government seldom run higher than "Maybe they won't do too much harm."

I am a conservative. I believe it is a healthy thing for Americans to be skeptical about the purposes and practices of public officials and to refrain from expecting too much from their government. Self-reliance is the ethic that made America great. But when healthy public skepticism becomes widespread cynicism bordering on alienation, conservative no less than liberal officeholders should recognize that we share the primary responsibility for convincing Americans that our government still embodies our national ideals. When the people come to believe that their government is so dysfunctional or even corrupt that it no longer serves basic constitutional ends, our culture could fragment beyond recognition.

Many, if not most, Americans believe we in government conspire to hold on to every political advantage we have, lest we jeopardize our incumbency by a single lost vote. They believe we would pay any price, bear any burden, to ensure the success of our personal ambitions, no matter how injurious the effect on the national interest. And who can blame them, when the wealthiest Americans and richest organized interests can make huge donations to political parties and gain the special access to power such generosity confers on the donor.

Were Congress and the president to agree to ban soft money—the five- and six-figure checks that have effectively nullified all legal limits on campaign contributions—even while agreeing to reasonable increases in hard money limits imposed more than a quarter of a century ago, we would remove one of the most durable impediments to achieving bipartisan consensus on reforming entitlements, the tax code, government spending, HMOs, education and tort law.

Soft money's practical effect on the legislative process is to elevate both parties' allegiance to their chief donors above our ideological distinctions and our responsibility to address pressing national priorities. Indeed, partisan deference to core supporters of both parties is a less significant cause of legislative gridlock than is our gratitude to the chief underwriters of our campaigns in elections that are less a battle of ideas than a test of political treasuries.

Trial lawyers, as major donors to the Democratic Party, prevent any reform of HMOs that doesn't encourage explosive increases in costly litigation, while insurance companies, as major donors to the Republican Party, resist even basic fairness in empowering patients to make life-or-death decisions regarding their own health care. Surely, we can do better than this.

When the new Congress and the new president are sworn in, let us remove soft money's negative effect on bipartisan cooperation and on our public discourse. Let us take this sensible first step on the long road to convincing the American people that their representatives in Congress and their president are patriots first and partisans second.

Argument Against, by Michael Barone

"How a company lets its cash talk," read the headline in the *New York Times* last month. The article tells of the success of Samuel Heyman, chairman of GAF Corp., in lobbying for a bill to change rules for asbestos lawsuits. The article sets out how much money Heyman, his wife, and GAF's political action committee have contributed to politicians and both parties, and the reader is invited to conclude that this billionaire and his company are purchasing legislation that will benefit them. Money buys legislation, which equals corruption: It is the theme articulated by John McCain in the Senate last month and on the campaign trail; it was the premise of questions asked at the Hanover, N.H., candidates' forum and taken for granted by Al Gore and Bill Bradley in their responses; it is the mantra of countless editorial writers and of Elizabeth Drew in her book *The Corruption of American Politics.*

But is it true? Careful readers of the *Times*'s "cash talks" story can find plenty of support for another conclusion: "Strong arguments talk." For 25 years, asbestos lawsuits have transferred billions of dollars from companies that once manufactured asbestos (it was banned in the 1970s) to workers exposed to asbestos and their lawyers. Asbestos causes sickness in some but by no means all workers many years after exposure. But most claimants who have recovered money are not sick and may never be, while those who are sick must often wait years for claims to be settled. The biggest winners in the current system are a handful of trial lawyers who take contingent fees of up to 40 percent and have made literally billions of dollars.

Heyman's proposal, altered somewhat by a proposed House compromise, would stop nonsick plaintiffs from getting any money, while setting up an administrative system to determine which plaintiffs are sick and to offer them quick settlements based on previous recoveries. The statute of limitations would be tolled, which means that nonsick plaintiffs could recover whenever signs of sickness appear. Sick plaintiffs would get more money more quickly, while companies would be less likely to go bankrupt; 15 asbestos firms are bankrupt now, and the largest pays only 10 cents on the dollar on asbestos claims. The two groups who lose, according to Christopher Edley, a former Clinton White House aide and Harvard Law professor who has worked on the legislation, would be nonsick plaintiffs who might get some (usually small) settlements under the current system and the trial lawyers who have been taking huge contingent fees.

These are strong arguments, strong enough to win bipartisan support for the bill, from Democratic Sens. Charles Schumer and Robert Torricelli as well as House Judiciary Chairman Henry Hyde and Senate Majority Leader Trent Lott. You would expect Hyde and Lott to support such a law, but for Schumer and, especially, Torricelli, it goes against political interest: Torricelli chairs the Senate Democrats' campaign committee, and Democrats depend heavily on trial lawyer money. One can only conclude that Schumer and Torricelli were convinced by strong arguments, which was certainly the case for Democrat Edley, who was writing about cases long before Heyman's bill was proposed. When McCain charged that the current campaign finance system was corrupt, Republican Mitch McConnell challenged him to name one senator who had voted corruptly. Certainly no one who knows the issues and the senators involved would have cited this case.

. . . When a government affects the economy, when it sets rules that channel vast sums of capital, people in the market economy are going to try to affect government. They will contribute to candidates and exercise their First Amendment right to "petition the government for a redress of grievances," i.e., lobby. Both things will continue to be true even if one of McCain's various campaign finance bills is passed. There is no prospect for full public financing of campaigns (Gore says he's for it, but he has never really pushed for it); one reason is that it leaves no way to prevent frivolous candidates from receiving public funds. (Look at the zoo of candidates competing for the Reform Party's $13 million pot of federal money.) Reformers speak of campaign advertisements as if they were a form of pollution and try to suppress issue ads as if no one but a candidate (or newspaper editorialist) had a First Amendment right to comment on politicians' fitness for office. And to communicate political ideas in a country of 270 million people you have to spend money.

The idea that the general public interest goes unrepresented is nonsense. There is no single public interest; reasonable people can and do disagree about every issue, from asbestos lawsuits to zoo deacquisitions. This country is rich with voluntary associations ready to represent almost anyone on anything; any interest without representation can quickly get some. Even when the deck seems stacked, as it has for trial lawyers on asbestos regulation, there will be a Samuel Heyman with, as Edley puts it, "the moxie to act on his convictions." Money talks, as it always will in a free society. But in America, and on Capitol Hill, strong arguments can talk louder, and do.

Argument in favor: ______________________________

____

Argument against: ______________________________

____

Editorial: ______________________________

____

____

____

____

____

____

____

____

6. a. Using the data in Table 5.5.1, calculate the percentage increase in soft-money contributions by party and election type from 1991 through 2000. Record your answers in the chart on the next page.

TABLE 5.5.1 SOFT-MONEY FUNDRAISING, MAJOR PARTIES, 1991–2000

	ELECTION CYCLE				
FUNDS RAISED BY	**1991–1992***	**1993–1994**	**1995–1996***	**1997–1998**	**1999–2000***
Democratic					
Federal party	$177.7	$139.1	$221.6	$160.0	$275.2
Nonfederal parties**	36.3	49.1	123.9	92.8	245.2
Total	214.0	188.2	345.5	252.8	520.4
Republican					
Federal party	267.3	245.6	416.5	285.0	465.8
Nonfederal parties**	49.8	52.5	138.2	131.6	249.9
Total	317.1	298.1	554.7	416.6	715.7

* Presidential election cycle.

** State party organizations.

Note: Figures are in millions.

SOURCE: All data are from the Federal Election Commission (www.fec.gov).

SOFT-MONEY CONTRIBUTIONS TO	PERCENTAGE INCREASE IN SOFT-MONEY CONTRIBUTIONS, 1991–2000
Democratic Party	
Federal elections	
Nonfederal elections*	
Total	
Republican Party	
Federal elections	
Nonfederal elections*	
Total	

* State and local elections.

b. Referring back to Reading 5.5.1, what likely accounts for the greater increase in soft-money contributions at the state (nonfederal) level?

____

____

____

____

7. a. According to the data in Table 5.5.1, is the accumulation of soft money greater in presidential election cycles (for example, 1999–2000) or in midterm election cycles (for example, 1997–1998)?

____

b. What is the most likely explanation for the difference?

____

____

____

8. Again referring to the data in Table 5.5.1, which political party has been more successful in raising soft money?

____

9. Many observers of Congress assert that party advantage is a better predictor of a roll call vote than principle is. That thinking, applied to campaign finance reform, suggests that members of the party that benefits most from soft money would be less likely to vote against abolishing it. Looking at Table 5.5.2 and your answer to question 8, was political party advantage a good indicator of the roll call vote in the Senate on the McCain–Feingold bill?

____

TABLE 5.5.2 SENATE VOTE ON THE BIPARTISAN CAMPAIGN REFORM ACT (S.27), APRIL 2, 2001

U.S. Senate roll call vote, 107th Cong., 1st sess. as compiled by the Senate bill clerk under the direction of the secretary of the Senate.

YEAS—59	YEAS—59 (continued)	NAYS—41
Akaka (D–Hawaii)	McCain (R–Ariz.)	Allard (R–Colo.)
Baucus (D–Mont.)	Mikulski (D–Md.)	Allen (R–Va.)
Bayh (D–Ind.)	Miller (D–Ga.)	Bennett (R–Utah)
Biden (D–Del.)	Murray (D–Wash.)	Bond (R–Mo.)
Bingaman (D–N.M.)	Nelson (D–Fla.)	Breaux (D–La.)
Boxer (D–Calif.)	Reed (D–R.I.)	Brownback (R–Kans.)
Byrd (D–W.Va.)	Reid (D–Nev.)	Bunning (R–Ky.)
Cantwell (D–Wash.)	Rockefeller (D–W.Va.)	Burns (R–Mont.)
Carnahan (D–Mo.)	Sarbanes (D–Md.)	Campbell (R–Colo.)
Carper (D–Del.)	Schumer (D–N.Y.)	Craig (R–Idaho)
Chafee (R–R.I.)	Snowe (R–Maine)	Crapo (R–Idaho)
Cleland (D–Ga.)	Specter (R–Pa.)	DeWine (R–Ohio)
Clinton (D–N.Y.)	Stabenow (D–Mich.)	Ensign (R–Nev.)
Cochran (R–Miss.)	Stevens (R–Alaska)	Enzi (R–Wyo.)
Collins (R–Maine)	Thompson (R–Tenn.)	Frist (R–Tenn.)
Conrad (D–N. Dak.)	Torricelli (D–N.J.)	Gramm (R–Tex.)
Corzine (D–N.J.)	Wellstone (D–Minn.)	Grassley (R–Iowa)
Daschle (D–S. Dak.)	Wyden (D–Ore.)	Gregg (R–N.H.)
Dayton (D–Minn.)		Hagel (R–Nebr.)
Dodd (D–Conn.)		Hatch (R–Utah)
Domenici (R–N.M.)		Helms (R–N.C.)
Dorgan (D–N. Dak.)		Hollings (D–S.C.)
Durbin (D–Ill.)		Hutchinson (R–Ariz.)
Edwards (D–N.C.)		Hutchison (R–Tex.)
Feingold (D–Wis.)		Inhofe (R–Okla.)
Feinstein (D–Calif.)		Kyl (R–Ariz.)
Fitzgerald (R–Ill.)		Lott (R–Miss.)
Graham (D–Fla.)		McConnell (R–Ky.)
Harkin (D–Iowa)		Murkowski (R–Alaska)
Inouye (D–Hawaii)		Nelson (D–Nebr.)
Jeffords (R–Vt.)*		Nickles (R–Okla.)
Johnson (D–S. Dak.)		Roberts (R–Kans.)
Kennedy (D–Mass.)		Santorum (R–Pa.)
Kerry (D–Mass.)		Sessions (R–Ala.)
Kohl (D–Wis.)		Shelby (R–Ala.)
Landrieu (D–La.)		Smith (R–N.H.)
Leahy (D–Vt.)		Smith (R–Ore.)
Levin (D–Mich.)		Thomas (R–Wyo.)
Lieberman (D–Conn.)		Thurmond (R–S.C.)
Lincoln (D–Ark.)		Voinovich (R–Ohio)
Lugar (R–Ind.)		Warner (R–Va.)

* In May 2001, Senator Jim Jeffords left the Republican Party and became an Independent. That action cost the Republicans control of the Senate.

SOURCE: http://senate.gov/legislative/vote1071/vote_00064.html.

10. Common Cause, a watchdog group, lobbies for legislation and regulations that keep political insiders and special interests from dominating the political system. This group has been at the forefront of those calling for reform of campaign finance. Common Cause maintains a Web site, Soft Money Laundromat (www.commoncause.org/laundromat), a searchable database on contributions to the two major parties. You'll find the answers to this question there.

a. For the 1999–2000 election cycle, list the ten largest soft-money donors to each political party and how much each donor gave. Be sure to list the main donors. (Look for the boldface amounts.)

DEMOCRATIC PARTY	AMOUNT	REPUBLICAN PARTY	AMOUNT
1.		1.	
2.		2.	
3.		3.	
4.		4.	
5.		5.	
6.		6.	
7.		7.	
8.		8.	
9.		9.	
10.		10.	

b. Identify at least one pattern that distinguishes the type of interests donating soft money to Democrats from those donating to Republicans.

____

____

____

c. Click on How to Shut Down the Soft Money Laundromat. What does Common Cause recommend for ending soft money?

____

____

____

____

____

____

____

INTEREST GROUPS

EXERCISE 6.1 THE AMERICAN SHEEP INDUSTRY ASSOCIATION AND WOOL SUBSIDIES: WHY IT'S SO DIFFICULT TO ELIMINATE PORK-BARREL SPENDING

BACKGROUND

Members of Congress often are accused of feathering their own nests—bringing federal dollars home to their districts or states—at the expense of the national interest. Political scientists call this use of federal funds *pork-barrel spending,* implying that the projects are wasteful and serve mainly to enhance the reelection prospects of the representative who is "bringing home the bacon."

Presidents are among the loudest critics of pork-barrel legislation. Because presidents are elected by the entire nation, they have a national perspective on budget priorities. They have less to lose by opposing spending that benefits narrow constituencies. Yet Congress often prevails in battles with the president over pork-barrel spending. Why? Two factors are particularly important in explaining how representatives protect their slice of the federal budget. First, members of Congress who hold positions on key committees and subcommittees have a built-in constituency: the groups whose special interests are protected by the actions of committee and subcommittee members. Congressional committees exercise immense power by determining which bills are left to die in committee and which are forwarded to the full chamber for a vote. And the quid for that quo? The special interests in the representative's district or state render support to the member of Congress at election time. Presidents find it difficult, if not impossible, to break the ties that bind powerful members of Congress to the people back home who are on the receiving end of the pork barrel.

Second, even though most members of Congress have no direct stake in any other member's particular pork-barrel agenda, they often are willing to vote for that agenda to ensure that their own pork-barrel programs are funded. This kind of reciprocal arrangement is called *logrolling.*

ASSIGNMENT

Reading 6.1, a case study of a classic pork-barrel program, points to the resiliency of pork-barrel programs despite the strategies presidents use to attack them. Questions 1 through 4 are based on the reading.

READING 6.1 Wool and Mohair Subsidies

In 1993, President Bill Clinton signed a bill abolishing agricultural subsidies for wool and mohair producers. It was the first subsidy program to be terminated since 1936.* It was a small program by federal standards, costing taxpayers about $100 million per year; but like other federal spending programs, it had powerful defenders in the American Sheep Industry Association (ASI) and in Congress.

The program was created in 1954 under the National Wool Act. Its goal was to provide government funds to the sheep industry, which was in trouble because of increasing imports of lower-cost wool from abroad. The mohair subsidy was added because similar problems plagued the goat industry. Members of Congress found the program appealing for two reasons: First, it allowed them to help an important agricultural interest in a number of districts and states and to earn, in return, the support of many constituents. Second, the program ensured a steady supply of wool for military uniforms. Without a reliable domestic supply, policymakers worried that the Pentagon would have to rely on wool imports from Australia and New Zealand.†

By 1960, the military had stopped classifying wool as a strategic material; still, Congress continued to appropriate money for the program. In 1982 and 1990, the General Accounting Office (GAO), which is responsible for auditing and evaluating the effectiveness of federal programs, issued reports concluding that the program had only limited success in increasing wool production and quality and had not effectively solved the sheep industry's problems. The GAO noted that wool production in the United States actually had dropped since the program's inception. And still Congress continued to fund the program. In fact, the Pentagon's reclassification of wool and the GAO's reports notwithstanding, the sheep and goat lobbies pressured Congress to increase the subsidies. The subsidies seemed to take on a life of their own.

Having pledged during the campaign to do something about rising budget deficits, President Clinton targeted the wool and mohair subsidies, among others, for elimination. Presidents since Jimmy Carter had tried to contain the spiraling cost of agricultural subsidies, but their efforts were blocked by a powerful coalition of interest groups and members of Congress on key committees. The main defenders of the subsidies held seats on the House and Senate agriculture committees, the committees that exercise life-and-death authority over agricultural spending. A particularly ardent defender of the programs was the powerful chair of the House Agriculture Committee, E. (Kika) de la Garza, a Democrat from Texas. Not surprisingly, Representative de la Garza's home state received more subsidies under the wool program than any other state in the nation.

The ties that bind members of Congress to their constituents' interests often are stronger than party loyalty. For this reason Clinton knew that many members of his own party in Congress would resist his efforts to eliminate the wool and mohair subsidies. To overcome that opposition, Clinton adopted a strategy of publicizing the waste in subsidy programs. In an environment of budget deficits, the president was hoping to embarrass proponents of the subsidies and put them on the defensive. He recognized that the more public the issue, the more likely congressional supporters of the subsidies would be accused of "feathering their own nests." The *New York Times* ran a front-page story criticizing the programs, and more critical coverage in the media followed. The negative publicity and some prodding from Clinton induced Senator Richard Bryan (D-Nev.) to assume an outspoken leadership role against the program. Vice President Al Gore lent support to the effort by singling out the wool subsidy program as an example of wasteful government spending in his National Performance Review on reinventing government.

READING SOURCE: Background information from James Risen, "Wool Subsidy's End Shows Vigor of Sacred Cows," *Los Angeles Times*, October 25, 1993, pp. A1, A16.

* Many more were abolished or slashed in the budget-cutting frenzy of the 104th Congress, 1995–1996.

† Many subsidies that seem specious today were justified during the cold war in the name of national security.

With Senator Bryan's help, the Senate voted to abolish the wool and mohair subsidies. The ASI and its congressional allies were furious, but they recognized that they were unlikely to prevail in the face of a determined president with friends in Congress, and widespread media coverage. Defenders of the subsidies, however, did win a reprieve. They managed to save the program for one more year and to have it phased out gradually, ending in 1996. On October 15, 1993, that compromise was approved by voice votes in the House and Senate.

The lobbyist for the ASI, Larry Meyers, had employed every resource at his command to defend the subsidies. Meyers, a skilled and knowledgeable insider, had even moved to Washington, D.C., to lead the battle. He rallied agricultural interest groups with no direct stake in the wool and mohair subsidies to defend the program. (Those groups were willing to lend support because they were afraid that their own subsidies might be next up for termination.) At Meyers's direction, the groups mobilized their members to write letters to key legislators asking that the subsidies be continued. The leaders of those groups met individually with members of Congress and attempted to call in whatever favors they were due. When an interest group mounts a campaign as extensive as the one Meyers mounted, it often wins. This time, however, Clinton and his allies were victorious.

---

1. Identify the combination of factors that made possible the elimination of the wool and mohair subsidies.

2. What sources of power can lobbyists and members of Congress call on to protect government spending programs?

3. There's an old saying in American politics: "Everyone wants a balanced budget, but nobody wants the balancing to be done at his or her expense." Does the wool-subsidy case study support that thinking? Explain your answer.

4. In a compromise between President Clinton and the Republican Congress, wool and mohair subsidies reappeared in the federal budget in 1998. What had happened to the combination of factors—see question 1—that made the elimination of the subsidies possible?

5. Interest groups develop close alliances with the members of Congress who sit on the committees or subcommittees that fund key programs and subsidies; they also establish close relationships with the departments and agencies that implement and administer those programs and subsidies. But those alliances don't stop lobbies from keeping a watchful eye on both Congress and the bureaucracy. The goal of that vigilance: to protect their interests. Go to the Web site of the American Farm Bureau Federation (www.fb.com), and explore the site and its many links. What evidence do you find that the American Farm Bureau Federation is keeping a watchful eye on Congress and the federal bureaucracy?

____

____

____

____

____

6. Because government departments and agencies administer the spending programs authorized by Congress, they have a vested interest in perpetuating those programs. When an agency must defend its services—and its authority—against congressional budget-cutters, the agency's clientele can be valuable allies. Interest groups call on their members to pressure Congress to maintain programs . . . and the groups' benefits. Go to the Web site of the Department of Veterans Affairs (www.va.gov), and explore the site and its many links. Do you find evidence that the department is cultivating its clientele? Explain your answer.

____

____

____

____

____

____

7. A number of watchdog groups are dedicated to battling government waste. One is Citizens Against Government Waste (CAGW). Go to the organization's Web site, at www.cagw.org, to answer these items.

a. Who is CAGW's Porker of the Month, and why was he or she nominated?

____

____

____

b. From the CAGW's home page, click on Pig Book database. Select a state and an appropriation category that interests you. For example, looking at Alabama under the agriculture category, you would find $500,000 in the fiscal year 2001 federal budget for research on peanut-allergy reduction. In the space below, identify two examples of pork-barrel spending. For each example, identify an interest group that would benefit from this slice of the federal pie.

____

____

____

____

____

____

EXERCISE 6.2 INTEREST GROUPS AND LITIGATION

BACKGROUND

It's common to think of interest groups pursuing their policy objectives in legislatures, in government agencies, even in the Oval Office; it's less common to think of them using the state and federal courts to advance their causes. Yet that is exactly what interest groups have been doing, especially since the 1960s. The strategy has been particularly effective for public interest groups—civil rights groups, consumer groups, environmental groups, women's groups—that find themselves at a disadvantage in legislatures, where well-financed, narrowly focused corporate and trade groups most often have the inside track.

An example: *Brown v. Board of Education of Topeka* (1954). The landmark school-desegregation case was financed and litigated by the National Association for the Advancement of Colored People (NAACP). More recently, the Sierra Club and other environmental groups have used the courts to block development plans that they believe violate federal and state laws and regulations.[1] The American Civil Liberties Union (ACLU), which was created to defend civil liberties and rights in the courts, recently obtained injunctions preventing the state of California from enforcing two initiatives.[2]

Litigation sponsored by interest groups is one way for average Americans to achieve equality under the law. Wealthy individuals and corporations have abundant resources to pursue their claims in court; but most Americans lack the means to support the lengthy, expensive process of litigation, especially through the appellate process. Interest groups make litigation possible for those who otherwise would be excluded.

Once the defenders of the status quo realized the advances that civil rights groups and other public interest groups were making in the courts, they tried to deny those groups further access to the courts. One such effort by the state of Virginia resulted in *NAACP v. Button* (1963), which is excerpted in Reading 6.2. In 1956, in reaction to the *Brown* decision, the Virginia legislature had passed a statute that contained a provision (Chapter 33) that made it illegal for an individual to solicit legal business for an organization "which retains a lawyer in any action to which it is not a party and in which it has no pecuniary interest or liability." The intent was to prevent the NAACP and other groups from encouraging citizens to bring suits that would be financed and litigated by the groups. Because the NAACP was the only group in Virginia at that time with an interest in and the resources to pursue desegregation lawsuits, the Virginia statute likely would have shut down future civil rights litigation in the state.

ASSIGNMENT

Refer to Reading 6.2 to answer the questions that follow it.

READING 6.2 FROM *NAACP v. BUTTON*, 371 U.S. 415 (1963)

Mr. Justice Brennan delivered the opinion of the Court:

. . . Chapter 33 as construed and applied abridges the freedoms of the First Amendment, protected against state action by the Fourteenth. More specifically, petitioner [NAACP] claims that the chapter infringes the right of the NAACP and its members and lawyers to associate for the purpose of assisting persons who seek legal redress for infringements of their constitutionally guaranteed and other rights. We think petitioner may assert this right on its own behalf, because, though a corporation, it is directly engaged in those activities, claimed to be constitutionally protected, which the statute would curtail. . . .

[1] See, for example, *Ohio Forestry Association v. Sierra Club* (1998).

[2] The cases were *Gregorio T. v. Wilson* (1995) and *Coalition v. Pete Wilson* (1997). One initiative deals with illegal immigrants (Proposition 187); the other, with affirmative action (Proposition 209).

Abstract discussion is not the only species of communication which the Constitution protects; the First Amendment also protects vigorous advocacy, certainly of lawful ends, against governmental intrusion. . . . In the context of NAACP objectives, litigation is not a technique of resolving private differences; it is a means for achieving the lawful objectives of equality of treatment by all government, federal, state and local, for the members of the Negro community in this country. It is thus a form of political expression. Groups which find themselves unable to achieve their objectives though the courts often turn to the ballot box. Just as it was true of the opponents of New Deal legislation during the 1930's, for example, no less is it true of the Negro minority today. . . . Litigation may well be the sole practicable avenue open to a minority to petition for the redress of grievances. . . .

There thus inheres in the statute the gravest danger of smothering all discussion looking to the institution of litigation on behalf of the rights of members of an unpopular minority. . . . In such circumstances, a statute broadly curtailing group activity leading to litigation may easily become a weapon of oppression, however evenhanded its terms appear. Its mere existence could well freeze out of existence all such activity on behalf of the civil rights of Negro citizens. . . . Resort[ing] to the courts to seek vindication of constitutional rights is a different matter from the oppressive, malicious, or avaricious use of the legal process for purely private gain [that states might have a reasonable interest in curtailing]. Lawsuits attacking racial discrimination, at least in Virginia, are neither very profitable nor very popular. They are not an object of general competition among Virginia lawyers; the problem is rather one of an apparent dearth of lawyers who are willing to undertake such litigation. There has been neither claim nor proof that any assisted Negro litigants have desired, but have been prevented from retaining, the services of other counsel. We realize that an NAACP lawyer must derive personal satisfaction from participation in litigation on behalf of Negro rights, else he would hardly be inclined to participate at the risk of financial sacrifice. But this would not seem to be the kind of interest or motive which induces criminal conduct [which would give the state reasonable grounds to regulate the practice of law].

. . . For the Constitution protects expression and association without regard to the race, creed, or political or religious affiliation of the members of the group which invokes its shield, or to the truth, popularity, or social utility of the ideas and beliefs which are offered.

---

1. On what grounds does Justice Brennan argue that the NAACP's activity, and interest group activity in general, is protected by the First Amendment?

____

____

____

2. The First Amendment reads: "Congress shall make no law respecting an establishment of religion, or prohibiting the free exercise thereof; or abridging freedom of speech, or of the press; or the right of the people peaceably to assemble, and to petition the government for a redress of grievances." Later the U.S. Supreme Court applied those protections to the states by way of the Fourteenth Amendment. Read the *Button* decision carefully. List the specific provisions of the First Amendment that the Court finds the Virginia statute violates.

____

____

____

____

____

____

3. The courts consistently have found that states have the right to regulate various professions to protect the public against shoddy or dangerous practices. How does Justice Brennan distinguish between that right and what Virginia was trying to do by regulating lawyers in this case?

4. To what extent does Justice Brennan's opinion suggest sympathy for the NAACP and its fight on behalf of black equality? Does he limit his defense of a group's First Amendment rights just to the NAACP? Explain and support your answer.

EXERCISE 6.3 THE CIVIL RIGHTS MOVEMENT AND CIVIL DISOBEDIENCE

BACKGROUND

When public opinion or the government or both are hostile to the goals of a group in society, that group may turn to the courts or take to the streets. In the 1950s, African Americans did both. Black leaders, concluding that Congress and the president were unlikely to respond to their concerns, supported the legal efforts of the NAACP and other civil rights organizations; they also embraced civil disobedience.

The quest of blacks for equal rights that began in the 1950s commonly is called the *civil rights movement.* The word *movement* suggests that new and different forces are at work, forces distinct from traditional interest groups. Movements are grassroots efforts: They mobilize people without the political clout or financial resources to influence government in traditional ways. Instead, the feeling that they have been denied some basic value—justice or equality, for example—drives those people to civil disobedience. Most movements advance broad moral or constitutional demands; interest groups, on the other hand, commonly focus on narrow economic concerns. But both movements and interest groups try to effect change by informing and mobilizing public opinion, to exert pressure on lawmakers to enact favorable legislation.

Essential to the success of the civil rights movement was the mass media's coverage of the actions it took to challenge segregation. Television was vital in showing the reality of the racial brutality that was pervasive in the South. Vivid, horrific images of the violence perpetuated by private citizens and public officials against peaceful civil rights demonstrators shocked many outside the South. More important, they were no longer able to avoid difficult questions about race relations in America. Television coverage accelerated the pace of social and economic change.

Interest groups—among them, the NAACP, the Urban League, the Southern Christian Leadership Conference, the Congress of Racial Equality, and the Student Nonviolent Coordinating Committee—formed an important component of the civil rights movement. Some of those groups pursued traditional strategies and tactics to advance the cause of civil rights. The legal arm of the NAACP, for example, challenged the constitutionality of state laws that required blacks and whites to attend separate schools. Thurgood Marshall, the lead attorney for the NAACP and later the first black to serve on the Supreme Court, pursued the issue to the High Court and, in *Brown v. Board of Education of Topeka* (1954), won.

Other groups relied on different tactics. The civil rights movement pioneered nonviolent resistance to racial segregation. Demonstrators defied unjust laws through sit-ins, marches, and boycotts—through *civil disobedience.* Demonstrators actually were trained not to respond in kind to violence. In the climate of racial relations in the South, those tactics were risky. The movement's leaders well knew that the commitment to nonviolence was in danger of straining to the breaking point, which could lead to widespread death and destruction, and to the alienation of public opinion.

Dynamic, bold, and charismatic leadership is an essential ingredient in the success of movements. That was especially true of the civil rights movement. Dr. Martin Luther King Jr. (1929–1968) was thrust into the civil rights struggle in 1955, while serving as pastor of a church in Montgomery, Alabama. After Rosa Parks, a black woman, was arrested for refusing to give up her seat on a bus to a white man—as the law of Alabama then required—King was asked to head up a bus boycott in Montgomery. The boycott went on for a year. It ended with the Supreme Court ruling that segregated buses are unconstitutional. King's inspiring presence, his speech, his commitment to nonviolence, and his tireless energy and determination made him a natural leader for the movement—and a target for its opponents. He was assassinated by a sniper on April 4, 1968.

Reading 6.3 is an excerpt from King's now-famous "Letter from a Birmingham Jail." The letter is perhaps his clearest statement of the principles of racial equality and nonviolence that guided the early stages of the civil rights movement. King wrote the letter on April 16, 1963, after the Birmingham police had jailed him for disobeying an Alabama state court injunction against sit-in demonstrations at lunch counters. King had come to Birmingham to participate in an ongoing effort to desegregate public accommodations in that city. (Later that year, the Supreme Court, in *Gober v. City of Birmingham,* declared Birmingham's segregation laws unconstitutional.) King wrote the letter in response to a public plea from a group of "moderate" white clergy who, although they expressed some sympathy for the

b. How did he respond to the clergymen's plea that he proceed more slowly and use more moderate tactics?

4. How did King justify breaking the law? That is, how did he distinguish the movement's lawbreaking from ordinary lawbreaking?

5. Suppose King's argument for civil disobedience had been advanced by a group whose goals and objectives you ardently oppose. Would the group's advocacy of civil disobedience change your view of civil disobedience? In other words, does it matter to you who advocates and practices civil disobedience? Or would you consistently defend or oppose the tactic for all groups that practice it?

EXERCISE 6.4 DOES MONEY BUY INFLUENCE? SENATOR ALAN CRANSTON AND THE KEATING FIVE

BACKGROUND

When you contribute to a campaign, are you paying for the candidate to carry out specific actions? The relationship between campaign contributions and the subsequent actions of elected officials is difficult to assess. Most studies show a fairly high correlation between campaign contributions and roll call votes in the national and state legislatures, especially when issues are both highly visible and important to constituents.[3] Finding a correlation, however, does not establish causation: It is difficult to show that a legislator cast a particular vote because of receiving a particular campaign contribution. Legislators claim, often with good reason, that they would have voted that way in any event and that it was the legislator's position on the issue in the first place that motivated the donor to make the contribution.

The legal standard for proving a causal relationship between a campaign contribution and a legislative vote requires evidence that the contribution was made explicitly in exchange for the legislator's taking some future action on behalf of the donor. Short of an outright admission by the legislator or contributor, that kind of evidence is difficult to obtain. The FBI has conducted sting operations in various states, having agents pose as wealthy contributors in hopes of getting a legislator to acknowledge—the agents are wearing hidden microphones—that the contribution is being made to secure a specific vote in the future. Widespread coverage in the media of sting operations no doubt gives legislators a powerful incentive to choose their words carefully when soliciting or acknowledging campaign contributions. And most campaign contributors would not admit publicly that they are buying influence. Instead, they say that they contribute because a particular candidate shares and represents their concerns; in return, they claim, they expect only "access"—a sympathetic ear, a representative who is willing to listen to their problems and consider their point of view.

Despite the reluctance of legislators to acknowledge it, access and influence are inextricably linked. By granting preferential access to contributors, legislators narrow the range of concerns and views they hear. Few average constituents can afford to make the contributions that provide entrée into the private offices of legislators. Hearing a particular point of view—to the exclusion of others—may lead a legislator to look more sympathetically on that cause or interest and even to act on its behalf.

One example of the relationship between access and influence is the cash nexus that tied former California Senator Alan Cranston to Charles Keating, a wealthy donor to Cranston's campaign and the campaigns of others.

Cranston, a Democrat, was first elected to the Senate in 1968. A savvy politician and a liberal, he was known for his determined efforts to promote California's interests in Congress. Over the years, Cranston received approximately $1 million in various forms of contributions from Keating, who owned Lincoln Savings and Loan Association in California. (Keating was actually a resident of Arizona; Lincoln Savings and Loan was owned by his Arizona corporation.) Keating, a registered Republican and a conservative, contributed money to the campaigns of Republicans and Democrats alike. He was also refreshingly honest, if not a bit cynical, in admitting that he made campaign contributions to obtain political influence.

In 1987, Keating sought the help of Cranston and four other senators, all of whom had received contributions from him. Regulators of the Federal Home Loan Bank Board (FHLBB), the federal agency that has jurisdiction over the savings and loan industry, were on Keating's trail, investigating his savings and loan (S&L) for alleged improprieties. Keating asked the five senators, later dubbed the *Keating Five,* to intervene on his behalf with Edward Gray, the head of the FHLBB. Keating was concerned that the FHLBB would issue new restrictive regulations challenging the high-risk investments Keating had made with the S&L's funds. The new regulations were necessary, according to Gray, because deregulation of the S&L industry had permitted high-risk investments in junk bonds and real estate that now jeopardized the survival of the industry.

Deregulation of the S&L industry had happened in the early 1980s, mostly in response to the industry's complaints that government regulation led to low profit margins. Deregulation allowed the

[3] See, for example, Jean Schroedel, "Campaign Contributions and Legislative Outcomes," *Western Political Science Quarterly* 39(1986): 371–389.

S&L industry to pay higher interest rates, which in turn attracted more capital; it also allowed the industry to invest depositors' funds with fewer restrictions. Many S&Ls capitalized on deregulation by funneling their new-found capital into high-risk investments. In 1989 and 1990, both the junk-bond and the real estate markets crashed, taking many S&Ls with them. The government intervened, bailing out the failed S&Ls and their depositors at a cost to taxpayers of approximately $500 billion.

Cranston, who actively solicited funds from Keating and who was the largest recipient of campaign donations from him, arranged to meet with Gray and the other four senators. Cranston had received warnings from several Senate colleagues and from some experts to stay away from Keating, but the California senator also had letters from several experts stating that Lincoln Savings and Loan was on sound footing. One of those experts was Alan Greenspan, later to serve as chairman of the Federal Reserve Board. The senators pitched Keating's case to Gray, insisting that Keating was being harassed by the FHLBB. No one is sure exactly what was said at the meeting, but we do know that the senators met later with federal regulators on Keating's behalf. At that meeting, the regulators warned the senators that criminal charges might be filed against Keating in the Lincoln Savings and Loan case. Still Cranston continued to advocate with the FHLBB on Keating's behalf, even making several telephone calls to regulators. Critics charged that the Keating Five's intervention with the FHLBB derailed the normal regulatory process and allowed the problems at Lincoln Savings and Loan to fester. The eventual crackdown by regulators did not come in time to save Lincoln Savings and Loan, which failed at a great loss to investors and at a cost to taxpayers of more than $2.5 billion.

After investigating the Keating Five's role in the Lincoln Savings and Loan debacle, the Senate Select Committee on Ethics reprimanded Cranston for linking fundraising with his official activities. The other four senators received milder rebukes. Cranston did not run for reelection in 1992, saying that he was suffering from prostate cancer. No criminal charges were filed against him. Charles Keating was convicted on both federal and state charges, but both convictions were later overturned on appeal.

ASSIGNMENT

Answer the questions that follow Readings 6.4.1 and 6.4.2.

READING 6.4.1 SENATOR ALAN CRANSTON IN HIS OWN DEFENSE

FROM A LETTER SENATOR CRANSTON ADDRESSED TO THE *LOS ANGELES TIMES*:*

Your article falsely charges that I revised my "story" about when I had first learned that federal regulators had filed a criminal referral relating to Lincoln Savings & Loan because it would be of great benefit to me if it appeared that I learned about the referral later rather than earlier.

This is pure yellow journalism.

The other four senators who have been under inquiry were informed at a meeting with regulators April 9, 1987, that a criminal referral had been filed against Lincoln Savings. I was not present when the regulators made this revelation. I discussed when I learned about the criminal referral in two paragraphs of my 23-page Jan. 15 affidavit, stating:

"I had originally thought, when endeavoring to reconstruct my memory of all this, that one of the senators who had attended the April 9 meeting told me about the criminal referral some weeks after the meeting. I have since learned that none of those senators recalls telling me about it, and that Ms. Jordan (one of my staffers) remembers bringing it to my attention after she read about it in a newspaper, much later in the year."

When I learned about the criminal referral is not really significant since the public record shows that I have always made plain that I did not stop my efforts when I heard about the referral.

The fact that some aspect of a business is the subject of a criminal referral does not make it improper for a senator to make status inquiries or to urge prompt and fair consideration of that business.

* August 4, 1991, p. B4.

Senator Cranston Speaking to the Members of the Ethics Committee:*

How many of you after really thinking about it, could rise and declare you've never, ever helped—or agreed to help—a contributor close in time to solicitation or receipt of a contribution? I don't believe any of you could say never. . . .

There is no precedent and there is no rule establishing that it is unethical for a senator to engage in legitimate constituent service on behalf of a constituent because it was close in time to a lawful contribution to the senator's campaign or to a charity the senator supports. . . . So let me ask: Since I have been singled out on access today, who among you can be sure you will not be singled out for a reprimand on access tomorrow? Here, but for the grace of God, stand you.

READING 6.4.2 From the Report of the Senate Select Committee on Ethics

Senator Cranston Contends That There Is No Evidence That Mr. Keating's Contributions Caused His Actions on Mr. Keating's Behalf

Senator Cranston contends that his conduct cannot be deemed improper absent a finding that Mr. Keating's contributions caused him to take official action on Mr. Keating's behalf, action that he would not otherwise have taken. Senator Cranston's standard requiring a "causal connection" between a contribution and official action appears to equate impropriety with illegality. This position fails to recognize that conduct that does not constitute illegal behavior may still be improper.

Senator Cranston's view of what constitutes improper conduct is at odds with the plain language of this Committee's authorizing legislation and is contradictory to the history of Senate disciplinary proceedings. Senate Resolution 338 confers on this Committee authority to investigate and recommend disciplinary action to the full Senate for violations of laws, Senate Rules and "improper conduct which may reflect upon the Senate." Moreover, the Committee is not required to find causation in order to find improper conduct.

. . . There is clear and convincing evidence before the Committee showing that Senator Cranston solicited and received contributions from Mr. [Keating] in a manner which linked the contributions with official notion.

Senator Cranston Argues That All His Contacts with the Bank Board Were Routine and Proper Constituent Service Status Inquiries

Senator Cranston contends that every contact he had with the Bank Board was a permissible constituent service "status inquiry" or request for careful consideration of matters involving Lincoln [Savings and Loan]. Although the evidence demonstrates that a number of Senator Cranston's contacts with the Bank Board cannot be characterized fairly as routine status inquiries, the Committee did not find any of Senator Cranston's contacts in and of themselves to be improper. It is the relationship of these interventions to Mr. Keating's contributions that was improper.

---

1. From the readings identify two arguments Senator Cranston makes in defense of his actions on Keating's behalf.

Argument 1: ____

____

____

---

* Quoted in Sara Fritz, "Cranston Harshly Rebuked," *Los Angeles Times,* November 21, 1991, p. A1.

READING SOURCE: Senate Select Committee on Ethics, *Investigation of Senator Alan Cranston,* no. 102-223, November 20, 1991.

Argument 2: ______________________________

____

____

2. Carefully examine the two arguments you identified in question 1. Decide if each is completely true, partly true, or completely false. Explain and support your analysis.

Argument 1: ______________________________

____

____

Argument 2: ______________________________

____

____

3. a. Why would someone like Keating, a conservative Republican businessman, give so much campaign money to someone like Cranston, a liberal Democrat, instead of contributing to Cranston's Republican opponents, people more likely to be sympathetic to Keating's business interests and ideology?

____

____

____

____

b. Why would someone like Cranston, a liberal committed to social and economic justice and a defender of regulatory agencies, take donations from someone like Keating and actively intervene against government regulators he usually supported?

____

____

____

____

4. The chairman of the Senate Ethics Committee, Senator Howell Heflin (D-Ala.), admitted that a connection between a particular contribution and a subsequent action by a senator on behalf of the contributor is difficult to establish. Then he added, "I know it when I see it."[4]

a. In your view, what would constitute a link between a donation and a lawmaker's behavior?

____

____

b. Do you think there was enough evidence to establish that Keating's contributions to Cranston *caused* Cranston to intervene on Keating's behalf? Explain and support your answer.

____

____

____

____

____

____

[4] Quoted in Sara Fritz, "Cranston Harshly Rebuked," *Los Angeles Times*, November 21, 1991, p. A1.

EXERCISE 6.5 POLITICAL ACTION COMMITTEES IN FEDERAL ELECTIONS

BACKGROUND

Most political action committees are the electoral arms of corporations, unions, or interest groups; some PACs, though, are only nominally affiliated with or are altogether independent of those entities. The primary mission of a PAC is to solicit voluntary contributions from a corporation's employees, a union's members, or the public at large and then to funnel that money to candidates the PAC supports.

Along with soft money (see Exercise 5.5), perhaps the most important development since the campaign finance reforms of the 1970s has been the growth in the role and power of PACs in federal elections. Remember that the Federal Election Campaign Act was lawmakers' response to revelations of gross abuses in the financing of President Nixon's reelection campaign in 1972. Although the intent of the law was to reign in campaign spending, the law had the opposite effect: inviting all manner of interests in society to undertake new ways of raising and distributing funds to favored candidates. Before the act was passed, PACs had been used only by labor unions. After the act was passed, corporations and other interests quickly formed their own PACs, eager to share the influence unions had on elections. And the law unwittingly created another incentive for the proliferation of PACs, allowing them to contribute more than individual donors could to federal candidates' campaigns. An individual could donate no more than $1,000 to any single candidate per election; a PAC could donate five times that amount. Furthermore, the reforms placed no limit on the total dollars a particular PAC could contribute in an election cycle. Finally, the law allowed unions and corporations with government contracts to form PACs, a practice that had been prohibited.

Two loopholes in the FECA undermined the law's ability to limit contributions by PACs and individual donors. The first was created in 1976, in *Buckley v. Valeo,* in which the Supreme Court ruled that limitations on independent spending by individuals or groups on behalf of a candidate were a violation of the First Amendment guarantee of free speech. *Independent spending* is spending on behalf of a candidate for federal office that is not funneled through the candidate's official campaign organization. The Court's decision opened the floodgates not only for PACs but also for interest groups, corporations, even wealthy individuals to spend any amount of money on direct mailings or television ads or other campaign expenses on behalf of federal candidates. Today, according to Federal Election Commission data, some union and single-issue PACs spend more money on independent campaigns on behalf of federal candidates than they do on direct contributions to the candidates' official campaign organizations. The second loophole, the subject of Exercise 5.5, is soft money, a means of funneling contributions in any amount through political-party organizations.

PACs have become so ubiquitous in federal campaigns that many observers fear the creation of a "special interest state," in which groups with financial means dominate and control the political agenda through campaign contributions and the access to policymakers those contributions afford.[5] Studies by political scientists demonstrate a high correlation between PAC contributions and congressional voting records, particularly on issues where the public is inattentive and where important votes take place in congressional committee.[6]

Reforming the PAC system would be difficult. Even if members of Congress were willing to bite the hand that feeds them by placing more limits on direct contributions to their campaigns, it is likely that PACs would respond by increasing their independent expenditures, which are protected by the Supreme Court's ruling in *Buckley.*

ASSIGNMENT

Answer the questions that follow the tables.

[5] For example, see the comments and writings of columnist David Broder, consumer advocate Ralph Nader, and Senator John McCain (R-Ariz.).

[6] See, for example, Laura Leighton, "PACs, Lobbies and Political Conflict: The Case of Gun Control," *Public Choice* 75(1993): 254–271.

TABLE 6.5.1 PAC ACTIVITY, 1986–2000

	1986–2000			
COMMITTEE TYPE	**NUMBER OF COMMITTEES**	**TOTAL RECEIPTS**	**TOTAL DISBURSEMENTS**	**CONTRIBUTIONS TO CANDIDATES**
CORPORATE				
1985–1986	1,906	$81,960,209	$79,277,456	$49,566,619
1987–1988	2,008	$96,917,153	$89,852,158	$56,155,259
1989–1990	1,972	$106,474,773	$101,055,267	$58,131,722
1991–1992	1,930	$112,517,482	$112,389,798	$68,430,976
1993–1994	1,875	$114,995,661	$116,814,143	$69,610,433
1995–1996	1,836	$133,793,654	$130,624,843	$78,194,723
1997–1998	1,821	$144,115,389	$137,570,423	$78,018,750
1999–2000	1,725	$164,454,559	$158,329,869	$91,525,699
LABOR				
1985–1986	417	$65,310,945	$57,881,815	$31,038,885
1987–1988	401	$78,509,139	$74,071,575	$35,495,780
1989–1990	372	$88,926,833	$84,615,373	$34,732,029
1991–1992	372	$89,935,941	$94,604,526	$41,357,222
1993–1994	371	$90,303,181	$88,437,349	$41,867,393
1995–1996	358	$104,059,450	$99,768,350	$47,980,492
1997–1998	353	$111,312,402	$98,247,303	$44,606,983
1999–2000	350	$136,011,151	$128,692,390	$51,573,364
INDEPENDENT				
1985–1986	1,270	$118,631,621	$118,423,473	$19,410,358
1987–1988	1,345	$106,254,069	$104,873,996	$20,330,050
1989–1990	1,321	$71,569,940	$71,382,835	$15,070,009
1991–1992	1,376	$73,810,989	$76,232,864	$18,326,404
1993–1994	1,318	$76,860,606	$75,060,494	$18,201,369
1995–1996	1,259	$81,165,399	$81,265,563	$23,960,110
1997–1998	1,326	$114,321,557	$107,775,031	$28,154,544
1999–2000	1,362	$144,266,748	$139,662,019	$37,297,383
TRADE/MEMBERSHIP/HEALTH				
1985–1986	789	$75,431,133	$73,291,156	$34,551,531
1987–1988	848	$89,538,894	$83,719,992	$41,213,596
1989–1990	801	$92,516,400	$88,095,809	$44,804,886
1991–1992	835	$95,740,556	$97,471,784	$53,870,702
1993–1994	852	$96,372,055	$94,122,563	$52,853,630
1995–1996	896	$105,956,146	$105,355,853	$60,153,725
1997–1998	921	$119,576,494	$114,365,202	$62,322,845
1999–2000	900	$142,870,952	$137,150,301	$71,802,756
COOPERATIVE*				
1985–1986	57	$4,697,153	$4,683,060	$2,671,545
1987–1988	61	$4,856,605	$4,520,516	$2,736,132
1989–1990	60	$4,974,122	$4,830,175	$2,950,960
1991–1992	61	$4,794,929	$4,891,433	$2,961,140
1993–1994	56	$4,377,763	$4,516,979	$3,035,003
1995–1996	45	$3,897,164	$4,195,374	$3,006,471
1997–1998	45	$4,468,403	$4,345,123	$2,411,076
1999–2000	41	$3,716,550	$3,297,957	$2,360,236

TABLE 6.5.1 (CONTINUED)

	1986–2000			
COMMITTEE TYPE	NUMBER OF COMMITTEES	TOTAL RECEIPTS	TOTAL DISBURSEMENTS	CONTRIBUTIONS TO CANDIDATES
CORPORATIONS WITHOUT STOCK				
1985–1986	157	$7,398,205	$6,397,186	$2,600,780
1987–1988	169	$8,541,233	$7,163,038	$3,312,424
1989–1990	151	$7,629,909	$7,669,098	$3,431,890
1991–1992	153	$8,730,610	$9,195,491	$3,981,324
1993–1994	149	$8,850,851	$9,151,115	$4,063,291
1995–1996	134	$8,500,508	$8,677,836	$4,535,098
1997–1998	133	$8,782,595	$8,527,765	$4,429,368
1999–2000	121	$13,591,109	$12,225,794	$5,270,336
TOTAL				
1985–1986	4,596	$353,429,266	$339,954,146	$139,839,718
1987–1988	4,832	$384,617,093	$364,201,275	$159,243,241
1989–1990	4,677	$372,091,977	$357,648,557	$159,121,496
1991–1992	4,727	$385,530,507	$394,785,896	$188,927,768
1993–1994	4,621	$391,760,117	$388,102,643	$189,631,119
1995–1996	4,528	$437,372,321	$429,887,819	$217,830,619
1997–1998	4,599	$502,576,840	$470,830,847	$219,943,566
1999–2000	4,499	$604,911,069	$579,358,330	$259,829,774

* These are smaller PACs that have pooled their resources for similar policy objectives.

SOURCE: All data are from the Federal Election Commission (www.fec.gov).

1. a. Based on the figures for 1999–2000 in Table 6.5.1, which committee type contributed the most to candidates?

____

b. What percentage of the total did that type of PAC contribute to candidates in 1999 and 2000?

____

c. What percentage of the total did labor PACs contribute to candidates in 1999 and 2000?

____

2. a. Based on the figures for 1985–1986 in Table 6.5.1, which committee type contributed the most to candidates?

____

b. What percentage of the total did that type of PAC contribute to candidates in 1985 and 1986?

____

c. What percentage of the total did labor PACs contribute to candidates in 1985 and 1986?

____

3. a. Between 1985–1986 and 1999–2000, which committee type had the largest percentage increase in contributions to candidates?

____

b. Between 1985–1986 and 1999–2000, what was the total percentage increase in PAC contributions to candidates?

____

4. a. Draw two pie charts (see Exercise 2.2, question 2), one depicting the percentage of total PAC contributions by each type of PAC in the 1985–1986 election cycle, and the other depicting the same information for the 1999–2000 cycle. Use a key, or label each chart clearly.

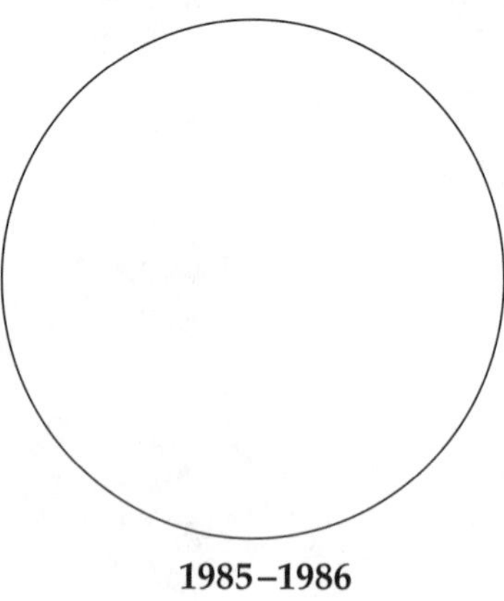

1985–1986

1999–2000

b. In a sentence or two, compare and contrast the two pie charts.

____

____

____

____

5. What might explain the discrepancy in Table 6.5.1 between the total-disbursements data and the contributions-to-candidates data? (You may need to review the background information to answer this question.)

____

____

____

____

6. a. Looking at Table 6.5.2, what percentage of PAC funds went to incumbents and what percentage went to challengers in 1994?

Incumbents: ____

Challengers: ____

b. What was the breakdown in 2000?

Incumbents: ____

Challengers: ____

7. a. Looking at Table 6.5.2, what percentage of corporate PAC funds went to incumbents and what percentage went to challengers in 1994?

Incumbents: ____

Challengers: ____

TABLE 6.5.2 PAC FUNDING BY CANDIDATE, 1994–2000

	1994–2000		
CANDIDATE	CORPORATE PACs	LABOR PACs	TOTAL*
INCUMBENT			
1994	$47,972,418	$27,273,752	$127,739,543
1996	$52,994,672	$23,536,516	$133,324,192
1998	$59,334,927	$30,258,097	$158,354,199
2000	$70,539,805	$32,596,929	$183,997,671
CHALLENGER			
1994	$4,885,278	$5,822,731	$18,444,744
1996	$4,329,085	$13,218,922	$28,336,104
1998	$4,640,602	$6,352,232	$21,474,504
2000	$3,797,707	$10,801,393	$26,987,927
OPEN SEAT			
1994	$11,505,128	$7,645,816	$33,408,102
1996	$12,422,341	$9,803,660	$39,816,592
1998	$7,146,002	$6,761,653	$26,983,424
2000	$11,495,266	$6,815,391	$36,939,795
DEMOCRAT			
1994	$31,430,922	$38,987,257	$112,134,640
1996	$19,096,942	$43,379,845	$93,961,914
1998	$23,067,243	$39,508,937	$98,390,372
2000	$27,132,353	$46,109,915	$116,914,373
REPUBLICAN			
1994	$32,872,432	$1,598,642	$67,149,974
1996	$52,057,218	$3,023,413	$109,143,907
1998	$48,039,663	$3,735,020	$108,173,607
2000	$58,547,850	$3,949,375	$130,477,308
OTHER PARTY			
1994	$59,470	$156,400	$307,775
1996	$181,150	$227,340	$783,102
1998	$14,625	$128,025	$248,148
2000	$152,575	$154,423	$533,712
TOTAL			
1994	$64,362,824	$40,742,299	$179,592,389
1996	$71,335,310	$46,630,598	$203,888,923
1998	$71,121,531	$43,371,982	$206,812,127
2000	$85,832,778	$50,213,713	$247,925,393

* Totals include other PAC funding in addition to corporate and labor PAC funding.

SOURCE: All data are from the Federal Election Commission (www.fec.gov).

b. What was the breakdown in 2000?

Incumbents: ____________________

Challengers: ____________________

8. a. Looking at Table 6.5.2, what percentage of labor PAC funds went to incumbents and what percentage went to challengers in 1994?

Incumbents: ____________________

Challengers: ____________________

b. What was the breakdown in 2000?

Incumbents: ____________________

Challengers: ____________________

9. a. According to Table 6.5.2, what percentage of their total contributions did corporate PACs give to incumbents and what percentage did they give to challengers in 2000?

Incumbents: ____________________

Challengers: ____________________

b. What percentage of their total contributions did labor PACs give to incumbents and what percentage did they give to challengers?

Incumbents: ____________________

Challengers: ____________________

c. Are corporate PACs or labor PACs more likely to fund incumbents?

____

10. a. Looking at Table 6.5.2, what percentage of PAC funds went to Democrats and what percentage went to Republicans in 1994?

Democrats: ____________________

Republicans: ____________________

b. What was the breakdown in 2000?

Democrats: ____________________

Republicans: ____________________

11. a. Looking at Table 6.5.2, what percentage of corporate PAC funds went to Democrats and what percentage went to Republicans in 1994?

Democrats: ____________________

Republicans: ____________________

b. What was the breakdown in 2000?

Democrats: ____________________

Republicans: ____________________

12. a. What percentage of labor PAC funds went to Democrats and what percentage went to Republicans in 1994?

Democrats: ____________________

Republicans: ____________________

b. What was the breakdown in 2000?

Democrats: ____________________

Republicans: ____________________

13. a. According to Table 6.5.2, what percentage of their total contributions in 2000 did corporate PACs give to Democrats and to Republicans?

Democrats: ____________________

Republicans: ____________________

b. In 2000, what percentage of their total contributions did labor PACs give to Democrats and to Republicans?

Democrats: ____________________

Republicans: ____________________

c. Are labor groups or corporate groups more likely to fund Republicans? Explain your answer.

____

____

____

____

14. In 2000, what percentage of PAC funds went to minor-party candidates?

____

15. a. In 2000, what percentage of total PAC funds came from labor PACs?

____

b. What percentage of total PAC funds did corporate PACs provide?

____

16. a. Based on your answers to questions 6 through 15, do corporate PACs tend to disburse their funds more on the basis of a candidate's party affiliation or incumbency? Explain your answer.

____

____

____

____

b. Based on your answers to questions 6 through 15, do labor PACs tend to disburse their funds more on the basis of a candidate's party affiliation or incumbency? Explain your answer.

____

____

____

____

17. Table 6.5.3 shows that PACs spend their money both for and against candidates, in positive and negative campaigns, and that the decision to promote or oppose candidates varies by campaign type and committee type.

a. In 1999–2000, which type of race—for the presidency, the U.S. Senate, or the U.S. House—was least negative?

____

b. Which type of PAC was most negative?

____

TABLE 6.5.3 INDEPENDENT EXPENDITURES, 1999–2000

RACE TYPE	POSITIVE	NEGATIVE	TOTAL
Presidential	$5,704,475	$427,007	$6,131,482
U.S. Senate	$4,533,830	$2,492,413	$7,026,243
U.S. House	$6,264,531	$1,619,533	$7,884,064
Total	$16,502,836	$4,538,953	$21,041,789

	POSITIVE*		NEGATIVE*		
COMMITTEE TYPE	NUMBER OF COMMITTEES	AMOUNT	NUMBER OF COMMITTEES	AMOUNT	TOTAL
Corporate	13	$95,305	3	$42,230	$137,535
Labor	24	$2,622,123	3	$203,717	$2,825,840
Independent	57	$4,711,107	24	$878,063	$5,589,170
Trade/membership/health	24	$8,949,143	7	$2,194,759	$11,143,902
Cooperative†	1	$4,958	0	$0	$4,958
Corporations without stock	6	$120,200	1	$1,220,184	$1,340,384
Total	125	$16,502,836	38	$4,538,953	$21,041,789

* Includes expenditures made in 1999–2000 for candidates involved in earlier elections.

† These are smaller PACs that have pooled their resources for similar policy objectives.

SOURCE: All data are from the Federal Election Commission (www.fec.gov).

18. a. In 1999–2000, what percentage of total independent expenditures was spent promoting candidates (on positive campaigns)?

b. What percentage was spent on negative campaigns?

19. What percentage of total PAC disbursements for 1999–2000 (see Table 6.5.3) was made up of independent expenditures (by committee type)?

TABLE 6.5.4 PAC FACTS

YEAR	NUMBER OF PACS	PERCENT OF CANDIDATES' FUNDS FROM PACS
1974*	608	16
1980	2,551	26
1990	4,667	38
2000	4,449	24

* The year of the reforms that allowed the development of PACs.

SOURCE: All data are from the Federal Election Commission (www.fec.gov).

20. Using the data in Table 6.5.4, create a graph showing the number of PACs in the United States between 1974 and 2000. Use the number of PACs as your vertical axis and the year as your horizontal axis.

21. Why do you think the number of PACs fell from 1990 to 2000?

22. Table 6.5.4 shows a decrease from 1990 to 2000 in the percentage of candidates' funds coming from PACs. But Tables 6.5.1 and 6.5.2 show that total PAC funding increased during the 1990s. How would you explain this apparent contradiction?

CONGRESS

EXERCISE 7.1 DEFINING THE EXTENT OF CONGRESSIONAL POWER

BACKGROUND

Congressional power, although defined in Article I, Section 8, of the Constitution, continues to evolve through political practice and occasional decisions of the Supreme Court.[1] What the Court has done is to interpret the often-ambiguous language of the Constitution. As Chief Justice John Marshall wrote in the landmark decision in *McCulloch v. Maryland* (1819), "It is a *constitution* we are expounding" (emphasis added).

Many of the extensive powers that Congress exercises today are not enumerated in the Constitution. That was the crux of Maryland's argument in *McCulloch:* that Congress had exceeded its constitutional power by establishing a national bank, that the Constitution did not specifically grant that power to Congress. The state's argument was strengthened by the Tenth Amendment, which reserves powers to the states (and whose language is quoted in the *McCulloch* decision). But the justices ruled that the enumerated powers of Congress should not be interpreted literally, that the necessary and proper clause (Article I, Section 8) gives Congress certain implied powers. Reading 7.1.1 describes the Court's reasoning for its broad interpretation of congressional powers in *McCulloch.*

ASSIGNMENT

Refer to Readings 7.1.1, 7.1.2, and 7.1.3 to answer the questions that follow them.

[1] Of course, Supreme Court decisions are themselves subject to modification and even reversal over time.

READING 7.1.1 FROM *McCULLOCH V. MARYLAND*, 4 WHEAT. 17 U.S. 316 (1819)

Mr. Chief Justice Marshall delivered the opinion of the Court:

The first question . . . is: Has the Congress power to incorporate a bank? . . .

Among the enumerated powers, we do not find that of establishing a bank or creating a corporation. But there is no phrase in the instrument which . . . excludes incidental or implied powers; and which requires that everything granted shall be expressly and minutely described. Even the Tenth Amendment, which was framed for the purpose of quieting the excessive jealousies which had been excited, omits the word "expressly" and declares only that the powers "not delegated to the United States . . . , nor prohibited to the states, are reserved to the states or to the people"; thus leaving the question, whether the particular power which may become the subject of contest, has been delegated to the one government, or prohibited to the other, to depend on a fair construction of the whole instrument. . . . A constitution, to contain an accurate detail of all the subdivisions of which its great powers will admit, and of all the means by which they may be carried into execution, would partake of the prolixity of a legal code, and could scarcely be embraced by the human mind. It would, probably, never be understood by the public. Its nature, therefore, requires that only its great outlines should be marked, its important objects designated, and the minor ingredients which compose those objects be deduced from the nature of the objects themselves. . . .

Although, among the enumerated powers of government, we do not find the word "bank," or "incorporation," we find the great powers, to lay and collect taxes; to borrow money; to regulate commerce [Article 1, Section 8]. . . . It may with great reason be contended, that a government, entrusted with such ample powers, on the due execution of which the happiness and prosperity of the nation so vitally depends, must also be entrusted with ample means for their execution. . . . That instrument does not profess to enumerate the means by which the powers that it confers may be executed; nor does it prohibit the creation of a corporation [or bank], if the existence of such a being be essential to the beneficial exercise of those powers. . . .

But the Constitution of the United States has not left the right of Congress to employ the necessary means for the execution of the powers conferred on the government to general reasoning. To this enumeration of powers is added that of making "all laws which shall be necessary and proper for carrying into execution the foregoing power, and all other powers vested by this Constitution in the government of the United States, or in any department . . . thereof" [Article 1, Section 8]. . . .

We admit . . . that the powers of the government are limited, and that its limits are not to be transcended. But we think the sound construction of the Constitution must allow to the national legislature that discretion, with respect to the means by which the powers it confers are to be carried into execution, which will enable that body to perform the high duties assigned to it, in the manner most beneficial to the people. Let the end be legitimate, let it be within the scope of the Constitution, and all means which are appropriate, which are plainly adapted to that end, which are not prohibited, but consistent with the Constitution, are constitutional. . . .

It being the opinion of the Court, that the act incorporating the bank is constitutional.

As the nation's problems became more complex, so did the process of legislating solutions. Limited by time and a lack of expertise in increasingly technical public policy, Congress began to delegate legislative power to the president, to federal agencies, even to private groups. The legality of that practice was the issue in *Schechter Poultry Corp. v. United States* (1935), which is excerpted in Reading 7.1.2. In the National Industrial Recovery Act (NIRA) of 1933, Congress had delegated to the president the power to issue codes by executive order for the purpose of promoting fair competition in various trades and industries. The codes would be proposed by private trade associations, then approved by the president, and then enforced against violators. When Schechter Poultry was convicted of violating a code, the owners challenged the NIRA on the grounds that Congress had delegated its legislative power unconstitutionally. The conservative Court agreed and reversed the conviction.

READING 7.1.2 FROM *SCHECHTER POULTRY CORP. V. UNITED STATES*, 295 U.S. 495 (1935)

Mr. Chief Justice Hughes delivered the opinion of the Court:

. . . First. . . . We are told that the provision of the [National Industrial Recovery Act] authorizing the adoption of codes must be viewed in the light of the grave national crisis [the Great Depression] with which Congress was confronted.* Undoubtedly, the conditions may call for extraordinary remedies. But the argument necessarily stops short of an attempt to justify action which lies outside the sphere of constitutional authority. Extraordinary conditions do not create or enlarge constitutional power. The Constitution established a national government with powers deemed to be adequate, as they have proved to be both in war and peace, but these powers of the national government are limited by the constitutional grants. Those who act under these grants are not at liberty to transcend the imposed limits because they believe that more or different power is necessary. Such assertions of extraconstitutional authority were anticipated by the explicit terms of the Tenth Amendment—"The powers not delegated to the United States by the constitution, nor prohibited to it by the States, are reserved to the States respectively, or to the people."

Second. The Question of the Delegation of Legislative Power. . . . The Constitution provides that "all legislative powers herein granted shall be vested in a Congress of the United States, which shall consist of a Senate and House of Representatives." Art. I, section 1. And the Congress is authorized "to make all laws which shall be necessary and proper for carrying into execution" its general powers. Art. I, section 3, par. 18. The Congress is not permitted to abdicate or to transfer to others the essential legislative functions with which it is thus vested. . . . We pointed out in [*Panama Refining Company* (1935)] that the Constitution has never been regarded as denying to Congress the necessary resources of flexibility and practicality, which will enable it to perform its function in laying down policies and establishing standards, while leaving to selected [executive agencies] the making of subordinate rules within prescribed limits.† . . . But we said that the constant recognition of the necessity and validity of such provisions, and the wide range of administrative authority which has been developed by means of them, cannot be allowed to obscure the limitations of the authority to delegate, if our constitutional system is to be maintained. . . .

But would it be seriously contended that Congress could delegate its legislative authority to trade or industrial associations or groups so as to empower them to enact the laws they deem to be wise and beneficent for the rehabilitation and expansion of their trade or industries? . . . Such a delegation of legislative power is unknown to our law and is utterly inconsistent with the constitutional prerogatives and duties of Congress. . . .

[Moreover] Congress cannot delegate legislative power to the President to exercise an unfettered discretion to make whatever laws he thinks may be needed or advisable for the rehabilitation and expansion of trade or industry. . . . In view of the scope of the broad declaration, and of the nature of the few restrictions that are imposed, the discretion of the President in approving or prescribing codes, and thus enacting laws for the government of trade and industry throughout the country, is virtually unfettered. We think that code-making authority thus conferred is an unconstitutional delegation of legislative power.

A few years later, however, the Court again allowed Congress to delegate its power. A stark statement of the Court's new position, one that dominated the Court's thinking from the late 1930s to the mid-1990s, can be found in Reading 7.1.3, excerpts from *United States v. Carolene Products Company* (1938).

---

* The codes were proposed by a trade organization to govern minimum prices and wages, trade practices, collective bargaining, and other practices.

† In this case, the Court ruled congressional delegation of power to the president unconstitutional.

READING 7.1.3 FROM *UNITED STATES V. CAROLENE PRODUCTS COMPANY*, 304 U.S. 144 (1938)

Mr. Justice Stone delivered the opinion of the Court:

. . . Regulatory legislation affecting ordinary commercial transactions is not to be pronounced unconstitutional unless in the light of the facts made known or generally assumed it is of such a character as to preclude the assumption that it rests upon some rational basis within the knowledge and experience of legislators.

[In a note (footnote 4 of the decision), Stone added this to the preceding paragraph:] There may be a narrower scope of the presumption of constitutionality when legislation appears on its face to be within a specific prohibition of the Constitution, such as those of the first ten Amendments. . . .

---

1. In one sentence, summarize the Supreme Court's decision in *McCulloch v. Maryland.*

____

____

2. Explain how Chief Justice Marshall's argument that the Constitution is not a legal code supports his broad view of congressional power.

____

____

____

____

3. The necessary and proper clause is commonly called the "elastic clause." What reasoning does Chief Justice Marshall use and what arguments does he advance to convert the necessary and proper clause into an elastic clause?

____

____

____

____

4. a. Rewrite the Tenth Amendment in a way that would make the necessary and proper clause less "elastic."

____

____

____

____

b. Explain why your revision would prove a greater obstacle to Chief Justice Marshall than the present wording of the Tenth Amendment.

____

____

____

____

5. In the *McCulloch* decision, Chief Justice Marshall notes that the Constitution grants enumerated powers to Congress "to lay and collect taxes; to borrow money; to regulate commerce." What is it about the enumerated powers that logically leads Marshall to conclude that incorporating a bank is constitutional?

6. In one sentence, summarize the Supreme Court's ruling in *Schechter Poultry Corp. v. United States.*

7. In *Schechter,* how does Chief Justice Hughes explain and justify limiting the national government's power even in a crisis as grave as the Great Depression?

8. Both Marshall (in *McCulloch*) and Hughes (in *Schechter*) use the Tenth Amendment to reach very different conclusions about the extent of congressional power under the Constitution. How is that possible?

9. Does the Court's decision in *Carolene* expand or limit the elasticity of the necessary and proper clause?

10. Some argue that the decision in *Carolene,* and others like it, nullifies the Tenth Amendment. They insist that the decision in effect says that Congress can do anything it wants to do so long as there is no specific constitutional prohibition, specifically in the Bill of Rights. On what language in the *Carolene* opinion is that argument based?

EXERCISE 7.2 WHAT IS THE PROPER ROLE OF THE REPRESENTATIVE?

BACKGROUND

All lawmakers must grapple with a question that goes to the heart of the legislative power vested in them by citizens in their district or state: On what basis should they cast their legislative votes? Should representatives vote the will of their constituents? Or should they vote for what they believe to be right, regardless of public opinion in their district or state?

The *delegate model* of legislative representation is most consistent with the tenets of democracy. According to this model, representatives look to the constituents in their district or state for instructions on what issues to promote and, ultimately, on how to cast their votes in the legislature. In this context, representatives act in place of the people who, for logistical reasons, are not able to act for themselves. Under the delegate model, representatives substitute for their constituents and do their bidding.

The delegate model of representation appears simple enough but raises several difficult issues. Should representatives be bound by the citizens who voted for them, or do they owe equal allegiance to the whole of their constituency? To what extent should campaign contributions—which come from a narrow segment of the constituency—factor into legislative decisions? Should representatives actively seek out constituent opinion, or should they simply respond to constituents' letters or phone calls? Should representatives be bound by the opinions and interests of their constituency on all legislative issues or only on those that most directly affect the state or district? Should representatives be especially responsive to constituents who have strong convictions on a particular issue? The realities of democratic politics complicate the delegate model of representation.

The *trustee model* of representation argues that representatives must transcend the short-term particular interests of their constituency and advocate for the long-term comprehensive interests of the nation. To make the trustee model compatible with democracy, its advocates necessarily make two assumptions. First, representatives must be accountable to their constituents: When they don't vote as their constituents would have them vote, representatives must be prepared to be voted out of office. Second, representatives must try to educate their constituents, to convince them that their thinking is wrong or to convince them to forgive the act of conscience that led the representatives to vote against the views of their constituents.

The trustee model also raises difficult issues. It assumes, for example, that the representatives' political judgment is better than that of their constituents, that the public interest is necessarily in safer hands. More important, the trustee model assumes that representatives who operate independently of their constituents are voting the public interest or their own conscience. It is possible, however, that the representatives might be responding to national interest groups with little or no support in the representatives' own district or state.

In practice, the dilemmas posed by the two models of representation are tempered by two realities. First, most voters in a district or state are likely to vote for someone who represents their political and cultural orientations and their economic interests. Second, the vast majority of constituents are unlikely to know much about the issue of a roll call vote, to hold strong views on the issue of a roll call vote, or even to know how their representative voted. Still, elected officials know all too well that an attentive group of constituents, by publicizing a vote it objects to, can make that vote a major issue in the next election.

ASSIGNMENT

1. Assume that a coalition of powerful interest groups has succeeded in bringing to the floor of the House a bill that would significantly tighten emission standards on automobiles. Many major automobile companies and their suppliers have factories in Michigan. Would a member of Congress from a district in Michigan be likely to follow the delegate or trustee model of representation? Explain and support your answer.

____

____

2. Nebraska shares many of the characteristics of midwestern farm states: Agriculture provides a significant portion of the state's income, even though fewer than 10 percent of its workers are employed in agriculture; the population is overwhelmingly white (Nebraska has a far lower percentage of minorities than the nation as a whole); and about a third of the state's population can be classified as rural.

a. On a vote to renew U.S. economic and military aid to Israel, would a U.S. senator from Nebraska more likely follow the delegate or trustee model? Explain and support your answer.

b. On a vote to sell wheat to the People's Republic of China, would a U.S. senator from Nebraska follow the delegate or trustee model? Explain and support your answer.

3. About 70 percent of the residents of Utah are members of the Mormon Church. Roman Catholics are the second largest denomination in the state. Republicans consistently dominate politics in Utah. On a vote to recognize same-sex marriages for federal employees, what model of representation would a U.S. senator from Utah likely follow? Explain and support your answer.

4. Oregon is a state with vast acreage of old-growth forests. The economy of the state is heavily dependent on the fortunes of the lumber industry. Oregon also has a strong environmental movement.

a. Would a U.S. senator from Oregon likely follow the delegate or trustee model in voting on a bill to ban cutting old-growth forests? Explain and support your answer.

b. Do you think the U.S. representative whose district includes most of Portland, the largest city in Oregon, would vote the same way? Explain and support your answer.

5. For each of the general issues identified below, indicate whether a U.S. representative would be more likely to follow the delegate or trustee model. Explain and support your answers.

a. Foreign policy

____

____

____

b. Civil rights

____

____

____

c. Highway construction funds

____

____

____

d. Social security

____

____

____

6. a. In the space below, write the number of your congressional district and the name of your representative in the U.S. House. (You can locate your representative by zip code at www.house.gov/house/MemberWWW.html.)

____

b. Identify an issue on which your representative would likely vote according to the delegate model of representation and an issue on which he or she would likely follow the trustee model. Explain and support your answer.

Delegate model: ____

____

____

Trustee model: ____

____

____

____

EXERCISE 7.3 WHY WE HATE CONGRESS BUT LOVE OUR MEMBER OF CONGRESS

BACKGROUND

Embedded in the controversy over legislative term limits is an underlying paradox about the voting behavior of many Americans: Americans may hate Congress, but they love their individual member of Congress. Pollsters consistently find that the public holds Congress in lower esteem than any other government institution, but election results show that voters consistently reelect their own member of Congress. Since 1945, on average, 90 percent of House members seeking reelection have been reelected, and about 80 percent of U.S. senators have been reelected.[2] Even in 1994, in the midterm election that gave Republicans control of both houses of Congress for the first time since 1954—and that was interpreted by many as an anti-incumbent election—slightly more than 90 percent of House members who were running for reelection were reelected.

Opponents of legislative term limits are understandably puzzled. Why do voters need term limits if it is possible every two years in the House and every six years in the Senate to vote incumbents out? Voters who are unhappy with their own representatives' performance have ample opportunities to even the score. But they hardly ever do. In fact, in an extraordinary number of congressional races, the incumbent wins with 60 percent or more of the vote—for the purposes of this exercise, an indicator of a noncompetitive election. Americans who want term limits seem to be saying that they want term limits for everyone else's representative but their own.

Proponents of term limits say the contradiction between Americans' disenchantment with Congress and their willingness to elect and reelect their own representatives has to do with the advantages of incumbency. After all, incumbents have more access to the media than challengers do, higher name recognition, and an easier time raising funds. Why? Because incumbents are able to perform casework for individual constituents and to deliver federal money for projects in the district. Incumbents use those tools to cement their relationship with voters. Term limits, then, may be a necessary response to the cumulative advantages incumbents enjoy—a tool to level the playing field and make elections competitive.

ASSIGNMENT

1. a. According to the data in Table 7.3.1, what percentage of incumbents in the House was reelected in 2000?

___

b. What percentage of incumbents won with 60 percent or more of the vote?

___

c. What was the average winning percentage in open races?

___

2. Free-market advocates tell us that competition helps make businesses accountable to consumers. In your view, does the dearth of competition in congressional elections pose a problem for representative democracy in the United States? Why or why not?

___

___

___

[2] See Susan Welch et al., *Understanding American Government*, 6th ed. (Belmont, Calif.: Wadsworth, 2001), p. 285 and figure 3.

TABLE 7.3.1 INCUMBENCY AND REELECTION TO THE HOUSE OF REPRESENTATIVES, 2000

STATE	DISTRICT	WINNER/PARTY	STATUS	PERCENT OF VOTE
Alabama	1	Callahan/R	Incumbent*	92
	2	Everett/R	Incumbent	69
	3	Riley/R	Incumbent*	88
	4	Aderholt/R	Incumbent	61
	5	Cramer/D	Incumbent*	90
	6	Bachus/R	Incumbent*	89
	7	Hilliard/D	Incumbent	75
Alaska	1	Young/R	Incumbent	71
Arizona	1	Flake/R	Open	54
	2	Pastor/D	Incumbent	69
	3	Stump/R	Incumbent	66
	4	Shadegg/R	Incumbent	64
	5	Kolbe/R	Incumbent	61
	6	Hayworth/R	Incumbent	61
Arkansas	1	Berry/D	Incumbent	59
	2	Snyder/D	Incumbent	58
	3	Hutchinson/R	Incumbent	100[+]
	4	Ross/D	Challenger	51
California	1	Thompson/D	Incumbent	66
	2	Herger/R	Incumbent	66
	3	Ose/R	Incumbent	57
	4	Doolittle/R	Incumbent	64
	5	Matsui/D	Incumbent	69
	6	Woolsey/D	Incumbent	65
	7	Miller/D	Incumbent	77
	8	Pelosi/D	Incumbent	85
	9	Lee/D	Incumbent	86
	10	Tauscher/D	Incumbent	53
	11	Pombo/R	Incumbent	58
	12	Lantos/D	Incumbent	75
	13	Stark/D	Incumbent	71
	14	Eshoo/D	Incumbent	71
	15	Honda/D	Open	55
	16	Lofgren/D	Incumbent	73
	17	Farr/D	Incumbent	69
	18	Condit/D	Incumbent	68
	19	Radanovich/R	Incumbent	65
	20	Dooley/D	Incumbent	53
	21	Thomas/R	Incumbent	72
	22	Capps/D	Incumbent	53
	23	Gallegly/R	Incumbent	54
	24	Sherman/D	Incumbent	67
	25	McKeon/R	Incumbent	63
	26	Berman/D	Incumbent*	85
	27	Schiff/D	Challenger	53
	28	Dreier/R	Incumbent	57
	29	Waxman/D	Incumbent	76
	30	Becerra/D	Incumbent	84
	31	Solis/D	Open	80
	32	Dixon/D	Incumbent	84
	33	Roybal-Allard/D	Incumbent	85
	34	Napolitano/D	Incumbent	72

(continued)

TABLE 7.3.1 (CONTINUED)

STATE	DISTRICT	WINNER/PARTY	STATUS	PERCENT OF VOTE
	35	Waters/D	Incumbent	87
	36	Harman/D	Challenger	49
	37	Millender-McDonald/D	Incumbent	83
	38	Horn/R	Incumbent	49
	39	Royce/D	Incumbent	63
	40	Lewis/R	Incumbent*	80
	41	Miller/R	Incumbent	59
	42	Baca/D	Incumbent	60
	43	Calvert/R	Incumbent*	74
	44	Bono/R	Incumbent	60
	45	Rohrabacher/R	Incumbent	62
	46	Sanchez/D	Incumbent	60
	47	Cox/R	Incumbent	66
	48	Issa/R	Open	61
	49	Davis/D	Challenger	50
	50	Filner/D	Incumbent	69
	51	Cunningham/R	Incumbent	64
	52	Hunter/R	Incumbent	65
Colorado	1	DeGette/D	Incumbent	69
	2	Udall/D	Incumbent	56
	3	McInnis/R	Incumbent	66
	4	Schaffer/R	Incumbent*	81
	5	Hefley/R	Incumbent*	83
	6	Tancredo/R	Incumbent	54
Connecticut	1	Larson/D	Incumbent	71
	2	Simmons/R	Challenger	51
	3	DeLauro/D	Incumbent	73
	4	Shays/R	Incumbent	58
	5	Maloney/D	Incumbent	54
	6	Johnson/R	Incumbent	63
Delaware	1	Castle/R	Incumbent	68
Florida	1	Scarborough/R	Incumbent*	100†
	2	Boyd/D	Incumbent	72
	3	Brown/D	Incumbent	58
	4	Crenshaw/R	Incumbent	67
	5	Thurman/D	Incumbent	64
	6	Stearns/R	Incumbent*	100†
	7	Mica/R	Incumbent	63
	8	Keller/R	Open	51
	9	Bilirakis/R	Incumbent*	82
	10	Young/R	Incumbent*	76
	11	Davis/D	Incumbent*	85
	12	Putnam/R	Open	57
	13	Miller/R	Incumbent	64
	14	Goss/R	Incumbent*	86
	15	Weldon/R	Incumbent	59
	16	Foley/R	Incumbent	61
	17	Meek/D	Incumbent*	100†
	18	Ros-Lehtinen/R	Incumbent*	100†
	19	Wexler/D	Incumbent	72
	20	Deutsch/D	Incumbent*	100†
	21	Diaz-Balart/R	Incumbent*	100†

TABLE 7.3.1 (CONTINUED)

STATE	DISTRICT	WINNER/PARTY	STATUS	PERCENT OF VOTE
	22	Shaw/R	Incumbent	50
	23	Hastings/D	Incumbent	76
Georgia	1	Kingston/R	Incumbent	69
	2	Bishop/D	Incumbent	53
	3	Collins/R	Incumbent	63
	4	McKinney/D	Incumbent	60
	5	Lewis/D	Incumbent	77
	6	Isakson/R	Incumbent	75
	7	Barr/R	Incumbent	54
	8	Chambliss/R	Incumbent	59
	9	Deal/R	Incumbent	75
	10	Norwood/R	Incumbent	63
	11	Linder/R	Incumbent*	100†
Hawaii	1	Ambercrombie/D	Incumbent	70
	2	Mink/D	Incumbent	62
Idaho	1	Otter/R	Incumbent	65
	2	Simpson/R	Incumbent	71
Illinois	1	Rush/D	Incumbent	88
	2	Jackson/D	Incumbent	90
	3	Lipinski/D	Incumbent	75
	4	Gutierrez/D	Incumbent	89
	5	Blagojevich/D	Incumbent*	88
	6	Hyde/R	Incumbent	59
	7	Davis/D	Incumbent	86
	8	Crane/R	Incumbent	61
	9	Schakowsky/D	Incumbent	76
	10	Kirk/R	Open	51
	11	Weller/R	Incumbent	56
	12	Costello/D	Incumbent	100†
	13	Biggert/R	Incumbent	66
	14	Hastert/R	Incumbent	74
	15	Johnson/R	Open	53
	16	Manzullo/R	Incumbent	67
	17	Evans/D	Incumbent	55
	18	LaHood/R	Incumbent	67
	19	Phelps/D	Incumbent	65
	20	Shimkus/R	Incumbent	63
Indiana	1	Visclosky/D	Incumbent	72
	2	Pence/R	Open	51
	3	Roemer/D	Incumbent	52
	4	Souder/R	Incumbent	63
	5	Buyer/R	Incumbent	61
	6	Burton/R	Incumbent	71
	7	Kerns/R	Open	65
	8	Hostettler/R	Incumbent	53
	9	Hill/D	Incumbent	55
	10	Carson/D	Incumbent	59
Iowa	1	Leach/R	Incumbent	62
	2	Nussle/R	Incumbent	56
	3	Boswell/D	Incumbent	63
	4	Ganske/R	Incumbent	62
	5	Latham/R	Incumbent	69

(continued)

TABLE 7.3.1 (CONTINUED)

STATE	DISTRICT	WINNER/PARTY	STATUS	PERCENT OF VOTE
Kansas	1	Moran/R	Incumbent*	90
	2	Ryun/R	Incumbent	68
	3	Moore/D	Incumbent	50
	4	Tiahrt/R	Incumbent	55
Kentucky	1	Whitfield/R	Incumbent	58
	2	Lewis/R	Incumbent	66
	3	Northup/R	Incumbent	53
	4	Lucas/D	Incumbent	55
	5	Rogers/R	Incumbent	74
	6	Fletcher/R	Incumbent	53
Louisiana	1	Vitter/R	Open	80
	2	Jefferson/D	Incumbent*	100†
	3	Tauzin/R	Incumbent	78
	4	McCrery/R	Incumbent	71
	5	Cooksey/R	Incumbent	69
	6	Baker/R	Incumbent	68
	7	John/D	Incumbent	84
Maine	1	Allen/D	Incumbent	60
	2	Baldacci/D	Incumbent	73
Maryland	1	Gilchrest/R	Incumbent	64
	2	Erlich/R	Incumbent	69
	3	Cardin/D	Incumbent	76
	4	Wynn/D	Incumbent	88
	5	Hoyer/D	Incumbent	65
	6	Bartlett/R	Incumbent	61
	7	Cummings/D	Incumbent	87
	8	Morella/R	Incumbent	52
Massachusetts	1	Olver/D	Incumbent	69
	2	Neal/D	Incumbent*	100†
	3	McGovern/D	Incumbent*	100†
	4	Frank/D	Incumbent	76
	5	Meehan/D	Incumbent*	100†
	6	Tierney/D	Incumbent	71
	7	Markey/D	Incumbent*	100†
	8	Capuano/D	Incumbent*	100†
	9	Moakley/D	Incumbent	78
	10	Delahunt/D	Incumbent	74
Michigan	1	Stupak/D	Incumbent	59
	2	Hoekstra/R	Incumbent	65
	3	Ehlers/R	Incumbent	65
	4	Camp/R	Incumbent	68
	5	Barcia/D	Incumbent	75
	6	Upton/R	Incumbent	68
	7	Smith/R	Incumbent	62
	8	Rogers/R	Open	49
	9	Kildee/D	Incumbent	62
	10	Bonior/D	Incumbent	65
	11	Knollenberg/R	Incumbent	56
	12	Levin/D	Incumbent	65
	13	Rivers/D	Incumbent	65
	14	Conyers/D	Incumbent	90
	15	Kilpatrick/D	Incumbent	90

TABLE 7.3.1 (CONTINUED)

STATE	DISTRICT	WINNER/PARTY	STATUS	PERCENT OF VOTE
	16	Dingell/D	Incumbent	71
Minnesota	1	Gutknecht/R	Incumbent	57
	2	Kennedy/R	Challenger	49
	3	Ramstad/R	Incumbent	68
	4	McCollum/D	Open	48
	5	Sabo/D	Incumbent	70
	6	Luther/D	Incumbent	50
	7	Peterson/D	Incumbent	69
	8	Oberstar/D	Incumbent	68
Mississippi	1	Wicker/R	Incumbent	71
	2	Thompson/D	Incumbent	65
	3	Pickering/R	Incumbent	74
	4	Shows/D	Incumbent	59
	5	Taylor/D	Incumbent	79
Missouri	1	Clay/R	Open	76
	2	Akin/R	Open	56
	3	Gephardt/D	Incumbent	58
	4	Skelton/D	Incumbent	67
	5	McCarthy/D	Incumbent	69
	6	Graves/R	Open	51
	7	Blunt/R	Incumbent	74
	8	Emerson/R	Incumbent	70
	9	Hulshof/R	Incumbent	60
Montana	1	Rehberg/R	Open	52
Nebraska	1	Bereuter/R	Incumbent	66
	2	Terry/R	Incumbent	67
	3	Osborne/R	Open	82
Nevada	1	Berkley/D	Incumbent	52
	2	Gibbons/R	Incumbent	65
New Hampshire	1	Sununu/R	Incumbent	54
	2	Bass/R	Incumbent	57
New Jersey	1	Andrews/D	Incumbent	77
	2	LeBiondo/R	Incumbent	67
	3	Saxton/R	Incumbent	58
	4	Smith/R	Incumbent	64
	5	Roukema/R	Incumbent	66
	6	Pallone/D	Incumbent	68
	7	Ferguson/R	Open	50
	8	Pascrell/D	Incumbent	68
	9	Rothman/D	Incumbent	68
	10	Payne/D	Incumbent	88
	11	Frelinghuysen/R	Incumbent	68
	12	Holt/D	Incumbent	49
	13	Menendez/D	Incumbent	79
New Mexico	1	Wilson/R	Incumbent	51
	2	Skeen/R	Incumbent	58
	3	Udall/D	Incumbent	67
New York	1	Grucci/R	Challenger	56
	2	Israel/D	Open	48
	3	King/R	Incumbent	60
	4	McCarthy/D	Incumbent	61
	5	Ackerman/D	Incumbent	68

(continued)

TABLE 7.3.1 (CONTINUED)

STATE	DISTRICT	WINNER/PARTY	STATUS	PERCENT OF VOTE
	6	Meeks/D	Incumbent*	100†
	7	Crowley/D	Incumbent	71
	8	Nadler/D	Incumbent	81
	9	Weiner/D	Incumbent	68
	10	Towns/D	Incumbent	90
	11	Owens/D	Incumbent	88
	12	Velazquez/D	Incumbent	86
	13	Fossella/R	Incumbent	65
	14	Maloney/D	Incumbent	74
	15	Rangel/D	Incumbent	91
	16	Serrano/D	Incumbent	96
	17	Engel/D	Incumbent	89
	18	Lowey/D	Incumbent	67
	19	Kelly/R	Incumbent	61
	20	Gilman/R	Incumbent	58
	21	McNulty/D	Incumbent	74
	22	Sweeney/R	Incumbent	69
	23	Boehlert/R	Incumbent	60
	24	McHugh/R	Incumbent	75
	25	Walsh/R	Incumbent	69
	26	Hinchey/D	Incumbent	62
	27	Reynolds/R	Incumbent	70
	28	Slaughter/D	Incumbent	66
	29	LaFalce/D	Incumbent	61
	30	Quinn/R	Incumbent	67
	31	Houghton/R	Incumbent	77
North Carolina	1	Clayton/D	Incumbent	66
	2	Etheridge/D	Incumbent	58
	3	Jones/R	Incumbent	62
	4	Price/D	Incumbent	62
	5	Burr/R	Incumbent*	93
	6	Coble/R	Incumbent*	92
	7	McIntyre/D	Incumbent	70
	8	Hayes/R	Incumbent	56
	9	Myrick/R	Incumbent	69
	10	Ballenger/R	Incumbent	69
	11	Taylor/R	Incumbent	55
	12	Watt/D	Incumbent	65
North Dakota	1	Pomeroy/D	Incumbent	54
Ohio	1	Chabot/R	Incumbent	54
	2	Portman/R	Incumbent	74
	3	Hall/D	Incumbent*	83
	4	Oxley/R	Incumbent	68
	5	Gillmor/R	Incumbent	70
	6	Strickland/D	Incumbent	58
	7	Hobson/R	Incumbent	68
	8	Boehner/R	Incumbent	71
	9	Kaptur/D	Incumbent	75
	10	Kucinich/D	Incumbent	76
	11	Tubbs-Jones/D	Incumbent	86
	12	Tiberi/R	Open	53
	13	Brown/D	Incumbent	65

TABLE 7.3.1 (CONTINUED)

STATE	DISTRICT	WINNER/PARTY	STATUS	PERCENT OF VOTE
	14	Sawyer/D	Incumbent	65
	15	Pryce/R	Incumbent	68
	16	Regula/R	Incumbent	70
	17	Traficant/D	Incumbent	50
	18	Ney/R	Incumbent	65
	19	LaTourette/R	Incumbent	70
Oklahoma	1	Largent/R	Incumbent	70
	2	Carson/D	Open	55
	3	Watkins/R	Incumbent	87
	4	Watts/R	Incumbent	65
	5	Istook/R	Incumbent	69
	6	Lucas/R	Incumbent	60
Oregon	1	Wu/D	Incumbent	59
	2	Walden/R	Incumbent	74
	3	Blumenauer/D	Incumbent	68
	4	DeFazio/D	Incumbent	69
	5	Hooley/D	Incumbent	57
Pennsylvania	1	Brady/D	Incumbent	88
	2	Fattah/D	Incumbent*	99
	3	Borski/D	Incumbent	69
	4	Hart/R	Open	59
	5	Peterson/R	Incumbent*	86
	6	Holden/D	Incumbent	67
	7	Weldon/R	Incumbent	65
	8	Greenwood/R	Incumbent	60
	9	Shuster/R	Incumbent*	100†
	10	Sherwood/R	Incumbent	53
	11	Kanjorski/D	Incumbent	66
	12	Murtha/D	Incumbent	71
	13	Hoeffel/D	Incumbent	53
	14	Coyne/D	Incumbent*	100†
	15	Toomey/R	Incumbent	53
	16	Pitts/R	Incumbent	67
	17	Gekas/R	Incumbent	72
	18	Doyle/D	Incumbent	69
	19	Platts/R	Open	73
	20	Mascara/D	Incumbent	64
	21	English/R	Incumbent	61
Rhode Island	1	Kennedy/D	Incumbent	67
	2	Langevin/D	Open	62
South Carolina	1	Brown/R	Open	60
	2	Spence/R	Incumbent	58
	3	Graham/R	Incumbent	68
	4	DeMint/R	Incumbent*	80
	5	Spratt/D	Incumbent	59
	6	Clyburn/D	Incumbent	73
South Dakota	1	Thune/R	Incumbent	74
Tennessee	1	Jenkins/R	Incumbent*	100†
	2	Duncan/R	Incumbent*	90
	3	Wamp/R	Incumbent	64
	4	Hilleary/R	Incumbent	66
	5	Clement/D	Incumbent	73

(continued)

TABLE 7.3.1 (CONTINUED)

STATE	DISTRICT	WINNER/PARTY	STATUS	PERCENT OF VOTE
	6	Gordon/D	Incumbent	63
	7	Bryant/R	Incumbent	70
	8	Tanner/D	Incumbent	72
	9	Ford/D	Incumbent*	100†
Texas	1	Sandlin/D	Incumbent	56
	2	Turner/D	Incumbent*	92
	3	Johnson/R	Incumbent	73
	4	Hall/D	Incumbent	61
	5	Sessions/R	Incumbent	55
	6	Barton/R	Incumbent*	89
	7	Culberson/R	Incumbent	74
	8	Brady/R	Incumbent*	92
	9	Lampson/D	Incumbent	60
	10	Doggett/D	Incumbent*	85
	11	Edwards/D	Incumbent	55
	12	Granger/R	Incumbent	63
	13	Thornberry/R	Incumbent	68
	14	Paul/R	Incumbent	60
	15	Hinojosa/D	Incumbent	89
	16	Reyes/D	Incumbent	69
	17	Stenholm/D	Incumbent	60
	18	Lee/D	Incumbent	77
	19	Combest/R	Incumbent*	92
	20	Gonzalez/D	Incumbent	88
	21	Smith/R	Incumbent	76
	22	DeLay/R	Incumbent	61
	23	Bonilla/R	Incumbent	60
	24	Frost/D	Incumbent	62
	25	Bentsen/D	Incumbent	60
	26	Armeny/R	Incumbent	73
	27	Ortiz/D	Incumbent	64
	28	Rodriguez/D	Incumbent	89
	29	Green/D	Incumbent	74
	30	Johnson/D	Incumbent*	92
Utah	1	Hansen/R	Incumbent	69
	2	Matheson/D	Open	56
	3	Cannon/R	Incumbent	59
Vermont	1	Sanders/I	Incumbent	70
Virginia	1	Davis/R	Open	58
	2	Schrock/R	Open	52
	3	Scott/D	Incumbent*	100†
	4	Sisisky/D	Incumbent*	100†
	5	Goode/I	Incumbent	68
	6	Goodlatte/R	Incumbent*	100†
	7	Cantor/R	Open	67
	8	Moran/D	Incumbent	64
	9	Boucher/D	Incumbent	70
	10	Wolf/R	Incumbent*	85
Washington	1	Inslee/D	Incumbent	55
	2	Larsen/D	Open	51
	3	Baird/D	Incumbent	57
	4	Hastings/R	Incumbent	61

TABLE 7.3.1 (CONTINUED)

STATE	DISTRICT	WINNER/PARTY	STATUS	PERCENT OF VOTE
	5	Nethercutt/R	Incumbent	58
	6	Dicks/D	Incumbent	65
	7	McDermott/D	Incumbent*	73
	8	Dunn/R	Incumbent	63
	9	Smith/D	Incumbent	62
West Virginia	1	Mollohan/D	Incumbent*	88
	2	Capito/R	Open	49
	3	Rahall/D	Incumbent*	92
Wisconsin	1	Ryan/R	Incumbent	66
	2	Baldwin/D	Incumbent	51
	3	Kind/D	Incumbent	64
	4	Kleczka/D	Incumbent	61
	5	Barrett/D	Incumbent	78
	6	Petri/R	Incumbent	65
	7	Obey/D	Incumbent	63
	8	Green/R	Incumbent	75
	9	Sensenbrenner/R	Incumbent	74
Wyoming	1	Cubin/R	Incumbent	67

Key: D = Democrat; R = Republican; I = Independent.

* Ran without opposition.

† Votes were not tallied officially. (In some states, when a race is uncontested, the winner is simply awarded 100 percent of the vote.)

Note: *Open* means no incumbent ran.

3. In 2000, the terms of thirty-four U.S. senators ended.

a. Twenty-six of those senators ran for reelection, and 76 percent of them won. How does that rate compare with the comparable rate in the House elections (see question 1)?

b. Sixteen of the twenty-six incumbents—that's 62 percent—won with 60 percent or more of the vote. How does that rate compare with the comparable rate in the House elections (see question 1)?

c. The average winning percentage in the open races was 53 percent. How does that rate compare with the comparable rate in the House elections (see question 1)?

4. Reelection rates in the House and Senate (see question 3) have differed consistently since 1945. What factors help explain the difference? Begin by thinking about how the constituency of a House member differs from that of a U.S. senator. Notice, too, that the reelection rate for incumbent senators from the largest states is about 6 or 7 points below that for senators from the smallest states.

____

____

____

____

____

____

5. What statistical support do you find in Tables 7.3.1 and 7.3.2 for the proposition that Americans hate Congress but love their own representative in Congress?

____

____

____

TABLE 7.3.2 PUBLIC OPINION OF THE PERFORMANCE OF CONGRESS, 1980–2000 (PERCENTAGE)

RESPONSE	1980	1982	1984	1986	1988	1990	1992	1994	1996	1998	2000*
Approve	34	34	53	44	52	36	28	32	46	48	45
Disapprove	48	49	35	38	24	55	63	60	47	43	44
Don't know	18	17	12	18	14	9	9	8	8	9	11

* August 2000.

SOURCE: The data are taken from "Poll Topics & Trends" on the Gallup Organization's Web site (www.gallup.com). Those data are now available only by subscription.

6. Political action committees are organizations whose sole purpose is to contribute money to candidates for election (see Exercise 6.5). Most PACs are associated with corporations, labor unions, or interest groups.

a. According to the data in Table 7.3.3, between 1999 and 2000, what was the average PAC contribution to incumbents, challengers, and candidates for open seats? (Get number of each from Table 7.3.1.)

Incumbents: ______________

Challengers: ______________

Candidates for open seats: ______________

TABLE 7.3.3 PAC CONTRIBUTIONS, 1985–2000 (IN MILLIONS)

	1985–1986	1987–1988	1989–1990	1991–1992	1993–1994	1995–1996	1997–1998	1999–2000
Incumbents	$96	$118	$126	$135	$137	$146	$171	$184
Challengers	$20	$19	$16	$23	$19	$32	$22	$27
Open seats	$24	$22	$17	$31	$33	$40	$27	$34

SOURCE: All data are from the Federal Election Commission (www.fec.gov).

b. How do these figures differ, and how would you explain the differences?

7. The Federal Election Commission maintains campaign finance data on all candidates for federal office. You can search that database at http://herndon1.sdrdc.com/fecimg/srssea.html. Go to the Web site and search for your member of the House of Representatives for the 1999–2000 election cycle. Click on the summary and then on contributions from nonparty or other committees. List the top ten PACs that gave money to his or her campaign and how much each gave.

8. In 1992, California voters passed Proposition 164, which limited the number of terms California's delegation in Congress could serve. Three years later, in *U.S. Term Limits, Inc., v. Thornton,* the Supreme Court declared that any attempt to impose term limits by state legislative action (with or without the initiative) was unconstitutional.[3] Arguments for and against Proposition 164, and the rebuttals to those arguments are reproduced in Reading 7.3.

READING 7.3 California Proposition 164: Arguments and Rebuttals

Argument in Favor of Proposition 164

Everybody is running for their own survival. The first priority of a member is to stay in office.

—Sixteen-year California Congressman Leon Panetta quoted in USA Today, *April 28, 1992*

Our founding fathers would be shocked at the abuses and attitudes of Congress today. While their policies were sending a record number of Californians to the unemployment line, members of the House voted themselves $40,000 in pay raises and Senate members $27,600. Each one of them now earns more than $129,000 a year. And most of them will be eligible for million dollar tax-subsidized pensions.

Our professional politicians in California's delegation have already given us a $4 trillion dollar national debt, a 9.5% California unemployment rate, 500,000 lost California jobs, banking and postal scandals, and the largest tax increase in U.S. history.

[3] By the mid-1990s, a number of states had imposed term limits on their congressional delegations. *U.S. Term Limits, Inc., v. Thornton,* an Alabama case, clarified the law in several states.

READING SOURCE: Voters' pamphlet, California, general election, November 1992.

Incumbent politicians have rigged the system to assure their re-election. The longer they are in Washington, the less our career representatives care about us. And the record shows that it's the long-term incumbents who are most likely to be caught in scandals.

California voters launched a national drive for term limits when we passed Prop. 140 in 1990. Term limits are an even better idea for Congress in 1992.

Prop. 164 will put term limits on California's Congressmembers. The terms of the President, the Governor and the California legislature are already limited; it's time to limit Congressional terms, too.

Prop. 164 will:

- *Increase California's clout in Congress.* Prop. 164 begins to break up the "good ol' boy" seniority system in Congress which rewards tenure not accomplishment and allows small states enormous power in Congress. With the largest delegation in the country, California's 54 representatives can work hard for California, instead of taking a back seat to politicians from Mississippi and West Virginia.
- *Give power back to the people of California.* Our representatives will be reminded they are public servants—not masters—who can serve for a definite time and then return home to *live under the laws they made.*
- *Reinvigorate Congress with new blood and new ideas* to tackle the tough problems facing our nation today.
- *Reintroduce courage and honesty* among our representatives by *weakening the hold of special interests, lobbyists and bureaucracy* on Congress. Prop. 164 will force our representatives to face facts, come clean on problems and propose bold new solutions.
- *Protect your right to vote and give you a real choice of candidates.* Incumbents dominate elections with free mail, huge staffs, free travel and PAC funding. Term limits will open up elections to competition and Prop. 164's special write-in provision will allow voters to re-elect exceptional representatives even if their terms have expired.

The dream of our founding fathers has not failed; the careerist politicians we've elected *have* failed. They put their own careers and multi-million dollar retirements ahead of the needs of California and the nation.

Prop. 164 will end political cronyism and reward merit, giving us a Congressional delegation that will solve problems, not add to them.

Rebuttal to Argument in Favor of Proposition 164

Proposition 164 won't make government more responsive. It will just give California citizens and taxpayers the short end of the stick.

Proposition 164 is biased against California unless the country has a national term limit law.

We'd rejoice to see them pass that (term limits) in California because it would give us relatively more power.

—Eighteen-year South Carolina Congressman Butler Derrick quoted in the Los Angeles Times, *June 10, 1992*

For California to set limits unilaterally . . . would just mean that Texas, Mississippi, Georgia and other Southern states would end up with most of the committee chairmanships.

—Twenty-year Texas Congressman Charlie Wilson quoted in the Los Angeles Times, *June 10, 1992*

We must revitalize Congress. The way to do that is by voting out those who are not doing their job and by passing legislation to reform campaign financing in Washington. Proposition 164 doesn't do either.

Proposition 164 doesn't "break up the 'good ol' boy' seniority system in Congress." It means we get left out. Senior politicians from New York and Florida will be in control while we have a revolving door of back benchers.

Here's what will happen:

- California will remain the largest source of Federal tax dollars, but senior members of Congress will grab those dollars for their states. We will get *less* than our fair share.

- California will lose jobs as powerful politicians from Texas, Illinois and elsewhere move government contracts to their states.

Let the people choose their representatives. Proposition 164 isn't reform, it's a disaster. *Vote no on Proposition 164.*

Argument Against Proposition 164

No matter how you feel about term limits, vote *no* on Proposition 164. It's not about term limits or Congressional reform; it's about destroying California's clout in Congress.

Proposition 164 will cost California thousands of jobs, weaken our environmental protections, and shift greater burdens onto the backs of California taxpayers.

Proposition 164 only affects *California's own* Members of Congress. It does not apply term limits to *all* Members of Congress.

What's so bad about that? The answer is that California *competes* with other states for Federal dollars—and we are sending more money to Washington than we get back in Federal dollars for California. Proposition 164 means we will pay hundreds of billions of dollars in Federal taxes and get less and less in return.

Powerful members of Congress decide how those Federal dollars are spent. How do they get to be powerful? They stay a long time in Congress. It's called the seniority system. If California limits our terms while Texas, Florida, and New York don't limit theirs, Californians will lose. Our clout in Congress will go to other states, and they will grab more of the hard earned dollars California taxpayers send to Washington.

We need strong California representation to get help for our struggling economy. What happens if we are devastated by another earthquake, or similar disaster? We need Congressional members on the major committees to see that we get help. With California-only term limits, we will end up with a delegation of low ranking members who can't fight for our state against the powerful interests from other states.

Hundreds of thousands of jobs are at stake as cutbacks continue. Who will fight to protect those jobs for California? The Texans, New Yorkers and Floridians will be there for their states. Where will California be?

The Governor's office and the Legislature agree that we need to fight for more Federal help to pay for the immigrant load on California. If we don't get Federal help, California taxpayers must bear a greater burden. Proposition 164 means those Federal dollars will go to other states.

This year we will be electing both U.S. Senators and all California Members of Congress. If we don't like the job incumbents are doing we can vote them out of office. Proposition 164 removes members of Congress without a vote of the people, whether or not they are doing a good job.

To quote the *Sacramento Bee:* "Seniority still counts for a lot in Washington, and if California members of the House are limited to only three two-year terms, and its U.S. Senators to only two six-year terms, the state will have doomed itself to be permanently represented by a bunch of back benchers."

With 54 Members in Congress—the most in the country—we should have the strongest delegation fighting for California in Washington. Proposition 164 assures that we have one of the weakest. Keep California strong. Vote *no* on Proposition 164.

Rebuttal to Argument Against Proposition 164

How much has California's congressional delegation done for you?

Opponents say California is "sending more money to Washington than we get back in Federal dollars for California." That's *true! And* that's a reason to *vote for Proposition 164.*

Career politicians have robbed California of our clout. Smaller states are constantly beating California for our fair share of Federal spending.

Washington, D.C. has a *cancer* that is eating away at the heart of America. This cancer's name is *career politicians.*

In 1991, nearly half—$182 million—of the $387 million allotted for special road projects in the Senate transportation appropriations bill went to West Virginia—all thanks to its senior Senator, Robert Byrd. That's $101 for every West Virginia resident and less than $1 for every Californian.

This is proof that the current seniority system has placed California at a disadvantage.

Other states are just as disenchanted with the career politicians' pork-barrel. California is not alone in the term limits fight. More than a dozen other states will be joining us *this year.*

In 1998, when California's term limits take effect, the seniority system in Congress will be long dead.

Since the career politicians invaded our capital, the seniority system has rewarded big-money lobbyists, big-spending bureaucrats, special interests and the politicians themselves.

Congress, quick to raise salaries to $129,500, is now dragging its feet on unemployment, medical insurance and the environment.

Let's reward merit and hard work—not seniority. *Return clout to California—vote yes on Proposition 164.*

---

8. a. In the space below, list what you think are the three most persuasive arguments on each side of the debate over Proposition 164.

For the proposition: ______________________

____

____

Against the proposition: ______________________

____

____

b. How would you have voted? Why?

____

____

____

____

____

EXERCISE 7.4 BLACKS IN CONGRESS

BACKGROUND

Like every other minority group in America, blacks always have been underrepresented in the U.S. Congress. The political strength of blacks in the national legislature has never been proportional to the number of blacks in the general population. Achieving proportional representation in Congress has long been a goal of minority groups because it increases the ability of minorities to influence the national agenda and address issues of concern. In addition, minorities in Congress function as role models, validating and encouraging the aspirations of others. Finally, representation in Congress may indicate a measure of the acceptance and respect accorded to minorities by society.

For some, minority representation in Congress should approximate a group's presence in the general population. Moving toward that goal requires that minority-group members have the right to vote and are able to exercise that right without interference. Only then can they elevate to office candidates who share their goals, concerns, and experiences.

Efforts by blacks to achieve proportional representation in Congress have been impeded by many factors, racism primary among them. The main problem facing African Americans in 1787 was not a lack of representation in Congress; it was that the vast majority of blacks were enslaved. *Slavery* was such an odious term that the framers did not use it in the Constitution—it first appeared in 1865, in the Thirteenth Amendment—but the practice was so deeply embedded in the new nation's economy and society that the framers could not escape addressing it. In Article I, Section 2, where the terms of the three-fifths compromise are specified, black slaves in the South are alluded to as "other Persons." In Article I, Section 9, which prohibited Congress from banning the slave trade before 1808, blacks are referred to as "such Persons." In Article IV, Section 2, which required the return of fugitive slaves, blacks are called persons "held to Service or Labour." The framers' euphemistic references to slaves notwithstanding, those three clauses in the Constitution recognized and explicitly protected slavery in the southern states. By the time the Constitution was ratified, in 1788, most northern states were in the process of freeing their slaves. But North or South, African Americans would have a long way to travel before achieving representation in Congress.

Black Representation in the House Any examination of the struggle of blacks to achieve representation in the House must begin with the position of blacks in the South.[4] The South did not elect a black to the House until 1870. Before the Civil War, the vast majority of African Americans in the South were slaves—property, not citizens. There was a substantial number of free blacks in the South before the Civil War, but most southern states prohibited them from voting. And, in any event, their number was not enough in any given congressional district to elect a black to the House.

In 1867 Republicans in Congress passed a series of laws, the Reconstruction Acts, mandating the use of federal power to protect the voting rights of the newly freed slaves. That application of federal power in the South on behalf of blacks, combined with the determination of newly enfranchised blacks to increase black representation in government, was directly responsible for the election of Joseph Rainey to the House in 1870, the first African American to take a seat there.[5] Rainey was born a slave in South Carolina, but his father later purchased the family's freedom. To avoid being drafted to work for the Confederate Army during the Civil War, Rainey escaped to the West Indies. He returned to South Carolina at the end of the war and held several political positions before being elected to the House. He was reelected four times.

Between 1870 and 1877, thirteen other blacks from southern states served in the House. Together, those fourteen men served a total of twenty-one terms. But those striking gains, the product of the application of federal military force in the South, were short lived. The commitment of whites in the North to the political equality of blacks in the South had always been weak, and the national government discontinued the application of force in 1877. Whites in the South, free to strip blacks of their voting rights,

[4] In this exercise, the *South* consists of the eleven states of the Confederacy: Alabama, Arkansas, Florida, Georgia, Louisiana, Mississippi, North Carolina, South Carolina, Tennessee, Texas, and Virginia.

[5] Rainey was elected in 1870 to fill a vacant seat. He joined the members of the Forty-First Congress, who had been elected in 1868.

instituted devices like the literacy test, the poll tax, and the grandfather clause to disfranchise blacks. Those devices, in combination with violence and economic intimidation, kept blacks from voting and running for office until well into the twentieth century.

Congress waited almost one hundred years before again using federal power to protect the voting rights of blacks in the South. The Voting Rights Act of 1965 authorized the president to send government officials to the South to ensure that blacks were allowed to vote without interference. President Lyndon Johnson aggressively enforced the new legislation. In 1965 only 6 percent of the blacks eligible to vote in Mississippi were registered; by 1968 that rate had increased to 44 percent.

Paradoxically, blacks in the North had to wait considerably longer than southern blacks to achieve representation in the House. From the time the Constitution was adopted until the Fourteenth and Fifteenth Amendments were ratified (in 1868 and 1870, respectively), determining who would vote was strictly a state prerogative. Northern states had a mixed record on black voting: Some allowed blacks to vote; others didn't. Even in northern states where blacks were allowed to vote, no black was elected to the House before the Civil War. During the period from the late 1780s to the late 1860s, blacks made up only a small proportion of the northern population—about 2 percent in 1840, for example—and the concentration of black voting power was not enough in any given House district to elect an African American.

After the Fourteenth and Fifteenth Amendments were ratified, voting by blacks in the north was widespread. But blacks there were not accorded the other rights of citizenship enjoyed by most white males. Blacks in the north faced segregation, race riots, and mob violence. And it was not until 1928 that Oscar De Priest became the first African American elected to the House from a northern district. De Priest was a Republican, elected from the First Congressional District in Illinois, on the south side of Chicago. De Priest served three terms in the House. He was defeated in 1934 by Arthur Mitchell, the first black Democrat elected to the House. The elections of De Priest and Mitchell were made possible, in large part, by the massive migration of blacks out of the South around the time of World War I. Many of those black migrants settled in burgeoning black communities in and around Chicago, New York, and Detroit, where their concentration in particular House districts made possible again black representation in the House.

Black Representation in the Senate The underrepresentation of blacks in the U.S. Senate has been staggering. With the adjournment of the 107th Congress late in 2002, the Senate will be 214 years old. Blacks have been represented in the Senate during just 25 of those years; and at no time has more than one seat in the Senate chamber been occupied by an African American. One important obstacle: the structure of the senatorial "district." U.S. senators run statewide. That means the electorate is usually more numerous and more diverse than the voters who elect U.S. representatives. In most states, blacks voters simply do not have the numbers to elect black candidates in statewide elections.

Hiram Revels was the first African American to serve in the U.S. Senate. He was born in North Carolina in 1827 to parents who were free blacks, which made him free also. After a career in the ministry, Revels settled in Mississippi and was elected to the state senate in 1869. The Mississippi legislature elected Revels in 1870 to fill one of the state's two vacant seats in the U.S. Senate. Revels served in the Senate from February 1870 until March 1871.[6]

Blanche Bruce, a Republican like Revels, was the second African American to serve in the U.S. Senate. Bruce held many local political offices in Mississippi, including registrar of voters and sheriff, and established himself as a wealthy cotton farmer. In 1874, the Mississippi legislature elected Bruce to a single term in the U.S. Senate; he took his seat in 1875. He was the first black to serve a full term in the Senate and the only former slave to serve.

Edward Brooke, the third black to serve in the U.S. Senate, was the first black elected to the Senate by popular vote and the first black to represent a northern state. Brooke served with distinction in World War II and pursued a career in law before winning election as the attorney general of Massachusetts in 1962. In 1966 he won election to the Senate as a Republican. He served two terms.

[6] Both of Mississippi's U.S. Senate seats had been empty since 1861, when Jefferson Davis and Albert Brown walked out of the Senate to signal Mississippi's secession from the Union. Those seats, and other southern seats, remained vacant for the duration of the Civil War and well into the period of reconstruction. Congress required that the southern states ratify the Fourteenth and, in some cases, the Fifteenth Amendments as a condition of readmission to the Union and to their vacant seats in the Senate. While the Senate seats of the southern states were vacant, the six-year term carried by all seats in the Senate continued to toll. The term for the seat Revels won was 1864–1870, which explains why Revels served just one year in the Senate.

Carol Moseley-Braun is the only black woman and the only black Democrat to serve in the U.S. Senate. Before her election to the Senate, Moseley-Braun had been a prosecutor for the U.S. attorney and had served in the Illinois legislature for ten years. In 1992 she won election to the Senate by defeating a white opponent. Moseley-Braun received 95 percent of the black vote and captured 48 percent of the white vote. She served a full term in the Senate and stood for reelection in 1998. Her bid for a second term was supported by 93 percent of African-American voters; but she attracted just 36 percent of the white vote. Her challenger in the election, Republican Peter Fitzgerald, capitalized on the scandals and controversies that plagued Moseley-Braun during her Senate term. He also outspent her two to one in the campaign.

ASSIGNMENT

Black representation in Congress has fluctuated dramatically since the Civil War. Blacks have at times achieved significant representation in the House and Senate only to see those gains erode or vanish. The questions below explore changes in the ability of African Americans to achieve and hold political power in the national legislature.

Blacks in the House of Representatives

Congress and Period*	Terms of Service in the House	Number of House Terms Blacks Served	Percentage of House Terms Blacks Served	Blacks as a Percentage of the Total National Population†
41st–44th 1869–1877	________	________	________	13
45th–56th 1877–1901	________	________	________	11–13
57th–70th 1901–1929	________	________	________	10–11
71st–90th 1929–1968	________	________	________	10–11
91st–106th 1969–2000	6,960	374	5.4	11–13
107th 2001–2002	435	37	8.5	13

* Before the Twentieth Amendment was ratified in 1933, an outgoing Congress typically would have its final meeting in the year that a newly elected Congress convened. So, for example, the 44th and the 45th Congresses were both in session at different times in 1877: The 44th early in the year and the 45th later. Since the amendment was ratified, Congress begins in January following the election.

† The black percentage of the nation's population has ranged from about 10 percent to 13 percent since the Civil War, but the distribution of the black population has changed dramatically during that period.

1. Use the data in Table 7.4.1 (on the next page) to complete the chart "Blacks in the House of Representatives." Notice that the data in Table 7.4.1 are grouped to correlate with the periods delineated in this chart. Your objective: to develop a quantitative measure of how the political power of blacks in the House has fluctuated since the Civil War (see the fourth column in the chart). The following information should help you complete the chart.

a. Determine the total terms of service in the House. Sessions of Congress run for two years and are numbered sequentially. The 107th Congress, for example, was elected in November 2000 and was seated in January 2001. All 435 House terms in the 107th Congress expire when that Congress adjourns sometime late in 2002. Since the 63d Congress (1913–1915), the number of seats in the House has been 435. So, for example, in the 91st through 106th Congresses (1969–2001), the total number of House terms was 6,960 (16 Congresses multiplied by 435 seats in each Congress).

TABLE 7.4.1 BLACKS IN THE HOUSE OF REPRESENTATIVES

ELECTION	CONGRESS*	SIZE OF HOUSE	NUMBER OF BLACKS ELECTED	PARTY	REGION
1868	41st	241	2	R	S
1870	42d	241	5	R	S
1872	43d	292	7	R	S
1874	44th	292	7	R	S
1876	45th	292	3	R	S
1878	46th	292	1	R	S
1880	47th	292	1	R	S
1882	48th	325	2	R	S
1884	49th	325	2	R	S
1886	50th	325	0		
1888	51st	325	3	R	S
1890	52d	325	1	R	S
1892	53d	356	1	R	S
1894	54th	356	1	R	S
1896	55th	356	1	R	S
1898	56th	356	1	R	S
1900	57th	356	0		
1902	58th	386	0		
1904	59th	386	0		
1906	60th	386	0		
1908	61st	386	0		
1910	62d	386	0		
1912	63d	435	0		
1914	64th	435	0		
1916	65th	435	0		
1918	66th	435	0		
1920	67th	435	0		
1922	68th	435	0		
1924	69th	435	0		
1926	70th	435	0		
1928	71st	435	1	R	N
1930	72d	435	1	R	N
1932	73d	435	1	R	N
1934	74th	435	1	D	N
1936	75th	435	1	D	N
1938	76th	435	1	D	N
1940	77th	435	1	D	N
1942	78th	435	1	D	N
1944	79th	435	2	D	N
1946	80th	435	2	D	N
1948	81st	435	2	D	N
1950	82d	435	2	D	N
1952	83d	435	2	D	N
1954	84th	435	3	D	N
1956	85th	435	4	D	N
1958	86th	435	4	D	N

TABLE 7.4.1 (CONTINUED)

ELECTION	CONGRESS*	SIZE OF HOUSE	NUMBER OF BLACKS ELECTED	PARTY	REGION
1960	87th	437†	4	D	N
1962	88th	435	5	D	N
1964	89th	435	6	D	N
1966	90th	435	6	D	N
1968	91st	435	10	D	N
1970	92d	435	11	D	N
1972	93d	435	16	D	2S 14N
1974	94th	435	16	D	3S 13N
1976	95th	435	16	D	3S 13N
1978	96th	435	17	D	2S 15N
1980	97th	435	18	D	2S 16N
1982	98th	435	21	D	2S 19N
1984	99th	435	20	D	2S 18N
1986	100th	435	22	D	4S 18N
1988	101st	435	24	D	5S 19N
1990	102d	435	27	1R 26D	6S 21N
1992	103d	435	39	1R 38D	18S 21N
1994	104th	435	41	2R 39D	17S 24N
1996	105th	435	39	1R 38D	16S 23N
1998	106th	435	35	1R 34D	19S 16N
2000	107th	435	37	1R 36D	16S 21N

Key: R = Republican; D = Democrat; S = southern state; N = nonsouthern state.

* Before the Twentieth Amendment was ratified in 1933, an outgoing Congress typically would have its final meeting in the year that a newly elected Congress convened. So, for example, the 44th and the 45th Congresses were both in session at different times in 1877: The 44th early in the year and the 45th later. Since the amendment was ratified, Congress begins in January following the election.

† To accommodate the admission of Alaska and Hawaii in 1959, the size of the House was increased temporarily to provide each of the new states with one seat. The size of the House returned to 435 after the apportionment based on the 1960 census.

SOURCE: Data come primarily from U.S. Senate, *Biographical Directory of the United States Congress, 1774–1989*, doc. 100-34 (Washington, D.C.: Joint Committee on Printing, 1989).

The calculations for the 91st through 106th Congresses, as well as those for the 107th Congress, have been completed for you. In making the calculations for the other periods, remember to factor in changes in the size of the House. Remember also that although the dates in Table 7.4.1 are important, when making the required calculations you should rely on the sessions of Congress specified by number in the second column of Table 7.4.1.

b. Determine the number of House terms blacks served in each period. You can find this information in the fourth column of Table 7.4.1. For each period, simply total the number of black representatives elected.

c. Determine the percentage of House terms blacks served. Now, working with the chart, simply divide the number of terms of service in any period into the number of terms blacks served. The quotient is the percentage of total House terms blacks served during that period.

That figure is useful for two reasons. First, it indicates how the political power of blacks in the House has changed since the Civil War. Second, we can compare it to the percentage of blacks in the total population to determine the extent to which black political strength in the House approximates the presence of blacks in the general population.

Looking at the percentage of total terms blacks served in the House is a more accurate measure of black political power than just counting the number of black representatives during a given period, a process that does not capture multiple terms. For example, between 1928 and 1944, a period that includes the 71st through 78th Congresses, two blacks were elected to the House: De Priest and Mitchell. But to say that two blacks served during this period is hardly an accurate measure of black representation because De Priest served three terms and Mitchell served four. Looking only at the number of black members who served in the House over a period of multiple Congresses, then, may underestimate the extent of black representation.

2. From 1869 to 1877, the national government protected black voting rights in the South. How did black representation in the House during that period compare with the succeeding period, from 1877 through 1901, when the power of the national government was withdrawn? To make the comparison, look at the quantitative measure of black political strength you developed filling in the chart in this assignment.

____

____

____

____

____

3. Looking at the data in Table 7.4.1 for the period 1901–1968, how effective were efforts by southern whites to strip blacks in the South of political power? Support your answer.

____

____

____

____

____

4. Looking at the chart you filled in, how did black representation in the House from 1929 to 1968 compare with the percentage of blacks in the total population?

____

____

____

5. There have been two periods since the Constitution was drafted when there was no African-American representation—from the North or South—in the House. Identify the beginning and ending dates of those periods.

Period 1: ______________________________

Period 2: ______________________________

6. Many believe that minority representation in Congress should approximate a minority's presence in the general population. In the 107th Congress, how far are blacks from achieving that goal? That is, how many more blacks would have to have been elected to the House in 2000 to make black representation there commensurate with black representation in the general population?

____

7. For the elections of 1968 through 2000, what number of Senate terms would have had to have been served by blacks to achieve black representation commensurate with the proportion of blacks in the general population? To calculate that figure, multiply the number of elections held during the period by the number of U.S. senators elected every two years. The product is the total number of Senate seats up for grabs over the period. Next, multiply that figure by the percentage of blacks in the total population over the period. Finally, compare that figure with the number of blacks actually elected to the Senate over the period.

____

8. Blanche Bruce's Senate term ended in 1881.

a. How many years would pass before Edward Brooke was elected to the Senate?

____

b. After Brooke served, how many more years would pass until another black senator was elected?

____

9. How many blacks serve in the U.S. Senate today?

____

10. Examine the data in Table 7.4.2. Notice that the population of congressional districts in Illinois is about 650,000. The total population of Illinois is about nineteen times that of any of its congressional districts. Candidates running to represent Illinois in the U.S. Senate face an electorate very different from that faced by candidates running for a seat in the House.

a. Calculate the percentage of blacks in the population for the First and Second Congressional Districts in Illinois, and for the state.

First Congressional District: ______________________________

Second Congressional District: ______________________________

State: ______________________________

b. How does the distribution of the black population within a state help explain why far more blacks have been elected to the House than to the Senate since the Civil War?

____

____

____

____

____

____

TABLE 7.4.2 ILLINOIS CONGRESSIONAL DISTRICTS, 106TH CONGRESS, BY RACE

DISTRICT	TOTAL POPULATION	WHITE	BLACK	AMERICAN INDIAN AND ALASKA NATIVE	ASIAN	NATIVE HAWAIIAN AND OTHER PACIFIC ISLANDER	SOME OTHER RACE	TWO OR MORE RACES	HISPANIC OR LATINO (OF ANY RACE)
First	560,239	128,823	393,738	1,017	7,632	150	20,261	8,618	41,866
Second	556,482	100,944	421,557	1,138	2,557	158	22,110	8,018	43,429
Third	629,597	494,324	28,447	1,900	10,439	199	76,261	18,027	153,021
Fourth	625,941	279,763	50,925	4,382	16,256	500	247,567	26,548	438,481
Fifth	635,824	488,185	12,604	2,082	38,819	355	70,734	23,045	159,220
Sixth	615,419	515,468	15,052	1,210	47,630	190	24,349	11,520	66,836
Seventh	569,470	159,378	360,548	890	27,334	305	12,389	8,626	29,724
Eighth	699,513	583,648	18,594	1,478	51,442	256	31,080	13,015	78,895
Ninth	593,205	396,198	72,486	1,838	71,738	480	29,218	21,247	72,793
Tenth	627,793	496,333	41,952	1,420	35,956	299	39,830	12,003	87,548
Eleventh	635,653	504,469	83,999	1,503	4,549	173	30,658	10,302	66,771
Twelfth	560,912	439,366	103,683	1,521	4,959	207	4,356	6,820	11,089
Thirteenth	759,124	651,412	34,298	1,096	46,969	194	13,344	11,811	41,223
Fourteenth	720,663	601,118	32,189	1,869	17,706	253	53,770	13,758	126,383
Fifteenth	595,833	509,612	52,563	1,186	15,652	163	8,303	8,354	17,743
Sixteenth	691,356	614,822	35,236	1,566	9,323	199	20,224	9,986	47,987
Seventeenth	567,712	523,622	21,026	1,145	3,718	134	11,015	7,052	26,098
Eighteenth	597,447	543,086	37,991	1,245	5,569	104	3,394	6,058	9,079
Nineteenth	575,769	539,061	26,604	1,201	2,226	132	1,737	4,808	5,537
Twentieth	601,341	555,839	33,383	1,319	3,129	159	2,112	5,400	6,539
Total	12,419,293	9,125,471	1,876,875	31,006	423,603	4,610	722,712	235,016	1,530,262

SOURCE: U.S. Census Bureau, *Census 2000 Redistricting Data,* summary file, matrices PL1 and PL2.

EXERCISE 7.5 LEGISLATIVE APPORTIONMENT

BACKGROUND

Lawmakers at the national, state, and local levels of government hold immense power over the lives of citizens. The issue here: Which citizens benefit from the exercise of legislative power? That depends largely on how seats in a legislature are distributed among citizens. Allocating seats in a legislature to constituents is called *legislative apportionment.* The basis for apportioning legislative seats is spelled out in constitutions, statutes, and judicial decisions. Because legislative apportionment ultimately distributes legislative power to citizens, to be exercised on the citizens' behalf by elected representatives, much is at stake politically in decisions on apportionment. And because the political fortunes of legislators and the future of democratic representation ride on matters of apportionment, those matters have been highly contested throughout American history.

The political conflict has centered on several difficult questions:

- Should every citizen receive an equal share of legislative power, or should some citizens receive more than others?
- On what basis should legislative power be allocated to citizens?
- Should the distribution be proportional to the number of people living in a legislative district?
- Should the allocation be based on the geographic size of a district?
- Are counties and other government units entitled to a fixed share of a state's legislative power?

Two strikingly different systems of representation are found in the U.S. Congress. In the House of Representatives, apportionment is population based. The Constitution allocates seats in the House to states in proportion to each state's share of the nation's population. Today the nation is divided into 435 House districts, each with a population of about 650,000, and each electing one member to the House. The Constitution envisioned that citizens, regardless of the House district in which they live, would be allocated an equal share of power in the House. This is not true of the system of representation the Constitution establishes for the U.S. Senate. The Constitution awards representation in the Senate equally to each state—two seats per state. In effect, the Constitution treats states as privileged political units entitled to representation simply because they exist as states. Before 1913, the Constitution assigned the power to choose U.S. senators to the members of each state's legislature. The Seventeenth Amendment transferred that power to the citizens themselves. After 1913, the citizens of each state chose their senators in direct elections. The Constitution's reassignment of the power to choose senators did not alter the way Senate seats are apportioned. The 495,304 citizens of Wyoming today have as much political power in the Senate as the 33,930,798 citizens of California.[7]

The Great Compromise at the Constitutional Convention in 1787 settled the matter of apportionment in Congress; but the framers did not prescribe a structure of representation for the state legislatures. The result: A number of structures have been employed. California's experience shows many of the difficult political questions surrounding legislative apportionment at the state level.

In 1849, California's first state constitution established a bicameral (two-house) legislature consisting of a state assembly and a state senate. Article I, Section 14, specified that "representation shall be apportioned according to population." In 1879, California's second constitution, in Article IV, Section 6, required that "for the purposes of choosing members of the Legislature, the State shall be divided into forty senate and eighty assembly districts, as nearly equal in population as may be." So the population of a senate district would be twice as great as that of an assembly district. Despite the difficulty of establishing legislative districts that are equal in population and despite the temptation to gerrymander (see Exercise 5.2), the framers of California's constitutions envisioned that legislative power in the state would be apportioned equally among citizens of the state.

Until the 1880s, northern California had the overwhelming majority of the state's citizens and hence the preponderance of political power in the state. By the 1920s, however, California's population had changed dramatically. The state's population was southern and urban. As California's population shifted, so did power in the state legislature. Rural interests perceived correctly that population-based

[7] The population numbers here are taken from the 2000 census.

apportionment worked against them, and they were afraid of being overwhelmed by the growing political power of urban centers, particularly in southern California. To preserve their political power, rural interests—represented by the California Farm Bureau Federation and other groups—sponsored Proposition 28, a ballot initiative to amend the state constitution. Approved by voters in November 1926, Proposition 28 fundamentally restructured apportionment by eliminating population-based representation in the state senate. (The assembly remained population based.) The new basis for representation in the California state senate mirrored that in the U.S. Senate: The state's counties would hold the same privileged position that states occupy in the U.S. Senate: California's counties, because they were discrete geographical and political units, were assigned a fixed amount of legislative power in the state senate whatever their population.

There was one problem: The size of the state senate in California was set at forty seats, and there were fifty-eight counties in the state. The difficulty was finessed by awarding one seat in the state senate to each of the more populous counties and grouping together the less populous counties—but only up to a maximum of three counties per senate district. As Table 7.5 makes apparent, twenty-seven senate districts were nothing more or less than the boundaries of a single county. Thirteen senate districts were made up of either two or three counties grouped together.

In 1964, in *Reynolds v. Sims,* in response to a legislative apportionment in Alabama, the Supreme Court declared that population parity, not geography, must be used to allocate seats in state legislatures. By 1966, California was again basing representation in the state senate on population.

ASSIGNMENT

The questions below explore the link between legislative apportionment and political advantage, the arguments for and against population-based apportionment, and the Supreme Court's verdict in 1964 on apportionment in state legislatures.

1. The sixteen smallest (by population) states in the nation are Alaska, Delaware, Hawaii, Idaho, Maine, Montana, Nebraska, Nevada, New Hampshire, New Mexico, North Dakota, Rhode Island, South Dakota, Vermont, West Virginia, and Wyoming. Each of these sixteen states has from 1 to 3 members in the House. Together, they have a total of 29 members in the House. Because there are 435 members in the House, these sixteen states have 6.7 percent of the seats in the House (435/29).

a. The nation's population according to the 2000 census is 281,424,177.[8] The population of the sixteen smallest states is 18,259,164. What percentage of the nation's total population do these sixteen states have?

---

b. Is the voting strength of these sixteen states in the House proportional to their share of the nation's population?

---

2. a. How many votes do the sixteen smallest (by population) states have in the U.S. Senate?

---

b. Looking at the census data in question 1, it's clear that the voting strength of these sixteen states in the Senate is not proportional to their share of the nation's population. To make the voting strength of the sixteen states proportional to their share of the nation's population, how many Senate seats in total would you assign to the states?

---

3. The four states with the largest populations in the nation are California, Florida, New York, and Texas. Together these four states have a total of 139 members in the House, or 32 percent of the seats in the House (435/139).

[8] This is the total apportionment population. The populations of the District of Columbia, Puerto Rico, and the U.S. Island Areas are excluded from the apportionment population because they do not have voting seats in the U.S. House of Representatives.

TABLE 7.5 POPULATION AND AREA OF CALIFORNIA STATE SENATE DISTRICTS, ESTABLISHED IN 1961

DISTRICT	COUNTIES	1960 POPULATION	AREA (SQUARE MILES)
1	Modoc, Lassen, Plumas	33,525	11,209
2	Del Norte, Siskiyou	50,656	7,315
3	Humboldt	104,892	3,573
4	Mendocino, Lake	64,845	4,763
5	Trinity, Shasta	69,174	6,989
6	Butte	82,030	1,663
7	Sierra, Nevada, Placer	80,156	3,360
8	Colusa, Glenn, Tehama	54,625	5,446
9	El Dorado, Amador	39,380	2,307
10	Yuba, Sutter	67,239	1,244
11	Napa, Yolo	131,617	1,792
12	Sonoma	147,375	1,579
13	Marin	146,820	520
14	San Francisco	740,316	45
15	Solano	134,597	827
16	Alameda	908,209	733
17	Contra Costa	409,030	734
18	Santa Clara	642,315	1,302
19	Sacramento	502,778	983
20	San Joaquin	249,989	1,409
21	San Mateo	444,387	454
22	Stanislaus	157,294	1,500
23	Santa Cruz, San Benito	99,615	1,835
24	Madera, Merced	130,914	2,144
25	Monterey	198,351	3,324
26	Calaveras, Mariposa, Tuolumne	29,757	4,756
27	Kings	49,954	1,395
28	Alpine, Inyo, Mono	14,294	13,842
29	San Luis Obispo	81,044	3,316
30	Fresno	365,945	5,964
31	Santa Barbara	168,962	2,738
32	Tulare	168,403	4,838
33	Ventura	199,138	1,851
34	Kern	291,984	8,152
35	Orange	703,925	782
36	San Bernardino	503,591	20,131
37	Riverside	306,191	7,177
38	Los Angeles	6,038,771	4,060
39	Imperial	72,105	4,284
40	San Diego	1,033,011	4,255

Note: The total population in California in 1960 was 15,717,204.

SOURCE: Adapted from Don A. Allen Sr., *Legislative Sourcebook* (Sacramento: Assembly of the State of California, 1965).

a. Again, the nation's total population according to the 2000 census is 281,424,177. The total population of the four largest states is 89,868,655. What percentage of the nation's total population do these four states have?

---

b. Is the voting strength of these four states in the House proportional to their share of the nation's population?

---

4. a. How many votes do the four most populous states have in the U.S. Senate?

---

b. Looking at the census data in question 3, it's clear the voting strength of these four states in the U.S. Senate is not proportional to their share of the nation's population. To make the voting strength of these four states proportional to their share of the nation's population, how many Senate seats in total would you assign to them?

---

5. a. Look at Table 7.5. Which state senate district had the lowest population?

---

b. Which district had the highest population?

---

c. What is the ratio of population variance between the two districts? (To perform this calculation, divide the smaller population figure into the larger one.)

---

6. The population variance you identified in question 5 is a measurement of the disparity in voting power between individual citizens in the two state senate districts. How many times greater is the weight of a vote cast by a citizen in the smallest district compared to one cast by a voter in the largest district?

---

7. In the early 1960s, the disparity in population in California's senate districts affected the impact of state spending programs. An example: Direct contributions and shared revenues that flow from state government coffers to California's counties are called *subventions.* In fiscal year 1963–1964, citizens in the Twenty-Eighth District (Alpine, Inyo, and Mono Counties) received an average per capita subvention of $255.24. In stark contrast, the citizens in the Thirty-Eighth District (Los Angeles County) received a per capita subvention of $77.08. Explain the relationship between the disparity in per capita subventions and the apportionment of the California state senate before the decision in *Reynolds v. Sims* (1964).

---

8. According to the 1960 census, California's total population was 15,717,204. The twenty-one state senate districts with the smallest populations had a combined population of 1,684,614.

a. What percentage of California's total population lived in the twenty-one smallest state senate districts?

---

b. What percentage of the total votes in the California state senate did the twenty-one smallest districts have?

____

c. What is your assessment of this distribution of political power?

____

____

____

____

____

____

READING 7.5 FROM *REYNOLDS V. SIMS,* 377 U.S. 533 (1964)

Mr. Chief Justice Warren delivered the opinion of the Court.

Legislators represent people, not trees or acres. Legislators are elected by voters, not farms or cities or economic interests. As long as ours is a representative form of government, and our legislatures are those instruments of government elected directly by and directly representative of the people, the right to elect legislators in a free and unimpaired fashion is a bedrock of our political system. It could hardly be gainsaid that a constitutional claim had been asserted by an allegation that certain otherwise qualified voters had been entirely prohibited from voting for members of their state legislature. And, if a State should provide that the votes of citizens in one part of the State should be given two times, or five times, or 10 times the weight of votes of citizens in another part of the State, it could hardly be contended that the right to vote of those residing in the disfavored areas had not been effectively diluted. It would appear extraordinary to suggest that a State could be constitutionally permitted to enact a law providing that certain of the State's voters could vote two, five, or 10 times for their legislative representatives, while voters living elsewhere could vote only once. And it is inconceivable that a state law to the effect that, in counting votes for legislators, the votes of citizens in one part of the State would be multiplied by two, five, or 10, while the votes of persons in another area would be counted only at face value, could be constitutionally sustainable. Of course, the effect of . . . state legislative districting schemes which give the same number of representatives to unequal numbers of constituents is identical. . . . Overweighting and overvaluation of the votes of those living here has the certain effect of dilution and undervaluation of the votes of those living there. The resulting discrimination against those individual voters living in disfavored areas is easily demonstrable mathematically. Their right to vote is simply not the same right to vote as that of those living in a favored part of the State. Two, five, or 10 of them must vote before the effect of their voting is equivalent to that of their favored neighbor. Weighting the votes of citizens differently, by any method or means, merely because of where they happen to reside, hardly seems justifiable. . . .

State legislatures are, historically, the fountainhead of representative government in this country. A number of them have their roots in colonial times, and substantially antedate the creation of our Nation and our Federal Government. In fact, the first formal stirrings of American political independence are to be found, in large part, in the views and actions of several of the colonial legislative bodies. With the birth of our National Government, and the adoption and ratification of the Federal Constitution, state legislatures retained a most important place in our Nation's governmental structure. But representative government is in essence self-government through the medium of elected representatives of the people, and each and every citizen has an inalienable right to full and effective participation in the political processes of his State's legislative bodies. Most citizens can achieve this participation only as qualified voters through the election of legislators to represent them. Full and effective participation by all citizens in state government requires, therefore, that each citizen have an equally effective voice in the election of members of his state legislature. Modern and viable state government needs, and the Constitution demands, no less.

Logically, in a society ostensibly grounded on representative government, it would seem reasonable that a majority of the people of a State could elect a majority of that State's legislators. To conclude differently, and to sanction minority control of state legislative bodies, would appear to deny majority rights in a way that far surpasses any possible denial of minority rights that might otherwise be thought to result. Since legislatures are responsible for enacting laws by which all citizens are to be governed, they should be bodies which are collectively responsive to the popular will. And the concept of equal protection has been traditionally viewed as requiring the uniform treatment of persons standing in the same relation to the governmental action questioned or challenged. With respect to the allocation of legislative representation, all voters, as citizens of a State, stand in the same relation regardless of where they live. Any suggested criteria for the differentiation of citizens are insufficient to justify any discrimination, as to the weight of their votes, unless relevant to the permissible purposes of legislative apportionment. Since the achieving of fair and effective representation for all citizens . . . is concededly the basic aim of legislative apportionment, we conclude that the Equal Protection Clause guarantees the opportunity for equal participation by all voters in the election of state legislators. Diluting the weight of votes because of place of residence impairs basic constitutional rights under the Fourteenth Amendment just as much as invidious discriminations based upon factors such as race . . . or economic status. . . . Our constitutional system amply provides for the protection of minorities by means other than giving them majority control of state legislatures. And the democratic ideals of equality and majority rule, which have served this Nation so well in the past, are hardly of any less significance for the present and the future. . . .

To the extent that a citizen's right to vote is debased, he is that much less a citizen. The fact that an individual lives here or there is not a legitimate reason for overweighting or diluting the efficacy of his vote. The complexions of societies and civilizations change, often with amazing rapidity. A nation once primarily rural in character becomes predominantly urban. Representation schemes once fair and equitable become archaic and outdated. But the basic principle of representative government remains, and must remain, unchanged—the weight of a citizen's vote cannot be made to depend on where he lives. Population is, of necessity, the starting point for consideration and the controlling criterion for judgment in legislative apportionment controversies. . . . A citizen, a qualified voter, is no more nor no less so because he lives in the city or on the farm. This is the clear and strong command of our Constitution's Equal Protection Clause. This is an essential part of the concept of a government of laws and not men. This is at the heart of Lincoln's vision of "government of the people, by the people, [and] for the people." The Equal Protection Clause demands no less than substantially equal state legislative representation for all citizens, of all places as well as of all races.

We hold that, as a basic constitutional standard, the Equal Protection Clause requires that the seats in both houses of a bicameral state legislature must be apportioned on a population basis. Simply stated, an individual's right to vote for state legislators is unconstitutionally impaired when its weight is in a substantial fashion diluted when compared with votes of citizens living in other parts of the State.

---

9. In *Reynolds v. Sims,* the plaintiffs argued that the apportionment of the Alabama state legislature deprived citizens of their rights under the equal protection clause of the Fourteenth Amendment. Certainly disparities among districts in population and political power were widespread in state legislatures across the nation in 1964, when the Supreme Court issued its decision. In the Alabama state senate, population variance ratios were as high as 40 to 1; in the state house of representatives, they were as high as 16 to 1. And those disparities were not nearly as large as those in California's state senate. Study the excerpt from *Reynolds* in Reading 7.5, and identify the reasons for the Court's ruling against geographic apportionment.

____

____

10. It is 1964, and you've been charged with applying the Supreme Court's ruling in *Reynolds v. Sims* to the California state senate. Begin by capping the number of seats in the state senate at forty. Explain the process you would use to allocate the forty seats in the legislative body to California's 15,717,204 citizens.

11. Why doesn't the *Reynolds v. Sims* decision apply to the U.S. Senate?

12. What would be necessary to make representation in the U.S. Senate conform to the "one person, one vote" standard?

CHAPTER

8

THE PRESIDENCY

EXERCISE 8.1 THE ELECTORAL COLLEGE

BACKGROUND

The 2000 presidential election demonstrated that the electoral college is no mere historical curiosity. Close observers of presidential elections have long noted the electoral college's power to shape the strategy of presidential campaigns. But that the electoral college could produce an unexpected outcome with its concomitant constitutional crisis and the potential for the abuse of power was thought by many to be a relic of the nineteenth century. And that the electoral college has installed in the Oval Office the runner-up in the popular vote has led many Americans to scrutinize this piece of the framers' handiwork.

The process for electing the president is set forth in Article II, Section 1, of the Constitution, but key elements of the system developed in the years following the Constitutional Convention of 1787. In fact, the term *electoral college* does not appear in the Constitution and did not become the official designation for the body until 1845.[1] The electoral college has been transformed over the past 200 years but without an overarching plan or philosophy to guide its metamorphosis. To many observers it is a peculiar, even bizarre, system for electing the person who will occupy the most powerful office on the planet. One scholar described the electoral college as "perhaps the world's most important governmental body that has neither meetings nor choices."[2]

How did the electoral college come into being? The delegates at the Constitutional Convention of 1787 considered four ways to choose a president: by direct popular election, through Congress, through the state legislatures, or through intermediate electors. Direct popular election was ruled out because the vast majority of delegates wanted to restrain—not expand—democracy. They believed that popular elections would arouse the passions and self-interest of people, destabilize the new government, undermine the public interest, and put demagogues in power. Democracy was so suspect in the framers'

[1] See *Presidential Elections, 1789–1992* (Washington, D.C.: Congressional Quarterly Press, 1995), for comprehensive information on the history and functions of the electoral college.

[2] Frank J. Sorauf, *Party Politics in America* (Boston: Little, Brown, 1984), p. 304.

minds that only the House was given to the citizens to elect directly, and even there, state laws restricted the franchise to adult, white, male property holders. Election of the president by Congress was rejected because the delegates feared it might compromise the independence of the executive branch. The delegates also rejected election by the state legislatures because they feared it might make the president beholden to the states and undermine the authority of the newly established central government.

For want of a better option, the delegates settled on vesting the power to choose the president in intermediate electors. Because the electoral college was a compromise negotiated among many, it's difficult to say precisely what the framers expected from the institution. But this much seems clear: They intended that the electors would select the president independent of public opinion. The framers assumed the electors would be educated and propertied men of talent and character, men who would be better able than the people at large to judge the qualifications of presidential candidates.

The electors, however, have never been as insulated from public opinion as the framers wanted. In the first presidential election, in 1789, four states held direct popular elections to choose their electors. In other states, the state legislatures picked the electors. As political parties developed and strengthened in the late 1790s, they began to offer voters slates of electors pledged to cast their ballots for the party's presidential and vice presidential candidates. The development of political parties essentially committed the electors to cast their ballots according to the popular will within their respective states. At the same time, direct popular election of electors spread widely and rapidly. By the election of 1836, South Carolina was the only state holding out against direct popular election of its electors: The South Carolina state legislature continued to pick the state's electors through the election of 1860. Since the Civil War, the direct popular election of electors has been virtually universal and has for the most part bound electors to the public will—precisely what the framers wanted to avoid.

In the Constitution, the framers allocated electoral college votes to the states by formula. Every state receives as many electoral votes as it has members in Congress. California, for example, since the 2000 reapportionment has 53 seats in the House and 2 seats in the Senate, netting it 55 electoral votes. The Twenty-Third Amendment, ratified in 1961, awarded 3 electoral votes to the citizens of Washington, D.C., bringing the total number of electoral votes to 538 (435 House seats plus 100 seats in the Senate plus 3 for the nation's capital).[3]

To win the presidency, a candidate must capture an absolute majority of the 538 electoral college votes. That magic number is 270. If no presidential candidate wins 270 votes, the Constitution requires a contingency election in the House of Representatives. The House chooses from among the three candidates who received the most electoral votes. In the House each state gets 1 vote. According to House rules, that vote is cast by the majority of the state's delegation in the House. The winner must receive a majority of the 50 votes cast by the state delegations. The election of 1824 is the best example of this constitutional provision in play. In that election, no candidate received a majority of the electoral college vote or, for that matter, a majority of the popular vote. Andrew Jackson had the most electoral votes and the most popular votes; John Quincy Adams was the runner-up in the electoral and popular vote; and William Crawford came in third. The House considered the three candidates and chose Adams as president. The Constitution does not require that the House choose the candidate with the most electoral or the most popular votes.

If no candidate for the vice presidency reaches the requisite 270 electoral college votes, the U.S. Senate chooses the vice president from the two candidates who have the most electoral votes. Each senator casts 1 vote, and a majority of the whole number of senators is required. Again, the Constitution does not require that the Senate select the candidate with the most electoral or the most popular votes.

Three elements of the electoral college are essential to understanding how candidates win the presidency. First, the electoral college is state centered. The general election for president is actually fifty separate state elections, and one in Washington, D.C., held on the same day. The national popular-vote total is irrelevant: All that counts is the popular-vote total in each state. Winning in a state requires a plurality of the popular vote. That's the second key element of the electoral college. Candidates do not need a majority of the popular vote in a state to win—only more popular votes than any other candidate. The third feature is winner-take-all. A state's electoral votes are not divided among the candidates according to the proportion of the popular vote they win. All of a state's electoral votes go to the can-

[3] The District was awarded the same number of votes as the number of seats in Congress it would be entitled to if it were a state.

didate who wins a plurality of the popular vote in the state. Winner-take-all is not required by the Constitution, but all states except Maine and Nebraska have implemented it.[4]

Interposed between the voters in a presidential election and the candidates seeking the presidency are the members of the electoral college. Some states make this explicit by printing the names of the electoral college members on the ballot under the name of the candidate to whom they are pledged. That would prove impractical, of course, in a large state like California, where there would be 55 electors named for each presidential candidate on the ballot.

How are electors chosen? How do they carry out their responsibility? State party organizations choose people to serve as electors based on their demonstrated loyalty and service to the party. Before the general election, each state party organization names a number of electors equal to the state's number of electoral votes. Each party's list of electors is called its *slate of electors.* The electors pledge to support the presidential and vice presidential candidates of the party. At this stage, the people named on each party's slate are only potential voting members of the electoral college. Whether they will cast an electoral college ballot depends on the results of the popular vote in their state.

On the first Monday after the second Wednesday in December, the electors pledged to the candidate who won the popular vote in each state go the state capital, where each elector casts one ballot for president and one ballot for vice president. On January 6, the current vice president counts the ballots cast by the members of the electoral college before a joint session of Congress.

The electors are not obligated by the Constitution or by federal law to cast their ballots for the candidate to whom they pledged their support. Electors who break ranks with their party are called *faithless electors.* The practice is not common, and no presidential election has turned on it. Still, many states have passed laws attempting to bind electors to their pledges. Whether those laws are enforceable has yet to be determined. In 1992, presidential candidate Ross Perot tried to bind the electors pledged to him by requiring them to sign notarized oaths promising allegiance. Perot worried more than the major-party candidates about faithless electors because his campaign had to recruit potential electors from the ranks of campaign volunteers who had only a short history of commitment to him.

ASSIGNMENT

Congress has charged the National Archives and Records Administration with managing the various functions and procedures of the electoral college. NARA's electoral college Web site is at www.nara.gov/fedreg/elctcoll/index.html. Information at the site should help you understand the electoral college and answer the questions below. Several of the questions below also require a careful reading of the Twelfth Amendment.

1. State party organizations choose people as electors because of their demonstrated loyalty to the party. Even so, some electors fail to cast their electoral votes as pledged. In 1956, W. F. Turner, an Alabama elector pledged to Democratic presidential candidate Adlai Stevenson, cast his vote for a local judge. (Who knows? Maybe they were fishing buddies.) In the 2000 election, Barbara Lett-Simmons, an elector from Washington, D.C., pledged to Al Gore, cast a blank ballot to protest the fact that the District of Columbia has no vote in Congress. What do you think could happen between the general election in November and the electoral vote in December that might lead the electors to install as president the candidate everyone thought had lost the election?

____

____

____

____

2. If no presidential candidate receives a majority of the electoral votes, the election is decided in the House. The development of a strong two-party system has made this contingency less likely:

[4] Both Maine and Nebraska award their electoral college votes according to what's called the *district system,* one electoral vote to each congressional district in the state. The candidate with a plurality of the popular vote in the district wins that electoral vote. Two electoral votes in each state—those that represent the states' Senate seats—are awarded to the plurality winner of the statewide popular vote.

Minor-party candidates are unlikely to win a plurality of the popular vote in enough states to deprive a major-party candidate of an electoral vote majority. In 1968, however, it seemed possible that third-party candidate George Wallace, an Independent, might do exactly that. And in 1992, at least before Perot dropped out of and then reentered the race, a viable third-party candidacy also seemed possible. (In that election, Perot ran as an Independent.) How do today's electoral conditions—weak political parties and little voter loyalty to the major parties—increase the possibility that a presidential election might again be decided in the House of Representatives?

____

____

____

____

____

____

3. In setting up the electoral college, the framers made a mistake. They assigned each elector two votes but did not require that the electors when casting their two votes specify whether they were voting for a candidate to be president or vice president. When the votes were tallied, the candidate with a majority became president and the runner-up became vice president. The framers apparently didn't anticipate—perhaps because they didn't want to contemplate fractious political parties—that a president elected under this system might have as his vice president his opponent in the election. That is exactly what happened in the election of 1796, when John Adams, a Federalist, became president and Thomas Jefferson, a Democratic Republican, became vice president. The Twelfth Amendment (1804) eliminated this politically difficult possibility by requiring that electors cast separate ballots for president and vice president. But the possibility remains that the electoral vote could install a president from one party and a vice president from another. Explain a sequence of events that would be required to produce that result. Begin with a situation in which the candidates for president and vice president receive fewer than 270 electoral votes and control of Congress is split between the Democrats and the Republicans.

____

____

____

____

____

____

4. In the 1980 presidential election, 41 electoral votes were at stake in New York. Ronald Reagan, the Republican Party candidate, received 2,893,831 popular votes statewide, or 46.7 percent of the popular vote. Jimmy Carter, the Democratic Party candidate, received 2,728,372 popular votes in the state, or 44.0 percent of the popular vote. John Anderson was the Independent Party candidate; he received 467,801 popular votes, or 7.5 percent of the popular vote.

a. According to the rules for awarding electoral college votes, how were New York's 41 electoral votes allocated to the candidates?

Reagan: ______________________________

Carter: ______________________________

Anderson: ______________________________

b. Suppose you knew nothing about the rules for awarding electoral votes and had no access to the popular-vote totals in this election. What does the distribution of electoral votes among the three candidates seem to indicate about each candidate's popular support in New York state?

____

____

____

____

5. Table 8.1.1 shows the popular vote by state in the 1976 presidential election. Jimmy Carter won a slim majority of the popular vote nationwide and 297 electoral votes. Gerald Ford received 240 electoral votes. Notice that 1 electoral vote is missing. Mike Padden, an elector in Washington state pledged to Ford, cast his electoral vote for Ronald Reagan.

Relatively small changes in the popular vote in 1976 could have given Ford the White House. For example, take 5,559 popular votes in Ohio—about one-tenth of 1 percent of the total votes cast in the state—and move them out of Carter's column and into Ford's. Then give Ford 3,687 of Carter's popular votes in Hawaii, about 1 percent of the total votes cast there.

a. What are the new electoral vote totals?

Carter: ____

Ford: ____

b. Who is president based on the new electoral college vote? Explain your answer.

____

____

____

____

c. Where would this election be decided? Why?

____

____

____

____

d. What three candidates have a chance to win the presidency? Explain your answer.

____

____

____

6. Table 8.1.2 shows the popular vote by state in the 2000 presidential election. Al Gore won a plurality of the popular vote nationwide. George W. Bush lost the popular vote to Gore but managed to win 271 electoral votes—1 more than he needed to be president. If just 269 of Bush's popular votes in Florida had gone to Gore, Gore would be president.

a. In what other state besides Florida did Bush have the smallest margin of victory in the popular vote total?

____

b. What is the minimum number of popular votes that if shifted from Bush's column to Gore's would have made Gore the winner of the state's electoral votes?

____

TABLE 8.1.1 POPULAR AND ELECTORAL COLLEGE VOTES, PRESIDENTIAL ELECTION 1976

		JIMMY CARTER (D)			GERALD FORD (R)		
STATE	TOTAL POPULAR VOTE	POPULAR VOTE	PERCENTAGE OF TOTAL POPULAR VOTE	ELECTORAL COLLEGE VOTE	POPULAR VOTE	PERCENTAGE OF TOTAL POPULAR VOTE	ELECTORAL COLLEGE VOTE
Alabama	1,182,850	659,170	55.7	9	504,070	42.6	
Alaska	123,574	44,058	35.7		71,555	57.9	3
Arizona	742,719	295,602	39.8		418,642	56.4	6
Arkansas	767,535	498,604	65.0	6	267,903	34.9	
California	7,867,117	3,742,284	47.86		3,882,244	49.4	45
Colorado	1,081,554	460,353	42.6		584,367	54.0	7
Connecticut	1,381,526	647,895	46.9		719,261	52.1	8
Delaware	235,834	122,596	52.0	3	109,831	46.6	
District of Columbia	168,830	137,818	81.6	3	27,873	16.5	
Florida	3,150,631	1,636,000	51.9	17	1,469,531	46.6	
Georgia	1,467,458	979,409	66.74	12	483,743	33.0	
Hawaii	**291,301**	**147,375**	**50.6**	**4**	**140,003**	**48.0**	
Idaho	344,071	126,549	36.8		204,151	59.3	4
Illinois	4,718,914	2,271,295	48.1		2,364,269	50.1	26
Indiana	2,220,362	1,014,714	45.7		1,183,958	53.3	13
Iowa	1,279,306	619,931	48.5		632,863	49.5	8
Kansas	957,845	430,421	44.9		502,752	52.5	7
Kentucky	1,167,142	615,717	52.8	9	531,852	45.6	
Louisiana	1,278,439	661,365	51.7	10	587,446	46.0	
Maine	483,216	232,279	48.1		236,320	48.9	4
Maryland	1,439,897	759,612	52.8	10	672,661	46.7	
Massachusetts	2,547,558	1,429,475	56.1	14	1,030,276	40.5	
Michigan	3,653,749	1,696,714	46.4		1,893,742	51.8	21
Minnesota	1,949,931	1,070,440	54.9	10	819,395	42.0	
Mississippi	769,361	381,309	49.6	7	366,846	47.7	
Missouri	1,953,600	998,387	51.1	12	927,443	47.5	
Montana	328,734	149,259	45.4		173,703	52.8	4
Nebraska	607,668	233,692	38.5		359,705	59.2	5
Nevada	201,876	92,479	45.8		101,273	50.2	3
New Hampshire	339,618	147,635	43.5		185,935	54.8	4
New Jersey	3,014,472	1,444,653	47.9		1,509,688	50.1	17
New Mexico	418,409	201,148	48.1		211,419	50.5	4
New York	6,534,170	3,389,558	51.9	41	3,100,791	47.5	
North Carolina	1,678,914	927,365	55.2	13	741,960	44.2	
North Dakota	297,188	136,078	45.8		153,470	51.6	3
Ohio	**4,111,873**	**2,011,621**	**48.9**	**25**	**2,000,505**	**48.7**	
Oklahoma	1,092,251	532,442	48.8		545,708	50.0	8
Oregon	1,029,876	490,407	47.6		492,120	47.8	6
Pennsylvania	4,620,787	2,328,677	50.4	27	2,205,604	47.7	
Rhode Island	411,170	227,636	55.4	4	181,249	44.1	
South Carolina	802,583	450,807	56.2	8	346,149	43.1	
South Dakota	300,678	147,068	48.9		151,505	50.4	4
Tennessee	1,476,345	825,879	55.9	10	633,969	42.9	
Texas	4,071,884	2,082,319	51.1	26	1,953,300	48.0	
Utah	541,198	182,110	33.7		337,908	62.4	4
Vermont	187,765	80,954	43.1		102,085	54.4	3
Virginia	1,697,094	813,896	48.0		836,554	49.3	12

(continued)

TABLE 8.1.1 (CONTINUED)

STATE	TOTAL POPULAR VOTE	JIMMY CARTER (D) POPULAR VOTE	PERCENTAGE OF TOTAL POPULAR VOTE	ELECTORAL COLLEGE VOTE	GERALD FORD (R) POPULAR VOTE	PERCENTAGE OF TOTAL POPULAR VOTE	ELECTORAL COLLEGE VOTE
Washington	1,555,534	717,323	46.1		777,732	50.0	8
West Virginia	750,964	435,914	58.1	6	314,760	41.9	
Wisconsin	2,104,175	1,040,232	49.4	11	1,004,987	47.8	
Wyoming	156,343	62,239	39.8		92,717	59.3	3
Totals	81,555,889	40,830,763	50.1	297	39,147,793	48.0	240

Note: The votes received by minor-party candidates are not noted.

SOURCE: *Dave Leip's Atlas of U.S. Presidential Elections,* "Past Presidential Election Results," at www.uselectionatlas.org.

c. Would winning this state's electoral votes have made Gore president?

7. Political science professors have long cautioned that in some future presidential election the winner of the popular vote would not be president. The 2000 election has given those instructors new credibility in the eyes of their students. Even so, it remains difficult for many students to understand how a candidate who loses the nationwide popular vote can win a majority of the electoral college vote. The answer, of course, is that the winner-take-all feature of the electoral college distorts the popular vote instead of taking an accurate account of it.

Careful analysis of the sample data below should reveal why in the elections of 1888 and 2000, the winners of the popular vote did not win the Oval Office. Apply the rules of the electoral college when answering the questions below.

- State X has 15 electoral votes. The Republican candidate received 255,000 popular votes; the Democratic candidate received 250,000 popular votes.
- State Y has 5 electoral votes. The Republican candidate received 50,000 popular votes; the Democratic candidate received 150,000 popular votes.

a. Which candidate won the popular vote?

b. Which candidate won a majority of the electoral vote?

c. To understand the reversal of the popular and electoral college votes, look for patterns in the popular-vote totals within each state and also between the two states. The Republican candidate in state X won a big prize in the electoral college vote by winning narrowly in the popular vote. The Democratic candidate in state Y won a small prize in the electoral college vote by capturing a very wide margin of popular votes. Explain in your own words why the winner of the popular vote did not win the electoral college vote.

TABLE 8.1.2 POPULAR AND ELECTORAL COLLEGE VOTES, PRESIDENTIAL ELECTION 2000

		George W. Bush (R)			Al Gore (D)		
State	Total Popular Vote	Popular Vote	Percentage of Total Popular Vote	Electoral College Vote	Popular Vote	Percentage of Total Popular Vote	Electoral College Vote
Alabama	1,666,272	941,173	56.5	9	692,611	41.6	
Alaska	285,560	167,398	58.6	3	79,004	27.7	
Arizona	1,532,016	781,652	51.0	8	685,341	44.7	
Arkansas	921,781	472,940	51.3	6	422,768	45.9	
California	10,965,856	4,567,429	41.7		5,861,203	53.5	54
Colorado	1,741,368	883,748	50.8	8	738,227	42.4	
Connecticut	1,459,525	561,094	38.4		816,015	56.0	8
Delaware	327,622	137,288	41.9		180,068	55.0	3
District of Columbia	201,894	18,073	9.0		171,923	85.2	2*
Florida	5,963,110	2,912,790	48.9	25	2,912,253	48.8	
Georgia	2,596,804	1,419,720	54.7	13	1,116,230	43.0	
Hawaii	367,951	137,845	37.5		205,286	55.8	4
Idaho	501,621	336,937	67.2	4	138,637	27.6	
Illinois	4,742,123	2,019,421	42.6		2,589,026	54.6	22
Indiana	2,199,302	1,245,836	56.7	12	901,980	41.0	
Iowa	1,315,563	634,373	48.2		638,517	48.5	7
Kansas	1,072,216	622,332	58.0	6	399,276	37.2	
Kentucky	1,544,187	872,492	56.5	8	638,898	41.4	
Louisiana	1,765,656	927,871	52.6	9	792,344	44.9	
Maine	651,817	286,616	44.0		319,951	49.1	4
Maryland	2,025,480	813,797	40.2		1,145,782	56.6	10
Massachusetts	2,702,984	878,502	32.5		1,616,487	59.8	12
Michigan	4,232,711	1,953,139	46.1		2,170,418	51.3	18
Minnesota	2,438,685	1,109,659	45.5		1,168,266	47.9	10
Mississippi	994,184	572,844	57.6	7	404,614	40.7	
Missouri	2,359,892	1,189,924	50.4	11	1,111,138	47.1	
Montana	410,997	240,178	58.4	3	137,126	33.4	
Nebraska	697,019	433,862	62.3	5	231,780	33.3	
Nevada	608,970	301,575	49.5	4	279,978	46.0	
New Hampshire	569,081	273,559	48.1	4	266,348	46.8	
New Jersey	3,187,226	1,284,173	40.3		1,788,850	56.1	15
New Mexico	598,605	286,417	47.9		286,783	47.9	5
New York	6,821,999	2,403,374	35.2		4,107,697	60.2	33
North Carolina	2,911,262	1,631,163	56.0	14	1,257,692	43.2	
North Dakota	288,256	174,852	60.7	3	95,284	33.1	
Ohio	4,701,998	2,350,363	50.0	21	2,183,628	46.4	
Oklahoma	1,234,229	744,337	60.3	8	474,276	38.4	
Oregon	1,533,968	713,577	46.5		720,342	47.0	7
Pennsylvania	4,913,119	2,281,127	46.4		2,485,967	50.6	23
Rhode Island	409,112	130,555	31.9		249,508	61.0	4
South Carolina	1,382,717	785,937	56.8	8	565,561	40.9	
South Dakota	316,269	190,700	60.3	3	118,804	37.6	
Tennessee	2,076,181	1,061,949	51.2	11	981,720	47.3	
Texas	6,407,637	3,799,639	59.3	32	2,433,746	38.0	
Utah	770,754	515,096	66.8	5	203,053	26.3	
Vermont	294,308	119,775	40.7		149,022	50.6	3
Virginia	2,739,447	1,437,490	52.5	13	1,217,290	44.4	

(continued)

TABLE 8.1.2 (CONTINUED)

		George W. Bush (R)			Al Gore (D)		
State	Total Popular Vote	Popular Vote	Percentage of Total Popular Vote	Electoral College Vote	Popular Vote	Percentage of Total Popular Vote	Electoral College Vote
Washington	2,487,433	1,108,864	44.6		1,247,652	50.2	11
West Virginia	648,124	336,475	51.9	5	295,497	45.6	
Wisconsin	2,598,607	1,237,279	47.6		1,242,987	47.8	11
Wyoming	218,351	147,947	67.8	3	60,481	27.7	
Totals	105,401,849	50,455,156	47.9	271	50,997,335	48.4	266

Note: The votes received by minor-party candidates are not noted.

* One Gore elector in Washington, D.C., abstained from voting.

SOURCE: *Dave Leip's Atlas of U.S. Presidential Elections,* "Past Presidential Election Results," at www.uselectionatlas.org.

8. The mechanics of the electoral college are peculiar. Presidential candidates must take careful account of those peculiarities and shape their electoral strategies around them. An *electoral strategy* is the plan a candidate follows to allocate the campaign's limited resources—the candidate's time and money, for example.

a. How do the mechanics of the electoral college influence candidates' decisions to target certain voters? Explain and support your answer.

b. Looking at Table 8.1.3, which reflects the reapportionment of the House based on the 2000 census, what is the minimum number of states a candidate would need to win to capture the White House? Remember that a state's electoral votes equal its representation in the House plus its two senate seats.

9. Research carried out by George W. Bush's campaign two months before the 2000 presidential election showed conclusively—barring some unforeseeable event—that whatever resources he might commit to the state, Bush had no chance of winning the popular vote in California on November 7. Bush's research was confirmed by independent public opinion polls taken in September, which showed Bush trailing Gore by about 13 percentage points in the state. There was precedent: George Bush Sr. in 1992 and Bob Dole in 1996—both Republicans—faced similar situations. Their positions on the environment and abortion, to name two examples, were out of sync with most voters in California; and they found it impossible to remake themselves or their views to win the support of a plurality of California's voters. In 1992, George Bush Sr. lost California to Clinton by 13 percentage points, 46 percent to 33 percent. In 1996, Dole lost the state to Clinton by 13 percentage points, 51 percent to 38 percent.

Assume the role of chief campaign adviser. Recognizing that George W. Bush is likely to meet a similar fate at the hands of California voters in November 2000, would you direct a substantial amount of

Table 8.1.3 Population and Representation in the House by State, 2000 Census Data

State	Population	Number of Representatives in the House
Alabama	4,461,130	7
Alaska	628,933	1
Arizona	5,140,683	8
Arkansas	2,679,733	4
California	33,930,798	53
Colorado	4,311,882	7
Connecticut	3,409,535	5
Delaware	785,068	1
Florida	16,028,890	25
Georgia	8,206,975	13
Hawaii	1,216,642	2
Idaho	1,297,274	2
Illinois	12,439,042	19
Indiana	6,090,782	9
Iowa	2,931,923	5
Kansas	2,693,824	4
Kentucky	4,049,431	6
Louisiana	4,480,271	7
Maine	1,277,731	2
Maryland	5,307,886	8
Massachusetts	6,355,568	10
Michigan	9,955,829	15
Minnesota	4,925,670	8
Mississippi	2,852,927	4
Missouri	5,606,260	9
Montana	905,316	1
Nebraska	1,715,369	3
Nevada	2,002,032	3
New Hampshire	1,238,415	2
New Jersey	8,424,354	13
New Mexico	1,823,821	3
New York	19,004,973	29
North Carolina	8,067,673	13
North Dakota	643,756	1
Ohio	11,374,540	18
Oklahoma	3,458,819	5
Oregon	3,428,543	5
Pennsylvania	12,300,670	19
Rhode Island	1,049,662	2
South Carolina	4,025,061	6
South Dakota	756,874	1
Tennessee	5,700,037	9
Texas	20,903,994	32
Utah	2,236,714	3
Vermont	609,890	1
Virginia	7,100,702	11
Washington	5,908,684	9
West Virginia	1,813,077	3
Wisconsin	5,371,210	8
Wyoming	495,304	1
Total	281,424,177*	435

*This is the total apportionment population. The populations of the District of Columbia, Puerto Rico, and the U.S. Island Areas are excluded from the apportionment population because they do not have voting seats in the U.S. House of Representatives.

the campaign's resources to California in the two months before the election? Cite specific features of the electoral college to explain and support your reasoning.

10. Dispense with the electoral college. Assume that the president is elected by a plurality of the popular vote nationwide. Under this system, every popular vote counts, whatever a candidate's prospects of winning a plurality of the popular vote in any particular state.

a. Consider again the situation posed in question 9. Under a plurality system, what factors would you weigh in deciding how much of the campaign's resources to direct to California in the two months before the election?

b. Why is your recommendation under the plurality system different from that under the electoral college system? Cite specific features of the electoral college to explain and support your reasoning.

11. Returning to the electoral college system for electing the president, assume you're managing George W. Bush's 2000 campaign in Texas. On October 7, one month before the election, your polling data show Bush with 60 percent of the popular vote in the state and Al Gore with 38 percent. At a meeting on October 8, the campaign's director of political advertising announces he has developed and tested a series of television advertisements designed to boost Bush's standing over the next four weeks. He claims that the ads will increase Bush's lead in the polls to 70 percent by the day of the election, reducing Gore's standing to 28 percent. The ads will cost $3 million. Assume the polling projections are accurate, that the campaign can afford the $3 million, and that you have it on good authority that Gore will not be presenting you with any surprises in Texas in the weeks before the election. Should you authorize the $3 million expenditure for the ads? Explain how your decision is derived from an understanding of how the electoral college operates.

12. Dispense again with the electoral college, and assume that the president is elected by a plurality of the popular vote nationwide.

a. Would you authorize the $3 million expenditure described in question 11?

b. Why is your recommendation under the plurality system different from that under the electoral college system?

EXERCISE 8.2 PRESIDENTIAL PARDONS

BACKGROUND

The presidential pardon is one of the enumerated powers of the president. Article II (the executive article), Section 2, states that the president "shall have Power to Grant Reprieves and Pardons for Offenses against the United States, except in Cases of Impeachment." A *reprieve* delays punishment; not surprisingly, reprieves are neither sought nor granted with any frequency. A *pardon,* on the other hand, restores all of the individual's civil rights.

The power of the pardon is as specific as Article II gets. Although some would say the pardon was motivated by the framers' sense of mercy, more likely it was included because the framers believed the power is a necessary part of the system of checks and balances. The presidential pardon is an executive check on the judicial branch. But there is no check on the president's grant, or denial, of a pardon.

Notice that the presidential pardon pertains only to crimes against the United States: It does not apply to crimes committed in violation of state or local laws or in civil matters. There is little in the writings of the framers to give us guidance on the extent of the power of the pardon as it applies to federal judicial proceedings. We know from the language itself that it does not apply to cases of impeachment, a political rather than judicial process. Otherwise there seem to be no restrictions on the power: It can be exercised before or after an indictment, during or after a trial, during incarceration, even after a punishment has run its course.[5]

Although there don't seem to be many rules governing presidential pardons, some pardons are controversial. An example: Jimmy Carter's pardon in 1977 of most Vietnam War draft resisters. There was such an outcry at the president's declaration of amnesty that the House of Representatives tried—albeit unsuccessfully—to withhold the funds necessary to establish the administrative apparatus to process the repatriation of Americans who had fled abroad. Also controversial was President Ford's pardon of Richard Nixon for any crimes against the United States that Nixon may have committed while he was in office. Nixon resigned from the presidency in 1974 while the House was voting on impeachment articles connected to the Watergate scandal. Some polling data suggest that Ford's pardon of Nixon might have cost Ford the 1976 election.

Contemporary presidents have been able to rely on the recommendation of the Justice Department's Office of the Pardon Attorney before making their decisions. The office reviews the merits of each pardon application and then submits its recommendations to the White House for action. The review often involves contact with the judge who presided over the defendant's trial and with the prosecuting attorneys. Over Bill Clinton's last several weeks in office, a large number of requests for pardons were made directly to the White House through executive branch officials, the president's advisers, and members of his extended family—bypassing the Office of the Pardon Attorney. Clinton used his power to pardon 140 people on the last day of his term. Some of the individuals who were pardoned, and the circumstances behind their pardons, created considerable controversy.[6]

After the pardon controversy broke, now citizen Bill Clinton wrote an article for the *New York Times* in which he justified his actions and defended the way the pardons, especially two particularly contentious ones, were handled.[7] He explained that there was no quid pro quo: No money or promises were made in exchange for a pardon. He also noted that the overall number of his pardons was consistent with those made by other presidents. Indeed, data from the Office of the Pardon Attorney show that Clinton granted a total of 395 pardons over his two terms, just 2 more than Reagan did during his eight years in office. By contrast, Harry Truman issued 1,913 pardons and Dwight D. Eisenhower 1,110.[8] What made several of Clinton's pardons so contentious was the fact that the petitioners had bypassed the Justice Department to make a direct appeal to the president.

---

[5] For example, in 1989, President Ronald Reagan pardoned New York Yankees owner George Steinbrenner, who had been convicted and paid a fine for illegal contributions to Richard Nixon's 1972 presidential campaign.

[6] Stephen Braun and Richard Serrano, "Clinton's Pardons: Ego Fed a Numbers Game," *Los Angeles Times,* February 25, 2001, p. A1.

[7] William Jefferson Clinton, "My Reasons for the Pardons," *New York Times,* February 18, 2001, p. 12.

[8] Office of the Pardon Attorney, reported in the *New York Times,* January 29, 2001, p. A6.

ASSIGNMENT

Reading 8.2 gives summaries of the cases of seven people who requested pardons from President Clinton during his last days in office. Not all the requests were granted.[9] Answer the questions that follow the reading.

READING 8.2 SEVEN APPLICATIONS FOR PARDONS

Vanessa Wade Wade was 19 years old when she carried 22 grams of cocaine for her boyfriend in 1990. She was arrested at a motel in possession of the drug, along with a 17-year-old male accomplice. Wade was prosecuted as a "lieutenant" involved in narcotics trade, in part because of the age of her accomplice. She was convicted on federal charges of conspiracy to distribute and possession with intent to distribute cocaine, and subsequently was sentenced to twenty-three years in prison. Her only work experience at the time of her arrest was as a waitress earning $226 a week at her boyfriend's restaurant. While she was in prison, she began taking classes toward a college degree. She also kept herself out of trouble with the other inmates and staff. The attorney representing Wade in her petition for a pardon said that she acknowledged her guilt but that ten years was enough. In the absence of a pardon, Wade faces eight more years before qualifying for early release based on good behavior.

Susan McDougal McDougal was summoned to answer questions before a federal grand jury in 1996 and 1998 by independent counsel Kenneth Starr, who was investigating charges that Bill and Hillary Clinton had been involved in illegal activity in a real estate deal in Arkansas. Both the McDougals (Susan and her then husband, James) and the Clintons had invested in what came to be known as Whitewater. The project never got off the ground. Investigators charged that Bill Clinton had pressured a judge to loan Susan McDougal $300,000. McDougal denied that Clinton knew of the loan. In 1998, she was sentenced to eighteen months in prison for failing to testify more fully before the grand jury. She was acquitted of obstruction of justice charges in 1999, charges that stemmed from her refusal to answer certain questions before the grand jury. Ultimately Starr brought no Whitewater-related charges against the president.

Leonard Peltier On June 25, 1975, two FBI agents were shot and killed during a fire fight on the Pine Ridge Indian Reservation in South Dakota. Activists on the reservation, members of the American Indian Movement (AIM), had faced off with the agents in various confrontations since AIM's violent takeover of a reservation village, Wounded Knee, several years earlier. Peltier admitted he exchanged shots with the authorities, but he denied shooting either of the agents who were killed. Peltier was one of four arrested for the murders. Two were acquitted, and charges against the third were dropped. Despite the absence of eyewitness testimony, and despite the prosecution's admission that it did not have evidence that Peltier fired the fatal shots, Peltier was convicted of murder and sentenced to two consecutive life terms. At the time he requested a pardon from President Clinton, he had been in prison for twenty-five years. Amnesty International was just one of the organizations that maintained that Peltier was not responsible for the deaths of the agents, that he had been targeted by the FBI for prosecution because he was an AIM leader. As Clinton considered the pardon request of the 56-year-old Peltier, FBI agents marched around the White House in silent protest of the pardon and in remembrance of their colleagues.

---

[9] Remind your instructor to tell you who did and did not get a presidential pardon from Clinton. (The answer is in the Instructor's Manual.)

READING SOURCES: Lisa Richardson, "A Prisoner's Plea to a President," *Los Angeles Times,* April 2, 2001, p. E1; Kevin McKiernan, "Put a Close to This Sad Chapter," *Los Angeles Times,* January 7, 2001, p. M2; Robert Rosenblatt and Debora Vrana, "Clinton Pardons McDougal and Hearst but Not Milken," *Los Angeles Times,* January 21, 2001, p. A1; William Carlsen, "The Kidnapping That Gripped the Nation," *San Francisco Chronicle,* February 4, 1999, A1; Walter Pincus, "No Decision on Altering Pollard's Sentence, White House Says," *Washington Post,* January 10, 1999, p. A4; James Thurman, "The Politics of Pardoning a Spy for Israel," *Christian Science Monitor,* December 7, 1998, p. 2; Stephen Braun and Richard A. Serrano, "In Clemency Inquiry, 'Pro' Proves Elusive," *Los Angeles Times,* March 18, 2001, p. A1; and Josh Getlin, "Clinton Pardons a Billionaire Fugitive and Questions Abound," *Los Angeles Times,* January 24, 2001, p. A1.

role in the exercise of the pardon power or that the president's role be restricted. Whatever you propose, be specific and explain why you think the proposed reform would achieve the stated objectives.

Reform 1: ____

Reform 2: ____

Reform 3: ____

4. a. In the space below, put a checkmark under the phrase that you feel best describes the gravity of each petitioner's offense (or alleged offense).

PETITIONER	VERY SERIOUS	SERIOUS	NOT VERY SERIOUS
Vanessa Wade			
Susan McDougal			
Leonard Peltier			
Michael Milken			
Patricia Hearst			
Jonathan Pollard			
Marc Rich			

b. Now go back and look at your pardon–no pardon decisions in question 1. What pattern emerges in your decisions when you consider the seriousness of the petitioners' offenses (or alleged offenses).

EXERCISE 8.3 EVALUATING PRESIDENTIAL PERFORMANCE

BACKGROUND

No one in the world is evaluated as searchingly, as frequently, or by so many as the president of the United States. A sitting president is scrutinized twenty-four hours a day. The product of all that scrutiny is public opinion, a fickle commodity at best. A president's public approval rating can shift dramatically during his term of office. Lyndon Johnson, for example, had a public approval rating of 76 percent in his first year in office. That rating fell as low as 39 percent in his fourth and fifth years in office, dragged down primarily by the widespread perception that the war in Vietnam had become a quagmire. And the scrutiny doesn't end when a president leaves office. The media may not be quite so persistent, but historians and political scientists are at the ready to dissect a former president's every action and decision for centuries to come.

All presidents are determined to shape the current and future assessments of their performance. Early in his first term, for example, Bill Clinton met in the Oval Office with Richard Reeves, an author and historian who had published a study of John Kennedy's presidency.[10] Clinton discussed with Reeves the elements that constitute presidential greatness, presumably with the purpose of shaping Clinton's own performance. To cement Kennedy's place in history, members of his family and his inner circle of advisers worked diligently after the assassination to perpetuate a number of myths about the Kennedy presidency. Richard Nixon, after resigning from office in disgrace, authored several books that he hoped would rehabilitate his reputation and encourage the public and scholars alike to see him as a great statesman.

People's perceptions of a president's performance in office are shaped by their expectations, which have increased dramatically since about 1900. In the nineteenth century, the national government played an insignificant role in the daily lives of most Americans. On a day-to-day basis, local and state governments provided the few services that governments rendered. It would not have occurred to most Americans to look to their president as the source of their prosperity and security.

Public expectations began to grow as Theodore Roosevelt, William Taft, and Woodrow Wilson led the national government to take on new responsibilities to ensure the social and economic welfare of the nation. Roosevelt, for example, led crusades against abuses by the meat-packing and drug industries, among others. Roosevelt's activism captured the imagination of many Americans and began to reshape their view of the presidency. But no president did more to inflate public expectations for presidential performance than Franklin Delano Roosevelt. FDR promised that under his leadership, the national government would restore security and stability to Americans mired in the Great Depression. Through his skillful use of press conferences and fireside chats broadcast on radio, FDR personalized the presidency. And he taught the nation to expect a great deal from the office and its occupant.

In time, inflated by the rhetoric of politicians and the constant glare of the media, public expectations of presidents became unrealistically high. Certainly there's something comforting about the thought of a president who can take the reins of power and dispatch the nation's problems with the stroke of an executive order. In reality, of course, a president's power is limited by the Constitution, by the legislative and judicial branches of government, by the power vested in state and local governments, by public opinion, and by myriad other factors. An electorate that expects the president to work miracles always is going to be disappointed.

We expect public opinion to change day to day. Not so historical opinion. Yet assessments by political scientists and historians of presidential performance can change dramatically over time. Early studies of Herbert Hoover, for example, portrayed him as a rigid ideologue who was overwhelmed by the economic collapse in 1929 and incapable of making a credible response to the subsequent crisis. In the 1970s, historians began to reexamine Hoover's performance in office.[11] Today, many scholars credit Hoover with making a vigorous if insufficient response to the crisis. Those scholars acknowledge the constraints Hoover faced and the unprecedented use he made of the tools available to him. What accounts for the change in thinking? With the passing of time have come perspective and judgment.

---

[10] *President Kennedy: Profile of Power* (New York: Simon & Schuster, 1993).

[11] For example, see Joan Hoff Wilson, *Herbert Hoover: Forgotten Progressive* (Boston: Little, Brown, 1975).

Until the 1970s, most scholars seemed unable to evaluate Hoover without comparing him with his successor, Franklin Delano Roosevelt. Roosevelt's unprecedented use of the national government—not to mention his personality, his charm, his charisma—obscured Hoover's innovative response to the crisis. Only decades after Hoover left office were historians able to bring him out from Roosevelt's shadow and judge him on his own merits.

For those making scholarly evaluations of presidential performance, time yields not only perspective and judgment but also more complete records—something essential to informed assessment. Executive branch departments and agencies, particularly the State Department and the CIA, are notoriously slow in declassifying documents. Eisenhower's two terms in office ended more than forty years ago, yet the documentary record of his presidency remains incomplete. As the documentary record is filled in, new information may lead scholars to reassess presidential performance. During the past decade, for example, the Kennedy and Johnson presidential libraries made available to researchers tape recordings secretly made in the Oval Office by the two presidents. Diligent historians have performed the difficult task of transcribing the tapes.[12] In Kennedy's case, the tapes reveal the president's skill and luck in negotiating the Cuban missile crisis and bringing the world back from the brink of nuclear destruction. In Johnson's case, the tapes point to the president's desperate search for a politically acceptable alternative to the mounting escalation of the war in Vietnam.

Political scientists, historians, and journalists have long debated which criteria to employ in assessing presidential performance, how to weigh those criteria to produce a balanced evaluation, and how to rank a president in relation to other presidents. The modern version of presidential assessment was pioneered in 1948, in a study by Arthur Schlesinger Sr. His son, Arthur Schlesinger Jr., produced a similar study in 1996.[13] More recently, C-SPAN and the *Wall Street Journal* ranked presidents based on surveys of presidential scholars.[14] C-SPAN surveyed fifty-eight scholars, asking them to evaluate the presidents on a number of criteria: public persuasion, crisis leadership, economic management, moral authority, international relations, administrative skills, relations with Congress, vision/agenda setting, pursuit of equal justice for all, and performance within the context of his times. The *Wall Street Journal*, working in conjunction with the Federalist Society, asked seventy-eight scholars to rank the presidents on criteria of each scholar's choosing.

ASSIGNMENT

Table 8.3 shows data from the C-SPAN and *Wall Street Journal* surveys and places the presidents from Lincoln on in historical context. Questions 1 through 5 are based on the table.

1. In the space below, list the presidents who served during periods when the level of crisis or challenge was low and who attained a near-great or great ranking.

____

____

2. What is the highest ranking achieved by a president who served when the level of crisis or challenge was low?

____

3. What connection exists between the crises or challenges a president faces in office and the possibility of his achieving near-great or great status?

____

____

[12] Ernest R. May and Philip D. Zelikow, *The Kennedy Tapes: Inside the White House During the Cuban Missile Crisis* (Cambridge, Mass.: Harvard University Press, 1997); and Michael R. Beschloss, *Reaching for Glory: Lyndon Johnson's Secret White House Tapes, 1964–1965* (New York: Simon & Schuster, 2001).

[13] "The Ultimate Approval Rating," *New York Times Magazine*, December 16, 1996, p. 46.

[14] Both surveys can be found on the Web: the C-SPAN survey at www.americanpresidents.org and the *Wall Street Journal* survey at www.opinionjournal.com/hail/.

TABLE 8.3 RANKINGS OF PRESIDENTIAL PERFORMANCE, 1860–2000

PERIOD	IMPORTANT ISSUES OR EVENTS	LEVEL OF CRISIS OR CHALLENGE	PRESIDENT	C-SPAN RANKING	WALL STREET JOURNAL RANKING	WALL STREET JOURNAL CATEGORY
1860–1865	Civil War	Extreme	Lincoln	1	2	Great
1865–1877	Reconstruction	High	Johnson	40	36	Failure
			Grant	33	32	Below average
1877–1900	Industrialization urbanization, westward expansion	Low	Hayes	26	22	Average
		Low	Garfield	29	*	*
		Low	Arthur	32	26	Average
		Low	Cleveland	17	12	Above average
		Low	Harrison	31	27	Below average
1896–1901	Spanish-American War	High	McKinley	15	14	Above average
1901–1912	Reform, foreign policy	High	Roosevelt	4	5	Near great
		Moderate	Taft	24	19	Average
1912–1920	Reform, World War I	Extreme	Wilson	6	11	Near great
1920–1928	Economic expansion	Low	Harding	38	38	Failure
			Coolidge	27	25	Average
1928–1932	Economic depression	High	Hoover	34	29	Below average
1932–1945	Great Depression, World War II	Extreme	Roosevelt	2	3	Great
1945–1952	Cold war, demobilization, Korean War	High	Truman	5	7	Near great
1952–1960	Cold war, economic expansion	Moderate	Eisenhower	9	9	Near great
1960–1963	Cold war, civil rights	High	Kennedy	8	18	Above average
1963–1968	Vietnam War, civil rights, Great Society	Very high	Johnson	10	17	Above average
1968–1974	Vietnam War, Watergate	Very high	Nixon	25	33	Below average
1974–1980	Cold war Economic recession, energy crisis	High	Ford	23	28	Below average
			Carter	22	30	Below average
1980–1988	Cold war	Moderate	Reagan	11	8	Near great
1988–1992	Gulf War, economic recession	Moderate	Bush	20	21	Average
1992–2000	Foreign policy, impeachment	Moderate	Clinton	21	21	Average

* James A. Garfield, elected in 1880, was shot several months into his term by a deranged office seeker and died two months later. Garfield served as president for a little over six months. His early death makes it difficult to evaluate and rank his performance.

SOURCE: Both surveys can be found on the Web: the C-SPAN survey at www.americanpresidents.org and the *Wall Street Journal* survey at www.opinionjournal.com/hail/.

4. The emergence of any single document or piece of information bearing on a president's performance is unlikely to decisively alter a scholar's assessment of that president. Of course, we can imagine exceptions to the general rule. For example, almost since the day the Japanese attacked Pearl Harbor (December 7, 1941), some have accused Franklin Delano Roosevelt of knowing in advance that the attack was coming and purposely leaving the nation vulnerable so as to galvanize public opinion and accomplish his objective: to join the world war on the side of the Allies and to defeat Hitler. A clear majority of Americans did not want to enter the war, and Roosevelt, so the argument goes, recognized that only an attack by a foreign power against U.S. territory and citizens—2,400 people died at Pearl Harbor—would shake the public from its isolationist stupor.

Most scholars agree that the charges against Roosevelt are contradicted by the documentary record and are unlikely ever to be substantiated. But suppose the scholars are mistaken; suppose the charges are proved true. In your view, how would the revelation that Roosevelt had prior knowledge of the attack on Pearl Harbor affect scholars' assessment of his presidency?

This question is not as simple as it seems at first glance. One author who believes Roosevelt did know about the attack in advance argues that the president was right to sacrifice Pearl Harbor to achieve a greater good: the defeat of Hitler.[15] Address this author's argument in your answer. Explain and support your position.

5. Evaluating presidential decision making is an important component of any overall assessment of presidential performance. Essential to a fair analysis of that decision making is the careful identification by scholars of the information presidents did and didn't have. Consider the case of Harry Truman and the decisions he made in the aftermath of World War II, which set the course of U.S.–Soviet relations for years to come.

Beginning in 1945, Truman used the economic and military power of the United States to protect Western Europe from what many feared were Soviet designs to expand communism. At the time, Truman knew very little about what the Soviets had in store for Western Europe. The Soviet Union was a totalitarian society that was difficult for Americans to penetrate. Because he didn't know with certainty what the Soviets' intentions were regarding Western Europe, Truman believed it only prudent to assume the worst and prepare to defend against a possible Soviet invasion of Western Europe. The president took the position that Western Europe was of vital interest to the United States, and that it had to be protected at all costs, even if that meant sacrificing America's cordial wartime relationship with the Soviet Union and waging a cold war against the country.

[15] Robert B. Stinnett, *Day of Deceit: The Truth about FDR and Pearl Harbor* (New York: Free Press, 2000). David Kahn published a devastating critique of Stinnett's book in the *New York Review of Books*, November 2, 2000.

Many historians praise Truman for the cost–benefit analysis that informed his decision to protect Western Europe. Melvyn Leffler, a prominent scholar in the field of cold war studies, wrote that officials in Truman's administration "manifested sagacity, sensitivity, and wisdom" in assessing and responding to the perceived Soviet threat against Western Europe.[16] As indicated in Table 8.3, Truman is ranked fifth in the C-SPAN survey and rated seventh and categorized as "near great" in the *Wall Street Journal* survey. In the C-SPAN survey, Truman received one of his highest scores on the international-relations criterion.

In the 1990s many documents from the Soviet era were opened to researchers. Imagine that several years from now, researchers uncover documentation that proves to everyone's satisfaction that the Soviet Union had no designs—territorial or otherwise—on Western Europe. That kind of revelation would mean that Truman incorrectly assessed the threat posed by the Soviet Union to vital U.S. interests, needlessly provoked and antagonized the Soviet Union, and unjustifiably launched the United States into a terribly dangerous and expensive cold war. How would such a revelation affect scholars' assessments of Truman's conduct of U.S. foreign policy and Truman's current ranking as a near-great president? Explain and support your answer.

6. To answer this question and questions 7 through 9, look at the *Wall Street Journal* survey at www.opinionjournal.com/hail/. Go to the site, click on Ranking Methodology, and read law professor James Lindgren's introduction to his essay. What methods did the *Wall Street Journal* employ to avoid bias in its survey?

7. Read the section of Lindgren's essay that covers America's most controversial presidents. Who are they, and what makes them controversial?

[16] Melvyn P. Leffler, *A Preponderance of Power: National Security, the Truman Administration, and the Cold War* (Stanford, Calif.: Stanford University Press, 1992), p. 502.

8. Read the section of Lindgren's essay titled "Comparing the Responses of Scholars in History, Law, and Political Science." Identify two systematic differences between the rankings assigned to presidents by law professors and those assigned by historians.

9. Read the section of Lindgren's essay on the most overrated presidents.

a. Who, according to Lindgren, is America's most overrated president?

b. Who is the second most overrated president?

c. Go back to www.opinionjournal.com/hail/, and scroll down to "Overrated Presidents." Click on Dynasty Dooms JFK by Akhil Reed Amar. Identify three arguments Amar makes in support of his thesis that Kennedy is overrated.

Argument 1:

Argument 2:

Argument 3:

10. You'll find the C-SPAN survey at www.americanpresidents.org. Scroll down and click on the C-SPAN Survey of Presidential Leadership and then Historian Survey Results. Notice that you can select a criterion and look at the ranking of every president based on that criterion. Or you can select a president and look at his ranking on all ten criteria.

a. Select Lyndon Johnson. On what criterion did he receive the highest final score?

b. On what criterion did he receive the lowest final score?

11. Select two other presidents. In the space below, identify the presidents and specify for each the category in which he achieved the highest and lowest final score.

President 1:

President 2:

EXERCISE 8.4 FIRES IN TEXAS, CROWDED CLASSROOMS IN FLORIDA, AND LIES IN DEBATES: DISTINGUISHING FACT FROM OPINION IN AN AMERICAN PRESIDENTIAL CAMPAIGN

BACKGROUND

The American public takes a dim view of its politicians. Many believe that politicians only want power and perks, and will say anything—even lie—to get elected. If we accept that that characterization is accurate at least sometimes, the difficulty becomes evaluating the truth of the statements made by candidates and officeholders. The line between fact and fiction is not always clear, and drawing that line demands more knowledge and understanding of politics and public policy than many citizens have or want to have. Yet democracy hinges on an educated citizenry.

Political campaigns illustrate the difficulty of separating fact from fiction. The first problem is that politicians exaggerate and distort, whether intentionally or unintentionally, to cast themselves in a favorable light and their opponents as creatures of the dark. Second, because media coverage of campaigns is often careless, candidate statements routinely are taken out of context or blown out of proportion. The third obstacle to drawing a clear line between fact and fiction is that many Americans are only marginally attentive to campaign coverage and rarely consult sources of information outside the mainstream media.

Voters and candidates often look at political campaigns from very different perspectives. Many voters want an absolute assessment: Is a candidate good or bad? Right or wrong? Telling the truth or lying? From a candidate's point of view, public policy issues are never this simple. Often a candidate speaking on an issue is not so much lying or telling the truth as taking positions based on an assessment of the evidence at hand. The citizens' job, then, is not to make an absolute distinction between truths and lies but to determine which candidate holds the better policy position.

The presidential campaign of 2000 offers several bizarre examples of the dilemmas citizens face in contemporary media-oriented campaigns. Two come from the first presidential debate between Gore and Bush, on October 3, 2000, in Boston.

The first example: Candidates Bush and Gore were asked about their ability to handle a crisis. Bush answered by citing his effective relationship as the governor of Texas with the Federal Emergency Management Administration (FEMA) when it responded to widespread wildfires in Texas in 1996. Before Gore gave his own account of successful crisis management, he said, "First I want to compliment the governor on his response to those fires and floods in Texas. I accompanied James Lee Witt [the director of FEMA] down to Texas when those fires broke out."[17] It eventually came out in the media, largely through the efforts of Bush staffers, that Gore had not surveyed the damage in Texas with Witt but with a lower-ranking FEMA official. Gore had been with the FEMA director eighteen times during his vice presidency to survey various catastrophes—but not this particular disaster.

The second example: In responding to a question about education, Gore argued that Bush's proposal to provide vouchers for families to send their children to private schools would draw needed funds away from the public schools, which Gore claimed already were strapped for funds. Gore then added this anecdote: "I got a letter today as I left Florida. . . . The guy who served me lunch gave me [the] letter. His name is Randy Ellis. He has a 15-year-old daughter. Her science class was supposed to be for 24 students. She's the 36th student in the classroom. They can't squeeze another desk in for her so she has to stand during the class. . . . I don't think private schools should have a right to take money away from public schools at a time when Ms. Ellis is standing in that classroom."[18]

In a bizarre chain of events, the principal of the school and the superintendent of the school district in Tampa, offended by the negative publicity, issued statements denying that Kailey Ellis was standing because students were sharing desks. Their statement faulted Gore for trying to score political points at the expense of one of the state's best school districts. The Bush campaign immediately went on the attack, issuing statements that questioned Gore's credibility and accused him of exaggerating evidence

---

[17] "Transcripts of the First Presidential Debate," *Los Angeles Times,* October 4, 2000, p. 12.

[18] Ibid., p. 10.

in support of his positions. Even Bush chimed in, saying that Gore's remark was "part of a disturbing pattern."[19]

As the story of the standing student became fodder for the talk shows, Gore's advisers and even the candidate himself appeared on television trying to extinguish the fires. The advisers were worried that Gore's alleged exaggerations and distortions, no matter how trivial, would prove significant in the campaign. One adviser said that the Republicans "will attempt to link Gore's exaggerations to the culture of the last eight years. It's dangerous because it reinforces a dangerous perception that Gore is just another arrogant politician, and we have eight more years of lies ahead of us."[20]

In the first example, Gore's story could be investigated and confirmed or refuted: Either the event in Texas happened as Gore described it or it didn't. A simple check of FEMA records or the vice president's schedule would verify the facts. As noted above, Gore did not travel with the FEMA director to Texas, but it wouldn't be surprising, given the number of times he had traveled with Witt, if Gore simply forgot the details of that trip to Texas. Gore later defended himself by reminding voters that his point in telling the story, after all, was to compliment the Texas governor's performance under pressure.

Gore's story about the student standing in the Florida classroom is more complex. It was true, as the school officials claimed, that Ms. Ellis had not been standing on the day Gore made his claim in the debate. However, she had been forced to stand one day, and her father had handed Gore a letter about the crowded classroom conditions. Kailey Ellis may not have been standing in class on the day of the debate, but that was because students in the overcrowded classroom had started sharing desks. Yes, Gore portrayed a single incident as a continuing problem. But as the student's father, a Republican, later pointed out, the real issue was the overcrowding in the school since a bond measure had been defeated. Polls at the time indicated that his two missteps undermined Gore's credibility in the view of many voters.[21]

When candidates' claims involve more complex issues, where evidence exists that supports as well as contradicts those claims, it becomes more difficult for voters to distinguish the truth. For example, in the first debate in 2000, during a discussion of campaign finance reform, Bush charged that Gore, who supported reform, was outspending Bush, who opposed reform. Federal Election Commission figures at the time of the first debate showed that Bush had spent overall more than double what Gore had spent—$124 million versus $61 million, but that Gore, with the help of soft money and independent spending by pro-Democratic groups, had spent slightly more on advertising.[22] By the end of the race, FEC figures showed that Bush significantly outspent Gore, even for advertising.[23] Which candidate benefited more from a system of campaign spending that had been under attack is an issue of manifestly greater consequence to the American people than whether or not Gore had traveled with the FEMA director on a particular day. Yet the accuracy of the FEMA claim received a great deal more attention than did the accuracy of the campaign-spending claim. Why? Because campaign spending is a much more complex issue than whether or not Gore had been with the FEMA director on a particular day, and therefore is a more difficult issue on which to focus the public's attention.

ASSIGNMENT

Reading 8.4 describes the differences between statements of fact and statements of opinion. Read the material and then read questions 1 through 10, a series of statements from the three debates between Bush and Gore in the election of 2000.[24] In the space below each question, note whether the statement is (a) a statement of fact—something that can be confirmed or refuted—or a statement of opinion. Then (b) explain and support your answer. (You do not have to decide whether or not the statements are true.)

---

[19] Maria L. LaGanga and Elizabeth Shogren, "Bush and Gore Campaigns Tally Up the Post-Debate Scores," *Los Angeles Times*, October 5, 2000, p. 22.

[20] David Von Drehle and Ceci Connolly, "GOP Homes in on Gore's Credibility," *Washington Post*, October 8, 2000, p. A1.

[21] Dan Balz, "Bush Overtakes Gore in Polls," *Washington Post*, October 11, 2000, p. A1.

[22] LaGanga and Shogren, "Campaigns Tally Up," p. 22. Because FEC totals run behind actual spending, the figures in the article dated from August 30, 2000.

[23] Figures are available at www.fec.gov.

[24] The quotes are taken from the Commission on Presidential Debates Web site (www.debates.org/pages/debhis2000.html).

READING 8.4 FACT OR OPINION?

A *statement of fact* can be verified as true or refuted as false. In the social sciences, fact and truth are not necessarily the same. According to one social scientist,

> facts are not to be confused with Truth. A fact is only as good as the means of verification used to establish it, as well as the frame of reference within which it requires meaning. A great deal of science consists of using methodological advances to reverse, modify, or even falsify "facts" . . . formerly verified.*

The social science definition of a factual statement would lead us to classify Gore's statements about his travel with the FEMA director and about Kailey Ellis standing in the classroom as statements of fact, as we would Bush's statement about his campaign spending. These statements are subject to verification by anyone using scientific methods of investigation.

A *statement of opinion* is based on personal values, ideology, or wishful prediction. With the passage of time, an opinion may turn out to be true, partially true, or false. But a statement of opinion at the time it's made cannot be verified or refuted scientifically. For example, in the election 2000 debates, Bush claimed that his proposed tax cuts would not eat up the budget surplus, and that claim was supported by arguments and even by impressive evidence from the budget. But the Gore campaign was able to muster opposing evidence and arguments that were just as impressive to many observers. Bush's position on tax cuts during the presidential campaign was nothing more than a statement of opinion about what he perceived as the need for tax cuts and their relationship to budget surpluses and deficits. Now that Bush is in office and a tax cut bill has been enacted, time will tell whether Bush's statement of opinion serves the national interest better than Gore's.[25] Of course, even if there are budget deficits during Bush's first term, the president and his advisers may attribute those deficits to something other than the tax cuts—for example, the Democratic Senate's refusal to go along with necessary spending cuts. At this writing, a budget deficit for fiscal year 2002 is in the offing. Charges and countercharges over who bears responsibility for the impending deficit already have begun.

In a political campaign, voters must recognize most statements by candidates about their positions on issues as statements of opinion, even when a candidate has abundant arguments and evidence to support the position. For example, a candidate who says that the media are destroying family values—but who does not preface the statement with "I believe"—is misrepresenting a statement of opinion as a statement of fact. There is no body of evidence or standard of measurement by which that statement of opinion can be verified or refuted.

---

1. Bush (Debate 1): "My opponent thinks the [budget] surplus is the government's money. That's not what I think. I think it's the hard-working people of America's money, and I want to share that money with you [in the form of tax cuts]. . . . It's a difference between government making decisions for you and you getting more of your money to make decisions for you."

a. Statement of fact or of opinion? ____________________

b. Why? ____________________

____

____

2. Bush (Debate 1): "I know we need to ban partial-birth abortions."

a. Statement of fact or of opinion? ____________________

b. Why? ____________________

____

____

---

* Kenneth Hoover and Todd Donovan, *The Elements of Social Scientific Thinking*, 7th ed. (Boston: Bedford, St. Martin's, 2001), p. 132.

[25] Economic Growth and Tax Relief Act of 2001, Public Law No. 107-16, June 6, 2001.

TABLE 8.4 VOTERS' KNOWLEDGE OF CANDIDATES' POSITIONS ON THE ISSUES, PRESIDENTIAL ELECTION 2000

BUSH				GORE			
ISSUE	FAVORS (PERCENT)	OPPOSES (PERCENT)	DIDN'T KNOW (PERCENT)	ISSUE	FAVORS (PERCENT)	OPPOSES (PERCENT)	DIDN'T KNOW (PERCENT)
Gun control	22	41	37	Vouchers	21	39	41
Cut defense spending	18	40	43	Ban on offshore oil drilling	35	16	48
Large, across-the-board tax cut	52	11	37	Americans should be able to invest portion of social security taxes privately	19	43	39
Ban on large contributions to political campaigns	22	19	59	Affirmative action	37	10	53
New restrictions on access to abortion	48	12	40	Restrictions on trade with China (human rights abuses)	18	14	68

Note: Some rows do not sum to 100 percent because of rounding.

SOURCE: Data for November 5, 2000, from the Joan Shorenstein Center on the Press, Politics and Public Policy, John F. Kennedy School of Government, Harvard University, Cambridge, Mass., 2001 (http://www.vanishingvoter.org/data/cand-knowledge.shtml).

BUSH

ISSUE	Plurality Perceived Position	
	Correctly	Incorrectly
Gun control		
Cut defense spending		
Large, across-the-board tax cut		
Ban on large contributions to political campaigns		
New restrictions on access to abortion		

GORE

ISSUE	Plurality Perceived Position	
	Correctly	Incorrectly
Vouchers		
Ban on offshore oil drilling		
Americans should be able to invest portion of social security taxes privately		
Affirmative action		
Restrictions on trade with China because of human rights abuses		

13. What do Table 8.4 and the chart in question 12 tell you about voters' understanding of candidates' positions on major issues?

____

____

____

____

____

____

EXERCISE 8.5 THE VICE PRESIDENCY

BACKGROUND

Despite all of the hoopla in the media about a presidential candidate's selection of a running mate, the choice has little to do with the outcome of presidential races, and the office itself has little constitutional power. Most vice presidents have been on the outside looking in, often relegated by the president's staff or by the president himself to ceremonial and symbolic functions.

John Adams, the nation's first vice president, wrote to his wife Abigail that "my country in its wisdom contrived for me the most insignificant office that ever the invention of man contrived or his imagination conceived."[26] John Nance Garner, one of Franklin Delano Roosevelt's vice presidents, after leaving office reportedly referred to the vice presidency as "not worth a warm pitcher of piss."[27] Lyndon Johnson, who had been one of the most powerful men in Washington as majority leader of the Senate, suffered a humiliating exile from the corridors of power as John Kennedy's vice president. George Bush Sr. asked by a reporter—half in jest—how he kept himself busy as vice president, supposedly replied that he attended lots of funerals in funny little countries whose names he couldn't remember.

One reason for the unhappy experience of so many vice presidents lies in the Constitution itself. The vice president's most important constitutional responsibility is to take the president's place if the president is unable to serve, a contingency addressed by the Twenty-Fifth Amendment (1967). The Constitution also assigns the vice president the task of breaking tie votes in the U.S. Senate (Article I, Section 3) and of counting the electoral college ballots every four years (the Twelfth Amendment, ratified in 1804), hardly enough to keep a vice president busy.

Actually, the tie-breaking duty kept John Adams busy throughout his two terms in office. Adams presided over the Senate on a daily basis and cast more tie-breaking votes during his tenure than any other vice president in history, using his power to protect the prerogatives and policy positions of President George Washington.

Today the Senate is managed informally from the floor of the chamber, so modern vice presidents have little incentive to preside over the body on a day-by-day basis as Adams did. But the power to cast a tie-breaking vote still allows the vice president to play a critical role in the Senate from time to time. For example, during the 107th Congress, which convened in January 2001, the Senate was divided equally between Republicans and Democrats. That led Vice President Dick Cheney to complain that he couldn't leave Washington to go fly fishing while the Senate was in session because the Republicans might need his tie-breaking vote at any moment.

Although the vice president has few constitutional powers, the officeholder is not necessarily relegated to the fringes of political power. Presidents have employed their vice presidents in a number of informal but powerful advisory and policymaking roles. Gore and Cheney are vice presidents who have had unlimited access to the president and who have exercised extraordinary power in shaping policy. Indeed, Cheney wields so much power within the Bush administration that some think of him as a co-president.

That so many vice presidents have been kept outside the president's inner circle is in part attributable to the politics of selecting vice presidential candidates. Until recently, vice presidents rarely have been selected for their policy expertise, for their demonstrated ability to work with the presidential candidate, or for their potential to serve as president should the need arise. Dan Quayle, for example, had never met George Bush Sr. before being asked to serve as Bush's running mate. Vice presidential candidates usually are chosen because they bring ideological balance to the ticket, because they come from a state considered crucial to the ticket's victory, or because they are unlikely to arouse controversy or opposition. That these political considerations would determine a presidential candidate's choice of a running mate is one of the great mysteries of American politics. Why? Because there is no evidence that a significant number of American voters cast their ballots based on who occupies the vice presidential slot on a ticket. Given the politics of selecting presidential running mates, it stands to reason that presidents would be reluctant to bestow on the vice president powers and responsibilities beyond those granted by the Constitution.

---

[26] Quoted in David McCullough, *John Adams* (New York: Simon & Schuster, 2001), p. 447.

[27] See Susan Welch et al., *Understanding American Government*, 6th ed. (Belmont, Calif.: Wadsworth, 2001), p. 344.

The selection of Gore and Cheney was a departure from the political criteria traditionally employed in selecting vice presidential candidates. Gore was an unlikely choice for Clinton because he, like Clinton, was from the South and was known as a political moderate. Also, Gore comes from Tennessee, a state with relatively few electoral votes. Cheney was an unlikely choice for Bush because the vice president hailed from Wyoming, a state with few electoral votes and one reliably in the Republican column under any circumstance. Cheney was not a particularly charismatic candidate, and he had a history of heart trouble. And his voting record in the House of Representatives was among the most conservative in that body, something of a problem for a presidential candidate styling himself as a compassionate conservative. Still, despite the lack of conventional wisdom in choosing their running mates, both Clinton and Bush won.

Some observers speculate that presidential candidates now recognize that vice presidential choices bring little, if any, electoral support to the ticket. If that is indeed the case, presidential candidates may feel free to cast political considerations aside and choose their running mates based on experience, expertise, compatibility, and the ability to fulfill the awesome responsibilities of the contemporary presidency. And whatever the nature of the office, many politicians would jump at the opportunity to serve as vice president. There is, of course, the honor, the prestige, and the possibility of access to the corridors of power. More important, perhaps, the vice presidency places politicians in a good position to lay claim to their party's nomination after the president leaves office.[28]

ASSIGNMENT

Answer the questions that follow Reading 8.5, a hypothetical description of a Democratic presidential candidate and his final list of possible running mates. Assume that any rumors about the possible candidates have been investigated but can neither be proved nor disproved.

READING 8.5 A Presidential Candidate and His Possible Running Mates

Presidential candidate White male, 53 years old, married, Protestant. Moderate liberal. From small eastern state; one-time governor of that state. Strongly pro-choice; favors death penalty and gun control. Limited experience in foreign policy. Good political skills but first national campaign. Not noted for speaking ability. Relatively unknown to American people. As governor earned respect for ability to balance state budget without major cutbacks in programs and to bring new business to state.

Running mate alternative 1 White female, 40 years old, married, nonpracticing Protestant. Liberal. From western state with large bloc of electoral votes. As U.S. senator has built national following for fiery defense of women's rights and affirmative action and opposition to death penalty. Candidate of choice for liberals and women in Democratic Party. Excellent speaker; skilled, energetic campaigner. Knows presidential candidate but not well; often has opposed him on issues and did not support his quest for party's nomination.

Running mate alternative 2 White male, 72 years old, divorced, Roman Catholic. Moderate. From midwestern state with large bloc of electoral votes. State considered crucial for Democratic victory, and race looks close. Currently serving in U.S. House. No strong identification with issues but is pro-choice; well respected in Congress for ability to fashion compromise, nonpartisanship, and knowledge of environmental and health-care policies. Low-keyed and soft spoken; adept with media but not charismatic. Has worked closely with presidential candidate on number of government commissions.

Running mate alternative 3 White male, 38 years old, Protestant. Unmarried—some rumors of womanizing—not much known about personal life. Moderate conservative. From eastern state with large

[28] Even the leg up vice presidents have on claiming the presidency tends to be overstated. In 1988, George Bush Sr. was the first sitting vice president to be elected president since Martin Van Buren in 1836.

bloc of electoral votes. No political experience but well known for earning billions from own software corporation. Extremely knowledgeable about public policy toward business and about technology, education, and trade policy. Some questions about propriety of certain business dealings and lobbying activities on behalf of business interests. No interest in social or moral issues; believes business of America is business. Viewed with suspicion by many within Democratic Party. Handsome and articulate. Knows presidential candidate well but is not a friend.

Running mate alternative 4 Black male, 55 years old, married, Protestant. Moderate liberal. From southern state with relatively large number of electoral votes. State has not gone Democratic in presidential election for decades (as is true of other southern states). Emerged in civil rights movement and later became first African American elected to U.S. Senate from South since Reconstruction. Strongly favored by minority groups within Democratic Party. Knows presidential candidate well and considers him a friend; they went to college together and worked together in variety of organizations. Reputation beyond reproach in both public and private life. Politically skilled and articulate, but identified nationally primarily with civil rights and welfare issues.

Running mate alternative 5 White female, 46 years old, married, Jewish. Moderate. From western state with huge number of electoral votes. State considered relatively safe for Democrats. First served in House of Representatives, then in U.S. Senate, and then as U.S. ambassador to United Nations during Republican presidency. Especially knowledgeable about foreign policy. Has reputation of being diplomatic to point of waffling on issues that matter to Democrats. Does not know presidential candidate.

---

1. If you were picking a vice presidential candidate for political reasons—in this case to strengthen the presidential candidate's appeal to voters—which running mate would you choose? Explain and support your answer.

____

____

____

2. Looking at the vice presidential candidates from a traditional perspective, which would be least likely to strengthen the presidential ticket? Explain and support your answer.

____

____

____

3. Now think about the Clinton and George W. Bush models of choosing a running mate. Which of the possible candidates is best qualified to help the president governing the nation? Explain and support your answer.

____

____

____

____

____

BUREAUCRACY AND THE REGULATORY PROCESS

EXERCISE 9.1 EXPLORING THE FEDERAL BUREAUCRACY ON THE INTERNET

BACKGROUND

When the executive branch of the national government was established in 1789, the federal bureaucracy consisted of just three Cabinet departments and the Office of the Attorney General, later to become the Justice Department. In 1789 the State Department had 9 employees, the War Department had 2, and the Treasury Department had 39. Today the State Department employs about 28,000 civilians, the Defense Department about 670,000, and the Treasury Department about 163,000. The federal bureaucracy today boasts fourteen Cabinet departments and dozens of agencies, commissions, and government corporations with a civilian workforce of more than 2.5 million. This bureaucratic behemoth exercises power and influence over virtually every facet of the nation's social and economic life. In the view of many observers, the power, reach, and independence of the federal bureaucracy demand that it be viewed as a fourth branch of government (see Exercise 9.4).

The size and scope of the federal bureaucracy are among the sources of its immense power; they also make the fourth branch difficult to conceptualize and understand. The Internet is a valuable tool for making sense of and gaining access to the myriad departments and agencies that constitute the federal bureaucracy.[1] In September 2000, the General Services Administration's Office of Governmentwide Policy (an agency in the federal bureaucracy) launched FirstGov, the official portal to more than 30 million pages of government information, services, and online transactions.

---

[1] It seems appropriate that we use the Internet to understand the federal bureaucracy. In 1969, the Department of Defense conducted research that laid the groundwork for the creation of the Net.

ASSIGNMENT

1. Begin exploring the federal bureaucracy by going to www.firstgov.gov. On the left side of the page, under the heading "Agencies," click on Federal and then Executive. FirstGov divides the executive branch into several segments. We've listed five of them below. Identify one specific department, agency, or office within each segment, and note its name.

Executive Office of the President: ______________________________

Cabinet departments: ______________________________

Independent agencies: ______________________________

Boards and commissions: ______________________________

Quasi-official agencies: ______________________________

2. Pick a Cabinet department and go to its Web site (use the link from FirstGov and then click again on the department name).

a. What department did you choose?

____

b. How does the department define its mission?

____

____

c. Does the department appear to serve any particular interest or group in society? Explain and support your answer.

____

____

____

d. Each department's Web site promotes the president of the United States or the secretary of the department—a recent proposal or accomplishment, for example. In the space below, briefly describe an example.

____

____

____

____

e. All of these Web sites list programs or services that are available to the public. In the space below, briefly describe an example.

____

____

____

____

f. Explore the job openings posted on the Cabinet department's Web site. In the space below briefly describe the typical position the department is trying to fill, including the salary range.

____

____

____

3. Continue your exploration of the federal bureaucracy by going to www.lib.lsu.edu/gov/fedgov, the Louisiana State University Library Federal Agencies Directory. At the top of the page, click on Complete U.S. Federal Government Agencies Directory (Hierarchical). Here are listed the Cabinet departments and independent agencies of the federal government and their various subunits. The subunits include bureaus, divisions, branches, offices, and services. Each line in the hierarchical list represents one subunit and is a link to that subunit's Web site.

a. Estimate the total number of subunits of the federal bureaucracy in this hierarchical list.

____

b. Explore several subunits. Based on your overview of the list and your examination of some of the subunits, identify and describe two characteristics of the federal bureaucracy.

Characteristic 1: ____

____

Characteristic 2: ____

____

4. The departments and agencies in the federal bureaucracy exercise immense power by making and implementing policy. Congress has delegated to the departments and agencies the quasi-legislative power of issuing rules and regulations that have the force of law. Because the regulations issued by the federal bureaucracy have the potential to affect every social and economic interest in the nation, Congress requires that proposed regulations, their justification, and the process used to formulate them be published in the *Federal Register.*[2] Generally, a proposed regulation does not take effect for thirty days after it's published in the *Federal Register.* During that period, concerned parties can express support or opposition to the suggested regulation.

a. Go the Government Printing Office Web site at www.access.gpo.gov and scroll down. Under "Quick Links," click on Federal Register. Use the browse feature to survey the proposed regulations. Find one that seems interesting. Summarize the rule in one or two sentences.

____

____

____

b. What agency is proposing the rule, and why does the agency claim the rule is needed?

____

____

____

____

c. Identify an interest or group in society that would be affected by this rule. Do you think that interest or group would support or oppose implementation of the rule? Explain why.

____

____

____

____

5. Departments and agencies in the federal bureaucracy gain power by developing expertise in particular policy areas. For example, subunits within the Department of Agriculture (USDA)—the Agricultural Research Service, the Economic Research Service, and the National Agricultural

[2] The *Federal Register* is published Monday through Friday; it is available on the Web at www.access.gpo.gov/su_docs.

Statistics Service, among them—conduct or sponsor research on every imaginable agricultural question. Farmers and agribusiness rely on information developed or collected by the USDA to keep the agricultural economy prosperous. The Census Bureau is an agency with just a single mission: to collect and disseminate information about the nation—who Americans are, where we are, and what we do. The Department of Defense, the CIA, and the National Security Agency collect and guard information that bears on national security. Deciding whether to release sensitive information is an important source of power for the executive branch departments and agencies that handle national security matters.

Go to FedStats (www.fedstats.gov), a Web site with links to the statistics collected by federal agencies and departments. Click on Agencies listed alphabetically, and select an agency with a policy area that interests you.

a. What is the agency?

____

b. What statistics does the agency collect? List three examples in the space below.

____

____

____

c. Look at the examples you listed. Who or what might use these statistics and for what purpose? Explain your answer.

____

____

____

____

EXERCISE 9.2 THE REAL WORLD OF REGULATION

BACKGROUND

In the real world of regulation, bureaucrats—officials who are not elected—make decisions every day that affect all aspects of Americans' lives, from defining a prune to determining how much arsenic a glass of drinking water can contain. To implement their decisions, departments and agencies in the executive branch issue rules and regulations that carry the force of law. Their authority to do so comes from the legislative power Congress delegates to the executive branch.

The interdependence of citizens in a modern industrial society has made the delegation of legislative authority to the federal bureaucracy necessary. As America's economy and society have grown increasingly complex and specialized, and as Americans have come increasingly to look to the national government to solve economic and social problems, Congress has not always been able to respond through lawmaking. The fact is that members of Congress do not have the time or the technical know-how to craft all the detailed legislation necessary to govern society today. And even if time and expertise were not issues, it would still be impossible to draft legislation that takes into account all the contingencies of living in complex and changing times. The latter explains why Congress often frames legislation in broad and sometimes ambiguous terms—identifying a general goal and then delegating to the federal bureaucracy the task of filling in the details. On occasion, the mandate Congress gives the bureaucracy is no more specific than *regulate in the public interest.* That kind of broad grant of authority confers on civil servants in the executive branch wide latitude to make policy by proposing and implementing the rules and regulations required to implement the will of Congress.

At times the delegation of legislative power has met with strong opposition. In 1935, in the early years of the New Deal, the Supreme Court ruled in *Schechter Poultry Corp. v. United States* that Congress's delegation of legislative power to the executive branch violated the principle of the separation of powers (see Exercise 7.1). Although the court did change its thinking within a few years, critics continue to charge today that the delegation of power is too broad and that the legislative branch in many cases is abdicating its duty to make difficult choices. When Congress steps aside, critics argue, the legislative power of the federal government devolves on nonelected, entrenched, often-invisible civil servants.

In a capitalist society, we might expect the most vocal opposition to the legislative delegation of powers, and the regulation it engenders, to come from business. But business often supports regulation because rules afford protection from unrestrained competition and the forces of the free market. More and more, business looks to government regulation to bring order to a chaotic marketplace and to guarantee a fair price for its products or services.

For business, the decision to support or oppose government regulation often stems less from a commitment to the free market than it does from self-interest: What would government regulation mean for the bottom line? In the 1970s, for example, the major airlines recognized that government regulation by the Civil Aeronautics Board kept prices stable and discouraged new airlines from entering the market. So, when Congress proposed to deregulate fares and routes, the industry strenuously opposed the plan. And, in the wake of the Airline Deregulation Act of 1978, many of the older airlines went bankrupt, profits generally fell, and some small cities lost service when airlines shed unprofitable routes. Agriculture is an industry that continues to rely on and support a wide array of government regulatory programs, including subsidies, parities, acreage allotments, and marketing standards. The Agricultural Marketing Service of the USDA, for example, serves a variety of agricultural interests by protecting and promoting their marketing efforts. The impact of the Agricultural Marketing Service is explored in Readings 9.2.1 and 9.2.2.

The process of developing and issuing federal regulations involves many actors. Before they draft proposed regulations, agencies and departments solicit the views of members of Congress, interest groups, and the segments of the public concerned with the issue at hand. The president, presidential commissions, and congressional staff members also may play a role in shaping proposed regulations. Once drafted, all proposed regulations are published in the *Federal Register,* so that those who would be affected by them have an opportunity to comment before the new regulations take effect. The Regulatory Flexibility Act (1980) requires that the economic impact of proposed regulations be evaluated before implementation. Proposed rules can be modified or even retracted based on comments from the public or from interest groups; but they seldom are challenged successfully. In the real world of regulation, departments and agencies continue to exercise power even after they issue rules and regulations, as they determine how and with what vigor to implement and enforce those rules and regulations.

ASSIGNMENT

Refer to Readings 9.2.1 and 9.2.2 to answer the questions that follow them.

READING 9.2.1 THE AGRICULTURAL MARKETING SERVICE: WHAT ARE MARKETING ORDERS, AND HOW DO THEY OPERATE?

Marketing orders and marketing agreements are [issued by the USDA and are] designed to help stabilize market conditions for fruit and vegetable products. The programs assist farmers in allowing them to collectively work to solve marketing problems. Industries voluntarily enter into these programs and choose to have Federal oversight of certain aspects of their operations. The Marketing Order Administration Branch of the Fruit and Vegetable Programs oversees the programs to make sure the orders and agreements operate in the public interest and within legal bounds. Presently, there are 36 active marketing agreement and order programs and an additional program for peanuts, which collect assessment fees from handlers to cover operation and administrative costs of the programs.

A marketing order is a legal instrument authorized by the U.S. Congress through the Agricultural Marketing Agreement Act of 1937. Marketing orders . . . are binding on all individuals and businesses who are classified as "handlers" in a geographic area covered by the order. . . .

Programs for fruits, vegetables and specialty crops are [initiated and developed by a steering committee of key industry people and are] administered by local administrative committees, which are made up of growers and/or handlers, and often a member of the public. Committee members are nominated by the industry and appointed by the Secretary of Agriculture (Secretary). The regulations are issued and become binding on the entire industry in the geographical area regulated if approved by at least two-thirds of the producers by number or volume and if approved by the Secretary.

Marketing orders and agreements may (1) maintain the high quality of produce that is on the market; (2) standardize packages and containers; (3) regulate the flow of product to market; (4) establish reserve pools for storable commodities; and (5) authorize production research, marketing research and development, and advertising.

READING 9.2.2 FRESH PRUNE IMPORT REGULATION

The Washington–Oregon Fresh Prune Committee is made up of local prune growers and handlers. The committee is organized under the authority of the Marketing Order Administration Branch of the Fruit and Vegetable Programs and regulates the handling and marketing of prunes in Washington and Oregon.

[a] Pursuant to section 8e of the Agricultural Marketing Agreement Act of 1937, as amended, the importation into the United States of any fresh prunes, other than the Brooks variety, during the period of July 15–September 30 of each year is prohibited unless such fresh prunes meet the following requirements:

[1] Such fresh prunes grade at least U.S. No. 1, except that at least two-thirds of the surface of the fresh prune is required to be purplish in color and such fresh prunes measure not less than 1¼ inches in diameter as measured by a rigid ring: Provided that the following tolerances, by count, of the fresh prunes in any lot shall apply in lieu of the tolerance for defects provided in the United States Standards for Grades of Fresh Plums and Prunes: A total of no more than 15 percent for defects, including therein not more than the following percentage for the defect listed:

READING SOURCE: From Agricultural Marketing Service, "What Are Marketing Orders, and How Do They Operate," www.ams.usda.gov/fv/moview.html.

READING SOURCE: From *Federal Register*, vol. 61, no. 153 (August 7, 1996), pp. 40956–40959.

[i] 10 percent for fresh prunes which fail to meet the color requirement;
[ii] 10 percent for fresh prunes which fail to meet the minimum diameter requirement;
[iii] 10 percent for fresh prunes which fail to meet the remaining requirements of the grade: Provided that not more than one-half of this amount, or 5 percent, shall be allowed for defects causing serious damage, including in the latter amount not more than 1 percent for decay. . . .

[c] The grade, size and quality requirements of this section shall not be applicable to fresh prunes imported for consumption by charitable institutions, distribution by relief agencies, or commercial processing into products, but such prunes shall be subject to the safeguard provisions in §944.350.
[d] The term "U.S. No. 1" shall have the same meaning as when used in the United States Standards for Grades of Fresh Plums and Prunes, the term "purplish color" shall have the same meaning as when used in the Washington State Department of Agriculture Standards for Italian Prunes (April 28, 1978), and the Oregon State Department of Agriculture Standards for Italian Prunes (October 5, 1977); the term "diameter" means the greatest dimension measured at right angles to a line from the stem to the blossom end of the fruit.
[e] The term "Prunes" means all varieties of plums, classified botanical as *Prunus domestica,* except those of the President variety.
[f] The term "importation" means release from custody of the United States Customs Service.
[g] Inspection and certification service is required for imports and will be available in accordance with the regulation designating inspection services and procedure for obtaining inspections and certification.
[h] Any lot or portion thereof which fails to meet the import requirements, and is not being imported for purposes of consumption by charitable institutions, distribution by relief agencies, or commercial processing into products, prior to or after reconditioning may be exported or disposed of under the supervision of the Federal or Federal–State Inspection Service with the cost of certifying the disposal of such fresh prunes borne by the importer. . . .

---

1. a. According to Reading 9.2.1, who or what initiates, develops, and administers market orders?[3]

____

____

____

b. Who issues market orders, and who is bound by them? Do market orders carry the force of law?

____

____

____

____

2. According to Reading 9.2.1, what are two benefits that accrue to fruit and vegetable producers from giving the Marketing Order Administration Branch of the Fruit and Vegetable Programs the authority to issue market orders?

____

____

____

3. Reading 9.2.2 is taken from a regulation issued by the Department of Agriculture and administered by the Washington–Oregon Fresh Prune Committee. Suppose you're in charge of communications for the committee. Explain to your members in one hundred words or less what the regulation is about.

---

[3] For additional information on the Agricultural Marketing Service's fruit and vegetable programs, visit its Web site at www.ams.usda.gov.

4. Identify two specific ways in which the prune import regulation protects fresh prune producers in Washington and Oregon from foreign competition.

5. According to the Fresh Prune Import Regulation, what is a prune?

EXERCISE 9.3 HOW MUCH REGULATION IS ENOUGH? HOW MUCH IS TOO MUCH?

BACKGROUND

The dizzying pace of change in biotechnology has generated conflict between those who see the promise of medical cures and corporate profits, and those who fear the damage emerging technologies might wreak on the public. For federal bureaucrats, the challenge is determining the right amount of regulation—rules that protect the general welfare without imposing undue delay on patients waiting for new treatments or undue costs on industry.

The problem of determining how much regulation is enough in the field of gene therapy was brought to light by the death in 1999 of an 18-year-old patient. Jesse Gelsinger had been undergoing gene therapy for a liver disease in a clinical trial at the University of Pennsylvania's Institute of Gene Therapy. (Many of the human subjects in clinical trials are suffering from life-threatening illnesses; the trials offer them their last hope of a cure.) Federal investigators later determined that the researchers had violated several federal regulations (see Reading 9.3.1).[4] Subsequently, the federal government proposed new regulations and guidelines for the practice of gene therapy.

Two government offices are responsible for monitoring gene therapy clinical trials. The Food and Drug Administration (FDA) is the primary watchdog; it tracks adverse reactions until the new therapy is approved. The second is the Recombinant DNA Advisory Committee (RAC) of the National Institutes of Health (NIH). The RAC was created to reassure Americans who are wary of genetic engineering; its role is primarily advisory, although it does approve the procedures for clinical trials.[5]

ASSIGNMENT

Please refer to Readings 9.3.1 and 9.3.2 to answer the questions that follow them.

READING 9.3.1 "Human Gene Therapy: Harsh Lessons, High Hopes"

A 4-year-old girl named Ashanthi DeSilva from the suburbs of Cleveland lay on crisp white hospital sheets with a needle stuck in a vein. She didn't mind; this happened all the time in her chronically sick childhood. At the other end of the intravenous hookup hung a clear plastic bag of very special cells: her own white blood cells, genetically altered to fix a defect she inherited at birth.

A strikingly thin middle-aged doctor stared anxiously at the tiny figure. W. French Anderson, M.D., and his colleagues R. Michael Blaese, M.D., and Kenneth Culver, M.D., all then working at the National Institutes of Health, crossed a symbolic threshold with Ashanthi DeSilva that day, becoming the first group to begin a clinical trial in the new frontier of medical treatment: human gene therapy.

The reason for the excitement was simple: Most diseases have a genetic component and gene therapy holds the hope of curing, not merely treating, a broad range of ailments, including inherited diseases like cystic fibrosis and even chronic conditions like cancer and infectious diseases like AIDS.

At least, that's the theory.

In the 10 years since that first genetic treatment on Sept. 14, 1990, the hyperbole has exceeded the results. Worldwide, researchers launched more than 400 clinical trials to test gene therapy against a wide array of illnesses. Surprisingly, cancer has dominated the research. Even more surprising, little has worked.

"There was initially a great burst of enthusiasm that lasted three, four years where a couple of hundred trials got started all over the world," says Anderson, now at the University of Southern California in Los Angeles. "Then we came to realize that nothing was really working at the clinical level."

---

[4] Marlene Simon, "Tougher Gene Therapy Protections Urged," *Los Angeles Times*, May 24, 2000, p. A6.

[5] Sheryl Gay Stolberg, "A Death Puts Gene Therapy under Increasing Scrutiny," *New York Times*, November 4, 1999, p. A1.

READING SOURCE: From Larry Thompson, "Human Gene Therapy: Harsh Lessons, High Hopes," *FDA Consumer Magazine*, September–October 2000 (www.fda.gov/fdac/features/2000/500_gene.html).

Abbey S. Meyers, president of the National Organization for Rare Disorders Inc., an umbrella organization of patients' groups, is much more blunt. "We haven't even taken one baby step beyond that first clinical experiment," Meyers says. "It has hardly gotten anywhere. Over the last 10 years, I have been very disappointed."

And then things got worse.

In September 1999, a patient died from a reaction to a gene therapy treatment at the University of Pennsylvania's Institute of Human Gene Therapy in Philadelphia. Jesse Gelsinger, an exuberant 18-year-old from Tucson, Arizona, suffered from a broken gene that causes one of those puzzling metabolic diseases of genetic medicine. An optimistic, altruistic Gelsinger went to Philadelphia to help advance the science that might eventually cure his type of illness. Instead, the experiment killed him.

In the aftermath of his death, there has been a flurry of activity to minimize the chance of future accidental deaths. The Food and Drug Administration, along with the National Institutes of Health, launched several investigations of the University of Pennsylvania studies and others. The inquiries provided disappointing news: Gene therapy researchers were not following all of the federal rules requiring them to report unexpected adverse events associated with the gene therapy trials; worse, some scientists were asking that problems not be made public. And then came the allegations that there were other unreported deaths attributed to genetic treatments, at least six in all.

"Probably the clearest evidence of the system not working is that only 35 to 37 of 970 serious adverse events from [a common type of gene therapy trial] were reported to the NIH" as required, says LeRoy Walters, the recently retired head of the Kennedy Institute of Ethics at Georgetown University and former chairman of NIH's Recombinant DNA Advisory Committee. "That is fewer than 5 percent of the serious adverse events."

The news hit the clinical trial community like a thunderclap. The consequences have been immediate and wide-ranging, and may threaten future research.

"Participation in gene therapy trials is way down because the public is not sure what to make of this," says Philip Noguchi, M.D., director of the Cellular and Genetic Therapy Division in FDA's Center for Biologic Evaluation and Research (CBER). "They want to know what the government is doing to help restore the confidence in this field."

Responding to the Crisis

The federal government moved quickly to do just that. FDA immediately shut down the trial in which Gelsinger had volunteered, and all clinical gene transfer trials at the University of Pennsylvania in January. The university went on to severely restrict the research of its once-high-flying gene therapy institute director James Wilson, M.D., announcing in May that all his work would be confined to animal and laboratory experiments and that he would be barred from conducting studies in people.

FDA also suspended gene therapy trials at St. Elizabeth's Medical Center in Boston, a major teaching affiliate of Tufts University School of Medicine, which sought to use gene therapy to reverse heart disease, because scientists there failed to follow protocols and may have contributed to at least one patient death. FDA also temporarily suspended two liver cancer studies sponsored by the Schering-Plough Corporation because of technical similarities to the University of Pennsylvania study.

Moreover, as nervousness spread through the field in the months after revelations about Gelsinger's death, some research groups voluntarily suspended gene therapy studies, including two experiments sponsored by the Cystic Fibrosis Foundation and studies at Beth Israel Deaconess Medical Center in Boston aimed at hemophilia. The scientists paused to review their studies and make sure they learned from the mistakes made at the University of Pennsylvania.

In March, the Department of Health and Human Services announced two initiatives by FDA and NIH. The Gene Therapy Clinical Trial Monitoring Plan is designed to ratchet up the level of scrutiny with additional reporting requirements for study sponsors. A series of Gene Transfer Safety Symposia was designed to get researchers to talk to each other, to share their results about unexpected problems and to make sure that everyone knows the rules.

In addition, FDA launched random inspections of 70 clinical trials in more than two dozen gene therapy programs nationwide and instituted new reporting requirements. "We see the need to get the concept across that this is for keeps," says FDA's Noguchi. "You can be sloppy when you are dealing with a scientific paper, but you can't be sloppy when you are dealing with a human. Everything matters."

So far, the inspections only suggest that one other program appears to be in trouble, he says, but by the fall, "We should be able to say accurately the state of the art of gene therapy and where it needs to improve."

Meanwhile, President Clinton announced more "new actions designed to ensure that individuals are adequately informed about the potential risks and benefits of participating in research . . . and steps designed to address the potential financial conflicts of interest faced by researchers." In addition, the President said in May, "We are also sending the Congress a new legislative proposal to authorize civil monetary penalties for researchers and institutions found to be in violation of regulations governing human clinical trials." If the legislation passes, FDA will, for the first time for drugs and biologics, have the power to essentially fine researchers and their institutions, up to $250,000 and $1 million, respectively.

"This is a clear message," HHS Secretary Donna E. Shalala, Ph.D., said in May, "that we intend to get serious." . . .

The Gelsinger Case

When Orkin and Motulsky reported on the technical limitations of gene transfer techniques five years ago, they virtually predicted problems in the clinic.* During that same December meeting at which Orkin and Motulsky made their disheartening report, the RAC approved the University of Pennsylvania gene therapy trial for ornithine transcarboxylase deficiency (OTCD). FDA, too, allowed the study to proceed.

The treatment idea was fairly straightforward. OTCD occurs when a baby inherits a broken gene that prevents the liver from making an enzyme needed to break down ammonia. With the OTCD gene isolated, the University of Pennsylvania researchers packaged it in a replication-defective adenovirus. To reach the target cells in the liver, the Philadelphia scientists wanted to inject the adenovirus directly into the hepatic artery that leads to that organ. Some members of the NIH RAC objected, fearing that direct delivery to the liver was dangerous. Nonetheless, after a vigorous public discussion with the University of Pennsylvania researchers, the RAC voted for approval of the study.

At age 18, Jesse Gelsinger was in good health, but was not truly a healthy teenager. He had a rare form of OTCD that appeared not to be linked to his parents, but the genetic defect arose spontaneously in his body after birth. During his youth, he had many episodes of hospitalization, including an incident just a year before the OTCD trial in which he nearly died from a coma induced by liver failure. But a strict diet that allowed only a few grams of protein per day and a pile of pills controlled his disease to the point where he appeared to be a normally active teenager. With the encouragement of his father, Paul Gelsinger, Jesse volunteered for the study, and when he was initially evaluated, his medical condition qualified him to participate.

Gelsinger received the experimental treatment in September 1999. Four days later, he was dead. No one is really sure exactly why the gene therapy treatment caused his death, but it appears that his immune system launched a raging attack on the adenovirus carrier. Then an overwhelming cascade of organ failures occurred, starting with jaundice, and progressing to a blood-clotting disorder, kidney failure, lung failure, and ultimately brain death.

In its investigation, FDA found a series of serious deficiencies in the way that the University of Pennsylvania conducted the OTCD gene therapy trial, some more serious than others. For example, researchers entered Gelsinger into the trial as a substitute for another volunteer who dropped out, but Gelsinger's high ammonia levels at the time of the treatment should have excluded him from the study. Moreover, the university failed to immediately report that two patients had experienced serious side effects from the gene therapy, as required in the study design, and the deaths of monkeys given a similar treatment were never included in the informed consent discussion.

FDA's discussions with the university remain ongoing.

Signs of Progress

Not all the news about gene therapy is bad. It's true that dramatic cures have not been seen to date, but there are tantalizing signs that important advances may be just around the corner.

---

*Orkin and Motulsky were two doctors who had been appointed to an FDA committee to review the efficacy of the NIH's investment in gene therapy trials.

Ashanthi DeSilva, the girl who received the first credible gene therapy, continues to do well a decade later. She suffered a type of inherited immune disorder called Severe Combined Immune Deficiency, or SCID (pronounced *skid*), that left her susceptible to every passing microorganism. Without gene therapy, DeSilva would be living like David, the Boy in the Bubble, who had a similar disorder. Instead, the NIH researchers inserted a normal copy of the broken gene into some of her white blood cells, healing them, helping them function normally to restore her immune system. Cynthia Cutshall, the second child to receive gene therapy for the same disorder as DeSilva, also continues to do well.

Scientists, however, have discounted the benefit of the first gene therapies because the girls began receiving a new drug treatment that replaces the missing enzyme just before receiving the genetic therapy. And they continue to receive the drug after the genetic treatment, though gene therapy pioneer Anderson argues that since the drug dose has remained the same while their bodies have grown substantially over the decade, it makes a negligible contribution to their well being.

In April, French scientists reported convincing evidence that they successfully treated a different form of SCID (X-linked severe combined immune deficiency, the type suffered by the boy in the bubble) with gene therapy. Four of the first five babies treated by Alain Fischer, M.D., of the Necker children's hospital in Paris have had "a complete or near complete recovery" of their immune systems after the treatment.

Meanwhile, researchers at Children's Hospital of Philadelphia, Stanford University and Avigen, Inc., a biotech company in Alameda, Calif., have reported promising results in hemophilia B patients. The team packaged a gene for Factor IX, a blood clotting protein, in a defective adeno-associated virus (AAV). They then used the AAV to insert the gene into patients who suffered abnormal blood clotting because they lack Factor IX. Normally, these hemophilia patients needed to inject Factor IX to prevent uncontrolled bleeding. In June, the researchers reported treating six patients with the Factor IX gene therapy. Even though the dose of the gene therapy was so low that no one expected it to help, it reduced the number of injections of Factor IX that these patients used on an ad hoc basis.

"The hemophilia studies are looking promising," says FDA's Noguchi, "but will need further study to know whether it is an effective product."

These two studies suggest the power of genetic treatments.

"We do seem to have turned the corner," says Anderson, "and there are a number of clinical trials that are starting to show success."

Even as FDA increases its scrutiny of the field to ensure patient safety, there is a sense of advancement. "There is good progress being made," Noguchi says. "FDA thinks that gene therapy will work, but we don't know for which disease. The recent events in France show that if you have the right disease, and can insert the right gene, you can obtain good results."

READING 9.3.2 Enhancing the Protection of Human Subjects in Gene Transfer Research at the NIH

Protocol Review

- Safety will be best protected if subjects are not enrolled in novel gene transfer trials until RAC [Recombinant DNA Advisory Committee] discussion has occurred and the investigator has responded to the RAC recommendations.
- The timing of review of gene transfer protocols by RAC, the local IRB [Institutional Review Board] and IBC [Institutional Biosafety Committee], and FDA should be altered to ensure that RAC can function as an effective advisory committee to investigators, institutional IRBs and IBCs, and FDA. Specifically,
- The requirement that the investigator obtain IRB approval prior to submission to OBA [Office of Biotechnology Activities]/RAC should be eliminated. This change would allow investigators to receive RAC input at an earlier stage of protocol development.

READING SOURCE: Advisory Committee to the Director, Working Group on NIH Oversight of Clinical Gene Transfer Research, "Executive Summary," in *Enhancing the Protection of Human Subjects in Gene Transfer Research at the National Institutes of Health,* July 12, 2000 (www.nih.gov/about/director/07122000.htm).

- IBC approval should be withheld until RAC review is complete. In the case of non-novel protocols, IBC approval can be granted as soon as the IBC is notified that the protocol has been deemed non-novel.
- In the case of novel protocols, IBC approval must be withheld until after RAC discussion and the investigator has responded to the review, thereby, preventing the initiation of a trial prior to RAC review.
- RAC should complete its review and revision of the definition of "novel" gene transfer protocols and the process/mechanism for determining whether or not a protocol is "novel." Public comment and input should be solicited.
- To clarify the types of research that are subject to the NIH Guidelines, RAC should complete its review and revision of the definition of gene transfer research to ensure that all applicable and appropriate areas of research are subject to oversight and review.

Serious Adverse Event Reporting

- Public discussion of serious adverse events is an important component of the oversight process.
- NIH/OBA should continue to receive from investigators reports of serious adverse events. The Working Group acknowledged that FDA is working on a proposed rule to make public some information regarding serious adverse events in gene transfer, and encourages the agency to move expeditiously in meeting this goal.
- Serious adverse events should not be considered trade secrets or proprietary, and must be reported to RAC.
- Data in aggregate made available to the public should be analyzed and interpreted.
- All reasonable measures must be taken to protect the privacy of the individual(s) who suffered the adverse event, without compromising the health of others in similar trials.
- A majority of the Working Group recommended that NIH and FDA must work together to simplify, streamline, and harmonize reporting of serious adverse events. This includes clarification of the timing requirements for reporting specific types of serious adverse events.
- NIH should work with FDA to expand and enhance education and outreach programs to investigators and sponsors conducting gene transfer research to inform them of their reporting obligations.
- NIH should explore ways for promoting the communication of serious adverse events to the relevant IBCs and IRBs.
- A standing body should be established to conduct ongoing analyses of adverse event data. This body should include basic scientists, clinicians, patient advocates, and ethicists. Additional ad hoc members can be appointed for their expertise on an as needed basis. This group would:
  —review all reports of adverse events,
  —analyze the data for trends,
  —develop a cumulative report that would be presented annually at a public RAC meeting and made available to the public, and
  —identify trends or even single events that may warrant further public discussion or federal action.

Professional and Public Education

- NIH/OBA should target education efforts at specialty clinical centers where gene transfer studies are likely to be conducted or subjects recruited, such as CF centers or hemophilia clinics. In addition, OBA/RAC should produce a pamphlet or brochure on gene transfer research targeted to families and consumers and post such information on its website.
- In collaboration with [Office for Human Research Protections (OHRP)] and other relevant groups, OBA should continue its initiatives for a series of workshops for IRBs and IBCs on gene transfer research.
- OBA should work with OHRP to encourage IRB cooperation in ensuring that human subjects are not enrolled in gene transfer trials until RAC deems a protocol non-novel, or if novel, the protocol has completed the RAC review process.

- NIH should work with OHRP to encourage the inclusion of additional resource sites for information regarding participation in clinical trials in the informed consent form. For gene transfer clinical trials, this information should include a reference to the RAC review process and directions regarding how to obtain relevant information from OBA/RAC.

---

1. Which federal rules did the gene therapy researchers who treated Jesse Gelsinger violate?

2. How did the FDA respond to the discovery of rule violations in gene therapy clinical trials?

3. Jesse Gelsinger volunteered for gene therapy in hopes of curing his liver disease. Gene therapy apparently has cured Ashanthi DeSilva and others of their genetic disorders. Families like the Gelsingers and the DeSilvas, along with researchers and biotechnology companies, often argue that increased federal regulations impede scientific progress and unduly limit the number of clinical trials available to people who are critically ill. Others argue that the federal government overreacted to Jesse Gelsinger's death when the FDA and NIH closed down the University of Pennsylvania's clinical trials and then issued new regulations and guidelines. Do you think the actions of the FDA and the NIH were justified? Explain and support your answer.

4. Would the NIH guidelines have prevented Jesse Gelsinger's death during the clinical trial? Explain and support your answer by citing specific guidelines.

EXERCISE 9.4 THE FOURTH BRANCH

BACKGROUND

The title *chief executive* suggests that the president, in principle, commands and controls the executive branch of the national government. Many presidents have embraced Franklin Delano Roosevelt's view that "the Presidency was established as a single strong Chief Executive in which was vested the entire executive power of the National Government."[6] The framers of the Constitution, however, refused to confer that much power on the president. Instead, the framers divided jurisdiction over the executive branch between Congress and the president, and assigned to Congress a substantial role in executive branch affairs. For example, to staff the highest positions in the executive branch, the president must secure the consent of the Senate. Congress also has the power to create executive branch agencies and departments, and to direct and fund their operations through legislation.

The Constitution clearly vests the executive power in the president (Article II, Section 1). But nowhere does it bestow the title *chief executive* on the president, and it has very little to say about the president's management of the executive branch. There are only three direct references in the Constitution to the president's power over the departments in the executive branch. Two are in Article II, Section 2: The first allows the president to "require the Opinion in writing, of the principal Officer in each of the executive Departments, upon any Subject relating to the Duties of their respective Offices." The second gives the president the power to appoint, subject to Senate approval, executive branch officers. The third reference to the president's executive powers is in Article II, Section 3, where the president is admonished to "take Care that the Laws be faithfully executed."

Throughout the nineteenth century, the president's position at the head of the executive branch would not have seemed to most Americans to be the source of much power. The national government was largely irrelevant to the conduct of most citizens' lives, and few had direct contact with it. At the time of the Civil War, for example, the federal bureaucracy consisted of just four Cabinet departments: war, state, treasury, and interior. Until well into the nineteenth century, the executive branch did little more than deliver the mail, guard the nation's coasts, fight Native Americans, and collect taxes.

In 1789 the president carried out his responsibility as head of the executive branch by supervising 50 civilian employees; by 1900, the number of civilian employees in the executive branch had gone up to about 240,000. By the end of the twentieth century, the federal bureaucracy had become more powerful than any nineteenth-century American could have imagined. Today the executive branch consists of fourteen Cabinet departments, dozens of agencies, commissions, and corporations, with more than 2.5 million civilian employees and a budget for fiscal year 2000 of about $1.7 trillion. When we speak today of the growth of the federal government, we are implicitly referring to the growth of the executive branch. The size and complexity of the federal bureaucracy raise important questions about the president's ability to oversee it. What does it mean to be the chief executive of the federal government? Is it possible for the president to command and control, or even manage and supervise, the federal bureaucracy? This exercise asks you to explore those questions.

ASSIGNMENT

1. Examine the organization chart of the executive branch in Figure 9.4.1. What do the vertical lines in the chart suggest about the president's position and power in the executive branch?

____

____

____

2. In Figure 9.4.1, the federal bureaucracy is connected by a vertical line to the Executive Office of the President. Locate the Department of Agriculture. In 2000, the USDA had about 95,000 employees

[6] Quoted in Richard M. Pious, *The American Presidency* (New York: Basic Books, 1979), p. 211.

FIGURE 9.4.1 THE EXECUTIVE BRANCH

PRESIDENT

Vice President

Executive Office of the President
White House Office
Council on Environmental Quality
Office of Management and Budget
Office of Science and Technology Policy
Council of Economic Advisors
National Security Council
Office of the United States Trade Representative
Office of Administration
Office of Policy Development

CABINET DEPARTMENTS

Department of Agriculture	Department of Commerce	Department of Defense	Department of Education	Department of Energy	Department of Health and Human Services	Department of Housing and Urban Development
Department of The Interior	Department of Justice	Department of Labor	Department of State	Department of Transportation	Department of The Treasury	Department of Veterans Affairs

INDEPENDENT ESTABLISHMENTS AND GOVERNMENT CORPORATIONS

ACTION
Administrative Conference of the U.S.
African Development Foundation
American Battle Monuments Commission
Appalachian Regional Commission
Board for International Broadcasting
Central Intelligence Agency
Commission on the Bicentennial of the United States Constitution
Commission on Civil Rights
Commission of Fine Arts
Commodity Futures Trading Commission
Consumer Product Safety Commission
Environmental Protection Agency
Equal Employment Opportunity Commission

Export-Import Bank of the U.S.
Farm Credit Administration
Federal Communications Commission
Federal Deposit Insurance Corporation
Federal Election Commission
Federal Emergency Management Agency
Federal Home Loan Bank Board
Federal Labor Relations Authority
Federal Maritime Commission
Federal Mediation and Conciliation Service
Federal Mine Safety and Health Review Commission
Federal Reserve System, Board of Governors of the
Federal Trade Commission
General Services Administration
Inter-American Foundation

Interstate Commerce Commission
Merit Systems Protection Board
National Aeronautics and Space Administration
National Archives and Records Administration
National Capital Planning Commission
National Credit Union Administration
National Foundation on the Arts and the Humanities
National Labor Relations Board
National Mediation Board
National Science Foundation
National Transportation Safety Board
Nuclear Regulatory Commission
Occupational Safety and Health Review Commission
Office of Personnel Management
Office of Special Counsel

Panama Canal Commission
Peace Corps
Pennsylvania Avenue Development Corporation
Postal Rate Commission
Railroad Retirement Board
Securities and Exchange Commission
Selective Service System
Small Business Administration
Tennessee Valley Authority
U.S. Arms Control and Disarmament Agency
U.S. Information Agency
U.S. International Development Cooperation Agency
U.S. International Trade Commission
U.S. Postal Service

and a budget of about $90 billion. In Figure 9.4.1, how significant a component of the executive branch does the USDA seem to be? Explain and support your answer.

---

3. Figure 9.4.2 shows the seven major subunits within the USDA, each headed by an undersecretary. Locate the undersecretary for natural resources and the environment. Notice that the Forest Service is one of the agencies charged with overseeing natural resources and the environment. How significant a component of the entire USDA does the Forest Service seem to be? Explain and support your answer.

---

4. Now go to the USDA's Web site, at www.usda.gov. Click on Agencies, Services, & Programs and locate the Forest Service under "Natural Resources & Environment." Click on the Forest Service link and then on Meet the Forest Service. Read the material there to better understand the size, scope, and mission of the Forest Service.

a. How many acres of land does the Forest Service administer?

---

b. What is the title of the head of the Forest Service?

---

c. How many people work for the Forest Service?

---

d. The Forest Service is a large and important agency by any standard, yet it doesn't appear in the organization chart of the executive branch (see Figure 9.4.1). What does its exclusion from that chart indicate about the executive branch?

---

5. In the 1930s, when Franklin Delano Roosevelt was president, the federal bureaucracy was less than half its present size. Even so, Roosevelt made the following complaint:

> The Treasury is so large and far-flung and ingrained in its practices that I find it almost impossible to get the action and results I want—even with Henry [Morgenthau] there. But the Treasury is not to be compared with the State Department. You should go through the experience of trying to get any changes in the thinking, policy, and action of the career diplomats and then you'd know what a real problem was. But the Treasury and the State Department put together are nothing compared with the Na-a-vy. The admirals are really something to cope with—and I should know. To change anything in the Na-a-vy is like punching a feather bed. You punch it

FIGURE 9.4.2 U.S. DEPARTMENT OF AGRICULTURE, 2002

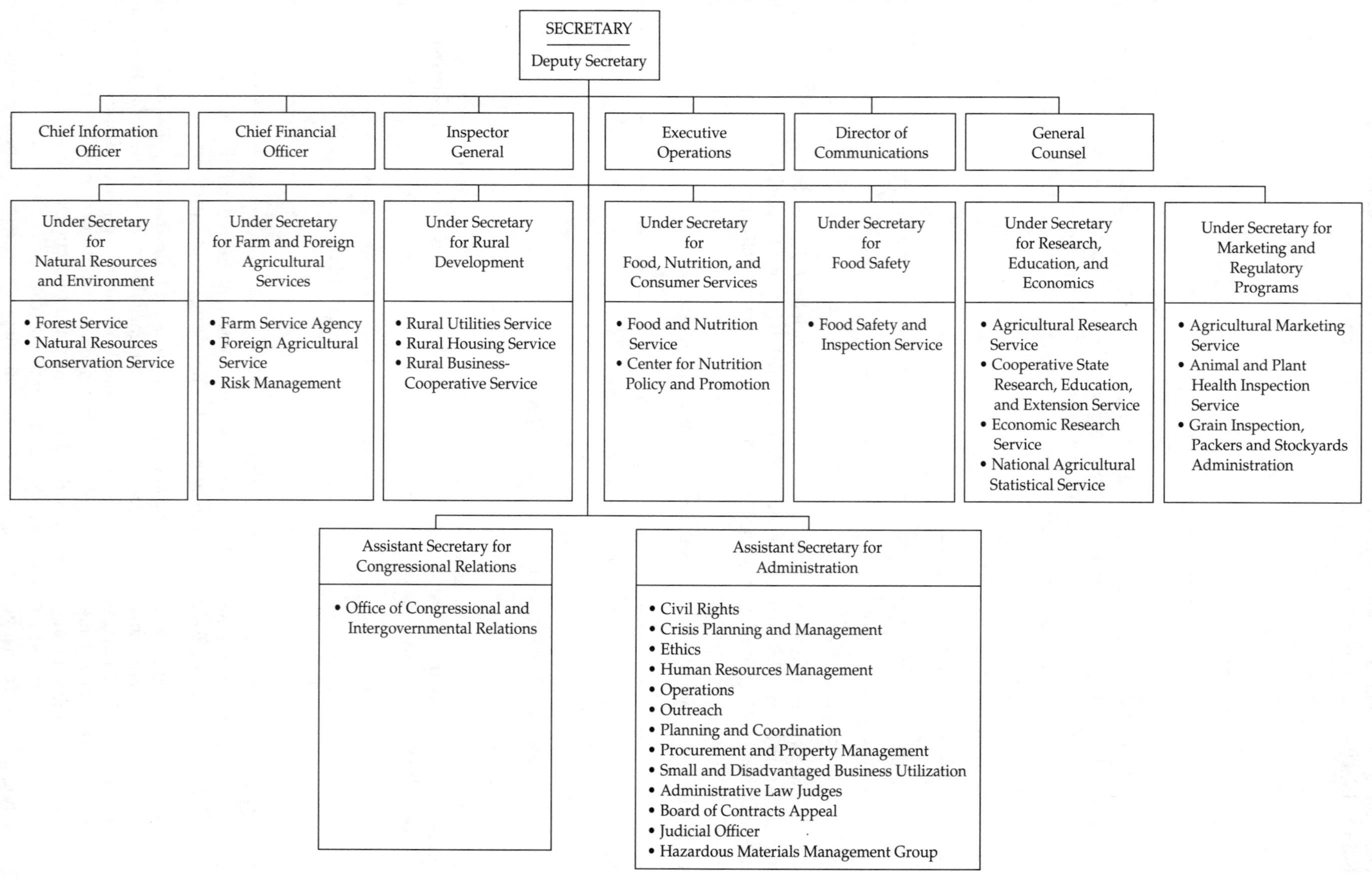

SECRETARY

Deputy Secretary

Chief Information Officer

Chief Financial Officer

Inspector General

Executive Operations

Director of Communications

General Counsel

Under Secretary for Natural Resources and Environment
- Forest Service
- Natural Resources Conservation Service

Under Secretary for Farm and Foreign Agricultural Services
- Farm Service Agency
- Foreign Agricultural Service
- Risk Management

Under Secretary for Rural Development
- Rural Utilities Service
- Rural Housing Service
- Rural Business-Cooperative Service

Under Secretary for Food, Nutrition, and Consumer Services
- Food and Nutrition Service
- Center for Nutrition Policy and Promotion

Under Secretary for Food Safety
- Food Safety and Inspection Service

Under Secretary for Research, Education, and Economics
- Agricultural Research Service
- Cooperative State Research, Education, and Extension Service
- Economic Research Service
- National Agricultural Statistical Service

Under Secretary for Marketing and Regulatory Programs
- Agricultural Marketing Service
- Animal and Plant Health Inspection Service
- Grain Inspection, Packers and Stockyards Administration

Assistant Secretary for Congressional Relations
- Office of Congressional and Intergovernmental Relations

Assistant Secretary for Administration
- Civil Rights
- Crisis Planning and Management
- Ethics
- Human Resources Management
- Operations
- Outreach
- Planning and Coordination
- Procurement and Property Management
- Small and Disadvantaged Business Utilization
- Administrative Law Judges
- Board of Contracts Appeal
- Judicial Officer
- Hazardous Materials Management Group

> with your right and you punch it with your left until you are finally exhausted, and then you find the damn bed just as it was before you started punching.[7]

In one sentence, using your own words, state the problem Roosevelt struggled with as head of the executive branch.

____

____

6. During Richard Nixon's term in office, this celebrated outburst by the president was recorded for posterity on the taping system he had secretly installed in the Oval Office:

> We have no discipline in this bureaucracy. We never fire anybody. We never reprimand anybody. We never demote anybody. We always promote the sons-of-bitches that kick us in the ass. . . . We are going to quit being a bunch of goddamn soft-headed managers. . . . When a bureaucrat deliberately thumbs his nose, we're going to get him. . . . The little boys over in [the State Department] particularly, that are against us [the Defense Department, the Department of Health, Education, and Welfare]—those three areas particularly. . . . There are many unpleasant places were civil service people can be sent. . . . When they don't produce in this administration, somebody's ass is kicked out. . . . Now, goddamn it, those are the bad guys—the guys down in the woodwork.[8]

a. What did Nixon likely mean by "the guys down in the woodwork"?

____

____

____

b. Identify the problem in contemporary government that triggered Nixon's anger.

____

____

____

____

7. In recent decades, many political scientists have come to think of the departments and agencies in the executive branch as a fourth branch of government. What evidence can you find in this exercise to support the characterization?

____

____

____

____

____

____

[7] Richard E. Neustadt, *Presidential Power: The Politics of Leadership from FDR to Carter* (New York: John Wiley and Sons, 1980), p. 33.

[8] J. Anthony Lukas, *Nightmare: The Underside of the Nixon Years* (New York: Viking Press, 1976), p. 18.

EXERCISE 9.5 THE NATIONAL SECURITY STATE

BACKGROUND

For most of their history, Americans have had to sacrifice comparatively little to maintain their national security. Much of the work was done for them by nature. Americans fortuitously built their nation in one of the most secure regions of the world. Vast oceans to the east and west have insulated the country for most of its history, protecting it from conflict and turmoil in Europe and Asia, and deterring would-be invaders from striking. U.S. national security has been bolstered as well by neighbors to the north and south that pose little threat to America.

That helps explain why many Americans view the military establishment and large standing armed forces with suspicion. For American colonists, the instruments of royal tyranny and the abridgement of their liberties were the British army and navy. Consequently, Americans in the early years of the Republic looked not to a national army to protect them but to their various state militias, whose importance was acknowledged in the Second Amendment to the Constitution. In 1787, the framers were careful to subordinate the military to civilian control and to vest two key powers in the hands of Congress instead of the executive: the power to raise armies and the power to declare war (Article I, Section 8). The president's role was limited to commanding the armies raised and authorized by Congress.[9]

Americans' sense of national security, their sense that they didn't need a large standing military force, was a casualty of the Japanese attack on Pearl Harbor on December 7, 1941. America was no longer a natural fortress. Japanese aircraft carriers had crossed the Pacific and penetrated both American defenses and confidence.

Technology had played a part in the Japanese attack; it would play a larger part in U.S. security concerns during the cold war. In 1949, the Soviet Union exploded its first atomic bomb and later threatened the United States with its capacity to deliver atomic weapons on intercontinental bombers. That threat paled in comparison with the development of the intercontinental ballistic missiles (ICBM) as a vehicle for delivering nuclear weapons. Because it was impossible to defend against incoming ICBMs, America was rendered utterly vulnerable to an attack by the Soviet Union. To limit its vulnerability, the United States adopted the doctrine of mutual assured destruction (MAD): A nuclear attack on the United States by the Soviet Union would trigger a massive nuclear counterattack by the United States. In a classic standoff, the Soviet Union made the same threat.

Today, more than ten years after the end of the cold war, the United States continues to grapple with the problem of vulnerability. President George W. Bush's altered version of Ronald Reagan's strategic defense initiative and his war against terrorism, launched in response to the destruction on September 11, 2001, of the World Trade Center towers and the attack on the Pentagon, are the latest in a long line of efforts to recover the sense of national security that Americans enjoyed before World War II.

One by-product of the Japanese attack on Pearl Harbor and the rise of the Soviet Union as a nuclear superpower was the belief that projecting military power abroad was essential to achieving national security at home. Adversaries had to be subdued overseas before they could carry their threat to American shores. Consequently, beginning in the late 1940s the United States developed a series of military alliances with nations in strategic areas of the world. In 1796, in his farewell address to the nation, President George Washington warned Americans of the dangers of permanent alliances with foreign powers. The nation heeded Washington's advice and avoided peacetime military alliances until 1949, when the country joined the North Atlantic Treaty Organization. For a nation so long averse to entangling itself with foreign powers, and so insistent on maintaining its freedom of action in foreign affairs, this was powerful evidence that Americans had embraced a new vision of national security.

When scholars describe the United States in the post–World War II era, many talk about the national security state. A *national security state* is permanently mobilized for war. That mobilization entails

[9] Many presidents have breached this constitutional barrier and made war without Congress's first declaring war. In 1973, Congress approved the War Powers Act, an attempt to curb the president's war-making power.

enormous social and economic costs to the nation, costs that Americans would never have accepted before World War II. The foundation of the national security state was laid in 1950, when President Harry Truman approved National Security Council Document 68 (NSC-68). NSC-68 was a blueprint for putting the nation on permanent wartime footing and for obtaining public and congressional approval for the sacrifices that would entail, primary among them a vast increase in military spending and maintenance of large standing military forces. NSC-68's recommendations for massive increases in defense spending were controversial, and Truman at first was reluctant to accept them. But the outbreak of the Korean War in June 1950 cinched the case for constructing the national security state.

The precise costs of the national security state are difficult to determine. Obviously, the national security state requires the maintenance of large standing military forces as well as the departments and agencies in the executive branch needed to sustain those forces. Other costs are less obvious. In the quest to develop and maintain a nuclear arsenal, the Departments of Energy and Defense contaminated vast swaths of land with nuclear and other wastes. The clean-up costs promise to run into the trillions of dollars. And there are the noneconomic costs. Opportunity costs are one example: The public resources dedicated to the national security state are not available for other uses. Social costs are another: In the postwar period, the national government trammeled the civil liberties and civil rights of some citizens in the name of national security. Sustaining the national security state undoubtedly entails other costs that have yet to be revealed.

ASSIGNMENT, PART A: PATTERNS OF MILITARY SPENDING

Table 9.5.1 lists data on U.S. military spending from 1791 to 1950 by year or by period. When a period is shown—for example, 1850–1859—the expenditure noted is the yearly average for that period. Notice that the dollar amount of military spending for each year or period is in current dollars, which means that the figures have not been adjusted for inflation. A dollar spent on the military in 1820, for example, would have purchased substantially more goods or services than a dollar spent in 1920. But the spending figures in Table 9.5.1 do not compensate for that erosion in value.[10]

1. Use the data in Table 9.5.1 to complete the chart that follows it. Your objective is to compare the average annual military spending in the years immediately preceding and following each war. To determine the *prewar average,* calculate the approximate average annual military spending over the five years preceding the war. The *wartime high* figure is just that, the highest amount spent on defense in any year during the war. To determine the *postwar average,* calculate the approximate average annual military spending during the four or five years following the war. In your calculation of the postwar average, don't include the figure for the year immediately following the war, the year labeled *demobilization.* Military spending may remain at wartime levels for a brief period after the fighting has stopped, reflecting the costs of demobilizing the forces. Finally, in the fourth column, note the ratio of prewar spending to postwar spending. Simply divide the prewar average into the postwar average, rounding the quotient to the nearest tenth. Notice that the ratio tells you how many times greater postwar spending was than prewar spending. We've given you a head start filling out the chart by entering the data for the War of 1812 and the Mexican War.

[10] Figures adjusted for inflation would allow more accurate comparisons of spending over time, but adjusted figures are not available for the years preceding 1945.

TABLE 9.5.1 U.S. MILITARY SPENDING, 1791–1950, IN CURRENT DOLLARS

YEAR OR PERIOD	MILITARY SPENDING PER YEAR	
1791–1799	2,013,000	
1800–1809	2,872,000	
1810	3,948,000	
1811	3,999,000	
1812	15,777,000	War of 1812 begins
1813	26,099,000	
1814	27,662,000	
1815	23,454,000	War of 1812 ends
1816	19,920,000	Demobilization
1817	11,319,000	
1818	8,577,000	
1819	10,350,000	
1820–1829	6,413,000	
1830–1839	12,041,000	
1840–1845	12,240,000	
1846	17,248,000	Mexican War begins
1847	46,207,000	
1848	34,910,000	Mexican War ends
1849	24,640,000	Demobilization
1850–1859	24,988,000	
1860	27,925,000	
1861	35,402,000	Civil War begins
1862	437,036,000	
1863	662,521,000	
1864	776,518,000	
1865	1,153,936,000	Civil War ends
1866	327,774,000	Demobilization
1867	126,258,000	
1868	149,023,000	
1869	98,503,000	
1870–1879	53,171,000	
1880–1889	51,756,000	
1890–1895	46,415,000	
1896	77,979,000	
1897	83,512,000	
1898	150,816,000	Spanish-American War
1899	293,783,000	Demobilization
1900	190,728,000	
1901	205,123,000	
1902	180,075,000	
1903–1915	291,294,000	
1916	337,030,000	
1917	617,574,000	U.S. enters World War I
1918	6,148,795,000	World War I ends
1919	11,011,387,000	Demobilization
1920	2,357,974,000	
1921	1,768,450,000	
1922	935,531,000	
1923	730,252,000	
1924–1935	768,382,000	
1936–1940	1,213,587,000	

TABLE 9.5.1 (CONTINUED)

YEAR OR PERIOD	MILITARY SPENDING PER YEAR	
1941	6,252,001,000	U.S. enters World War II
1942	22,905,097,000	
1943	63,413,912,000	
1944	75,975,964,000	
1945	80,537,254,000	World War II ends
1946	40,184,000,000	Demobilization
1947	13,205,000,000	
1948	10,151,000,000	
1949	11,241,000,000	
1950	11,674,000,000	

Note: Current dollars have not been adjusted for inflation.

SOURCE: Adapted from Census Bureau, *Historical Statistics of the United States* (Washington, D.C.: U.S. Government Printing Office, 1975).

WAR	MILITARY SPENDING			
	PREWAR AVERAGE	WARTIME HIGH	POSTWAR AVERAGE	PREWAR AVERAGE: POSTWAR AVERAGE
War of 1812	$3,300,000	$27,662,000	$11,000,000	1:3.3
Mexican War	$12,000,000	$46,000,000	$25,000,000	1:2.1
Spanish-American War				
Civil War				
World War I				
World War II				

2. How did the six wars listed in the chart affect the long-term pattern of military spending? Use data from the chart to support your answer.

____

____

____

____

3. Again looking at the chart in question 1, does spending after any of the wars listed ever drop to the prewar spending average? Formulate a hypothesis to explain why or why not.

4. Table 9.5.2 shows data on military spending since 1945. The amounts in the table are constant 2002 dollars: They've been adjusted for inflation. A dollar adjusted for inflation would purchase the same amount of military supplies or services in 1945 as it would in 2002. Looking at the table, describe briefly and in general terms the trend in annual military spending since the end of the Korean War.

5. a. Estimate the average annual military expenditure since the end of the Korean War. To avoid skewing the average, exclude from your estimate the years 1966 to 1972, when spending on the Vietnam War escalated. Also exclude from your average the president's defense spending request for 2003.

b. How does that average compare with military spending in 1945, at the height of World War II?

c. What does that comparison indicate about the budget requirements of the national security state?

6. The cold war between the United States and the Soviet Union ended in 1991 with the collapse of the Soviet Union. Many observers at the time predicted that the end of the cold war would bring a "peace dividend," that spending on the national security state would be cut and the savings redirected to education, the environment, medical care, even reducing taxes.

a. Compare yearly military expenditures in the 1980s with those in the 1990s. What is the average annual peace dividend since 1990?

b. What percentage of yearly military spending in the 1980s does the annual peace dividend represent? To make the calculation, simply divide the average annual peace dividend by the average yearly military expenditure in the 1980s.

c. What factors might explain that relatively meager peace dividend?

TABLE 9.5.2 U.S. MILITARY SPENDING, FISCAL YEARS 1945–2003, IN CONSTANT 2002 DOLLARS

YEAR	MILITARY SPENDING PER YEAR	
1945	1,030,629,000,000	World War II ends
1946	560,290,000,000	Demobilization
1947	171,764,000,000	
1948	127,260,000,000	
1949	135,191,000,000	
1950	132,203,000,000	Korean War begins
1951	198,443,000,000	
1952	350,952,000,000	
1953	379,422,000,000	Korean War ends
1954	357,078,000,000	Demobilization
1955	310,447,000,000	
1956	296,674,000,000	
1957	303,010,000,000	
1958	295,566,000,000	
1959	298,382,000,000	
1960	297,142,000,000	
1961	300,304,000,000	
1962	325,485,000,000	
1963	330,485,000,000	
1964	329,172,000,000	
1965	302,145,000,000	Johnson escalates Vietnam War
1966	331,942,000,000	
1967	388,989,000,000	
1968	424,032,000,000	
1969	413,380,000,000	
1970	383,626,000,000	
1971	350,095,000,000	
1972	326,198,000,000	
1973	299,483,000,000	U.S. troops leave Vietnam
1974	293,533,000,000	
1975–1979	284,993,000,000	
1980–1989	373,832,000,000	
1990–1999	323,051,000,000	
2000	297,693,000,000	
2001	292,200,000,000	
2002	312,963,000,000	
2003	379,000,000,000*	

Note: The amounts here have been adjusted for inflation.

* President Bush requested $379 billion for defense spending in fiscal year 2003 (October 1, 2002–September 30, 2003). In addition, he asked for $38 billion for homeland security.

SOURCE: U.S. Department of Defense, Office of the Undersecretary of Defense; and Center for Defense Information, www.cdi.org.

system that the Kremlin is brought at least to the point of modifying its behavior to conform to generally accepted international standards.

It was and continues to be cardinal in this policy that we possess superior overall power in ourselves or in dependable combination with other likeminded nations. One of the most important ingredients of power is military strength. In the concept of "containment," the maintenance of a strong military posture is deemed to be essential for two reasons: (1) as an ultimate guarantee of our national security and (2) as an indispensable backdrop to the conduct of the policy of "containment." Without superior aggregate military strength, in being and readily mobilizable, a policy of "containment"—which is in effect a policy of calculated and gradual coercion—is no more than a policy of bluff. . . .

IX. Possible Courses of Action . . .

D. THE REMAINING COURSE OF ACTION—A RAPID BUILD-UP OF POLITICAL, ECONOMIC, AND MILITARY STRENGTH IN THE FREE WORLD

A more rapid build-up of political, economic, and military strength and thereby of confidence in the free world than is now contemplated is the only course which is consistent with progress toward achieving our fundamental purpose. The frustration of the Kremlin design requires the free world to develop a successfully functioning political and economic system and a vigorous political offensive against the Soviet Union. These, in turn, require an adequate military shield under which they can develop. It is necessary to have the military power to deter, if possible, Soviet expansion, and to defeat, if necessary, aggressive Soviet or Soviet-directed actions of a limited or total character. . . .

A comprehensive and decisive program to win the peace and frustrate the Kremlin design should be so designed that it can be sustained for as long as necessary to achieve our national objectives. It would probably involve:

1. The development of an adequate political and economic framework for the achievement of long-range objectives.
2. A substantial increase in expenditures for military purposes. . . .
3. A substantial increase in military assistance programs. . . .
4. Some increase in economic assistance programs. . . .
5. Development of programs designed to build and maintain confidence among other peoples in our strength and resolution, and to wage overt psychological warfare calculated to encourage mass defections from Soviet allegiance and to frustrate Kremlin design in other ways.
6. Intensification of affirmative and timely measures and operations by covert means in the fields of economic warfare and political and psychological warfare with a view to fomenting and supporting unrest and revolt in selected strategic satellite countries.
7. Development of internal security and civilian defense programs.
8. Improvement and intensification of intelligence activities.
9. Reduction of Federal expenditures for purposes other than defense and foreign assistance. . . .
10. Increased taxes.

Conclusions and Recommendations

Conclusions

In summary, we must, by means of a rapid and sustained build-up of the political, economic, and military strength of the free world, and by means of an affirmative program intended to wrest the initiative from the Soviet Union, confront it with convincing evidence of the determination and ability of the free world to frustrate the Kremlin design of a world dominated by its will. Such evidence is the only means short of war which eventually may force the Kremlin to abandon its present course of action and to negotiate acceptable agreements on issues of major importance.

The whole success of the proposed program hangs ultimately on recognition by this Government, the American people, and all free peoples, that the cold war is in fact a real war in which the survival of the free world is at stake. Essential prerequisites to success are consultations with Congressional leaders designed to make the program the object of non-partisan legislative support, and a presentation to the public of a full explanation of the facts and implications of the present international situation. The prosecution of the program will require of us all the ingenuity, sacrifice, and unity demanded by the vital importance of the issue and the tenacity to persevere until our national objectives have been attained.

Recommendations

That the President:

a. Approve the foregoing Conclusions.
b. Direct the National Security Council, under the continuing direction of the President, and with the participation of other Departments and Agencies as appropriate, to coordinate and insure the implementation of the Conclusions herein on an urgent and continuing basis for as long as necessary to achieve our objectives. For this purpose, representatives of the member Departments and Agencies, the Joint Chiefs of Staff or their deputies, and other Departments and Agencies as required should be constituted as a revised and strengthened staff organization under the National Security Council to develop coordinated programs for consideration by the National Security Council.

---

1. What assessment did the authors of NSC-68 make of Soviet intentions and capabilities? In your answer, address the basis for their assessment.

____

____

____

2. According to the authors of NSC-68, what were the intentions and capabilities of the United States?

____

____

____

3. In your own words, summarize the course of action recommended in NSC-68.

____

____

____

____

____

4. What costs and risks to the American public would the course of action charted in NSC-68 entail?

____

____

____

5. What indications are there in NSC-68 that the recommended course of action might be open-ended?

____

____

____

ASSIGNMENT, PART C: BUREAUCRATIC COMPONENTS OF THE NATIONAL SECURITY STATE

Carrying out a national task or meeting a national objective in a modern industrial society demands the use of modern forms of bureaucratic organization. The national security state has more than its share of government departments and agencies supporting it. Here are the Web addresses of several of those departments and agencies:

CIA: www.cia.gov

Department of Defense: www.defenselink.mil

Energy Department: www.energy.gov

Joint Chiefs of Staff: www.dtic.mil/jcs

National Security Agency: www.nsa.gov

National Security Council: www.whitehouse.gov/nsc/index.html.

Visit any two of them and determine the role they play in the national security state. Then summarize their mission and functions in the space below.

Department/agency 1: ____________________

____

____

____

Department/agency 2: ____________________

____

____

____

CHAPTER 10

THE JUDICIARY

EXERCISE 10.1 JUDICIAL ACTIVISM VERSUS JUDICIAL RESTRAINT: THE SUPREME COURT AND THE DEATH PENALTY

BACKGROUND

The debate between the proponents of judicial activism and the proponents of judicial restraint is as old as the Republic. The debate centers on this question: What is the proper role of the federal courts, particularly the Supreme Court, in the American constitutional system? The answer to this question cannot be found in the Constitution because the framers did not spell out the judicial powers. In fact, even judicial review—the extraordinary power of the federal courts to decide the constitutionality of legislative and executive branch actions—is not noted in the Constitution. It was Chief Justice John Marshall, ruling in *Marbury v. Madison* (1803), who bestowed judicial review on the courts.

That decision sparked an early debate about the role of the Supreme Court, detractors claiming that the Court had overreached itself in declaring an act of Congress unconstitutional and in claiming for itself a power that is nowhere specified in the Constitution. Controversy over the role of the Supreme Court in the constitutional system continued to flare. In 1857 the Court waded into the great controversy of the day, the question of slavery in the western territories. In *Scott v. Sanford* the High Court ruled that slaves are not citizens of the United States under the provisions of the Constitution and went on to declare the Missouri Compromise unconstitutional.[1] For the first time since *Marbury,* the Court exercised the power of judicial review, and it ignited a firestorm of controversy that would help drag the nation into a civil war. It would take the Civil War and the Thirteenth and Fourteenth Amendments (ratified in 1865 and 1868, respectively) to fix what judicial activism had broken.

The debate between judicial activism and judicial restraint continues. The modern controversy can be traced back to 1953, when Earl Warren took over leadership of the Court. On Warren's watch, from

[1] The Missouri Compromise (1820) had established a boundary between free states and territories, and slave states and territories. Because the law had made some areas free that were formerly slave areas, the Court ruled that property holders (slave holders) had been deprived of their property without due process of law. Ironically, the Missouri Compromise had been repealed in 1850.

1953 to 1969, a solid majority of the Court initiated extraordinary changes in our understanding of constitutional liberties and rights, especially the rights of the accused. And for the first time, the Court ruled that a number of provisions of the Bill of Rights must be applied to protect citizens from the actions of state governments. Inevitably the Court's activism generated a political reaction. Conservatives, who felt the Court was undermining law and order, called for Warren's impeachment. In 1968 presidential candidate Richard Nixon ran on a promise to appoint "strict constructionists" to the federal courts, by which he meant judges who would not read their own political agenda into the language of the Constitution and who generally would defer to the will of the people—or at least to the will of elected officials. Later Ronald Reagan, George Bush Sr., and George W. Bush would echo Nixon's pledge.

In *Bush v. Gore* (2000), the Court voted to exercise jurisdiction over the contested presidential election in Florida. In this case, conservative justices—who often appear to be advocates of judicial restraint—supported the Court's putting an end to the recount, while the liberal justices—who often appear to be advocates of judicial activism—vehemently opposed the decision to stop the recount. In a 5–4 vote, the conservative justices prevailed, handing the election to Bush.

Among the tenets of judicial activism are the following:

- *The Constitution is a living document.* The meaning of its language is not always clear, nor can its meaning always conform to the intentions of its authors. The principles set forth in the Constitution are timeless, but the language of the document must be adapted to new times and conditions. The framers purposely left the language ambiguous to allow future generations of Americans to create their own politics. They did not intend for the Constitution to become a straitjacket.
- *A constitutional system ultimately depends on the federal courts to protect minority and individual rights.* Elected officials need to be in sync with the majority to get reelected. It's not surprising, then, that they may neglect minority and individual rights. Because federal judges are appointed, not elected, and because they have life tenure as long as they behave well, they are less likely to succumb to the tyranny of the majority. In the long run, the judiciary is the only branch of government that can be counted on to protect minority and individual rights.

The tenets of judicial restraint include the following:

- *The job of judges is to apply laws, not make them.* When judges interpret the Constitution, often with scant regard for the language in the document and the intentions of those who wrote it, they are likely to read their own political agenda into the Constitution. The best way to interpret the Constitution is to adhere to the language in the document—not to make inferences from that language—and, when necessary, to the intentions of the men who wrote it.
- *Judges must defer to the elected representatives of the people and to the people themselves.* Unless a law clearly violates specific language in the Constitution, democracy requires that judges defer to the elected representatives of the people. Judges cannot and should not protect the people from poorly conceived laws; in the spirit of democracy, the people themselves must act to correct laws that they consider unwise. There is a manifest difference between bad public policy and unconstitutional public policy. Republican government will not long survive if the people look to the courts for redress rather than to themselves and to their elected representatives. In James Madison's words in "Federalist No. 10," "The ultimate repository of liberty is in the people."

The significant philosophical differences between judicial activism and judicial restraint often are blurred in everyday politics. Most people—citizens and politicians—applaud the courts for doing what they like and criticize the courts for doing what they don't like. Now that the Supreme Court under the leadership of Chief Justice William Rehnquist has become markedly more conservative than it was during the Warren years, conservatives rarely criticize the Court for its willingness to nullify federal and state laws. And today liberals, knowing that the Court is likely to make conservative decisions, are advocating judicial restraint.

Reading 10.1, from the Court's decision in *Furman v. Georgia* (1972), shows the conflict between judicial activism and judicial restraint. In *Furman*, the justices consolidated three capital punishment appeals into one case and ruled 5–4 that the death penalty in Texas and Georgia was unconstitutional because it was applied in an "arbitrary and capricious" manner, violating the Eighth Amendment's prohibition against cruel and unusual punishment. That ruling effectively invalidated the death sentence in the thirty-five states that allowed capital punishment at the time. Since *Furman,* thirty-eight states have revised their capital punishment laws to meet the guidelines set forth in subsequent High Court decisions on the death penalty.[2]

ASSIGNMENT

Refer to Reading 10.1 to answer questions 1-5 that follow it. Then read the instructions that follow question 5 to determine whether you should answer question 6 or 7.

READING 10.1 FROM *FURMAN V. GEORGIA,* 408 U.S. 238 (1972)

Mr. Justice Brennan, concurring:

. . . We know "that the words of the Clause are not precise, and that their scope is not static." * We know, therefore, that the Clause "must draw its meaning from the evolving standards of decency that mark the progress of a maturing society." That knowledge, of course, is but the beginning of the inquiry. . . .

At bottom, then, the Cruel and Unusual Punishments Clause prohibits the infliction of uncivilized and inhuman punishments. The State, even as it punishes, must treat its members with respect for their intrinsic worth as human beings. A punishment is "cruel and unusual," therefore, if it does not comport with human dignity. . . .

The primary principle is that a punishment must not be so severe as to be degrading to the dignity of human beings. Pain, certainly, may be a factor in the judgment. The infliction of an extremely severe punishment will often entail physical suffering. . . .

More than the presence of pain, however, is comprehended in the judgment that the extreme severity of a punishment makes it degrading to the dignity of human beings. The barbaric punishments condemned by history, "punishments which inflict torture, such as the rack, the thumbscrew, the iron boot, the stretching of limbs, and the like," are, of course, "attended with acute pain and suffering." † . . .

In determining whether a punishment comports with human dignity, we are aided also by a second principle inherent in the Clause—that the State must not arbitrarily inflict a severe punishment. This principle derives from the notion that the State does not respect human dignity when, without reason, it inflicts upon some people a severe punishment that it does not inflict upon others. Indeed, the very words "cruel and unusual punishments" imply condemnation of the arbitrary infliction of severe punishments. . . .

A third principle inherent in the Clause is that a severe punishment must not be unacceptable to contemporary society. Rejection by society, of course, is a strong indication that a severe punishment does not comport with human dignity. In applying this principle, however, we must make certain that the judicial determination is as objective as possible. . . .

The final principle inherent in the Clause is that a severe punishment must not be excessive. A punishment is excessive under this principle if it is unnecessary: The infliction of a severe punishment by the State cannot comport with human dignity when it is nothing more than the pointless infliction of suffering. . . .

---

[2] See, for example, *Gregg v. Georgia* (1976).

* *Clause* refers to the prohibition of cruel and unusual punishment in the Eighth Amendment. The quoted material comes from *Trop v. Dulles* (1958).

† *O'Neil v. Vermont* (1892).

The progressive decline in, and the current rarity of, the infliction of death demonstrates that our society seriously questions the appropriateness of this punishment today. The States point out that many legislatures authorize death as the punishment for certain crimes and that substantial segments of the public, as reflected in opinion polls and referendum votes, continue to support it. Yet the availability of this punishment through statutory authorization, as well as the polls and referenda, which amount simply to approval of that authorization, simply underscores the extent to which our society has in fact rejected this punishment. When an unusually severe punishment is authorized for wide-scale application but not, because of society's refusal, inflicted save in a few instances, the inference is compelling that there is a deep-seated reluctance to inflict it. Indeed, the likelihood is great that the punishment is tolerated only because of its disuse. The objective indicator of society's view of an unusually severe punishment is what society does with it, and today society will inflict death upon only a small sample of the eligible criminals. Rejection could hardly be more complete without becoming absolute. At the very least, I must conclude that contemporary society views this punishment with substantial doubt. . . .

Mr. Justice Blackmun, dissenting:

Cases such as these provide for me an excruciating agony of the spirit. I yield to no one in the depth of my distaste, antipathy, and, indeed, abhorrence for the death penalty, with all its aspects of physical distress and fear and of moral judgment exercised by finite minds. That distaste is buttressed by a belief that capital punishment serves no useful purpose that can be demonstrated. . . . Were I a legislator, I would vote against the death penalty for the policy reasons argued by counsel for the respective petitioners and expressed and adopted in the several opinions filed by the Justices who vote to reverse these judgments. . . .

To reverse the judgments in these cases is, of course, the easy choice. It is easier to strike the balance in favor of life and against death, It is comforting to relax in the thoughts—perhaps the rationalizations—that this is the compassionate decision for a maturing society; that this is the moral and the "right" thing to do; that thereby we convince ourselves that we are moving down the road toward human decency. . . .

This, for me, is good argument, and it makes some sense. But it is good argument and it makes sense only in a legislative and executive way and not as a judicial expedient. As I have said above, were I a legislator, I would do all I could to sponsor and to vote for legislation abolishing the death penalty. And were I the chief executive of a sovereign State, I would be sorely tempted to exercise executive clemency. . . . There—on the Legislative Branch of the State or Federal Government, and secondarily, on the Executive Branch—is where the authority and responsibility for this kind of action lies. The authority should not be taken over by the judiciary in the modern guise of an Eighth Amendment issue.

I do not sit on these cases, however, as a legislator, responsive, at least in part, to the will of constituents. Our task here, as must so frequently be emphasized and re-emphasized, is to pass upon the constitutionality of legislation that has been enacted and that is challenged. This is the sole task for judges. We should not allow our personal preferences as to the wisdom of legislative and congressional action, or our distaste for such action, to guide our judicial decision in cases such as these. The temptations to cross that policy line are very great. In fact, as today's decision reveals, they are almost irresistible. . . .

---

1. In *Furman,* every justice who voted with the majority wrote his own explanation, called a *concurring opinion,* for his decision. Based on your examination of Justice Brennan's concurring opinion, would you identify him as a practitioner of judicial restraint or judicial activism? Cite specific language in his concurring opinion to support your position.

____

____

____

____

____

2. In *Furman*, Justice Blackmun did not vote with the majority; he offered his explanation for his decision in a *dissenting opinion*. Based on your examination of Justice Blackmun's opinion, would you identify him as a practitioner of judicial restraint or judicial activism? Cite specific language in the opinion to support your position.

3. In his dissenting opinion, Justice Blackmun writes that he opposes capital punishment and would vote to abolish it if he were a state legislator. Yet he voted to uphold the use of capital punishment. In the opinion, how did he resolve this apparent contradiction?

4. In your view, should the Supreme Court justices factor public opinion into their decisions on the death penalty and other controversial issues? Explain and support your position.

5. In your view, what role should the Supreme Court play in the American political system? Should the justices practice judicial activism or judicial restraint? Explain and support your position.

If in your answer to question 5 you wrote that you believe in judicial activism, answer question 6. If in your answer to question 5 you wrote that you support judicial restraint, answer question 7.

6. Identify a value or belief that you hold dear. Suppose that an activist Supreme Court ruled against that value or belief. Would that ruling lead you to reevaluate your support for judicial activism? Explain your answer.

____

____

____

____

____

7. Identify a value or belief that you hold dear. Suppose that value or belief is being violated on a daily basis by the behavior of individual citizens or by some institution. You bring a case before the Supreme Court pleading that in the interest of truth and justice, the behavior be stopped. But the Court refuses to hear your case, citing the principle of judicial restraint. Would that refusal lead you to reevaluate your support for judicial restraint? Explain your answer.

____

____

____

____

____

EXERCISE 10.2 DO THE CHARACTERISTICS OF JUDGES TELL US ANYTHING ABOUT JUDICIAL DECISION MAKING?

BACKGROUND

Among the many intriguing aspects of the 2000 presidential election was the role played by the judiciary. The courts traditionally do not get involved in electoral disputes. But in 2000, both the Florida Supreme Court and the U.S. Supreme Court played dominant roles, with the High Court ultimately making the 5–4 decision that gave Florida's presidential electors, and the election, to George W. Bush.

The several decisions of the two courts continue to be debated, in part because the two courts were at odds with each other in terms of how the vote-counting process should work. The courts also appeared to be mirror images of each other: Six of the seven judges on the Florida Supreme Court were appointed by Democratic governors; and seven of the nine justices on the U.S. Supreme Court were appointed by Republican presidents.[3] According to pundits, the Florida court often was described in the media as a "liberal Democratic court" and the U.S. Supreme Court as a "conservative Republican court." But can the courts' decisions be attributed to the political affiliations of the justices?

Most social scientists believe that people's personal characteristics (age, race, gender, education, work, income) and their experience (growing up poor or rich, spending time in the Peace Corps, serving in the military) are fairly reliable predictors of their political ideology and behavior. That general rule applies whether a person is a city councilor, a mayor, even a Supreme Court justice. It would be unrealistic to expect a Supreme Court justice to come to the bench a blank slate.

Justices on the U.S. Supreme Court are nominated by the president and then confirmed by a majority of the U.S. Senate. Once confirmed, the justices serve for life.[4] Typically but not always, presidential nominees to the High Court are men and women whose politics are not unlike the president's politics. Once serving, though, justices sometimes vote much more independently than the president expected.

Justices on the Florida Supreme Court are selected by means of a merit plan, a procedure designed to limit the politics in judicial appointments. Under the plan, a nonpartisan commission of citizens, judges, and attorneys reviews applications from lawyers interested in serving as an appellate court judge. When there's a vacancy, the commission recommends three to five individuals to the governor. The governor then selects one of those individuals to fill the vacancy. The person appointed to the position appears on a ballot for a public vote—ratification—in an upcoming election.

ASSIGNMENT

The following questions are based on Table 10.2, which shows the characteristics and experience of the jurists who heard the arguments in *Bush v. Gore* (U.S. Supreme Court) and *Gore v. Harris* (Florida Supreme Court).

1. Listed below are several personal characteristics. In the space provided, describe how each characteristic might shape a judge's ruling on a controversial question when that characteristic is an important component of the question. For example, a young, black, female judge might be expected to be more sensitive to a plaintiff claiming race-gender discrimination than an older, white male judge.

Age: ____

____

____

[3] One of the Florida justices was appointed jointly by the outgoing Democratic governor and the incoming Republican governor.

[4] Justices can be impeached and removed for misconduct or because of mental or physical incapacity.

TABLE 10.2 THE JUSTICES ON TWO APPELLATE COURTS, 2002

U.S. Supreme Court

William Rehnquist: Born 1924; white; Lutheran; Republican; B.A. and M.A., Stanford; M.A., Harvard; J.D., Stanford; Army Air Corps (World War II); formerly in private practice and assistant U.S. attorney general; nominated to the Court by President Nixon, confirmed in 1971; elevated to chief justice by President Reagan in 1986.

John Paul Stevens: Born 1920; white; Republican; B.A., University of Chicago; J.D., Northwestern; Navy (World War II); formerly federal court of appeals judge; nominated to the Court by President Ford, confirmed in 1975.

Sandra Day O'Connor: Born 1930; white; Episcopalian; Republican; B.A. and J.D., Stanford; formerly state legislator (Ariz.) and state trial and appellate court judge (Ariz.); nominated to the Court by President Reagan, confirmed in 1983; first woman on the Court.

Antonin Scalia: Born 1936; white; Catholic; Republican; B.A., Georgetown; J.D., Harvard; formerly with a corporate law firm, law professor, assistant U.S. attorney general, and federal court of appeals judge; nominated to the Court by President Reagan, confirmed in 1988.

Anthony Kennedy: Born 1936; white; Catholic; Republican; B.A., Stanford; J.D., Harvard; formerly federal appeals court judge; nominated to the Court by President Reagan, confirmed in 1988.

David Souter: Born 1939; white; Episcopalian; Republican; B.A. and J.D., Harvard; Rhodes Scholar (Oxford); formerly state attorney general (N.H.) and trial and appellate court judge (N.H.); nominated to the Court by President George Bush Sr., confirmed in 1990.

Clarence Thomas: Born 1948; black; Episcopalian; Republican; B.A., Holy Cross; J.D., Yale; formerly on staff of U.S. Senator John Danforth (R-Mo.), Department of Education, Equal Opportunity Commission, and federal appeals court judge; nominated to the Court by President George Bush Sr., confirmed in 1991.

Ruth Bader Ginsburg: Born 1933; white; Jewish; Democrat; B.A., Cornell; J.D., Columbia; formerly law professor, general counsel of the American Civil Liberties Union, founder and counsel of the Women's Rights Project, and federal court of appeals judge; nominated to the court by President Clinton; confirmed in 1993.

Stephen Breyer: Born 1938; white; Democrat; B.A., Stanford; J.D., Harvard; formerly assistant special prosecutor, Watergate Special Prosecution Force (1973), law school professor, and federal court of appeals judge; nominated to the court by President Clinton, confirmed in 1994.

Florida Supreme Court

Leander Shaw: Born 1930; black; Democrat; J.D., Howard; U.S. Army (Korean War); formerly assistant public defender and prosecutor, courts of appeals; appointed to the state supreme court in 1983.

Major B. Harding: Born 1936; white; Presbyterian; Republican; J.D., Wake Forest; formerly in private practice, county juvenile judge, and appellate court judge; appointed to the state supreme court in 1991.

Charles Wells: Born 1939; white; Methodist; Democrat; J.D., University of Florida; U.S. Army; formerly in private practice and attorney, U.S. Department of Justice; appointed to the state supreme court in 1994.

Harry Lee Anstead: Born 1937; white; Catholic; Democrat; J.D., University of Florida; formerly in private practice, court of appeals; appointed to the state supreme court in 1994.

Barbara Pariente: Born 1948; white; Democrat; B.A., Boston University; J.D., George Washington; formerly in private practice, court of appeals; appointed to the state supreme court in 1997.

R. Fred Lewis: Born 1947; white; Democrat; B.A., Florida Southern; J.D., University of Miami; U.S. Army; formerly in private practice; appointed to the state supreme court in 1998.

Peggy Quince: Born 1948; black; Baptist; Democrat; B.S., Howard; J.D., Catholic University; formerly in private practice, Fla. attorney general's office, and court of appeals; appointed to the state supreme court in 1998; first African American woman on court.

Note: The justices are listed in order of their confirmation or appointment to the courts.

Education: ____

Gender: ____

Religion: ____

2. What are three characteristics that distinguish justices on the U.S. Supreme Court from those on the Florida Supreme Court?

3. You are a career counselor advising a group of Florida high school seniors who are interested in becoming judges one day.

a. What advice would you give them to maximize their chances of serving on the Florida Supreme Court?

b. What advice would you give them to maximize their chances of serving on the U.S. Supreme Court?

4. a. Looking only at the personal characteristics shown in Table 10.2, which U.S. Supreme Court justice is likely the most liberal? Explain and support your answer.

b. Again, looking only at the personal characteristics shown in Table 10.2, which U.S. Supreme Court justice is likely the most conservative? Explain and support your answer.

5. Based on the information in Table 10.2, how valid is the charge that the U.S. Supreme Court is conservative and that the Florida Supreme Court is liberal?

EXERCISE 10.3 SENTENCING BEHAVIOR IN CRIMINAL COURTS

BACKGROUND

The crime rate in the United States increased dramatically from the mid-1960s to the early 1990s and then leveled off. Indications in the first years of the new century are that certain types of violent crime are on the rise. The public is understandably worried about the level of crime, especially violent crime. Crime rates are substantially higher in the United States than in other western nations. Although Congress and presidents have waged wars on crime at various times over the past three decades, controlling crime is at base a responsibility of the states. Over 90 percent of all criminal activity involves violation of state laws; and when suspects in that activity are charged, their trials are held in state courts.[5]

The FBI collects data from local law enforcement agencies on the number of crimes reported in their jurisdictions. The crime rate, calculated on the number of crimes per 100,000 population, is based on just seven categories of crime: murder, rape, robbery, aggravated assault, burglary, larceny-theft, and auto theft. (Obviously, many criminal offenses—drug trafficking among them—are not part of the bureau's crime index.) The FBI issues periodic reports on the fluctuation in crime rates across the county, by region, and within individual states.

The states have toughened their anticrime policies, primarily by adopting strict sentencing laws for those found guilty of criminal offenses. Underlying that response is the premise that strict sentences deter at least certain would-be criminals. And implied in that response is the assumption that the leniency of judges is a factor in rising crime rates. In reality, the vast majority of criminal cases are settled through *plea bargaining:* A defendant agrees to forgo a trial and plead guilty to a lesser charge that carries a lesser sentence.[6] Among the other components of anticrime laws are policies that

- reduce the number of convicted felons released from prison under parole.
- require prisoners to serve more time before becoming eligible for release because of good behavior.
- make prison sentences mandatory for conviction of specific serious and/or violent crimes.
- put repeat offenders behind bars for extended sentences, up to life (the "three strikes and you're out" laws).

Table 10.3 shows data on the average duration of felony sentences handed down in state courts. Notice that the data in the table are organized by sentence (prison, jail, probation), by offense, and by method of conviction (jury trial, bench trial, guilty plea).[7]

ASSIGNMENT

Use the data in Table 10.3 to answer the following questions.

1. In the space at the top of p. 249, create a table that shows the mean prison sentences for those convicted of each category of crime—violent, property, and drug offenses—according to whether they were convicted by a judge or a jury, or entered a guilty plea.

[5] See David W. Neubauer, *America's Courts and the Criminal Justice System,* 7th ed. (Stamford, Conn.: Wadsworth, 2002), pp. 68 and 92.

[6] Henry Glick, *Courts, Politics & Justice* (New York: McGraw-Hill, 1993), p. 206.

[7] The seriousness of the offense usually, but not always, dictates whether the guilty party is sentenced to probation, jail, or prison. Probation often is given to first-time offenders convicted of nonviolent crimes when the judge feels the defendant is a good risk not to commit other crimes. A person on probation usually has to report periodically to a probation officer, and violation of the terms of probation can result in the individual's being sent to jail. Jail is an option for those convicted of misdemeanors (nonfelonies); the sentence is usually less than a year. Those convicted of serious offenses usually are sentenced to prison and to a mandatory term of more than one year. The national government and some states now make prison terms mandatory for first-time offenders found guilty of drug trafficking.

TABLE 10.3 AVERAGE LENGTH OF SENTENCES, STATE COURTS, 1990

Most Serious Conviction Offense	Maximum Sentence Length (in Months) for Convictions by Trial									
	Jury		Bench		Total		Guilty Plea		Total	
	Mean	Median	Mean	Median	Mean	Median	Mean	Median	Mean	Median
Sentences to Prison										
Violent offenses	228	120	148	96	205	120	102	60	119	72
Murder	368	264	236	180	337	240	215	180	243	180
Rape	281	180	179	144	252	180	137	90	160	108
Robbery	222	144	158	120	204	144	100	72	115	72
Aggravated assault	133	84	117	60	128	72	69	48	78	48
Other	160	60	55	31	126	48	72	60	85	60
Property offenses	112	60	93	48	104	60	62	48	65	48
Burglary	138	84	118	60	129	72	76	54	80	54
Larceny	76	54	68	36	72	48	46	36	49	36
Fraud	78	48	68	36	72	36	56	36	58	36
Drug offenses	140	84	91	60	118	60	58	42	66	48
Possession	136	84	72	48	99	48	45	30	49	30
Trafficking	141	72	97	60	122	72	64	48	74	48
Weapons offenses	80	60	70	60	74	60	46	36	50	36
Other offenses	89	48	71	60	82	60	41	30	44	30
All offenses	**166**	**84**	**104**	**60**	**142**	**72**	**67**	**48**	**75**	**48**
Sentences to Jail										
Violent offenses	12	6	11	6	12	6	9	6	10	6
Murder	110	12	6	6	102	12	22	12	37	12
Rape	9	1	8	9	9	1	9	6	11	6
Robbery	9	6	11	9	11	8	12	12	12	11
Aggravated assault	6	3	12	6	9	4	8	5	9	6
Other	16	12	6	6	13	12	6	4	7	4
Property offenses	6	6	6	3	6	4	7	5	8	5
Burglary	5	6	7	6	6	6	8	6	9	6
Larceny	7	6	5	2	6	3	7	4	7	4
Fraud	9	6	4	2	7	6	5	3	6	3
Drug offenses	9	6	6	2	7	3	8	6	9	5
Possession	5	5	3	1	4	2	5	3	6	3
Trafficking	13	9	8	3	9	4	10	6	10	6
Weapons offenses	6	5	3	2	4	3	5	3	7	3
Other offenses	5	6	6	4	6	5	7	4	9	4
All offenses	**9**	**6**	**6**	**3**	**7**	**4**	**8**	**6**	**8**	**5**
Sentences to Probation										
Violent offenses	55	36	49	36	52	36	44	36	46	36
Murder	115	120	33	12	61	30	64	60	67	60
Rape	72	60	48	36	62	48	57	54	61	60
Robbery	51	40	59	48	56	40	49	48	50	48
Aggravated assault	47	30	48	24	47	30	41	36	43	36
Other	73	48	56	36	66	48	43	36	45	36
Property offenses	38	30	69	36	53	30	43	36	44	36
Burglary	44	36	78	36	65	36	47	36	48	36
Larceny	37	30	56	30	47	30	40	36	41	36
Fraud	34	30	74	36	48	30	42	36	43	36
Drug offenses	51	48	48	30	49	36	40	36	42	36
Possession	54	48	40	24	46	30	37	36	39	36
Trafficking	48	36	51	36	50	36	43	36	44	36
Weapons offenses	35	30	27	24	30	24	34	24	34	24
Other offenses	34	30	37	25	35	30	40	36	39	36
All offenses	**43**	**30**	**53**	**30**	**48**	**30**	**41**	**36**	**42**	**36**

SOURCE: U.S. Department of Justice, Bureau of Statistics, *National Judicial Reporting Program*, 1990 (Washington, D.C., 1993), pp. 45–46.

2. What is the difference between the median number of years a man would serve behind bars if he was convicted of a drug-trafficking offense that carries a prison term as opposed to a drug-trafficking offense that carries a jail sentence?

___

3. You have committed a violent crime. You know the prosecutor has solid evidence that you are guilty of the crime, which carries a prison term of ten to twenty years. Would you want your case decided by a judge or by a jury, or would you enter a plea bargain? Explain why you chose the one you did instead of the other two.

___

___

___

___

EXERCISE 10.4 CIVIL JURY AWARDS

BACKGROUND

Most legal cases in the United States involve either criminal or civil law. In a *criminal case,* the prosecution—the state or the national government—alleges that a crime has been committed (murder, drunk driving, assault and battery, rape). If no plea agreement is entered, the case goes to trial, where a judge or a jury determines the defendant's guilt and sentence. Sentences for crimes include incarceration, community service, probation, and fines. *Civil cases* are disputes between "private individuals involving either a breach of an agreement or a breach of a duty imposed by law."[8] Notice that both plaintiff and defendant are *private individuals,* which can mean corporations or businesses as well as people; the government is not a party. Civil suits also are heard by a judge or a jury, which decides who is legally responsible for the injury alleged by the plaintiff. Common civil actions include divorce, breach of contract, medical malpractice, and automobile accident cases. Although criminal law makes for exciting television shows, motion pictures, and books, most people are much more likely to be a party in a civil suit.

When a defendant is found guilty in a civil case, the judge or jury awards the plaintiff some amount of money. (A prison term isn't an option for a defendant who loses a civil suit.) Awards fall into two categories: *Compensatory awards* repay the victim for financial losses suffered—loss of wages, for example, or the costs of doctor, hospital, and rehabilitation. *Punitive awards* are designed to discourage similar behavior.

From time to time, what seems to be an excessive jury award makes the news. That was the case in 1994, when a jury awarded $2.7 million in punitive damages to an 81-year old woman in Albuquerque. The woman had stopped at a McDonald's and bought a container of coffee to go. As the car she was a passenger in left the restaurant, the coffee spilled and scalded her legs. The plaintiff maintained that McDonald's served its coffee at a dangerously high temperature and that the fast-food chain was aware from previous lawsuits that people could be burned as a result. The jury based the award on the plaintiff's medical bills, the profit McDonald's made from the sale of its coffee, and the many suits filed against the company over the high temperature of its coffee—a higher temperature than that of coffee served by other fast-food outlets. To much less fanfare, an appellate court did reduce the punitive damages in the case to $480,000; it did not, however, change the $160,000 the jury had awarded in compensatory damages.

In 1995, the Supreme Court for the first time invalidated a punitive award on the grounds that the award was excessive. In its ruling in *BMW of North America v. Gore,* the justices identified guideposts state courts can use to check the reasonableness of an award. Among those guideposts: "the degree of reprehensibility of the defendant's conduct, the relationship between the award and the actual damages to the defendant, and the difference between the award and the civil or criminal sanctions that could be imposed for comparable misconduct."[9]

In reality, most civil cases are settled out of court: They never go to trial.[10] But big awards capture the headlines, fostering the misleading impression that huge jury awards are the norm, not the exception. It's that impression that has sparked efforts in many states and in Congress to cap punitive damages so that they are not grossly out of line with the actual damages sustained by plaintiffs.

ASSIGNMENT

Reading 10.4 summarizes the relevant details in six civil suits. As you answer the questions that follow the reading, bear in mind the guideposts identified by the Supreme Court:

- The degree of negligence on the part of the defendant
- The relationship between the award and the actual damages to the defendant

[8] Harold J. Grillot and Frank A. Schubert, *Introduction to Law and the Legal System,* 5th ed. (Boston: Houghton Mifflin, 1992), p. 46.

[9] Tyler Cunningham, "Huge Punitives Growing—Judges Trim Them," *Los Angeles Daily Journal,* October 6, 2000, p. 4.

[10] G. Alan Tarr, *Judicial Process and Judicial Policymaking,* 2d ed. (Stamford, Conn.: Wadsworth, 1999), p. 223.

- The difference between the award and the sanctions that could be imposed for similar misconduct.

Where appropriate, also consider the difference between actual damages (based on medical fees, lost pay, and replacement costs) and intangible damages (for pain and suffering, disfigurement, and other factors, like quality of life or impact). Obviously calculating a specific dollar amount in intangible damages must be subjective.

READING 10.4 Six Civil Cases

Case 1

In January 1990, a doctor bought a brand-new BMW 535i from a dealer in Alabama. Nine months later, the doctor took the car in to be serviced, and a mechanic told him that the car had been repainted. Apparently, at some point between the car's leaving the plant and arriving at the showroom, acid rain had marred the original finish and the car was repainted. The doctor was not told about the paint job at the time he bought the car. Believing that the dealer's paint job would be inferior to the factory paint job, and angry that he had been deceived, the doctor filed suit. An Alabama jury awarded him $4,000 in compensatory damages and $4 million in punitive damages. The punitive award was based at least in part on the fact that other "new" BMWs were sold to buyers who were unaware that the cars—for similar reasons—had been repainted. BMW filed an immediate appeal contesting the size of the punitive award.

Case 2

In 1999, a jury ordered General Motors to pay $4.9 billion in damages to two women and their four children who were burned when their 1979 Chevrolet Malibu was struck by a drunk driver six years earlier. The Malibu's gas tank exploded in the rear-end collision, burning the trapped occupants of the car. The jury awarded the six victims a total of $107 million to compensate them for their pain, suffering, and disfigurement. The jurors also hit GM for $4.8 billion in punitive damages on the grounds that the gas tank explosion might not have occurred had the company installed a device that cost less than $9 to prevent fuel-fed fires. GM blamed the fire, and the injuries to the victims, on the drunk driver who was traveling at 70 miles per hour when he hit the Malibu (the victims' car was stopped at a traffic signal). The trial court judge subsequently reduced the punitive damages to $1.2 billion. GM, the world's largest carmaker, announced it would appeal the award.

Case 3

In a 1999 case, three plaintiffs alleged they were overcharged for two satellite dishes they had bought several years earlier. It seems the salesman had told the plaintiffs they would have to pay $34 a month per dish for three years. But the contract was written to run for four and a half years. A jury in Birmingham, Alabama, awarded the three plaintiffs $975,000 for mental anguish and $580 million in punitive damages.

Case 4

In 2001 a jury in Seattle held Abbott Laboratories and the University of Washington liable for $8.1 million each for a misdiagnosis of cancer that led to unnecessary surgery and chemotherapy for a female patient. The woman had used a pregnancy test produced by Abbott; the results falsely indicated she had a deadly form of cancer. Abbott had failed to warn physicians that a false-positive reading for cancer was not an uncommon result of the pregnancy test. The subsequent surgery—a hysterectomy—and treatment were carried out by physicians at the University of Washington.

Case 5

The adult children of a California man were awarded $1.5 million by a jury in 2001 because their father died under unnecessarily painful circumstances. The 85-year-old man, who died in 1998, was suffering from bone fractures and probably lung cancer. The children's attorney charged that the attending physician was recklessly negligent and was guilty of elder abuse because he undermedicated the patient. The physician promised to appeal the award.

Case 6

In an unusual case that received national attention and was the subject of a made-for-television movie, a 16-year-old boy filed a lawsuit in 2000 for $1 million against his local school district and town authorities. The suit charges that the district and the authorities did not take the necessary steps to stop his relationship with a teacher even after they learned of it. The affair between the boy and his 30-year-old teacher began when the boy was 13; it produced one child. The teacher was prosecuted (for having sex with a minor) and sentenced to six months in jail in 1997. When she was released, the romance resumed, and she and the boy had a second child. The former teacher was prosecuted again and this time was sentenced to seven years in prison. In his lawsuit, the teenager claims emotional suffering, lost income, and the cost of raising the two children (who are in the custody of his mother).

---

1. a. Members of the jury in case 2 should have asked two questions to determine GM's liability for a 14-year-old car. What are those two questions?

Question 1: ______________________________

____

Question 2: ______________________________

____

b. Why are the two questions critical to determining the carmaker's liability?

____

____

____

____

____

____

2. a. Looking at case 3, how much would the two satellite dishes cost over three years?

____

b. How much would the two dishes cost over four and a half years?

____

c. How much did the company actually overcharge the plaintiffs?

____

d. What was the ratio of the amount overcharged to the award for mental anguish?

____

3. One of the Supreme Court guidelines for determining the reasonableness of punitive damages is the "degree of reprehensibility of the defendant's conduct."

a. What does *reprehensibility* mean?

____

____

b. How would you as a juror determine a defendant's reprehensibility? What specific criteria would you employ?

4. a. What intangible damages have been alleged in cases 1, 2, and 3?

Case 1:

Case 2:

Case 3:

b. What is the basis for awarding actual damages in cases 1, 2, and 3? Explain and support your answer.

5. Suppose you are the lead attorney for the plaintiff in case 6. What are the two strongest arguments you would advance in court on behalf of your client, the 16-year-old boy? Explain why you think those arguments are particularly potent.

6. Do you think the school district in case 6 should file a suit against the teenager or his mother for not taking the necessary steps to stop a relationship that they knew was improper? Explain your answer.

7. If you were the plaintiff's attorney in case 6, what specific information would you offer the jury to support the case for damages based on something as subjective as emotional suffering?

8. Suppose you are a judge on an appellate court that's been asked to review the jury awards in each of the cases described in Reading 10.4. Which award would you find most suspect and be least likely to uphold in your ruling? Explain and support your answer.

EXERCISE 10.5 CHANGING PRODUCT-LIABILITY LAWS

BACKGROUND

As several of the examples in Exercise 10.4 show, when a business loses a civil suit, it may be asked to pay millions in damages. In response to large awards made to consumers based on problems with items they bought from stores, many manufacturers now place warning labels on their products to inform consumers of proper use and the consequences of misuse. So, for example, a child's Batman costume for Halloween is likely to come with a tag reminding the buyer that the mask and cape are for play only and that neither allows the user to fly. Or the paper screens drivers place on the inside of their windshield to block the sun when the car is parked carry the warning that serious injury may result if a car is driven with the screen in place.

Interest groups that advocate on behalf of businesses in the corridors of state and federal government—the National Association of Manufacturers and other lobbies, the chambers of commerce, and state chapters of the National Federation of Independent Businesses—have pressed for changes in product-liability law at both the state and federal levels. They want three fundamental changes in the law:

- A cap on pain-and-suffering awards
- A federal law governing product-liability awards that will render the numerous and various state laws on product liability unenforceable
- Elimination of retail stores as possible defendants in product-liability lawsuits, on the grounds that selling a product should not make a business liable for defects in the product or for improper use by the consumer[11]

Not surprisingly, advocates and opponents of changing product-liability law disagree profoundly on the value of the suggested reforms. Reform advocates claim large awards translate into higher prices that then are passed on to consumers. Yet those who feel the process works fine as it is now say that only 2 percent of the cases filed nationally in the mid-1990s involved product-liability claims and that, on average, fewer than two punitive-damages verdicts are handed down each year.[12]

To date, product-liability reform efforts have not been successful. Even where states have changed their laws, courts have overturned the legislation.[13] In 1996, President Bill Clinton vetoed a major product-liability reform bill on the grounds that it would have rewritten product liability rules for all businesses and capped punitive damages in all cases. Interestingly, the National Conference of State Legislatures opposed the bill because it would have preempted state laws.

ASSIGNMENT

With the backing of the business community, a scaled-down version of the 1996 legislation was introduced into Congress in 1999 as HR 2366.[14] One significant change: HR 2366 applies exclusively to *small businesses*, which the proposal defines as businesses having twenty-five or fewer employees. A summary of HR 2366 appears in Reading 10.5. Refer to the reading to answer the questions that follow it.

READING 10.5 HR 2366: SMALL BUSINESS LIABILITY REFORM ACT OF 1999

Note: The provisions of this bill apply to businesses with twenty-five or fewer employees.

---

[11] Few stores have been sued successfully on the basis of product liability, but being named as a defendant in a product-liability case can translate into significant financial cost.

[12] Dan Lawton, "Torts Need No Reform; Law Already Protects Real Victims," *Los Angeles Daily Journal*, September 4, 2001, p. 6.

[13] Milo Geyelin, "Liability Limits Encounter Roadblocks in State Courts," *Wall Street Journal*, December 10, 1996, p. B3.

[14] To date, the bill has not been passed.

READING SOURCE: Bill Summary and Status for the 106th Congress.

TITLE I: SMALL BUSINESS LAWSUIT ABUSE PROTECTION

Allows punitive damages to be awarded against a small business only if the claimant establishes by clear and convincing evidence that conduct carried out by the defendant through willful misconduct or with a conscious, flagrant indifference to the rights or safety of others was the proximate cause of the harm that is the subject of the action. Limits such punitive damages to the lesser of two times the amount awarded for economic and noneconomic losses, or $250,000.

Sec. 104. States that, in any civil action against a small business: (1) each defendant shall be liable only for the amount of the noneconomic loss allocated to that defendant in direct proportion to the percentage of responsibility of that defendant for the harm caused to the plaintiff; and (2) the court shall render a separate judgment against each defendant describing such percentage of responsibility.

Sec. 105. Exempts from such liability limitations any misconduct of a defendant: (1) that constitutes a crime of violence, international terrorism, or a hate crime; (2) that results in liability for damages under specified provisions of the Oil Pollution Control Act of 1990 or the Comprehensive Response, Compensation, and Liability Act of 1980; (3) that involves a sexual offense or violation of a Federal or State civil rights law; or (4) caused by being under the influence of intoxicating alcohol or a drug.

Sec. 106. Preempts inconsistent State law.

TITLE II: PRODUCT SELLER FAIR TREATMENT

States that this title governs any product liability action brought in any Federal or State court. Excludes from this title actions for commercial loss, negligent entrustment, negligence per se concerning firearms and ammunition, and actions brought under a dram-shop or third-party liability arising out of the sale or provision of alcohol to an intoxicated person or a minor.

Sec. 204. Mandates that, in any product liability action covered by this Act, a product seller other than a manufacturer shall be liable to a claimant only if such claimant establishes that: (1) the product that caused the harm was sold, rented, or leased by the seller, the seller failed to exercise reasonable care with respect to the product, and such failure was the proximate cause of harm to the plaintiff; (2) the seller made an express warranty applicable to such product, the product failed to conform to the warranty, and such failure caused the harm to the plaintiff; or (3) the product seller engaged in intentional wrongdoing (as determined under applicable State law), and such wrongdoing caused the harm to the plaintiff. States that a seller shall not be considered to have failed to exercise reasonable care with respect to a product based upon a failure to inspect if: (1) there was no reasonable opportunity to inspect; or (2) such inspection would not have revealed the aspect of the product that allegedly caused the claimant's harm. Allows a seller to be liable as a manufacturer if: (1) the manufacturer is not subject to appropriate service of process; or (2) the court determines that the claimant is or would be unable to enforce a judgment against the manufacturer. Provides limited liability for persons engaged in the business or renting or leasing a product.

---

1. a. Which groups or interests would likely benefit should HR 2366 pass and be signed into law?

____

____

____

b. Which groups or interests would likely suffer should HR 2366 pass and be signed into law?

____

____

____

2. Identify three words or phrases in HR 2366 that though important to the bill are vague and would likely be disputed in court when attorneys attempt to resolve questions about a plaintiff's behavior or a defendant's liability. For example, the phrase "if the product seller engaged in intentional wrongdoing" is vague because *intentional* is open to interpretation.

____

____

____

3. A plaintiff wins a $150,000 liability award from Shoddy Ladders Inc. because of injuries she suffered when one of Shoddy's ladders collapsed (poor welds). Under HR 2366, what is the maximum punitive award this plaintiff could receive? Explain your answer.

____

____

4. A woman buys an over-the-counter nasal spray and suffers a severe adverse reaction to the medication. Neither the store (one of a national chain of drugstores) nor the pharmaceutical company warned consumers of the possible side effect. Would HR 2366 limit the punitive damages this woman might receive from the drugstore chain? Cite specific language in the bill to support your answer.

____

____

____

____

____

5. Under HR 2366, can the seller of a product be held liable for damages if the buyer used the product in a prescribed way but was injured nonetheless? Cite specific language in the bill to support your answer.

____

____

____

____

6. a. Make two arguments: one in favor of leaving product-liability laws to the states and one in favor of having a federal law determine the matter.

State law: ______________________________

____

____

____

Federal law: ______________________________

____

____

____

b. Which argument do you find more persuasive? Explain and support your answer.

____

____

____

7. In general, do you support liability reform of the type represented by HR 2366? Why or why not?

CHAPTER 11

CIVIL RIGHTS

EXERCISE 11.1 MANDATING RACIAL SEGREGATION BY STATE LAW

BACKGROUND

Blacks liberated from slavery by the Civil War defined *freedom* in expansive terms, arguing that freedom necessarily includes the right to vote and hold political office, equality before the law, and the ownership of land. Many whites, North and South, defined *freedom* for blacks in the most narrow, restrictive terms, arguing that freedom is nothing more than the absence of slavery. The battle over the meaning of *freedom* for blacks raged during the late nineteenth century and throughout the twentieth, and goes on in the twenty-first century as the United States continues its painful and drawn-out adjustment to the end of slavery.

In 1867, Congress under the leadership of the Radical Republicans passed the Reconstruction Acts, legislation that secured for blacks in the South the right to vote and a measure of legal equality. African Americans were elected to political office throughout the South and in 1870, for the first time, took seats in the U.S. House of Representatives and Senate (see Exercise 7.4). Those gains were made possible by the use of military power on behalf of African Americans in the South. In 1877, the North pulled its troops out of the South. Unencumbered, southerners reasserted white supremacy by passing a series of state laws to disfranchise and segregate blacks. Among the devices employed to strip blacks of their voting rights were the literacy test, the poll tax, the grandfather clause, and the white primary. Jim Crow laws buttressed white supremacy by mandating the separation of whites and blacks in almost every public and private area of life. Blacks were sent to separate schools and had to use separate restrooms, parks, restaurants, hotels, trains, streetcars, swimming pools, even cemeteries.

In 1890 the Louisiana state legislature required railroads to provide "equal but separate accommodations for the white and colored races" and prohibited travelers from riding in rail cars designated for the other race. A group of blacks from New Orleans challenged the law in court. They received some support from railroad companies that objected to the additional expense of providing separate cars for black and white passengers. The dispute eventually made its way to the Supreme Court. There, in *Plessy v. Ferguson* (1896), a majority of the justices ruled that the doctrine of separate but equal was constitutional.

In 1909, blacks and whites alarmed at the deteriorating position of African Americans, formed an interest group called the National Association for the Advancement of Colored People. Its mission: to secure full rights of citizenship for black Americans. The legal arm of the NAACP filed a series of lawsuits challenging the system of racial separation mandated by state law in the South. Those suits made inroads against segregation in the South, particularly in the areas of graduate education and interstate transportation, but progress was slow. Segregation was pervasive and firmly entrenched.

Beginning in the late 1940s, the NAACP challenged segregation in public schools. One case, *Briggs v. Elliott* (1952), was initiated by black parents in Clarendon County, South Carolina, where the school board in the 1949–1950 term spent $43 per black child and $179 per white child. The Supreme Court consolidated *Briggs* with three other challenges to school segregation under the name of a case from Kansas, *Brown v. Board of Education of Topeka* (1954). The case was argued before the Court by Thurgood Marshall, the lead attorney for the NAACP's Legal and Educational Defense Fund, who was later appointed by President Lyndon Johnson to a seat on the Supreme Court. Earl Warren, the Chief Justice who engineered the Court's unanimous decision in *Brown*, had been appointed to the Court by President Dwight Eisenhower in 1953.

ASSIGNMENT

Refer to Readings 11.1.1 and 11.1.2 to answer the questions that follow them.

READING 11.1.1 *PLESSY V. FERGUSON*, 163 U.S. 537 (1896)

Mr. Justice Brown delivered the opinion of the court.

The constitutionality of this act is attacked upon the ground that it conflicts both with the thirteenth amendment of the constitution, abolishing slavery, and the fourteenth amendment, which prohibits certain restrictive legislation on the part of the states.

1. That it does not conflict with the thirteenth amendment, which abolished slavery and involuntary servitude, except a punishment for crime, is too clear for argument. . . .

2. . . . The object of the [fourteenth] amendment was undoubtedly to enforce the absolute equality of the two races before the law, but, in the nature of things, it could not have been intended to abolish distinctions based upon color, or to enforce social, as distinguished from political, equality, or a commingling of the two races upon terms unsatisfactory to either. Laws permitting, and even requiring, their separation, in places where they are liable to be brought into contact, do not necessarily imply the inferiority of either race to the other, and have been generally, if not universally, recognized as within the competency of the state legislatures in the exercise of their police power. The most common instance of this is connected with the establishment of separate schools for white and colored children, which have been held to be a valid exercise of the legislative power even by courts of states where the political rights of the colored race have been longest and most earnestly enforced. . . .

We think the enforced separation of the races, as applied to the internal commerce of the state, neither abridges the privileges or immunities of the colored man, deprives him of his property without due process of law, nor denies him the equal protection of the laws, within the meaning of the fourteenth amendment. . . .

In this connection, it is also suggested by the learned counsel for the plaintiff in error that the same argument that will justify the state legislature in requiring railways to provide separate accommodations for the two races will also authorize them to require separate cars to be provided for people whose hair is of a certain color, or who are aliens, or who belong to certain nationalities, or to enact laws requiring colored people to walk upon one side of the street, and white people upon the other, or requiring white men's houses to be painted white, and colored men's black, or their vehicles or business signs to be of different colors, upon the theory that one side of the street is as good as the other, or that a house or vehicle of one color is as good as one of another color. The reply to all this is that every exercise of the police power must be reasonable, and extend only to such laws as are enacted in good faith for the promotion of the public good, and not for the annoyance or oppression of a particular class. . . .

We consider the underlying fallacy of the plaintiff's argument to consist in the assumption that the enforced separation of the two races stamps the colored race with a badge of inferiority. If this be so, it is not by reason of anything found in the act, but solely because the colored race chooses to put that construction upon it. The argument necessarily assumes that if, as has been more than once the case, and is not unlikely to be so again, the colored race should become the dominant power in the state legislature, and should enact a law in precisely similar terms, it would thereby relegate the white race to an inferior position. We imagine that the white race, at least, would not acquiesce in this assumption. The argument also assumes that social prejudices may be overcome by legislation, and that equal rights cannot be secured to the negro except by an enforced commingling of the two races. We cannot accept this proposition. If the two races are to meet upon terms of social equality, it must be the result of natural affinities, a mutual appreciation of each other's merits, and a voluntary consent of individuals. . . . Legislation is powerless to eradicate racial instincts, or to abolish distinctions based upon physical differences, and the attempt to do so can only result in accentuating the difficulties of the present situation. If the civil and political rights of both races be equal, one cannot be inferior to the other civilly or politically. If one race be inferior to the other socially, the constitution of the United States cannot put them upon the same plane. . . .

Mr. Justice Harlan dissenting. arguments?

In respect of civil rights, common to all citizens, the constitution of the United States does not, I think, permit any public authority to know the race of those entitled to be protected in the enjoyment of such rights. . . . Indeed, such legislation as that here in question is inconsistent not only with that equality of rights which pertains to citizenship, national and state, but with the personal liberty enjoyed by every one within the United States.

It was said in argument that the statute of Louisiana does not discriminate against either race, but prescribes a rule applicable alike to white and colored citizens. But this argument does not meet the difficulty. Every one knows that the statute in question had its origin in the purpose, not so much to exclude white persons from railroad cars occupied by blacks, as to exclude colored people from coaches occupied by or assigned to white persons. Railroad corporations of Louisiana did not make discrimination among whites in the matter of accommodation for travelers. The thing to accomplish was, under the guise of giving equal accommodation for whites and blacks, to compel the latter to keep to themselves while traveling in railroad passenger coaches. No one would be so wanting in candor as to assert the contrary. The fundamental objection, therefore, to the statute, is that it interferes with the personal freedom of citizens. . . . If a white man and a black man choose to occupy the same public conveyance on a public highway, it is their right to do so; and no government, proceeding alone on grounds of race, can prevent it without infringing the personal liberty of each.

It is one thing for railroad carriers to furnish, or to be required by law to furnish, equal accommodations for all whom they are under a legal duty to carry. It is quite another thing for government to forbid citizens of the white and black races from traveling in the same public conveyance, and to punish officers of railroad companies for permitting persons of the two races to occupy the same passenger coach. . . .

Our constitution is color-blind, and neither knows nor tolerates classes among citizens. In respect of civil rights, all citizens are equal before the law. The humblest is the peer of the most powerful. The law regards man as man, and takes no account of his surroundings or of his color when his civil rights as guaranteed by the supreme law of the land are involved. It is therefore to be regretted that this high tribunal, the final expositor of the fundamental law of the land, has reached the conclusion that it is competent for a state to regulate the enjoyment by citizens of their civil rights solely upon the basis of race. . . .

The destinies of the two races, in this country, are indissolubly linked together, and the interests of both require that the common government of all shall not permit the seeds of race hate to be planted under the sanction of law. What can more certainly arouse race hate, what more certainly create and perpetuate a feeling of distrust between these races, than state enactments which, in fact, proceed on the ground that colored citizens are so inferior and degraded that they cannot be allowed to sit in public coaches occupied by white citizens? That, as all will admit, is the real meaning of such legislation as was enacted in Louisiana. . . .

The arbitrary separation of citizens, on the basis of race, while they are on a public highway, is a badge of servitude wholly inconsistent with the civil freedom and the equality before the law established by the constitution. It cannot be justified upon any legal grounds.

READING 11.1.2 *Brown v. Board of Education of Topeka*, 347 U.S. 483 (1954)

Mr. Chief Justice Warren delivered the opinion of the Court.

These cases come to us from the States of Kansas, South Carolina, Virginia, and Delaware. They are premised on different facts and different local conditions, but a common legal question justifies their consideration together in this consolidated opinion.

In each of the cases, minors of the Negro race, through their legal representatives, seek the aid of the courts in obtaining admission to the public schools of their community on a nonsegregated basis. In each instance, they had been denied admission to schools attended by white children under laws requiring or permitting segregation according to race. This segregation was alleged to deprive the plaintiffs of the equal protection of the laws under the Fourteenth Amendment. In each of the cases other than the Delaware case, a three-judge federal district court denied relief to the plaintiffs on the so-called "separate but equal" doctrine announced by this Court in *Plessy v. Ferguson.* Under that doctrine, equality of treatment is accorded when the races are provided substantially equal facilities, even though these facilities be separate. . . .

The plaintiffs contend that segregated public schools are not "equal" and cannot be made "equal," and that hence they are deprived of the equal protection of the laws. Because of the obvious importance of the question presented, the Court took jurisdiction. Argument was heard in the 1952 Term, and reargument was heard this Term on certain questions propounded by the Court.

Reargument was largely devoted to the circumstances surrounding the adoption of the Fourteenth Amendment in 1868. It covered exhaustively consideration of the Amendment in Congress, ratification by the states, then existing practices in racial segregation, and the views of proponents and opponents of the Amendment. This discussion and our own investigation convince us that, although these sources cast some light, it is not enough to resolve the problem with which we are faced. At best, they are inconclusive. The most avid proponents of the post-War Amendments undoubtedly intended them to remove all legal distinctions among "all persons born or naturalized in the United States." Their opponents, just as certainly, were antagonistic to both the letter and the spirit of the Amendments and wished them to have the most limited effect. What others in Congress and the state legislatures had in mind cannot be determined with any degree of certainty.

An additional reason for the inconclusive nature of the Amendment's history, with respect to segregated schools, is the status of public education at that time. In the South, the movement toward free common schools, supported by general taxation, had not yet taken hold. Education of white children was largely in the hands of private groups. Education of Negroes was almost nonexistent, and practically all of the race were illiterate. In fact, any education of Negroes was forbidden by law in some states. Today, in contrast, many Negroes have achieved outstanding success in the arts and sciences as well as in the business and professional world. It is true that public school education at the time of the Amendment had advanced further in the North, but the effect of the Amendment on Northern States was generally ignored in the congressional debates. Even in the North, the conditions of public education did not approximate those existing today. The curriculum was usually rudimentary; ungraded schools were common in rural areas; the school term was but three months a year in many states; and compulsory school attendance was virtually unknown. As a consequence, it is not surprising that there should be so little in the history of the Fourteenth Amendment relating to its intended effect on public education. . . .

In the instant cases, that question [of whether *Plessy v. Ferguson* should be held inapplicable to public education] is directly presented. Here . . . there are findings below that the Negro and white schools involved have been equalized, or are being equalized, with respect to buildings, curricula, qualifications and salaries of teachers, and other "tangible" factors. Our decision, therefore, cannot turn on merely a comparison of these tangible factors in the Negro and white schools involved in each of the cases. We must look instead to the effect of segregation itself on public education.

In approaching this problem, we cannot turn the clock back to 1868 when the Amendment was adopted, or even to 1896 when *Plessy v. Ferguson* was written. We must consider public education in the light of its full development and its present place in American life throughout the Nation. Only in this way can it be determined if segregation in public schools deprives these plaintiffs of the equal protection of the laws.

Today, education is perhaps the most important function of state and local governments. Compulsory school attendance laws and the great expenditures for education both demonstrate our recognition of the importance of education to our democratic society. It is required in the performance of our most basic public responsibilities, even service in the armed forces. It is the very foundation of good citizenship. Today it is a principal instrument in awakening the child to cultural values, in preparing him for later professional training, and in helping him to adjust normally to his environment. In these days, it is doubtful that any child may reasonably be expected to succeed in life if he is denied the opportunity of an education. Such an opportunity, where the state has undertaken to provide it, is a right which must be made available to all on equal terms.

We come then to the question presented: Does segregation of children in public schools solely on the basis of race, even though the physical facilities and other "tangible" factors may be equal, deprive the children of the minority group of equal educational opportunities? We believe that it does. . . .

To separate [children in grade and high schools] from others of similar age and qualifications solely because of their race generates a feeling of inferiority as to their status in the community that may affect their hearts and minds in a way unlikely ever to be undone. The effect of this separation on their educational opportunities was well stated by a finding in the Kansas case by a court which nevertheless felt compelled to rule against the Negro plaintiffs:

"Segregation of white and colored children in public schools has a detrimental effect upon the colored children. The impact is greater when it has the sanction of the law; for the policy of separating the races is usually interpreted as denoting the inferiority of the negro group. A sense of inferiority affects the motivation of a child to learn. Segregation with the sanction of law, therefore, has a tendency to [retard] the educational and mental development of negro children and to deprive them of some of the benefits they would receive in a racial[ly] integrated school system."

Whatever may have been the extent of psychological knowledge at the time of *Plessy v. Ferguson*, this finding is amply supported by modern authority. Any language in *Plessy v. Ferguson* contrary to this finding is rejected.

We conclude that in the field of public education the doctrine of "separate but equal" has no place. Separate educational facilities are inherently unequal. Therefore, we hold that the plaintiffs and others similarly situated for whom the actions have been brought are, by reason of the segregation complained of, deprived of the equal protection of the laws guaranteed by the Fourteenth Amendment. . . .

It is so ordered.

---

1. In one sentence, summarize the Supreme Court's decision in *Plessy v. Ferguson.*

2. Briefly describe what you think are the most important arguments made by the majority to justify its decision in *Plessy.*

3. Briefly describe what you think are the most important arguments made by Justice John Marshall Harlan in his dissent in *Plessy.*

4. How does the majority opinion in *Plessy* differ from Justice Harlan's dissent on the important question of the Louisiana state legislature's intent in enacting the law that segregated rail cars?

5. In one sentence, summarize the Supreme Court's decision in *Brown v. Board of Education of Topeka.*

6. Briefly describe what you think are the most important arguments made by the Supreme Court to justify its decision in *Brown.*

______

______

______

______

______

______

7. Before *Brown* reached the Supreme Court, many school districts in the South dramatically increased their spending on black schools, hoping to stop the justices from ruling that segregated schools are unconstitutional. The strategy didn't work: Despite an influx of funds, most black schools were patently inferior to white schools. In 1954, for example, public funding per pupil for black schools in the South was only 60 percent of that per pupil for white schools.

But what if the strategy had worked? Suppose that southern whites had spent enough to make black schools the equivalent of white schools. Suppose that the defendants in *Brown* were able to demonstrate conclusively to the justices on the Supreme Court that schools for blacks across the South were in every tangible and measurable way equal to schools for whites. In their decision, do the justices indicate whether real equality between black and white schools would have altered their decision? Cite language from *Brown* to support your answer.

______

______

______

______

______

______

______

______

______

______

8. In the early 1950s, the judiciary was the only branch of the national government to act against segregation in the South. Both the executive and the legislative branches studiously avoided the issue. And when the Supreme Court ruled in *Brown,* its decision was vehemently opposed in the South. What characteristics of the Court give it the freedom to make unpopular decisions?

______

______

______

______

EXERCISE 11.2 RACE RELATIONS: HOW PERSISTENT A PROBLEM?

BACKGROUND

Many countries around the world have experienced internal conflict between groups of citizens over religious, linguistic, and ethnic differences. Most often, those whose characteristics put them in the majority enjoy more rights—economic, legal, political, and social—than those in the minority. The United States is no exception. And still a dilemma for Americans is the legacy of racial discrimination.

At the time the Constitution was ratified, black Americans were prohibited from voting by the states and were denied most rights granted to white citizens. The Civil War amendments aimed to extend basic rights to blacks in this country. The Thirteenth Amendment (1865) abolished slavery; the Fourteenth (1868) gave citizenship and the "equal protection of the laws" to black Americans; and the Fifteenth (1870) granted voting rights to all citizens except women. But Congressional actions and Supreme Court rulings significantly diminished the impact of the amendments in the period of Reconstruction. And in 1896, in *Plessy v. Ferguson,* the Supreme Court gave its imprimatur to segregation, holding that separate-but-equal facilities for whites and blacks do not constitute race discrimination, just "race distinction."

Race distinction was very much the rule into the new century. Discrimination was most evident in the South, where more than 90 percent of the country's black population lived until the early twentieth century.[1] In 1905, for example, Georgia prohibited blacks and whites from using the same public park facilities; in 1915, Oklahoma voted for separate telephone booths for blacks and whites; and all southern states had laws on their books mandating separate restrooms and drinking fountains for blacks and whites. Not until 1940 did the municipal zoo in Atlanta open its gates to black and white visitors at the same time.[2]

By midcentury, though, change was coming. In 1948, President Harry Truman ordered the integration of the armed services. In 1954, the decision in *Brown* signaled the Supreme Court's willingness to end the legal barriers that supported race discrimination. The refusal of school districts in the South to integrate in compliance with *Brown* spurred the intervention of the national government and black protest marches.

The modern civil rights movement began with the boycott of the Montgomery, Alabama, bus system in 1955 (see Exercise 6.3). By the early 1960s, black activists were taking part in sit-ins at segregated lunch counters and marches to protest their second-class status.

The executive had acted; the judiciary had acted. Finally, the legislature did its part. In 1964, Congress passed a law that dismantled the system of segregation in the South and throughout the country. The Civil Rights Act of 1964 was the most significant piece of federal legislation to address racial inequalities in the nation. The following year, Congress passed the Voting Rights Act. Together, the two pieces of legislation began to make real the promises of the Fourteenth and Fifteenth Amendments.

Still the conflict between whites and blacks did not disappear. The late 1960s saw riots in cities across America; and after the assassination of Dr. Martin Luther King Jr. in April 1968, race riots broke out in some one hundred cities. The violence subsided in the 1970s and 1980s, but racial polarization was still a part of the American experience. Witness the rioting in Los Angeles in 1992 following the acquittal of four police officers who had been videotaped beating a black motorist named Rodney King.

Although allegations of abuse at the hands of law enforcement officers kept tension high between blacks and whites in many cities in the 1990s, racial equality did not have a place on the public agenda for much of the decade. It was an issue in Reverend Jesse Jackson's unsuccessful campaign for the presidency in 1992; but four years later, neither Bill Clinton nor Bob Dole addressed the plight of the minority underclass in their campaigns. And the issue also was neglected in the 2000 presidential contest.

---

[1] National Advisory Commission on Civil Disorders, *Report* (New York: Bantam, 1968), pp. 236–237.

[2] Robert Weisbolt, *Freedom Bound: A History of America's Civil Rights Movement* (New York: Plume, 1991), p. 5.

ASSIGNMENT

The question: Do you think that relations between blacks and whites will always be a problem for the United States, or that solutions will eventually be worked out? Table 11.2.1 shows how Americans—by gender, age, and other characteristics—answered that question in 1995. Table 11.2.2 shows responses by race to the question in 1963, 1993, and 1995. Use the two tables to answer the following questions.

1. What influence does education appear to have on attitudes about racial problems?

2. What do you think accounts for the different responses of black men and women to the question?

3. What impact could age have on responses to the question?

4. Use the data in Table 11.2.1 to create a profile of a person who is most likely to believe that black–white relations will always be a problem.

5. Look at the data in Table 11.2.2.

a. How did the attitudes of whites change between 1963 and 1995?

b. How did the attitudes of blacks change between 1963 and 1995?

c. Formulate two hypotheses to explain the changes from 1963 to 1995. Those hypotheses should consider historical events and generational changes.

Hypothesis 1: __________

Hypothesis 2: __________

TABLE 11.2.1 ATTITUDES ABOUT BLACK–WHITE RELATIONS, BY DEMOGRAPHICS, 1995

DEMOGRAPHICS	ALWAYS A PROBLEM (PERCENT)	WILL FIND SOLUTIONS (PERCENT)
Gender		
Male	54	41
Female	55	40
Age		
18–29 years	58	37
30–49 years	56	41
50–64 years	51	46
65 and older	52	40
Region		
East	50	46
Midwest	55	42
South	57	37
West	56	39
Race		
White	55	40
Black	55	41
Race/gender		
White male	55	41
White female	54	41
Black male	46	48
Black female	62	36
Education completed		
High school or less	59	36
Some college	54	41
Bachelor's degree	51	45
College postgraduate	41	57
Political party		
Republican	61	35
Democrat	50	43
Independent	53	43
National	**54**	**41**

Notes: Respondents were asked, "Do you think that relations between blacks and whites will always be a problem for the United States, or that solutions will eventually be worked out?" The table does not show all the categories in the original Gallup Poll; nor does it show the percentage of respondents who did not have an opinion.

SOURCE: *Gallup Poll Monthly*, October 1995, p. 9.

TABLE 11.2.2 ATTITUDES ABOUT BLACK–WHITE RELATIONS, BY RACE, 1963, 1993, AND 1995

	ALWAYS A PROBLEM (PERCENT)	WILL FIND SOLUTIONS (PERCENT)
1963		
White	44	53
Black	26	70
1993		
White	53	44
Black	55	44
1995		
White	55	40
Black	55	41

Notes: Respondents were asked, "Do you think that relations between blacks and whites will always be a problem for the United States, or that solutions will eventually be worked out?" The table does not show all the categories in the original Gallup Poll; nor does it show the percentage of respondents who did not have an opinion.

SOURCE: *Gallup Poll Monthly*, October 1995, p. 9.

EXERCISE 11.3 ASSESSING MINORITY ECONOMIC GAINS

BACKGROUND

The urban riots in the late 1960s were a grim reminder that the American dream didn't always come true. After racial disorders in Newark and Detroit in July 1967, President Johnson appointed the Commission on Civil Disorders to examine the causes of the riots and to recommend actions that might prevent their recurrence. The commission quickly became known as the Kerner Commission, after its chair, Illinois governor Otto Kerner. Although the details and the findings of the commission's final report rarely are cited today, one of its conclusions spoke briefly but eloquently to the racial divisions in American society: "Our nation is moving toward two societies, one black, one white—separate and unequal."[3]

Chapter 7 of the Kerner Commission report focused on unemployment, the family structure, and social disorganization in the black community. The commission identified three major "Negro economic groups":

- A small middle- and upper-income group made up of individuals who share educational, occupational, and cultural characteristics with whites in the same socioeconomic class
- The largest category, African Americans whose incomes are above poverty level but who do not share educational or occupational characteristics with middle-class Americans
- A subpoverty-level group characterized by very "low educational, occupational, and income attainments"[4]

Social scientists use income as one measure of the comparative status of blacks and other minority groups in the United States to whites. The assumption underlying that index: The historical effects of discrimination have relegated many minority groups to lower economic ranks. Social scientists would argue that income is associated with education, which in turn is linked to employment: The better educated the individual, the more likely he or she is to work in a higher-paying profession. It follows, then, that for minority groups to improve their economic standing, discriminatory barriers have to be eliminated. And by extension, income is a reliable gauge of discriminatory practices in society.

ASSIGNMENT

Table 11.3 shows median household income in current and constant dollars for several racial or ethnic groups from 1980 to 1998. Remember that current dollars have not been adjusted for inflation; the constant dollars in the table are the inflation-adjusted value of the 1998 dollar.

1. The median income in current dollars for all households increased almost 120 percent between 1980 and 1998. What was the percentage increase for whites, blacks, and Hispanics over the same period?

Whites: ______________________________

Blacks: ______________________________

Hispanics: ______________________________

2. The median income in current dollars was higher for Hispanics than for blacks from 1980 to 1998, yet the percentage increase over the period was substantially higher for blacks. How do you explain this apparent contradiction?

____

____

____

[3] National Advisory Commission on Civil Disorders. *Report* (New York: Bantam Books, 1968), p. 1.

[4] Ibid., p. 251.

TABLE 11.3 MEDIAN HOUSEHOLD INCOME BY RACE/ETHNICITY, 1980–1998

	MEDIAN INCOME									
	CURRENT DOLLARS*					CONSTANT DOLLARS*				
YEAR	ALL HOUSEHOLDS ($)	WHITE ($)	BLACK ($)	ASIAN, PACIFIC ISLANDER ($)	HISPANIC ($)	ALL HOUSEHOLDS ($)	WHITE ($)	BLACK ($)	ASIAN, PACIFIC ISLANDER ($)	HISPANIC ($)
1980	17,710	18,684	10,764	NA	13,651	35,076	37,005	21,319	NA	27,037
1985	23,618	24,908	14,819	NA	17,465	31,717	33,450	19,901	NA	23,454
1988	27,225	28,781	16,407	32,267	20,359	33,255	35,155	20,041	39,413	24,868
1989	28,906	30,406	18,083	36,102	21,921	33,685	35,433	21,073	42,070	25,545
1991	30,126	31,569	18,807	36,449	22,691	31,962	33,493	19,953	38,670	24,074
1992	30,786	32,368	18,660	38,153	22,848	31,708	33,337	19,219	39,295	23,532
1993	31,241	32,960	19,533	38,347	22,886	31,241	32,960	19,533	38,347	22,866
1995	34,076	35,766	22,393	40,614	22,860	36,466	38,254	23,951	43,439	24,450
1998	38,885	40,912	25,351	46,637	28,330	38,885	40,912	25,351	46,637	28,330

* Current dollars are not adjusted for inflation; constant dollars have been adjusted as of 1993.

NA = not available.

SOURCE: *Statistical Abstract of the United States, 2000,* table 737, p. 466.

3. Look at the data from 1988 to 1998 for median income in constant dollars.

a. In the space below, indicate the percentage loss or gain for whites, blacks, and Hispanics over the period.

Whites: ______

Blacks: ______

Hispanics: ______

b. Compare your results for the three groups to the change in all households over the same period. (Calculate the constant-dollar change from 1988 to 1998 for all households and for each of the three groups. Then indicate how much higher or lower the all-household figure is than the equivalent figure for each of the three groups).

Whites: ______

Blacks: ______

Hispanics: ______

4. Formulate three hypotheses that explain why the median income for Hispanics lags so far behind the median income for all households. In your answers, guard against using ethnic or racial stereotypes as the bases for your hypotheses.

Hypothesis 1: ______

Hypothesis 2: ______

Hypothesis 3: ______

EXERCISE 11.4 THE GENDER WAGE GAP

BACKGROUND

Women in the United States have long been denied the economic, legal, political, and social standing granted men in American society. And they have been challenging those inequalities since the Republic came into being.

In 1920, women won a notable victory in the political realm with ratification of the Nineteenth Amendment, which gave women the right to vote. Still, tradition and stereotyping continued to relegate women to the domestic sphere, a world separate from the public and political world dominated by men. That changed—at least for a time—during World War II, when government and society asked women to leave the domestic sphere and work in the factories and at other nontraditional jobs as replacements for men who had gone off to war. After the war, though, millions of the women who had responded to wartime appeals to serve their nation were pressured once again to make a full-time commitment to home and family.

The status of women in American society finally began to change in the 1950s. Women were entering the workforce in greater numbers. Rising divorce rates had something to do with that. More important, a new generation of women was emerging from college with the goal of establishing professional careers. In 1963, Congress passed the Equal Pay Act to equalize the wages of men and women who performed the same jobs. Title VII of the Civil Rights Act of 1964 gave women the right to sue for gender discrimination. And in 1971, in *Reed v. Reed,* the Supreme Court issued a ruling that prohibits gender-based classification unless there is a valid reason for such classification. In *Reed,* an Idaho woman wanted to be appointed the administrator of her adopted son's estate following his death. At that time, Idaho law provided that when two equally qualified administrators sought appointment, the man should be designated over the woman. The Court held that the Idaho law was "the very kind of arbitrary legislative choice forbidden by the Equal Protection Clause." Although the states failed to ratify the proposed Equal Rights Amendment by the 1982 deadline, other Supreme Court decisions made it clear that women were no longer presumed inferior.[5]

Women have made enormous strides toward equality over the past forty years. They are winning elections; they are working in most professions; they are combat soldiers and officers in the military. Even our language reflects their new status in society: Editors delete all instances of gender stereotyping, and a phrase like *members of Congress* replaces the ubiquitous and no longer accurate *congressmen.* But economic discrimination remains a formidable problem for women in the workplace. Some claim that a glass ceiling prevents women from moving up to top-executive jobs; others charge that women are paid less than men for comparable work. According to the Department of Labor, for every dollar a man earned in 1979, a woman was paid 60 cents, 60 percent of what a man earned. By 2000, the rate had gone up to 72 percent.[6] Throughout the twentieth century, most women in professional fields found themselves limited to teaching or nursing. At the beginning of the twenty-first century, the largest group of women professionals is still teachers, but the number of women in managerial positions has increased tenfold.[7]

ASSIGNMENT

Table 11.4 shows data from 1988 and 1998 on selected occupations by gender. You'll need to refer to the table when answering the questions below. Then refer to Reading 11.4 to answer the questions that follow it.

1. a. According to the data in Table 11.4, in 1988 what was the ratio of the total median earnings for women to the total median earnings for men?

---

[5] For example, in 1975 the Court held that state laws that discourage women from serving on juries were unconstitutional (*Taylor v. Louisiana*). See David O'Brien, *Constitutional Law and Politics*, 2d ed., vol. 2 (New York: Norton, 1995), pp. 1446–1451, for other cases supporting the rights of women.

[6] Department of Labor, "Women's Earnings as a Percent of Men's, 1979–2000."

[7] Department of Labor, "Women at the Millennium, Accomplishments and Challenges Ahead."

TABLE 11.4 SELECT OCCUPATIONS AND SALARIES BY GENDER, 1988 AND 1998

	1988				1998			
	WOMEN		MEN		WOMEN		MEN	
OCCUPATIONAL CATEGORY	NUMBER (IN THOUSANDS)	MEDIAN EARNINGS	NUMBER (IN THOUSANDS)	MEDIAN EARNINGS	NUMBER (IN THOUSANDS)	MEDIAN EARNINGS	NUMBER (IN THOUSANDS)	MEDIAN EARNINGS
Executive, administrative, and managerial	4,880	$23,356	7,860	$36,759	7,125	$34,755	9,438	$51,351
Professional specialty	4,882	$25,789	6,458	$37,490	6,922	$36,261	7,768	$51,654
Technical and related support	1,208	$21,039	1,563	$30,369	1,612	$27,849	1,737	$40,546
Sales	3,273	$15,474	5,490	$27,022	4,182	$23,197	6,397	$37,248
Administrative support, including clerical	9,452	$16,676	2,706	$24,399	9,697	$23,835	3,004	$31,153
Precision, production, craft, and repair	799	$16,869	9,759	$25,746	927	$23,907	11,064	$31,631
Machine operators, assemblers, and inspectors	2,329	$13,289	3,741	$21,382	1,955	$19,015	3,953	$27,890
Transportation and material moving	169	$13,021	3,205	$23,453	268	$21,449	3,671	$30,422
Handlers, equipment cleaners, helpers, and laborers	372	$13,397	2,071	$17,042	544	$16,550	2,633	$21,871
Service workers	3,665	$11,032	3,655	$18,648	5,262	$15,647	4,881	$22,515
Private household	224	$7,299	13	*	245	$11,840	9	*
Other	3,441	$11,232	3,642	$18,670				
Farming, forestry, and fishing	194	$9,926	1,687	$14,300	235	$15,865	1,739	$18,855
Total	**31,237**	**$17,606**	**48,285**	**$26,656**	**38,785**	**$25,862**	**56,951**	**$35,345**

* Data are missing or too small to note.

SOURCES: *Statistical Abstract of the United States* (Washington, D.C.: Government Printing Office, 1990), p. 411; and *Statistical Abstract of the United States* (Washington, D.C.: Government Printing Office, 2000), p. 438.

b. According to the data in Table 11.4, what was the ratio in 1998?

c. Describe and characterize the change.

2. In what occupational category did the ranks of women increase most over the ten-year period?

3. a. According to the data in Table 11.4, in which occupational categories in 1988 did women make up less than 15 percent of the workforce?

b. What was the wage gap between men and women in those occupations in 1988? The wage gap is the difference—expressed as a percentage—between the average earnings of men and women in the same occupational category. To calculate the wage gap in a category, subtract the median earnings of women from the median earnings of men, and then divide the result by the median earnings of men. For example, the wage gap in the technical and related support category in 1988 was 31 percent:

$$\$30{,}369 - \$21{,}039 = \$9{,}330 \div \$30{,}369 = 0.31$$

4. a. According to the data in Table 11.4, in which occupational categories in 1998 did women make up less than 15 percent of the workforce?

b. What was the wage gap between men and women in those occupations in 1998?

5. Compare the wage gap for each of the occupational categories in your answers to questions 3 and 4.

a. Between 1988 and 1998, in which categories did the wage gap widen?

b. Between 1988 and 1998, in which categories did the wage gap narrow?

READING 11.4 THE FAIR PAY ACT OF 2001 (HR 1362)

SECTION 1. SHORT TITLE AND REFERENCE

(a) SHORT TITLE—This Act may be cited as the "Fair Pay Act of 2001."

(b) REFERENCE—Except as provided in section 8, whenever in this Act an amendment or repeal is expressed in terms of an amendment to, or repeal of, a section or other provision, the reference shall be considered to be made to a section or other provision of the Fair Labor Standards Act of 1938.

SECTION 2. FINDINGS

Congress finds the following:

(1) Wage rate differentials exist between equivalent jobs segregated by sex, race, and national origin in Government employment and in industries engaged in commerce or in the production of goods for commerce.

(2) The existence of such wage rate differentials—

(A) depresses wages and living standards for employees necessary for their health and efficiency;

(B) prevents the maximum utilization of the available labor resources;

(C) tends to cause labor disputes, thereby burdening, affecting, and obstructing commerce;

(D) burdens commerce and the free flow of goods in commerce; and

(E) constitutes an unfair method of competition.

(3) Discrimination in hiring and promotion has played a role in maintaining a segregated work force.

(4) Many women and people of color work in occupations dominated by individuals of their same sex, race, and national origin.

(5) (A) A General Accounting Office analysis of wage rates in the civil service of the State of Washington found that in 1985, of the 44 jobs studied that paid less than the average of all equivalent jobs, approximately 39 percent were female-dominated and approximately 16 percent were male dominated.

(B) A study of wage rates in Minnesota using 1990 Decennial Census data found that 75 percent of the wage rate differential between white and nonwhite workers was unexplained and may be a result of discrimination.

(6) Section 6(d) of the Fair Labor Standards Act of 1938 prohibits discrimination in compensation for "equal work" on the basis of sex.

(7) Title VII of the Civil Rights Act of 1964 prohibits discrimination in compensation because of race, color, religion, national origin, and sex. The Supreme Court, in its decision in *County of Washington v. Gunther* (1981) held that title VII's prohibition against discrimination in compensation also applies to jobs that do not constitute "equal work" as defined in section 6(d) of the Fair Labor Standards Act of 1938. Decisions of lower courts, however, have demonstrated that further clarification of existing legislation is necessary in order effectively to carry out the intent of Congress to implement the Supreme Court's holding in its *Gunther* decision.

(8) Artificial barriers to the elimination of discrimination in compensation based upon sex, race, and national origin continue to exist more than 3 decades after the passage of section 6(d) of the Fair Labor Standards Act of 1938 and the Civil Rights Act of 1964. Elimination of such barriers would have positive effects, including—

(A) providing a solution to problems in the economy created by discrimination through wage rate differentials;

(B) substantially reducing the number of working women and people of color earning low wages, thereby reducing the dependence on public assistance; and

(C) promoting stable families by enabling working family members to earn a fair rate of pay.

SECTION 3. EQUAL PAY FOR EQUIVALENT JOBS

(a) AMENDMENT—Section 6 is amended by adding at the end the following:

"(h) (1)(A) Except as provided in subparagraph (B), no employer having employees subject to any provision of this section shall discriminate, within any establishment in which such employees are employed, between employees on the basis of sex, race, or national origin by paying wages to employees in such establishment in a job that is dominated by employees of a particular sex, race, or national origin at a rate less than the rate at which the employer pays wages to employees in such establishment in another job that is dominated by employees of the opposite sex or of a different race or national origin, respectively, for work on equivalent jobs.

"(B) Nothing in subparagraph (A) shall prohibit the payment of different wage rates to employees where such payment is made pursuant to—

"(i) a seniority system;

"(ii) a merit system;

"(iii) a system that measures earnings by quantity or quality of production; or

"(iv) a differential based on a bona fide factor other than sex, race, or national origin, such as education, training, or experience, except that this clause shall apply only if—

"(I) the employer demonstrates that—

"(aa) such factor—

"(AA) is job-related with respect to the position in question; or

"(BB) furthers a legitimate business purpose, except that this item shall not apply if the employee demonstrates that an alternative employment practice exists that would serve the same business purpose without producing such differential and that the employer has refused to adopt such alternative practice; and

"(bb) such factor was actually applied and used reasonably in light of the asserted justification; and

"(II) upon the employer succeeding under subclause (I), the employee fails to demonstrate that the differential produced by the reliance of the employer on such factor is itself the result of discrimination on the basis of sex, race, or national origin by the employer.

"(C) The Equal Employment Opportunity Commission shall issue guidelines specifying criteria for determining whether a job is dominated by employees of a particular sex, race, or national origin. Such guidelines shall not include a list of such jobs.

"(D) An employer who is paying a wage rate differential in violation of subparagraph (A) shall not, in order to comply with the provisions of such subparagraph, reduce the wage rate of any employee. . . ."

6. Review sections 1 through 3 of the Fair Pay Act of 2001 (Reading 11.4). In no more than two sentences, state the purpose of HR 1362.

7. Read Section 2 of HR 1362, Findings. In your view, what are the three most damaging results of wage rate differentials between women and men?

8. Read Section 3 of HR 1362, Equivalent Pay for Equivalent Jobs. In your own words, explain when the payment of different wage rates is permitted under the bill.

9. Go to the Employment Policy Foundation home page at www.epf.org. Click on Research and then on EPF Research Listed by Topic. Select "Comparable Worth and Pay Equity" and then the May 4, 2000, article, "Background on Comparable Worth," by Anita U. Hattiangadi. Identify two important objections Hattiangadi raises against pay equity and comparable-worth legislation.

10. According to Hattiangadi, what factors beside gender discrimination in the workplace account for the pay gap between men and women?

11. Go to the AFL-CIO home page at www.aflcio.org. Click on Working Women and then on How Much Will the Pay Gap Cost YOU? At the bottom of the page, click on The Case for Equal Pay. Summarize the AFL-CIO's case for equal pay.

12. In "The Case for Equal Pay," the AFL-CIO identifies several arguments against equal pay and counters each of those arguments.

a. In your view, for which argument against equal pay is the AFL-CIO's counterargument most persuasive? Explain and support your answer.

b. In your view, for which argument against equal pay is the AFL-CIO's counterargument least persuasive? Explain and support your answer.

EXERCISE 11.5 THE END OF AFFIRMATIVE ACTION?

BACKGROUND

One of the most controversial methods of compensating for discriminatory practices has been the use of affirmative-action policies. President Franklin Roosevelt acknowledged racial discrimination in the workplace in 1941, when he issued Executive Order 8802, which established the Fair Employment Practices Commission, a federal board. But it was not until 1965, when President Johnson issued Executive Order 11246, that affirmative action became an official policy. Initially, affirmative action was targeted at blacks; but in time its application was expanded to members of other minority groups and to women—to what activists called *underrepresented groups.* Where discriminatory practices had closed doors to members of minority groups seeking admission to colleges and universities and employment in the public and private sectors, affirmative action was intended to open those doors. Under affirmative action, when everyone in the applicant pool has similar qualifications, members of minority groups are favored over white male applicants. The assumption was always that as minority representation in colleges and universities and in the workplace increased, the need for affirmative-action policies would disappear.

Affirmative-action programs never enjoyed popular support for two basic reasons. First, many whites believed that they were now the victims of reverse discrimination, that they were now at a disadvantage in education and employment because of discriminatory practices that were prevalent years, if not generations, before they were born. Second, some of the early affirmative-action programs set quotas for minority representation. So, for example, a medical school might reserve a certain number of first-year slots exclusively for members of minority groups, in the process denying admission to what might have been better-qualified white applicants. Even after the Supreme Court declared the use of quotas unconstitutional in most cases, opponents of affirmative action insisted that quotas were still in effect—now under the guise of goals.

The U.S. Supreme Court first addressed affirmative action in 1978, in *Regents of the University of California v. Bakke.* Alan Bakke was twice rejected for admission to the UC-Davis medical school. The university had reserved sixteen of the one hundred openings for applicants who were economically or educationally "disadvantaged." Because some minority applicants who were statistically less qualified were accepted under the special-admissions program, Bakke charged that his equal protection rights under the Fourteenth Amendment had been violated. The Court agreed with Bakke. A majority of the justices held that quotas were unacceptable, although they also agreed that race and other nonacademic factors could be considered in the admissions process.[8] In other Supreme Court rulings, the justices upheld affirmative-action programs when there was clear evidence of past discrimination against minorities or women, when the remedial programs to counter that discrimination were voluntary, and when those programs were of limited duration.[9] A defeat for affirmative action in higher education came in 1996, in *Hopwood v. Texas,* when a federal court of appeals held that the admissions policies of the University of Texas law school denied equal protection to white applicants.

There is no doubt that affirmative action has opened many doors to underrepresented groups, but as one political scientist has noted, black males have not been the prime beneficiaries of affirmative action, at least in employment: "By and large white men have been displaced by white women, Asians, and black women. Except for two blue-collar occupations—electricians and sheet-metal workers—black men made smaller gains than members of those other groups."[10] Some critics charge that affirmative-action programs would garner more support if they were directed toward the underclass, people of all races and ethnicities who are mired in poverty, instead of focusing on race and ethnicity.

In 1995, the University of California Board of Regents voted to end affirmative-action admissions at the state's public universities. The move was led by Ward Connerly, an African American who had been appointed a regent by Republican Governor Pete Wilson. Wilson and Connerly also became instrumental in qualifying the California Civil Rights Initiative (CCRI) for the November 1996 general

---

[8] Lee Epstein and Thomas G. Walker, *Constitutional Law for a Changing America: Rights, Liberties, and Justice* (Washington, D.C.: CQ Press, 1992), pp. 557–563.

[9] See, for example, *United Steelworkers of America v. Weber* (1979) and *Johnson v. Transportation Agency* (1987).

[10] Andrew Hacker, "Goodbye to Affirmative Action?" *New York Review of Books,* July 11, 1996, p. 27.

election. The CCRI did not mention affirmative action by name, although the main thrust of the measure was to abolish affirmative-action programs in public education, government employment, and government contracting (see Reading 11.5). Proponents of the measure argued that the initial goals of affirmative action had been subverted over the years, that thirty years of affirmative-action programs had leveled the playing field, and that the programs were largely demeaning to minorities. Opponents countered that women and minorities benefited from the programs because of past and present discrimination and that the CCRI promoted racial divisiveness.[11] California voters approved the initiative, Proposition 209, with 54 percent of the vote. Shortly thereafter, the University of California initiated a policy of guaranteeing admission to one of its nine campuses to the top 4 percent of the graduating class of each high school in the state, so long as the prerequisite courses had been completed successfully. When this policy failed to maintain diversity at the most competitive campuses in the system, the university decided in 2001 to replace the Scholastic Aptitude Test, on which minorities commonly have low scores, with achievement tests that measure subject matter and skill preparation. Additionally, the university is engaging in a more comprehensive review of applicants, a review that includes other indicators of potential—for example, difficulties overcome—not just grades and test scores.

ASSIGNMENT

The CCRI is reprinted in Reading 11.5. The questions that follow the reading are based on the ballot measure.

READING 11.5 THE CALIFORNIA CIVIL RIGHTS INITIATIVE

PROPOSED AMENDMENT TO ARTICLE I [of the California Constitution]

SEC. 31. (a) The state shall not discriminate against, or grant preferential treatment to, any individual or group on the basis of race, sex, color, ethnicity, or national origin in the operation of public employment, public education, or public contracting.

(b) This section shall apply only to action taken after the section's effective date.

(c) Nothing in this section shall be interpreted as prohibiting bona fide qualifications based on sex which are reasonably necessary to the normal operation of public employment, public education, or public contracting.

(d) Nothing in this section shall be interpreted as invalidating any court order or consent decree which is in force as of the effective date of this section.

(e) Nothing in this section shall be interpreted as prohibiting action which must be taken to establish or maintain eligibility for any federal program, where ineligibility would result in a loss of federal funds to the state.

(f) For the purposes of this section, "state" shall include, but not necessarily be limited to the state itself, any city, county, city and county, public university system, including the University of California, community college district, school district, special district, or any other political subdivision or governmental instrumentality of or within the state.

(g) The remedies available for violations of this section shall be the same, regardless of the injured party's race, sex, color, ethnicity, or national origin, as are otherwise available for violations of then-existing California antidiscrimination law.

(h) This section shall be self-executing. If any part or parts of this section are found to be in conflict with federal law or the United States Constitution, the section shall be implemented to the maximum extent that federal law and the United States Constitution permit. Any provision held invalid shall be severable from the remaining portions of this section.

---

1. The CCRI prohibits preferential treatment based on a number of characteristics, but it does not mention economic class. Would it be possible under the CCRI for a public university in California to

[11] A. G. Bloc, "Proposition 209: Affirmative Action," *California Journal*, September 1996, pp. 8–10.

give admission preference to applicants from "economically disadvantaged backgrounds" in any of its undergraduate or graduate programs? Cite the initiative to support your answer.

____

____

____

____

____

____

2. Do you think it's appropriate for a state university system to use economic disadvantage as a criterion for admissions to diversify its professional programs—for example, its engineering and law programs? Explain and support your answer.

____

____

____

____

____

____

3. Clause (c) of the CCRI allows gender-based discrimination that is "reasonably necessary." In the space below, give two examples of situations in which gender-based discrimination might be reasonably necessary, and explain why it would be justified.

Example 1: ____

____

____

Example 2: ____

____

____

CIVIL LIBERTIES

EXERCISE 12.1 DRUG TESTING AND THE RIGHT TO PRIVACY

BACKGROUND

All of the states and the national government have increased the criminal penalties for those found guilty of possessing or selling drugs. The sole exception: the laws that govern possession of small amounts of marijuana. In some states, possession of a few ounces of marijuana is just a citable offense or a misdemeanor. Alaska is the only state that allows the cultivation of marijuana for personal use. But it is clear that penalties for possessing or selling hard drugs are considerably tougher today than they were several decades ago.

The intent of the tougher penalties is to discourage drug use. Whether these penalties have reduced the recreational use of cocaine and other stimulants is debatable. For example, over the past several decades there have been periods when teenage use of drugs has gone down only to go back up after several years. Drugs became an issue in the 1996 presidential campaign, when Republican challenger Bob Dole criticized President Bill Clinton for not doing enough to combat drug use. As Dole noted, marijuana use had decreased yearly between 1985 and 1991—for most of those years, there was a Republican in the White House—but then increased dramatically among 12- to 17-year-olds beginning in 1992.[1] Dole's issue did not win him the election in 1996; nor did it find much of an audience in the 2000 presidential contest.

According to civil libertarians, efforts to curb drug use pose threats to individual privacy. One privacy issue involves drug testing and the language in the Fourth Amendment that protects people "against unreasonable searches and seizures" except where there is probable cause. According to the Supreme Court, drug testing is reasonable for employees in "safety-sensitive" jobs—railroad engineers and airline pilots, for example—as well as for those who carry firearms.[2] The Court also recognizes that some forms of drug testing are more intrusive than others. For example, breath and urine tests are

---

[1] Christopher Wren, "Youths Confide Buying Drugs as Easy as Beer," *New York Times*, October 10, 1996, p. A1.

[2] *Skinner v. Railway Labor Executives Association* (1989); and *Treasury Employees v. Von Raab* (1989).

less intrusive than blood tests, which require penetration of the skin. Many companies routinely test prospective employees for drugs as a condition for working. But the Court has not given a green light to drug testing under all circumstances. In 1997, in *Chandler v. Miller,* the Court struck down a Georgia law that required candidates for public office to pass a drug test to qualify for a spot on the ballot. According to the Court, Georgia offered no proof of a drug problem among its political candidates, and so the testing was not reasonable. In 2000, in *Ferguson v. City of Charleston,* the Court invalidated drug testing for indigent pregnant women who were using the medical services of a city hospital. A public hospital in Charleston, South Carolina, was giving drug tests to pregnant women—without the women's knowledge—as a way to check for crack babies. The results of all positive tests were passed on to the police. In a 6–3 decision, the justices held that the hospital's failure to inform the women of the test and that positive results were being forwarded to the police constituted an infringement of their rights under the Fourth Amendment.

ASSIGNMENT

Reading 12.1 describes a random drug-testing policy in an Oregon school district and the outcome of a lawsuit challenging that policy. Refer to the reading to answer the questions that follow it.

READING 12.1 JUNIOR HIGH SCHOOL ATHLETES AND DRUG TESTING

Teachers and administrators in an Oregon school district were concerned about the increased use of drugs and disciplinary problems among junior high school students. Because they knew that drug use by students in athletics often resulted in sports-related injuries, and because they suspected that some athletes were using drugs, school district officials called a meeting with parents. In September 1989, parents gave their unanimous approval to a urine drug-test proposal with these conditions:

- Students who wanted to participate in interscholastic athletics had to sign a form agreeing to the drug test. (Their parents also had to sign the form.)
- All athletes were to be tested at the beginning of their team's season.
- Ten percent of the athletes would be subject to a random urine test at various times during the season.

In the fall of 1991, a seventh-grade student was not allowed to take part in the district's football program because he and his parents refused to sign the consent form. The student and his parents filed suit seeking an injunction to halt the drug testing on the grounds that it violated the Fourth Amendment to the Constitution. School district officials maintained that the testing was reasonable and appropriate, given their concern about sports safety. They also argued that participation in the sports programs was voluntary and that the drug testing was done in a manner that respected individual privacy. Moreover, the school district argued that public school students do not enjoy the same level of constitutional protection that adults do.

In a 6–3 decision, the Supreme Court agreed. That the Court supported the drug-testing policy is typical of its deference to public school authorities, who, according to the Court, have a "compelling interest" in the educational program and the safety of its underage participants. The Court generally strikes down a school district policy or action only if that policy or action is an unreasonable exercise of authority. And since the Court ruled in this case, the federal courts have allowed random drug testing of participants in all extracurricular activities.

---

1. Identify at least two reasons why the Oregon school district would argue that the random drug testing was reasonable.

____

____

READING SOURCE: From *Vernonia School District v. Acton,* 132 L.Ed. 2d (1995).

2. Identify at least two reasons why the student's parents would argue that the random drug testing was unreasonable.

3. The random drug testing in Oregon developed out of a concern about drug use among all students, not just the athletes. The test was imposed on athletes because of their increased risk of injury. Do you think drug testing would be more reasonable if all students were tested at the beginning of the year and then randomly tested throughout the academic year? Explain your answer.

4. In your view, would it be morally and legally more acceptable to use student informants to identify and report drug use among specific students than to have all student athletes subjected to the drug test? Why or why not?

5. This particular drug-testing policy has been held constitutional for public school athletes, who are minors. Do you think it would be reasonable to implement a similar policy among public school teachers on the grounds that adults also use illegal drugs, that the behavior and lifestyles of teachers have significant influence on students, and that teachers cannot very well educate and protect the safety of students when they themselves might be using illegal drugs? Explain and support your answer.

EXERCISE 12.2 DEFINING OBSCENITY: IS THERE AN ANSWER?

BACKGROUND

The wording of the First Amendment should be familiar:

> Congress shall make no law respecting an establishment of religion, or prohibiting the free exercise thereof; or abridging the freedom of speech, or of the press; or the right of the people peaceably to assemble, and to petition the Government for a redress of grievances.

The generalities in the amendment have forced the Supreme Court to define each of the rights noted there. A few examples: Is *religion* a national church or any religious belief? Can *speech* be an action—burning the flag, for example? Does *press* include television and motion pictures?

One major headache for the Supreme Court has been distinguishing between speech that is protected from speech that does not fall within the freedom of the First Amendment. The justices consistently have held that obscenity is not protected speech, but they have not been able to define exactly what constitutes obscenity. Until 1934, U.S. courts tended to adhere to the test established in an English case, *Regina v. Hicklin* (1868): "The test of *obscenity* is this, whether the tendency of the matter charged as *obscenity* is to deprave and corrupt those whose minds are open to such immoral influences, and into whose hands a publication of this sort may fall." In 1934 a court of appeals rejected the *Hicklin* test because it focused on isolated passages of a work as they might be interpreted by the most suggestible person in the country. At issue in the case was James Joyce's classic, *Ulysses.* Said Judge Augustus Hand: "The proper test of whether a given book is obscene is its dominant effect. . . . For works of art are not likely to sustain a high position with no better warrant for their existence than obscene content."

In 1957, Justice Brennan enunciated a new standard in *Roth v. United States:* "Whether to the average person, applying contemporary community standards, the dominant theme of the material taken as a whole appeals to prurient interests."[3] In short order, the *Roth* test created problems of its own because of the ambiguity of *average person, contemporary community standards,* and *prurient interests.* In 1964, in *Jacobellis v. Ohio,* Brennan wrote that *obscenity* is expression that is "utterly without redeeming social importance." That definition didn't prove particularly useful either, and the Court continued to hear obscenity-conviction appeals, asking for clarification. In 1973, Chief Justice Warren Burger entered the fray in *Miller v. California.* Burger, writing the majority opinion, wanted clearly defined rules for pornography prosecutions. To that end he

- retained the prurient-interest test.
- rejected the utterly-without-redeeming-social-importance test.
- redefined the idea of community standards to mean local standards.
- created a new criterion—"whether the work taken as a whole lacks serious literary, artistic, political, or scientific value."

Warren's decision didn't still the debate over the definition of obscenity, but it moved the arena to the state courts.[4]

One difficulty in defining *obscenity* is that obscenity changes. Sometimes that change reflects changing social standards. Before World War II, for example, most states had laws prohibiting the utterance of certain expletives in front of women. Today, none do. Sometimes the change is a product of technology. A case in point: monitoring material on the Internet. Guidelines and censors work effectively to control what's shown on television and in the movies; but there is no equivalent system on the Net. The problem is compounded by the accessibility of the Net: A computer and a phone line connect the user—any user, no matter how young—to thousands of sites. And to date, neither filters nor codes work effectively to allow adults access to certain material while blocking children's access to the same material.

---

[3] Lee Epstein and Thomas G. Walker, *Constitutional Law for a Changing America: Rights, Liberties, and Justice* (Washington, D.C.: CQ Press, 1992), pp. 230–232.

[4] See David O'Brien, *Constitutional Law and Politics,* 2d ed., vol. 2 (New York: Norton, 1995), pp. 420–424.

ASSIGNMENT

Reading 12.2 is a hypothetical example of a law that attempts to regulate what can be transmitted on the Internet. Refer to the reading to answer the questions that follow it.

READING 12.2 A Hypothetical Decency Law for the Internet in the State of Old Hampshire

In an effort to protect children from sexually oriented material on the Internet, the legislators of Old Hampshire passed, and the governor signed into law, the Communications Decency Act of 1997. There are two key provisions in the act:

> Section 1. Any person who makes, creates, solicits, or initiates the transmission of any comment, request, suggestion, proposal, image, or other communication that is obscene, indecent, lewd, or lascivious, knowing the recipient of the communication is under 18 years of age, shall be criminally fined or imprisoned.
>
> Section 2. It is a crime to use an interactive computer service to send or display to a person under age 18 any communication that, in context, depicts or describes, in terms patently offensive as measured by contemporary community standards, sexual or excretory activities or organs, regardless of whether the user of such service placed the call or initiated the communication.

Louise Thomas, a 35-year-old sexual consultant in Onetwothree, Old Hampshire, was charged and convicted of violating the law after she sent graphic images and explicit descriptions of sexual intercourse between an adult male and an adult female and between two adult males to seven minors, ages 13 to 17, in a nearby community. The Old Hampshire Supreme Court upheld Thomas's conviction despite her claims that she had asked the seven teenagers via e-mail if they were adults. At trial, the teens all acknowledged that they had said they were adults.

Thomas has appealed her conviction to the U.S. Supreme Court on the grounds that the Old Hampshire decency law violates her First Amendment rights.

---

1. Onetwothree, Old Hampshire, is a city of 39,000, down from almost 70,000 thirty-five years ago. The population shrunk after most of the light-manufacturing businesses in the city closed. Most of the citizens of Onetwothree are over age 54. Section 2 of the decency law refers to "contemporary community standards." What are two credible ways of determining those standards in Onetwothree?

Method 1: ______________________________

____

Method 2: ______________________________

____

2. Thomas asked the seven teenagers if they were adults, and they all lied and said yes. Should she be held legally responsible for sending information to the teens after they lied to her about their ages? Explain and support your answer. Remember that it would have been legal to disseminate the information to the seven teens if they were the adults they claimed to be.

____

____

____

____

____

3. Apply one of the obscenity tests set forth by Chief Justice Burger in *Miller* to the material disseminated by Thomas. Would the material pass or fail the obscenity test? Explain and support your answer.

4. Assume that contemporary community standards in Onetwothree would find that the materials Thomas sent over the Internet are obscene, but that standards 100 miles away in Berkeley, the home of liberal Old Hampshire State University, would not find the material obscene. Would it be sound policy for the U.S. Supreme Court to uphold the decency law when the standards might vary from one community to another? Explain and support your answer.

5. Assume that the seven teenagers lived in a neighboring state that does not have an Internet decency act. Could Thomas still be prosecuted for transmitting her material on the Internet from Old Hampshire to those under 18 in another state? Explain and support your answer with reference to the constitutional principle of federalism.

EXERCISE 12.3 HOMOSEXUALS, PRIVACY, AND THE SUPREME COURT

BACKGROUND

The Constitution addresses the right of privacy only by implication, and only in the Fourth Amendment: "The right of the people to be secure in their persons, houses, papers, and effects, against unreasonable search and seizures."[5] Not surprisingly, then, the Supreme Court has had to grapple with the concept of privacy. In *Griswold v. Connecticut* (1965), the High Court held that a married couple's right to privacy was violated by a state law that prohibited them from obtaining information about the use of contraceptives. In *Stanley v. Georgia* (1969), the Court found that people can watch sexually explicit movies in their own homes. The Court also has found that the concept of privacy supports a woman's right to an abortion (*Roe v. Wade,* 1973), but that there is no expectation of privacy for the contents of trash bags left at the curb for pickup (*California v. Greenwood,* 1988).

Here, too, changing social standards have posed problems for the Court, especially in cases involving sexual behavior between consenting adults. As tolerance for private sexual behavior has grown, the Court has applied privacy rights to consensual heterosexual sex between adults. But it has yet to extend privacy rights to homosexuals. Although many states have struck down their own anti-gay laws, the legal rights of gays are still being contested.

The gay rights movement began with a riot in New York City in 1969, when city police raided the Stonewall Inn, a gay bar. At that time, it was illegal for people of the same gender to dance together. Like those who fought for civil rights and women's rights, gay rights activists pushed for equality along a number of fronts. Their successes have been modest: In 1973, the American Psychiatric Association removed homosexuality from its list of psychiatric disorders; in 1975, California passed a law allowing all private sexual acts between consenting adults. In 1993, President Clinton failed to persuade Congress to repeal its ban on homosexuals in the military, but he was able to get a "Don't ask, don't tell" policy enacted. Gays can still be discharged from the military for homosexual acts, but they can't be discharged for simply being homosexual. That policy angered many gay rights activists, who claim that it doesn't work because it's enforced in a discriminatory manner.

At the local level, many cities and businesses have adopted domestic-partner policies that extend medical insurance and other benefits to those in same-sex relationships. In 2000, Vermont became the first state to enact legislation that gave recognition to same-sex unions, with legal benefits similar to those of marriage. Florida is the only state that prohibits gays from adopting children, although it does allow gays to serve as foster parents.

The U.S. Supreme Court has not supported the rights of gays. In *Boy Scouts of America v. Dale* (2000), the Court held that the Boy Scouts could ban gays because it is a private organization and because its creed prohibits homosexuality.

The Court's ruling in *Bowers v. Hardwick* (1986), which is excerpted in Reading 12.3, still stands as a landmark decision on sexual privacy. In August 1982, a police officer in Atlanta went to the home of Michael Hardwick to serve him with an arrest warrant for failure to appear in court on a charge of drinking in public.[6] A roommate responded to the officer's knock, said he didn't know if Michael was home or not, and invited the officer in to check. As the officer walked down a hallway, he noticed a bedroom door ajar and inside saw Michael and another male engaged in oral sex. The officer ticketed the two for violating Georgia's sodomy statute, a law prohibiting oral or anal sex that had been passed in 1816 and that carried a twenty-year prison term. Then the officer searched the bedroom and uncovered a small amount of marijuana. The two men were arrested, taken to the police station, and booked. The arrest warrant that brought the police officer to Hardwick's home in the first place was never served. It turned out that Hardwick had paid the $50 fine for his public drinking charge; the warrant should have been canceled.

Hardwick subsequently pleaded guilty to misdemeanor possession of marijuana and paid a fine. He was not tried on the sodomy offense. The American Civil Liberties Union had been watching for a

[5] The Court has said that there are "penumbras" (shadows) in other amendments that support the idea of a constitutional right of privacy. Those other amendments include the First, Third, Fourth, Ninth, and Tenth.

[6] The fascinating background to Michael Hardwick's arrest and challenge to the Georgia sodomy law is found in Peter Irons, *The Courage of Their Convictions* (New York: Penguin, 1990), chap. 16.

case to challenge the constitutionality of the Georgia sodomy statute. Attorneys for the ACLU convinced Hardwick that his was that case. Because the district attorney never brought Hardwick's sodomy offense to the grand jury for indictment, the ACLU got the case before a federal judge. The attorneys argued that Hardwick's rights of privacy and due process, and freedoms of expression and association had been violated. The attorneys lost in the federal trial court, but they were successful before a federal appellate court, which found that private sexual activity between consenting adults was protected. The state of Georgia appealed that ruling to the U.S. Supreme Court. In 1986, the justices in a 5–4 vote, upheld the constitutionality of the sodomy statute. In late 1998, the Georgia Supreme Court held the state's sodomy statute an unconstitutional invasion of privacy.

In 1998, Matthew Shepard, a 21-year-old University of Wyoming student, was savagely beaten and left tied to a fence one night. He died five days later. Although the two young men who killed Shepard denied they attacked him because he was gay, his death outraged gays and sympathetic straights across the nation.

ASSIGNMENT

Portions of the majority and dissenting opinions in *Bowers v. Hardwick* are found in Reading 12.3. Georgia's attorney general, Michael Bowers, was the plaintiff in the appeal. Refer to the reading to answer the questions that follow it.

READING 12.3 *Bowers v. Hardwick*, 478 U.S. 186 (1986)

Justice White (opinion of the Court):

This case does not require a judgment on whether laws against sodomy between consenting adults in general, or between homosexuals in particular, are wise or desirable. It raises no question about the rights or propriety of state legislative decisions to repeal their laws that criminalize homosexual sodomy, or of state court decisions invalidating those laws on state constitutional grounds. The issue presented is whether the Federal Constitution confers a fundamental right upon homosexuals to engage in sodomy and hence invalidates the laws of the many States that still make such conduct illegal and have done so for a very long time. The case also calls for some judgment about the limits of the Court's role in carrying out its constitutional mandate.

Striving to assure itself and the public that announcing rights not readily identifiable in the Constitution's text involves much more than the imposition of the Justices' own choice of values on the States and the Federal Government, the Court has sought to identify the nature of the rights qualifying for heightened judicial protection. In *Palko v. Connecticut*, . . . (1937), it was said that this category includes those fundamental liberties that are "implicit in the concept of ordered liberty," such that "neither liberty nor justice would exist if [they] were sacrificed." A different description of fundamental liberties appeared in *Moore v. East Cleveland*, . . . (1977) . . . , where they are characterized as those liberties that are "deeply rooted in this Nation's history and tradition. . . ."

It is obvious to us that neither of these formulations would extend a fundamental right to homosexuals to engage in acts of consensual sodomy. Proscriptions against that conduct have ancient roots. Sodomy was a criminal offense at common law and was forbidden by the laws of the original thirteen States when they ratified the Bill of Rights. In 1868, when the Fourteenth Amendment was ratified, all but 5 of the 37 States in the Union had criminal sodomy laws. In fact, until 1961, all 50 States outlawed sodomy, and today, 24 States and the District of Columbia continue to provide criminal penalties for sodomy performed in private and between consenting adults. Against this background, to claim that a right to engage in such conduct is "deeply rooted in this Nation's history and tradition" or "implicit in the concept of ordered liberty" is, at best, facetious.

Nor are we inclined to take a more expansive view of our authority to discover new fundamental rights imbedded in the Due Process Clause. The Court is most vulnerable and comes nearest to illegitimacy when it deals with judge-made constitutional law having little or no cognizable roots in the language or design of the Constitution.

Justice Powell (concurring):

I join the opinion of the Court. I agree with the Court that there is no fundamental right—i.e., no substantive right under the Due Process Clause—such as that claimed by respondent, and found to exist by the Court of Appeals. This is not to suggest, however, that respondent may not be protected by the Eighth Amendment of the Constitution. The Georgia statute at issue in this case . . . authorizes a court to imprison a person for up to 20 years for a single private, consensual act of sodomy. In my view, a prison sentence for such conduct—certainly a sentence of long duration—would create a serious Eighth Amendment issue. . . .

In this case, however, respondent has not been tried, much less convicted and sentenced. Moreover, respondent has not raised the Eighth Amendment issue below. For these reasons this constitutional argument is not before us.

Justice Blackmun (joined by Justice Brennan, Justice Marshall, and Justice Stevens, dissenting):

This case is no more about "a fundamental right to engage in homosexual sodomy," as the Court purports to declare, than *Stanley v. Georgia,* . . . (1969) was about a fundamental right to watch obscene movies. . . . Rather, this case is about "the most comprehensive of rights and the right most valued by civilized men," namely, "the right to be left alone." . . .

In a variety of circumstances we have recognized that a necessary corollary of giving individuals freedom to choose how to conduct their lives is acceptance of the fact that different individuals will make different choices. For example, in holding that the clearly important state interest in public education should give way to a competing claim by the Amish to the effect that extended formal schooling threatened their way of life, the Court declared: "There can be no assumption that today's majority is 'right' and the Amish and others like them are 'wrong.' A way of life that is odd or even erratic but interferes with no rights or interests of others is not to be condemned because it is different." *Wisconsin v. Yoder,* . . . (1972). The Court claims that its decision today merely refuses to recognize a fundamental right to engage in homosexual sodomy; what the Court really has refused to recognize is the fundamental interest all individuals have in controlling the nature of their intimate associations with others.

Justice Stevens (joined by Justice Brennan and Justice Marshall, dissenting):

Our prior cases make two propositions abundantly clear. First, the fact that the governing majority in a State has traditionally viewed a particular practice as immoral is not a sufficient reason for upholding a law prohibiting the practice; neither history nor tradition could save a law prohibiting miscegenation from constitutional attack. Second, individual decisions by married persons concerning the intimacies of their physical relationship, when not intended to produce offspring, are a form of "liberty" protected by the Due Process Clause of the Fourteenth Amendment. . . .

If the Georgia statute cannot be enforced as it is written—if the conduct it seeks to prohibit is a protected form of liberty for the vast majority of Georgia's citizens—the State must assume the burden of justifying a selective application of its law. Either the persons to whom Georgia seeks to apply its statute do not have the same interest in "liberty" that others have, or there must be a reason why the State may be permitted to apply a generally applicable law to certain persons that it does not apply to others.

. . . A policy of selective application must be supported by a neutral and legitimate interest—something more substantial than a habitual dislike for, or ignorance about, the disfavored group. Neither the State nor the Court has identified any such interest in this case. . . .

1. a. What does Justice Byron White, who wrote the majority opinion, identify as the constitutional issue in *Bowers v. Hardwick?*

b. How did White's definition of the constitutional issue predetermine the ruling in the case?

2. What does Justice Harry Blackmun's dissenting opinion identify as the constitutional issue in the case?

3. In his concurring decision, Justice Lewis Powell notes that he would have been troubled if Hardwick had been found guilty of sodomy and sentenced to prison. What is the Eighth Amendment issue in this case?

4. Consider this point made by Justice John Paul Stevens in his dissenting opinion: "Either the persons to whom Georgia seeks to apply its statute do not have the same interest in 'liberty' that others have, or there must be a reason why the State may be permitted to apply a generally applicable law to certain persons that it does not apply to others."

a. What does Stevens mean? What Fourteenth Amendment issue is he raising?

b. Do you agree or disagree with the justice's position? Explain and support your answer.

EXERCISE 12.4 LIBEL

BACKGROUND

The Supreme Court consistently has held that libel is not protected expression under the First Amendment. *Libel* is the defamation of character in print or by other visual means; *slander* is oral defamation. The problem for the Court has been defining *defamation* in a way that does not jeopardize material that is "merely offensive" and that therefore is protected by the First Amendment.

Most libel cases are filed as civil claims: Plaintiffs seek compensatory and/or punitive damages from those responsible for the defamatory material. *Compensatory damages* are intended to compensate the injured party for actual financial losses—say a loss of employment or earning power. *Punitive damages* are intended to compensate the victim for suffering and to inflict financial loss on the libeler, to prevent libel's happening again.

The Supreme Court has established three categories of libel as it applies to individuals:

- *Public officials* are those who are elected or appointed to public office. In a landmark decision, *New York Times v. Sullivan* (1964), the Court held that a public official could not recover damages for libel unless that individual could prove actual malice or that an article was printed or a statement made "with knowledge that it was false or with reckless regard of whether it was false or not." The Court's decision was based on the principle that public debate about a public official needs to be free, open, and uninhibited, even if that means a public official's reputation is tarnished. The necessity of a free press in a free society means that the public's right to know prevails over a public official's reputation.
- A second category is reserved for *public figures,* movie stars and other celebrities. In general, the *Sullivan* test also applies to public figures, although public figures may have a better chance of proving libelous conduct if they can show that a reporter did not try to verify a story.
- The *Sullivan* standard does not apply to the third category, *private individuals.* In *Gertz v. Welch* (1974), a 5–4 majority of the Court held that private individuals do not have to prove malice in a libel action. The effect of *Gertz* is to give private citizens more protection from defamatory statements than public officials or public figures have.[7] In a libel or slander suit, private individuals need prove only that a statement was defamatory and false.

ASSIGNMENT

Refer to Reading 12.4 to answer the questions that follow it. Don't let the Supreme Court's decision in *Hustler Magazine v. Falwell* influence your answers.

READING 12.4 REVEREND JERRY FALWELL AND *HUSTLER* MAGAZINE

Hustler magazine is best known for its photographs of naked women in explicit sexual poses, not for satire. But in 1983, *Hustler* published a parody of an ad for Campari, an alcoholic beverage. The original series of Campari ads, which appeared in a number of magazines but never in *Hustler,* featured celebrities who, in interview format, talked about their "first time." At first glance, it looked as though the "first time" was referring to the interviewee's first sexual experience, but it was clear in reading the ads that the interviewees actually were talking about the first time they had experienced Campari.

In the *Hustler* parody, Reverend Jerry Falwell was the celebrity and his answers to the interviewer's questions were of a decidedly sexual nature. In the parody, Falwell spoke of getting drunk on Campari and having sex with his mother in an outhouse. He also was quoted saying he often got drunk before delivering his Sunday sermons. At the bottom of the ad, in small but legible print, ran this statement: **AD PARODY—NOT TO BE TAKEN SERIOUSLY.**

---

[7] For an overview of the Supreme Court's rulings on libel, see O'Brien, *Constitutional Law and Politics*, pp. 489–518.

READING SOURCE: Based on material in Lee Epstein and Thomas G. Walker, *Constitutional Law for a Changing America: Rights, Liberties, and Justice* (Washington, D.C.: CQ Press, 1992), pp. 261–265. A reprint of the *Hustler* parody appears on page 262 of the book.

Not surprisingly, Falwell, a televangelist and conservative commentator on politics and morality, took issue with the parody. He filed suit against *Hustler* and its publisher, Larry Flynt, seeking damages for invasion of privacy, libel, and intentional infliction of emotional distress. A U.S. district court judge in Virginia dismissed the invasion-of-privacy allegation, and the jury found the parody was not libelous because no reader would have believed the words or the behavior attributed to Falwell in the ad. But the jury awarded Falwell $200,000 in damages for "the intentional infliction of emotional distress." After the award was upheld by a court of appeals, Flynt appealed to the U.S. Supreme Court. In *Hustler Magazine v. Falwell* (1988), Chief Justice William Rehnquist posed the legal issue for the Court:

> This case presents us with a novel question involving First Amendment limitations upon a State's authority to protect its citizens from the intentional infliction of emotional distress. We must decide whether a public figure may recover damages for emotional harm caused by the publication of an ad parody offensive to him, and doubtless gross and repugnant in the eyes of most.

In the end, the Supreme Court reversed the award for emotional distress in an 8–0 vote. *

---

1. If you were on the federal court jury in Virginia, would you have supported the $200,000 award to Falwell for emotional distress? Why or why not? In your answer, consider the effect of the emotional-distress standard on freedom of speech and of the press.

2. The *Hustler* parody depicted Reverend Falwell as an incestuous drunk. Even though it was unlikely that anyone would believe the parody, does this sort of depiction warrant protection under the First Amendment freedom of expression? Explain and support your answer.

3. Do you think it's fair that public officials and public figures do not enjoy the same protection against damaging statements that private individuals do? Why or why not?

---

* Justice Anthony Kennedy did not join in consideration or decision of the case.

4. Do you think the satirical ad would have been found libelous if the warning—the parody disclaimer—had been omitted? Why or why not?

EXERCISE 12.5 REGULATING HATE SPEECH ON UNIVERSITY CAMPUSES

BACKGROUND

In 1977, the Chicago suburb of Skokie was the unlikely setting for a First Amendment controversy. That year, Frank Collins, the head of the Nationalist Socialist Party of America, announced that his pro-Nazi organization was going to hold a march in the community. Almost half of Skokie's 70,000 residents were Jews, among them 5,000 Holocaust survivors. Community leaders denounced the planned march and enacted several ordinances to prevent it from taking place. One of the ordinances required a parade permit; another mandated that groups obtain a $350,000 insurance bond; and a third prohibited passing out any information that intentionally "promotes and incites hatred against persons by reason of their race, national origins, or religion." The ACLU challenged the ordinances on the grounds that they violated the free-speech guarantees of the First Amendment. The community obtained an injunction against the march, but it was overturned by an Illinois appellate court that ruled the march could proceed but that no swastikas could be displayed. Early in 1978, the Illinois Supreme Court held that the neo-Nazis could wear swastikas. Finally, a federal court ruled that the ordinance prohibiting language that intentionally incites "hatred" was overly broad and so unconstitutional.[8]

The U.S. Supreme Court refused to hear the appeal in the Skokie case; in 1992 it did hand down an important ruling in a hate-speech case originating from St. Paul, Minnesota. Three years earlier, St. Paul had passed a city ordinance making it illegal to place on public or private property a burning cross, swastika, or other symbol, including graffiti that "one knows or has reasonable grounds to know arouses anger, alarm, or resentment in others on the basis of race, color, creed, religion or gender." A white teenager was arrested and charged with violating the ordinance after he and several of his friends burned a cross on the lawn of a black family. The state juvenile court dismissed the charge because it felt the ordinance was overly broad and therefore unconstitutional. But the Minnesota Supreme Court reversed the dismissal, ruling that the ordinance sought to prohibit only "fighting words," which fall outside the protection of the First Amendment.[9] The teenager's attorney appealed to the U.S. Supreme Court. In a unanimous decision in *R.A.V. v. St. Paul,* the Court held that the ordinance was unconstitutional because "it has proscribed fighting words of whatever manner that communicate messages of racial, gender, or religious intolerance. Selectivity of this sort creates the possibility that the city is seeking to handicap the expression of particular ideas." The Court's opinion made clear that the justices regarded burning a cross in front of a black family's home to be "reprehensible," but it said there were other means to punish this type of conduct without resorting to the ordinance in question.[10]

The examples from Skokie and St. Paul illustrate the dilemma facing those who cherish the freedoms in the First Amendment: Just how repugnant, hateful, or disturbing must public utterances be to be illegal? We know that when behavior accompanies speech—when a person yells, "Death to all Taoists," and then assaults several Taoists—that the individual is committing a crime (assault). But what about someone who puts a bumper sticker on his car that reads "Stalin Was Right, All Taoists Should Be Exterminated"? Because there is no shortage of derogatory terms for people of different religions, ethnicities, and races, you can easily substitute some other group in place of Taoists to understand just how offensive a bumper sticker can be.

Beginning in the 1980s, many colleges and universities created speech codes to inhibit the use of racial, ethnic, and sexual slurs in campus discourse. At a time when new and old hate groups appeared to be undermining civility, it seemed appropriate for institutions of higher learning to do what they could to discourage students from denigrating other students. But the constitutionality of the codes is an issue, particularly at public institutions. Private colleges and universities have much greater leeway in defining prohibited behavior.

---

[8] See H. L. Pohlman, *Constitutional Debate in Action: Civil Rights and Liberties* (New York: HarperCollins, 1995), pp. 224–229.

[9] In 1942, in *Chaplinsky v. New Hampshire,* the Court ruled on fighting words. The justices originally defined *fighting words* as expressions that "have a direct tendency to cause acts of violence by the persons to whom, individually, the remark is addressed." One interest the Court has in cases involving fighting words is the reaction provoked by the expression of the words, not just the words themselves. Usually offensive speech that is general, that is not directed at one individual or group, does not constitute fighting words.

[10] For the background to this case and the Court's abbreviated opinion, see O'Brien, *Constitutional Law and Politics,* pp. 477–487.

ASSIGNMENT

Read the three cases in Reading 12.5, and then answer the questions that follow it.

READING 12.5 REGULATING OFFENSIVE EXPRESSION

In each of the three examples here, a university's efforts to discourage certain types of expression are pitted against the First Amendment.

CASE 1

A fraternity at a private East Coast university held an "ugly woman" contest. One of the contest participants wore a black wig with curlers, painted his face black, and used pillows to simulate a bust and buttocks. Several weeks later, the university dean, at the urging of several student leaders, disciplined the fraternity for engaging in behavior that perpetuated racial and sexual stereotypes. The fraternity appealed the discipline on the grounds that the First Amendment protects this harmless conduct. University rules specifically prohibit speech and conduct that demean others on the basis of race, ethnicity, sexual orientation, or gender. A hearing has been scheduled for the appeal.

CASE 2

A professor in the English Department of a West Coast community college was charged with violating the school's sexual harassment policy. A female student complained that the professor's continual references to sexual topics and use of profanity in class constituted sexual harassment under the college's new sexual-harassment policy. That policy reads in part: "Conduct is prohibited that has the purpose or effect of unreasonably interfering with an individual's academic performance or creating an intimidating, hostile, or offensive learning environment." The faculty did not receive specific notice of the new policy, but the policy was printed in the manual that is distributed to every faculty member. The professor acknowledged that his teaching style is sometimes provocative and confrontational but argued that he has taught this way effectively for years. The college administration put the professor on unpaid leave for one semester and required that he attend sensitivity-training workshops. After a lower court upheld the administration's actions, the professor appealed on the grounds that his First Amendment rights had been violated under the college's sexual-harassment policy.

CASE 3

A public university in the Midwest adopted a code prohibiting certain kinds of expressive conduct. The key part of the code holds:

> For racist or discriminatory comments, epithets or other expressive behavior directed at an individual or on separate occasions at different individuals, or for physical conduct, if such comments, epithets or other expressive behavior or physical conduct intentionally:
>
> 1. Demean the race, sex, religion, color, creed, disability, sexual orientation, national origin, ancestry or age of the individual or individuals; or
>
> 2. Create an intimidating, hostile or demeaning environment for education, university-related work, or other university-authorized action.

A student at the university was expelled after he called out, "Shut up, you water buffalos," to a group of black sorority sisters who were singing late at night below his dormitory window. The student challenged the expulsion in federal court on the grounds that the code was overly broad and vague, and violated the First Amendment. The university defended the code on the grounds that it simply prohibited fighting words.

---

1. Suppose five black students at the East Coast university (Case 1) testify at the hearing that they think the depiction of a black woman in the contest was in poor taste, but that the contest was funny and they did not feel demeaned. Among those who speak for the university's policy are two white students and a black professor, all women, who were deeply offended by the sexual and racial stereotypes. You are the university official who has been asked to take action in this matter. Do you (a) tell the fraternity to clean up its act in the future; (b) tell the complaining students (and faculty member) that they are adults and could simply leave if they did not enjoy the contest; (c) sanction the fraternity; or (d) take some other form of action? Explain and justify your decision.

____

____

____

____

____

____

2. If you were the judge hearing the professor's appeal in Case 2, would you rule (a) that obscene language and repeated references to sexual topics are not part of professorial academic freedom and that the professor was properly sanctioned; (b) that the school cannot sanction the professor because the charge of sexual harassment was based solely on the complaint of one student; (c) that the punishment is fitting because the professor's use of obscenities is not protected by the First Amendment; or (d) that the punishment is not permissible because the college did not take appropriate steps to notify the professor that his long-standing teaching style was now inappropriate. Explain and justify your answer.

____

____

____

____

____

____

____

____

3. a. In Case 3, do you think the university's hate-speech code was sufficiently clear that the student could have anticipated his words would be prohibited under it? Why or why not?

____

____

____

b. Do you think the student's words were fighting words? That is, the code aside, would his words be protected under the First Amendment? Explain and support your answer.

____

____

____

____

____

4. How do the cases in Reading 12.5 point to a conflict between freedom and equality?

____

____

CHAPTER 13

PUBLIC POLICIES

EXERCISE 13.1 PROMOTING PUBLIC SAFETY

BACKGROUND

One of the functions of government is to serve the public welfare—on that most people agree. But there often is considerable controversy over just how far the government should go, and what public policies it should enact, to fulfill that mandate.

Public policies fall into three broad categories:[1]

- *Distributive policies* extend goods and services to all citizens, and the costs of the policies are shared by all. Government expenditures for public education, highways, and public safety are examples of distributive policies.
- *Regulatory policies* seek to minimize or eliminate harmful practices. Most environmental policies whose goal is to reduce air or water pollution are regulatory in nature.
- *Redistributive policies* take "benefits" from one group and give them to another. For instance, luxury taxes—a traditional favorite with liberals—redistribute tax money collected on luxury items (fur coats, yachts) on services for the poor.

Virtually all public policies have costs and benefits. A pivotal part of the decision-making process about which public policies to enact revolves around the costs and benefits of those policies. For example, most people support the idea of public education even if they don't have children in public schools. Why? Because an educated population benefits the country as a whole. But public education is not free, which means there often is controversy over who should be taxed, and at what rates, to pay for this public good. Similarly, clean air and water are public goods that most people value. The controversy arises when government sets a "price" and creates standards for clean air and water.

One category of regulatory policy is transportation safety. Over the years, the national government has established rules to promote the safety of citizens while they travel. The Federal Aviation Administration promotes safe air travel by regulating the licensing of air carriers, mandating procedures for

[1] See Charles O. Jones, *An Introduction to the Study of Public Policy,* 3d ed. (Monterey, Calif.: Brooks/Cole, 1984).

the certification of pilots, and requiring safety equipment at airports. In the 1960s, Congress passed a law that required that all vehicles sold in the United States be equipped with safety belts. By the 1990s, a number of states had passed laws requiring that passengers use seatbelts or face a fine for not doing so. Most states now have laws mandating that children under a certain age or weight be secured in child carriers in vehicles. Some states say no passengers in the back of pickup trucks. The goal of these rules is to reduce the likelihood of accidents and of injury in the event of an accident. Because the cost to carmakers to install seatbelts is low and the success of passenger restraints to reduce injury in common accidents is high, seatbelts are thought of as cost-effective—that is, their benefits outweigh their costs.

How far should the government's concern over transportation safety extend? A number of states require that riders operate their motorcycles with the headlights on, and half the states require that riders, including passengers, wear helmets. California enacted a mandatory helmet law in 1991 that went into effect January 1, 1992. In previous years, similar legislation had stalled at the state house or been vetoed by the governor; but in 1991 a majority of lawmakers and the governor were persuaded that the law would reduce fatalities and head injuries to motorcyclists as a result of accidents. Additionally, law enforcement groups and health-care professionals claimed the state would save between $65 million and $100 million in medical costs from uninsured and helmetless riders. Opponents of the law charged that helmets reduce visibility and impair the hearing of riders. But their main contention was that the proposed law was Big Brother at work, yet another instance of the government's intrusion into the lives of adults who should decide for themselves whether or not to wear helmets. This last claim is interesting because it points to a symbolic cost, the loss of a right—not a financial cost that can be measured by the price of a helmet or by a hospital bill. Of course some would argue that all costs, including symbolic costs, need evaluating in any cost–benefit analysis policymakers conduct.

ASSIGNMENT

Tables 13.1.1 and 13.1.2 show data on motorcyclists in California. Use the data to answer the following questions.

1. Looking at Table 13.1.1, what was the chance that a motorcyclist would be involved in an accident (injury or fatality) in 1986 versus 1993? To calculate the figures, add the injuries and fatalities for the given year and then divide that total by the number of licensed motorcyclists.

1986: One in ______________ motorcyclists.

1993: One in ______________ motorcyclists.

2. According to Table 13.1.1, what were the chances of a motorcyclist's dying as the result of an accident in 1986 versus 1999?

1986: One in ______________ motorcyclists.

1999: One in ______________ motorcyclists.

3. Looking at the data for helmet use in 1991 and 1999 in Table 13.1.2, it would appear that a motorcyclist is better off not wearing a helmet. Is that a valid deduction based on the data, or is there a better explanation? Support your answer.

____

____

____

____

____

____

TABLE 13.1.1 MOTORCYCLE INJURIES AND FATALITIES, CALIFORNIA, 1982–1999

			MOTORCYCLISTS	
YEAR	POPULATION	LICENSED MOTORCYCLISTS	INJURIES	FATALITIES
1982	24,724,000	765,845	23,116	681
1984	25,622,000	735,174	23,851	845
1986	26,980,000	778,083	25,846	848
1988	28,314,500	822,416	21,556	603
1990	29,976,000	842,145	18,578	569
1993	31,740,400	825,350	11,043	303
1999	34,036,000	844,011	6,933	230

SOURCE: Department of California Highway Patrol, *Annual Report of Fatal and Injury Motor Vehicle Traffic Accidents* (Sacramento, selected years).

TABLE 13.1.2 HELMET USE AND MOTORCYCLE INJURIES AND FATALITIES, CALIFORNIA, 1988–1999

	FATALITIES		INJURIES	
YEAR	USED	NOT USED	USED	NOT USED
1988	121	482	4,739	16,817
1989	124	496	4,564	14,963
1990	94	475	4,538	14,040
1991	99	413	4,439	12,471
1993	219	84	7,741	3,302
1999	174	56	5,658	1,275

SOURCE: Department of California Highway Patrol, *Annual Report of Fatal and Injury Motor Vehicle Traffic Accidents* (Sacramento, selected years).

4. Do the data from Table 13.1.1 support a claim that the helmet law has had the wanted effect in reducing injuries and fatalities? (To answer this question, analyze the number of injuries or fatalities in relation to the number of motorcyclists.)

5. If you were a legislator in a state that was considering passage of a helmet law, would the data in Tables 13.1.1 and 13.1.2 convince you that the law would be cost-effective? Or is there a philosophical consideration that would lead you to make the decision quite apart from the data? Explain and support your answer.

EXERCISE 13.2 THE WAR ON TERRORISM

BACKGROUND

Terrorist attacks on U.S. territory or the country's leaders leave behind not only death and destruction but also a permanent imprint on the lives of citizens. Many older Americans remember where they were when word came December 7, 1941, of the Japanese attack on Pearl Harbor, an attack that resulted in a devastating loss to the Pacific naval fleet and led the United States to enter World War II. Others remember what they were doing when the news of President John Kennedy's assassination on November 22, 1963, was announced. And you likely will remember for the rest of your life what you were doing on the morning of September 11, 2001, when reports and pictures of the terrorist attacks on the World Trade Center and the Pentagon were broadcast.

Since World War II, the planet has endured a bewildering variety of violent conflicts. They have included rebellions to achieve independence from colonizing powers, wars fought by the proxies of superpowers to spread or contain communism, sporadic clashes between neighboring developing countries, and struggles within nations between culturally distinct peoples. Assassinations and assassination attempts have become part of the American political fabric. But the terrorist assault on September 11, 2001, was unprecedented in its audacity, the magnitude of destruction, and the immediate political and economic effects. That evening, President George W. Bush in a televised address to the nation said that "our way of life, our very freedom came under attack." In a speech to Congress nine days later, he promised that the United States would "pursue nations that provide aid or safe haven to terrorism."

Wars are fought between or within nations. Acts of terrorism usually are carried out by organizations. Don't confuse terrorism with the guerilla warfare that the United States confronted in Vietnam. Guerrilla attacks usually focus on military and government centers; and their ultimate goal is to seize power. Terrorists attacks civilian targets; and their goal is to disrupt society by inflicting maximum damage. More people died in the terrorist actions on September 11 than died at Pearl Harbor sixty years earlier. The attacks on the twin towers of the World Trade Center and the Pentagon killed approximately 3,000.

Terrorism escalated in the late 1960s, when radical Middle Eastern groups began hijacking commercial airliners. In 1972, terrorists murdered eleven Israeli athletes at the Olympic games in Munich, Germany. Groups like Hamas, Hezbollah, and Islamic Jihad have terrorized the Middle East for years. Their members are extremists who oppose Israel in particular and Western values in general. The United States felt the pain of terrorism directly in 1988, when Pan American flight 103 exploded over Lockerbie, Scotland, with a loss of 270 lives, including a number of U.S. college students who were returning from a holiday vacation. Six people died in the first terrorist attack on the World Trade Center in February 1993. For radical Islamic groups, the World Trade Center was a symbol of U.S. imperialism.

Terrorism is an attractive weapon for groups that lack the resources of the state to mount conventional attacks. Modern industrial societies offer terrorists many targets, particularly for suicide bombers hoping to instill fear and command media attention. As one authority notes, terrorism "is a strategy that involves a low risk to perpetrators and a good chance of success. Whereas outsiders may view terrorists as thugs and hoodlums, they are seen by their supporters as heroes and, in death, martyrs."[2]

President Bush held Al Qaeda responsible for the September 11 tragedy. The organization, which began in 1988 and is thought to operate in sixty countries today, is loosely organized by millionaire militant Osama bin Laden. The United States supported the Saudi-born bin Laden when he led the successful resistance against the Soviet invasion of Afghanistan in the 1980s. The Soviets were defeated, and eventually a fundamentalist Islamic regime, the Taliban, took control over most of the impoverished, land-locked country. The hostile terrain and mountains in and surrounding Afghanistan have served as barriers against outside aggressors for over two centuries. And fierce Afghan resistance to outside aggression has been as formidable as the terrain. The deployment of U.S. forces to Saudi Arabia in 1990 and the international effort to drive Iraqi troops out of Kuwait led bin Laden to redirect his wrath to the United States, in part because U.S. troops were on Islamic holy ground in Saudi Arabia.

---

[2] Randal Cruikshanks, "Conflict Resolution in the Other World," in *The Other World*, ed. Joseph Weatherby (New York: Longman, 2000), pp. 86 and 88.

ASSIGNMENT

Reading 13.2 describes six scenarios for combating terrorism. Use the material there to answer the questions that follow the reading. Although the questions focus on Afghanistan and Osama bin Laden, in your answers consider the problem of terrorism in general, the available responses to terrorism, the prospects for achieving the stated goals, and the cost and likely consequences of each option.

READING 13.2 COMBATING TERRORISM: SIX SCENARIOS

Each scenario below offers different options for pursuing a war on terrorism. Those options relate to the scope of the response, the involvement of allies, the intensity of battle and the anticipated level of casualties, and the degree to which information about the war is made public.

SCENARIO 1

Provide the rebels with sophisticated weapons to use against the Taliban government; station supporting U.S. troops on the border inside Pakistan, although the U.S. and Pakistani governments will deny knowledge of their existence; and have U.S. operatives flood the country with counterfeit Afghan currency.

Goals Destabilize the Taliban government by forcing it to direct its limited resources against rebels; cause internal rebellion; and disrupt the meager Afghan economy.

SCENARIO 2

Insert small groups of elite forces into Afghanistan to search for and seize Osama bin Laden; to disrupt Taliban operations wherever possible by covert action against military targets and strategic resources; and to help rebel forces currently operating in Afghanistan. The U.S. government would not acknowledge the operations or publicize their successes or failures.

Goals Capture or assassinate the leadership of Al Qaeda; and disrupt the Taliban government and weaken Afghanistan's, and thereby Al Qaeda's, infrastructure.

SCENARIO 3

Mount a coordinated multilateral effort, with the support of as many Middle Eastern and South Asian countries as possible, to destabilize the Taliban government through nonmilitary strategies. Among those strategies: isolating the Taliban government politically, disrupting all economic activity in Afghanistan, prohibiting all loans to the country from the United Nations or the International Monetary Fund, seizing shipments of strategic materials to Afghanistan, and limiting the emergency food and medical supplies allowed into the country.

Goals Isolate the Taliban government politically and economically from the region and the rest of the world through an international alliance; and slowly force concessions from the Taliban, or squeeze the government until it collapses.

SCENARIO 4

Insert elite forces—U.S. and allied troops—into Algeria, Iran, Iraq, Syria, and Afghanistan, all countries with governments hostile to the West and linked to the support of terrorism, to attack oil refineries and curtail production; to flood the countries with counterfeit currency; and to mobilize and support internal opposition groups.

Goals Disrupt the normal functioning of governments that support terrorism, to make those governments respond to disorders—real or possible—in their own countries and thereby limit their ability to support terrorist activities overseas.

Scenario 5

With allies, engage in direct military action against the Taliban government in Afghanistan and Saddam Hussein's government in Iraq, both sponsors of global terrorism. Among the military actions: Direct massive air strikes at military, government, and infrastructure targets (after warning civilians of the bombing and urging them to seek refuge); supply Kurdish forces in Iraq with military equipment to use against the Iraqi troops; and follow up the air strikes with ground forces. In addition, assure the Middle Eastern countries that once the Afghan and Iraqi governments have been overthrown, independent democratic governments not controlled by the West would be established; and that the West would require only that the new governments not present a destabilizing force in the region.

Goal Overthrow pro-terrorist governments in Afghanistan and Iraq.

Scenario 6

Insert elite troops into Afghanistan and Iraq to disrupt all aspects of political, economic, and social activities in the countries by cutting power supplies, contaminating water resources, blowing up bridges, disrupting oil production, and placing explosives in public areas for maximum exposure of the population.

Goal Use terrorism directly against governments that themselves sponsor the use of terrorism against the United States, to destabilize those governments.

---

1. a. Why is the level of public awareness important in each of the six scenarios?

____

____

____

b. What are the advantages and disadvantages of providing accurate information to the American public about the war on terrorism?

____

____

____

2. Plot the scenarios on the chart below according to the number of participating allies (vertical axis) and the intensity of the conflict (horizontal axis). *Intensity of conflict* refers to the expected number of military and civilian casualties. Scenario 1 has been plotted as an example.

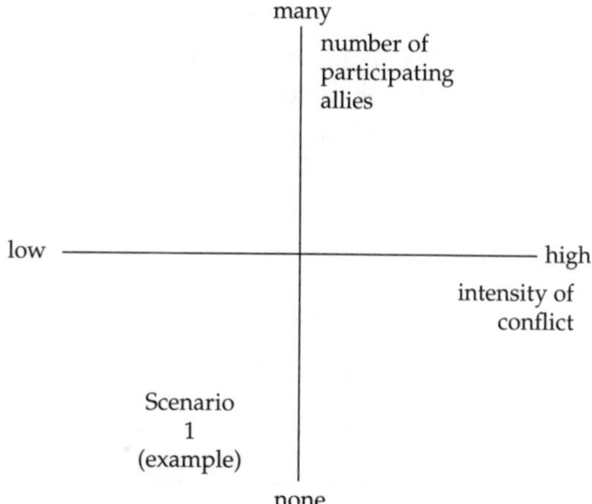

3. What do you think are two advantages to the United States of coordinating a war on terrorism with as many allies as possible?

Advantage 1: ______

Advantage 2: ______

4. Identify two advantages of unilateral action by the United States in a war on terrorism.

Advantage 1: ______

Advantage 2: ______

5. Which of the six scenarios identified in Reading 13.2 appears to have the best chance of succeeding with minimal casualties to U.S. military personnel? Explain and support your choice.

______

6. Which scenario has the least chance of achieving its stated goal(s)? Explain and support your choice.

______

7. Identify three important geographical factors that need to be considered in deciding which scenario to pursue. Explain the importance of each factor.

Factor 1: ______

Factor 2: ______

Factor 3: ______

EXERCISE 13.3 WHAT TO DO ABOUT CASTRO?

BACKGROUND

U.S. foreign policy is often the result of compromises agreed to by members of Congress, the president, and officials in the State Department and the military. Every policy takes into account the opinions and expertise not only of those officials but also of business leaders and officials in the governments of U.S. allies. Of course, U.S. foreign policy is based on the national interest. But that doesn't mean that it can't serve other purposes as well.

ASSIGNMENT

Reading 13.3 describes the evolution of American foreign policy toward Cuba after Fidel Castro came to power. Refer to the reading to answer the questions that follow it.

READING 13.3 THE EVOLUTION OF AMERICAN FOREIGN POLICY TOWARD CASTRO'S CUBA

In early 1952, Fulgencio Batista overthrew the government of Cuba and installed himself as dictator. His corrupt reign, supported by the United States, lasted several years, until a rebellion forced him to flee; in 1959 a young guerrilla leader, Fidel Castro, assumed the presidency. Today, more than forty years later, Castro is still running Cuba—despite repeated attempts of the U.S. government to topple his regime militarily or economically.

Cuba had been under the influence of the United States through the first half of the twentieth century, in large part because of its proximity to the United States. The island lies just 70 miles off the Florida coast. When he assumed control of Cuba, Castro was not a friend of the United States; but he also was not closely allied with the Soviet Union. After taking power, Castro sought to sever Cuban dependence on the United States: He rejected tentative offers of U.S. economic aid in 1959. The Soviet Union offered to exchange Soviet oil for Cuban sugar in a trade agreement in 1960, but U.S. and British oil refineries in Cuba refused to process the oil. Congress authorized President Dwight Eisenhower to cut U.S. imports of Cuban sugar. In response, Castro nationalized all U.S. properties in Cuba without compensating their owners. The United States retaliated by issuing a trade embargo on all Cuban goods and prohibiting U.S. companies from doing business with the Cuban government. *

The following year the ill-fated Bay of Pigs invasion took place. Secretly sponsored by the Central Intelligence Agency, Cuban exiles landed in a swampy area where the ragtag force was quickly defeated. The United States was humiliated, and President John Kennedy was left with a foreign policy debacle on his hands.

Cuban–U.S. relations grew worse as the Soviet Union strengthened its ties with Castro. In 1962, a U.S. spy plane photographed sites in Cuba that were being prepared for Soviet nuclear missiles and long-range bombers. The United States already was troubled by Castro's policy of sowing the seeds of revolution in Central America; but now, facing land-based missiles that could strike American cities, the country's cold war fears intensified. President Kennedy immediately established a naval blockade around Cuba and demanded that Soviet Premier Nikita Khrushchev remove all offensive weapons from the island. Kennedy warned Khrushchev that the United States would stop any Soviet ships carrying missiles from entering Cuban waters. The two nuclear superpowers were on the brink of a nuclear confrontation over Cuba. Khrushchev eventually backed down, agreeing to a United Nations inspection team that would verify the removal of the weapons from Cuba, and the United States pledged not to invade the island.

Castro had a love–hate relationship with the Soviet Union. On the one hand, he depended on Soviet economic aid; on the other, he did not want to be thought of as a lackey of the Kremlin. Moreover,

* Jaime Suchlicki, *Cuba from Columbus to Castro*, 2d ed. (New York: Pergamon-Brassey, 1986), p. 163.

U.S.–Soviet relations gradually improved after the Cuban missile crisis, which made Castro wonder about secret agreements between the United States and the Soviet Union that could threaten his position in Cuba.

Over the next two decades, Cuba under Castro became a showcase for social services. But the Cuban economy, overwhelmingly dependent on sugar exports, languished. Cuba's economic problems became more acute after the breakup of the Soviet Union in 1991 and the end of economic aid from Moscow. Politically, Castro never tried to institute a democratic regime. As long as the United States was perceived as a threat to Cuban sovereignty, Castro was able to justify his dictatorial control over the island.

Cuba-initiated revolutions never materialized in Latin America, and the leading proponent of revolutionary efforts, Che Guevera, was killed in Bolivia in 1967. But Castro did dispatch Cuban troops to Angola and Ethiopia in the 1970s to help rebels attempting to overthrow the governments of those African countries. All Cuban troops had withdrawn from Africa by the early 1990s.

Since the mid-1960s, Cubans who flee the island have been granted automatic asylum in the United States, a status not conferred on illegal immigrants from other countries. In 1980, the Mariel Boat Lift brought tens of thousands of Cubans to the United States, including a number of criminals whom Castro had released from prison. Later Castro reluctantly agreed to accept the return of some of those criminals. Again in 1994, thousands of Cubans took to small boats to escape to the United States. President Clinton was able to persuade Castro to contain the exodus in return for allowing 20,000 Cubans to immigrate legally to the United States each year.

Since 1987, the U.S. Information Agency has spent $11 million annually to beam news and entertainment shows into Cuba via TV Marti. The Cuban government regularly jams the signal.

According to one scholar, U.S. policies toward Cuba reflected the concern that the Soviet Union would militarize Cuba and thereby threaten U.S. security.* In the 1960s, the United States set two conditions that Cuba had to meet to restore relations with the United States. First, Cuba had to abandon its efforts to spread revolution abroad. Second, Cuba had to cut its military ties with the Soviet Union. In the late 1970s, the Carter administration added two other conditions: greater respect for human rights and the withdrawal of Cuban troops from Africa. President George Bush Sr. added yet another requirement: democratic elections. In 2002, Cuba has met all of these conditions with the exception of open elections.

The United States maintains diplomatic and trade relations with a number of countries whose governments are not democratic, among them China, Vietnam, and Saudi Arabia. But there has been no softening of U.S. policy toward Cuba. In fact, in 1996 Congress passed the Helms-Burton Act, which allows Americans to sue foreign companies that invest in property seized by Castro's government. (Part of this bill, Title III, enables the president to either waive or enforce its provisions every six months.) President Clinton refused to invoke the law; and in 2001, President George W. Bush quietly refused to do so as well.

The months-long saga of young Elian Gonzalez (see Exercise 3.4) reminded Americans about the U.S. policy of isolating Cuba. By the time Elian was returned to Havana in June 2000, Americans thought of Fidel Castro as a long-winded dictator but not a military threat to the United States. Television news clips from Havana showed the island as an economically depressed country whose hardworking people were suffering because of the U.S. economic embargo.

The United States certainly could benefit from a rapprochement with Cuba. Many U.S. business leaders have proposed an end to the economic embargo of Cuba and the Helms-Burton Act. As one scholar observes:

> In this post–cold war era, Cuba poses no threat to the United States, nor does it present any problem that could possibly outweigh in importance relations with countries such as Canada, Mexico, France, Great Britain, and Russia. Still, a substantial number of United States leaders seem willing to risk disrupting those relations in an effort to force the issue against Castro. †

* Much of this summary of U.S. foreign policy toward Cuba is derived from Wayne S. Smith, "Shackled to the Past: The United States and Cuba," *Current History* 95 (February 1996): 49–54.

† Ibid., p. 49.

---

1. In one sentence, summarize U.S. foreign policy toward Castro's regime in Cuba.

2. a. What did the United States hope to achieve through its cold war policies toward Cuba?

b. What, in fact, did the United States achieve?

3. a. In your view, have U.S. policies toward Cuba advanced American interests in any way?

b. If so, identify those interests and explain and support your position. If not, explain what interests the United States should have been hoping to advance and what tactics the country should have employed.

4. Now that the cold war is over, what interest, if any, does the United States have in pursuing its anti-Castro foreign policies? If you think there is an interest, identify it and explain why it should drive policy toward Cuba. If you do not think a valid interest is served by continuing America's cold war policies toward Cuba, explain how you would reshape American foreign policy toward the island.

EXERCISE 13.4 DEVELOPING A COUNTERTERRORISM POLICY

BACKGROUND

Many Americans think of the horrifying events of September 11, 2001, and the subsequent incidents of biological terrorism through the U.S. postal system, as abrupt departures from traditional national security concerns. The exposure of the homeland to violence from elusive foreign adversaries seems unprecedented in any number of ways, among them the attack on American civilians in their own country, the problems of detecting and responding to deadly biological toxins, and the difficulty of directing American military might at nonstate actors.

In reality, with the exception of the use of airplanes as deadly missiles, experts on terrorism had anticipated a wide range of threats to American national security, including the use of biological and chemical agents. For example, in June 2000, a national advisory commission foresaw the increased likelihood of terrorist attacks against the United States and made specific recommendations for an antiterrorist strategy (see Reading 13.4.1). Similarly, in April 2000, a task force within the Centers for Disease Control (CDC) issued a report calling for increased preparedness against biological and chemical attacks (see Reading 13.4.2). Neither report received much play in the print media and even less on radio and television. The government's failure to respond adequately to these reports and to other warnings of the terrorist threat likely will be the subject of congressional inquiries and investigative commissions.

ASSIGNMENT

Examine the warnings in the reports that make up Readings 13.4.1 and 13.4.2, and their impact on national spending to combat terrorism. Answer the questions that follow the readings.

COUNTERING THE CHANGING THREAT OF INTERNATIONAL TERRORISM

FOREWORD

Six months ago, the National Commission on Terrorism began its Congressionally mandated evaluation of America's laws, policies, and practices for preventing and punishing terrorism directed at American citizens. After a thorough review, the Commission concluded that, although American strategies and policies are basically on the right track, significant aspects of implementation are seriously deficient. Thus, this report does not attempt to describe all American counterterrorism activities, but instead concentrates on problem areas and recommended changes. We wish to note, however, that in the course of our assessment we gained renewed confidence in the abilities and dedication of the Americans who stand on the front lines in the fight against terrorism. . . .

Throughout our deliberations, we were mindful of several important points:

- The imperative to find terrorists and prevent their attacks requires energetic use of all the legal authorities and instruments available.
- Terrorist attacks against America threaten more than the tragic loss of individual lives. Some terrorists hope to provoke a response that undermines our Constitutional system of government. So U.S. leaders must find the appropriate balance by adopting counterterrorism policies which are effective but also respect the democratic traditions which are the bedrock of America's strength.
- Combating terrorism should not be used as a pretext for discrimination against any segment of society. Terrorists often claim to act on behalf of ethnic groups, religions, or even entire nations. These claims are false. Terrorists represent only a minuscule faction of any such group.

READING SOURCE: National Commission on Terrorism, *Report*, June 5, 2000 (www.fas.org/irp/threat/commission.html).

- People turn to terrorism for various reasons. Many terrorists act from political, ideological, or religious convictions. Some are simply criminals for hire. Others become terrorists because of perceived oppression or economic deprivation. An astute American foreign policy must take into account the reasons people turn to terror and, where appropriate and feasible, address them. No cause, however, justifies terrorism.

Terrorists attack American targets more often than those of any other country. America's pre-eminent role in the world guarantees that this will continue to be the case, and the threat of attacks creating massive casualties is growing. If the United States is to protect itself, if it is to remain a world leader, this nation must develop and continuously refine sound counterterrorism policies appropriate to the rapidly changing world around us.

Executive Summary

International terrorism poses an increasingly dangerous and difficult threat to America. This was underscored by the December 1999 arrests in Jordan and at the U.S./Canadian border of foreign nationals who were allegedly planning to attack crowded millennium celebrations. Today's terrorists seek to inflict mass casualties, and they are attempting to do so both overseas and on American soil. They are less dependent on state sponsorship and are, instead, forming loose, transnational affiliations based on religious or ideological affinity and a common hatred of the United States. This makes terrorist attacks more difficult to detect and prevent.

Countering the growing danger of the terrorist threat requires significantly stepping up U.S. efforts. The government must immediately take steps to reinvigorate the collection of intelligence about terrorists' plans, use all available legal avenues to disrupt and prosecute terrorist activities and private sources of support, convince other nations to cease all support for terrorists, and ensure that federal, state, and local officials are prepared for attacks that may result in mass casualties. The Commission has made a number of recommendations to accomplish these objectives:

Priority one is to prevent terrorist attacks. U.S. intelligence and law enforcement communities must use the full scope of their authority to collect intelligence regarding terrorist plans and methods.

- CIA guidelines adopted in 1995 restricting recruitment of unsavory sources should not apply when recruiting counterterrorism sources.
- The Attorney General should ensure that FBI is exercising fully its authority for investigating suspected terrorist groups or individuals, including authority for electronic surveillance.
- Funding for counterterrorism efforts by CIA, NSA, and FBI must be given higher priority to ensure continuation of important operational activity and to close the technology gap that threatens their ability to collect and exploit terrorist communications.
- FBI should establish a cadre of reports officers to distill and disseminate terrorism-related information once it is collected.

U.S. policies must firmly target all states that support terrorists.

- Iran and Syria should be kept on the list of state sponsors until they stop supporting terrorists.
- Afghanistan should be designated a sponsor of terrorism and subjected to all the sanctions applicable to state sponsors.
- The President should impose sanctions on countries that, while not direct sponsors of terrorism, are nevertheless not cooperating fully on counterterrorism. Candidates for consideration include Pakistan and Greece.

Private sources of financial and logistical support for terrorists must be subjected to the full force and sweep of U.S. and international laws.

All relevant agencies should use every available means, including the full array of criminal, civil, and administrative sanctions to block or disrupt nongovernmental sources of support for international terrorism.

Congress should promptly ratify and implement the International Convention for the Suppression of the Financing of Terrorism to enhance international cooperative efforts. Where criminal prosecution is not possible, the Attorney General should vigorously pursue the expulsion of terrorists from the United States through proceedings which protect both the national security interest in safeguarding classified evidence and the right of the accused to challenge that evidence.

A terrorist attack involving a biological agent, deadly chemicals, or nuclear or radiological material, even if it succeeds only partially, could profoundly affect the entire nation. The government must do more to prepare for such an event.

The President should direct the preparation of a manual to guide the implementation of existing legal authority in the event of a catastrophic terrorist threat or attack. The President and Congress should determine whether additional legal authority is needed to deal with catastrophic terrorism.

- The Department of Defense must have detailed plans for its role in the event of a catastrophic terrorist attack, including criteria for decisions on transfer of command authority to DoD in extraordinary circumstances.
- Senior officials of all government agencies involved in responding to a catastrophic terrorism threat or crisis should be required to participate in national exercises every year to test capabilities and coordination.
- Congress should make it illegal for anyone not properly certified to possess certain critical pathogens and should enact laws to control the transfer of equipment critical to the development or use of biological agents.
- The President should establish a comprehensive and coordinated long-term research and development program for catastrophic terrorism.
- The Secretary of State should press for an international convention to improve multilateral cooperation on preventing or responding to cyber attacks by terrorists.

The President and Congress should reform the system for reviewing and funding departmental counterterrorism programs to ensure that the activities and programs of various agencies are part of a comprehensive plan.

- The executive branch official responsible for coordinating counterterrorism efforts across the government should be given a stronger hand in the budget process.
- Congress should develop mechanisms for a comprehensive review of the President's counterterrorism policy and budget.

READING 13.4.2 Biological and Chemical Terrorism: Strategic Plan for Preparedness and Response

U.S. Vulnerability to Biological and Chemical Terrorism

Terrorist incidents in the United States and elsewhere involving bacterial pathogens, nerve gas, and a lethal plant toxin (i.e., ricin) have demonstrated that the United States is vulnerable to biological and chemical threats as well as explosives. Recipes for preparing "homemade" agents are readily available, and reports of arsenals of military bioweapons raise the possibility that terrorists might have access to highly dangerous agents, which have been engineered for mass dissemination as small-particle aerosols. Such agents as the variola virus, the causative agent of smallpox, are highly contagious and often fatal. Responding to large-scale outbreaks caused by these agents will require the rapid mobilization of public health workers, emergency responders, and private health-care providers. Large-scale outbreaks will also require rapid procurement and distribution of large quantities of drugs and vaccines, which must be available quickly. . . .

Recommendations

Implementing CDC's strategic preparedness and response plan by 2004 will ensure the following outcomes:

- U.S. public health agencies and health-care providers will be prepared to mitigate illness and injuries that result from acts of biological and chemical terrorism.

READING SOURCE: Centers for Disease Control, Strategic Planning Workgroup, *Recommendations*, April 21, 2000 (www.cdc.gov/mmwr/preview/mmwrhtml/rr4904a1.htm).

- Public health surveillance for infectious diseases and injuries—including events that might indicate terrorist activity—will be timely and complete, and reporting of suspected terrorist events will be integrated with the evolving, comprehensive networks of the national public health surveillance system.
- The national laboratory response network for bioterrorism will be extended to include facilities in all 50 states. The network will include CDC's environmental health laboratory for chemical terrorism and four regional facilities.
- State and federal public health departments will be equipped with state-of-the-art tools for rapid epidemiological investigation and control of suspected or confirmed acts of biological or chemical terrorism, and a designated stock of terrorism-related medical supplies will be available through a national pharmaceutical stockpile.
- A cadre of well-trained health-care and public health workers will be available in every state. Their terrorism-related activities will be coordinated through a rapid and efficient communication system that links U.S. public health agencies and their partners.

Conclusion

Recent threats and use of biological and chemical agents against civilians have exposed U.S. vulnerability and highlighted the need to enhance our capacity to detect and control terrorist acts. The U.S. must be protected from an extensive range of critical biological and chemical agents, including some that have been developed and stockpiled for military use. Even without threat of war, investment in national defense ensures preparedness and acts as a deterrent against hostile acts. Similarly, investment in the public health system provides the best civil defense against bioterrorism. Tools developed in response to terrorist threats serve a dual purpose. They help detect rare or unusual disease outbreaks and respond to health emergencies, including naturally occurring outbreaks or industrial injuries that might resemble terrorist events in their unpredictability and ability to cause mass casualties (e.g., a pandemic influenza outbreak or a large-scale chemical spill). Terrorism-preparedness activities described in CDC's plan, including the development of a public health communication infrastructure, a multilevel network of diagnostic laboratories, and an integrated disease surveillance system, will improve our ability to investigate rapidly and control public health threats that emerge in the twenty-first century.

---

1. In its report, the National Commission on Terrorism issued several warnings about the U.S. response to terrorism (Reading 13.4.1). Identify one benefit or one drawback, or both, of heeding each of the warnings below.

a. "Some terrorists hope to provoke a response that undermines our Constitutional system of government. So U.S. leaders must . . . respect the democratic traditions which are the bedrock of America's strength."

Benefit: ______________________________

____

Drawback: ______________________________

____

b. "Combating terrorism must not be a pretext for discrimination against any segment of society."

Benefit: ______________________________

____

Drawback: ______________________________

____

c. "An astute American foreign policy must take into account the reasons people turn to terror and, where appropriate and feasible, address them."

Benefit: ______________________________

Drawback:

2. a. With the benefit of hindsight, which of the commission's conclusions (printed in bold in Reading 13.4.1, in the Executive Summary) anticipated the events of September 11 and afterward?

b. Which of the conclusions now appear to have misjudged the threat?

3. a. With the benefit of hindsight, which of the CDC workgroup's recommendations anticipated the problems created by the anthrax attacks in the fall of 2001?

b. Which of the recommendations appear to have misjudged the threat?

4. None of the workgroup's recommendations had been acted on at the time of the anthrax attacks in the fall of 2001. Realistically, do you think it was possible for the recommendations to have been accepted and implemented some eighteen months after the report was issued? Explain and support your answer by citing specific recommendations.

5. Looking at Table 13.4, what percentage of total federal funding to combat terrorism in fiscal year 2001 was for defense against weapons of mass destruction (WMD)?

TABLE 13.4 FEDERAL FUNDING TO COMBAT TERRORISM, FISCAL YEARS 1998–2001

	FISCAL YEARS			
CATEGORY OF SPENDING	1998	1999	2000	2001*
Total funding for defense against WMD	$645.30	$1,238.40	$1,453.70	$1,550.00
Law enforcement and investigative activities	$2,654.70	$2,686.80	$2,820.00	$3,025.50
WMD figure	$71.80	$102.30	$93.80	$142.50
Physical security of government facilities/ employees	$2,983.70	$4,356.40	$3,637.50	$4,259.20
WMD figure	$175.10	$199.40	$200.60	$185.40
Physical protection of national population/ infrastructure	$146.70	$256.80	$249.90	$266.80
WMD figure	$3.40	$3.80	$3.60	$3.60
Preparing for and responding to terrorist acts	$417.80	$930.20	$984.40	$947.00
WMD figure	$155.30	$564.20	$618.70	$633.50
– Equipment for first responders	$15.10	$98.40	$95.20	$102.20
– Federal planning exercises	$3.50	$6.10	$7.60	$8.60
– First-responder training and exercises	$13.30	$86.10	$90.40	$104.00
– Medical-responder training and exercises	—	$3.00	$1.00	$2.00
– Other planning and assistance to state/local	$18.80	$60.00	$52.40	$66.70
– Public health infrastructure/surveillance	—	$62.00	$88.60	$91.40
– Special response units	$99.20	$191.50	$224.50	$191.40
– Stockpile of vaccines and therapeutics	—	$51.00	$52.00	$52.00
– Other	$5.40	$5.90	$7.10	$15.20
Research and development	$403.10	$527.00	$727.90	$812.80
WMD figure	$239.80	$368.80	$537.00	$589.90
– Basic research	$70.50	$31.00	$48.00	$92.30
– Detection/diagnostics	$17.80	$59.00	$78.30	$97.00
– Modeling, simulation, and system analyses	$3.60	$10.60	$16.70	$16.70
– Personal/collective protection	$12.00	$10.00	$30.00	$28.20
– Personal/environmental decontamination	$1.80	$9.30	$20.30	$24.20
– Therapeutics/treatments	—	$16.00	$20.90	$26.60
– Vaccines	$2.90	$35.70	$82.60	$99.20
– Other	$131.20	$197.20	$240.30	$205.80
Total funding	**$6,516.10**	**$8,757.30**	**$8,419.70**	**$9,311.30**

WMD = weapons of mass destruction (atomic, biological, chemical).

* Requested (budgeted).

Note: All figures are in millions of dollars.

SOURCE: Adapted with permission. Copyright is held by the Center for Nonproliferation Studies at the Monterey Institute of International Studies.

6. a. By what percentage did federal funding to combat terrorism increase between fiscal year 1998 and fiscal year 2001?

____

b. By what percentage did federal funding for defense against WMD increase over the same period?

____

7. a. Looking at Table 13.4, in which fiscal year did total federal funding to combat terrorism go up by the largest percentage?

---

b. In which fiscal year did total federal funding for defense against WMD go up by the largest percentage?

---

8. a. In which category of spending was the percentage increase for federal funding to combat terrorism the largest between fiscal years 1998 and 2001?

---

b. For which category of spending was the percentage increase for defense against WMD the largest between fiscal years 1998 and 2001?

---

9. Overall, do the budget figures for fiscal year 2001 suggest that the report of the National Commission on Terrorism had an impact on the allocation of federal dollars? Explain and support your answer.*

---

* Whatever you conclude will be necessarily tentative. The budget figures for fiscal year 2001 are requested only and may have been subsequently supplemented.

EXERCISE 13.5 TO DRILL OR NOT TO DRILL? THE ARCTIC NATIONAL WILDLIFE REFUGE

BACKGROUND

In 1980, Congress passed the Alaska Lands Act, which designated 104 million acres of new parks and wilderness refuges in Alaska. Included under the act is the Arctic National Wildlife Refuge (ANWR), which encompasses 19 million acres. The ANWR is located in the most northeastern part of Alaska, in a region with few roads (none of which are open year-round) and several small native settlements. It is home to more than 180,000 caribou, polar bears, wolves, and other Arctic animals. Under provisions of the Alaska Lands Act, Congress can authorize oil drilling on 1.9 million acres of the ANWR. That segment of land is some 150 miles from Prudhoe Bay, where oil has been extracted and pumped through the Alaska pipeline to Valdez, a port in the southwestern part of the state. From there the oil is loaded onto tankers destined for refineries in the lower United States. One of those tankers, the *Exxon Valdez,* foundered on rocks in 1989, spilling more than 11 million gallons of oil into pristine Prince William Sound.

On several occasions, bills have been introduced in Congress to give the go-ahead for oil and gas exploration and development of the 1.9 million acres in the ANWR. The bills either have not passed or have passed and then been vetoed—as President Clinton did in 1996, citing potential harm to the environment. Yet Alaska's two senators and one member of the House are adamant supporters of the plan to extract oil from the area. Apparently the citizens of the state also support oil drilling. Two political scientists explain:

> One might think the beauty of the land would unite Alaskans in support of preservationist values. It does not. A majority of the population values development and believes it can proceed without much harm to the environment. Only a minority are "environmentalists" in the sense commonly used in American politics. But in coalition with national environmental groups, this minority has been able to stall an onslaught on Alaska's remaining wilderness.[3]

Those who back oil drilling in the ANWR, including President George W. Bush, cite Alaska's dependence on oil revenues to finance the state government and the services it provides. Virtually 85 percent of the state's general budget comes from oil revenues that are in jeopardy as the supply of oil from Prudhoe Bay drops off. In addition, because of the oil revenues, Alaskans do not pay a sales tax or personal income tax. And, the drilling would create several hundred thousand jobs (although it's not clear how many of them actually would be in Alaska). Drilling proponents also argue that oil development in the ANWR would lessen U.S. dependence on oil imported from foreign countries. That argument became more vehement in the wake of fuel shortages and rapidly increasing fuel costs in California and other western states during the spring and early summer of 2001. And the argument was invoked again after the September 11 attacks highlighted for many the need to reduce U.S. dependence on Middle Eastern oil.

Opponents of the drilling proposal counter that the potential damage to the environment is not worth the cost, especially because the estimated oil reserves represent only about a six months' supply of oil under the present rate of consumption in the United States. They insist that if Congress would increase the fuel-efficiency requirements for new vehicles by 3 miles a gallon, that savings would translate into the same amount of oil in ANWR.[4] Moreover, according to some analysts, the United States already has abundant oil reserves in California, Oklahoma, and Texas, making the need for additional development in a wilderness area unnecessary. And the economic argument for allowing drilling is faulty, say opponents. ANWR is federal land, so oil lease and royalty money would not accrue to the state government—although the state would benefit from the construction aspects of drilling and extraction.

---

[3] Gerald A. McBeath and Thomas A. Morehouse, *Alaska Politics & Government* (Lincoln: University of Nebraska Press, 1994), p. 26.

[4] "Arctic Drilling Is Still Bad Idea," *Los Angeles Times,* September 28, 2001, p. B16.

ASSIGNMENT

1. What percentage of the total land area of the ANWR is made up by the area where drilling can take place?

2. What does President Bush have to gain or lose politically by supporting legislation to allow oil drilling in the ANWR? In your answer, consider who supports and who opposes the drilling.

3. In your view, should Congress (a) approve drilling as soon as possible, (b) prohibit drilling now and in the future, or (c) prohibit drilling now but revisit the issue in five years? Explain and support your answer.

4. In your view, who should decide the drilling issue: Congress or the residents of Alaska? Explain and support your answer.

APPENDIX

1

TOOLS IN POLITICAL ANALYSIS

NORMATIVE AND EMPIRICAL THEORIES

Social scientists formulate theories to explain relationships between events and behaviors. Usually expressed as a generalization or a proposition, a *theory* offers a coherent explanation of "why events occur in the manner that they do."[1] The value of a theory is twofold: It explains behavior, and it can be tested. In political science, the acid test of a theory is its ability not only to explain but also to predict.

There is no shortage of theories to explain why voters are apathetic, why reform-minded candidates seem to moderate their views once elected, why some presidents are more effective than others, or why courts in one region of the country are more receptive to environmental litigation than are courts in other regions. Just as medical researchers develop theories of how lifestyle, blood pressure, age, and eating habits produce (or inhibit) certain kinds of illnesses, political scientists construct theories about the political behaviors of people, institutions, and governments.

Two dominant theoretical approaches guide how political scientists explain political behavior. The first, *normative theories,* focus on values: how people should behave, what governments should do, and how countries should interact with each other under different conditions. By contrast, *empirical theories* address what actually takes place, making no value judgments about the behavior under study. Because normative theories are value based, they cannot be tested scientifically, the way empirical theories can.

The line between the two approaches is not always clear. Much of social science research blends the two, ascribing certain expectations to behavior and then testing to see if those expectations are valid. Political scientist Darrell West's study of television ads in election campaigns, for example, combined empirical and normative approaches. West examined the television ads run by candidates in several presidential primaries and general elections, and in U.S. Senate campaigns. He wanted to determine what impact, if any, the ads had on voters. West's theoretical foundation was what others had written about the effects of the media on ordinary citizens, in particular the assumption that television campaign ads have more influence on voters than does television news coverage of elections and candidates. West began his study by analyzing earlier research and articles in several prominent newspapers, data on the number and substance of television campaign ads, and public opinion polls. His empirical

[1] Kenneth Hoover and Todd Donovan, *The Elements of Social Scientific Thinking* (New York: St. Martin's Press, 1995), p. 38.

finding: Political ads do shape voters' perceptions of the candidates. West proceeded to discuss the implications of candidates being able, through television ads, to shape citizens' perceptions of them. His normative conclusion: Campaign ads, which usually focus on the personal characteristics of candidates, not their policies, are important, but their influence "is not always positive from the standpoint of representative democracy."[2]

HYPOTHESES AND VARIABLES

Hypotheses guide scientific research. *Hypotheses* (singular: *hypothesis*) suggest relationships between two or more variables in which one variable is thought to influence the others. Hypotheses are derived from common sense and casual observation. For example, medical scientists for years have studied the effects of smoking on health. Their initial hypothesis would have been something like "smoking has negative consequences on a person's health." More specifically, they might have hypothesized that "smoking has a negative effect on a person's cardiovascular and respiratory systems." Then they would have designed their research to test their hypothesis. They would begin with an examination of the physical condition of smokers and nonsmokers. In this instance, smoking or not smoking would be one variable, and the subjects' cardiovascular and respiratory health would be another. Of course other variables might influence a person's physical health, among them weight, age, eating and drinking habits, cholesterol level, exercise, and heredity. And the researcher must *control for*—account for or factor in—those variables. That can be a formidable task. Even in medical research, even under laboratory conditions, establishing a causal relationship between variable *X* (smoking) and variable *Y* (health) is no easy matter.

In trying to develop a theory of voting behavior, political scientists examine *independent variables,* the characteristics of voters—age, race or ethnicity, religion, income, education, gender, geographic location, for example—that can influence their decision. That decision—whether an individual votes for a Democratic or Republican presidential candidate, say—is the *dependent variable.* In other words, we hypothesize that independent variables (voters' characteristics) influence the dependent variable (party preference at the polls). If we look at race and party preference, we see that blacks are much more likely to vote for Democratic presidential candidates. It makes sense, then, to assume that race does influence voting behavior.

The critical feature of any variable is that it can be used to classify something along a dimension. For example, gender is a variable in many studies: That is, many studies divide participants into male and female subsets to see if behaviors differ along the gender dimension. Other studies group people by age or by religion.

Some of the variables that affect voting behavior are linked. For example, we can examine party preference (Democrat or Republican) by education (high school diploma, some college, college degree, graduate degree) and by income level (low, middle, high). Of course we know that education and income are linked: In general, the better educated the individual, the higher his or her income.

We need to add three cautionary notes here. First, in most research involving political behavior and attitudes, we are not talking about causation. Research in the social sciences is not like research in the natural sciences. A chemist, for example, can strictly control and isolate variables in the laboratory—adding one compound to another and then measuring what happens when a third compound is added to the mix. The chemist has control over *intervening variables.* Not so the social scientist: The variables that affect human behavior cannot be controlled for or reproduced in a laboratory. And because human behavior is the product of a large number of influences, it is very difficult to prove that just one or two variables cause a particular behavior. In most cases, political scientists, like most social scientists, can establish only that particular independent variables are more or less likely to explain a particular dependent variable. Political scientists usually have to be content with establishing correlation rather than causation.

Second, social scientists do not prove hypotheses. After testing a hypothesis with empirical evidence (data), they might accept or reject the hypothesis; but they can't prove it.

Third, a hypothesis must be based on a reasonable connection between the variables under study. Political scientists might be able to show that a candidate whose last name has seven letters has been

[2] Darrell M. West, "Television Advertising in Election Campaigns," *Political Science Quarterly* 109 (Winter 1994–1995): 789–809.

elected governor of a state every twenty-four years, but they wouldn't be able to demonstrate that causation is at work here. Why? Because there's no plausible reason for hypothesizing a connection between the number of characters in the last names of gubernatorial candidates and voting behavior. Yet they could hypothesize that an odd-sounding name might cost a candidate votes. Candidates' names offer subtle cues about their ethnicity, gender, even religion—factors that do shape voters' behavior.

CASE STUDIES AND COMPARATIVE STUDIES

Studies that focus on the dynamics of one political contest, the impact of one anticrime program, the record of a particular mayor or governor or president, or the political and social views of students on one college campus are called *case studies.* Case studies focus on behavior in a narrow environment. Case studies abound in social science research in large part because they're both economical and interesting.

Case studies also can serve as the theoretical foundation for subsequent studies that compare behaviors in two or more environments. For example, a case study of the Reagan presidency (1981–1988) might assess the foreign and defense policies of the administration during a period of economic and political change in the United States and rapid change in the Soviet Union. For a more comprehensive picture of Reagan's foreign policy, a comparative study might include the foreign and defense policies of other contemporary presidents. The comparative perspective is valuable because it increases our ability to make generalizations about political behavior.

CREATING AN INDEX

An *index* is a single value that summarizes a number of related variables. For example, suppose you were the chair of a college committee assigned the task of selecting "the outstanding senior of the year" for special recognition at commencement exercises. Of course you could simply identify the graduating senior with the highest grade point average. But suppose you want the honor to reflect more than scholastic achievement. Suppose you're also interested in students' community service or achievement in extracurricular activities.

To create an index for the outstanding senior of the year based on multiple criteria, you would begin by identifying several categories and assigning a number to each level in those categories. That would allow you to summarize and compare the candidates' scores across categories. Consider grade point average. Let's say you break down the category into five levels: very high (3.75–4.00), high (3.50–3.74), above average (3.00–3.49), average (2.50–2.99), and below average (below 2.50). Then you assign each level a number from 5 (very high) to 1 (below average). You'd do the same in each of the other categories. Then, for each student, you'd add the numbers in all the categories and divide the total by the number of categories. The quotient is the student's index. And the outstanding senior would be the student with the highest index.

The consumer price index (CPI) is a summary score that measures the changing price of consumer goods over a given period. In the United States, the CPI is based on the prices of four hundred items measured monthly in eighty-five cities. This index tells us whether inflation is up, down, or holding steady compared with inflation in previous periods. Similarly, the FBI's crime index is based on eight categories of serious crimes reported to the police monthly. FBI analysts summarize the frequency of those crimes—usually the rate of crime per 100,000 people—and issue reports that show whether crime in general is up, down, or unchanged compared with crime in some previous period. Those reports also allow cities and states to compare crime rates.

MEASURES OF CENTRAL TENDENCY

The mode, median, and mean are common statistics in the analysis of data. These *measures of central tendency*—each a single number—give us basic information about patterns in data.

The *mode* is the element that occurs most often in a distribution. In Table A.1, the mode is 78: More students received a grade of 78 than any other grade.

The *median* is the middle value in a distribution; that is, an equal number of elements lie above and below the median. The median grade in Table A.1 is 79.5: There are forty scores above that grade and

TABLE A.1 GRADE DISTRIBUTION ON EXAMINATION 1

POINTS	NUMBER OF STUDENTS
66	1
70	3
72	4
75	3
76	6
77	9
78	12
79	2
80	7
81	1
82	2
83	5
84	4
85	2
86	5
87	3
88	2
89	3
90	1
91	1
92	1
93	2
95	1

forty scores below it. (The median looks at the number of data points in the distribution; it doesn't matter if a value is repeated.) The formula we used to calculate the median in Table A.1 is $(N + 1)/2$, where N is the number of values in the distribution. Notice that the result is not the median but the rank of the value that is the median.

The *mean* is just the average of the values. It is calculated by taking all of the values in the distribution, adding them together, and dividing the sum by the number of values. In Table A.1, the average score is 78.5: the total of the scores (6,280) divided by the number of students who took the exam (80).

It is easy to be overwhelmed by statistics, especially those derived from complex models and tests. The exercises in this workbook that require data analysis employ elementary statistics, like those described here.

THE UNITED STATES CONSTITUTION

We the People of the United States, in Order to form a more perfect Union, establish Justice, insure domestic Tranquility, provide for the common defence, promote the general Welfare, and secure the Blessings of Liberty to ourselves and our Posterity, do ordain and establish this Constitution for the United States of America.

ARTICLE I.

Section 1 All legislative Powers herein granted shall be vested in a Congress of the United States, which shall consist of a Senate and House of Representatives.

Section 2 The House of Representatives shall be composed of Members chosen every second Year by the People of the several States, and the Electors in each State shall have the Qualifications requisite for Electors of the most numerous Branch of the State Legislature.

No Person shall be a Representative who shall not have attained to the Age of twenty five Years, and been seven Years a Citizen of the United States, and who shall not, when elected, be an Inhabitant of that State in which he shall be chosen.

Representatives and direct Taxes shall be apportioned among the several States which may be included within this Union, according to their respective Numbers, which shall be determined by adding to the whole Number of free Persons, including those bound to Service for a Term of Years, and excluding Indians not taxed, three fifths of all other Persons.

The actual Enumeration shall be made within three Years after the first Meeting of the Congress of the United States, and within every subsequent Term of ten Years, in such Manner as they shall by Law direct. The Number of Representatives shall not exceed one for every thirty Thousand, but each State shall have at Least one Representative; and until such enumeration shall be made, the State of New Hampshire shall be entitled to chuse three, Massachusetts eight, Rhode Island and Providence Plantations one, Connecticut five, New York six, New Jersey four, Pennsylvania eight, Delaware one, Maryland six, Virginia ten, North Carolina five, South Carolina five and Georgia three.

When vacancies happen in the Representation from any State, the Executive Authority thereof shall issue Writs of Election to fill such Vacancies.

The House of Representatives shall chuse their Speaker and other Officers; and shall have the sole Power of Impeachment.

Section 3 The Senate of the United States shall be composed of two Senators from each State, chosen by the Legislature thereof, for six Years; and each Senator shall have one Vote.

Immediately after they shall be assembled in Consequence of the first Election, they shall be divided as equally as may be into three Classes. The Seats of the Senators of the first Class shall be vacated at the Expiration of the second Year, of the second Class at the Expiration of the fourth Year, and of the third Class at the Expiration of the sixth Year, so that one third may be chosen every second Year; and if Vacancies happen by Resignation, or otherwise, during the Recess of the Legislature of any State, the Executive thereof may make temporary Appointments until the next Meeting of the Legislature, which shall then fill such Vacancies.

No person shall be a Senator who shall not have attained to the Age of thirty Years, and been nine Years a Citizen of the United States, and who shall not, when elected, be an Inhabitant of that State for which he shall be chosen.

The Vice President of the United States shall be President of the Senate, but shall have no Vote, unless they be equally divided.

The Senate shall chuse their other Officers, and also a President pro tempore, in the absence of the Vice President, or when he shall exercise the Office of President of the United States.

The Senate shall have the sole Power to try all Impeachments. When sitting for that Purpose, they shall be on Oath or Affirmation. When the President of the United States is tried, the Chief Justice shall preside: And no Person shall be convicted without the Concurrence of two thirds of the Members present.

Judgment in Cases of Impeachment shall not extend further than to removal from Office, and disqualification to hold and enjoy any Office of honor, Trust or Profit under the United States: but the Party convicted shall nevertheless be liable and subject to Indictment, Trial, Judgment and Punishment, according to Law.

Section 4 The Times, Places and Manner of holding Elections for Senators and Representatives, shall be prescribed in each State by the Legislature thereof; but the Congress may at any time by Law make or alter such Regulations, except as to the Place of Chusing Senators.

The Congress shall assemble at least once in every Year, and such Meeting shall be on the first Monday in December, unless they shall by Law appoint a different Day.

Section 5 Each House shall be the Judge of the Elections, Returns and Qualifications of its own Members, and a Majority of each shall constitute a Quorum to do Business; but a smaller number may adjourn from day to day, and may be authorized to compel the Attendance of absent Members, in such Manner, and under such Penalties as each House may provide.

Each House may determine the Rules of its Proceedings, punish its Members for disorderly Behavior, and, with the Concurrence of two-thirds, expel a Member.

Each House shall keep a Journal of its Proceedings, and from time to time publish the same, excepting such Parts as may in their Judgment require Secrecy; and the Yeas and Nays of the Members of either House on any question shall, at the Desire of one fifth of those Present, be entered on the Journal.

Neither House, during the Session of Congress, shall, without the Consent of the other, adjourn for more than three days, nor to any other Place than that in which the two Houses shall be sitting.

Section 6 The Senators and Representatives shall receive a Compensation for their Services, to be ascertained by Law, and paid out of the Treasury of the United States. They shall in all Cases, except Treason, Felony and Breach of the Peace, be privileged from Arrest during their Attendance at the Session of their respective Houses, and in going to and returning from the same; and for any Speech or Debate in either House, they shall not be questioned in any other place.

No Senator or Representative shall, during the Time for which he was elected, be appointed to any civil Office under the Authority of the United States which shall have been created, or the Emoluments whereof shall have been increased during such time; and no Person holding any Office under the United States, shall be a Member of either House during his Continuance in Office.

Section 7 All bills for raising Revenue shall originate in the House of Representatives; but the Senate may propose or concur with Amendments as on other Bills.

Every Bill which shall have passed the House of Representatives and the Senate, shall, before it become a Law, be presented to the President of the United States; If he approve he shall sign it, but if not he shall return it, with his Objections to that House in which it shall have originated, who shall enter the Objections at large on their Journal, and proceed to reconsider it. If after such Reconsideration two thirds of that House shall agree to pass the Bill, it shall be sent, together with the Objections, to the other House, by which it shall likewise be reconsidered, and if approved by two thirds of that House, it shall become a Law. But in all such Cases the Votes of both Houses shall be determined by Yeas and Nays, and the Names of the Persons voting for and against the Bill shall be entered on the Journal of each House respectively. If any Bill shall not be returned by the President within ten Days (Sundays excepted) after it shall have been presented to him, the Same shall be a Law, in like Manner as if he had signed it, unless the Congress by their Adjournment prevent its Return, in which Case it shall not be a Law.

Every Order, Resolution, or Vote to which the Concurrence of the Senate and House of Representatives may be necessary (except on a question of Adjournment) shall be presented to the President of the United States; and before the Same shall take Effect, shall be approved by him, or being disapproved by him, shall be repassed by two thirds of the Senate and House of Representatives, according to the Rules and Limitations prescribed in the Case of a Bill.

Section 8 The Congress shall have Power To lay and collect Taxes, Duties, Imposts and Excises, to pay the Debts and provide for the common Defence and general Welfare of the United States; but all Duties, Imposts and Excises shall be uniform throughout the United States;

To borrow money on the credit of the United States;

To regulate Commerce with foreign Nations, and among the several States, and with the Indian Tribes;

To establish an uniform Rule of Naturalization, and uniform Laws on the subject of Bankruptcies throughout the United States;

To coin Money, regulate the Value thereof, and of foreign Coin, and fix the Standard of Weights and Measures;

To provide for the Punishment of counterfeiting the Securities and current Coin of the United States;

To establish Post Offices and Post Roads;

To promote the Progress of Science and useful Arts, by securing for limited Times to Authors and Inventors the exclusive Right to their respective Writings and Discoveries;

To constitute Tribunals inferior to the supreme Court;

To define and punish Piracies and Felonies committed on the high Seas, and Offenses against the Law of Nations;

To declare War, grant Letters of Marque and Reprisal, and make Rules concerning Captures on Land and Water;

To raise and support Armies, but no Appropriation of Money to that Use shall be for a longer Term than two Years;

To provide and maintain a Navy;

To make Rules for the Government and Regulation of the land and naval Forces;

To provide for calling forth the Militia to execute the Laws of the Union, suppress Insurrections and repel Invasions;

To provide for organizing, arming, and disciplining the Militia, and for governing such Part of them as may be employed in the Service of the United States, reserving to the States respectively, the Appointment of the Officers, and the Authority of training the Militia according to the discipline prescribed by Congress;

To exercise exclusive Legislation in all Cases whatsoever, over such District (not exceeding ten Miles square) as may, by Cession of particular States, and the acceptance of Congress, become the Seat of the Government of the United States, and to exercise like Authority over all Places purchased by the Consent of the Legislature of the State in which the Same shall be, for the Erection of Forts, Magazines, Arsenals, dock-Yards, and other needful Buildings; And

To make all Laws which shall be necessary and proper for carrying into Execution the foregoing Powers, and all other Powers vested by this Constitution in the Government of the United States, or in any Department or Officer thereof.

Section 9 The Migration or Importation of such Persons as any of the States now existing shall think proper to admit, shall not be prohibited by the Congress prior to the Year one thousand eight hundred and eight, but a tax or duty may be imposed on such Importation, not exceeding ten dollars for each Person.

The privilege of the Writ of Habeas Corpus shall not be suspended, unless when in Cases of Rebellion or Invasion the public Safety may require it.

No Bill of Attainder or ex post facto Law shall be passed. No capitation, or other direct, Tax shall be laid, unless in Proportion to the Census or Enumeration herein before directed to be taken.

No Tax or Duty shall be laid on Articles exported from any State.

No Preference shall be given by any Regulation of Commerce or Revenue to the Ports of one State over those of another: nor shall Vessels bound to, or from, one State, be obliged to enter, clear, or pay Duties in another.

No Money shall be drawn from the Treasury, but in Consequence of Appropriations made by Law; and a regular Statement and Account of the Receipts and Expenditures of all public Money shall be published from time to time.

No Title of Nobility shall be granted by the United States: And no Person holding any Office of Profit or Trust under them, shall, without the Consent of the Congress, accept of any present, Emolument, Office, or Title, of any kind whatever, from any King, Prince or foreign State.

Section 10 No State shall enter into any Treaty, Alliance, or Confederation; grant Letters of Marque and Reprisal; coin Money; emit Bills of Credit; make any Thing but gold and silver Coin a Tender in Payment of Debts; pass any Bill of Attainder, ex post facto Law, or Law impairing the Obligation of Contracts, or grant any Title of Nobility.

No State shall, without the Consent of the Congress, lay any Imposts or Duties on Imports or Exports, except what may be absolutely necessary for executing it's inspection Laws: and the net Produce of all Duties and Imposts, laid by any State on Imports or Exports, shall be for the Use of the Treasury of the United States; and all such Laws shall be subject to the Revision and Controul of the Congress.

No State shall, without the Consent of Congress, lay any duty of Tonnage, keep Troops, or Ships of War in time of Peace, enter into any Agreement or Compact with another State, or with a foreign Power, or engage in War, unless actually invaded, or in such imminent Danger as will not admit of delay.

ARTICLE II.

Section 1 The executive Power shall be vested in a President of the United States of America. He shall hold his Office during the Term of four Years, and, together with the Vice-President chosen for the same Term, be elected, as follows:

Each State shall appoint, in such Manner as the Legislature thereof may direct, a Number of Electors, equal to the whole Number of Senators and Representatives to which the State may be entitled in the Congress: but no Senator or Representative, or Person holding an Office of Trust or Profit under the United States, shall be appointed an Elector.

The Electors shall meet in their respective States, and vote by Ballot for two persons, of whom one at least shall not lie an Inhabitant of the same State with themselves. And they shall make a List of all the Persons voted for, and of the Number of Votes for each; which List they shall sign and certify, and transmit sealed to the Seat of the Government of the United States, directed to the President of the Senate. The President of the Senate shall, in the Presence of the Senate and House of Representatives, open all the Certificates, and the Votes shall then be counted. The Person having the greatest Number of Votes shall be the President, if such Number be a Majority of the whole Number of Electors appointed; and if there be more than one who have such Majority, and have an equal Number of Votes, then the House of Representatives shall immediately chuse by Ballot one of them for President; and if no Person have a Majority, then from the five highest on the List the said House shall in like Manner chuse the President. But in chusing the President, the Votes shall be taken by States, the Representation from each State having one Vote; a quorum for this Purpose shall consist of a Member or Members from two-thirds of the States, and a Majority of all the States shall be necessary to a Choice. In every Case, after the Choice of the President, the Person having the greatest Number of Votes of the Electors shall be the Vice President. But if there should remain two or more who have equal Votes, the Senate shall chuse from them by Ballot the Vice-President.

The Congress may determine the Time of chusing the Electors, and the Day on which they shall give their Votes; which Day shall be the same throughout the United States.

No person except a natural born Citizen, or a Citizen of the United States, at the time of the Adoption of this Constitution, shall be eligible to the Office of President; neither shall any Person be eligible to that Office who shall not have attained to the Age of thirty-five Years, and been fourteen Years a Resident within the United States.

In Case of the Removal of the President from Office, or of his Death, Resignation, or Inability to discharge the Powers and Duties of the said Office, the same shall devolve on the Vice President, and the Congress may by Law provide for the Case of Removal, Death, Resignation or Inability, both of the President and Vice President, declaring what Officer shall then act as President, and such Officer shall act accordingly, until the Disability be removed, or a President shall be elected.

The President shall, at stated Times, receive for his Services, a Compensation, which shall neither be increased nor diminished during the Period for which he shall have been elected, and he shall not receive within that Period any other Emolument from the United States, or any of them.

Before he enter on the Execution of his Office, he shall take the following Oath or Affirmation:

"I do solemnly swear (or affirm) that I will faithfully execute the Office of President of the United States, and will to the best of my Ability, preserve, protect and defend the Constitution of the United States."

Section 2 The President shall be Commander in Chief of the Army and Navy of the United States, and of the Militia of the several States, when called into the actual Service of the United States; he may require the Opinion, in writing, of the principal Officer in each of the executive Departments, upon any subject relating to the Duties of their respective Offices, and he shall have Power to Grant Reprieves and Pardons for Offenses against the United States, except in Cases of Impeachment.

He shall have Power, by and with the Advice and Consent of the Senate, to make Treaties, provided two thirds of the Senators present concur; and he shall nominate, and by and with the Advice and Consent of the Senate, shall appoint Ambassadors, other public Ministers and Consuls, Judges of the Supreme Court, and all other Officers of the United States, whose Appointments are not herein otherwise provided for, and which shall be established by Law: but the Congress may by Law vest the Appointment of such inferior Officers, as they think proper, in the President alone, in the Courts of Law, or in the Heads of Departments.

The President shall have Power to fill up all Vacancies that may happen during the Recess of the Senate, by granting Commissions which shall expire at the End of their next Session.

Section 3 He shall from time to time give to the Congress Information of the State of the Union, and recommend to their Consideration such Measures as he shall judge necessary and expedient; he may, on extraordinary Occasions, convene both Houses, or either of them, and in Case of Disagreement between them, with Respect to the Time of Adjournment, he may adjourn them to such Time as he shall think proper; he shall receive Ambassadors and other public Ministers; he shall take Care that the Laws be faithfully executed, and shall Commission all the Officers of the United States.

Section 4 The President, Vice President and all civil Officers of the United States, shall be removed from Office on Impeachment for, and Conviction of, Treason, Bribery, or other high Crimes and Misdemeanors.

ARTICLE III.

Section 1 The judicial Power of the United States, shall be vested in one Supreme Court, and in such inferior Courts as the Congress may from time to time ordain and establish. The Judges, both of the supreme and inferior Courts, shall hold their Offices during good Behavior, and shall, at stated Times, receive for their Services a Compensation which shall not be diminished during their Continuance in Office.

Section 2 The judicial Power shall extend to all Cases, in Law and Equity, arising under this Constitution, the Laws of the United States, and Treaties made, or which shall be made, under their Authority; to all Cases affecting Ambassadors, other public Ministers and Consuls; to all Cases of admiralty and maritime Jurisdiction; to Controversies to which the United States shall be a Party; to Controversies between two or more States; between a State and Citizens of another State; between Citizens of different States; between Citizens of the same State claiming Lands under Grants of different States, and between a State, or the Citizens thereof, and foreign States, Citizens or Subjects.

In all Cases affecting Ambassadors, other public Ministers and Consuls, and those in which a State shall be Party, the Supreme Court shall have original Jurisdiction. In all the other Cases before mentioned, the Supreme Court shall have appellate Jurisdiction, both as to Law and Fact, with such Exceptions, and under such Regulations as the Congress shall make.

Trial of all Crimes, except in Cases of Impeachment, shall be by Jury; and such Trial shall be held in the State where the said Crimes shall have been committed; but when not committed within any State, the Trial shall be at such Place or Places as the Congress may by Law have directed.

Section 3 Treason against the United States, shall consist only in levying War against them, or in adhering to their Enemies, giving them Aid and Comfort. No Person shall be convicted of Treason unless on the Testimony of two Witnesses to the same overt Act, or on Confession in open Court.

The Congress shall have power to declare the Punishment of Treason, but no Attainder of Treason shall work Corruption of Blood, or Forfeiture except during the Life of the Person attainted.

ARTICLE IV.

Section 1 Full Faith and Credit shall be given in each State to the public Acts, Records, and judicial Proceedings of every other State. And the Congress may by general Laws prescribe the Manner in which such Acts, Records and Proceedings shall be proved, and the Effect thereof.

Section 2 The Citizens of each State shall be entitled to all Privileges and Immunities of Citizens in the several States.

A Person charged in any State with Treason, Felony, or other Crime, who shall flee from Justice, and be found in another State, shall on demand of the executive Authority of the State from which he fled, be delivered up, to be removed to the State having Jurisdiction of the Crime.

No Person held to Service or Labour in one State, under the Laws thereof, escaping into another, shall, in Consequence of any Law or Regulation therein, be discharged from such Service or Labour, But shall be delivered up on Claim of the Party to whom such Service or Labour may be due.

Section 3 New States may be admitted by the Congress into this Union; but no new States shall be formed or erected within the Jurisdiction of any other State; nor any State be formed by the Junction of two or more States, or parts of States, without the Consent of the Legislatures of the States concerned as well as of the Congress.

The Congress shall have Power to dispose of and make all needful Rules and Regulations respecting the Territory or other Property belonging to the United States; and nothing in this Constitution shall be so construed as to Prejudice any Claims of the United States, or of any particular State.

Section 4 The United States shall guarantee to every State in this Union a Republican Form of Government, and shall protect each of them against Invasion; and on Application of the Legislature, or of the Executive (when the Legislature cannot be convened) against domestic Violence.

ARTICLE V.

The Congress, whenever two thirds of both Houses shall deem it necessary, shall propose Amendments to this Constitution, or, on the Application of the Legislatures of two thirds of the several States, shall call a Convention for proposing Amendments, which, in either Case, shall be valid to all Intents and Purposes, as part of this Constitution, when ratified by the Legislatures of three fourths of the several States, or by Conventions in three fourths thereof, as the one or the other Mode of Ratification may be proposed by the Congress; Provided that no Amendment which may be made prior to the Year One thousand eight hundred and eight shall in any Manner affect the first and fourth Clauses in the Ninth Section of the first Article; and that no State, without its Consent, shall be deprived of its equal Suffrage in the Senate.

ARTICLE VI.

All Debts contracted and Engagements entered into, before the Adoption of this Constitution, shall be as valid against the United States under this Constitution, as under the Confederation.

This Constitution, and the Laws of the United States which shall be made in Pursuance thereof; and all Treaties made, or which shall be made, under the Authority of the United States, shall be the supreme Law of the Land; and the Judges in every State shall be bound thereby, any Thing in the Constitution or Laws of any State to the Contrary notwithstanding.

The Senators and Representatives before mentioned, and the Members of the several State Legislatures, and all executive and judicial Officers, both of the United States and of the several States, shall be bound by Oath or Affirmation, to support this Constitution; but no religious Test shall ever be required as a Qualification to any Office or public Trust under the United States.

ARTICLE VII.

The Ratification of the Conventions of nine States, shall be sufficient for the Establishment of this Constitution between the States so ratifying the Same.

Done in Convention by the Unanimous Consent of the States present the Seventeenth Day of September in the Year of our Lord one thousand seven hundred and Eighty seven and of the Independence of the United States of America the Twelfth. In Witness whereof We have hereunto subscribed our Names.

Go Washington—President and deputy from Virginia
New Hampshire—John Langdon, Nicholas Gilman
Massachusetts—Nathaniel Gorham, Rufus King
Connecticut—Wm Saml Johnson, Roger Sherman
New York—Alexander Hamilton
New Jersey—Wil Livingston, David Brearley, Wm Paterson, Jona. Dayton
Pensylvania—B Franklin, Thomas Mifflin, Robt Morris, Geo. Clymer, Thos FitzSimons, Jared Ingersoll, James Wilson, Gouv Morris
Delaware—Geo. Read, Gunning Bedford jun, John Dickinson, Richard Bassett, Jaco. Broom
Maryland—James McHenry, Dan of St Tho Jenifer, Danl Carroll
Virginia—John Blair, James Madison Jr.
North Carolina—Wm Blount, Richd Dobbs Spaight, Hu Williamson
South Carolina—J. Rutledge, Charles Cotesworth Pinckney, Charles Pinckney, Pierce Butler
Georgia—William Few, Abr Baldwin
Attest: William Jackson, Secretary

Amendment I Congress shall make no law respecting an establishment of religion, or prohibiting the free exercise thereof; or abridging the freedom of speech, or of the press; or the right of the people peaceably to assemble, and to petition the Government for a redress of grievances.

Amendment II A well regulated Militia, being necessary to the security of a free State, the right of the people to keep and bear Arms, shall not be infringed.

Amendment III No Soldier shall, in time of peace be quartered in any house, without the consent of the Owner, nor in time of war, but in a manner to be prescribed by law.

Amendment IV The right of the people to be secure in their persons, houses, papers, and effects, against unreasonable searches and seizures, shall not be violated, and no Warrants shall issue, but upon probable cause, supported by Oath or affirmation, and particularly describing the place to be searched, and the persons or things to be seized.

Amendment V No person shall be held to answer for a capital, or otherwise infamous crime, unless on a presentment or indictment of a Grand Jury, except in cases arising in the land or naval forces, or in the Militia, when in actual service in time of War or public danger; nor shall any person be subject for the same offense to be twice put in jeopardy of life or limb; nor shall be compelled in any criminal case to be a witness against himself; nor be deprived of life, liberty, or property, without due process of law; nor shall private property be taken for public use, without just compensation.

Amendment VI In all criminal prosecutions, the accused shall enjoy the right to a speedy and public trial, by an impartial jury of the State and district wherein the crime shall have been committed, which district shall have been previously ascertained by law, and to be informed of the nature and cause of the accusation; to be confronted with the witnesses against him; to have compulsory process for obtaining witnesses in his favor, and to have the Assistance of Counsel for his defence.

Amendment VII In Suits at common law, where the value in controversy shall exceed twenty dollars, the right of trial by jury shall be preserved, and no fact tried by a jury, shall be otherwise re-examined in any Court of the United States, than according to the rules of the common law.

Amendment VIII Excessive bail shall not be required, nor excessive fines imposed, nor cruel and unusual punishments inflicted.

Amendment IX The enumeration in the Constitution, of certain rights, shall not be construed to deny or disparage others retained by the people.

Amendment X The powers not delegated to the United States by the Constitution, nor prohibited by it to the States, are reserved to the States respectively, or to the people.

Amendment XI The Judicial power of the United States shall not be construed to extend to any suit in law or equity, commenced or prosecuted against one of the United States by Citizens of another State, or by Citizens or Subjects of any Foreign State.

Amendment XII The Electors shall meet in their respective states, and vote by ballot for President and Vice-President, one of whom, at least, shall not be an inhabitant of the same state with themselves; they shall name in their ballots the person voted for as President, and in distinct ballots the person voted for as Vice-President, and they shall make distinct lists of all persons voted for as President, and of all persons voted for as Vice-President and of the number of votes for each, which lists they shall sign and certify, and transmit sealed to the seat of the government of the United States, directed to the President of the Senate;

The President of the Senate shall, in the presence of the Senate and House of Representatives, open all the certificates and the votes shall then be counted;

The person having the greatest Number of votes for President, shall be the President, if such number be a majority of the whole number of Electors appointed; and if no person have such majority, then from the persons having the highest numbers not exceeding three on the list of those voted for as President, the House of Representatives shall choose immediately, by ballot, the President. But in choosing the

President, the votes shall be taken by states, the representation from each state having one vote; a quorum for this purpose shall consist of a member or members from two-thirds of the states, and a majority of all the states shall be necessary to a choice. And if the House of Representatives shall not choose a President whenever the right of choice shall devolve upon them, before the fourth day of March next following, then the Vice-President shall act as President, as in the case of the death or other constitutional disability of the President.

The person having the greatest number of votes as Vice-President, shall be the Vice-President, if such number be a majority of the whole number of Electors appointed, and if no person have a majority, then from the two highest numbers on the list, the Senate shall choose the Vice-President; a quorum for the purpose shall consist of two-thirds of the whole number of Senators, and a majority of the whole number shall be necessary to a choice. But no person constitutionally ineligible to the office of President shall be eligible to that of Vice-President of the United States.

Amendment XIII 1. Neither slavery nor involuntary servitude, except as a punishment for crime whereof the party shall have been duly convicted, shall exist within the United States, or any place subject to their jurisdiction.

2. Congress shall have power to enforce this article by appropriate legislation.

Amendment XIV 1. All persons born or naturalized in the United States, and subject to the jurisdiction thereof, are citizens of the United States and of the State wherein they reside. No State shall make or enforce any law which shall abridge the privileges or immunities of citizens of the United States; nor shall any State deprive any person of life, liberty, or property, without due process of law; nor deny to any person within its jurisdiction the equal protection of the laws.

2. Representatives shall be apportioned among the several States according to their respective numbers, counting the whole number of persons in each State, excluding Indians not taxed. But when the right to vote at any election for the choice of electors for President and Vice-President of the United States, Representatives in Congress, the Executive and Judicial officers of a State, or the members of the Legislature thereof, is denied to any of the male inhabitants of such State, being twenty-one years of age, and citizens of the United States, or in any way abridged, except for participation in rebellion, or other crime, the basis of representation therein shall be reduced in the proportion which the number of such male citizens shall bear to the whole number of male citizens twenty-one years of age in such State.

3. No person shall be a Senator or Representative in Congress, or elector of President and Vice-President, or hold any office, civil or military, under the United States, or under any State, who, having previously taken an oath, as a member of Congress, or as an officer of the United States, or as a member of any State legislature, or as an executive or judicial officer of any State, to support the Constitution of the United States, shall have engaged in insurrection or rebellion against the same, or given aid or comfort to the enemies thereof. But Congress may by a vote of two-thirds of each House, remove such disability.

4. The validity of the public debt of the United States, authorized by law, including debts incurred for payment of pensions and bounties for services in suppressing insurrection or rebellion, shall not be questioned. But neither the United States nor any State shall assume or pay any debt or obligation incurred in aid of insurrection or rebellion against the United States, or any claim for the loss or emancipation of any slave; but all such debts, obligations and claims shall be held illegal and void.

5. The Congress shall have power to enforce, by appropriate legislation, the provisions of this article.

Amendment XV 1. The right of citizens of the United States to vote shall not be denied or abridged by the United States or by any State on account of race, color, or previous condition of servitude.

2. The Congress shall have power to enforce this article by appropriate legislation.

Amendment XVI The Congress shall have power to lay and collect taxes on incomes, from whatever source derived, without apportionment among the several States, and without regard to any census or enumeration.

Amendment XVII The Senate of the United States shall be composed of two Senators from each State, elected by the people thereof, for six years; and each Senator shall have one vote. The electors in each State shall have the qualifications requisite for electors of the most numerous branch of the State legislatures.

When vacancies happen in the representation of any State in the Senate, the executive authority of such State shall issue writs of election to fill such vacancies: Provided, That the legislature of any State may empower the executive thereof to make temporary appointments until the people fill the vacancies by election as the legislature may direct.

This amendment shall not be so construed as to affect the election or term of any Senator chosen before it becomes valid as part of the Constitution.

Amendment XVIII 1. After one year from the ratification of this article the manufacture, sale, or transportation of intoxicating liquors within, the importation thereof into, or the exportation thereof from the United States and all territory subject to the jurisdiction thereof for beverage purposes is hereby prohibited.

2. The Congress and the several States shall have concurrent power to enforce this article by appropriate legislation.

3. This article shall be inoperative unless it shall have been ratified as an amendment to the Constitution by the legislatures of the several States, as provided in the Constitution, within seven years from the date of the submission hereof to the States by the Congress.

Amendment XIX The right of citizens of the United States to vote shall not be denied or abridged by the United States or by any State on account of sex.

Congress shall have power to enforce this article by appropriate legislation.

Amendment XX 1. The terms of the President and Vice President shall end at noon on the 20th day of January, and the terms of Senators and Representatives at noon on the 3d day of January, of the years in which such terms would have ended if this article had not been ratified; and the terms of their successors shall then begin.

2. The Congress shall assemble at least once in every year, and such meeting shall begin at noon on the 3d day of January, unless they shall by law appoint a different day.

3. If, at the time fixed for the beginning of the term of the President, the President elect shall have died, the Vice President elect shall become President. If a President shall not have been chosen before the time fixed for the beginning of his term, or if the President elect shall have failed to qualify, then the Vice President elect shall act as President until a President shall have qualified; and the Congress may by law provide for the case wherein neither a President elect nor a Vice President elect shall have qualified, declaring who shall then act as President, or the manner in which one who is to act shall be selected, and such person shall act accordingly until a President or Vice President shall have qualified.

4. The Congress may by law provide for the case of the death of any of the persons from whom the House of Representatives may choose a President whenever the right of choice shall have devolved upon them, and for the case of the death of any of the persons from whom the Senate may choose a Vice President whenever the right of choice shall have devolved upon them.

5. Sections 1 and 2 shall take effect on the 15th day of October following the ratification of this article.

6. This article shall be inoperative unless it shall have been ratified as an amendment to the Constitution by the legislatures of three-fourths of the several States within seven years from the date of its submission.

Amendment XXI 1. The eighteenth article of amendment to the Constitution of the United States is hereby repealed.

2. The transportation or importation into any State, Territory, or possession of the United States for delivery or use therein of intoxicating liquors, in violation of the laws thereof, is hereby prohibited.

3. The article shall be inoperative unless it shall have been ratified as an amendment to the Constitution by conventions in the several States, as provided in the Constitution, within seven years from the date of the submission hereof to the States by the Congress.

Amendment XXII 1. No person shall be elected to the office of the President more than twice, and no person who has held the office of President, or acted as President, for more than two years of a term to which some other person was elected President shall be elected to the office of the President more than once. But this Article shall not apply to any person holding the office of President, when this Article was proposed by the Congress, and shall not prevent any person who may be holding the office of President, or acting as President, during the term within which this Article becomes operative from holding the office of President or acting as President during the remainder of such term.

2. This article shall be inoperative unless it shall have been ratified as an amendment to the Constitution by the legislatures of three-fourths of the several States within seven years from the date of its submission to the States by the Congress.

Amendment XXIII 1. The District constituting the seat of Government of the United States shall appoint in such manner as the Congress may direct: A number of electors of President and Vice President equal to the whole number of Senators and Representatives in Congress to which the District would be entitled if it were a State, but in no event more than the least populous State; they shall be in addition to those appointed by the States, but they shall be considered, for the purposes of the election of President and Vice President, to be electors appointed by a State; and they shall meet in the District and perform such duties as provided by the twelfth article of amendment.

2. The Congress shall have power to enforce this article by appropriate legislation.

Amendment XXIV 1. The right of citizens of the United States to vote in any primary or other election for President or Vice President, for electors for President or Vice President, or for Senator or Representative in Congress, shall not be denied or abridged by the United States or any State by reason of failure to pay any poll tax or other tax.

2. The Congress shall have power to enforce this article by appropriate legislation.

Amendment XXV 1. In case of the removal of the President from office or of his death or resignation, the Vice President shall become President.

2. Whenever there is a vacancy in the office of the Vice President, the President shall nominate a Vice President who shall take office upon confirmation by a majority vote of both Houses of Congress.

3. Whenever the President transmits to the President pro tempore of the Senate and the Speaker of the House of Representatives his written declaration that he is unable to discharge the powers and duties of his office, and until he transmits to them a written declaration to the contrary, such powers and duties shall be discharged by the Vice President as Acting President.

4. Whenever the Vice President and a majority of either the principal officers of the executive departments or of such other body as Congress may by law provide, transmit to the President pro tempore of

the Senate and the Speaker of the House of Representatives their written declaration that the President is unable to discharge the powers and duties of his office, the Vice President shall immediately assume the powers and duties of the office as Acting President.

Thereafter, when the President transmits to the President pro tempore of the Senate and the Speaker of the House of Representatives his written declaration that no inability exists, he shall resume the powers and duties of his office unless the Vice President and a majority of either the principal officers of the executive department or of such other body as Congress may by law provide, transmit within four days to the President pro tempore of the Senate and the Speaker of the House of Representatives their written declaration that the President is unable to discharge the powers and duties of his office. Thereupon Congress shall decide the issue, assembling within forty eight hours for that purpose if not in session. If the Congress, within twenty one days after receipt of the latter written declaration, or, if Congress is not in session, within twenty one days after Congress is required to assemble, determines by two thirds vote of both Houses that the President is unable to discharge the powers and duties of his office, the Vice President shall continue to discharge the same as Acting President; otherwise, the President shall resume the powers and duties of his office.

Amendment XXVI 1. The right of citizens of the United States, who are eighteen years of age or older, to vote shall not be denied or abridged by the United States or by any State on account of age.

2. The Congress shall have power to enforce this article by appropriate legislation.

Amendment XXVII No law, varying the compensation for the services of the Senators and Representatives, shall take effect, until an election of Representatives shall have intervened.

Lawrence Barkley / Christine Sandoval

Grammar and Usage, Naturally

CENGAGE Learning®

Australia • Brazil • Mexico • Singapore • United Kingdom • United States

Grammar and Usage, Naturally
Lawrence Barkley,
Christine Sandoval

Product Director: Annie Todd

Associate Content Developer: Elizabeth Rice

Product Assistant: Luria Rittenberg

Marketing Manager: Lydia Lestar

Content Project Manager: Dan Saabye

Art Director: Faith Brosnan

Manufacturing Planner: Betsy Donaghey

Rights Acquisition Specialist: Ann Hoffman

Production Service:
Cenveo® Publisher Services

Text Designer: Shawn Girsberger

Cover Designer: Sarah Bishins - sarahbdesign

Cover Image: © Tungphoto/ShutterStock.com

Compositor: Cenveo® Publisher Services

Library of Congress Control Number: 2013948778

ISBN-13: 978-1-285-44586-1

ISBN-10: 1-285-44586-4

Cengage Learning
200 First Stamford Place, 4th Floor
Stamford, CT 06902
USA

Printed in the United States of America
1 2 3 4 5 6 7 17 16 15 14 13

From Larry Barkley

To my colleagues in the Menifee English Department—Michelle Stewart, Ricki Rycraft, Yvonne Atkinson, Lorrie Ross, and Ted Blake—and my colleague in Anthropology, Erik Ozolins: Thank you for your continual support and encouragement. Y'all are truly wonderful people.

To my mother and father: Thank you for being my role models, people I am proud to emulate.

To Christine: The wait was truly worthwhile. Thank you.

To Susan: I dedicate this book to you, darlin'. Thank you for overlooking all the weekends I spent working on it; your patience would embarrass Job.

From Christine Sandoval

To Mom and Dad: Thank you for always making it clear that you expected I could accomplish anything I put my mind to. Mom, I wish you were here to see the final product, but I have a feeling you're bragging to your celestial friends.

To Alec and Toby: Thank you for allowing me the time to work and for cheering me on. A mother could never ask for better sons.

To Victor: Thank you for being my best friend and my greatest support. This book is for you.

And to Larry: Thank you for seeing in me what I had not noticed, and thank you for inviting me on this wild ride. I have enjoyed every minute of it.

CONTENTS

I THE FUNDAMENTALS 1

PREFACE

TO THE INSTRUCTOR: CULTIVATING YOUR STUDENTS' SUCCESS

As developmental English instructors, we take the time each semester to reevaluate our instructional methods, teaching strategies, activities, and assignments, and we ask ourselves if we should make changes for the next semester. We swap mediocre paragraph and essay prompts for better ones, we rethink our explanations of grammatical concepts, and we ask our colleagues for ideas to better instruct our students in the art of writing.

Part of this semesterly tradition of course evaluation is choosing a textbook. We flip through dozens of books, comparing approaches and structures, hoping to find that one text that will fulfill all of our students' needs. What inevitably happens is that we choose a textbook that *almost* does. We may rearrange chapters because the book's concepts aren't ordered in the way we would order them, or we may follow the structure but exchange our terminology for the book's. More times than not, we choose the best of the not-good-enough. Of course, the problem lies in that we want something that does not exist: we want a text that will miraculously impart all necessary knowledge to all students so they will then have all of the skills needed to be strong writers and editors.

Our goal in writing *Grammar and Usage, Naturally* is to get as close as possible to creating a text that will allow our students to communicate as skilled, confident writers and editors.

DISTINCTIVE FEATURES OF *GRAMMAR AND USAGE, NATURALLY*

A Flexible Organization

Grammar and Usage, Naturally is divided into three sections. Section I: "The Fundamentals" and Section III: "Enhancing the Fundamentals" both support Section II: "The Elements of Composition." In order to achieve proficiency and competency (as well as confidence) in their writing and editing, students must know the grammatical concepts in the nine chapters in Section I. Once they are familiar with those concepts and have begun their writing practice, the chapters in Section III allow them to develop a more sophisticated, mature writing style. Both Sections I and III augment Section II. Furthermore, the tripartite structure allows instructors, should they wish, to begin *en medias res*, in the middle of things. Since each section is self-contained, should instructors wish to begin their classes by teaching Section II initially, the tripartite organization allows them to do so. Overall, the three-way structure allows for greater flexibility in teaching *Grammar and Usage, Naturally*.

We organized Section I, "The Fundamentals," to reflect an organic approach to learning the basics of grammar. When learning the concepts of language, one concept is born of another; a natural progression exists, a growth of ideas. One can imagine a seed bursting open underground, a vine working its way through the dirt, sprouting leaves, one after another, as it reaches toward the sun. Too many developmental English books assume the seed has already been planted or the sprouts can grow without the first initial push through the dirt. This growth has to happen organically, naturally. Why do so many developmental books present the parts of speech chapter at the end of the text when these core concepts are crucial for a student to understand sentence structure? Words, phrases, clauses, and their functions are only truly understood once students understand the parts of speech.

As an example of this organic approach, imagine young students learning to play the piano. First, they learn the notes A through G, both as they appear on paper and as they appear on the white keys of the instrument. Once the children understand the white keys, they learn the black keys, the sharps and flats. They play scales to produce dexterity in their fingers. Finally, they learn how to place notes together to form melodies. The piano instructor teaches the concepts necessary for growth in the young pianists; she does not place a composition by Beethoven in front of the students and expect them to play it well. The teacher does not say, "Oh, by the way, if you need it, there's an explanation of the notes in the back of your book." Such an approach is exactly what many basic grammar textbooks take.

A Comprehensive Approach to Grammar

The second distinctive feature of *Grammar and Usage, Naturally* is that it differs from other basic skills texts in three important ways.

- *Grammar and Usage, Naturally* thoroughly examines the foundations of grammar: the parts of speech. Truly understanding the parts of speech and how each one contributes to the structure of a sentence allows students to become confident, skilled writers and editors. Students must have a solid foundation before they can begin composing, for they must not only compose but also edit their writings.
- *Grammar and Usage, Naturally* explores all grammatical concepts in depth, making sure students understand not only the fundamentals but

also the subtleties of the concepts, for students must first understand the concept and its functions to be able to understand how sentences may be controlled to best communicate ideas.

- *Grammar and Usage, Naturally* further establishes the foundations of grammar by using terminology commonly used in the field of composition and rhetoric. In no other field of study do the participants forego the use of the field's professional vocabulary. So why do basic skills instructors claim that using the vocabulary of grammar is too daunting for basic skills students? We have found that integrating the vocabulary of grammar without apologizing for it or replacing it with vague generalizations allows our students to participate in the grammatical conversation as well as ensure they will understand any instructor or tutor with whom they come in contact to discuss writing.

Numerous, Comprehensive Exercises

The final distinctive feature is the use of sentence combining and two types of exercises—(1) the chapter exercises and (2) "Components at Work"—to actively engage students in the writing process.

- *Grammar and Usage, Naturally* asks students to use the skill of sentence combining throughout the text in many chapters after we introduce the concept in Chapter 9. The sentence combining exercises use the grammatical concepts students learn as they progress through the book. For example, students may combine two sentences into one and include a prepositional phrase, participial phrase, or an infinitive phrase. Alternatively, they may turn one clause into a subordinate clause.
- *Grammar and Usage, Naturally* has students write more and identify less. Research shows that writing, not simply identifying a concept in a pre-composed sentence, helps students better remember an idea; *Grammar and Usage, Naturally* provides students the opportunity to apply the grammar concept to their own writing.
- *Grammar and Usage, Naturally*'s "Components at Work" incorporates three unique exercises: "Using Your Skills in Sentences," "Using Your Skills in Reading," and "Using Your Skills in Composition." In "Using Your Skills in Sentences," students are asked to write sentences using grammatical concepts from the chapter they are currently studying as well as review concepts from previous chapters. For example, in Chapter 4, "Subjects," students compose sentences that include adjectives, adverbs, prepositional phrases, and subject and object pronouns, concepts from the previous two chapters. In Chapter 9, "Clauses," students compose main clauses that use the different types of verbs discussed in

Chapter 6, "Verbs." While the exercises within any given chapter allow students to practice a specific grammatical concept, the "Using Your Skills in Sentences" exercises are particularly important because the students continually review and build upon skills learned up to that point.

- "Using Your Skills in Reading" presents students a paragraph that illustrates the grammatical concept discussed in the current chapter. Students read through the paragraph once for understanding and comprehension and then re-read the paragraph and identify a specific grammatical concept(s). For example, in Chapter 5, "Subjects That Don't Look like Subjects," students read a paragraph on the Salem Witch Trials and underline all common nouns, proper nouns, pronouns, one gerund, one infinitive, one indefinite pronoun, and one imperative/understood *you* that function as subjects of the paragraph's sentences.
- "Using Your Skills in Composition" asks students to compose a paragraph on a topic similar to the one in "Using Your Skills in Reading" and to use the grammatical concept they studied in the chapter in their composition. The directions for Chapter 5's "Using Your Skills in Composition," for instance, read

> On a separate piece of paper, write a paragraph discussing the case of an individual or a group of people who have been unjustly accused of something. You may write about yourself, someone you know personally, or someone you have read about in the newspaper or heard about on the news. When you are finished, cross out all prepositional phrases and then, underline all of your subjects. Look back at your subjects and highlight any that are gerunds, infinitives, and indefinite pronouns. If you cannot find any of these subjects in your paragraph, revise a few sentences to include a gerund, an infinitive, and an indefinite pronoun as the subjects. If you find one or more sentences where you have used the understood *you*, revise the sentence to eliminate the second person point of view.

Overall, the "Components at Work" asks students, first, to practice a grammatical concept at the sentence level, second, to identify the grammatical concept within a reading (so that the student can see the concept in a context), and, third, to use the grammatical concept in their writing.

A Focus on Correctness

Last, *Grammar and Usage, Naturally* places the emphasis on "how to" over "how not to." Rather than emphasize errors with separate chapters on fragments and run-ons, for example, *Grammar and Usage, Naturally* accentuates clear and correct writing, relegating errors to an online appendix entitled "Common Writing Errors." The text focuses on teaching students to build correct sentences that clearly communicate their ideas. Relegating errors to a subordinate location is far more sensible than relegating the parts of speech—the basic building blocks of learning to write proficiently—to a subordinate location. *Grammar and Usage, Naturally* emphasizes correct writing over incorrect writing.

CLASS TESTED

Grammar and Usage, Naturally is unique in one additional way: the text was classroom tested for two years before publication. We tested and revised the book's organization, the chapters' content, and exercises based on our students' comments and feedback during and at the end of each semester. Literally hundreds of students have contributed to the development of this text.

ADDITIONAL RESOURCES

Instructor's Manual and Test Bank for Grammar and Usage, Naturally includes sample syllabi for eighteen-week, sixteen-week, and eight-week sessions; classroom activities to engage your students; reproducible quizzes for each grammatical concept; and mapping to **Aplia for Basic Writing Levels 1 and 2**. Aplia™ is dedicated to improving learning by increasing student effort and engagement. Aplia is an online, auto-graded homework solution that keeps your students engaged and prepared for class and has been used by more than 850,000 students at over 850 institutions. Aplia's online solutions provide developmental writing students with clear, succinct, and engaging writing instruction and practice to help them build the confidence they need to master basic writing and grammar skills. Aplia for Basic Writing: Level 1 (sentence to paragraph) and Aplia for Basic Writing: Level 2 (paragraph to essay) feature ongoing individualized practice, immediate feedback, and grades that can be automatically uploaded, so instructors can see where students are having difficulty (allowing for personalized assistance). Visit www.aplia.com/cengage for more details.

Instructor Companion Website for *Grammar and Usage, Naturally* features the Instructor Manual and Test Bank, PowerPoint slides, and access to student companion website content. The instructor companion website is accessible through login.cengage.com.

Student Companion Website for *Grammar and Usage, Naturally* includes the following additional appendices: "Fundamental Spelling Rules,"

"Common Writing Errors," and "Confusing and Misused Word Pairs." Also included are online flashcards for on-the-go practice and a downloadable spelling error chart.

ACKNOWLEDGMENTS

We are tremendously grateful to Cengage Learning's Annie Todd, a righteously cool editor and person, who gave her unyielding support to *Grammar and Usage, Naturally*. We also thank Elizabeth Rice, our editor, for her encouragement, critical observations, thoughtful supervision, and continuous enthusiasm.

We wish also to thank our many colleagues who gave of their time to review *Grammar and Usage, Naturally* and who provided lucid, insightful feedback that has helped shape and inform the text.

Karen Abele, Sauk Valley Community College
Melissa Barrett, Portland Community College and Clark Community College
Thomas Beery, Rhodes State College
Jolan Bishop, Southeastern Community College
Delmar Brewington, Piedmont Technical College
Steven Budd, Los Medanos College
Marie Calderoni, Penn State Berks
Dorothy Chase, College of Southern Nevada
Lucia Cherciu, Dutchess Community College
Judy Covington, Trident Technical College
Darin Cozzens, Surry Community College
Barbara Davis, Yavapai College
Dolores de Manuel, Nassau Community College
Margie Dernika, Southwest Tennessee Community College
Phyllis Dircks, LIU Post
Susan Edele, Lindenwood University
Karen Feldman, Seminole State College
Bonnie Flaig Prinsen, Rochester Community and Technical College
Holly French Hart, Bossier Parish Community College
Lilian Gamble, Delgado Community College
Sally Gearhart, Santa Rosa Junior College
Dustin Greene, Caldwell Community College and Technical Institute
Judith Harper, SUNY Adirondack
Elizabeth Huergo, Montgomery College
Kimberlie Johnson, North Idaho College
Jacquelyn Lyman, Anne Arundel Community College
Shirley Kahlert, Merced College
Irma Luna, San Antonio College
Tony Luu, Mt. San Jacinto College
Alissa Martinka, Ridgewater College
James McCormick, Rochester Community and Technical College
Katherine McEwen, Cape Fear Community College
Samadhi Metta Bexar, Arizona Western College
Laura Meyers, Hawkeye Community College
David Nelson, Glendale Community College
Thomas Nicholas, Prairie State College
Erika Olsen, New Hampshire Technical Institute
Eliana Osborn, Arizona Western College
Brit Osgood-Treston, Riversity City College
Sarah Pett, Miles Community College

Dyanna Rajala, San Bernardino Valley College
Patrick Reichard, Prairie State College
Barbara Rohrich, Cankdeska Cikana Community College
Marsha Rutter, Southwestern College
Hale Savard, Los Angeles Harbor College
Vicki Strunk, National College
Suba Subbarao, Oakland Community College
Lisa Tittle, Harford Community College
Karen Tuggle, Victory University
Dr. Charles F. Warren, Salem State University
Lynn Watson, Santa Rosa Junior College
Tammy White, Forsyth Technical Community College

We would especially like to thank Anthony Campos, Miguel Cea, Luis Martinez, and Jennifer Morales, who generously allowed their work to be used in *Grammar and Usage, Naturally*. We are also grateful to Patrick and Cheryl Duffy, the owners of Jammin' Bread in Riverside, California, who allowed us to take up space at their café while we worked on the book and who serve the best cinnamon rolls we've ever tasted.

I

The Fundamentals

1 YOUR GRAMMATICAL ROOTS

Nouns, Pronouns, and Verbs

Every word in our language has a meaning and a function, and some words have more than one. When discussing **parts of speech**, you are referring to the way words are categorized to make clear exactly how you are using them in language. When you give a label to a word—for instance, when you call the word *rocks* a **noun**—you are defining how you are using it. But you could also call the word *rocks* a **verb**. This means you are using the word differently than if you were using it as a noun. Look at these two sentences.

> Geology is more than the study of rocks.
>
> The father rocks his baby to sleep at night.
>
> In the first sentence, *rocks* means *stones*, hard masses of dirt and minerals. Most of you remember from elementary school that a noun is a person, place, living creature, thing, or idea. *Rocks* in the first sentence fits into that category.
>
> However, in the second sentence, *rocks* means no such thing. *Rocks* in the second sentence is describing the action of the father, showing us how he moves the baby back and forth in his arms, and an action is a verb.

The 2nd edition of the *Oxford English Dictionary* has 171,476 entries for words in current use. These words can function in different ways to create different meanings. Just as the word *rocks* has different meanings, the word *ditch* does as well. *Ditch* can be a noun when you are talking about a trench or furrow and a verb when you are talking about leaving a friend behind. The word *page* can be a noun when you are referring to a piece of paper in a book or a verb when you are referring to the action of summoning or calling someone. In *Webster's New World Dictionary of the American Language, Second College Edition,* the word *run* has 86 definitions, covering the way *run* is used as a noun, verb, and adjective.

The importance of the first three chapters is this: Chapters 1, 2, and 3 will help you understand the eight different categories into which words are placed in order to understand their meaning and purpose. If you take the time to learn and understand the parts of speech, all other grammar principles will fall into place. This first chapter focuses on the three most basic parts of speech, the parts of speech that can create complete sentences: noun, pronoun, and verb.

NOUNS

A **noun** is a person, place, thing, living creature, or idea. An *idea* is a concept, belief system, or philosophy.

Common and Proper Nouns

There are two types of nouns: common and proper. **Common nouns** name **general** people, places, things, living creatures, and ideas. These nouns are not capitalized. **Proper nouns** name **specific** people, places, living creatures, and belief systems, and they are capitalized. In texting and tweeting, many people have stopped paying attention to the rules of capitalization. While the lack of capitalization is acceptable in informal social networking and texting, it is **not** acceptable in academic or business writing. Refer to "Appendix A: Capitalization," for further discussion. Below are some examples of common nouns (**Table 1.1**) and proper nouns (**Table 1.2**):

TABLE 1.1
Common nouns

Person	Place	Thing	Living Creature	Idea
grandmother	desert	desk	zebra	religion
doctor	canyon	purse	leopard	justice
professor	beach	pencil	giraffe	passion
flight attendant	prairie	computer	butterfly	anger
cousin	high school	patio chair	lizard	democracy

EXERCISE 1.1: Common Nouns

Now, on the lines below, add your own nouns for each category.

Person	Place	Thing	Living Creature	Idea
___________	___________	___________	___________	___________
___________	___________	___________	___________	___________
___________	___________	___________	___________	___________
___________	___________	___________	___________	___________
___________	___________	___________	___________	___________

TABLE 1.2
Proper nouns

Person	Place	Thing	Living Creature	Idea
Aunt Irene	New York City	Bic	Pomeranian	Catholicism
Doctor Jackson	Grand Canyon	Mac	Siberian Tiger	Buddhism
Bob	Myrtle Beach	Nikon D3100	Silver Pheasant	Islam
Professor Smith	Europe	Chevrolet	Eastern Gorilla	English
Barack Obama	Uganda	Droid	Metallic Weevil	Chinese

EXERCISE 1.2: Proper Nouns

Again, on the lines below, add your own nouns for each category. Since you are now dealing with **specifically named** people, places, things, creatures, and ideas, be sure to capitalize.

Person	Place	Thing	Living Creature	Idea
______	______	______	______	______
______	______	______	______	______
______	______	______	______	______
______	______	______	______	______
______	______	______	______	______

EXERCISE 1.3: Common and Proper Nouns

For each common noun, write a proper noun in the space provided. For each proper noun, write a common noun in the space provided. Remember to capitalize all proper nouns. Use the example as your model.

Example: ballpark ←→ Wrigley Field

Example: band ←→ The Rolling Stones

1. ______________ ←→ Yellowstone National Park
2. high school ←→ ______________
3. college ←→ ______________
4. ______________ ←→ German Shepherd
5. religion ←→ ______________
6. language ←→ ______________
7. ______________ ←→ France
8. continent ←→ ______________
9. president ←→ ______________
10. document ←→ ______________
11. ______________ ←→ Abraham Lincoln
12. ______________ ←→ *Moby Dick*
13. magazine ←→ ______________
14. ______________ ←→ *Los Angeles Times*
15. ______________ ←→ Sahara

USAGE NOTE

The articles *a*, *an*, and *the* are sometimes called *noun markers* since they frequently precede a common or proper noun. The noun may not appear immediately after the *a*, *an*, or *the* because other words, such as adjectives, may appear between the article and the noun. Look at the following sentences.

A girl stared at the large, striped zebra.

In the above sentence, *A* announces the noun *girl*, and *the* announces the noun *zebra* even though *large* and *striped* come between *the* and *zebra*.

The Statue of Liberty is an important tourist attraction in New York.

In the above sentence, *The* introduces *Statue of Liberty* while *an* points to the noun *attraction*.

EXERCISE 1.4: Common and Proper Nouns

In the sentences below, underline each noun you find. Then, above each noun write a *C* if the noun is a common noun and a *P* if the noun is a proper noun.

Example: Two cats (C) and one dog (C) slept on the porch (C) of the Huntington House (P).

1. Every child in the classroom gave a presentation on Mount Rushmore, the Lincoln Memorial, or the Statue of Liberty.

2. In Native American culture, a fetish is a carving of an animal in wood, stone, antler, bone, or shell that represents the spirit and influence of the animal.

3. The state of Hawaii is made up of eight main islands: Ni'ihau, Kaua'i, O'ahu, Moloka'i, Lana'i, Kaho'olawe, Maui, and the big island of Hawaii.

4. When I vacation in Yosemite National Park, I hike in the lush mountains, swim in the streams, and photograph the deer, sheep, eagles, and other wildlife.

5. Dr. Hanson wrote a prescription for Xanax, a popular medication for anxiety.

EXERCISE 1.5: Common and Proper Nouns

Write five sentences, making sure each sentence has at least two common nouns and at least one proper noun. Write a *P* above your proper nouns and a *C* above your common nouns.

1. ____

____

2. ____

____

3. ____

____

4. ____

____

5. ____

____

PRONOUNS

A **pronoun** takes the place of a noun so you are not continually repeating yourself when you speak or write.

Look at these two sentences:

> Suzy left Suzy's purse in Suzy's car, so Suzy needs to run back to the parking lot.
>
> Suzy left her purse in her car, so she needs to run back to the parking lot.

While you will study a variety of pronouns in following chapters, for now, you will focus solely on subject pronouns and object pronouns.

Making flashcards and studying them on a regular basis can help you remember concepts and terms. Get some index cards and write one pronoun per card, putting subject pronouns in one color and object pronouns in another color. Carry the flashcards in your purse or back pack, and pull them out to study when waiting for the bus, standing in line at the grocery store, or waiting in the doctor's office. Use them to quiz your classmates, and have your classmates quiz you as well. If you don't want to carry around a stack of cards, consider downloading a flashcard app to your smart phone. A variety of flashcard apps exists to help you study and learn the various grammatical concepts you will learn in this textbook. Just a few minutes each day will help you memorize these pronouns, and having them memorized will benefit you greatly as you move forward in your grammar studies.

Subject and Object Pronouns

The chapter preview noted that this first chapter covers the parts of speech that create a sentence: subjects and verbs. Remember, the word *subject* describes how the noun or pronoun functions in the sentence; *subject* is not a part of speech. The two parts of speech that can function as a subject of a sentence are nouns and pronouns.

Two groups of pronouns you need to know now are subject and object pronouns (**Table 1.3**). You need to know the difference between subject and object pronouns because frequently people use object pronouns as subjects, and you don't want to make the same mistake.

TABLE 1.3
Subject and object pronouns

Subject Pronouns	Object Pronouns
I	Me
You	You
He/She	Him/Her
It	It
We	Us
They	Them

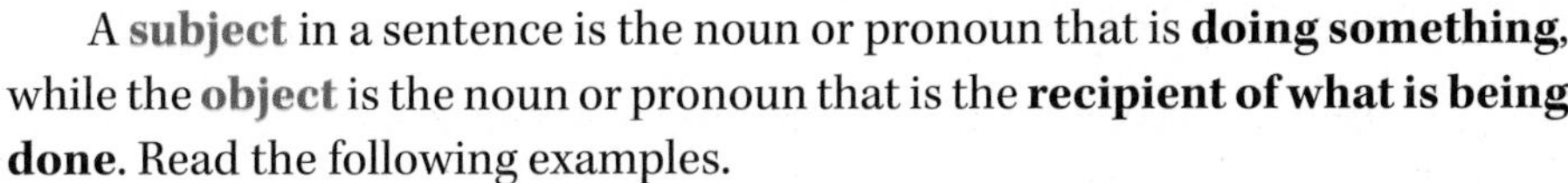

A **subject** in a sentence is the noun or pronoun that is **doing something**, while the **object** is the noun or pronoun that is the **recipient of what is being done**. Read the following examples.

> Sarah gave the ball to Andrew.
>
> *Sarah* is the subject. She is the one who did something; she gave the ball to Andrew. *Ball* and *Andrew* are both objects; the ball was being given, and Andrew was the person to whom the ball was given. Neither the ball nor Andrew did anything in the sentence.

Now, if you used pronouns in place of the nouns in the sentence above, you would need to be careful to use a subject pronoun for the subject and object pronouns for the objects. The sentence would then look like this:

> She gave it to him.
>
> *She* is the correct subject pronoun to take the place of *Sarah* and *it* is the correct object pronoun to take the place of *ball*. *Him* is the correct object pronoun to take the place of *Andrew*.

At this point, if you do not already know the subject and object pronouns, you need to learn them. The subject pronouns always function as subjects, and the object pronouns always function as objects. The previous table shows you that *I*, *he*, *she*, *we*, and *they* are **always** subjects. *Me*, *him*, *her*, *us*, and *them* are **always** objects. *You* and *it* can be both; it is necessary to ask yourself if the pronoun *you* is doing something or having something done to it. Is the pronoun *it* the performer of the action or the receiver of the action?

EXERCISE 1.6: Subject and Object Pronouns

Write an *S* above any subject pronoun and an *O* above any object pronoun. Remember that *you* and *it* can be either a subject or an object, so you must read carefully to see how they function in the sentence.

S O S

Example: You need to give the glass to me; you do not want to drop

O

and break it.

1. You scared me when you crept by me while I was watching a horror movie.
2. You and I need to meet with them to discuss the group presentation.
3. He gave us the book so that we could study for the test.
4. They planned a surprise anniversary party for us.

5. She threw the ball to him, and then he threw the ball to her.
6. He read the bedtime story to me when I was a little girl.
7. I will lend you the CD if you promise to give it back to me by Saturday.
8. You need to give him the books and then hope he doesn't lose them before he needs to return them to you.
9. We must remember to call her so she will know when we are meeting.
10. It is so funny when he imitates you.

VERBS

Most of you will remember from elementary school or from the *Grammar Rock* musical videos that verbs show action. **Verbs** show what the subject of the sentence is doing. However, to have only one definition of a verb will simply limit your ability to recognize verbs in a sentence. Actually, three types of verbs exist, and this section of the chapter will help you recognize all of them.

Action Verbs

Action verbs show action. An action verb refers to anything you can physically or mentally do. Read the following sentences.

> Carla jogs through Central Park every Tuesday and Thursday evening.
>
> The ambulance siren blared through the night.
>
> A puppy in the pet store window wagged his tail and barked for attention.
>
> I think frequently about all the assignments due in my three classes.

All the words written in green in the examples show some type of physical or mental activity. While *think* may not elicit a picture of movement or action, *think* is an undertaking, a development of thought, which shows growth or progress.

USAGE NOTE Do not confuse the construction TO + VERB, for example, *to dance*, *to trim*, or *to rake*, for an action verb. These are called infinitives. Even though they include a verb, they can **never** be the verb of a sentence.

EXERCISE 1.7: Action Verbs

Underline all action verbs in the sentences below. If you are having trouble finding the verb, simply ask yourself, "What does/did the person or animal or thing DO?" Some sentences may have more than one verb. Read carefully.

Example: The sycamore trees shaded the children as they threw the Frisbee back and forth.

1. Circus clowns scare my nephew but delight my niece.
2. The trial lawyer questions the defendant.
3. The accused bank robber defended himself and offered an alibi.
4. Shamu jumps out of the water, flips in the air, and splashes back down into the pool.
5. Several detectives swarmed the crime scene.

EXERCISE 1.8: Action Verbs

Provide an action verb for each sentence below.

Example: Medical researchers ___work___ daily in the lab.

1. The gymnasts __________________ their routines all afternoon.
2. Spelling Bee contestants __________________ into the auditorium.
3. My grandmother __________________ the best Italian food and __________________ me her recipes whenever I ask.
4. The campers __________________ by the fire all night.
5. Every Saturday afternoon, my aunt and uncle __________________ at the senior center.

Linking Verbs

The job of **linking verbs** is simply to link (to connect) the subject of the sentence (which is always a noun or a pronoun) to another word. Forms of the verb *to be* (is, am, are, was, were) are linking verbs as well as the forms of the verbs *to seem, to taste, to feel, to appear, to sound,* and *to smell.* You will learn more about linking verbs in Chapter 6. A linking verb connects the subject to

- another noun that **renames** the subject.
- a pronoun that **renames** the subject.

- an adjective that **describes** the subject.
- a prepositional phrase that **names the location of** the subject.

> My late great uncle was a commander in World War II.
>
> The verb *was* is a form of the *to be* verb and links the noun *uncle* to the noun *commander*. The verb *was* links the subject to another noun that **renames** the subject.
>
> The woman on the phone was she.
>
> The verb *was* links the subject *woman* with the pronoun *she*. The pronoun *she* **renames** the subject.
>
> Miss Jackson seems upset today.
>
> The linking verb *seems* connects the subject, *Miss Jackson,* to a description of Miss Jackson. The adjective *upset* **describes** the subject.
>
> The chocolate chip cookies are in the cupboard.
>
> The verb *are* links the subject *cookies* to the prepositional phrase *in the cupboard*. The verb *are* connects the subject with the prepositional phrase that **names the location** of the subject.

 EXERCISE 1.9: Linking Verbs

Underline the linking verb in each sentence below.

Example: The supervisor was angry at my co-worker's insubordinate attitude.

1. That fish smells funny.
2. My grandmother's homemade minestrone tastes delicious.
3. Her article on climate change appeared in the *New Yorker*.
4. Mrs. Loomis felt betrayed by her husband's indiscretions.
5. King Tut's tomb was a major discovery in the nineteenth century.

 EXERCISE 1.10: Linking Verbs

Provide a linking verb for each sentence below. Vary your use of linking verbs.

Example: That child by the swing set seems lost.

1. Barack Obama ____________ the 44th president of the United States.
2. His entire music collection ____________ on his iPod.

3. His violin music ____________ beautiful.

4. This milk ____________ sour.

5. This fossil ____________ to be a fake.

Helping (Auxiliary) Verbs

Helping verbs show

- when something happened or will happen.
- if something should happen.
- the circumstances needed for something to happen.

The following words are always helping verbs; they can never function as main verbs.

could	may	can
would	might	will
should	must	shall

> Danny will mow the lawn before noon. (when something happened or will happen)
>
> I should ask Connie to the dance. (if something should happen)
>
> If you attend your tutoring session, you may go to the party. (the circumstances needed for something to happen)

When forms of the verbs *to be*, *to have*, and *to do* stand on their own, they are main verbs. When placed before another verb, they act as helping verbs. Read the examples below.

> I am having a difficult time with this subject.
>
> The verb *am* is functioning as a helping verb here because it comes before the main verb *having*.
>
> She has been absent three times this week.
>
> The verb *has* is functioning as a helping verb here because it comes before the main verb *been*.
>
> Larry does not enjoy the beach.
>
> The verb *does* is a helping verb here because it comes before the main verb *enjoy*. Remember that the adverb *not* is **never** part of the verb.

A helping verb and the main verb are called the **complete verb.** If you add a helping verb to an action verb, for example, *must exercise*, the complete verb is still considered an action verb. If you add a helping verb to a linking verb, for example, *should seem*, the complete verb is considered a linking verb.

EXERCISE 1.11: Helping Verbs

Put a rectangle around each helping verb and circle each main verb. Then, after each sentence, write an *A* if the complete verb is an action verb or an *L* if the complete verb is a linking verb. Use the model sentence as your example.

Example: Sheryl should enjoy the concert tonight. __A__

1. The sixth graders will have much homework this week. _____
2. The party should be a success. _____
3. Shashawna does not want ketchup on her hot dog. _____
4. The ink in the printer has run low this week. _____
5. Mr. Pritchett can do over a hundred push-ups without stopping. _____

EXERCISE 1.12: Helping Verbs

Provide a helping verb before each main verb below.

Example: All students __must__ complete the application.

1. Kelly ______________ babysitting the kids this weekend.
2. The sun ______________ setting over the ocean.
3. You ______________ begin your report now.
4. My two-year-old nephew ______________ recite the alphabet.
5. Her daughter ______________ finish her chores before she ______________ go to the party.

- The two necessary components of a complete sentence are a ________________ and a ________________.
- The two parts of speech that can be subjects are ________________ and ________________.
- The three types of verbs are ________________, ________________, and ________________.
- The word ________________ is never part of a verb.

COMPONENTS AT WORK

USING YOUR SKILLS IN SENTENCES I

Add subjects to each sentence by filling in each blank with a noun. Use either a common noun or a proper noun. Remember to capitalize your proper nouns. After you have supplied the subject, underline the verb twice. Then, above the verb, write *A* for action or *L* for linking. If there is a both a helping verb and main verb, write *H* above the helping verb and *L* or *A* above the main verb. Use the example sentences as your model.

> H A
> Example: My mother has shopped at the mall all afternoon.
>
> L
> Example: Yosemite National Park in California is my favorite place to camp.

1. Nearby, the ______________________ swung in the trees.
2. The ______________________ has many activities for children.
3. Next Tuesday, ______________________ will be in town.
4. ______________________ struggles in his math classes.
5. The ______________________ stopped at midnight.
6. Before any vacation, ______________________ washes all of her clothes.
7. ______________________ has acted strangely all day.
8. In the back of the classroom, ______________________ had posted all of the students' final exam grades.
9. ______________________ has the best beaches in the United States.
10. ______________________ completed his project before everyone else.
11. Toby's ______________________ goes to obedience training this summer.
12. ______________________ always confuses me.
13. Many times this semester, ______________________ went to the writing center for help.
14. Before graduation, ______________________ must send out her party invitations.
15. Grandma's ______________________ tastes too salty.

USING YOUR SKILLS IN SENTENCES II

Carefully read each sentence below and write a subject pronoun or an object pronoun that renames the highlighted words.

> Example: After Harold read the book, he loaned it to me so I could read it.

1. The dogs ran around the back yard, and __________ chased one another's tails.
2. Macias could not work his shift, so __________ called Luis.
3. Before the paramedic closed her bag, __________ checked __________ to make sure __________ had all the necessary supplies.
4. As the racecar driver swerved his car to the right, __________ heard __________ make a screeching sound.
5. While my friends and I collected litter on the beach, __________ shook our heads in disgust at people's disrespect.

USING YOUR SKILLS IN READING

Carefully read the following paragraph "Fossils." Read it once for understanding, which includes looking up unfamiliar words; then read it again. If there are any words that are unfamiliar to you, try to figure out their meaning through context clues, looking at the words surrounding the unfamiliar word. Those context clues can help you figure out the meaning of a word. Other times, you may need to use a dictionary or your smart phone to look up the word. Write the definitions to unfamiliar words in the margins to help you remember them. Do not merely skip over a word you do not know. A single word can change the meaning of an entire sentence.

After rereading the paragraph, first, underline all the nouns, both common and proper, once. Then, place a *C* above all common nouns and a *P* above all proper nouns. Second, underline all verbs—action, linking, and helping—twice. Then, label actions verbs *A*, linking verbs *L*, and helping verbs *H*. Finally, draw circles around all subject and object pronouns, and label the subject pronouns *S* and the object pronouns *O*.

Fossils

Fossils can spark the imagination. They show us a moment in the past when a plant or animal died and was preserved. Most children (and many adults) let their imaginations carry them back to the past when they see the skeletons of dinosaurs, such as Tyrannosaurus Rex and Triceratops, in museums. But smaller fossils, such as trilobites, prehistoric ferns, and small fish, from what were once inland seas, can also excite children's imaginations. Finding a prehistoric shark's tooth in a slab of shale from the Jurassic Period or the Triassic Period can be exciting and lead children to other discoveries.

USING YOUR SKILLS IN COMPOSITION

Write at least four sentences about one of the following topics: (1) a cell phone, (2) a reality TV show, (3) a college class you are currently taking, (4) a teacher you currently have or have had in the past, or (5) your favorite place to eat. In your sentences, name the person, place, or thing you are writing about. Describe the person, place, or thing as specifically as possible. Then go back through the four sentences and identify the nouns, pronouns, and verbs in the same way you did in the "Using Your Skills in Reading" exercise. If you do not find any pronouns, revise a sentence to include a subject or object pronoun that renames one of the nouns you used.

CULTIVATING YOUR GRAMMATICAL ROOTS I

Adjectives and Adverbs

Chapter PREVIEW

In this chapter, you will learn about adjectives and adverbs, the parts of speech that modify—describe and enrich—other parts of speech, creating more vivid, sophisticated sentences.

ADJECTIVES

Adjectives are words that describe a noun or a pronoun. Adjectives are sometimes referred to as *modifiers* because they modify (change) how the reader pictures your noun or pronoun. Look at these sentences.

> That movie left an impression on us.
>
> That horror movie left a disturbing impression on us.
>
> In the first sentence, you could have seen any movie and could have been affected in many ways. Your readers simply don't know because the sentence lacks modifiers. In the second sentence, you make clear exactly what type of movie you saw and what type of impression the movie made on you. The modifiers **changed** how your readers understand the event.

Adjectives answer these questions:

- Which one?
- What kind?
- How many?
- Whose?

Adjectives can be descriptive words, such as *beautiful*, *hairy*, *terrified*, or *difficult*, and in most situations, the adjective will precede the noun or pronoun it modifies.

beautiful ballerina
hairy tarantula
terrified child
difficult exam

As you learned in Chapter 1,the adjective (or modifier) may follow a linking verb. In the following examples, the noun being modified is highlighted in green.

> The pencil jar appears cracked.
>
> The picture is blurry.
>
> The judge seems distracted.

USAGE NOTE The articles *a*, *an*, and *the* function as adjectives. The word *the* indicates a specific item, whereas the words *a* and *an* indicate a generic or general item.

Comparative and Superlative Adjectives

Comparatives are adjectives used to show the difference between two things, and **superlatives** are adjectives used to show the difference among three or more things.

> My neighbor's house is bigger than my house.
>
> The word *bigger* is an adjective comparing the two houses. You add *-er* to comparative adjectives.
>
> The house on the corner is the biggest house in the neighborhood.
>
> The word *biggest* is an adjective comparing all of the houses in the neighborhood. You add *-est* to superlative adjectives.

For words of two or more syllables, you do not add *-er* or *-est*, but rather use the words *more* and *most.*

> peaceful = more peaceful (**not** peacefuler)
>
> careful = most careful (**not** carefulest)

However, if the two-syllable word ends in a *y*, you change the *y* to *i* and add *-er* or *-est.*

pretty = prettier
happy = happier

For a complete explanation of spelling rules for comparative and superlative adjectives, see "Fundamental Spelling Rules" on the student companion site at cengagebrain.com.

However, some adjectives are irregular; for these you can't add *-er* or *-est,* nor can you add *more* or *most.* These adjectives change form.

bad ---- worse ---- worst
good --- better --- best
far --- farther --- farthest
little --- less --- least

Less and Fewer

You use the word *less* with non-count nouns (nouns you cannot count, such as *sand* or *skin*) and *fewer* with count nouns (nouns that are plural and that you can count, such as *cups, snakes,* or *coins*). Read the following sentences.

Fewer cookies are in that jar.

I have fewer pets than my friend Jamie.

Since the modified nouns, *cookies* and *pets,* are count nouns, use *fewer.*

It takes less time to get to Anaheim than it does to get to Los Angeles.

Drake has less facial hair than his father.

You use *less* in these sentences because the modified nouns, *time* and *hair,* are non-count nouns.

Lately I have been drinking less milk, so I am buying fewer bottles of milk.

Use the word *less* because you **cannot** count milk, and use the word *fewer* because you **can** count bottles.

Possessive as Adjectives

When a possessive word appears before a noun, that word is functioning as an adjective because it answers the question *whose.*

Jessica's horse Windy came in first place.

The word *Jessica's* is an adjective because it is telling us **whose** horse came in first place. The word *Jessica's* is modifying the noun *horse.*

We eagerly anticipated Mr. Johnson's lectures on the Civil War.

The word *Mr. Johnson's* is an adjective because it modifies the word *lectures.* The word *Mr. Johnson's* tells us **whose** lectures.

EXERCISE 2.1: Adjectives

Underline the adjectives in the following sentences.

Example: <u>The</u> <u>tattered</u> book sat on <u>the</u> <u>dusty</u> shelf.

1. A decrepit old woman waited for the rickety bus to take her to distant lands.
2. Twelve silly monkeys entertained the inquisitive school children.
3. Loud music reverberated from the dilapidated house.
4. Across the lush meadow lies a verdant valley with many varieties of wild flowers.

5. My youngest nephew always wants the newest technological gadget.
6. Suzie's presentation was the most thoughtful presentation of all.
7. I usually choose Italian food when my husband takes me to a romantic restaurant.
8. Sandy has less time to study because of her demanding job.
9. The sweaty boy with the curly hair cried when his plastic squirt gun broke.
10. Hundreds of screaming fans ran toward the bright lights of the crowded arena.

EXERCISE 2.2: Adjectives

Look at this picture of an elephant in Figure 2.1. What words could you use to describe this elephant? Any word you use in the blank should be an adjective.

This is a(n) ________________ elephant.

So, for instance, you could fill in the words *huge, gigantic, mean, cuddly, funny,* and *smelly*. Any of these words would make sense in the sentence above. There are hundreds more. Write all the adjectives you can think of around the elephant. Two adjectives have been provided to help you get started.

FIGURE 2.1
What adjectives describe this elephant?

©Talvi/Shutterstock.com

ADVERBS

Adverbs, like adjectives, also describe, or modify, other words. While adjectives describe nouns and pronouns, adverbs describe verbs, adjectives, and other adverbs. Because adverbs describe three different parts of speech and because they have more uses than adjectives, you may have more difficulty identifying them. But once you understand the questions adverbs answer, identifying them will be much easier.

Adverbs answer these questions:

- how?
- in what manner?
- when?
- how often?
- where?
- to what extent?

The question *how?* is answered when the adverb describes a verb. Study the following sentences:

How did I walk to the store?

I briskly walked to the store.

I walked quickly to the store.

I slowly walked to the store.

I walked hesitantly to the store.

As you can see, the adverb explains **how** I walked, **in what manner** I walked. You can also see that the adverb may be placed before or after the verb. Sometimes, adverbs are placed even further away from the verb as in the sentence below.

Excitedly, I walked to the store.

EXERCISE 2.3: Adverbs

Fill in the blanks in the following sentences with a word that answers the question *how* or *in what manner*.

Example: In the emergency room, the nurse _efficiently_ cleaned the patient's wound.

Because you are describing **how** the nurse *cleaned*, you are using the adverb to describe a verb.

Example: Below the bridge, the homeless man hid _silently_ from society.

Silently describes **in what manner** the homeless man *hid*. You modified a verb when you modified *hid* with *silently*.

1. The rain poured ________________ onto the sidewalk.
2. The telephone rang ________________ all afternoon.
3. ________________, the puppy jumped all over his master.
4. Before the school bell rang, the children ________________ played a game of tag.
5. Every night before a big exam, Jeremy studies _____________ until he falls asleep.

USAGE NOTE While many adverbs end in *-ly*, not all adverbs do. Don't get in the habit of identifying adverbs based on a word ending in *-ly*. If you do, you will make many mistakes. Many words end in *-ly* that aren't adverbs. *Lovely*, for instance, is an adjective. In the examples below, you will see many adverbs that do **not** end in *-ly*. Be careful!

When using adverbs to answer the question *when?*, you are once again using them to describe a verb because you are describing **when** the action occurred or **how often** the action occurs.

When did I walk to the store? How often do I walk to the store?

> Yesterday I walked to the store.
>
> I always walk to the store.
>
> I never walk to the store.
>
> I often walk to the store.

Here are some common adverbs to memorize that answer the questions *when* or *how often*.

already	never	often	always	soon
seldom	still	now	then	rarely

Create flashcards for these adverbs to familiarize yourself with them.

EXERCISE 2.4: Adverbs

Fill in the blanks in the following sentences with an adverb that answers the question *when* or *how often.* Refer to the listed common adverbs and to your flashcards. Make sure to read carefully and choose a logical adverb for the context of the sentence.

Example: Victoria __always__ teases her little brother.

1. We ___________ see snow in our area until after Thanksgiving.
2. I ______________ turned in my science report, and ______________ I will finish my essay on *Hamlet.*
3. Mrs. Robinson _________________ goes to the mall because she doesn't like crowds.
4. He __________________ goes to the movies to escape from his dismal reality.
5. I ______________ visit my grandmother even though I live 30 miles away.

Adverbs can also tell you *where* the action took place.

> Nearby, several squirrels were gathering acorns.
>
> I need you to place the boxes there.
>
> Please put your assignments here.

When adverbs answer the question *to what extent,* they are describing adjectives and other adverbs. Remember that elephant you were describing earlier? If you said to me, "That is a grumpy elephant!" and I asked, "How grumpy is he?" I would be asking "To what extent is he grumpy?" You could answer, "Very grumpy!" or "Incredibly grumpy!" Look at the following sentences:

> His grandfather was too lonely in the nursing home.
>
> His grandfather was very lonely in the nursing home.
>
> His grandfather was somewhat lonely in the nursing home.
>
> His grandfather was incredibly lonely in the nursing home.
>
> His grandfather was extremely lonely in the nursing home.
>
> Each sentence above gives the reader a different image of the grandfather's loneliness because of the adverb used.

EXERCISE 2.5: Adverbs

Go to the elephant image on page 23. Look at all of the adjectives you wrote around that elephant. On the lines here, make a list of five of those adjectives and place an adverb before each one. For instance, if you wrote *hairy*, ask yourself, "**How** hairy is that elephant?" Try to write a different adverb for each adjective. Provided are a few examples:

> *very* hairy *rather* hairy *especially* hairy

1. ______________________________
2. ______________________________
3. ______________________________
4. ______________________________
5. ______________________________

Good and Well

Good is an adjective and *well* is an adverb. The only time *well* is an adjective is when *well* refers to health and well being.

> Josh is a good singer.
>
> The word *good* modifies the noun *singer*, so the word *good* has been used correctly. *Good* is an adjective, so it must modify a noun.

Remember, you can use adjectives after linking verbs; see page 12 in Chapter 1. *Smells, tastes,* and *feel* in the following sentences are all linking verbs.

> The stew smells good.
>
> The soup tastes good.
>
> I feel good.
>
> *Good* is modifying the subjects of these sentences. *Stew* and *soup* are nouns, and *I* is a pronoun. Adjectives modify nouns and pronouns.
>
> Josh sings well.
>
> The word *well* is an adverb. You need an adverb here because you are modifying the word *sings*, which is a verb. If you wrote, *Josh sings good*, you would have a grammatically incorrect sentence.

> After a week in the hospital, Aunt Mary feels well now.
>
> Here, *well* is functioning as an adjective, not an adverb, because you are discussing Aunt Mary's health.

EXERCISE 2.6: Good or Well

Fill in the blanks with either *good* or *well*. Read carefully to determine if you need an adjective or an adverb.

1. David is a ____________ first baseman.
2. David plays baseball very ____________.
3. Laquisha is a ____________ dancer.
4. Laquisha dances extremely ____________.
5. Maria felt ill last week, but this week she is ____________.
6. Mr. Perkins is a ____________ history teacher.
7. He lectures very ____________.
8. Grandma Rosy is not a ____________ driver.
9. Grandpa Jim, however, drives ____________.
10. I do not sing very ____________, but I am a ____________ drummer.

Chapter SUMMARY

- Adjectives modify ____________ and ____________.
- Adjectives answer the questions ____________, ____________, ____________, and ____________?
- Adverbs modify ____________, ____________, and other ____________.

- Adverbs answer the questions ______________, ______________, ______________, and ______________?
- The word *good* is always an ______________ because it describes ______________ and ______________.
- The word *well* is an ______________ because it describes ______________ unless it is referring to health, in which case it is an ______________.
- The word *less* is used to describe ______________ nouns, and the word *fewer* is used to describe ______________ nouns.

COMPONENTS AT WORK

USING YOUR SKILLS IN SENTENCES

Many words can function as more than one part of speech. Remember the example of the word *rocks* at the beginning of Chapter 1? Let's look again at those two sentences:

> Geology is more than the study of rocks.
>
> The father rocks his baby to sleep at night.
>
> In the first sentence the word *rocks* is a noun because the word is referring to minerals, to objects you can hold in your hands. In the second sentence, the word *rocks* is a verb because the word is discussing an action. Look at the following sentences with the word *light*.
>
> Every night, the stars light the sky.
>
> Before I read, I need to turn on the light.
>
> The baby's hair was a light blonde.

Fill in the blanks identifying the correct part of speech:

In the first sentence, *light* is a ________________ because it describes the **action** of the stars.

In the second sentence, *light* is a ________________ because it is an **object** that helps you see your book.

In the third sentence, *light* is an ________________ because it **describes** the color of the baby's hair.

Try the same exercise with the following words. Write three sentences using the italicized word. In the first space use the word as a *verb*; in the second space use the word as a *noun*; in the third space use the word as an *adjective.*

Top:

1. ____

2. ____

3. ____

Book:

1. ____

2. ____

3. ____

Text:

1. ____

2. ____

3. ____

Box:

1. ____

2. ____

3. ____

Now, think of two other words that you can use as a noun, a verb, and an adjective. Then, write a sentence using each word correctly as the given part of speech.

Word: ____________________

Part of speech: ________________________

1. ____

Part of speech:________________________

2. ____

Part of speech: ______________________

3. ____

Word: ____________________

Part of speech: __________________

1. ____

Part of speech: __________________

2. ____

Part of speech: __________________

3. ____

The exercises for "Using Your Skills in Reading" and "Using Your Skills in Composition" for this chapter appear in a combination "Using Your Skills in Reading" and "Using Your Skills in Composition" exercise at the end of Chapter 3.

CULTIVATING YOUR GRAMMATICAL ROOTS II

Conjunctions, Prepositions, and Interjections

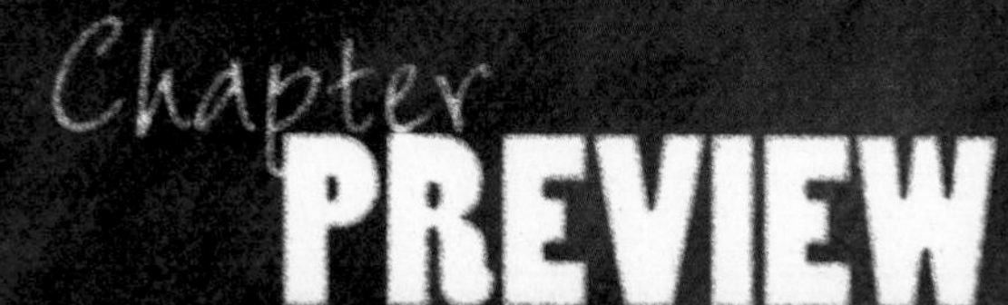

In this chapter you will learn the last three parts of speech—conjunctions, prepositions, and interjections. Conjunctions and prepositions connect words and show relationships between words. Interjections show emotion or excitement.

CONJUNCTIONS

Conjunctions are words that connect. They may connect words, phrases, or clauses (you will learn more about phrases and clauses in Chapters 9, 13, and 14). For now, you are still learning the parts of speech, the language of grammar. Later when you are learning how to connect clauses to avoid fragments and run-on sentences, how to place commas, or how to create sentence variety, your knowledge of these conjunctions will make learning more challenging concepts easier. There are four types of conjunctions: coordinating, correlative, subordinating, and adverbial.

Coordinating Conjunctions

There are seven **coordinating conjunctions**. Your previous English instructors may have called them *joining words* or *FANBOYS*. They are called *FANBOYS* because each letter of the word *FANBOYS* is the first letter of each of the coordinating conjunctions. If you are not already familiar with coordinating conjunctions, take the time to learn them. Get some index cards (or download a flashcard app) and write one conjunction per card, including the relationship the conjunction conveys. Carry the flashcards with you, and pull them out to study when you have a few extra minutes. Use them to quiz your classmates, and have your classmates quiz you as well. Just a few minutes each day will help you memorize these conjunctions, and having them memorized will benefit you greatly as you move forward in your grammar studies.

For
And
Nor
But
Or
Yet
So

Each coordinating conjunction conveys a distinct relationship.

For = cause
And = addition
Nor = negation
But = contrast
Or = alternative
Yet = contrast
So = purpose

There are only seven coordinating conjunctions in English. Once you have learned these seven, you will know all the coordinating conjunctions.

EXERCISE 3.1: Coordinating Conjunctions

Underline all of the coordinating conjunctions in the sentences below.

> Example: Tabitha and Alex have hiked in the Iao Valley in Maui, and they have snorkeled in the Bahamas.

1. Mr. Phillips collects foreign money and stamps, but he does not have any coin from China, nor does he have a stamp from India.
2. The school dance was postponed, for the gym was damaged by the wind and rain.
3. The city council needs to decide to cut from the education budget or from the public safety budget.
4. Zeima had a migraine today, yet she went to school anyway, for she needed to turn in her science report.
5. The principal ballerina needed emergency surgery, and her understudy had a sprained ankle, so the ballet was cancelled.

Correlative Conjunctions

Correlative conjunctions are always pairs. These pairs must always be used together.

> not only . . . but also
>
> both . . . and
>
> neither . . . nor
>
> either . . . or
>
> whether . . . or

Read the following sentences.

> You must either scrub the showers or mow the lawn before you are allowed to go out with friends tonight.
>
> Notice how the correlative conjunctions are followed by the same parts of speech, in this case, verbs.
>
> Every night Sherry studies not only chemistry but also math.
>
> Here, the correlative conjunctions are both followed by nouns. The correlative conjunctions join together two like sentence elements.

EXERCISE 3.2: Correlative Conjunctions

Insert correlative conjunctions in each sentence below. Make sure the conjunctions you use are logical. Read carefully.

Example: Sheryl studies not only architecture but also art history.

1. I like ________ sushi ________ gazpacho.
2. ________ you go ________ not, you still need to send a gift.
3. ________ wash the car ________ wash the dog.
4. The nurse ________ drew my blood ________ took my temperature.
5. Samuel enjoys ________ classical music ________ rap.

Subordinating Conjunctions

Subordinating conjunctions are sometimes also called *dependent words* or *dependent conjunctions* because they create subordinate clauses when you place the subordinating conjunctions before a subject and a verb. While you will learn about subordinate clauses in Chapter 9, right now, familiarize yourself with these conjunctions because the earlier you start learning them, the faster you will be able to learn and to create subordinate clauses in Chapter 9.

The following subordinating conjunctions are organized according to their meanings and usage (**Table 3.1**).

TABLE 3.1 Subordinating conjunctions

Cause and Effect	Concession	Condition	Comparison and Contrast	Manner	Opposition	Place	Time
as	although	even if	as	as if	although	where	after
because	as if	if	as if	as	though	wherever	before
in order that	even though	in case (that)	although	though	even though		since
now that	though	only if	even though		whereas		when
since	while	provided that	whereas		while		whenever
so		unless	while				while
so that		until					until
		whether or not					as
							as . . . as
							once

There are many more subordinating conjunctions, but these are some of the more common ones. Create flashcards to help you learn both subordinating and adverbial conjunctions now to benefit you when you begin your study of clauses in Chapter 9. To help you more easily remember the different groups of conjunctions, you might consider using a different color for each group, for example, coordinating conjunctions could be blue, correlative conjunctions green, subordinating conjunctions red, and adverbial conjunctions orange. Pick your favorite colors or use different colored index cards.

Adverbial Conjunctions

Adverbial conjunctions are also called *conjunctive adverbs* and sometimes merely *transitions*. Many words could be considered transitions, so avoid the term *transitions* for identifying this particular type of conjunction. Learn the correct terminology so you can communicate with any English teacher when you have future questions or concerns. When a tutor or instructor refers to *transitions*, make sure to ask if he or she means adverbial conjunctions. That way, you're talking about the same concept.

Adverbial conjunctions are often used between two complete thoughts. When you use an adverbial conjunction between two sentences, the adverbial conjunction needs either a semicolon or a period preceding it. Look at these example sentences:

> My sister needs to get to work; however, her car's battery died.
>
> Dr. Jenkins is an expert in the field of cardiology. In fact, he has won several awards for his research.

The following adverbial conjunctions are organized according to their meanings and usage (**Table 3.2**).

TABLE 3.2 Adverbial conjunctions

Time and Chronology	Cause and Effect	Comparison and Contrast	Additional Information	Emphasis
finally	therefore	on the other hand	additionally	certainly
then	as a result	however	for example	in fact
next	thus	likewise	for instance	still
meanwhile	accordingly	in contrast	furthermore	
	hence	nonetheless	also	
	consequently	instead	besides	
		nevertheless	in addition	
			moreover	

As noted earlier, you will learn much more about the uses of these conjunctions in Chapter 9. Right now, you only need to familiarize yourself with the names and types of conjunctions and the conjunctions themselves. Remember that for now you are learning the language of grammar, the terminology. Once you have learned how to **speak** grammar, you will much more easily be able to learn how to **use** grammar.

EXERCISE 3.3: Coordinating, Correlative, Subordinating, and Adverbial Conjunctions

In the following sentences, write *C* over any coordinating conjunctions, *CC* over any correlative conjunctions, *S* over any subordinating conjunctions, and *A* over any adverbial conjunctions. There may be more than one conjunction in a sentence, so read carefully.

1. Terry is seeking a job at the hospital, and she needs two letters of recommendation.
2. Smoking not only causes emphysema but also causes lung cancer.
3. Because a large storm is coming, we need to fill sandbags to protect our home.
4. Students in my philosophy course are allowed to work in groups; however, we must make sure our work is our own.
5. Whenever there is an accident, traffic gets backed up, and Doug's daily commute can take up to an hour longer.
6. Mekhong is a Thai rum that is distilled from sugar cane and infused with Thai herbs and spices; as a result, it tastes of toffee, citrus, nuts, and vanilla.
7. Writing an essay can be a long process, but the end result can be immensely satisfying.
8. All campers must bring either a flashlight or a lantern.
9. In this age of ever-changing technology, there is disagreement among the blind over whether Braille should be abolished or preserved.
10. Since the budget crisis began in California, many community colleges have cut classes, and students are having a difficult time graduating in a timely manner.

PREPOSITIONS

Prepositions are words that relate a noun or pronoun to another word. Prepositions show a relationship of location, direction, time, or condition.

In the following sentences, each preposition shows a different relationship between the hamster and the box; these prepositions indicate location or place.

> The hamster jumped in the box.
>
> The hamster jumped over the box.
>
> The hamster jumped around the box.

Some other prepositions that show a relationship of location or place are

above against about between by next to on through at
below from beneath over aboard across beside beyond
inside into upon out of to

Now, read the following two sentences about a mother and daughter. The two prepositions show different relationships between the mother and daughter. One indicates the mother wants to be with her daughter, and the other indicates the mother wants to get away from her daughter.

> The mother rushed toward her daughter.
>
> The mother rushed from her daughter.

These prepositions show a relationship of direction, the direction the mother is rushing in relation to the daughter. Some other prepositions that show a relationship of direction are as follows:

> in into on onto through past over in front of out of
> in back of

One way to help remember prepositions of location, place, and direction is to think of a rabbit and a chair. Whatever the rabbit's relationship is to the chair is a preposition. Read the following example.

> The rabbit jumped on the chair.

The preposition *on* tells us the rabbit's relationship to the chair. Rather than jump under it, over it, or near it, he jumped on it. The preposition *on* tells us about the relationship between the rabbit and the chair.

EXERCISE 3.4: Prepositions

Draw arrows to indicate the rabbit's relationship to the chair in **Figure 3.1**. Then, write the prepositions next to their arrows.

FIGURE 3.1
What is the rabbit's relationship to the chair?

Other prepositions show relationships of time and condition. Here is a list:

after before until of without according to because of except like during concerning for in addition to owing to past with

USAGE NOTE Some prepositions are composed of two words, three words, or even four words, for example, *next to*, *in spite of*, or *in the middle of*. You would identify all the words as the preposition. Also, the word *to* can appear before a verb, for example, *to paint*, *to garden*, *to work*. When *to* comes immediately before a verb, you call the structure an *infinitive*. An infinitive is a type of verbal, which is discussed in Chapters 5 and 13.

You can use some of the prepositions listed previously as adverbs. If the word is showing a relationship between a noun/pronoun and another word in the sentence, then it is a preposition. If the word is modifying a verb and answers the question *where*, then it is an adverb. Look at the following examples:

The little boy looked down the hall.

The word *down* here is a preposition because it helps to explain the relationship between the boy and the hall.

The boy looked down.

Here, the word *down* is an adverb. *Down* is describing **where** the boy looked. *Down* is not showing a relationship; it is not connected to another word.

EXERCISE 3.5: Prepositions

Underline all of the prepositions you see in the sentences below.

Example: El Bulli is located <u>in</u> Roses, Spain, and has been voted "The Best Restaurant <u>in</u> the World" a record <u>of</u> five times.

1. A wild boar is a type of pig brought here from Europe by Spanish explorers in the 1500s.
2. In the cupboard above the drawers, you will find the glasses on the bottom shelf.
3. I am going to France with my husband for our 25th wedding anniversary.
4. Across the street from the market is the best Mexican restaurant in town.
5. Like his father, Frank is a lover of all sports.
6. Wildflowers grow in the high Sierras between April and September.
7. The graduation ceremony will be held at the Ramona Bowl in Hemet from 6:00 p.m. to 8:00 p.m.
8. Without an explanation, the waitress threw her apron against the wall and stormed into the kitchen.
9. We sat beside the stream beneath the trees and thought about our future.
10. The cup of tea sitting on the desk had become cold.

While you will learn about different types of phrases in Chapters 13 and 14, learning about **prepositional phrases** now will help you in Chapters 4, 5, and 6 when you learn about subjects and verbs because you will **never** find the subject and the verb of a sentence in a prepositional phrase.

A prepositional phrase consists of a preposition, a noun or pronoun, and any words that may modify the noun or pronoun. The noun or pronoun is called the **object of the preposition**. Study the following examples. Each prepositional phrase begins with a preposition and ends with a noun or pronoun (the object of the preposition). Remember that if you end a prepositional phrase with a pronoun, it **must** be an object pronoun: *me, you, him, her, it, us, them, whom.*

at home   to him   with sympathy   in time

You can also place an article or possessive pronoun between the preposition and the object of the preposition. Read the examples below.

in	the	cupboard	by	the	stream
(preposition)	(article)	(object)	(preposition)	(article)	(object)

with	my	friend	for	his	mother
(preposition)	(possessive pronoun)	(object)	(preposition)	(possessive pronoun)	(object)

A prepositional phrase may also have compound objects.

with my mother and father
after the trials and tribulations
to the doctor and nurse

You can also place adjectives within the prepositional phrase as in the following examples:

over the fluffy white clouds
beyond the distant horizon
from my cruel Aunt Betty

Prepositional phrases can even include adjectives and compound objects:

to the generous volunteers and benefactors
with her close relatives and friends

USAGE NOTE While articles, possessive pronouns, and adjectives may appear in a prepositional phrase, the first word of a prepositional phrase is **always** a preposition, and the last word of a prepositional phrase is **always** a noun or pronoun.

EXERCISE 3.6: Prepositional Phrases

Draw a line through the prepositional phrase in the sentences below.

Example: The boy jumped ~~from the tree~~ ~~to the top~~ ~~of the house~~ and then ~~to the ground~~.

1. The bird flew up into the tree and settled in its nest.
2. Over the top of the hill crawled a gigantic spider.
3. The tall stack of books on the messy desk soon fell over.
4. The clock on the wall is an antique and came from Germany.
5. In her yard, she had planted many varieties of drought tolerant plants.
6. Down the street from his house, around the corner, in an alley, Tom found his lost cat.
7. At the gym, Kelsey sweated through her daily workout.
8. The trees and plants around his home attracted many varieties of birds.
9. Above the building, a UFO hovered silently in the air.
10. Between appointments, the oncologist searched through his files for an important article on cancer treatments.

Use this list of prepositions to check your answers for this chapter's exercises and to use for your own writing. An asterisk indicates that the preposition may also be used as a subordinating conjunction.

aboard
about
above
absent
according to
across
*after
against
ahead of
all over
along
alongside
amid or amidst
among
around
*as
as of
as to
as early as
as late as
as often as
aside
astride
at
away from
because of
*before
behind
below
beneath
beside
besides
between
beyond
but
by
by the time of
circa
close by
close to
concerning
considering
despite
down
due to
during
except
except for
excepting
excluding
failing
for
from
given
in
in between
in front of
in keeping with
in the middle of
in place of
in spite of
in view of
including
inside
instead of
into
less
like
minus
near
near to
next to
notwithstanding
of
off
on
on top of
onto
opposite
other than
out
out of
outside
over
past
pending
per
plus
regarding
respecting
round
save
saving
similar to
*since
than
through
throughout
till
to
toward or towards
under
underneath
unlike
*until
unto
up
upon
up to
versus
via
wanting
with
within
without

EXERCISE 3.7: Prepositional Phrases

Using the previous list of prepositions as a reference, look at **Figure 3.2** and imagine a rabbit entering the landscape in the picture. Think about the relationship between the rabbit and the bench, the rocks, the stream, the grass, etc., and finish the ten sentences below with prepositional phrases.

FIGURE 3.2 What is the relationship between the rabbit and the landscape?

Example: The rabbit scurries across the lawn.

1. The rabbit jumps ______________________.
2. The rabbit scampers ______________________.
3. The rabbit creeps ______________________.
4. The rabbit sits ______________________.
5. The rabbit hops ______________________.
6. The rabbit digs ______________________.
7. The rabbit hides ______________________.
8. The rabbit inches ______________________.
9. The rabbit stands ______________________.
10. The rabbit stares ______________________.

INTERJECTIONS

Interjections are words that stand alone to express emotion and are usually followed by an exclamation mark. They have no grammatical relation to the rest of the sentence. You will not be using these words much in your academic writing. Following are some examples:

> Ouch! That hammer landed right on my thumb.
>
> Hooray! We graduate this Thursday.
>
> You really passed your math class? Wow!

As you can see, interjections create a much more casual form of communication, and you will not be using them much, if at all, in your academic writing.

Chapter SUMMARY

- ____________________, ____________________, ____________________, and ____________________ are the four kinds of conjunctions.
- Conjunctions join ____________________, ____________________, and ____________________.
- Prepositions are words that ____________________ a noun or pronoun to another word.
- Prepositions show relationships of ____________________, ____________________, ____________________, and ____________________.

COMPONENTS AT WORK

USING YOUR SKILLS IN SENTENCES I

Part 1: Fill in each blank with a logical preposition. Do not use any preposition more than once.

1. ______________ the fence
2. ______________ our yard
3. ______________ the waves
4. ______________ his mother
5. ______________ my girlfriend
6. ______________ the sink
7. ______________ the bed
8. ______________ the night
9. ______________ her nightstand
10. ______________ the question
11. ______________ their heads
12. ______________ many years
13. ______________ my car
14. ______________ the store
15. ______________ my friend
16. ______________ the counter
17. ______________ the show
18. ______________ a storm
19. ______________ my professor
20. ______________ the beach

Part 2: Using the prepositional phrases you created in Part 1 of this exercise and using each prepositional phrase only once, write five sentences that include at least one prepositional phrase each on the lines provided.

1. ____
2. ____
3. ____
4. ____
5. ____

USING YOUR SKILLS IN SENTENCES II

Read each sentence carefully and supply a needed adverb, adjective, or preposition. After you fill in the blanks, label each part of speech. Be prepared to explain your choices and your labeling.

> Example: The women's sale at (prep) the crowded (adj) department store lasted all weekend.
>
> Example: Behind (prep) the rock, a scraggly (adj) coyote patiently (adv) waited for his prey.

1. The ______________ old woman ______________ stared ______________ the window.
2. ______________ pine trees towered ______________ our campsite.
3. Plastic storage containers ______________ the garage held many ______________ memories.
4. A ______________ doctor ______________ threw his patient's file ______________ the desk.
5. The ______________ eagle flew ______________ the ______________ clouds.
6. The ______________ flowers ______________ my neighbors' front door needed watering.

7. Two ________________ puppies ________________ chased the ball ________________ the dog park.
8. The ________________ author worked ________________ the night to finish her ________________ manuscript.
9. A ________________ soccer ball ________________ rolled ________________.
10. ________________ the store, the ________________ crowds ________________ waited for the newest phone to go on sale.

USING YOUR SKILLS IN READING

Read the following paragraph "Her Desk." First, read the paragraph for understanding. If there are any words that are unfamiliar to you, try to figure out their meaning through context clues, looking at the words surrounding the unfamiliar word. Many times, those context clues can help you figure out the meaning of a word. However, there may be times when context clues do not help, so make sure to have a dictionary or your smart phone nearby in case you need to look up a word. Do not merely skip over a word you do not know. A single word can change the meaning of an entire sentence.

After reading through it once for understanding, read it again and draw a line through all prepositional phrases. Then, highlight all adjectives in one color and all adverbs in another color. Once you finish highlighting all of your adjectives and adverbs, grab your conjunctions flashcards so you have them as a resource. Read through the paragraph again, circling all of the conjunctions.

Her Desk

Against the east wall of the room rests a three drawer oak computer desk. The top of her desk is rather cluttered. On the left bottom corner of the desk is a pile of seven hastily stacked VHS and DVD tapes that explore Tai Chi—the Chinese system of slow, meditative physical exercises—and the history of Blues music. Next to the tapes lies a small stack of various papers meant to remind her of things she must do; her daily calendar sits on top of this pile. A third stack houses various writing projects, and a pile of books balances precariously on the bottom right corner of the desk. Along the back of the desk are empty jelly jars and cracked coffee cups holding pens and pencils; an apothecary jar with the caption “Pro Dolore” (“For Pain”) holds paper clips, and an old, black desk stapler waits patiently for use. Toward the back of the desk is a wooden carving of William Shakespeare, which stands about ten inches high. He stands with his left hand to the middle of his chest and his right hand holds a sword, gently pointing to the ground. He seems ready to perform a monologue from one of his plays. Beside Shakespeare stands a small (about 4 1/2" tall and 4" long) matte black metal silhouette of an Osborne Bull, a memento of Spain. In the spare, open spaces between stacks of books and papers, a stack of 3 × 5 cards, a phone charger, several thumb drives, and a couple of drink coasters have found resting places. The LCD computer monitor takes up the remainder of the desktop, about the back one-third. Anyone looking at the desktop would enthusiastically claim the area an utter mess. But I imagine for her, she can find what she is looking for quickly, well . . . pretty quickly, sometimes.

Using Your Skills in Composition

Compose a descriptive paragraph about an object or item you are able to examine, for example, the interior of your refrigerator, your car’s interior, your bedroom, a place you enjoy hanging out, etc. Try to use at least five to ten adjectives to modify your nouns and pronouns and three to five adverbs to modify your verbs, adjectives, and other adverbs. Highlight all your adjectives in one color and your adverbs in another color. Then, read through your paragraph again and see if there are any places you could add prepositional phrases to make your paragraph more descriptive.

SUBJECTS

Chapter PREVIEW

In this chapter you will learn about the first major component in a complete thought or a complete sentence: the subject. You will learn about single subjects, compound subjects, and subject pronouns.

SUBJECTS

As briefly discussed in Chapters 1 and 2, the two necessary parts to a complete thought are the subject and the verb. If one of those parts is missing, you no longer have a complete thought or a complete sentence. Chapters 4 and 5 will focus on subjects, and Chapter 6 will focus on verbs.

The **subject** of a sentence is what you can call the *do-er* or actor of the sentence. The subject is the thing or person or living creature that did something, does something, is doing something, or will do something. Sometimes the subject is doing nothing more than existing, but still the subject is the *do-er* of the existing. Read the following examples.

> Rodney surfed all afternoon.
>
> *Rodney* is the subject of this sentence. He is the person who surfed all afternoon.
>
> Our waitress forgot to bring our drinks.
>
> *Waitress* is the subject of this sentence. She is the person who forgot to bring our drinks.
>
> After the challenging tennis match, the winner broke down and cried.
>
> *Winner* is the subject of this sentence. The winner is the person who broke down and cried.
>
> The raindrops are pelting my car windshield.
>
> *Raindrops* is the subject of this sentence. They are pelting the windshield.
>
> Mrs. Calhoun is my next door neighbor.
>
> *Mrs. Calhoun* is the subject of this sentence. In this sentence, the linking verb *is* links the subject, *Mrs. Calhoun*, to the noun *neighbor*. In sentences with linking verbs rather than action verbs, in order to locate the subject ask yourself what noun or pronoun is being renamed or described.

SINGLE SUBJECTS

As the word *single* implies, when a sentence has a single subject, the sentence has one subject. All of the above sentences have single subjects.

Most of the time, there are many nouns in one sentence, but not every noun is a subject. How can you recognize the subject? Remember: the subject is the noun that *did* something, *does* something, or is *doing* something. In the case of the linking verb, however, the subject is the word being linked to either a noun, pronoun, adjective, or prepositional phrase.

Another way to help identify the subject is by process of elimination. One way to eliminate other nouns that are not subjects is by identifying prepositional phrases. In Chapter 3, you learned about prepositions and prepositional phrases. Remember that the nouns in prepositional phrases are **always** objects; a subject will **never** be found in a prepositional phrase. Read the following examples.

> ~~For hours and hours~~, the Great Dane galloped ~~in the backyard~~.
>
> In the sentence, *Great Dane* is the subject because the dog is the living creature that is doing something in the sentence; it is galloping. Also, crossing out the other nouns that were part of prepositional phrases (*hours and hours* and *backyard*), eliminated any confusion over which noun might be the subject of the sentence.
>
> The garlic ~~in the spaghetti sauce~~ was too strong ~~for my taste~~.
>
> When you cross out the prepositional phrases, you realize the subject is *garlic*, **not** *sauce*. *Sauce* is the object of the preposition *in*.

Either . . . Or and *Neither . . . Nor* and *Or*

When subjects are connected by *or*, *either . . . or*, or *neither . . . nor*, they are still considered single subjects because you are thinking about **one or the other** or **one at a time**. Read the examples below.

> Dr. Meyers or Dr. Chang will be assisting you today.
>
> Even though two names are presented in the sentence, the sentence still has a single subject because you are talking about **one or the other** doctor.
>
> Either Juan's brother or father is going to help coach the team.
>
> Even though you see two people named—Juan's brother and Juan's father—the sentence has a single subject because you are discussing **one or the other** as helping, not both.
>
> Neither the hummingbird nor the whippoorwill nested in my garden this spring.
>
> This sentence has a single subject because you are talking about the birds as single entities, and neither **one** has nested this year.

EXERCISE 4.1: Single Subjects

Underline the single subject once in each sentence below. You may first want to cross out any prepositional phrases. Some sentences have more than one prepositional phrase.

Example: The bank teller ~~behind the glass partition~~ quickly counted the money.

Example: Neither the playground supervisor nor the teacher would believe my story ~~about the bullies.~~

1. His little sister or his next-door neighbor left the bike in the front yard.
2. A frustrated student stomped out of the long line at the bookstore.
3. In the middle of the most romantic scene of the movie, a cell phone started ringing.
4. In the Louvre Museum in Paris, the *Mona Lisa* attracts thousands of visitors a month.
5. Adrien Brody won an Oscar for Best Actor for his portrayal of Wladyslaw Szpilman in *The Pianist.*
6. In the city of Dubai in the United Arab Emirates, the Burj Khalifa stands as the tallest building in the world.
7. In the chair at the dentist's office, Mary started to shake from nervousness.
8. Ana Maria is the youngest of six siblings.
9. According to the newspaper's food critic, either Spencer's or Lighthouse Inn would be perfect for a wedding reception.
10. My brother or my mother will pick me up from work tonight.

EXERCISE 4.2: Single Subjects

Supply a single subject for each sentence.

Example: After the basketball game, Donna asked me to go out for pizza.

1. ____________________ struggled to remember the combination to his locker.
2. ____________________ diagnosed the patient.

3. ____________________ or ____________________ needs to empty the dishwasher and take out the trash.

4. Between the books and the lamp ____________________ found the letter.

5. During his favorite movie, ____________________ snacked on popcorn and licorice.

6. ____________________ always loses her sunglasses and car keys.

7. ____________________ needs to take the placement exam.

8. Around the corner from his house, ____________________ stumbled upon a lost puppy.

9. Either ____________________ or ____________________ should be able to perform that experiment.

10. After the game, the ____________________ will collect all of the equipment.

COMPOUND SUBJECTS

When more than one subject is completing the action or existing in the sentence, the subject is a compound subject. Read the following examples.

> Keisha, Lily, and Jasmine decorated the gym for the homecoming assembly.
>
> *Keisha*, *Lily*, and *Jasmine* all decorated the gym. All the girls completed the action as one unit.
>
> *The Lightning Thief* and *The Last Olympian* were my two favorite novels in Rick Riordan's series.
>
> Both books were favorites. Since the titles are joined together by *and*, both book titles form a compound subject.
>
> History 101 and Anatomy 120 are Armando's most difficult classes this semester.
>
> Again, the classes are joined together by *and* and form a compound subject.

As Well As and *Along With*

When a single subject is followed by the phrase *as well as* or *along with*, the single subject remains single. *As well as* and *along with* do **not** function in the same way as *and*. *As well as* and *along with* are prepositions and begin prepositional phrases; *and* is a conjunction and therefore can join subjects to create a compound subject. Read the following examples.

> The executive chef, along with his sous chef, will cook the president's meal.
>
> Remember: *along with* is a preposition, so *sous chef* is an object of a preposition, **not** a subject.
>
> After the lecture, the professor, as well as his assistant, is going to dinner with the chancellor.
>
> *As well as* is **not** functioning like the word *and* here; rather than join the nouns together, *as well as* is more like an afterthought. Also, *as well as* is a preposition, so *assistant* is the object of a preposition, **not** a subject.

The above sentences both have single subjects, so do not confuse this type of sentence construction with the usage of compound subjects.

EXERCISE 4.3: Single and Compound Subjects

Underline each subject in the sentences below; then, write an *S* next to sentences with single subjects and a *C* next to sentences with compound subjects. Cross out any prepositional phrases.

Example: C Cumin, coriander, and tamarind are common spices ~~in Indian food~~.

1. _____ The counselor advised me of my options.
2. _____ Over the hill and beyond the barn, the beautiful mare ran freely.
3. _____ Antibiotic ointment, bandages, and tweezers should be in every hiker's backpack.
4. _____ Movie rental companies, such as Blockbuster and Hollywood Video, are struggling to compete against Netflix.
5. _____ Piles of magazines and stacks of bills covered the woman's desk.
6. _____ My sister, as well as her daughter, will perform in the play tonight.
7. _____ Waves crashed upon the black sand beach.
8. _____ iPods, iTouches, and iPads sold out quickly this Christmas season.

9. _____ The Chilean president, along with his aide, answered the reporter's questions.

10. _____ During the scary movie, thunder and lightning raged outside our window.

EXERCISE 4.4: Compound Subjects

Write five sentences in which you use compound subjects joined by the word *and*. Use the verb supplied for you.

Example: Grandma Rosie and Aunt Cecilia cooked an Italian dinner last night.
(use the verb *cooked*)

1. ____________________
____
(use the verb *swim*)

2. ____________________
____
(use the verb *battled*)

3. ____________________
____
(use the verb *practice*)

4. ____________________
____
(use the verb *studied*)

5. ____________________
____
(use the verb *painted*)

SUBJECT PRONOUNS

As you learned in Chapter 1, certain pronouns exist in English that are **always** subjects. Learn these pronouns.

I (singular)
He/she (singular)

We (plural)
They (plural)

Any time you see any of these pronouns, you can be sure they are subjects. Being subjects is their purpose. Read the following examples.

> Before the big exam, they studied their notes and their flashcards.
>
> *They* is the subject. *They* are the ones who studied, who completed the action in the sentence.

As you learned in Chapter 1, *you* and *it* can be either subjects or objects. If *you* or *it* is completing the action, the pronoun is functioning as a subject; if *you* or *it* is receiving the action, the pronoun is functioning as an object. Read the following examples.

> Before the presentation, you must give your report to the supervisor.
>
> Here, *you* is the subject of the sentence because *you* is the person completing the action, the person who must give the report to the supervisor.
>
> Before the presentation, the supervisor will give the report to you.
>
> Here, *you* is not a subject. *You* is an object in this sentence because *you* is the receiver of the action; the report is being given to *you*. Also, notice that *you* comes after the preposition *to*, which makes *you* the object in a prepositional phrase.

EXERCISE 4.5: Subject Pronouns

First, cross out any prepositional phrases you see in the sentences below. Then, underline the subject pronouns in each sentence.

1. They understand the importance of safety in their job.
2. After each game, we celebrate with pizza and ice cream.
3. In the face of his friends' insistence, he refused to join a social networking site.
4. Before a tough exam, I relax by my pool with my flashcards and notes.
5. Every day at the same time, she boards the bus at Hayward and Vine.

EXERCISE 4.6: *You* and *It*—Subject or Object?

In each sentence below, determine if *you* and *it* are being used as subjects or objects. Write an *S* above the pronoun if it is functioning as a subject, and write an O above the pronoun if it is functioning as an object. First, identify the prepositional phrases since pronouns that are part of prepositional phrases will always be object pronouns. Remember, however, that not all object pronouns will be in prepositional phrases.

S
Example: You teach every Wednesday at 4:00 p.m.

O
Example: Harry placed it in the cupboard.

1. Like your Uncle Spike, you have a wonderful sense of humor.

2. To become a civil engineer, you must earn good grades in math.

3. You need to put it in the trash can.

4. It rained all day and all night.

5. Ms. Howard will see you after her meeting.

Chapter SUMMARY

- The two necessary components for a complete thought, or a complete sentence, are the ________________ and the ________________.
- If one subject is in a sentence, you call this a ________________ subject.
- If more than one subject is joined together by the word *and*, you call this a ____________________ subject.

- If two subjects are joined together by *neither . . . nor* or *either . . . or*, you have a ________________ subject.
- If two subjects are joined together by *or*, you have a ________________ subject.
- *Along with* and *as well as* create ____________________ phrases.

COMPONENTS AT WORK

Using Your Skills in Sentences

Compose sentences following the directions. When you are finished, trade with a classmate and label the components in each other's books. Be prepared to justify your labeling. Use the first one as a model.

> Example: Compose a sentence with one adjective, one adverb, and a single subject. Use the verb *fished*.
>
> S Adv. V Adj.
>
> Mr. Ortiz patiently fished in the shimmering lake.

1. Compose a sentence with a prepositional phrase and a compound subject. Use the verb *threw*.

   ____

   ____.

2. Compose a sentence with an adjective, a prepositional phrase, and a subject pronoun. Use the verb *dance*.

   ____

   ____.

3. Compose a sentence with a single subject, an adverb, and a prepositional phrase. Use the verb *drove*.

   ____

   ____.

4. Compose a sentence in which *you* is a subject and *it* is an object. Add a prepositional phrase. Use the verb *fixed.*

____

____.

5. Compose a sentence with a compound subject, one adjective, one adverb, and a prepositional phrase. Use the verb *ate.*

____

____.

The exercises for "Using Your Skills in Reading" and "Using Your Skills in Composition" for this chapter appear in a combination "Using Your Skills in Reading" and "Using Your Skills in Composition" exercise at the end of Chapter 5.

5 SUBJECTS THAT DON'T LOOK LIKE SUBJECTS

Chapter PREVIEW

This chapter focuses on words and phrases that do not look or appear to be subjects of the sentence, such as indefinite pronouns, but, indeed, they are. Two other disguised subjects are imperatives (the understood you) and verbals (gerunds and infinitives).

INDEFINITE PRONOUNS

Indefinite pronouns are words that refer to someone or something that is not specific. For instance, in the sentence *Someone left his or her backpack in the classroom,* the indefinite pronoun *someone* is not explicit.

Table 5.1 includes three lists of indefinite pronouns. The indefinite pronouns in the first group are always singular. The indefinite pronouns in the second group are always plural. The indefinite pronouns in the third group may be either singular or plural, depending upon the object of the preposition in the prepositional phrase that follows the pronoun. Knowing whether an indefinite pronoun is either singular or plural will be necessary when you study subject-verb agreement in Chapter 8.

TABLE 5.1
Indefinite pronouns

Singular Indefinite Pronouns

someone	something	something	each
everyone	everything	everybody	each one
anyone	anything	anybody	either
no one	nothing	nobody	neither

Plural Indefinite Pronouns

both	many	few	several

Singular or Plural Indefinite Pronouns

some	all	any	half	more	most

To determine if the indefinite pronouns *some, all, any, half, more,* or *most* are singular or plural, look at the prepositional phrase (discussed in Chapter 3) that follows them.

> All of the ice cream is gone.
>
> *All* here is singular because the object of the preposition *ice cream* is singular.
>
> All of the ice cream bars are gone.
>
> *All* here is plural because the object of the preposition *ice cream bars* is plural.

You follow the same rule to determine if the remaining indefinite pronouns in this group—*some, any, half, more,* and *most*—are singular or plural: look at the object of the preposition in the prepositional phrase that follows the indefinite pronoun.

Confusion arises in identifying indefinite pronouns as subjects because frequently, as in the examples you just read, if an indefinite pronoun is placed before a prepositional phrase you may mistake the object of the preposition for the subject of the sentence, forgetting a phrase does not contain a subject or a verb. Below are more examples of indefinite pronouns, in green, placed before prepositional phrases, in italics.

> Neither *of my brothers* has a decent job.
>
> Each *of his cousins* is a mechanical engineer.
>
> Someone *on the baseball team* stole the opposing team's mascot.
>
> Everyone *in my family* has a great sense of humor.

In Chapter 3 you learned that prepositional phrases include, at a minimum, a preposition and a noun or pronoun functioning as the object of the preposition. You also learned that you will never find the subject of a sentence in a phrase. Read the following sentence.

> Each ~~of my brothers~~ has a degree in criminal justice.
>
> In this sentence, *each* is functioning as the subject. *Brothers* **cannot** be the subject because it is the object of the preposition *of.*

EXERCISE 5.1: Indefinite Pronouns

In each sentence below, underline the indefinite pronoun that functions as the subject. First, cross out any prepositional phrases. Model your answers on the example sentence.

Example: Nothing ~~in the refrigerator or pantry~~ satisfied my craving ~~for chocolate~~.

1. Everything about the restaurant was second rate.
2. Everyone in Professor Chow's class needs to write a research paper.
3. On the wall above the filing cabinet, many of my wedding pictures form a collage.
4. Snuggling next to each other, neither of the puppies has opened its eyes yet.
5. Each of the assignments was worth 100 points.
6. Behind the swing set, several of the children play Power Rangers during recess.
7. Some of the first grader's teeth were missing.

8. All of the clean clothes need to be folded and put away sometime today.
9. Many of the magazines can be donated to the senior center.
10. After school, both of the finalists need to practice their acceptance speeches.

THE UNDERSTOOD *YOU* OF IMPERATIVES

Imperatives are sentences that give commands or convey directions. In imperatives, the subject *you* is understood; in other words, while you don't say or write the word *you*, the word is implied. Read the following examples.

> Please get me a pencil.
> Henry, clean your room!
> Place the research papers on my desk.
> Eat your dinner.

You can see that while each of the above imperatives contains verbs—*get, clean, place,* and *eat*—the word groups do not seem to include a subject. But each **does** include a subject. The subject for each imperative is an unwritten *you.*

Think of imperatives this way: when you are giving an order, you are saying, "Hey, you, get me a pencil" or "Hey, you, put your research paper on my desk." While you do not say or write *you*, the subject is understood to be in the command.

Remember, however, that you will not be using imperative sentences much in your academic writing. Imperatives are in second person point of view, which is an informal and conversational point of view, so is generally not accepted in academic prose. Therefore, when you edit your writing, be on the lookout for imperatives that you may have used inadvertently.

EXERCISE 5.2: The Implied *You*

Write five commands and/or directions below in which *you* is the implied subject. Refer to examples above if you need help getting started.

1. ______________________________.
2. ______________________________.
3. ______________________________.
4. ______________________________.
5. ______________________________.

VERBALS: GERUNDS AND INFINITIVES

Verbals are verb forms that can function as nouns and modifiers but can never stand alone as the complete verb of a sentence. Because verbals seemingly look like verbs, you may become confused over their true function. Two verbals that can function as subjects are **gerunds** and **infinitives**.

Gerunds

A **gerund** is a verb form ending in *-ing* that functions as a noun, so a gerund can be either a subject or an object. For the purposes of this chapter, gerunds will be discussed as subjects. Read the following sentences.

> Raising a pet can teach a child responsibility.
>
> What can teach a child responsibility? Raising a pet can. *Raising* is the subject.
>
> Dusting is my least favorite chore.
>
> What is my least favorite chore? Dusting is. *Dusting* is the subject.

USAGE NOTE If you see an *-ing* word without a helping verb, the *-ing* word is **not** a verb. Read the following word group.

Nicholas swimming in the mountain lake.

Swimming is not a verb. The above word group is not a complete thought because the word group does not contain a verb. By placing a period after the word group, only part of a sentence has been created, a fragment (see "Common Writing Errors" on the student companion site at cengagebrain.com). *Is swimming* and *had been swimming* are both verbs because a helping verb precedes the *-ing* word. Read the following sentences.

Nicholas is swimming in the mountain lake.

Nicholas had been swimming in the mountain lake.

Nicholas was swimming in the mountain lake.

All three examples are complete sentences because they contain both a subject and a verb.

EXERCISE 5.3: Gerunds as Subjects

Underline the gerunds that function as subjects. Crossing out prepositional phrases first may help you identify the gerund. Model your answers on the example sentence.

> Example: Fencing became an Olympic sport ~~during the first modern Olympiad in 1896~~.

1. During high school, saving 10 percent of each paycheck from any part-time job or summer job is a smart way to amass funds for college.
2. Cheering and screaming at the concert gave Amy a sore throat.
3. Speed skating requires great technical skill and concentration.
4. Snorkeling is one of Keisha's favorite activities whenever she is on vacation in Cancun.
5. Traveling around the globe would be such a fabulous learning experience.

EXERCISE 5.4: Gerunds as Subjects

Add a logical gerund to supply each sentence with a subject.

1. For families with pools, ______________________________ is a necessary skill for young children.
2. After midnight, the ______________________________ will begin.
3. ______________________________ is my favorite way to unwind after a stressful day.
4. ______________________________ is one way Arnold prepares for his toughest exams.
5. Last night, ______________________________ from the neighbor's garage woke us up.
6. ______________________________ is a serious addiction for many people.

Infinitives

You create an **infinitive** by placing *to* in front of the base form of any verb. *To skate, to wander, to type*, and *to cook* are all infinitives. Remember, though, infinitives are **not** verbs. They can, however, like gerunds, function as nouns, so they can function as subjects. Read the following sentences.

> To make an eight-course meal requires careful planning and preparation.
>
> What requires careful planning and preparation? To make an eight-course meal does. *To make* is the subject.
>
> To invent the next greatest surgical robot was Dr. Garrett's objective.
>
> What was Dr. Garrett's objective? To invent the next greatest surgical robot. *To invent* is the subject.

Remember this point: If you see the word *to* before a verb, the two-word group is **not** a verb. *To swim* is not a verb. *Swim* is a verb.

> Jerry wants to swim across the English Channel.
>
> In this sentence, the verb is *wants. To swim* is an infinitive, not the verb.
>
> The campers swim every afternoon at three o'clock.
>
> In this sentence, *swim* is the verb. *Swim* is what the campers do, and *swim* is not preceded by *to.*

USAGE NOTE Remember not to confuse an infinitive with a prepositional phase. An infinitive is a verbal created when you precede the stem form of the verb with *to*: *to write, to sing, to laugh, to jog, to whistle, to discuss.*

The word *to* may also function as a preposition. If *to* is functioning as a preposition, the word immediately following *to* will be a noun or pronoun or an adjective followed by a noun or pronoun (*to home, to the local store, to her*).

EXERCISE 5.5: Infinitives as Subjects

In the sentences below, underline the infinitives that function as subjects, and then double underline the verb. Crossing out prepositional phrases first may help you identify the subjects and verbs. Use the example as a model.

Example: <u>To swim</u> ~~across the English Channel in 6 hours and 30 minutes~~ <u>was</u> his goal.

1. Until the end of time, to find true love will be the princess's ultimate goal.

2. With recipes, to substitute one ingredient for another can change the way a recipe turns out.
3. To write the great American novel motivates Amos.
4. To lose eighteen pounds was the contestant's primary objective.
5. Since 1965, to win the "Best Barbecue Sauce" title has been the chef's dream.

EXERCISE 5.6: Infinitives as Subjects

Add a logical infinitive to supply each sentence with a subject.

1. ________________________ his study skills was a necessity for Darren.
2. ________________________ a starring role in the movie would certainly improve Justin's prospects.
3. ________________________ another round of medical tests seemed too much for the patient to handle.
4. ________________________ the last one standing would fill the soldier with pride.
5. ________________________ sentences with infinitives as subjects is not an easy task.

Chapter SUMMARY

- ________________________ pronouns can function as subjects of sentences.
- Subjects will never be found in ________________________ phrases.
- In ________________________ sentences (commands), the implied subject is ________________________.

- ________________________ are forms of verbs that do not function as verbs.
- ________________________ and ________________________ are verbals that can function as nouns, which means they can function as ________________________.

COMPONENTS AT WORK

Using Your Skills in Sentences

Compose five of your own imperatives. Once you are finished, trade papers with a classmate. Have your classmate insert the subject *you* between parentheses where it is implied in your imperatives and do the same to your classmate's imperatives.

> Examples: Please, staple the pages together.
> Please, (you) staple the pages together.
>
> Go to your room!
> (You) go to your room!

1. ____.
2. ____.
3. ____.
4. ____.
5. ____.

Using Your Skills in Reading I

Read the following paragraph and cross out all prepositional phrases. Then, underline any indefinite pronoun, gerund, or infinitive functioning as a subject. Highlight the sentence in which *you* is the implied subject. Read the paragraph carefully; some sentences will not be touched.

Lindsey Vonn

Skiing is Lindsey Vonn's greatest thrill. Vonn started skiing at the age of three, and she hasn't stopped since. All of her siblings took skiing lessons as well. However, none skied with the passion of Lindsey. Vonn pushed herself to be the best. Everyone would agree. To win five gold medals was her goal in the 2010 winter Olympics. Losing three of the events only motivated her to work harder. She won one gold medal and one bronze medal. Follow your dreams and work hard. Pushing yourself will result in great outcomes.

Using Your Skills in Reading II

Carefully read the following paragraph, "The Salem Witch Trials." This paragraph has more challenging sentences than the previous paragraph, and many sentences have more than one subject. After reading through it once for understanding, which includes looking up words you do not understand or recognize, read it again. If there are any words that are unfamiliar to you, try to figure out their meaning through context clues, looking at the words surrounding the unfamiliar word. Many times, those context clues can help you figure out the meaning of a word. However, there may be times when context clues do not help, so make sure to have a dictionary or your smart phone nearby in case you need to look up a word. Do not merely skip over a word you do not know. A single word can change the meaning of an entire sentence.

After rereading the paragraph for understanding, read through it again, crossing out each prepositional phrase. Then, underline all subjects. Along with common nouns, proper nouns, and pronouns, the subjects include one gerund, one infinitive, one indefinite pronoun, and one understood *you.*

The Salem Witch Trials

The Salem Witch Trials occurred during a shameful period of American Colonial history between February of 1692 and May of 1693, but this episode was not the first time innocent people had been accused and executed for witchcraft. The belief in demons and in Satan's earthly existence began in Europe around the 1400s. Outcasts of various sorts had been blamed for poor crops, bad weather, and unfortunate accidents and were subsequently put to death for their dealings with the devil. Believing in witches was common among immigrants, and this belief combined with citizen rivalry and fanatic religious leadership created the perfect climate for mass hysteria. The hysteria began when Salem minister Samuel Parris' daughter and niece, ages 9 and 11, began to have fits. They would throw things, scream strange sounds, and convulse on the ground. Doctors could find nothing physically wrong with them, and the girls began to blame others in the town for working with the devil to torture them. Then, other young women in the vicinity also began to throw fits, and the hysteria increased. A homeless beggar, along with a non-church-going woman and a slave, was accused of witchcraft, and townspeople were hesitant to stand up for them because of their lower class standing. Later, however, even upstanding citizens were accused. In addition, anyone defending the accused would end up accused as well. Thus, the paranoia and fear spread rapidly. The judges would spare from execution those who confessed to being witches, so many innocent people confessed, thus perpetuating the belief that witches did, indeed, exist. All in all, twenty one people were found guilty of witchcraft and executed; many more were accused. One of the most infamous cases was that of four-year-old Dorothy Good. She was arrested and held in jail for nine months until her father could afford her bond. During questioning, the little girl inadvertently implicated her mother, Sarah Good, and Sarah Good was hanged on July 19, 1692. Thankfully, during the trials, ministers, judges, and other influential leaders from surrounding regions expressed their dismay at the lack of due process rights and lack of evidence. Finally, Sir William Phips, Governor of Massachusetts, stopped further arrests and ordered the release of those still in jail. In 1711, the colony passed a bill that pardoned those accused of witchcraft during the Salem Witch Trials and offered 600 pounds to their heirs in an attempt to make up for the pain and suffering those families had to endure. Remember this shameful and illogical conduct of our forebears. To reflect on past behavior is to learn from it.

Using Your Skills in Composition

On a separate piece of paper, write a paragraph discussing the case of an individual or a group of people who have been unjustly accused of something. You may write about yourself, someone you know personally, or someone you have read about in the newspaper or heard about on the news. When you are finished, cross out all prepositional phrases, and then underline all of your subjects. Look back at your subjects and highlight any that are gerunds, infinitives, and indefinite pronouns. If you cannot find any of these subjects in your paragraph, revise a few sentences to include a gerund, an infinitive, and an indefinite pronoun as the subjects. If you find one or more sentences where you have used the understood *you,* revise the sentence to eliminate the second person point of view.

The copier ______________. The house ______________.

The horn ______________. The alarm ______________.

Now that you have added various action verbs to your subjects, think about how important choosing the correct verb is to convey your point. For instance, *The woman walks down the beach* is not as visual as the sentence could be, and because *walks* is a nonspecific verb and can be interpreted many ways, your readers will be left to envision for themselves exactly how the woman walks. What if you said the woman *strolls*? Or the woman *swaggers*? Or the woman *frolics*? *Strolls*, *swaggers*, and *frolics* all create different pictures. Strong, specific action verbs help your writing come alive, and your readers will be more interested and more engaged in what you have to say.

EXERCISE 6.3: Specific Action Verbs

Part 1. Choose one action verb from Exercise 6.1 and think of five similar, specific action verbs that could create a more vivid picture.

Example: I laugh.

I giggle. I cackle. I snort. I howl. I guffaw.

I ______________________

I ______________ I ______________ I ______________

I ______________________ I ______________________

Part 2. Choose one action verb from Exercise 6.2 and think of five specific action verbs that could create a more vivid picture. Use the example as a model for your answers.

Example: The toilet flushes

The toilet clogs. The toilet floods. The toilet reeks.

The toilet backs up. The toilet cracks.

The ______________________

The ______________ The ______________ The ______________

The ______________________ The ______________________

LINKING VERBS

Because linking verbs do not show action, they are sometimes more difficult to identify. But once you understand the function of linking verbs and take some time to learn them, you will be able to identify linking verbs confidently.

As you learned in Chapter 1, the job of the linking verb is simply to link, or to connect, the subject of the sentence, which is always a noun or a pronoun, to another word. A linking verb connects the subject to

- another noun that **renames** the subject
- a pronoun that **renames** the subject
- an adjective that **describes** the subject
- a prepositional phrase that **names the location of** the subject

When a linking verb connects a subject to a noun or pronoun that renames the subject, think of the linking verb as an equals sign (=). Also, when a linking verb links a subject to a noun that renames the subject, typically the articles, *a*, *an*, or *the*, will follow the linking verb.

Here are some examples:

My neighbor is a fireman.

The linking verb *is* connects *neighbor* and *fireman. Fireman* is a noun that renames *neighbor. Neighbor* = *fireman.*

His front yard is a clutter of weeds, junked cars, and litter.

The linking verb *is* connects *yard* and *clutter. Clutter* is a noun that renames *yard. Yard* = *clutter.*

In formal writing, when a pronoun appears after a linking verb, you use a subject pronoun to rename the subject. Study the following examples.

The young woman who won the 100 yard dash is she.

The linking verb *is* connects the pronoun *she* to the noun *woman. She* renames *woman. Woman* = *she.*

It is I.

The linking verb *is* connects the pronoun *I* to the noun *It. It* renames *I. It* = *I.*

The person on the phone was she.

The linking verb *was* connects the pronoun *she* to the noun *person. She* renames *person. Person* = *she.*

The following example shows a linking verb connecting a subject to an adjective that describes the subject.

Doctor Harrison seems preoccupied today.

The linking verb *seems* links *Dr. Harrison* with the adjective *preoccupied. Preoccupied* describes *Dr. Harrison.*

That little boy in the middle of the mall appears lost.

The linking verb *appears* links *boy* with the adjective *lost. Lost* describes the *little boy.*

Finally, these last examples show a linking verb connecting a subject to a prepositional phrase that indicates the subject's location.

The drinking glasses are in the cupboard above the toaster.

The linking verb *are* links *glasses* with their location *in the cupboard above the toaster.*

Hawaii is in the middle of the Pacific Ocean.

The linking verb *is* links *Hawaii* with its location *in the middle of the Pacific Ocean.*

Professor Connelley was at the conference in Tennessee.

The linking verb *was* links *Professor Connelley* with his location *at the conference in Tennessee.*

USAGE NOTE In Chapter 2, you learned that adjectives appear before the nouns or pronouns they describe. However, an adjective can also come after the noun or pronoun the adjective describes **if** the adjective is connected to the noun or pronoun by a linking verb. Adjectives placed after linking verbs are called **predicate adjectives**. Here are four examples:

This soup tastes salty.

The dog was scruffy.

The little girl feels lonely.

That elephant was ferocious.

To refresh your memory on adjectives, see pages 20–23.

All forms of the verbs *to be*, *to seem*, and *to become* are true linking verbs. The forms of the verbs *to taste*, *to feel*, *to appear*, *to sound*, and *to smell* and several more may be linking verbs or action verbs.

To check if the verb is acting as a linking verb or an action verb, apply the following test: if you can replace the verb in a sentence with the words *am*, *is*, or *are*, and the sentence still makes sense, still sounds correct, then the verb in the sentence is a linking verb. Look at the following sentences.

The teacher feels ill. The teacher is ill.
The dogs sound lonely. The dogs are lonely.

> The food tastes salty. The food is salty.
> I appear short in that photo. I am short in that photo.
> Your perfume smells lovely. Your perfume is lovely.

But if you replace the verb with *am*, *is*, or *are*, and the sentence does not make sense, then the verb is an action verb. Read the following sentences.

> Mom always tastes her food before she serves it. Mom always is/are/am her food.
> I smell smoke in the air. I is/am/are smoke in the air.
> He felt the sides of the box for an opening. He is/are/am the sides of the box.
>
> Because the sentences with *is*, *am*, and *are* do not make sense, you know that *tastes*, *smell*, and *felt* are functioning as action verbs in the sentences.

The forms of *to be* and other linking verbs change depending upon the subject and the verb tense. Following are the various forms of *to be:*

Am	Been	Was being
Is	Has been	Were being
Are	Have been	Will be
Was	Had been	Will have been
Were	Am being	Shall be
Be	Is being	Shall be being
Being	Are being	Shall have been

Following are some forms of *to become*. The forms of the remaining linking verbs are similar to *to become*.

Become	Had become	Was becoming
Becomes	Am becoming	Were becoming
Has become	Is becoming	Will become
Have become	Are becoming	Shall become

EXERCISE 6.4: Linking Verbs

Underline the linking verbs in the following sentences. Then, draw an arrow from the subject to the word or words the linking verb joins to the subject.

Example: Luke became a vegan.

1. That archeology class seems interesting to me.
2. The clouds were billowy and white.
3. His grandfather is a Navajo.
4. This milk tastes sour.
5. That little boy looks afraid of the roller coaster.
6. The composer's music sounds uplifting and inspiring.
7. His favorite snacks are in the back of the cabinet behind the canned goods.
8. Those scented candles smell fruity.
9. The person chatting on MySpace was he.
10. The couple appears happy with the purchase of their new couch.

EXERCISE 6.5: Using Linking Verbs

Use a different linking verb in each sentence.

1. Compose a sentence that uses a linking verb to link the subject to another noun that renames the subject.

   ___

   ___

2. Compose a sentence that uses a linking verb to link the subject to a pronoun that renames the subject.

   ___

   ___

3. Compose a sentence that uses a linking verb to link the subject to an adjective that describes the subject.

4. Compose a sentence that uses a linking verb to link the subject to a prepositional phrase that tells the location of the subject.

5. Compose a sentence that uses the verb *taste, smell,* or *sound* as a linking verb, not as an action verb.

HELPING (AUXILIARY) VERBS

Helping verbs show

- when something happened or will happen,
- if something should happen, or
- the circumstances needed for something to happen.

The following words are always helping verbs; they can **never** function as main verbs.

could	may	can
would	might	will
should	must	shall

Place helping verbs in front of main verbs. Each helping verb has its own meaning, so the meaning of the sentence will depend on which helping verb you use. Read the following examples and notice how, even though the main verb remains the same, the meaning of each sentence changes because of the helping verbs. The main verbs are underlined, and the helping verbs are in green.

> Jackie <u>studies</u> every night.
>
> The verb *studies* shows that Jackie regularly studies. No helping verb exists in this sentence.

Jackie may study every night.

The helping verb *may* indicates that Jackie is considering the possibility of studying every night.

Jackie will study every night.

The helping verb *will* indicates that Jackie does not study every night right now, but she intends to in the future.

Jackie should study every night.

The helping verb *should* tells the reader that Jackie does not study every night, nor does she have plans to study every night, but it is something that would be a good idea according to the writer's attitude.

Jackie can study every night.

The helping verb *can* shows that Jackie has the ability but doesn't make clear whether she does or doesn't study every night.

Also, remember that a main verb can have more than one helping verb:

Jackie should have studied every night.

Jackie should have been studying every night.

Jackie might have been studying every night.

USAGE NOTE Sometimes, the helping verbs are distanced from the main verb or other helping verbs. Adverbs, such as *always*, *never*, *not*, and *also*, can come between the helping verb and the main verb. Look at the examples below.

- Maria has never met her grandparents.
- New York, New York, will always be Mark's favorite city.
- Music and art should not have been taken out of the elementary school curriculum.

To Be, To Have, and To Do

The verbs *to be*, *to have*, and *to do* can function as **both** main verbs and helping verbs. When standing alone, they are main verbs. When placed before another verb, they are helping verbs. Study the following examples.

Guillermo has two midterms this week.

The verb *has* is alone and, thus, the main verb of this sentence.

Guillermo has written two essays this week.

The verb *has* is placed before the verb *written. Has* is the helping verb and *written* is the main verb.

Judge Haggerty is one of the oldest judges in this district.

The verb *is* stands alone. It is the main verb.

Judge Haggerty is known as one of the toughest judges in this district.

The verb *is* is placed before the verb *known. Is* is the helping verb and *known* is the main verb.

Doctor Chang does ten surgeries a week.

The verb *does* stands alone. It is a main verb in this sentence.

Doctor Chang does not perform more than ten surgeries a week.

The verb *does* is placed before the verb *perform. Does* is the helping verb and *perform* is the main verb.

Following are the forms of the verbs *to be, to have*, and *to do* that typically function as helping verbs.

To Be: am, is, are, was, were, been
To Have: has, have, had
To Do: do, does, did

 EXERCISE 6.6: Helping Verbs

In the following sentences, write HV above each helping verb and MV above each main verb. To locate the verbs more easily, first, cross out the prepositional phrases.

HV MV
Example: Noise ~~from the nearby factory~~ can be irritating.

1. Raccoons might have been rummaging in the garbage cans.
2. Our neighbors should have cleaned up after their wild party.
3. Lemon wedges should be added to ice water for a tangier flavor.
4. Fundraisers can help student athletes pay for equipment.
5. A 7.0 earthquake has destroyed many of Haiti's buildings and homes.

6. My sister's husband may have been feeling ill.

7. Telephone books have become obsolete.

8. Volunteers were needed to sell the carwash tickets.

9. Chickens are raised on his uncle's farm.

10. At the beach, the weather has been balmy.

EXERCISE 6.7: Helping Verbs

1. In the space provided, compose a sentence that uses the helping verb *should* with the action verb *exercise.*

   ____

   ____

2. In the space provided, compose a sentence that uses the helping verb *may* with the action verb *mow.*

   ____

   ____

3. In the space provided, compose a sentence that uses the helping verb *will* with the action verb *study.*

   ____

   ____

4. In the space provided, compose a sentence in which you use a form of the verb *to do* as a helping verb.

   ____

   ____

5. In the space provided, compose a sentence in which you use a form of the verb *to have* as a helping verb.

   ____

   ____

There are three types of verbs: action, linking, and helping.

- Action verbs show ______________________.
- A linking verb links the subject to a word or phrase that ____________ the subject, ____________ the subject, or tells the ____________ of the subject.
- A helping verb is also known as an ____________ verb and shows ____________, ____________, or ____________.

COMPONENTS AT WORK

Using Your Skills in Sentences

Part 1

With each verb below, create as many combinations as you can think of with different helping verbs.

> Example: Wash: <u>is washing, was washing, am washing, are washing, were washing, have washed, had washed, did wash, does wash, have been washing, has been washing, had been washing, could wash, would wash, should wash, may wash, might wash, must wash, can wash, will wash, shall wash</u>

1. Swim: ____

____

____

2. Write: ______________________________

____

____

3. Run: ______________________________

____

____

4. Teach: ______________________________

____

____

5. Juggle: ______________________________

____

____

Using Your Skills in Sentences

Part 2

Now choose one verb form from each group you created and compose five sentences in the designated spaces, using the five forms you chose.

Example: He has been washing clothes all day.

1. ______________________________

2. ______________________________

3. ______________________________

4. ______________________________

5. ______________________________

Using Your Skills in Reading I

In the following paragraph, cross out all prepositional phrases; then underline all the verbs. Write *A* above action verbs and *L* above linking verbs. For any verb groups that contain both helping verbs and main verbs, write *HV* above the helping verbs, *MVA* above main verbs that show action, and *MVL* above main verbs that are linking the subject to a noun, adjective, or prepositional phrase.

Gossip

People in all countries and in all walks of life have gossiped for centuries. Psychologists have studied both the positive and negative impacts of this form of human communication. According to some researchers, gossip reinforces moral boundaries in a community. Gossip can also foster a sense of belonging to a certain group. However, gossip has many negative effects as well. Gossip can be used as a tool to isolate and ostracize people. When singled out and embarrassed by harmful rumors, individuals become depressed and lonely. Gossip exists in the workplace, in school, and in social groups. Seemingly, gossip will never go away. We must do our best to rise above it. We must refuse to participate in such damaging communication.

Using Your Skills in Reading II

Carefully read the following paragraph "Niagara Falls and Daredevils." If there are any words that are unfamiliar to you, try to figure out their meaning through context clues by looking at the words surrounding the unfamiliar word. Many times, those context clues can help you figure out the meaning of a word. However, there may be times when context clues do not help, so make sure to have a dictionary or your smart phone nearby in case you need to look up a word. Do not merely skip over a word you do not know. A single word can change the meaning of an entire sentence.

The sentences in this paragraph are more challenging than the sentences in the paragraph "Gossip," so read carefully. First, cross out all prepositional phrases. Then, underline all verbs, writing an *A* above action verbs and an *L* above linking verbs. For any verb groups that contain both helping verbs and main verbs, write *HV* above the helping verbs and *MVA* above main verbs that show action and *MVL* above main verbs that are linking the subject to a noun, adjective, or prepositional phrase. Remember: infinitives, *to* plus the base form of the verb (*to smile, to draw, to type, etc.*), are **not** verbs, but verbals. Also, present participles, *-ing* forms of the verbs (*leaving, dancing, turning, etc.*), are **not** verbs, but verbals as well. Remember that *–ing* words are only verbs when helping verbs precede them. Remember that infinitives, participles, and gerunds are verbals, **not** verbs.

Niagara Falls and Daredevils

Niagara Falls straddles the border between the Canadian province of Ontario and the state of New York, and throughout the decades this group of waterfalls has been the site of many stunts. The power of the falls beckons daredevils to test their courage and skill, and the hordes of tourists offer a captive audience. The first person to prove her bravery was Annie Taylor. In 1901, the 63-year-old teacher strapped herself and her cat into a wooden barrel, and assistants tossed the barrel into the river rapids. As fascinated onlookers gaped at the scene, the barrel violently ricocheted between the rapids, plunged over 100 feet down the waterfall, and then bobbed and flowed to the shore. Amazingly, when friends opened the barrel, Ms. Taylor was alive. Many other daredevils followed in Taylor's footsteps, but not all of them survived to tell their tales. Some people attempted to brave the rapids in boats; others swam through the rapids. More people flung themselves over the falls in barrels, and others walked across the falls on a high wire. The first high wire artist to cross the falls was Jean Francois Gravelet, also known as The Great Blondin. Gravelet not only walked across the wire, but he also rode a bicycle, pushed a wheelbarrow, and carried his manager, Harry Colcord, on his back. All of the stunting through the years began to create a carnival-like atmosphere around the falls, so the Niagara Falls Commission eventually outlawed any daredevil activities. Recently, however, the commission agreed to allow Nik Wallenda, of the trapeze group The Flying Wallendas, to cross the falls on a high wire, instigating appeals from many other stunters wanting to perform their acts. The commission then decided to allow one qualified stunt every twenty years. Any person attempting a crazy stunt without permission will be fined $10,000.

Using Your Skills in Composition

Write a paragraph about a courageous stunt you performed or one you have read about or witnessed. Try to use as many specific active verbs as possible. Once you are finished writing, cross out all prepositional phrases and underline all verbs.

7 IRREGULAR VERBS

Chapter PREVIEW

In this chapter you will learn how irregular verbs differ from regular verbs. You will also learn the four principal parts of irregular verbs. Finally, the chapter explains three troublesome pairs of verbs: to lie / to lay, to sit / to set, and to rise / to raise.

Verbs can be identified not only as *action, linking,* or *helping,* but they can also be divided into *regular* and *irregular.* **Regular verbs** follow a consistent pattern in forming the past by adding *-ed* or *-d.* For example, *dance* becomes *danced* or *mow* becomes *mowed; practice* becomes *practiced* and *laugh* becomes *laughed.* This pattern—adding *-d* and *-ed*—holds true for all regular verbs.

Irregular verbs, on the other hand, do not follow this pattern. For example, *write* does not become *writed,* but *wrote,* and *drive* does not become *drived,* but *drove.*

PRINCIPAL PARTS OF A VERB

The **four principal parts of a verb** (all forms of the verb can be made from these four forms) are the present, the past, the past participle, and the present participle.

The **present** is the base form of a verb, the infinitive form without the word *to.* For example, take the infinitive *to grow,* remove the *to,* and you have the base form of the verb: *grow.*

The **past** is the simple past tense form of a verb, a specific time at which an event occurred before now, for example, *typed, wrote, paused,* or *froze.*

The **past participle** is a verb form preceded by a form of the verb *to have* or a form of the verb *to be,* for example, *has painted* or *was brought.* Other helping verbs may also occur, for example, *could have painted* or *might be brought.*

The **present participle** is the *-ing* form of the verb, such as *dancing.*

USAGE NOTE Remember, when you use an *-ing* form as a main verb of a sentence, you must include a helping verb(s). Notice the helping verbs in the following examples.

He will be dancing in the next performance.

The storm has been damaging the beach front.

An *-ing* word without a helping verb preceding it is NOT the verb of the sentence; it may look like a verb, but it is actually functioning as a noun or adjective. Look at the following sentence:

Janice was afraid of swimming in the churning water.

In this sentence, as the object of the preposition *of,* swimming is a noun. *Churning* is an adjective because the word modifies the noun *water.* See "Fundamental Spelling Rules" on the student companion site at cengagebrain.com for spelling rules that explain when to drop letters when adding suffixes, such as, *-ing.*

Since formal communication and academic writing should reflect proper English usage, you need to learn the correct forms of irregular verbs you do not know. Following is a list of many common irregular verbs in their four principal parts (**Table 7.1**).

TABLE 7.1
Common irregular verbs

Use the check boxes to indicate the verb groups you need to study.

	Present	Past	Past Participle	Present Participle
☐	arise	arose	arisen	arising
☐	be	was/were	been	being
☐	bear (to carry)	bore	borne	bearing
☐	bear	bore	born	bearing
☐	beat	beat	beat	beating
☐	become	became	become	becoming
☐	begin	began	begun	beginning
☐	bend	bent	bent	bending
☐	bet	bet	bet	betting
☐	bid	bid/bade	bid/bidden	bidding
☐	bind	bound	bound	binding
☐	bite	bit	bitten/bit	biting
☐	bleed	bled	bled	bleeding
☐	blow	blew	blown	blowing
☐	break	broke	broken	breaking
☐	bring	brought	brought	bringing
☐	broadcast	broadcast	broadcast	broadcasting
☐	build	built	built	building
☐	buy	bought	bought	buying
☐	burn	burned/burnt	burned/burnt	burning
☐	catch	caught	caught	catching
☐	choose	chose	chosen	choosing
☐	clothe	clothed/clad	clothed/clad	clothing
☐	come	came	come	coming
☐	cost	cost	cost	costing
☐	creep	crept	crept	creeping
☐	cut	cut	cut	cutting
☐	dig	dug	dug	digging
☐	dive	dived/dove	dived	diving

TABLE 7.1
Common irregular verbs *(continued)*

Use the check boxes to indicate the verb groups you need to study.

	Present	Past	Past Participle	Present Participle
☐	do	did	done	doing
☐	drag	dragged	dragged	dragging
☐	draw	drew	drawn	drawing
☐	dream	dreamed/dreamt	dreamt	dreaming
☐	drink	drank	drunk	drinking
☐	drive	drove	driven	driving
☐	drown	drowned	drowned	drowning
☐	eat	ate	eaten	eating
☐	fall	fell	fallen	falling
☐	feed	fed	fed	feeding
☐	feel	felt	felt	feeling
☐	fight	fought	fought	fighting
☐	find	found	found	finding
☐	fit	fit	fit	fitting
☐	flee	fled	fled	fleeing
☐	fly	flew	flown	flying
☐	forbid	forbade	forbidden	forbidding
☐	forget	forgot	forgotten	forgetting
☐	forgive	forgave	forgiven	forgiving
☐	forsake	forsook	forsaken	forsaking
☐	freeze	froze	frozen	freezing
☐	get	got	got/gotten	getting
☐	give	gave	given	giving
☐	go	went	gone	going
☐	grow	grew	grown	growing
☐	hang*	hung	hung	hanging
☐	have	had	had	having
☐	hear	heard	heard	hearing
☐	hide	hid	hidden	hiding
☐	hit	hit	hit	hitting
☐	hold	held	held	holding

*Use *to hang* and its forms *hang, hung, hung, hanging* with any object that can be suspended, for example, *I hung the plant from the ceiling* or *The TV has been hung on the wall.* Use *to hang* and its forms *hang, hanged, hanged, hanging* when you are describing the execution of a person.

TABLE 7.1 Common irregular verbs *(continued)*

Use the check boxes to indicate the verb groups you need to study.

	Present	Past	Past Participle	Present Participle
☐	hurt	hurt	hurt	hurting
☐	keep	kept	kept	keeping
☐	kneel	knelt	knelt	kneeling
☐	know	knew	known	knowing
☐	lay	laid	laid	laying
☐	lead	led	led	leading
☐	leave	left	left	leaving
☐	lend	lent	lent	lending
☐	let	let	let	letting
☐	lie	lay	lain	lying
☐	light	lighted/lit	lighted/lit	lighting
☐	lose	lost	lost	losing
☐	make	made	made	making
☐	mean	meant	meant	meaning
☐	meet	met	met	meeting
☐	overcome	overcame	overcome	overcoming
☐	overtake	overtook	overtaken	overtaking
☐	overthrow	overthrew	overthrown	overthrowing
☐	pay	paid	paid	paying
☐	prove	proved	proved/proven	proving
☐	put	put	put	putting
☐	quit	quit	quit	quitting
☐	read	read	read	reading
☐	ride	rode	ridden	riding
☐	ring	rang	rung	ringing
☐	rise	rose	risen	rising
☐	run	ran	run	running
☐	say	said	said	saying
☐	see	saw	seen	seeing
☐	seek	sought	sought	seeking
☐	sell	sold	sold	selling
☐	send	sent	sent	sending
☐	set	set	set	setting
☐	shake	shook	shaken	shaking

TABLE 7.1
Common irregular verbs *(continued)*

Use the check boxes to indicate the verb groups you need to study.

	Present	Past	Past Participle	Present Participle
☐	shine**	shone	shone	shining
☐	shoot	shot	shot	shooting
☐	show	showed	shown	showing
☐	shut	shut	shut	shutting
☐	sing	sang	sung	singing
☐	sink	sank	sunk	sinking
☐	sit	sat	sat	sitting
☐	sleep	slept	slept	sleeping
☐	slide	slid	slid	sliding
☐	sneak	sneaked/snuck	sneaked/snuck	sneaking
☐	speak	spoke	spoken	speaking
☐	speed	sped	sped	speeding
☐	spend	spent	spent	spending
☐	spring	sprang	sprung	springing
☐	stand	stood	stood	standing
☐	steal	stole	stolen	stealing
☐	stick	stuck	stuck	sticking
☐	sting	stung	stung	stinging
☐	stink	stank	stunk	stinking
☐	strike	struck	struck	striking
☐	swear	swore	sworn	swearing
☐	sweep	swept	swept	sweeping
☐	swim	swam	swum	swimming
☐	swing	swung	swung	swinging
☐	take	took	taken	taking
☐	teach	taught	taught	teaching
☐	tear	tore	torn	tearing
☐	tell	told	told	telling
☐	think	thought	thought	thinking
☐	throw	threw	thrown	throwing
☐	understand	understood	understood	understanding
☐	use	used	used	using

**Use *to shine* and its forms *shine, shone, shone, shining* when you are discussing the release of a light beam, for example, *The light shone over a large area.* Use *to shine* and its forms *shine, shined, shined, shining* when you are discussing polishing an object, for example, *He shined his car once a month.*

TABLE 7.1
Common irregular verbs *(continued)*

Use the check boxes to indicate the verb groups you need to study.

	Present	Past	Past Participle	Present Participle
☐	wake	woke/waked	woken/waked/ woke	waking
☐	wear	wore	worn	wearing
☐	weep	wept	wept	weeping
☐	win	won	won	winning
☐	write	wrote	written	writing

USAGE NOTE When an irregular verb has the same forms for the present, past, and past participle, for example, *put* or *set*, remember that the past participial form must be preceded by a form of *to have* or *to be.*

She set the table. (past)

She had set the table. (past participle)

 EXERCISE 7.1: Irregular Verb Forms

Underline the correct verb form in the parentheses.

1. The gift was (hid / hidden) in the back of the closet.
2. The sprinter (ran / run) in three different events.
3. By the time I turned on TV, the parade had (began / begun).
4. The young man (drew / drawn) water from a well with an old bucket.
5. The bell that hung in the tower (rang / rung) each hour.
6. By the time she was twenty-two, she had (flew / flown) around the world twice.
7. By next month, Martha will have (swam / swum) in fourteen competitions.
8. Standing by the window, Ralph (saw / seen) the rain begin to fall.
9. To get the apples from the tree, the twins (shook / shaken) the tree.
10. Nell had (fell / fallen) three times by the end of her ice skating lesson.

EXERCISE 7.2: Irregular Verb Forms

Compose sentences following the directions. Refer to the list of irregular verbs on pages 92-96 if you need to review the principal parts of a verb.

1. Compose a sentence that includes the past tense of the verb *bind.*

____

____

2. Compose a sentence that includes the past tense of the verb *creep.*

____

____

3. Compose a sentence that includes the past tense of the verb *sink.*

____

____

4. Compose a sentence that includes the past participle of the verb *hide.*

____

____

5. Compose a sentence that includes the past participle of the verb *stink.*

____

____

6. Compose a sentence that includes the past participle of the verb *wear.*

____

____

7. Compose a sentence that includes the present participle of the verb *shut.*

____

____

8. Compose a sentence that includes the present participle of the verb *pay*.

____

____

9. Compose a sentence that includes the present participle of the verb *weep*.

____

____

10. Compose a sentence that includes the past participle of an irregular verb of your choice.

____

____

EXERCISE 7.3: Irregular Verb Forms

In the space provided, insert either the past tense form or the past participial form of the verb indicated in parenthesis.

When the UFO landed in the city park, at first I (think) __________ the whole event was a joke. But after I (see) __________ the military and the media arrive, I (know) __________ I was witnessing an historical event. First, the military (set) __________ up a perimeter around the space craft. Civilians were (tell) __________ to leave the immediate area, but I had (hide) __________ behind a car that was (park) __________ near the area. Nothing happened for about an hour. Then a bell inside the space craft (ring) __________ and a door (begin) __________ to open. While waiting, I had (become) __________ tired and seemingly fell asleep, but the bell startled me, and I (peek) __________ over the back of the car to see who or what would exit the UFO. But I never (find) __________ out since my alarm awakened me from my dream.

THREE PAIRS OF TROUBLESOME VERBS

Three pairs of verbs that have proven more difficult than others are the verbs *to lie* and *to lay*, *to sit* and *to set*, and *to rise* and *to raise*.

Lie and *Lay*

The verb *to lie* means to rest or to recline, and the verb's principal parts are *lie*, *lay*, *lain*, and *lying*.

> They lie on the couch every day to watch television. (Present)
>
> They lay on the couch yesterday for most of the day. (Past)
>
> They have lain on the couch for most of the day. (Past Participle)
>
> They are lying on the couch even as we speak. (Present Participle)

The verb *to lay* means to put or to place something or someone, and the verb's principal parts are *lay*, *laid*, *laid*, and *laying*.

> We lay the flowers on the table. (Present)
>
> We laid the flowers on the table yesterday. (Past)
>
> We have laid the flowers in the same spot for the last two weeks. (Past Participle)
>
> We will be laying the flowers next to the candles. (Present Participle)

Sit and *Set*

The verb *to sit* means to seat oneself, and the four principal parts are *sit*, *sat*, *sat*, and *sitting*.

> I sit in the same spot each morning when I eat breakfast. (Present)
>
> I sat in the same spot for several months to eat breakfast. (Past)
>
> I have sat in the same spot for several weeks now. (Past Participle)
>
> I was sitting in my favorite chair when the phone rang. (Present Participle)

The verb *to set* means to put or to place something or someone, and the four principal parts are *set*, *set*, *set*, and *setting*.

> We set the dishes in the cupboard. (Present)
>
> We set the dishes in the cupboard yesterday. (Past)

> We have set the dishes where you said to set them. (Past Participle)
>
> We were setting the dishes down when you walked in. (Present Participle)

Rise and Raise

The verb *to rise* means to stand or to reach a greater height/altitude, and the four principal parts are *rise, rose, risen,* and *rising.*

> People rise when the president enters the room. (Present)
>
> People rose when the president entered the room. (Past)
>
> People have risen as a show of respect since as far back as biblical times. (Past Participle)
>
> People are rising when they need a break from sitting. (Present Participle)

The verb *to raise,* a regular verb, means to elevate something or someone or to increase in amount, and its four principal parts are *raise, raised, raised,* and *raising.*

> The soldiers raise the flag each morning. (Present)
>
> The young boy raised his blinds when he awoke. (Past)
>
> The player has raised the ante in the poker game. (Past Participle)
>
> I am raising the height of the chimney for better draw. (Present Participle)

EXERCISE 7.4: Lay/Lie; Sit/Set; Rise/Raise

Insert the correct **past** or **past participial** form of the verb indicated in parenthesis.

1. The young woman has (raise) ______________ rabbits for breeding and show.
2. Yesterday Timmy (lie) ______________ down for a nap.
3. When I came home, I (set) ______________ the mail on the table.
4. When I came home yesterday, I (sit) ______________ down to rest for fifteen minutes.
5. Because she (lay) ______________ the coat on the floor, the cat slept on it.

6. I (rise) ______________ when my new boss entered the room.
7. The toddler had (set) ______________ the toy down and crawled away.
8. My ill daughter has (lie) ______________ in bed all day.
9. The clerk had (sit) ______________ at his desk for most of the day.
10. I have (rise) ______________ at 5 a.m. each morning for the last six months.

EXERCISE 7.5: Pasts and Past Participles of Lie/Lay, Sit/Set, and Rise/Raise

Compose one sentence each for the present (PR), past (PAST), and past participial (PP) forms of the verbs *Lie, Lay, Sit, Set, Rise,* and *Raise*. Do not hesitate to review the forms.

Lie — PR ____

Lie — PAST ____

Lie — PP ____

Lay — PR ____

Lay — PAST ____

Lay — PP ____

Sit — PR ____

Sit — PAST ____

Sit — PP ____

Set — PR ____

Set — PAST ____

Set — PP ____

Rise — PR ____

Rise — PAST ______________________________

Rise — PP ______________________________

Raise — PR ______________________________

Raise — PAST ______________________________

Raise — PP ______________________________

- You form the present participle by adding ____________ to the base form.
- The past participle form of the verb must be preceded by the verb ____________ or ____________.

COMPONENTS AT WORK

Using Your Skills in Sentences

Compose sentences according to the directions. Do not hesitate to return to previous chapters if you need to review earlier lessons.

1. Compose a sentence that uses the past participle of the verb *hide* and includes a prepositional phrase.

   ____

   ____

2. Compose a sentence that uses the past participle of the irregular verb *drive* and includes an infinitive phrase.

   ____

   ____

3. Compose a sentence that uses the present participle of the irregular verb *creep* and an adverb and an adjective.

   ____

   ____

4. Compose a sentence that uses the past tense of the verbs *chase* and *give*.

   ____

   ____

5. Compose a sentence that includes an infinitive and the adjective *fewer*.

   ____

   ____

6. Compose a sentence that uses the past tense of the irregular verbs *bind* and *take*.

   ____

   ____

7. Compose a sentence that uses the past participial form of the verb *teach* and a prepositional phrase.

____

____

8. Compose a sentence that uses the present participle of the verb *weep*.

____

____

Using Your Skills in Reading

Carefully read the following short fairy tale. After reading through it once for understanding, which includes looking up words you do not understand or recognize, read it again. If there are any words that are unfamiliar to you, try to figure out their meaning through context clues, looking at the words surrounding the unfamiliar word. Many times, those context clues can help you figure out the meaning of a word. However, there may be times when context clues do not help, so make sure to have a dictionary or your smart phone nearby in case you need to look up a word. Do not merely skip over a word you do not know. A single word can change the meaning of an entire sentence.

After rereading the fairy tale, read the story again and underline or highlight all the **past**, **past participial**, and **present participial** verbs. Identify each form: P = past, PP = past participial, PSP = present participial.

The Magical Shoes

Once upon a time a little girl lived in a great forest in the middle of an enchanted kingdom. Since the little girl had no brothers or sisters, she was friends with the animals in the forest. The girl was poor and had few possessions. But she did own a pair of magic shoes.

The shoes had always belonged to the little girl, even when she was only a baby. Wonderfully, the shoes had never worn out and had grown larger as the girl grew. But there was more magic in the shoes than just never wearing out or growing in size. With the correct magic words, the shoes allowed the girl to run faster than any animal in the forest.

The little girl never knew about the shoes' magic until one day when she had taken her shoes off and was dangling her feet in a stream. A beautiful woman with long golden hair, blue eyes, and wearing a purple gown suddenly appeared beside her. She told the girl the magic verse that would allow her to run faster than the animals in the forest: "Shoes on my feet, wind at my back, now I can run faster than that." The girl had always thought the spell was rather silly, but regardless, the spell worked.

But the little girl was not the only person who dwelt in the woods. In the exact center of the forest lived a wicked witch. The witch had twice seen the little girl running through the forest, and the witch decided she wanted the shoes for herself. Even though the witch did not know the spell that would allow her to run faster than any animal in the forest, she was a powerful witch, and she thought she would first steal the shoes and then figure out how they worked. But since the girl took her shoes off only to sleep and to bathe, the witch knew she had to be patient and wait for the right time.

One summer day, the little girl had been running through the forest when she decided to stop by a stream and dip her feet in the water. On this particular day, the witch had been watching the little girl and was nearby when she sat by the stream, took her shoes off, and put her feet in the cool water.

The witch knew this might be her best chance to obtain the shoes, so she cast a sleeping spell on the girl. Soon the little girl closed her eyes and fell asleep on the mossy bank, so the witch sneaked over, took the shoes, and hurried back to her cottage in the center of the forest.

When the little girl awoke, she saw her magic shoes were gone, and she began to cry. As she was crying, she heard a voice ask her, “Why are you crying?”

She looked up to see the beautiful woman who had given her the magic spell.

The little girl answered, “I fell asleep, and when I awoke, my shoes were gone.”

“The witch who lives in the center of the forest stole them for herself. And even though she doesn’t know the spell to make them work, she is a powerful witch and will soon learn the spell. You must get the shoes back quickly.”

The little girl thanked the woman and set off to regain her shoes.

After walking for three days, the little girl found the witch’s cottage in the center of the forest. She sneaked up to the cottage and peeked in the window. The little girl could see her shoes sitting on a table in the middle of the room. She could also see the witch standing over a cauldron and mixing a magic potion. The little girl knew she was not fast enough to run into the cottage, grab the shoes, put them on, say the spell, and run off before the witch caught her. So she crept away and hid behind a tree and thought about what she could do.

Soon she had a plan, and she called her friends, the birds and the raccoons, and explained to them the plan. When the little girl gave the signal, the birds flew into the cottage and flew around and around and around the witch, interrupting her magic work. While the witch was busy trying to chase the birds out of the cottage, two raccoons waddled into the cottage, climbed up on the table, and grabbed one shoe each. They then hurried back out of the cottage and took the shoes to the little girl. As soon as the little girl put the shoes on her feet, she said the magic words, “Shoes on my feet, wind at my back, now I can run faster than that,” picked up the two raccoons, and ran off through the forest.

The little girl had learned her lesson, and she never again removed the shoes unless she was safe and alone at home.

Using Your Skills in Composition

Recall a favorite fairy tale (*Cinderella, Hansel and Gretel, Jack and the Beanstalk,* etc.) or a favorite movie based on a fairy tale (*Enchanted; Mirror Mirror; Snow White and the Huntsman; Hansel and Gretel: Witch Hunters,* etc.), and retell the fairy tale in a paragraph or two. Be sure in your retelling to use the past, past participial, and present participial forms of verbs.

8 SUBJECT-VERB AGREEMENT

Chapter PREVIEW

In this chapter, you will learn thirteen rules to make sure the subjects and verbs in your sentences agree in number.

SUBJECT-VERB AGREEMENT

Simply put, **subject-verb agreement** is making sure the subject and verb of the sentence agree in number. In other words, if the subject is singular, the verb must be singular. If the subject is plural, the verb must be plural. Look at the two sentences below; pay close attention to the words written in green:

> The young girl skips happily down the sidewalk.
>
> The young girls skip happily down the sidewalk.
>
> In the first sentence, the subject *girl* is singular and the verb *skips* is also singular because it ends in *-s*. In the second sentence, the subject *girls* is plural and the verb *skip* is plural because it does **not** end in *-s*.

For some, subject-verb agreement is confusing because when you apply an *-s* or an *-es* to a noun, you create a plural noun. For example, *boy* becomes *boys,* and *fox* becomes *foxes,* but when you apply an *-s* or *-es* to a verb, you create a singular verb, such as *he paints* or *she explores*. Look at the next pair of sentences. Again, pay attention to the words written in green:

> The peach sits on the kitchen counter.
>
> The peaches sit on the kitchen counter.
>
> In the first sentence, the singular subject *peach* agrees in number with the singular verb *sits* since both are singular. In the second sentence, the plural subject *peaches* agrees in number with the plural verb *sit* since both are plural.

The following rules will help you make sure your subjects and verbs agree in number. You may already be familiar with some of the rules. Those you are not familiar with, you will need to learn.

While this chapter presents and explains thirteen rules concerning subject-verb agreement, these rules mostly pertain to the present tense, with the exception of the past tense forms of the verb *to be*. As you read and study each rule, note the verbs. Faulty subject-verb agreement, when a subject and a verb do not agree in number, rarely occurs outside of present tense.

THIRTEEN RULES FOR SUBJECT-VERB AGREEMENT

RULE #1. Even if a word or group of words comes between the subject and verb, the subject and verb must still agree in number.

> The can of soda sitting by the newspapers is not open.
>
> The verb *is* agrees with the subject *can,* not *newspapers*, which is the object of the preposition *by.*

> The boxes of cookies stuffed into our backpack take up too much room.
>
> The verb *take* agrees with the subject *boxes,* not *backpack,* which is the object of the preposition *into.*

USAGE NOTE Remember, if after you have written a sentence, you are unsure you have correct subject-verb agreement, go back and identify any prepositional phrases in the sentence and line them out because, as you learned in Chapter 3, phrases cannot contain either a subject or a verb. Having marked out any prepositional phrases in your sentence, you have a better chance of correctly identifying the subject and verb to make sure they agree in number.

EXERCISE 8.1: Subject-Verb Agreement Rule 1

Correct the subject-verb agreement errors in the following sentences by drawing an X through the incorrect verb and writing in the correct one above it. One sentence is correct. Indicate the correct sentence with *C*. To help identify the subject and verb, you may wish to line out any phrases.

Example: The small, neighborhood grocery store ~~down the street from two large chain markets~~ ~~are~~ is closing next month.

1. The children playing stickball in the street seems unconcerned about the traffic.
2. Standing before their mother, the twin girls, who were finger painting the living room walls, look worried.
3. The students from the afternoon class of third semester Italian is looking forward to their six week trip to Italy.
4. The managers in the sales department is going on a retreat next month.

5. Bicycling, whether on a stationary bike or on a traditional bike where you

   can ride outside for miles and miles, are good cardiovascular exercise.

RULE #2. Subjects in a sentence joined by the conjunction *and* usually take a plural verb.

> Bright flowers and butterflies always bring a smile to my face.
>
> *Flowers* and *butterflies* create a compound subject so you need a plural verb, *bring*.
>
> A thick crust pizza, sweet iced tea, and cheesecake for dessert are the perfect meal.
>
> *Pizza*, *tea*, and *cheesecake* are the three subjects, so you need a plural verb, *are*.

The exception to this rule occurs when a compound subject is considered by usage a single group or unit. Then you need to use a singular verb.

> Bacon and eggs is my usual breakfast.
>
> Peanut butter and jelly is a favorite sandwich for children.

RULE #3. When two or more singular subjects in a sentence are joined by the conjunction *or* or *nor*, the subjects take a singular verb. When both subjects are plural, the verb is plural.

> The bright red pickup truck or the teal green car is going to be my next ride.
>
> The books in the front room or the boxes of pictures in the garage need to be moved.

RULE #4. If a singular subject and a plural subject are joined by *or* or *nor*, the subject closer to the verb determines whether the verb is singular or plural.

> The coaches or the player is the person responsible.
>
> The player or the coaches are the people responsible.

USAGE NOTE When a sentence contains a singular subject and a plural subject, some writers prefer always to place the plural subject closer to the verb so that the verb is always plural.

EXERCISE 8.2: Subject-Verb Agreement Rules 2, 3, and 4

Correct the subject-verb agreement errors in the following sentences by drawing an X through the incorrect verb and writing in the correct one above it. One sentence is correct. Indicate the correct sentence with *C*. To help identify the subject and verb, you may wish to line out any phrases.

1. A rabbit and a parrot, either one a possible pet, is in my yard.
2. Neither the apple trees nor the apricot tree, all of which are dying, are producing fruit.
3. The young boy, ten years old, and the young girl, his twin, skate happily in the park.
4. Either the laundry or the windows needs to be washed today.
5. The statues or the paintings reminds me of my father's fondness for museums.
6. Under the bridge, the toad, the frog, and the cricket, small creatures every one, sings merrily.
7. Kerosene lamps or candles, both of which people use to light their way at night, is dangerous if not used properly.
8. Neither the teacher nor his students, each one listening intently to the speaker, hears the bell.
9. The children or the parents or the grandparents, all of whom attended the award ceremony, wants to help when they are able.
10. Flashing lights and loud noise is expected at a rave.

RULE #5. When the subject of the sentence is (1) the title of a book, magazine, newspaper, short story, song, etc., (2) a business, or (3) a word or concept you are describing or defining, the verb remains singular even if the subject contains a plural noun.

> Even though the novel is 320 pages long, *Pride and Prejudice and Zombies* reads quickly.
>
> Sears makes shopping for tools easy.
>
> *Peoples* is a way to describe a group of human beings who identify with each other, for example, "the native peoples of North America."

RULE #6. When a sentence begins with *Here* or *There*, the subject comes after the verb.

> Here in the box are the six bags of chips you wanted.
>
> The plural subject of the sentence, *bags,* follows the verb *are.*
>
> There is the book Vicki wanted for her birthday.
>
> The singular subject of the sentence, *book,* follows the verb *is.*

RULE #7. In questions, the subject may come in between the helping (auxiliary) verb and the main verb or the subject may follow the verb.

> Does Jeremy know what he wants for dinner?
>
> The subject, *Jeremy,* separates the helping verb *Does* and the main verb *know.*
>
> Where are Faye and her friends?
>
> The compound subject *Faye* and *friends* follow the plural verb *are.*

EXERCISE 8.3: Subject-Verb Agreement Rules 5, 6, and 7

Correct the subject-verb agreement errors in the following sentences by drawing an X through the incorrect verb and writing in the correct one above it. One sentence is correct. Indicate the correct sentence with *C.* To help identify the subject and verb, you may wish to line out any prepositional phrases.

1. There are in the downstairs' bedroom Grayson's favorite toy.

2. Do the cat, which is Skye's pet, know it is going to the vet?

3. Macy's, a nationwide department store, are having a holiday sale.

4. *The Sorcerer and His Magic Spells* are one of my son's favorite books.

5. Here in the window is the pies your grandmother made this morning.

6. Where is the last pieces for the jigsaw puzzle?

7. Zora Neal Hurston's *Of Mules and Men* are one of my favorite books.

8. Sara's article on the homeless, "Programs That Work," appear in Sunday's paper.

9. Are there any peaches left in the refrigerator?

10. *136 Fast and Easy Meals* are a cookbook every single male should own.

RULE #8. Singular indefinite pronouns (see Chapter 5) will always require a singular verb.

The singular indefinite pronouns include

someone	everyone	anyone	no one	each
something	everything	anything	nothing	each one
somebody	everybody	anybody	nobody	either / neither

> Someone is knocking at the door.
>
> Anybody has the ability to laugh.
>
> Everything is in working order.
>
> Each of the children wants to walk in front.
>
> In this last sentence, even though the word *children* is plural, *children* is the object of the prepositional phrase *of the children*, so the subject is *Each.*

RULE #9. Some indefinite pronouns can be either singular or plural depending on the context in which you use the pronoun. These pronouns include

some all any half more most none

Two quick ways exist for you to determine if the pronoun is singular or plural. First, look at the object of the preposition in the prepositional phrase that follows the indefinite pronoun. If the object of the preposition is singular, the verb will be singular; if the object of the preposition is plural, the verb

will be plural. When the verb following the prepositional phrase contains a helping verb created from either *to be*, *to do*, or *to have*, only the helping verb changes its spelling, not the main verb. Read the following examples.

> Most of the cake has been eaten.
>
> Most of the cakes have been eaten.
>
> All of the class wants to go on a field trip.
>
> All of the classes want to go on a field trip.

USAGE NOTE Do not be confused if the preposition in the prepositional phrase following the indefinite pronoun is omitted. The same rules apply. Look at the two sentences below:

All the workers wear shorts on Fridays.

Half the children want chocolate milk for lunch.

Although the words *the workers* and *the children* do not appear to be prepositional phrases, the preposition *of* is implied in both.

The same is true for a sentence like *Several people want off of the plane.* While seemingly no prepositional phrase follows *Several*, the phrase *of the people* is implied.

The second way to determine if the indefinite pronouns *some*, *all*, *any*, *half*, *more*, *none*, or *most* are singular or plural is to identify the object of the preposition in the prepositional phrase that immediately follows the indefinite pronoun. If the noun tells *how much*, the verb is singular. If the noun tells *how many*, the verb is plural.

> Most of the milk is gone.
>
> How much?
>
> Some of the cookies are gone.
>
> How many?
>
> All of the book is marked up.
>
> How much?
>
> All of the books are marked up.
>
> How many?

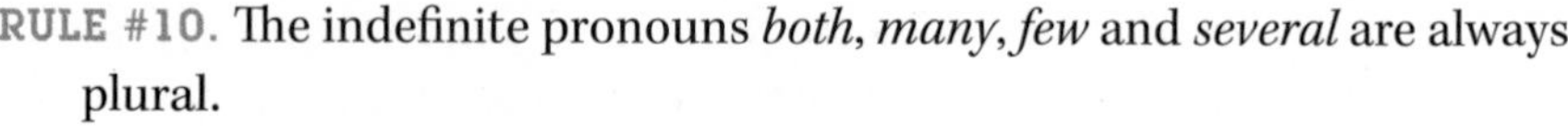

RULE #10. The indefinite pronouns *both, many, few* and *several* are always plural.

> Two men were invited to speak. Both are late.
>
> With the millions of clocks in the world, few ever show the same time.
>
> We ordered a large pizza, which has twelve pieces. Several remain in the box.

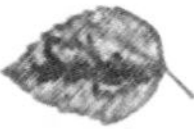

EXERCISE 8.4: Subject-Verb Agreement Rules 8, 9, and 10

Correct the subject-verb agreement errors in the following sentences by drawing an X through the incorrect verb and writing in the correct one above it. One sentence is correct. Indicate the correct sentence with *C*. To help identify the subject and verb, you may wish to line out any prepositional phrases.

1. Everybody at the festivals are enjoying the wide variety of music.
2. Half of the pies in the refrigerator is missing.
3. Several of the men down by the loading dock is looking for work.
4. Most of the plants in my neighbor's yard is California native plants.
5. Nothing in the living room, dining room, or bedrooms are painted blue.
6. Both of my siblings, who live in Washington, D.C., work at the State Department.
7. More of the building down the street from the town's only two gas stations have been repaired and repainted.
8. Each of the children in the play have a chance to recite a poem.
9. After a flight is canceled, a few people in the airport seeks another flight.
10. During the dance, anybody who happens to be wearing red shoes receive a special prize.

RULE #11. A number of words in the English language appear to be plural in form but are often singular in meaning. This group of words includes *athletics, aeronautics, economics, electronics, linguistics, mathematics, measles, molasses, mumps, news, physics, politics,* and *statistics.* The names of places may also appear plural but may be singular, for example, *United States, Honduras,* or *Philippines.* As you see in the examples below, these nouns require singular verbs.

> Mathematics is an important field of study.
>
> Statistics requires a fundamental understanding of mathematics.
>
> The news has upset my brother.
>
> Molasses makes a wonderful sweetener.

Be aware that depending upon the context, many of these words can also be plurals. For instance, *economics* is singular when using the word to refer to a field of study as in the following sentence: *Economics is difficult for many students.* But the term is plural when you use it as a financial reference: *The couple's economics are the reason they refinanced their home.* If you are unsure whether the usage of the word is singular or plural, check your dictionary.

RULE #12. Another group of words, **collective nouns**, may appear plural because they name groups of things but are often singular when they act as a collective, singular unit. Literally hundreds of collective nouns exist in the English language. More familiar collective nouns include *army, audience, class, committee, crowd, family, fleet, group, panel, squad,* and *team.* As you see in the examples below, these nouns require singular verbs.

> The class laughs at the art instructor's stick figure drawings.
>
> The committee votes on agenda items during each meeting.
>
> The fleet sails tomorrow.
>
> The panel develops guidelines for the quality of food.

RULE #13. When you write about money, distance, time, or measurements as a single unit and use the information as the subject of the sentence, the verb is singular.

> Twenty dollars is all I have.
>
> Fifteen miles makes for a long day's hike.

> Four hours without a break is a long time to study.
>
> Two yards of cloth was not enough for the shirt I was sewing.

EXERCISE 8.5: Subject-Agreement Rules 11, 12, and 13

Correct the subject-verb agreement errors in the following sentences by drawing an X through the incorrect verb and writing in the correct one above it. One sentence is correct. Indicate the correct sentence with *C.* To help identify the subject and verb, you may wish to line out any prepositional phrases.

1. The Bahamas are a group of twenty-nine islands in the Caribbean Sea.
2. The crowd surrounding the speaker's platform are awaiting the company CEO.
3. Seven dollars are too much for a hamburger and a small drink.
4. After the performance, the audience claps and whistles its appreciation.
5. Measles are a dangerous childhood disease.
6. Jeremy thought, "Eight yards of material for this shirt seem like way too much."
7. While Sophie does well in math, statistics are a difficult subject for her.
8. Each Friday the class vote on which book to read the following week.
9. A flock of magpies on its way to its roost in the evening make a loud noise.
10. Sixteen hours are too long a time for one person to drive alone in one day.

Chapter SUMMARY

- Simply put, subject-verb agreement is making sure ________________ ____.
- By adding *-s* or *-es* to a noun, you make the noun ________________.
- By adding *-s* or *-es* to a verb, you make the verb ________________.
- Subjects joined by the conjunction *and* usually take ________________ ____.
- When a sentence begins with *There* or *Here*, the subject comes ____.
- Singular indefinite pronouns will always require a ________________ verb.
- The indefinite pronouns *both, many, few*, and *several* will always require a ________________ verb.
- When a sentence contains a singular subject and a plural subject joined by *or* or *nor*, ________________________________ determines whether the verb is singular or plural.

COMPONENTS AT WORK

Using Your Skills in Sentences I

Correct the subject-verb agreement errors in the following sentences by lining out the incorrect verb and inserting the correct one.

1. By early afternoon, half of the peaches in the refrigerator was eaten.

2. *The New York Times*, a major U.S. newspaper with a Sunday circulation of over two million people, have the second largest Sunday circulation in the United States.

3. Neither the police nor the defendant's attorneys, all of whom are packed into the court room, wants to discuss the case with the press.

4. Each of the avocadoes cost $2.

5. When I was a child, mumps were a common and dangerous disease.

6. Without a rest, six hours are a long time to exercise.

7. The video tapes, which sit along with a number of DVDs on the desk, is covered with dust.

8. Either the pick-up truck, which has 32,000 miles on it, or the compact, which has fewer miles, are a good buy.

9. There on the table, next to the salt and pepper shakers, are the piece of pie you wanted.

10. Booing the players, the crowd, almost everyone standing up and waving towels, are unhappy with the players' performance.

Using Your Skills in Sentences II

Compose sentences according to the directions. Remember to keep your verbs in present tense.

1. Compose a sentence that exhibits S-V agreement Rule #1 and includes an adjective and a prepositional phrase.

 ____

 ____

2. Compose a sentence that exhibits S-V agreement Rule #4 and includes an action verb and an adverb.

 ____

 ____

3. Compose a sentence that exhibits S-V agreement Rule #5 and includes a form of *to be, to do,* or *to have* as a helping verb.

 ____

 ____

4. Compose a sentence that exhibits S-V agreement Rule #8 and includes a linking verb.

 ____

 ____

5. Compose a sentence that exhibits S-V agreement Rule #13 and includes an adverb and a prepositional phrase.

 ____

 ____

Using Your Skills in Reading

Carefully read the following short essay "Camping and Backpacking Preparations." After reading through it once for understanding, which includes looking up words you do not understand or recognize, read it again. If there are any words that are unfamiliar to you, try to figure out their meaning through context clues, looking at the words surrounding the unfamiliar word. Many times, those context clues can help you figure out the meaning of a word. However, there may be times when context clues do not help, so make sure to have a dictionary or your smart phone nearby in case you need to look up a word. Do not merely skip over a word you do not know. A single word can change the meaning of an entire sentence.

After rereading the essay, correct the subject-verb agreement errors by drawing an X through the incorrect verb and writing the correct one above it. To help you identify the subject and verb, you may want to line out any prepositional phrases in the sentence.

Camping and Backpacking Preparations

Camping and backpacking in our family, which includes my wife and two daughters, ages 7 and 9, is not chaotic, disorganized activities. On the contrary, once we decide that we are going on a camping or backpacking trip, the preparations for the excursion is methodical and organized.

There are a number of steps we follow to make sure the trip is more fun than work. First, the family, whether we are camping or backpacking and depending on where we are going and how long we will be gone, develop a chart that identifies how many meals we will need to fix. The girls, independently of each other, make a list that include breakfasts, lunches, dinners, and snacks. Also *Easy and Simple Backpacking Meals*, a book my wife and I picked up several years ago, offer a variety of high energy, filling meals.

Once we have developed our meal plan, my wife or I, depending on who has the most free time, begin to gather our gear. Again we have a list of equipment that we pick and choose from, depending on the type and duration of the outing. For example, if we are car camping, we can pack cots to sleep on rather than light sleeping pads. If we take the car, I can pack my cast iron frying pan and a three-burner propane stove, neither of which I want to carry when backpacking. Also, if we are car camping, we usually pitch camp in a campground that provides potable water for the campers, so we don't have to concern ourselves about carrying sufficient water with us like we do when we are backpacking.

After we choose all the gear that we plan to take, everyone who is going on the adventure, for not everyone in the family goes on all the trips, are involved in checking the equipment to make sure everything we are using, for example, stove, sleeping pads, tent, packs, lights, etc., are clean and working. If my wife or the girls or I find a problem with any of the equipment, we either repair the problem then or replace the piece of gear. We don't want our trip spoiled because of a piece of faulty equipment.

When we are backpacking, my wife and I must also take into account who is going on the trip. For example, while my wife and I may find walking fifteen miles in a day an acceptable pace, fifteen miles are too far for our daughters to walk in a day. As the girls grow older, they will be able to walk further, but right now ten miles a day are all they are only able to walk comfortably.

The news are also an important part of our planning. We check *www.noaa.gov/wx.html* and *www.weather.com* for the area we will be camping to help us decide on the type of clothing we need to pack. For warm, sunny weather, hats, long sleeve but light weight shirts, and a pair or two of shorts is included. If the weather prediction is for rain, a rain jacket with a hood as well as a backpack cover is part of our gear. The weather can also influence the food we take because if the weather is cold, the girls, who do not particularly enjoy cold weather, asks us to pack additional instant hot chocolate.

Last, each person who is going on the outings are required to check to make sure she or he has all her or his gear. We pack the night before so that our preparations in the morning is limited to having a bite to eat, brushing our teeth, and setting out on our trip.

While some people enjoy the adventure of a quickly planned camping or backpacking trip, my wife, the girls, and I prefers to follow an organized preparation so that we spend our time enjoying our trip rather than forgetting something or repairing our equipment.

Using Your Skills in Composition

Write a well developed paragraph on a trip you have taken. Within the paragraph, include at least five sentences that illustrate five of the subject-verb agreement rules presented in this chapter. After the sentences where you have applied the five subject-verb agreement rules, indicate in parenthesis the rule you are illustrating in that sentence.

CLAUSES

Chapter PREVIEW

In this chapter you will learn to recognize main and subordinate clauses, to punctuate them, and to combine both types of clauses with main clauses to create effective sentences. You will also learn to use restrictive and nonrestrictive clauses.

CLAUSES

When you assemble the various parts of speech and grammatical structures you studied in Chapters 1-8, you have the ability and the knowledge to create clauses.

A **clause** is a group of related words that contains **both** a subject and a verb. Clauses may be either a main clause (also called an independent clause) or a subordinate clause (also called a dependent clause).

A **main clause** can exist by itself because the word group has a subject and verb and expresses a complete thought or idea. A main clause is a sentence. Look at the following examples:

> The young woman walked happily down the grocery aisle.
>
> A puppy and a kitten chased each other around the couch.
>
> The student studied Sunday afternoon for his Monday morning exam.
>
> Early in the morning, the rain pelted the bedroom window and awoke Stacie.
>
> Each one of the above sentences has a core idea created by the subject and the verb: *woman walked, puppy... kitten chased, student studied,* and *rain pelted... awoke.* The rest of the information in each sentence provides readers additional information about the subject and verb. For example, in the first sentence, readers discover that the woman is *young* (adjective), that she walked *happily* (adverb), and that she walked *down the grocery aisle* (prepositional phrase).

In contrast to a main clause, a **subordinate clause** is **not** a complete idea. Even though a subordinate clause contains a subject and verb, the word group cannot stand by itself as a complete thought. Therefore, a subordinate clause **cannot** be a sentence.

USAGE NOTE A subordinate clause is an incomplete idea. When you punctuate a subordinate clause as a sentence, you create a fragment. For additional information on fragments, see "Common Writing Errors" on the student companion site available at CengageBrain.com.

Because a subordinate clause is an incomplete idea, readers require more information.

When the band began playing "Pomp and Circumstance."

When the band began playing "Pomp and Circumstance," what happened?

Because the fire in the living room fireplace went out.

Because the fire in the living room fireplace went out, what occurred?

Since his computer failed to save the document.

Since his computer failed to save the document, what did he do?

EXERCISE 9.1: Main and Subordinate Clauses

Identify the following clauses as either a main clause (M) or a subordinate clause (S).

1. _____ Because he knew the owner.
2. _____ The soda sat unsteadily on the stack of papers.
3. _____ Book shelves filled the walls of the couple's living room.
4. _____ Since the rain had been falling hard for several hours.
5. _____ Which happens every evening at this time.
6. _____ The student's curious nature led him to read widely.
7. _____ Whom Rose introduced as her brother.
8. _____ While the clock ticked.
9. _____ The poster of the mountains was taped to the wall.
10. _____ If you are not able to attend the party.

ADJECTIVE AND ADVERB SUBORDINATE CLAUSES

The two types of subordinate clauses are adjective clauses and adverb clauses. An **adjective subordinate clause** (also called a relative clause) begins with a relative pronoun. The relative pronouns are

That	Who	Whoever
Which	Whose	Whomever
Where	Whom	

Adjective subordinate clauses modify nouns and pronouns, just as adjectives modify nouns and pronouns. Furthermore—and this is important—a subordinate adjective clause should always be placed immediately after the noun or pronoun it modifies.

> The picture that hangs on the wall depicts a desert sunrise.
>
> The adjective subordinate clause *that hangs on the wall* modifies the noun *picture.*
>
> The woman who lives next door was my fifth grade teacher.
>
> The adjective subordinate clause *who lives next door* modifies the noun *woman.*
>
> The shed, which was destroyed in the storm, held all my garden tools.
>
> The adjective subordinate clause *which was destroyed in the storm* modifies the noun *shed.*
>
> The glass of soda sat on the desk that was piled high with papers and books.
>
> The adjective subordinate clause *that was piled high with papers and books* modifies the noun *desk.*
>
> The restaurant where my husband proposed is just down the street from here.
>
> The adjective subordinate clause *where my husband proposed* modifies the noun *restaurant.*

Adverb subordinate clauses, on the other hand, begin with a subordinating conjunction. Here are some common subordinating conjunctions arranged according to the relationships they signify (**Table 9.1**).

TABLE 9.1 Common subordinating conjunctions

Cause and Effect	Concession	Condition	Comparison and Contrast	Manner	Opposition	Place	Time
as	although	even if	as	as if	although	where	after
because	as if	if	as if	as	though	wherever	before
in order	even though	in case (that)		though	even though		since
that	though	only if			whereas		when
now that	while	provided that			while		whenever
since		unless					while
so		until					until
so that		whether or not					as
							as . . . as
							once

USAGE NOTE Some subordinating conjunctions can express different relationships between clauses. For example, you can use the subordinating conjunction *since* to show **cause and effect** as well as **time**.

Since I am cold standing in the snow, I'm going home. (cause and effect)

He has been living with his grandmother since he turned three years old. (time)

Similar to adverbs, adverb subordinate clauses modify verbs, adverbs, adjectives, and phrases and clauses.

> The movie patrons jumped when the zombie lunged from behind the bushes.
>
> The adverb subordinate clause *when the zombie lunged from behind the bushes* modifies the verb *jumped.*
>
> The athlete was still healthy after seventeen years of playing because he slept eight hours each night and avoided fatty foods.
>
> The adverb subordinate clause *because he slept eight hours each night and avoided fatty foods* modifies the adjective *healthy.*
>
> Since I was the last one home, I had to make sure the cat was in and fed.
>
> The adverb subordinate clause *Since I was the last one home* modifies the main clause, *I had to make sure the cat was in and fed.*

USAGE NOTE

There are several subordinating conjunctions that may also function as prepositions. These words include *after*, *as*, *before*, *for*, *since*, and *until*. Look at the following sentences.

After the game, everyone met at the local pizza place.

After functions as a preposition in the prepositional phrase *After the game*, because only a noun, *game*, follows the subordinating conjunction *After*, not both a noun and verb.

(continued)

After the game ended, everyone met at the local pizza place.

After functions as a subordinating conjunction because both a subject and verb, *game ended*, follow the subordinating conjunction.

As the only son, my father felt intense pressure from his family to succeed.

As functions as a preposition *As the only son*, because only a noun, *son*, follows the subordinating conjunction *As*, not both a noun and a verb.

As I left the house, I realized I had forgotten my wallet.

As functions as a subordinate conjunction in the subordinate clause *As I left the house. As* functions as a subordinating conjunction here because both a subject and a verb, *I left*, follow the subordinating conjunction.

EXERCISE 9.2: Adjective and Adverb Clauses

Identify the underlined clause in each sentence as either an adjective (ADJ) subordinate clause or an adverb (ADV) subordinate clause. If the clause is an adjective subordinate clause, draw an arrow from the clause to the noun it modifies. Remember: adjective subordinate clauses begin with relative pronouns and adverb subordinate clauses begin with a subordinating conjunction.

1. _____ The red envelope <u>that sat on the desk</u> was partially hidden by a picture.

2. _____ My neighbor, <u>who is 85 years of age</u>, tells me frequently about growing up in Texas.

3. _____ <u>Since Stella was over six feet tall</u>, she was recruited to play both volleyball and basketball.

4. _____ I stayed inside and looked out at the porch, <u>which was covered in snow</u>.

5. _____ I was walking down the grocery aisle when I met an old high school friend.

6. _____ Because I wear my hair in braids and have a beard, I am often mistaken for Willie Nelson, the singer.

7. _____ Teresa was late for work even though she left the house earlier than normal.

8. _____ Although the sun was shining, the thermometer read 36 degrees.

9. _____ The ladder that leaned against the house seemed too unstable to climb.

10. _____ Mindy smiled as she walked across the stage to receive her diploma.

EXERCISE 9.3: Adjective and Adverb Clauses

1. Compose a sentence that includes an adjective subordinate clause that modifies the word *pen.*

____

____

2. Compose a sentence that includes an adjective subordinate clause that modifies the word *mouse.*

____

____

3. Compose a sentence that includes an adjective subordinate clause that modifies the word *building.*

____

____

4. Compose a sentence that includes an adverb subordinate clause that begins with the subordinating conjunction *whenever.*

____

____

5. Compose a sentence that includes an adverb subordinate clause that begins with the subordinating conjunction *while.*

____

____

6. Compose a sentence that includes an adverb subordinate clause that begins with the subordinating conjunction *after* (be sure you compose a subordinate clause, not a prepositional phrase).

____

____

PUNCTUATING ADVERB CLAUSES

Because incorrectly punctuated clauses can lead to misinterpretation or miscommunication, punctuating clauses correctly is just as important as writing them correctly. Follow these three punctuation rules when inserting subordinate adverb clauses into your sentences.

1. Use a comma to separate introductory subordinate clauses from main clauses.

> While the child slept, her parents wrapped her presents.
>
> Because the temperature dropped below 32 degrees, I wrapped my roses in blankets.
>
> Until Trevor cleaned his room, his mom would not let him play outside.
>
> While her coffee cooled, Yvonne warmed her cinnamon roll in the microwave.
>
> Until he could no longer sleep, James stayed in bed.

2. Subordinate clauses that follow the main clause **generally** are not separated from the main clause by a comma.

> Jenny's parents wrapped her presents while she slept.
>
> I wrapped my roses in blankets because the temperature dropped below 32 degrees.
>
> Trevor's mom would not let him play outside until he cleaned his room.

> Yvonne warmed her cinnamon roll in the microwave while her coffee cooled.
>
> James stayed in bed until he could no longer sleep.

3. **However**, subordinate clauses that (1) follow the main clause but contradict or oppose the idea in the main clause or (2) are incidental to the information in the main clause are separated from the main clause by a comma.

> Stephen's mom bought the tee shirt, even though Stephen did not like the color or the logo.
>
> The shirt described in the concluding subordinate clause is not a shirt Stephen would have bought, but his mom purchased it anyway, so the concluding subordinate clause contradicts or opposes the main clause and is set off with a comma.
>
> Stephen's mom bought a neon green tee shirt with an unknown band's logo for her son, after she bought herself a purse.
>
> The concluding subordinate clause presents additional information that does not influence the meaning of the main clause, so the information in the concluding clause is incidental and set off with a comma.

EXERCISE 9.4: Punctuating Adverb Clauses

First, insert commas in those sentences that require punctuation. Then, in the space provided, write the number of the comma rule (1, 2, or 3) that applies to the subordinate clause.

1. _____ Even though Sheila ran track she found the sprinting in basketball quite tiring.
2. _____ After the parents bathed the baby and put her to bed they ate dinner.
3. _____ Tommy played in the sandbox while his sister drew on the sidewalk.
4. _____ The pizza looked terrific on the box whereas it was tasteless and soggy when cooked.
5. _____ Since the painting hung in an out-of-the-way alcove visitors rarely saw it.

6. _____ Photography was her true passion even though she worked as a bouncer.

7. _____ Jim was late for his dental appointment because he was stuck in a traffic jam.

8. _____ Until he apologized for yelling Lonny was grounded.

9. _____ As he walked down the street texting Truman almost walked into a light pole.

10. _____ Yolanda almost fell when she tripped on her son's toy.

RESTRICTIVE AND NONRESTRICTIVE ADJECTIVE SUBORDINATE CLAUSES

You should be familiar with two types of adjective subordinate clauses: restrictive (also called essential) and nonrestrictive (also called nonessential).

A **restrictive adjective subordinate clause** provides information essential and necessary for understanding (1) the noun the adjective clause modifies and (2) the sentence's meaning. Look at this sentence.

> The book that is sitting on the hallway table belongs to my neighbor.
>
> The adjective clause *that is sitting on the hallway table* is necessary to identify the *book* that *belongs to my neighbor*. Without the restrictive adjective clause, the sentence would read, *The book belongs to my neighbor*. And a reader would want to know, "What book belongs to the neighbor?" The adjective clause identifies and makes specific which book, the one *that is sitting on the hallway table*. Hence, the adjective clause is essential and provides meaning for the rest of the sentence. Here is another example.
>
> The woman who survived being struck by lightning twice is writing a book about her experience.
>
> If you remove the subordinate adjective clause modifying *woman*, you are left wondering what woman is writing a book. The adjective clause is essential for identifying which *woman*. The adjective clause modifies and provides meaning to the rest of the sentence. Because the information in the subordinate clause is necessary to understand the modified noun and the sentence, you do **not** place commas around the restrictive adjective clause.

In contrast, a **nonrestrictive adjective subordinate clause** provides information **not** essential, **not** necessary for understanding or clarifying the modified noun or the main clause. If you were to remove the clause, the sentence would still have the same meaning.

A nonrestrictive adjective clause merely adds interesting, incidental information that isn't needed to understand the noun it modifies. Since the information is not needed and does not change the meaning of the sentence, you should surround nonrestrictive adjective clauses with commas. Think of the commas as hooks that you can use to drag the information in the adjective clause out of the sentence because it isn't needed. Look at this sentence.

> J. K. Rowling, who lives in Scotland, wrote the Harry Potter series.
>
> You do not need the subordinate adjective clause *who lives in Scotland* to identify the modified proper noun, *J. K. Rowling*. Nor is the information essential to understand J. K. Rowling wrote the Harry Potter series.

Consider this example:

> The *Mona Lisa*, which measures only 30 by 21 inches, hangs in the Louvre in Paris, France.
>
> Here the adjective clause, *which measures only 30 by 21 inches,* may provide interesting information, but the painting's dimensions are not necessary to the meaning of the main idea, *The Mona Lisa hangs in the Louvre in Paris, France.*

Please note that while the above examples all show the restrictive or nonrestrictive adjective clauses following the subject of the sentence, restrictive and nonrestrictive adjective clauses may appear after any noun in a sentence.

Study the examples below. The restrictive or nonrestrictive clauses are in green and arrows have been drawn to the modified noun.

Terry enjoyed his soda, which he sipped slowly.

Jordan found her car keys, which had fallen between the cushions on the couch.

Simon glanced at the watch that he received for his birthday.

Jessica lunged for the book that was falling toward the water puddle.

Samuel took the mirror, which was cracked, and placed it in the trash.

Manny drove the car that needed a tune-up to the local garage.

In fact, you can compose sentences in which an adjective subordinate clause modifies a noun in a previous adjective subordinate clause.

> The boy walked down to the barn that was near the river that had recently flooded.
>
> The first restrictive adjective subordinate clause *that was near the river* is positioned to modify the noun *barn*, and the second restrictive adjective subordinate clause *that had recently flooded* modifies the noun *river*.
>
> The picture that hung on the wall, which was badly cracked, depicted a ballet dancer at the barre.
>
> The first restrictive adjective subordinate clause *that hung on the wall* modifies the noun *picture*, and the second nonrestrictive adjective subordinate clause modifies the noun *wall*.

USAGE NOTE Historically, when writers began an adjective subordinate clause with the relative pronoun *that*, they intended their audiences to understand the clause to be a restrictive clause. If writers began the clause with the relative pronoun *which*, they meant their audience to read the clause as a nonrestrictive clause. While some writers do not follow this historical pattern, most good writers do.

The following flow chart shows the relationship among the different types of clauses discussed in this chapter.

- Clause = a group of words with a subject and verb
  - Main clause (independent) = a sentence
  - Subordinate clause (dependent) = a fragment
    - Adjective clause = begins with relative pronoun
      - Restrictive = provides necessary information to identify a noun or pronoun and makes meaning within the sentence; does not include commas
      - Nonrestrictive = provides incidental information that may be omitted from the sentence; requires commas
    - Adverb clause = begins with subordinating conjunction

EXERCISE 9.5: Restrictive and Nonrestrictive Adjective Subordinate Clauses

First, underline the adjective subordinate clauses in the following sentences; then in the lines provided, identify the adjective subordinate clause as either restrictive (R) or nonrestrictive (NR). Last, place commas around the nonrestrictive adjective clauses when the clause is positioned in the middle of the sentence or before the clause when the clause ends the sentence. Two sentences have more than one adjective subordinate clause.

1. _____ The woman who accepted the award spoke eloquently of her parents' help.
2. _____ The Empire State Building which is located in New York is a focal point in many movies.
3. _____ Michael Jackson who was known as the King of Pop died in 2009.
4. _____ The car that is blocking the driveway belongs to my friend who is missing.
5. _____ A shopper whom Bob believed to be his neighbor turned out to be a complete stranger.
6. _____ A calendar that I received from my local market comes with stickers to mark special days.
7. _____ Cynthia Robins whom Miguel introduced founded her own company.
8. _____ The first set of landscaping plans which the company submitted excluded drought tolerant plants.
9. _____ The painting by Picasso that is titled *Corrida de toros, 1934* hangs in the Museo Thyssen-Bornemisza, which also houses the paintings of Salvador Dali, Francisco de Goya, and John Singer Sargent.
10. _____ My calculator which is solar powered doesn't work in the dark.

EXERCISE 9.6: Restrictive and Nonrestrictive Adjective Subordinate Clauses

Compose your own sentences according to the following directions. Do not hesitate to review the information in this chapter if you need help to compose your sentences. In your sentences, insert commas when needed.

1. Compose a sentence that includes a restrictive adjective clause that modifies the noun *bowl.*

2. Compose a sentence that includes a restrictive adjective clause that modifies the noun *paperclip.*

3. Compose a sentence that includes a restrictive adjective clause that modifies the noun *neighbor.*

4. Compose a sentence that includes a nonrestrictive adjective clause that modifies *elm tree.*

5. Compose a sentence that includes a nonrestrictive adjective clause that modifies *University of Texas.*

6. Compose a sentence that includes a nonrestrictive adjective clause that modifies *Chicago.*

SENTENCE COMBINING AND ADJECTIVE AND ADVERB SUBORDINATE CLAUSES

Sentence combining is a writing strategy you use to join word groups in various ways to create effective sentences. Look at the following sentences.

> Abbie ran to the store. Abbie forgot her purse. Abbie forgot her grocery list.
>
> As written, the three main clauses are repetitious because each sentence repeats not only the subject, *Abbie*, but also, in two cases, the verb *forgot*. In addition, the three sentences are short, only four or five words. This combination of repetition and brevity can be monotonous and bore readers.

To provide readers greater sentence variety and to create sentences that communicate more effectively, you can combine the three sentences a number of different ways. For example, you can change one of the main clauses into an adverb subordinate clause that begins or ends the sentence:

> When Abbie ran to the store, she forgot her purse and grocery list.
>
> Although Abbie ran to the store, she forgot her purse and grocery list.
>
> As Abbie ran to the store, she forgot her purse and grocery list.
>
> Abbie forgot her purse and grocery list when she ran to the store.
>
> Abbie forgot her purse and grocery list although she ran to the store.
>
> Abbie forgot her purse and grocery list as she ran to the store.

And instead of *when*, you can add other subordinating conjunctions, for example, *even though*, *since*, *though*, *while*, *whereas*, etc., to create additional sentences.

Your choice of a subordinating conjunction to begin the subordinate clause will depend upon the relationship between the subordinate clause and the main clause. To review the functions of subordinating conjunctions, see page 128.

You can also change one of the main clauses into an adjective subordinate clause:

> Abbie, who ran to the store, forgot her purse and grocery list.
>
> Abbie, who forgot her purse and grocery list, ran to the store.

Sentence combining allows you to manipulate sentences to eliminate repetition and unnecessary words in order to create effective sentences, sentences that communicate successfully.

But sentence combining does more than just eliminate repetition and create more complex ideas. Sentence combining also allows you to arrange your ideas in a hierarchy. Look again at the three sentences with which you started.

> Abbie ran to the store. Abbie forgot her purse. Abbie forgot her grocery list.

Which idea is the most important? Abbie's going to the store? Abbie's forgetting her purse? Abbie's forgetting her grocery list? By using main and subordinate clauses, you create a hierarchy of information **because the information in a main clause is more important than the information in a subordinate clause.** So if you want to emphasize that going to the store is more important than forgetting the purse or shopping list, you place that information in the main clause:

> Abbie, who forgot her purse and grocery list, ran to the store.
>
> Abbie ran to the store, although she forgot her purse and grocery list.

On the other hand, if you wanted to emphasize that Abbie forgot her purse and grocery list, you would place that information in the main clause.

> Abbie, who ran to the store, forgot her purse and grocery list.
>
> Although she ran to the store, Abbie forgot her purse and grocery list.

Therefore, when you place information in either main clauses or subordinate clauses, you are letting your readers know what has primary importance (main clause) and what has secondary importance (subordinate clauses).

EXERCISE 9.7: Sentence Combining

1. Combine the following two sentences to create a single sentence in which sentence A is the main clause and sentence B is the subordinate clause that begins with *because.*

   A. Eli scratched his neck.

   B. Eli's neck itched.

   ____

   ____

2. Combine the following two sentences to create a single sentence in which sentence B is the main clause and sentence A is the subordinate clause that begins with *when.*

   A. Sophie left the back door open.

   B. The family cat ran out.

   ____

   ____

3. Combine the following two sentences to create a single sentence in which sentence A is the main clause and sentence B is a nonrestrictive adjective subordinate clause that modifies the noun *clock.*

   A. The clock hung on the wall.

   B. The clock was two hours slow.

   ____

   ____

4. Combine the following two sentences to create a single sentence in which sentence B is the main clause and sentence A is a restrictive adjective subordinate clause that modifies the noun *clock.*

   A. The clock hung on the wall.

   B. The clock was two hours slow.

   ____

   ____

5. Combine the following two sentences to create a single sentence in which sentence A is the main clause and sentence B is a restrictive adjective subordinate clause that modifies the noun *baby.*

   A. The baby has ocean-blue eyes.

   B. The baby was smiling.

   ____

   ____

6. Combine the following two sentences to create a single sentence in which sentence A is the main clause and sentence B is a nonrestrictive adjective subordinate clause that modifies the noun *Mr. Macginty.*

   A. Mr. Macginty is a retired magician.

   B. Mr. Macginty enjoys drinking tea.

   ____

   ____

Chapter SUMMARY

Fill in the blanks to review this chapter's information.

- Clauses are ____ ____.
- Main clauses contain ____ ____.
- Subordinate clauses contain ____ ____.
- There are two types of subordinate clauses: ______________________ and ____.
- Adjective subordinate clauses modify ______________________ and ______________________ and are placed ______________________ ____.
- Adverb subordinate clauses modify ____ ____.
- Restrictive adjective clauses provide information required/necessary to identify the modified noun and ______________________ be enclosed in commas.
- Nonrestrictive adjective clauses provide information that is not necessary or required to identify the modified noun and ______________________ ______________________ be enclosed in commas.

COMPONENTS AT WORK

Using Your Skills in Sentences I

1. In the space below, compose one main clause that uses the action verb *strain.*

____

____

2. In the space below, compose one main clause that uses the action verb *flip.*

____

____

3. In the space below, compose one main clause that uses the linking verb *become.*

____

____

4. In the space below, compose one main clause that uses *taste* as a linking verb.

____

____

5. In the space below, compose one main clause that uses the verb *is* as a helping verb, not a main verb.

____

____

6. In the space below, compose one main clause that uses *has* as a helping verb, not a main verb.

____

____

7. In the space below, compose one main clause that uses the helping verb *can.*

8. In the space below, compose one main clause that uses the helping verb *would.*

Using Your Skills in Sentences II

1. Combine the following sentences to create a single sentence that makes the second sentence an adverb subordinate clause that begins with the subordinate conjunction *where.*

   a. Susan looked under the couch.

   b. Susan found her keys.

2. Combine the following sentences to create a single sentence that makes the first sentence an adverb subordinate clause that begins with the subordinating conjunction *when.*

   a. Steven walked in the house after work.

   b. Steven had to begin dinner.

3. Combine the following sentences to create a single sentence that includes an adverb subordinate clause.

   a. The weather outside was cold and damp.

   b. Stella decided not to weed her garden.

4. Combine the following sentences to create a single sentence that includes an adverb subordinate clause.

   a. Lydia was late for class.

   b. Lydia's car would not start.

   ____

   ____

5. Combine the following sentences to create a single sentence that includes an adverb subordinate clause.

   a. The water in the tea kettle heated.

   b. Latoya toasted her bagel.

   ____

   ____

6. Combine the following sentences to create a single sentence that creates a nonrestrictive adjective subordinate clause from one of the two sentences.

   a. The Grand Canyon can be seen from outer space.

   b. The Grand Canyon is located in Arizona.

   ____

   ____

7. Combine the following sentences to create a single sentence that creates a nonrestrictive adjective subordinate clause from one of the two sentences.

   a. Mr. Jones has lived in Tucson for twenty-five years.

   b. Mr. Jones is my next door neighbor.

   ____

   ____

8. Combine the following sentences to create a single sentence that creates a restrictive adjective subordinate clause from one of the two sentences.

   a. The ruins are a Roman amphitheatre.

   b. The ruins are located in Merida, Spain.

   ____

   ____

9. Combine the following sentences to create a single sentence that creates a restrictive adjective subordinate clause from one of the two sentences.

   a. The house stood on the corner of 5th and Vine.

   b. The house was haunted by a family of ghosts.

   ____

   ____

10. Combine the following sentences to create a single sentence that creates a restrictive adjective subordinate clause from one of the two sentences.

    a. The book contained stories from people who have seen ghosts on the London underground.

    b. The book is sitting on the table near the lamp.

    ____

    ____

Using Your Skills in Reading

Carefully read the following paragraph "Molokai's History with Hansen's Disease." After reading through it once for understanding, which includes looking up words you do not understand or recognize, read it again. If there are any words that are unfamiliar to you, try to figure out their meaning through context clues, looking at the words surrounding the unfamiliar word. Many times, those context clues can help you figure out the meaning of a word. However, there may be times when context clues do not help, so make sure to have a dictionary or your smart phone nearby in case you need to look up a word. Do not merely skip over a word you do not know. A single word can change the meaning of an entire sentence.

After rereading the paragraph, underline all adverb subordinate clauses and adjective subordinate clauses, circling the subordinating conjunctions and relative pronouns that begin the clauses.

Molokai's History with Hansen's Disease

When most people imagine living in Hawaii, they picture sunbathing on long stretches of white sand beaches, frolicking in dazzlingly clear water, and sipping cocktails adorned with pineapple and mango slices. However, their fantasy is far from the reality of the Hawaiians with Hansen's Disease (formerly known as leprosy) who were forced between 1865 and 1969 to live in settlements on the north shore of the island of Molokai. Because more and more foreign traders and visitors were visiting the islands in the 1800s, many Hawaiians found themselves suffering from illnesses and diseases that they had never before experienced. One of these diseases was Hansen's Disease, which was thought to be highly contagious and incurable. To stop the spread of this disease, King Kamehameha V approved the Hawaiian legislature's "Act to Prevent the Spread of Leprosy," and the government quarantined all Hawaiians with Hansen's Disease to the settlements of Kalaupapa and Kalawao on the island of Molokai. The north shore of Molokai is surrounded on three sides by ocean, and the last side is a steep mountain ridge that isolates the inhabitants from the rest of the island. Small airplanes and boats can reach the settlements over the water, but the only way to reach the settlements by land is to ride a mule down the steep mountain ridge. One of the most famous inhabitants of the colonies was Father Damien, a Belgian Catholic priest who ministered to the afflicted. Father Damien helped the people build a church, build homes, and organize community events. He also helped to nurse the sick and bury the dead. Father Damien contracted Hansen's Disease in 1884 and died in 1889 at the age of 49. During the 104-year quarantine, the government sent approximately 8,000 Hawaiians to Molokai; today, forty are still there. When the quarantine was lifted in 1969 due to greater knowledge of the disease and the creation of antibiotics, some inhabitants left to join family and re-begin their lives, but many Hawaiians who had been living in isolation were fearful to leave and chose to remain where they felt safe from ridicule and prejudice. Small airplanes regularly fly in supplies, such as fresh meat, dairy, and newspapers, and once a year a barge brings in heavy items, such as television sets, kitchen appliances, and furniture. The average age of the few Hawaiians who still live in the settlements is 75, and soon the "leper colony" of Molokai will exist only in our history books.

Using Your Skills in Composition

Write a paragraph discussing a time when you, someone else, or a group of people was isolated from others. You may use examples from your own life, from the lives of people you know, or from stories you have read in the newspaper or heard on the news. Use both main and subordinate clauses in your writing, and try to use both adjective subordinate clauses and adverb subordinate clauses.

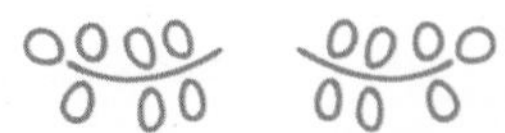

REVIEWING YOUR GROWTH

In this chapter you will review all the information from the first nine chapters—parts of speech, subjects, verbs, and clauses—focusing on how these various components work together to form grammatically correct word groups and sentences.

PARTS OF SPEECH

EXERCISE 1: Adjectives

Place an adjective before each noun. Do not use any adjective more than once. Adjectives are discussed on pages 20-23.

Example: furry cat wooden table soggy noodles refreshing water

________ movie	________ painting	________ book	________ picture
________ drink	________ teacher	________ car	________ dress
________ couch	________ meal	________ ocean	________ warrior
________ child	________ canyon	________ valley	________ airport
________ monkey	________ chef	________ report	________ spy

EXERCISE 2: Adverbs

Place an adverb before or after each verb. Do not use any adverb more than once. Adverbs are discussed on pages 24-28.

Example: always walked gently cooed cried hysterically walks regularly

_______ swam	_______ yelled	cooks _______	writes _______
_______ drove	_______ dances	laughs _______	cleaned _______
_______ chops	_______ crashed	screams _______	lectured _______
_______ hikes	_______ paints	babbled _______	swings _______
_______ celebrates	_______ inspected	trailed _______	sniffles _______

Now, place an adverb before each adjective. Try to use as many different adverbs as you can.

Example: extremely pretty

_______ large	_______ distasteful	_______ tall	_______ funny
_______ short	_______ lovely	_______ respectful	_______ easy
_______ gross	_______ spicy	_______ fancy	_______ rude
_______ likeable	_______ aromatic	_______ challenging	_______ far
_______ pleasant	_______ hysterical	_______ salty	_______ narrow

EXERCISE 3: Linking Verbs

Place a different linking verb between each subject and adjective. Linking verbs are discussed on pages 11-13 and pages 76-81.

Example: Sheryl _is_ sad.

1. That child ___________ scared.
2. Aunt Myra ___________ hilarious.
3. This soup ___________ salty.
4. Officer Gonzalez ___________ brave.
5. Dr. Chung ___________ conscientious.
6. My mother ___________ thrilled.
7. His cousin ___________ studious.
8. Her song ___________ mellow.
9. These papers ___________ wet.
10. David ___________ ill.

Now, place a linking verb between each subject and noun. Try to use as many different linking verbs as you can.

1. Keisha and Lily ___________ cheerleaders.
2. Uncle Sherman ___________ a lawyer.
3. I ___________ an academic.
4. You ___________ the shift leader.
5. He ___________ the captain.
6. They ___________ interns.
7. We ___________ musicians.
8. Mrs. Lee ___________ a nurse.
9. Professor Ramapuram ___________ a history buff.
10. This song ___________ his favorite.

EXERCISE 4: Prepositional Phrases

Place a prepositional phrase or two in each of the following sentences. Prepositional phrases are discussed on pages 41-44.

Example: Squirrels jumped from tree to tree.

Example: My grandmother made spaghetti sauce with bell peppers and garlic.

1. All____________________ the cars raced ______________________.
2. ____________________________________ flowed the flood waters.
3. The tornado tore ____.
4. The paper clips and rubber bands are _________________________.
5. ______________________ and ______________________ ran the escaped convicts.
6. Each girl ___________________ has a flower ____________________.
7. All ___________________________ graduated from University ____.
8. ______________________________ soared the eagle.
9. Any boy ___________________ is able to join ____________________.
10. ______________________ the surfer rode _______________________.
11. A squad _______________________ rushed ______________________.
12. The group ____________________ sang carols ____________________.
13. __________________________________ crashed the motorcycle.
14. The family ______________________ cuddled ______________________.
15. ______________________________ tumbled the bear cub.

EXERCISE 5: Subject and Object Pronouns

Complete each sentence with either a subject pronoun or an object pronoun. Decide if you need the do-er of the verb (subject) or the receiver of the verb (object). Choose from these pronouns, and make sure to vary your choices:

Subject: I, he, she, we, they
Object: me, him, her, us, them

Remember, *you* and *it* can be either subjects or objects, so we are leaving them out for the purpose of this exercise.

1. Daryl and ________________ decided to run in the Boston Marathon.
2. That secret is just between Steven and ________________.
3. The coach awarded trophies to Luis and ________________.
4. Professor Hahn and ________________ lectured on the evolution of parrots.
5. After the wedding, the best man and ________________ went out dancing.
6. During the graduation ceremony, the student speaker and ________________ sat to the right of the school president.
7. The nurse told ________________ to sit still and stop wiggling.
8. Near the top of the tower sat the princess and ________________.
9. The tennis coach handed racquets to Lily and ________________.
10. ________________ practiced scales on the piano.

SUBJECTS AND VERBS

EXERCISE 1: Single Subjects

Supply each verb with a single subject (noun or subject pronoun). You may use an article before the subject if necessary.

1. ____________________ waits.
2. ____________________ sing.
3. ____________________ tumbles.
4. ____________________ cry.
5. ____________________ wonders.
6. ____________________ howl.
7. ____________________ build.

8. ______________________ asks.

9. ______________________ studies.

10. ______________________ dance.

EXERCISE 2: Compound Subjects

Supply each verb with a compound subject. You may use nouns (Aunt Maria and Uncle Rugilio) or subject pronouns (He and I). You may place an article before the subject if necessary.

1. ____ read.

2. ____ write.

3. ____ jump.

4. ____ swim.

5. ____ sail.

6. ____ exercise.

7. ____ sleep.

8. ____ relax.

9. ____ shake.

10. ____ dream.

EXERCISE 3: Subjects and Adverbs

Before each verb, place first an adjective and then a subject (noun or subject pronoun), and after each verb place an adverb.

Example: The grouchy neighbor yells frequently.

1. ______________________________ ran ______________________________.

2. ______________________________ skips ______________________________.

3. ______________________ brags ______________________.

4. ______________________ painted ______________________.

5. ______________________ smiles ______________________.

6. ______________________ cooked ______________________.

7. ______________________ began ______________________.

8. ______________________ chose ______________________.

9. ______________________ wakes ______________________.

10. ______________________ jiggles ______________________.

EXERCISE 4: Sentences

Compose sentences following the directions. Label each component requested in the directions and be ready to justify your labeling.

1. Write a sentence with a single subject, a linking verb, and a prepositional phrase.

   ____

   ____.

2. Write a sentence with a compound subject, an action verb, an adverb, and a prepositional phrase.

   ____

   ____.

SUBJECTS THAT DON'T LOOK LIKE SUBJECTS

EXERCISE 1: Indefinite Pronouns

Supply an indefinite pronoun for each verb listed as follows. Be careful to determine if you need a singular or plural indefinite pronoun.

Example: Everyone struggles.

1. __________ loses.
2. __________ dances.
3. __________ paints.
4. __________ smells.
5. __________ shop.
6. __________ falls.
7. __________ studies.
8. __________ cook.
9. __________ writes.
10. __________ dine.

EXERCISE 2: Imperative Sentences

Write two imperative sentences. Place the understood subject *you* in parentheses.

Example: Before the exam begins, (you) turn in your homework.

1. ____

   ____

2. ____

   ____

EXERCISE 3: Gerunds

Supply a gerund to act as the subject for each sentence below.

Example: Baking always makes me feel better when I am down.

1. ______________________ is very good exercise.
2. Before a big test, ______________________ helps me to calm down.
3. ______________________ was one of Albert's talents.
4. A long time ago, ______________________ was considered taboo.
5. ______________________ keeps me organized.

EXERCISE 4: Infinitives as Subjects

Write five sentences in which you use an infinitive as a subject.

Example: To clean my room was the first goal of the day.

1. ____

____

2. ____

____

3. ____

____

4. ____

____

5. ____

____

EXERCISE 5: Composing Sentences

Write sentences according to the following directions. Label each component and be ready to justify your labeling.

1. Write a sentence that has an indefinite pronoun as a subject. The sentence must also have a helping verb with a main verb, an adjective, and a prepositional phrase.

   ____

   ____

2. Write an imperative sentence with an adverb and an adjective.

   ____

   ____

3. Write a sentence with a gerund as a subject. The sentence must also have a linking verb and a prepositional phrase.

   ____

   ____

4. Write a sentence with an infinitive as a subject. Also, add an action verb, an adverb, an adjective, and a prepositional phrase.

   ____

   ____

5. Write a sentence of your own design, using the components we have discussed thus far. Make sure to label all components.

   ____

   ____

CLAUSES

EXERCISE 1: Adjective and Adverb Subordinate Clauses

Compose subordinate clauses according to the directions. Do not write complete sentences.

1. Compose an adjective subordinate clause beginning with *that.*

____

____

2. Compose an adjective subordinate clause beginning with *which.*

____

____

3. Compose an adjective subordinate clause beginning with *who.*

____

____

4. Compose an adjective subordinate clause beginning with *where.*

____

____

5. Compose an adjective subordinate clause beginning with *whom.*

____

____

6. Compose an adverb subordinate clause beginning with *because.*

____

____

7. Compose an adverb subordinate clause beginning with *until.*

____

____

8. Compose an adverb subordinate clause beginning with *although.*

____

____

9. Compose an adverb subordinate clause beginning with *before*.

10. Compose an adverb subordinate clause beginning with *if*.

EXERCISE 2: Adjective and Adverb Subordinate Clauses

Follow the directions below to compose sentences that include subordinate clauses.

1. Compose a sentence that includes an adjective subordinate clause that modifies the word *photograph*.

2. Compose a sentence that includes an adjective subordinate clause that modifies the word *lunch*.

3. Compose a sentence that includes an adjective subordinate clause that modifies the word *computer*.

4. Compose a sentence that includes an adverb subordinate clause that begins with the subordinating conjunction *unless.*

____

____

5. Compose a sentence that includes an adverb subordinate clause beginning with the subordinating conjunction *whereas.*

____

____

6. Compose a sentence that includes an adverb subordinate clause beginning with the subordinating conjunction *since.* Be sure you compose a subordinate adverb clause, not a prepositional phrase.

____

____

EXERCISE 3: Punctuating Subordinate Adjective and Adverb Clauses

Using commas only, punctuate the following sentences according to the rules you studied in Chapter 9.

1. Because we were going away for a week we stopped the mail and newspaper.
2. Mick Jagger who is 70 years old is the lead singer for the Rolling Stones.
3. Sandy enjoys the beach whereas Harry prefers the mountains.
4. The bookcases which were made of oak lined the entire south side of the room.
5. Although he was unable to sleep Wilbert stayed in bed.
6. The sergeant followed orders even though he knew the command was a bad idea.
7. If you decide to play you must bring your own equipment.

8. Westminster Abbey which is located in London is the burial place for a number of famous English poets.
9. John Muir whose photographs are prized by collectors was born in Dunbar, East Lothian, Scotland, in 1838.
10. While Cassy set up the tent Cory unrolled the sleeping bags.

DEMONSTRATING YOUR GROWTH

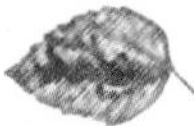

EXERCISE 1: Sentences

In the spaces provided, compose sentences according to the directions.

1. Compose a sentence that includes a single subject, an adjective, and a prepositional phrase.

 ____

2. Compose a sentence that begins with a subordinate adverb clause and includes an adverb that modified the sentence's main verb.

 ____

3. Compose a sentence that includes a restrictive adjective subordinate clause.

 ____

4. Compose a sentence that includes a multiple subject, a helping verb, and an adverb.

 ____

5. Compose a sentence that uses a subject pronoun for the subject of the sentence and an adjective that modifies a noun.

 ____

6. Compose a sentence that includes a single subject and a nonrestrictive adjective subordinate clause.

 ____

7. Compose a sentence that includes multiple subjects, multiple verbs, an adjective, and an adverb.

____

8. Compose a sentence that ends with a subordinate adverb clause that begins with *whereas.*

____

9. Compose a sentence that includes a subject pronoun and an object pronoun.

____

10. Compose a sentence that includes a helping verb and an adverb.

____

11. Compose a sentence that includes a subordinate adverb clause. Include an adverb in the subordinate adverb clause.

____

12. Compose a sentence that includes a single subject and multiple verbs.

____

13. Compose a sentence that includes a subject pronoun in the adjective subordinate clause.

____

14. Compose a sentence that includes a restrictive adjective subordinate clause that modifies the word *fish.*

____

15. Compose a sentence that uses the subject pronoun *he* as the subject of the sentence and the object pronoun *us* as the object of a prepositional phrase.

____

10 WRITING PARAGRAPHS

Chapter PREVIEW

In this chapter, you will learn about the issues you must consider when writing a paragraph: the topic and the topic sentence, the audience, and the purpose of the paragraph.

THE PARAGRAPH

When an instructor asks you to write a paragraph, what pops into your mind? A piece of writing that has to have five sentences? That has to be one hundred words? That must include examples? That can't be in second person? That must have a topic sentence? That must have a beginning, middle, and end? That can only be three sentences? That is indented at the beginning? That makes three points, with each point illustrated by an example? Ask any classmate, and you'll receive these answers and more. So what is a paragraph?

A **paragraph** can be defined as a series of sentences that focus on a single topic or subject. This definition allows flexibility because not all paragraphs are the same. Not all paragraphs have five sentences or one hundred words, nor are they all written in first person.

Most paragraphs in academic prose have a few common traits. For example, the first sentence is indented, the paragraph contains a topic sentence, evidence exists to support the topic sentence, the paragraph contains two or more sentences, and the information in the paragraph is coherent and unified. However, most paragraphs differ in content, length, sentence structure, and vocabulary.

What determines a paragraph's content and length depends upon three elements:

- the topic (the subject of the paragraph)
- the audience (the readers of the paragraph)
- the purpose of the paragraph (narrative, expository, descriptive, or persuasive).

THE TOPIC AND TOPIC SENTENCE

A paragraph's topic (or subject) is what the paragraph is about. Writers typically identify the paragraph's topic in the **topic sentence**, a sentence that makes an observation or comment on the topic. Study the following topic sentences.

William Shakespeare's life prior to 1590 is largely a mystery.

In this topic sentence the topic is *William Shakespeare's life*. The observation is that prior to 1590, his life *is largely a mystery*.

For their size, hummingbirds are extremely aggressive birds.

In this topic sentence, the subject is *hummingbirds* and the comment on the topic is they are *extremely aggressive birds*.

Exercise helps eliminate or control a number of diseases.

Texting while driving is becoming more common and causing numerous accidents.

What are the topics for the third and fourth sentences?

____

What observations or comments do the topic sentences make?

____

DIRECT AND CLIMACTIC PARAGRAPHS

Placement of a topic sentence in a paragraph depends upon how you structure your paragraph. In English prose, most paragraphs exhibit one of the two basic structures: the direct paragraph and the climactic paragraph.

In a **direct paragraph**, you place the topic sentence at the beginning or near the beginning of the paragraph. Composing a paragraph using this structure quickly tells your reader the intent of the paragraph.

The following paragraph is an example of a direct paragraph. The topic sentence is underlined.

> The impact of the telegraph was global and immediate. On November 14, 1847, market quotations from the London Stock Exchange were telegraphed to Manchester, England, and financial markets would never be the same. In 1849 journalist Paul Julius Reuter instituted a press wire service, and by 1855 telegraphs printed words. The telegraph did its first military duty during the Crimean War. By the end of the Civil War, the American telegraph network had grown to cover 200,000 miles. By 1866 a telegraph cable traversed the Atlantic Ocean, and by 1861—eight years before the first transcontinental railroad—the telegraph lines of Western Union stretched coast to coast, putting the Pony Express out of business.

from National Geographic Society's
Inventors and Discovers Changing Our World, pp. 53-54

In a **climactic paragraph**, the topic sentence comes near the end or at the end of the paragraph. You may choose to use a climactic structure in order to compile examples and evidence before presenting the observation or opinion that ties the information together.

The following paragraph is an example of a climactic paragraph. Again, the topic sentence is underlined.

> Vaccination of dogs and cats is the most important action that can be taken to protect the public from exposure to rabies. Even in urban settings, pets come into contact with wild and feral animals that can be infected. Also, it is essential that people, especially children, be cautioned about the potential dangers of contact with unfamiliar animals. They should be warned that any bat that can be caught is more likely than others to be sick and that it should not be handled. The same caution applies to all wild mammals. Even among sick bats, the vast majority is not rabid, but one should not take unnecessary chances with a fatal disease. In the event of any animal bite, medical advice should be sought immediately. <u>Strictly following these precautions will make the danger of contracting rabies incalculably small.</u>
>
> from Merlin Tuttle's
> *America's Neighborhood Bats*, p. 21

Since a paragraph's topic sentence states the subject on which you are going to write and the opinion or attitude you hold on the topic, you need to be sure all the information in the paragraph focuses on the paragraph's subject and the overall controlling idea. If you include information that does not relate to the subject and controlling idea of the topic sentence, you create a digression. In other words, you have wandered away from your topic and have begun discussing another idea.

Three elements that will help you stay focused on the main point of the paragraph include **unity**, **support**, and **coherence**.

When you need or want to communicate ideas to others, it is imperative that the people to whom you are speaking or writing understand you. If you send a company a cover letter with a resume, for instance, it is important that you clearly state why you are perfect for the position and why the company should hire you. If the points in your letter go off in unrelated directions, the prospective employer will either lose interest or decide immediately that your lack of focus means you are not right for the position.

Unity, support, and coherence are three elements in good writing that help ensure your audience will follow your thoughts and understand exactly what you are saying. Unity, support, and coherence hold a paragraph together, present your points in a logical manner, and show that you can focus on one idea at a time without your mind wandering in unnecessary and irrelevant directions.

UNITY

Unity ensures parts of the whole are successfully combined into one. When a paragraph is unified, every sentence in it serves the purpose of supporting one main idea. The main idea is stated or clearly implied in the topic sentence, and the rest of the sentences in the paragraph work to explain, illustrate, or prove that main idea. If any of the sentences in the paragraph veer off topic, the paragraph lacks unity.

Earlier on page 167, the topic sentence was described as the topic of the paragraph along with an observation about that topic. Every piece of writing has a purpose, whether that purpose is to explain, prove, or enlighten; the topic sentence presents that purpose to your readers. Look at the following topic sentence.

> Three study habits are essential for school success.
>
> The topic is *three study habits*, and the observation or comment is that these study habits *are essential for school success.* The purpose of the paragraph is to convince the readers that the three study habits you will discuss are necessary for academic success. With the word *essential*, readers know that you want them to follow your advice and adopt these habits.

A strong topic sentence, one that holds together or unifies a paragraph, will make your purpose clear. If your topic sentence is unclear, you appear unsure of your purpose, and if you are not absolutely certain of your purpose, you will have difficulty achieving paragraph unity.

EXERCISE 10.1: Topic Sentences

In the following topic sentences, draw a circle around the topic, and then underline the observation about the topic.

Example: (A deficiency in vitamin B12) <u>causes many health problems</u>.

1. The electric battery was the most important invention of the early nineteenth century.
2. Social networking sites do more harm than good.
3. Exercise is necessary for cardiovascular health.
4. The Harlem Renaissance provided a sense of self-determination for African-Americans in the early 1900s.

5. College graduation requirements should include community service hours.
6. The "No Tolerance for Bullying" policy saved my life in middle school.
7. Reality television shows are popular because of our desire to live vicariously through others.
8. Caring for a pet is a good way for a child to learn responsibility and commitment.
9. Taking music out of the elementary school curriculum will have detrimental effects.
10. Air travel has become much more difficult since September 11, 2001.
11. Cellular telephones make being out of touch challenging.
12. Holidays are not always festive occasions.
13. Eating out can be a monthly family adventure.
14. Computers can be both beneficial and detrimental.
15. Developing fully electric cars is an important step in energy conservation.

Each of the previous fifteen topic sentences has both a topic and an observation about that topic—the point that will be explained, proved, or illustrated in the sentences that develop the paragraph. When you have a topic sentence with both components—topic and observation—you are better able to keep the paragraph unified because you have a clear purpose in mind. Because the purpose is clear in your mind, it is easier for you to compose sentences that are meant to prove or explain the main point.

On the other hand, if the topic sentence is lacking either the topic or the comment on the topic, you may become confused about your purpose.

This confusion causes lack of focus, which leads to a lack of unity in the paragraph. Again, look at the following topic sentence.

> Social networking sites, though popular, do more harm than good.

The purpose of this paragraph, as presented in the topic sentence, is to show that even though these sites are popular, they can also be harmful. Every sentence that follows the topic sentence needs to illustrate this point. For example, if you were to begin discussing the history of social networking sites, the paragraph would stray off topic; the information digresses from the paragraph's main point.

 EXERCISE 10.2: Paragraph Unity

Carefully read the two paragraphs below, paying special attention to the topic sentences. Keeping the paragraphs' purposes in mind, underline the sentences that stray off topic and create a lack of unity within the paragraphs.

Paragraph #1

My Self-Imposed Obstacle to Student Success*

Prioritizing other activities over schoolwork gets in the way of my academic success. For example, when I sit down in the evening to do homework, if my best friend Pamela calls and asks me to come over, I set my homework aside and drive over to spend time with her. By the time I leave her house late at night, I am too tired to finish my assignments. Pamela, on the other hand, is a great student and earns top scores in all of her classes. Another activity I prioritize over my schoolwork is shopping, especially Internet shopping. I will sit down at my computer to work on an essay, and I end up visiting my favorite online stores such as Amazon.com and Overstock.com. Last year I bought my sister a beautiful pearl necklace from Overstock.com for under twenty dollars. Most often, I put my desire to spend time with my boyfriend over my need to finish schoolwork. For instance, last week he had a day off work and wanted to go to the beach, and even though I had a calculus test the next day, I went to the beach instead. Needless to say, I didn't do so well on that test; I earned a D. I was happy, then, when I earned an A on my history test the next day. If I want to succeed and achieve my goals, I need to start prioritizing work over play.

---

*Reprinted by permission of Jennifer Morales.

Paragraph #2

Most Beneficial Item*

An iPod is one of the most beneficial products ever invented because it holds thousands of songs, provides access to a variety of entertainment, makes checking social networking sites easy, and is incredibly small. Depending upon the number of gigabites, an iPod can hold between 1,000 and 40,000 songs. Currently, I have 418 songs on my iPod, and that's only one half of what it can hold. I also have a collection of old vinyl records, but I don't listen to them much. However, with just the movement of my thumb, I can listen to groups from different generations, such as the Beatles, the Rolling Stones, Aerosmith, Guns N' Roses, Nirvana, and the Black Keys. Of course, there have been other music devices that have this feature as well, but this iPod allows me to input lyrics, album art, and even videos. Second, with an iPod, finding entertainment is easy. People can access the world of the Internet where they can watch YouTube videos, check the Internet Movie Data Base for movie trailers for upcoming movies, and download a variety of game apps. My iPod has only one app, *Temple Run*, because I prefer to listen to music for entertainment rather than play games. Next, an iPod allows easy access to social networking sites. With one push, I can access sites, such as *Facebook*, *Twitter*, *LinkedIn*, which is a business and networking site, and *fubar*, an online bar for people eighteen and over. With such easy access to social networking sites, keeping up with family, friends, and colleagues is easy. Checking *Facebook* is the reason most of my friends have an iPod. A few of my friends, though, believe *Facebook* is a dangerous place and do not have accounts. The last reason an iPod is beneficial is because it's incredibly small and weighs no more than a CD case. My iPod is easily protected in my pocket, and no one can hear my iPod, so it isn't a distraction in public. I take my iPod with me everywhere I go, even when I run. Because of its versatility, an iPod has to be one of the most beneficial products available to people.

SUPPORT

Support in a paragraph is the information you include to illustrate, to explain, and/or to argue for the paragraph's topic sentence. The support you provide in your paragraph needs to be specific and sufficient.

The more specific your support, the more alive and vivid your examples, the more engaging your writing. Examples are called *illustrations* because the reader should be able to picture exactly what you are explaining or describing.

---

*Reprinted by permission of Miguel Cea.

If your support is vague and unclear, the reader will have trouble picturing or understanding your examples. As a result, you have done little to prove your point. Read the paired sentences below.

> **General**: My kindergarten teacher said mean things to me.
>
> **Specific**: On the first day of school and in front of all of the other students, my kindergarten teacher, Mrs. Humplenuff, told me that my handwriting looked worse than chicken scratch.
>
> **General**: The dog ran across the yard.
>
> **Specific**: The fluffy white Poodle bounded like a jackrabbit across the overgrown lawn.

The first sentence of each pair gives a general description of an event. The second sentence in each pair takes that same event and makes it come alive with vivid, specific wording.

When you set out to prove a point or explain an idea, the more concrete and specific your vocabulary, the more effective your explanation. When your wording is vague and general, the reader loses interest and your explanation loses effectiveness.

When you are trying to think of specific examples to support your topic sentence, think of this situation: if you asked your friend to get something for you at the store, what would happen if you said, "Grab me something"? Your friend would have no idea what to pick up, and he would be wandering the aisles trying to decide what to buy. If you asked for "lunch meat," your friend would wander the deli aisle, wondering if he should get you turkey, ham, corned beef, pastrami, bologna, chicken breast, olive loaf, or salami. If you were more specific and asked for turkey, he would know *what* to get, but would have no idea what brand. The more specific you are with your shopping list, the more apt you are to get exactly what you want. The more specific you are with your examples and details in your paragraphs, the more convincing your writing.

 EXERCISE 10.3: Specific Support

Look at the following illustration. The more general the word or phrase, the farther it is to the left, and the more specific the word or phrase, the farther is to the right.

Example: General ________________________________ Specific

snake → a brown snake → a rattlesnake → a slithering, hissing rattlesnake

Below, on the left, are five common words. As in the snake example, see how specific you can be with each word in order to provide a more compelling illustration.

1. School: General ____________________ Specific
2. Building: General ____________________ Specific
3. Teacher: General ____________________ Specific
4. Car: General ____________________ Specific
5. Tree: General ____________________ Specific

COHERENCE

In composition, *coherence* refers to the connectivity and organization of ideas in a paragraph.

If a paragraph is coherent, its points are logically organized according to the nature of the assignment, and the points are connected with appropriate **transitions** that create rational connections between ideas. Transitions allow you to express to your readers a clear understanding of the relationships among the ideas in your writing.

Following are some common transitions categorized by their use or purpose (**Table 10.1**).

TABLE 10.1 Transitions

Chronological or Time Order	Spatial Order	Emphatic Order	Comparison	Contrast	Addition
After	Near	First	Similarly	Yet	Also
While	Across	First of all	Likewise	But	In addition
Before	Beside	Second	On the one hand	On the other hand	Further
Later	Diagonally	Third	Also	In contrast	Furthermore
First	Under	Also	In comparison	However	Moreover
Now	On top	Another		Although	Besides
Second	To the left	Finally		By comparison	And
Soon	To the right	Most importantly			Next
Since	Over	Most important			First
Often	Beneath				Second
Next	Next to				Third
During					
Then					
As					
Finally					
Last					

 EXERCISE 10.4: Transitions

In the paragraph below, underline or highlight the transitions that connect the supporting points.

Surviving a Tornado

The most violent tornadoes are capable of tremendous destruction, but much can be done to prepare for such a storm. First, develop an evacuation plan for yourself and your family for home, work, school, and outdoors. Make sure to have frequent drills for all of your plans. Second, if you do not own an NOAA (National Oceanic and Atmospheric Administration) Weather Radio with a warning alarm, purchase one for your home so that you and your family can receive tornado warnings. Furthermore, listen to radio and television for weather information and, if traveling outdoors, listen to the latest forecast to see if threatening weather is possible. If a warning is issued or if threatening weather is approaching, move to a designated shelter, such as a basement. If an underground shelter is not available, move to an interior room or hallway on the lowest floor and get under a sturdy piece of furniture. Also, make sure to stay away from windows. If you are in a car, do not try to outrun the tornado; instead, get out of your car immediately and lie flat in a nearby ditch or depression. Tornadoes can occur any time of year, so it is important to be prepared and watchful.

Adapted from "What to Do in Case of a Tornado"
www.gohsep.la.gov/factsheets

 EXERCISE 10.5: Adding Transitions

In the following paragraph, create a more coherent paragraph by inserting necessary and appropriate transitional words and phrases where necessary.

Surviving a Broken Heart

Recovering from a break-up is never easy, but there are certain things you can do to help ease the transition back into single life. ________________________, let yourself wallow in the heartbreak and have a good cry. Do not try to repress your emotions; they will only come back later with a vengeance. Allow yourself to release the anger and sadness so you can move on. ________________________, surround yourself with supportive friends. Choose people who are positive and encouraging, people who do not dwell on the past but look forward to the future. ________________________, make an empowering playlist of music and listen to it often, when you are driving in your car, cleaning the house, or doing laundry. Choose artists and songs that tout independence and strength. Women, ______________________, may like Pat Benetar, Kelly Clarkson, Pink, and Aretha Franklin. Men, ______________________, may prefer The Rolling Stones, Cee Lo Green, Johnny Cash, and Blink 182. ______________________, after the music starts to sink in and you feel better, take up a new hobby or get back to one you neglected while you were involved with your ex. ______________________, if you used to play the paino or paint, start up again. If you always wanted to run a marathon but were too afraid to try, grab a friend and start training. Before you know it, you will feel emotionally and physically stronger than ever. ______________________, as Neil Sedaka said, "Breaking up is hard to do," but these suggestions can help you navigate through the pain so you can feel joy again.

AUDIENCE AND AUDIENCE ANALYSIS

When you write, you need to be aware that someone will be reading your words. And because your readers help shape your writing, you need to ask yourself who your readers are.

Your audience can be a single person, for example, an employer reading a perspective employee's application; a few people, for example, a committee reading a scholarship letter; or thousands of individuals reading an article in a popular magazine or academic journal. For you, your academic writing will be largely for the classes in which you are enrolled. So who are your readers?

In a typical academic classroom, your reader is more than likely your instructor or your peers in the classroom. But with any academic writing assignment you undertake, if the directions do not clearly indicate a specific audience, you should ask your instructor for whom you are writing: the instructor? Your peers in the classroom? Yourself? Someone else?

Regardless of your audience, there are a series of questions you can ask and answer that will help you focus your writing for not only the readers but also for yourself.

Following are twelve questions that will help provide information you need to better communicate clearly with your readers. For many of the questions, no right or wrong answer exists. And with many of the questions, you will have to make an educated guess in order to answer the questions. But once you have answered the questions, the understanding you will have of your audience will help you compose a paragraph that is far more likely to communicate clearly.

1. What is the subject of your paragraph?
(For this question, merely identify your topic.)

2. Who are your readers, specifically?
(Identify the individual or individuals who are going to read your paragraph, for example, classroom peers, home owners association board members, scholarship committee.)

3. What are some essential characteristics of your readers?
(Age, sex, ethnic background, economic status, education, occupation, etc.; the more you are able to describe your readers, the more real they will become.)

4. For what reason are your readers going to read your writing?
(Readers typically read for one of five reasons: information, entertainment, opinion, self-expression, or a combination of the previous four; identify the reason or reasons you believe your readers will read your paragraph.)

5. How do your readers feel about your subject?
(This question addresses your readers' feelings; what do you think your readers' emotional response is toward your topic; for example, are they hostile, neutral, positive, open, inquisitive, apathetic, angry, etc.?)

6. How do you want them to feel when they have finished reading what you have written?
(Do you want your readers to feel anger, excitement, sadness, curiosity, interest, etc.?)

7. How can you make them feel that way?
(What type of information are you going to provide in your paragraph to evoke the emotional response you're seeking to achieve?)

8. What is the main point you want to make to your readers?
(This question asks for your paragraph's topic sentence ; if you cannot answer this question, you need to take the time to develop a clear topic sentence because without one your paper will ramble and lack unity and focus).

9. What knowledge do your readers already have of your subject?
(How much does your audience already know about your topic: nothing, a little, some, much? The answer to this question is going to help you determine how much information you need to include in your paragraph.)

10. What information does your audience need to know to clearly understand your subject?
(What fundamental information do you need to include in your paper to be sure your readers understand your topic?)

11. What will be your basic writing strategy?
(Some fundamental methods to present information include narrative, cause and effect, comparison/contrast, division/classification, example, description, process analysis.)

12. What type of sentence structure is most appropriate to your readers? (Depending upon your readers, will you use mainly simple, compound, complex, or compound-complex sentences? See Chapters 15 and 16 for a discussion of sentence types.)

As you can see, some of the questions require specific, concrete answers, for example, "Name your specific readers," "What is the main point you want to make to your readers?" or "What will be your basic writing strategy?" Other questions require you to make some educated guesses about your readers, for example, "Give a concise description of your readers" or "What information does your audience need to know to understand your subject?" And some of the questions require you to consider the readers' position and/or attitude toward the paper's subject, for example, "How do your readers feel about your subject?"

Answering each of these questions as specifically and thoughtfully as possible will help you better understand your purpose in writing the paper and the person or people who will read your paper. And the better you understand the paper's purpose and your readers, the better you will be able to craft your paper to communicate your ideas clearly and effectively.

THE PURPOSE OR INTENT OF THE PARAGRAPH

Regardless of what you write, ultimately you write to convey information and share ideas. And regardless of the paragraph's subject and the opinion on the subject, the paragraph's intent is meant to accomplish one of four actions: to narrate, to describe, to explain, or to persuade.

Narration

When you narrate, you recount a series of events or tell a story. The events or story are usually told chronologically, starting with the earliest event and ending with the latest or last event.

Narrations range from simple explanations (for example how a friend acquired the tickets to an upcoming, anticipated concert: "Dude, I camped out in front of the box office from Tuesday through Saturday when the tickets went on sale."). Other narratives require extensive, complex accounts of personal experiences (for example, the possible trauma, fear, frustration, joy, and exaltation one may have experienced during a tour of military duty in Iraq or Afghanistan).

In the following paragraph, Norman Hammond, while visiting a Mayan ruin in Guatemala, recounts his experience during a total lunar eclipse.

> In the brilliant moonlight of a tropical night at Eastertide, I sat in the Great Plaza of Tikal, the largest Classic Maya ruin in Guatemala. It was my first visit. The pale walls of the towering pyramids echoed the noises of the jungle around: a constant racket of howler monkeys, an occasional gruff sound that could have been a jaguar. Then, slowly, it all stopped. The moon dimmed, and the animals went into suspenseful stillness. Nobody had told me there would be a total eclipse of the moon that night, and I sat entranced while in my mind's eye, the ghosts of the ancient Maya passed to and fro between the temples.
>
> from Norman Hammond's "Mesoamerica," in National Geographic Society's *Builders of the Ancient World*, p. 72

Description

When you describe, you explain the topic using the physical senses: what does it look like? How does it smell? How does it taste? How does it feel? What does it sound like?

Typically, descriptions are either objective or subjective or a combination of the two. **Objective descriptions** focus almost exclusively on the measurable or quantifiable characteristics of the topic. For example, you could describe a quarter by measuring the coin and providing readers its dimensions, by telling readers its weight in grams or ounces, by describing the images and words on the coin, by describing the appearance and feel of the coin's textured edge, etc.

Or you could describe the coin subjectively. **Subjective descriptions** are more an emotional response to the topic. That same quarter could evoke memories of the first sale at a summer lemonade stand when you were a child or of the coin as a gift from a grandparent or other important family member. Subjective descriptions are generally less about the topic than the emotional response the topic evokes.

In the following paragraphs from her essay "The Vibrations of Djoogbe," Barbara Kingsolver describes the activity outside the window of her Benin, South Africa, hotel, which she calls "a concrete shell of a building," as vendors head toward the local market.

> A first light, the commerce outside my window rose to fever pitch. The first travelers of the morning were half a dozen small girls driving a herd of pigs; the second, two young men zooming across the bridge on a motorcycle, carrying upright between them a five-foot-square pane of naked glass.

> Women crossed the bridge at a more stately pace and moved toward the market balancing gigantic burdens on their heads: bolts of cloth; a mountain of bread; a basket of live chickens with their wings draped over the side, casual as an elbow over the back of a chair. Nearly everyone in Benin dresses in magnificently printed wax cloth, West Africa's trademark garb. Women wrap great rectangles of it around their bodies and heads; men wear it tailored into pajamalike suits or embroidered caftans. The central market is a roar of color, scent, and sound. Next to a pile of dried fish, a tailor works at his open-air table. A woman selling tapioca also does coiffure: a client at her feet can get her hair wrapped with black thread into dozens of pointed, upright sprigs. The market's outskirts grade into industrial zones: cooking fires and small foundries. Beyond this, pigs devoutly work the riverbank garbage dumps.
>
> from Barbara Kingsolver's *High Tide in Tucson*, p. 182

Explanation

Academic writing frequently asks for some type of explanation. For example, a history prompt may require you to "explain the causes and effects of the Norman invasion of England in 1066"; a cultural anthropology paper may require you to "compare and contrast marriage rituals in two or more cultures"; a biology paper may ask you to "divide and classify a species by its genotype"; a sociology class may ask you to "define the term *social constructionism* and provide an example." Familiarizing yourself with the various ways of explaining a topic will benefit you in your other college courses.

When you explain, you are attempting to make your topic clear and understandable to your readers.

To explain your topic, you have a number of approaches from which to choose, including

- illustration,
- cause and effect,
- comparison and contrast,
- division and classification,
- definition, and
- process analysis

Illustration/Example

Illustration provides examples that explain and clarify your topic sentence. Depending on your audience, you may be able to clarify your topic sentence by providing a single extended example, or you may need to include several shorter examples to be sure your readers fully understand your topic. For example, if a paragraph had the following topic sentence: "For their size, hummingbirds are extremely aggressive birds," readers would expect one or more examples that clearly show the hummingbirds' aggressive behavior.

The following direct paragraph provides the reader five examples that illustrate the topic sentence.

> The vast and varied wild habitats of Central Spain are home to the richest avifauna [the birds of a specific region] in the peninsula. White storks' nests are a common sight on the church towers and chimneypots of towns. Grebes, herons, and shovelers can be seen in the marshlands; the distinctive hoopoe is often spotted in woods; and grasslands are the nesting grounds of bustards and cranes. The mountains and high plains are the domain of birds of prey, such as the imperial eagle, peregrine falcon, and vultures. Today, almost 160 bird species are the subject of conservation initiatives.
>
> from *Eyewitness Travel: Spain*, p. 342

Cause and Effect

Cause and effect explains why something occurred and the results of the occurrence. While the two ideas—cause and effect—are frequently considered together, you can compose a paragraph that explains only the causes of an event, just as you can also have a paragraph that explains only the effects of the event. For example, you might examine the causes—the reasons—behind a person's decision to drop out of high school. You could also explore the effects of dropping out of high school. Likewise, you could study the causes of the American Revolution and investigate the effects the war had on the United States.

The paragraphs that follow explore possible causes for getting a tattoo and the possible effects of being tattooed.

> **Causes for Getting Inked**
>
> Tattoos can be painful. Tattoos can also be expensive. And tattoos are virtually permanent. Yet a 2012 Harris Poll discovered that 21 percent of Americans have tattoos; in other words, over 66 million people currently living in the United States have at least one tattoo. Obviously tattoos are no longer sported by only criminals and military personnel, so with the great number of people wearing tattoos, why do people decide to get inked? First, people frequently get a tattoo to memorialize the death of a family member, close friend, or pet. From the individual's name to a portrait, the tattoo honors the individual's or pet's passing. People also get tattooed to memorialize events. After 9-11, a number of people had images of the Twin Towers

tattooed on their bodies. And I know a young man who celebrated his twenty-first birthday in Las Vegas, and to memorialize this rite of passage, he had prominent Las Vegas Strip landmarks tattooed on his back. Individuals also get inked to announce their affiliations. From gangs to military units to fraternities and sororities, people want others to know with whom they associate. Furthermore, people get tattooed to express their religious beliefs. Tattoos of the Virgin Mary, Jesus Christ, Our Lady of Guadalupe, a cross, a Bible, a Torah, etc. all express an individual's faith. Love also inspires people to get a tattoo. Having a tattoo of the names of one's spouse or loved one expresses the belief that the relationship is pretty permanent. And I have several friends who have their children's names and portraits tattooed on their bodies as an expression of their love for their children. Finally, people also get inked because they see tattoos as a form of art and their body as a living canvas. From simple flowers and butterflies to entire landscapes and collages, some people want to be a living *objets d'art*. The reasons people decide to get inked are just as varied as the tattoos people display.

Effects of Getting Inked

With over 66 million people in the United States having at least one tattoo, one would think that the public no longer sees tattoos in a negative way. And, to a point, that idea is correct. Yet, while tattoos have become more mainstream, there are still a number of negative effects associated with them. For example, potential employers in the hospitality (hotels and restaurants) and retail (especially high-end department stores) markets may look negatively on tattoos since appearance in these markets is important. Also, a person who has been tattooed is nine times more likely to contract hepatitis C (a type of liver disease) than individuals who have never been inked. In addition, recent studies suggest that the inks tattoo artists use may contain toxic elements that may lead to certain types of cancer. Furthermore, while getting a tattoo was once a rite of passage of being in the military, new military regulations prohibit tattoos that are visible on the head, face, and neck. Depending on the tattoo and/or its location, an individual may be charged with insubordination for having visible tattoos. Finally, I have both male and female friends who still believe that any male with a tattoo is a thug or a criminal, and any girl who gets inked is promiscuous. In fact, the term *tramp stamp* has been given to a tattoo that is etched on a girl's back at the base of her spine. So while tattoos do not have the stigma attached to them they once did, getting inked is not without negative consequences.

Comparison and Contrast

Comparison explains how items are similar; **contrast** explains how items are different. You may use comparison and contrast together to explain the similarities and differences of the subject, or you may use each concept separately and explain only the similarities or only the differences.

You often use comparison and contrast, for example, to evaluate products. An article in an auto magazine might compare and contrast the newest models of two pick-up trucks, or a movie reviewer might compare and contrast a movie's sequel to the first film. The following paragraph contrasts taking a course over summer versus taking that same course over a semester.

> Taking a college class over summer rather than over a full semester can be challenging; however, for some students, completing a course in just six weeks is also more rewarding. Because the pace of a summer class is fast and furious compared to the unhurried pace of a regular semester, college students often find they actually retain more information and achieve higher grades. While the quick pace is not for everyone, some students thrive under the pressure. First, when students are forced to do homework every day rather than letting days go in between assignments, they remember concepts and key terms more easily and then understand the next concept more readily. For instance, summer school students don't have time to forget the function of an adverb before the next lesson on the adverb clause is introduced. Hence, understanding the adverb clause is easy. Also, summer students' study sessions are closer together because tests are closer together rather than weeks apart as in a regular semester. Back-to-back study sessions allow for greater retention of ideas. Last, the momentum of a summer class helps students tune out distractions; the idle time of a sixteen- or eighteen-week course allows for bad habits to form. When students are given the chance to slow down, they browse websites, post on social networking sites, watch TV, and party with friends, telling themselves they have plenty of time to finish their school work. They then find that the due date of an important assignment has come and gone. While summer classes seem daunting, their difficulties may be outweighed by their benefits.

Division

Division typically takes one item and divides the item into its various components or parts to help your readers understand the item. For example, you could choose a restaurant as your subject and divide it into its various components, which may include the parking lot, the inner dining area, the patio dining area, the bar, the kitchen, the restrooms, etc. Or if you were trying to explain how the US government works, you could begin by dividing the government into its three branches, the legislative branch, with the House of Representatives and Senate; the executive branch, with the president and vice president; and the judicial branch, with the Supreme Court. By dividing an item into its various parts, readers are better able to understand how the item works or functions, how it operates.

The following paragraph is the introductory paragraph from a longer essay that discusses the human body's ten bodily systems.

> Organs of the body that perform similar functions are organized into a body system. Again, as an example, the stomach joins with the mouth, throat, esophagus, and the small and large intestines to make up the alimentary tract of the digestive system. The alimentary tract combines with the teeth, tongue, salivary glands, liver, pancreas, and the gallbladder to form the total digestive system. The other systems of the body, which will be discussed individually, are the integumentary, skeletal, muscular, respiratory, circulatory, urinary, nervous, endocrine, and reproductive systems.
>
> from Lucile Keir et. al. *Medical Assisting.* 6th ed. p. 333

Classification

Classification takes a number of elements and groups them according to similar criteria. For example, you could take all restaurants in a specific area and classify them according to the type of food they serve, their location, their meal costs, or their atmosphere. If you were setting out to landscape your yard, you could identify plants by how much water they require or how much sun or shade they need or how frequently they bloom in order to decide where you are going to plant the flowers and shrubs.

The following paragraph discusses the current classification of clouds.

> Clouds, regardless of the type (and there are at least nine), are composed entirely of water droplets. Meteorologists, people who study the atmosphere, especially the weather, have classified clouds into three large groups: lower level clouds, middle level clouds, and higher level clouds. Each of these three levels is further subclassified. For example, lower level clouds, which generally form below 6,500 feet, comprise cumulus, stratocumulus, and stratus clouds. Middle level clouds, which occur between 6,500 and 20,000

> feet, include altocumulus, altostratus, and nimbostratus. And higher level clouds, which occur above 20,000 feet, are called cirrus and cirrostratus, cirrocumulus, and cumulonimbus. Even with nine categories of clouds at a variety of heights in the sky above us, most every cloud we look at is formed in the troposphere, the lowest layer of the Earth's atmosphere, starting at the Earth's surface and rising to approximately 5 to 12 miles above sea level depending where on Earth we are standing.

Definition

When you define your subject, you can compose either a denotative definition or a connotative definition. **Denotative definitions** provide precise, dictionary-type definitions; denotative definitions are objective in that they provide an unprejudiced and neutral meaning for the word or concept.

Connotative definitions, on the other hand, are more subjective and will frequently add personal, individual meanings to the literal meaning.

The following paragraph provides both denotative and connotative definitions for the word *happiness*.

> What is *happiness*? As a part of speech, the word *happiness* is a noun since happiness is a concept or idea. *Happiness* is also the feeling of being happy, a state of enjoyment and pleasure. *Happiness* can be characterized by a feeling of contentment. And contentment is what I feel when riots of children are running around the back yard, laughing and playing utterly freely. Or when after a long day's hike I delight in a panoramic view of the mountains and valleys through which I am hiking, I am happy and content. But I am most happy when I am merely walking hand in hand with my girlfriend, whether down some sleepy street on our way to dinner or through a crowded and hectic mall. Happiness, whether defined by the dictionary or by one's adventures, is an indispensable human need, an essential condition we should all seek more often.

Process Analysis

Process analysis is sometimes called a "how to" paper. In other words, process analysis tells readers how to do something or how something works. Paragraphs using process analysis must be carefully thought out since all steps in the process must be accounted for and included in the process. For example, a paper for an archaeology class might explain the sequence of steps one follows when excavating artifacts from a dig site so that a novice archaeologist does not inadvertently corrupt the area.

The following paragraph provides readers a step-by-step process for a successful interview.

> A formal interview can be an anxiety-inducing experience, but a prospective employee can calm her nerves by taking certain measures that build and exude self-confidence. First, before ever setting foot in the manager's office, the applicant should research the particulars of the company or organization, such as when it was founded, where the parent office is located, what its recent accomplishments have been, and what its current challenges are. When an applicant is armed with up-to-date information about the company, she will be prepared if asked about the organization. A manager will be impressed that she took the time to investigate. This initial step shows a boss she is tenacious and motivated. Another aspect of the interview to consider before entering the manager's office is the interview outfit. An applicant should present herself as a professional and respectful individual. When choosing the outfit, she should consider the type of organization: an interview with a fashion design company or music studio may allow for more creative clothing, but an interview with an accounting company would require a conservative suit. Armed with information and a professional look, the applicant is ready to meet the management. Upon entering the office, the applicant should offer her hand and give a firm hand shake while smiling and making eye contact. Eye contact and good posture during the interview exude confidence. During the interview, if she does not know an answer to a question, she should ask for a moment to think rather than offer a quick, and potentially wrong, answer. If the answer does not come to her, she should say, "That is a very good question, one that I would like to investigate. Please let me get back to you as soon as I find the answer." Admitting ignorance and offering to educate oneself is much better than faking knowledge and getting caught later. An employer does not want an impulsive employee. When the interview is coming to a close, usually the interviewer will ask if the applicant has any questions, so she should be prepared with intelligent questions about the company. A person with no questions appears apathetic, and an employer does not want an apathetic employee. When the interview is over, the applicant should give a firm hand shake again, make eye contact, express her sincere desire to join the company, and thank her interviewer for his or her time. To further showcase her professionalism, she should send a thank-you card to her interviewer within the week. Even if she does not get the job, she will know she did her best and will have gained valuable experience for her next interview.

PERSUASION

When you persuade, you argue. You seek to convince your readers that your opinion about the topic is a feasible position. For example, you may want to persuade your readers that states that are experiencing extreme droughts should pass a law that limits the amount of sod people are allowed to plant. Or you may wish to argue that since eighteen-year-olds are able to vote and serve in the military, they should also be allowed to drink.

Persuasion involves presenting readers with logical evidence, evidence that supports the position you stated in your topic sentence. You cannot persuade rationally by being biased and subjective; you must provide your readers verifiable facts, statistics, and evidence from authorities.

The following paragraph uses a narrative format to present an argument on the importance of reading.

> Walking across campus yesterday, I overheard a piece of a conversation. A student was complaining to another about an assignment and said, "I have all this reading to do, pages and pages. I don't have time to read all this stuff. Besides, reading isn't as important as teachers think it is." I disagree. Reading is one of the most important activities people will ever learn. First, any subject individuals wish to study or learn about, they can. All they need to do is pick up a book and read. Granted, people may be able to find a video on Youtube.com concerning the subject, but no video can provide the in-depth investigation and consideration that a book can. Second, reading allows people the opportunity to get away. Books on other countries and cultures may be found in any bookstore or library, and the Internet provides instant access to information. All one must be able to do is read. If travel is not an activity of interest, just sitting down with a good novel or short story provides the opportunity to escape for a little while. Most importantly, reading helps people learn to think. As they read, they must consider—based on the author's evidence and support—the validity or invalidity of what the author is writing; they must evaluate the text and decide what to accept and what to discard. Thinking allows individuals to become more responsible and conscientious. Contrary to the student's opinion, reading is important.

In Chapters 11 and 12, you will be introduced to a process that will lead you, step by step, from generating ideas to editing and submitting the paragraph.

Chapter SUMMARY

- When you sit down to write, you need to identify ____________________,

  ______________________________, and ______________________________

  since these three elements are the foundation of your writing.
- A topic sentence should include ______________________________ and

  ____.
- A direct paragraph places the topic sentence _______________________

  ____.
- A climactic paragraph places the topic sentence ____________________

  ____.
- When a paragraph is unified, ____________________________________

  ____.
- Support in a paragraph should be ______________ and ______________.
- If a paragraph is coherent, its points are __________________________.
- A paragraph's purpose is to __________________, __________________,

  ______________________________, or ______________________________.

INVENTING AND ORGANIZING

Chapter PREVIEW

In this chapter you will learn the first two steps of the writing process we recommend you follow in developing your compositions: inventing and organizing. Inventing will teach you strategies to generate ideas. Organizing will provide you with methods to structure those ideas.

THE WRITING PROCESS

Frequently, when students sit down to write a paper, they just begin writing, trying to accomplish in one step what should take several steps.

If you were asked to take a morning shower, dress for the day, eat your breakfast, brush your teeth, collect your books and papers, and drive to school **all at the same time**, you would laugh at the improbability of performing all those actions simultaneously.

Yet many students set out trying to perform a variety of tasks all at once when they sit down to write. Given a writing assignment, many students try to limit the topic, compose a topic sentence, develop an organizational structure, generate support for the main idea, use appropriate sentence structures, maintain a consistent vocabulary, edit the grammar and mechanics, and proofread all in one sitting.

Trying to perform all the stages of writing a paper at once is difficult and frustrating. Rather than attempting to complete a writing assignment in one sitting, you should follow a process that leads you step by step to a finished composition.

The process taught in this textbook includes five steps:

- Inventing
- Organizing
- Drafting
- Revising
- Editing/Proofreading

Following this process will enable you to compose paragraphs and essays that are thoughtful and well written rather than rushed and insubstantial. And one of the benefits not only of learning this process but also of using it regularly is this: you can adapt the process to most any writing situation, including in-class midterms and final exams, because the process is generic and meant to be applied to most any type of writing assignment.

But before you read about each step in the process, you need to understand that the writing process does not go in a straight line, from Step 1 straight to Step 5. As you compose, you may find yourself going back to previous steps. Returning to a previous step should not concern you, for you are rethinking, reconsidering your options and ideas. Returning to a previous step is standard practice for good writers.

To help you focus on each step of the process, you should incorporate the following suggestions into your writing routine.

1. Work in a comfortable environment. *Comfortable* may mean you need to have music playing, or it may mean you need complete silence. Create a work space in which you can think and create.

2. Work in chunks of time. Don't sit down thinking, "I'm not moving until this paper is finished." Give yourself a break periodically. For example, write for fifty minutes and take a break for ten minutes.
3. If you are easily distracted by noise, wear headphones to cut down on disrupting noises around you.
4. If you are composing on your personal computer, do not open your email or log into any social networking sites so that you are not tempted to stop your writing and respond to a recently received email or comment on someone's post.
5. And last, turn off your phone and put it out of sight. Use that ten-minute break mentioned in suggestion #2 to check your phone.

STEP 1: INVENTING

Simply stated, inventing is generating ideas. Students can use invention techniques to discover a tentative topic sentence or ideas for a paragraph.

While numerous invention strategies exist, the following are five basic but effective methods:

- Brainstorming
- Freewriting
- Journalistic Questioning
- Clustering
- Cubing

Please be aware that not every invention technique will come easily to you. But as you work through the five techniques, you will find one or two of the techniques more effective than the others. Use the method or methods that work best for you in helping you generate the most ideas.

Also, as you work through an invention technique, keep the following guidelines in mind.

- Don't worry about repetition.
- Write as much as you can in response to any step in the technique.
- Forget about grammar, spelling, and mechanics.
- Reward yourself when you have finished.

Finally, always keep the following in mind: **the only wrong answer in invention is an empty page.**

Brainstorming

With brainstorming, your goal is to generate a list of ideas. You can use brainstorming in two ways:

- to generate topics on which to write.
- to generate ideas about a topic.

Generally, when instructors assign a paper, they provide a writing prompt. But every once in a while, instructors will assign a paper and allow you to choose the topic. You can use brainstorming to help you come up with a topic on which to write.

First, set a specific amount of time that you will write; usually four to five minutes can generate a large number of topics.

After you have decided upon a time limit, take out a sheet of paper (lined paper will keep your list neater) or open a blank document in your word processor, and when you are ready, begin listing subjects that interest you. Do not judge or think about the topics you list. Just write the subject down and move on. Keep listing topics until your time runs out. If your time expires and you are still jotting down topics, don't stop listing until you have run out of ideas.

While you are listing your topics, do not stop to consider how much or how little you like the topic; don't worry about how much you know or don't know about the topic. Just keep listing topics and subjects, whether or not the topic interests you. Just list.

After your time has ended, you can then return to your list and begin to identify those topics that you find most interesting.

You may wish to organize your topics from most interesting to least interesting or from those you know the most about to those you know only a little. You can identify topics that interest you with a symbol, such as a star, a smiley face, or an exclamation point. Topics that you find uninteresting, you can cross out. Keep editing your list until you have narrowed your topics to the top three to five. From these several topics pick the one you like the most.

You can also use brainstorming to generate a list of ideas on a topic. First, write your topic across the top of the paper on which you will brainstorm. Then, using the above techniques, begin listing your ideas on the subject. You can use single words, phrases, dates, statistics—anything that is associated with your topic. One idea may generate more ideas, so keep listing until you can think of nothing else to add.

Freewriting

Freewriting is a writing strategy in which you write nonstop for a specific period of time without worrying about spelling, grammar, sentence structure,

or punctuation. The main focus behind freewriting is to put your ideas on paper. The order of the ideas, the number of ideas, and the development of the ideas are not important at this point. Since ideas can quickly evaporate, freewriting allows you to put ideas in a place where you can come back and find them.

While both brainstorming and freewriting help you generate ideas, the fundamental difference between the two invention techniques is how you deliver your ideas: brainstorming presents ideas as lists; freewriting presents ideas in longer groups of words, such as clauses. For example, someone brainstorming on hummingbirds might write

Hummingbirds
Small
Colorful
Fast
Aggressive
Territorial

While someone who is freewriting might write

Hummingbirds–small colorful birds; they dart quickly from one place to another; are aggressive and territorial, will drive away other hummers and bigger birds from their feeding area.

Once you have a topic, you can use freewriting in the same way you used brainstorming, to narrow your subject and produce ideas about it. Again, set a prescribed amount of time. Since you are now beginning to develop your topic, you should spend five or ten minutes freewriting ideas; write everything you can think of about your topic. With freewriting you are **not** listing; you are trying to write in generally complete thoughts.

But, as noted above, don't worry about your spelling; don't worry about your grammar; don't worry about your sentence structure. Your goal at this point in the writing process is to get your ideas down on paper. Keep writing until your time ends. If, when your time ends, you are still producing ideas, keep writing.

If, on the other hand, you seem to have run out of ideas before your time runs out, don't stop writing. Write your last idea over again if you need to. Write, "I don't know what to say anymore" or "I need to keep writing because my teacher said to." By continuing to write, even if you are not generating ideas on your topic, you are allowing your brain a chance to dredge up additional information on your topic and make it available to you. If you stop and begin rereading what you have written, you are shutting down the idea-generating process. While writing the same thing over and over again or writing down information unrelated to your topic may seem nonproductive, you may be surprised at how quickly new information about your topic may spring to mind.

If you compose on a computer, one interesting way to freewrite is to open your word processor to a blank document and then turn off your monitor. **Be sure to turn off the monitor, not the computer**. Once you start typing, you will not be able to see what you are writing. Since you will no longer be able to see what you are writing, you cannot focus on the page and the words in front of you. You focus more on the ideas swirling around in your head. Once you turn the monitor back on, what you see may not be pretty, but all the ideas you had about your topic are now available for you to consider at a later time. One warning though: before you start typing with your monitor off, be sure your fingers are on the correct keys.

There are two important points to remember when you are brainstorming and freewriting. First, don't think. For these activities, you do not want to spend time contemplating the value or importance of the ideas you are writing down. You merely want to put them in a concrete form so that you can come back to them later.

Second, once you start writing, don't stop. Don't stop to think about what you have written; don't stop to consider the merit of your ideas; don't stop to correct a spelling or grammar error. Even if you believe you have put on paper everything you have to say about the topic and you have time left, don't stop listing or writing. Write about something related to your topic; write about anything that pops into your head. Ultimately, you don't want to interrupt the process of putting your ideas on the page. Again, once your time ends, you can go back and begin to edit and organize the ideas you have generated.

Journalistic Questioning

Asking journalistic questions about your topic can help you generate ideas that you may use in developing your paper. Six traditional questions journalists typically ask when composing a story are *who, what, why, when, where,* and *how*. These questions largely ensure you are able to explore most features of your topic.

1. When you ask the question *who*,
   - remember that *who* does not need to be a person; *who* refers to the main idea of your paragraph, which could be a person, event, or idea.
   - include all persons and ideas involved with your topic.
   - ask what their roles in your topic are.
2. When you ask the question *what*,
   - include any actions involved with your subject.
3. When you ask the question *why*,
   - explore the causes behind your topic.
4. When you ask the question *when*,
   - include present, past, and/or future dates and times associated with your topic.
5. When you ask the question *where*,
   - include any place or places involved with your topic.
6. When you ask the question *how*,
   - include any processes, techniques, approaches, systems, or procedures associated with your topic.

Look at the information that one student generated on the topic "Study Abroad Programs."

> **Who?** Students and instructors. Family I will be staying with. Who are they? Will they be nice? Do they have any kids? Will I be with another study abroad student? Mom and Dad—they will have to help me with some of the expenses (but they said they would. They are excited for me and scared at the same time).
>
> **What?** What do I have to do? I will have to take classes in London. What classes? I will find out at the orientation. I will have to fly to England. I will have to come up with money to cover cost of program plus money for other expenses. I will have to submit the application and come up with money. I will be gone for 12 weeks, so I will have to pack (make sure I have my camera). What will I pack? Maybe orientation will help.
>
> **Why?** Why should I participate? Going abroad for twelve weeks will be awesome. Get to see things I've never seen before (except

> in pictures or on TV). Get a chance to spend some time in other countries. Learn about other cultures. Drink some foreign beer.
>
> **When?** When does the program occur? Will be gone spring semester, from early February to mid May. About 12 weeks. So the weather should be pretty nice, but I've heard that the weather in England can change quickly. When I told one of my instructors about going to study in London, he told me he was in London one spring, and he walked from the British Museum to a café to have lunch, and in the six blocks he walked, it rained, hailed, the wind blew, and the sun shined. Sounds like I'll have to carry a suitcase full of clothes when I go out.
>
> **Where?** Where are we going? We will be studying in London. But that puts us really close to the rest of Europe. So when we have time, we can hop over to Italy or Germany or France or Spain (I might get a chance to use the Spanish I've been studying for two years). We are also going on field trips in England. I don't know where in London I will be staying because I don't know what family I'm staying with. If I had an address I could look it up on mapquest. Where do we take classes? In a school? Where will I be living? I really need an address.
>
> **How?** How will we get there and once there how will I get around? We are going to fly from LAX to London. How long will the plane ride take? Will we have to stop and change planes? How much can I carry on the plane? Once there I imagine we will take busses and the underground around London. I can't wait to use the underground. I imagine we will take busses or vans when we go on our field trips, but if we're in London, maybe we'll walk or take the underground.

Clustering

A fourth invention technique that you will find helpful is clustering. Clustering involves grouping together (clustering) your ideas on a subject. When you cluster, you create a visual map of your ideas.

To begin, take a sheet of paper and orient it to a landscape position to give yourself more room to draw. Next, write your topic in the middle of the page and draw a circle or oval around it. As ideas about your topic come to mind, write the ideas around the middle circle. After you have created an initial circle of ideas—these are your primary ideas on your topic—jot down your thoughts and observations on your primary ideas. These thoughts are your secondary ideas on your topic. You can continue to add additional views to your secondary thoughts, essentially narrowing your primary subject to a more specific, concrete topic.

Once you have an overview of your topic and its subtopics, then you can take another sheet of paper, place a subtopic or secondary idea that interests you in the middle, and begin creating bubbles appropriate to your subject. The process continues until you have sufficient ideas to begin organizing them into a paragraph or essay.

Here are the results of a clustering activity from a student who wanted to write about amusement parks.

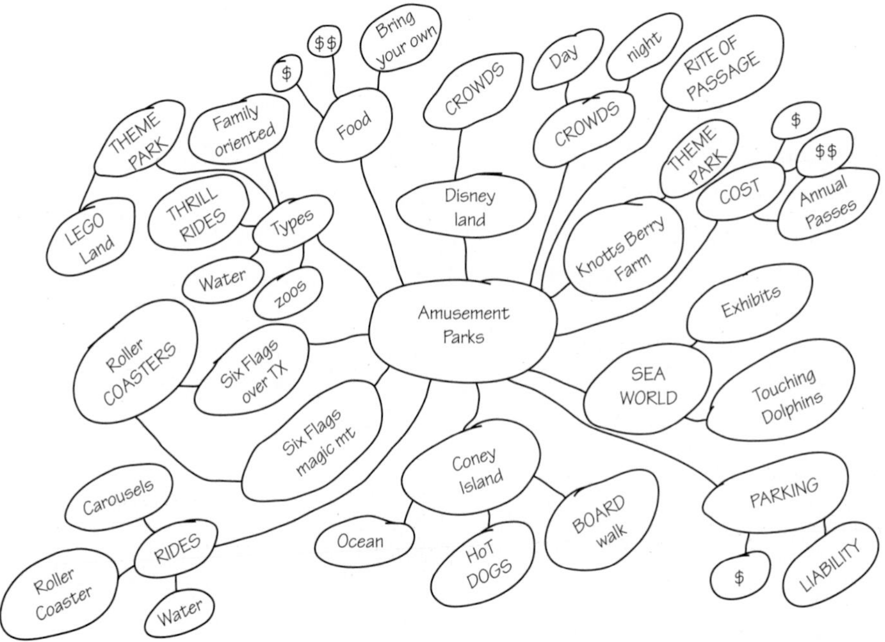

Cubing

Cubing takes its name from the fact that a cube has six sides. In this activity, you have six ways to consider your topic:

1. When you **describe** your topic, consider
   - the subject's color, shape, age, dimensions, locations, sequence, contents, substance, style of construction, origin, nationality, etc.
2. When you **compare** your topic, ask
   - what is it similar to? What is it different from?
3. When you **associate** your topic, ask
   - what does my topic remind me of?
   - how does it connect with my individual life, with the life of my family or community?
   - what events, ideas, concepts, persons, times, places do I associate with my topic?

4. When you **analyze** your topic, inquire
   - what is it made of?
   - how does it work?
   - how do the parts of your topic relate to one another?

5. When you **apply** your topic, examine
   - what it is used for.
   - what it could be used for.
   - who uses it.

6. When you **argue** for or against your topic, ask
   - is it a good idea or a bad idea?
   - are there features to the idea that are both good and bad?
   - are the ideas neither good nor bad?

Asking the above questions of a topic like amusement parks and other concrete or physical subjects can generate answers rather easily. But when the topic is more abstract or large, for example, patriotism or the environment, generating ideas may take you more time. Don't give up.

Just because you cannot immediately think of an answer does not mean no answer exists. Follow these guidelines when working with cubing: (1) Consider each side of the cube and the associated questions for four to five minutes. Don't just sit; think, consider, ponder, reflect, ask the questions out loud, ask your roommate or a member of your family. If, at the end of the time, you still have not thought of anything, move to the next side of the cube. (2) Once finished, go back and reconsider that side or those sides of the cube you did not answer. Cubing is a wonderful invention strategy, and if you take your time, you can generate many useful ideas about any topic.

EXERCISE 11.1: Invention Techniques

Below are twenty general topics. Choose one and use each of the five invention techniques above to generate ideas on the topic. Follow the guidelines for each invention strategy. Be prepared to share your completed exercises with your instructor and classmates.

1. Skateboarding
2. Paintball
3. Raves
4. MORPGs (Massive Online Role Playing Games)
5. Facebook or other social networking website

6. Anime
7. Movies
8. Fashions
9. Amusement parks
10. Tattoos
11. WWF (World Wrestling Federation)
12. Street racing
13. Pilates or yoga
14. The living dead (vampires, zombies, or werewolves)
15. Photography
16. Scrapbooking
17. A holiday (New Year's Eve, Thanksgiving, Kwanza, Ramadan, Veteran's Day, etc.)
18. Pollution (light, water, noise, air)
19. Study abroad programs
20. The economy

STEP 2: ORGANIZING

Once you have generated a number of ideas regarding your topic, you need to arrange them in a logical manner; in other words, you need to organize your thoughts.

Organizing techniques range from various forms of outlines—such as formal outlines, scratch outlines, and topic sentence outlines—to the rhetorical modes—including narrative, description, examples, cause and effect, comparison and contrast, process analysis, division and classification, and definition. Several of the previous organizational structures may be unfamiliar. But organizing techniques merely reflect the ways people think, so while you may believe you are not familiar with organizing strategies, the truth is you have been using them all your life.

Since you will be writing papers and exams for a variety of classes, the more organizational structures you are familiar with, the better opportunity you will have to organize your ideas in a logical manner and write a successful paper.

Following are some of the more commonly used methods for organizing information, including general to specific, specific to general, order of importance, order of familiarity, and time or space order. After you read about the various patterns of organization, you will learn how to put them in an outline to help you evaluate their effectiveness.

General to Specific

A paragraph using a general to specific structure typically begins with a broad or wide-ranging idea that is followed by information that provides specific details to illustrate the generalization. A direct paragraph (see page 168) is an example of a piece of writing using a general to specific organization.

Specific to General

A paragraph developed following a specific to general organizational pattern begins with specific, detailed information and ends with a generalization arising from the specifics. A climactic paragraph (see page 168) is an example of writing that uses a specific to general organization.

Order of Importance

An order of importance writing assignment organizes the information from either least important to most important or from most important to least important. It is up to you to decide what is least important or most important.

What is important to remember with these two organizational patterns is that you must choose appropriate transitions that alert your readers to the structure you are using. For example, transitions, such as *most importantly* or *most important* along with such transitional words as *first, next, also* announce to readers the various points you are making and their importance among all the points you make.

The paragraph below, using a *most important* to *least important* structure, explores some of the benefits of doing crossword puzzles. The transitions that indicate the order of importance are in bold. Transitions that identify examples and details and identify the paragraph's conclusion are underlined.

> The benefits of doing crossword puzzles, whether online or in the daily newspaper, are several. **First, and most important**, crossword puzzles help people expand their vocabularies. The majority of clues in crossword puzzles ask for synonyms (words having the same or similar meaning as the clue word) and sometimes antonyms (a word meaning the opposite of the clue word) for their answers. For people who do not read widely or who are non-native speakers, working crossword puzzles is more inviting than simply learning vocabulary lists. **Second**, working crossword puzzles promotes close reading.

> Noun clues presented in singular form will have a singular answer, while noun clues presented in the plural will have a plural answer. For example, a clue might read "Earthen pot" and the answer is "olla" or "Earthen pots" and the answer is "ollas" with an "s." The reader must be attentive to the number of the noun. Also, verb clues are typically in the verb tense in which the answer will be. A present tense clue will require a present tense answer. Similarly, a past tense clue will require a past tense answer. For example, "Wished undone" = "rued" or "Writes on glass" = "etches." **Third**, crossword puzzles also familiarize people with geographical places, for instance, Pharaoh's river (Nile) or Europe-Asia range (Ural) and people, Explorer Polo (Marco) or Latin historian (Cato). **Finally**, crossword puzzles provide people practice in grammar. Perhaps the clue may ask for a comparative or superlative form of an adjective. For instance, if the clue is "More aloof" the answer might be "icier," or the clue "Most pleasant" might be seeking the answer "nicest." Overall, crossword puzzles provide a variety of reading and writing skills to people who do them on a daily basis.

Order of Familiarity

When you organize information following order of familiarity, you can arrange details from least familiar to most familiar or from most familiar to least familiar. If you organize your writing following an order of familiarity structure, you need to know who your readers are so that you are relatively sure what information is and is not familiar to them. The audience analysis found in Chapter 10 will go a long way to helping you identify your readers so that you can be more confident in choosing the most appropriate structural strategy.

The paragraph below discusses different types of guard dogs, the most familiar breeds introduced first. The transitions that indicate the paragraph is structured from most familiar to least familiar are in bold. Transitions that identify examples and details are underlined.

> When people hear the words "guard dogs," they **generally** envision German Shepherds or Doberman Pinschers since these two breeds of dogs are **typically** seen in movies and on television acting as watch dogs. Nevertheless, other breeds of dogs also make excellent watch dogs, for example, a Rottweiler. A Rottweiler is both smart and brave. And while they are gentle around their family, Rottweilers are fiercely protective. **Another less well known** breed that makes good guard dogs are Komondors, dogs that have been described as looking like a four-legged mop or a dog covered

> in dreadlocks. However, despite its appearance, a Komondor is a courageous dog that will become aggressive when it believes its master or property is threatened. **Probably least well known** as a guard dog is the Kuvasz. The breed's name comes from the Turkish word meaning "guard" or "protector." While not a particularly big dog, a Kuvasz is extremely territorial and protective.

Chronological Order

A chronological organization arranges events in time order, typically from the earliest event to the latest or last event. Necessary and appropriate transitional words and phrases help the reader follow the sequence of events.

In the following paragraph, the various time signals are bolded to help you follow the author's morning routine.

> **During the week**, my morning routine is pretty repetitive and unexciting, but it helps get me get out the door and to school on time. My alarm goes off at 6:30 a.m. Moaning and grousing to anyone who will listen (even though there is no one in the apartment but me), I climb out of bed and head for the shower. **After** a fifteen-minute shower, I dress for the day, but I don't put on whatever shirt I'm wearing that day since I don't want to chance spilling breakfast or spattering toothpaste on it. **After dressing**, I head out to the kitchen to eat. Breakfast is a fried egg, bagel, and juice or cold cereal topped with a banana and strawberries or oatmeal with raisins, dried cranberries, and brown sugar. **While I eat**, I read the paper, comics first. **Following breakfast**, I brush my teeth, rinse my mouth, and put on my shirt. **Then** it's back out to the kitchen to make my lunch since my classes do not end until mid-afternoon. **Once** I've made my lunch, I gather my books, put my lunch in my backpack, and I'm out the door around 8 a.m. While not a particularly adventurous way to start my weekday mornings, my routine virtually guarantees I'm in class on time.

Spatial Order

A spatial organization is typical in descriptive writing. Spatial organization mimics the way you commonly look at something: top to bottom, one side to another side, near to far.

When you use spatial organization, you generally pick a specific perspective and describe the object, person, or scene from that viewpoint. For example, if someone asked you to describe a room in your house or apartment, you might choose your living room. Where you choose to mentally sit or stand to view the room is the viewpoint from which you are going to describe the room.

You might decide to stand in one corner of the room or in the doorway or in the middle of the room. Once you have your perspective, you then must decide in what order you will describe the room: from left to right, right to left, from near to far, from the ceiling to the floor, from the floor to the ceiling. Or if you choose to stand in the middle of the room, you may describe the room in a circular fashion.

While the perspective you choose to describe the room is your choice, your description must follow a logical development. You do not want to begin describing the room starting on the left and moving to the right only to suddenly move to the floor or the opposite side of the room.

In the following paragraph, notice how the writer announces her position and then leads the reader across the room left to right. The various spatial signals are bolded.

> I stopped in the doorway, amused by what confronted me. The **left** side of the room, **near** the closet, was largely clean and free of clutter. But as my gaze moved **across** the room, the **closer** I got to a desk that sat **against** the **right** wall, the messier and more disorderly the room became. Three stacks of books stood guard **at** the **left** end of the desk. The stacks rose about 2 to 2 ½ feet in the air; one stack looked as if it were about to topple over. **On** the desk top several stacks of paper completely covered the writing area. **Toward** the back of the desk top rested a dusty tape dispenser, an antique stapler, and several cups and empty jelly jars filled with pens and pencils. A computer monitor took up position **at** the **far** end of the desk. The desk drawers were blocked by two boxes full of papers and books. Several more boxes formed a short wall that allowed the user a pathway **from** the doorway **to** the chair **at** the desk.

Outline

You can use an outline to help you organize and visualize any paragraph or essay regardless of the organizational pattern you choose. An outline provides extensive details and illustrates the ways ideas are arranged in relation to each other. Developing an outline of your pattern of organization helps you see any areas that need improvement, such as organizational unity or lack of support, before you begin to compose your draft.

The following pattern illustrates a simple paragraph outline.

I. Main Idea
    A. First Supporting Point
        1. Example or Detail
            a. Specific illustration of example or detail

        2. Example or Detail
            a. Specific illustration of example or detail
    B. Second Supporting Point
        1. Example or Detail
            a. Specific illustration of example or detail
        2. Example or Detail
            a. Specific illustration of example or detail

An outline for a paragraph on the topic of hummingbirds and their aggressive behavior might look like the following:

I. Hummingbirds for their size are an aggressive bird
    A. Defends territory
        1. Feeding places
            a. Will chase other hummingbirds as well as much larger birds from flowers and feeders.
        2. Nesting areas
            a. Once hummingbirds have found a good nesting site, they will keep all other birds away from the area by flying at them and chasing them away
    B. Attacks much larger creatures
        1. Will attack not only other hummingbirds, but also larger birds and some animals
            a. For example, mockingbirds and cats
        2. Not afraid of humans
            a. Hummingbirds will dive bomb both adults and children

- The first two steps in the writing process are ______________________ and ______________________.
- Five helpful invention strategies are (1) ______________________, (2) ______________________, (3) ______________________, (4) ______________________, and (5) ______________________.
- Six organizing methods are (1) ______________________, (2) ______________________, (3) ______________________, (4) ______________________, (5) ______________________, and (6) ______________________.

DRAFTING, REVISING, AND EDITING

Chapter PREVIEW

In Chapter 11 you learned the first two steps in the writing process: inventing and organizing. In this chapter, you will learn the final three steps—drafting, revising, and editing—that will prepare you to write well-developed papers for your classes. This chapter concludes with guidelines for submitting academic writing.

STEP 3: DRAFTING

Once you have developed a number of ideas and composed a working topic sentence or thesis and decided upon an organizational structure, you draft. Your first draft should be all about getting your ideas down on paper following the structure you developed in the second step and not about editing and proofreading. Ideas can quickly disappear and to spend time trying to edit—concerning yourself with spelling, punctuation, and mechanics—at this step is wasted time. You need to take the ideas you generated during the invention phase and commit them to paper.

The draft is for you only. So, don't worry about mistakes. Just write. You want your ideas, all your ideas, on paper so that they are available should you wish to look back and consider previous ideas.

Some writers find starting the draft the most difficult part of writing, so if you find yourself having difficulty beginning your draft, try one of the following:

1. Since you have a working organization, divide your paper into sections—for example, the introduction, various points in the body, and the conclusion—and begin with a section where you are most confident or that you know best.
2. Start in the middle or at the end of your paper. You do not need to start your draft at the beginning.
3. Just begin writing on the topic without worrying about a specific organization. The ideas you generated during the invention step will help keep you focused, and as you place your ideas about the topic on the page, you will begin to see that one organizational structure may be more effective than another.

When you begin drafting, keep the following guidelines in mind:

1. Keep writing. Remember, this is a draft. Sentence level errors at this point don't count, so don't worry about them. Don't go back to correct spelling or capitalization.
2. If you come to a spot in your paper that you find difficult or challenging, write what you can and move on. You can always come back. If you have to stop writing, try to stop with an idea you feel you know well so that when you return, you can pick up the thread of the idea and continue writing.

Remember, drafting is your initial effort to place your ideas on paper, so stay open to where your ideas may take you, but focused enough to avoid leaving your subject completely.

STEP 4: REVISING

The word *revise* comes from the Latin *revisere*, which means *to visit again.* When you revise your paper, you are going back to reconsider what you have said and how you have written what you have said.

Following is a body paragraph from a student's essay as the student first wrote it. The writer, arguing for a student cell phone ban in K-12 schools, was unhappy with the way the information in one paragraph sounded. His original text lacked development because he only had one supporting point, which was vague because his one point lacked enough specific details. In addition, his language was repetitive, and his word choice lacked sophistication.

A copy of the student's revision of the paragraph follows the original paragraph. You will notice the student has crossed out information, rewritten sentences, and used different vocabulary. As noted above, revision involves rethinking (**Figure 12.1**).

Last is the paragraph as the student revised it. As you will see, after he revised his text, the paragraph includes another supporting point and is also further developed with more specific examples. The student also has elevated his vocabulary so his writing is not only more academic but also more engaging.

Original Paragraph from *Cell Phones on Campus**

Another negative effect that K-12 students come across is that when they have their cell phone at school they rely on it for everything. It cannot be stressed enough when we say that independence is vital when a young adult enters into the real world. When a student is growing up with a cell phone, his or her independence is affected in a harmful way. The reason why is because every time that student has a problem, he or she would turn to their cell phone to either contact his or her mom or dad. For example, if the student forgot his or her P.E. clothes for gym class, the student can call his or her parents to bring the clothes, and many times the parents do just that. When students contact their parents, they are not learning how to solve problems on their own or face the consequence of their mistakes. If a child doesn't have any consequences from a mistake they have done the first time, how will he or she learn from it? If cell phones are banned, children would have to be responsible for their daily responsibilities or deal with the consequences. Students that cannot remember something as simple as to bring their gym clothes to school will never be responsible enough to be in charge of a much bigger task as they grow to become adults.

*Reprinted by permission of Anthony Campos.

FIGURE 12.1 The purpose of this example is to show you what a revision might look like. Notice how this student asked questions, wrote notes, and made comments on the paper. Revision requires you to evaluate your own writing—and sometimes it's messy.

Original Paragraph

Secondly, when K-12 students have cell phones available all day, they do not learn problem-solving skills because the cell phone offers non-stop access to Mom and Dad, and every time parents step in to handle their children's problems, ... (something about growth / independence).

~~Another negative effect that K-12 students come across is that when they have their cell phone at school they rely on it for everything. It cannot be stressed enough when we say that independence is vital when a young adult enters into the real world. When a student is growing up with a cell phone, his or her independence is affected in a harmful way. The reason why is because every time that student has a problem, he or she would turn to their cell phone to either contact his or her mom or dad.~~ For example, if the student forgot his or her P.E. clothes for gym class, the student can call his or her parents to bring the clothes, and many times the parents do just that. The parents don't want little Johnny to get in trouble so that all When students it takes is a phone call for their parents to come to the rescue, ~~contact their parents~~, they are not learning how to solve problems on their own or face the consequence of their mistakes. ~~If a child doesn't have any consequences from a mistake they have done the first time, how will he or she learn from it?~~ If cell phones are banned, children would have to be responsible for their daily responsibilities or deal with the consequences. Students that cannot remember something as simple as to bring their gym clothes to school will never be responsible enough to be in charge of a much bigger task as they grow to become adults. such as? responsibilities for college? responsibilities for career? Add before social problem examples

I don't like topic sentence - rework!!

do not ask question - make a statement

put at end of paragraph

Reorganize - 1st: consequences for mistakes 2nd: social problem solving

Calls mom + dad when teacher is mean or kids are teasing, or when girlfriend / boyfriend breaks up with him or her - doesn't figure out how to handle tough social situations or challenging emotional experiences.

Revised Paragraph

Secondly, when K-12 students have cell phones available all day, they do not learn problem-solving skills because the cell phone offers non-stop access to Mom and Dad, and every time parents step in to handle their children's problems, those children are denied the opportunity for mental and emotional growth. For example, if a child forgets his P.E. clothes for gym class, he or she can call Mom or Dad to bring them, and many times parents, not wanting little Johnny or Janie to get in trouble, will come to the rescue. When students see that all it takes is a phone call for their parents to come to the rescue, they are not learning how to solve problems on their own or how to accept the consequences for their mistakes. Students who cannot remember something as simple as bringing their gym clothes to school will never be responsible enough to be in charge of much bigger tasks as they grow into adulthood, such as remembering materials for a college course or going prepared to a job. When the cell phone is so readily available, students also tend to call their parents when they are experiencing emotional stress, and again, avoid tough situations that can teach them how to face social and emotional problems. For instance, if a girl feels her teacher is being mean, she can call her parents to come to the school and handle the issue instead of figuring out how to communicate with her teacher to come to an understanding. Or if a boy gets rejected by a girl he asked to a dance and is then teased by his classmates, he can call his parents to come and pick him up from school instead of learning how to continue on with responsibilities even though he is sad or angry. Students need to learn coping mechanisms as they grow up, and easy access to parental involvement only gets in the way of their learning these important social skills. If cell phones were banned from K-12 campuses, students would be forced to accept the consequences of their actions and to learn ways of coping.

Micro and Macro Revisions

When you revise, you should divide your revision into two parts: macro revisions and micro revisions (some instructors refer to these stages as *global* and *local*). During a macro revision, you should focus on the paper's organization and content. At this point, you should consider your readers. Does the paper's structure address the need of your readers? Would restructuring the information better address the audience's needs? Is the paper's content sufficient for the audience's knowledge of your subject? Do you need to provide additional information? Have you included too much information?

When you are satisfied with your paper's organization and content, turn your attention to the micro revision: sentence structure and diction. Ask yourself, "Is the sentence structure I use appropriate for my readers? Do I need to provide greater variety in my sentence structure?"

As part of the micro revision, consider your paper's diction, its vocabulary. Again, is the vocabulary you use in your paper appropriate for your readers? Do you need to define words or provide synonyms? You do not want to lose your readers because they do not understand your vocabulary or, conversely, because they find your choice of words inappropriate or immature.

REVISION CHECKLIST

- ☐ Does my paragraph have a clear topic sentence?
- ☐ Is the purpose of my paragraph (narration, description, explanation, or persuasion) clear to my reader?
- ☐ Is the organizational structure for my paragraph clear?
- ☐ Is there enough information in my paragraph to support the main idea?
- ☐ Did I use necessary and appropriate transitions between my supporting ideas?
- ☐ Does each sentence have a subject, a verb, and a complete thought?
- ☐ Is the meaning of each one of my sentences clear?
- ☐ Will my readers understand what I am saying in each of my sentences the first time they read them?
- ☐ Have I used a variety of sentence types: simple, compound, complex, compound/complex?
- ☐ Am I able to combine any of my sentences to avoid using only simple sentences? Can I combine simple sentences to create compound (coordination) or complex (subordination) sentences?
- ☐ Does my concluding sentence bring my paragraph to a logical close, providing a sense of completeness?
- ☐ If I wrote more than one paragraph, did I include an appropriate transition between my paragraphs?

STEP 5: EDITING/PROOFREADING

Once you are sure that your paper is organized logically for your readers, that your paper's content is sufficiently developed, and that your paper's sentence structure and vocabulary are appropriate for your audience, read your paper for spelling, grammar, and mechanical errors.

Word processors have become more adept at identifying spelling, grammar, and mechanical errors, but don't rely too heavily on the red and green wavy lines you may find in your paper. Remember, word processors are programmed to look for patterns and are not actually reading your paper. For example, your word processor may be programmed to mark as misspellings words with British spellings, such as theatre or colour. Or you may have used the wrong word and spelled the word correctly; for example, you may have meant to write *their afternoon lunch* but instead wrote *there afternoon lunch.* Your word processor will not flag the incorrect word. While your word processor may help you identify obvious errors, ultimately you must proofread your paper yourself.

While numerous proofreading tips exist, the following are suggestions that students have found most useful and effective:

1. Proofread when you are rested. If you try to proofread when you are tired, you will miss errors.

2. Manage your time so that you can put your paper aside for 24 to 48 hours before you proofread it.

3. Print your paper out, and read it out loud, slowly, reading every word.

4. Have someone read your paper out loud to you.

5. Read your paper backward sentence by sentence.

6. Use a blank sheet of paper to cover the material you have not yet proofread.

7. Don't proofread for every type of error at once. Proofread once for spelling errors and misused words. Proofread a second time for punctuation. Proofread a third time for other errors you know you are prone to make.

PROOFREADING AND EDITING CHECKLIST

- ☐ Have I eliminated any repetition and/or wordiness?
- ☐ Do all of my sentences illustrate subject-verb agreement?
- ☐ Are my verb tenses consistent? Do I change my verb tense for seemingly no reason?
- ☐ Do all my pronouns have clear, appropriate references?
- ☐ Do I have any misplaced or dangling modifiers?
- ☐ Are my sentences in active voice?
- ☐ Have I used vocabulary appropriate to my readers?
- ☐ Have I checked my spelling and not relied only on my word processor's spell checker?
- ☐ Have I capitalized the first word in each sentence and all proper nouns?
- ☐ Is all my punctuation correct?

Following the process of inventing, drafting, revising, and editing/proofreading will ultimately lead you to becoming a confident, competent writer and editor, one who approaches a writing assignment with assurance rather than apprehension and frustration.

SUBMITTING YOUR PAPER

After you have proofread your paper and are ready to submit the paper, be sure you format your paper according to the following guidelines. Although the guidelines are standard, check with your instructor to be sure they meet his or her criteria for submitting a paper.

1. Use 8 ½ × 11 paper. Write or type on one side only.
2. Double-space your writing or typing. If you are handwriting your paper, write on every other line. If you are typing your paper, set your word processor's line spacing to "Double" or "2."
3. Keep margins to 1" to 1 ½" on the top, bottom, and sides.

4. If your instructor allows you to handwrite your paper, (a) do not use pencil for the copy you submit; use a dark ink, such as black or blue, (b) make your letters distinct, and (c) distinguish between capital and lowercase letters.
5. Place your name, the date, the assignment, and the name of your instructor in the upper left corner of the paper.
6. Center your title on the first page. Generally you do not underline your own title or place your title in quotation marks. Capitalize all major words in your title; do not capitalize articles or prepositions unless they begin your title.
7. Indent new paragraphs five spaces (if typing) or one inch if writing by hand.
8. If you handwrite your paper, make your punctuation marks clear.
9. If you handwrite your paper, do not break or divide a word at the end of a line.

Chapter SUMMARY

- The final three steps in the writing process are (1) ________________ ____, (2) __________ ____, and (3) ____.
- Drafting allows you to commit all your ____________ to paper so that you do not forget them.
- The two parts of revision are (1) ______________________________ and (2) ____.

- When you proofread/edit your paper, you are checking your paper for

  (1) ______________________________,

  (2) ______________________________, and

  (3) ______________________________ errors.

- When you submit a paper, generally you do not ____________________ your title or place your title in ______________________________.

- You must ______________________________ all major words in your title; do not capitalize ______________________________ or ______________________________ unless they begin your title.

Enhancing the Fundamentals

13 VERB PHRASES

Infinitive and Participial Phrases

Chapter **PREVIEW**

In this chapter you will learn to recognize and use phrases, word groups without a subject and/or a verb. Specifically, you will learn three phrases built around verbs: infinitive phrases, present participial phrases, and past participial phrases.

In previous chapters, you learned about subjects, verbs, and clauses, three necessary components to form a complete thought. However, while *the lion attacks* may form a complete thought (and does, by itself, form a complete sentence), it lacks details, which is where phrases help because phrases add detail to sentences.

Different types of phrases exist in our language, and you can use them in your writing to expand, to describe, and to elaborate on the main idea of your sentence.

INFINITIVE PHRASES

Chapter 5 discussed infinitives as subjects. In this chapter, you will learn about **infinitive phrases**, word groups that consist of an infinitive, which is the simple form of the verb preceded by *to*, and its modifiers—words that describe the infinitive or tell you more about the infinitive. Here are some examples:

> to save money   to eat more healthfully   to hear the story
>
> Each infinitive phrase begins with an infinitive and is followed by words that tell readers more about the infinitive. These additional words modify or complement the infinitive. For example, in the infinitive phrase *to hear the story*, *to hear* is the infinitive, and *the story* modifies the infinitive because it tells readers what is being heard.

Infinitive phrases can act as adjectives, adverbs, or nouns (as in Chapter 5 when you learned that infinitives can function as subjects). Read the following examples.

> The lawyer's plan to exonerate his client would set a precedent in his field of law.
>
> The infinitive phrase *to exonerate his client* functions as an **adjective** because it describes the noun *plan*. The infinitive phrase tells us **which** plan.
>
> Mrs. Rodriguez went to the store to purchase the dinner's ingredients.
>
> The infinitive phrase *to purchase the dinner's ingredients* functions as an **adverb** because it modifies the verb *went*. The infinitive phrase explains **why** Mrs. Rodriguez went to the store.

The councilman voted to cut city services by 20 percent.

The infinitive phrase *to cut city services by 20 percent* functions as a **noun** because it is the object of the verb *voted*. It tells you **what** the councilman voted. Notice also that the infinitive phrase ends with the prepositional phrase *by 20 percent*. Prepositional phrases can be embedded within infinitive phrases.

The little boy's dream is to become a professional football player.

The infinitive phrase *to become a professional football player* functions as a **noun** because it renames the subject *dream*. The infinitive phrase tells you **what** the dream **is**.

EXERCISE 13.1: Infinitive Phrases

Draw a line through each infinitive phrase in the sentences below. On the line before each sentence, write *ADJ* if the infinitive phrase is functioning as an adjective, write *ADV* if the infinitive phrase is functioning as an adverb, and write *N* if the infinitive phrase is functioning as a noun. Be prepared to explain your answers to the class.

Example: Adv The boy stood by the window ~~to watch the snow fall gently on the lawn~~.

The infinitive phrase *to watch the snow fall gently on the lawn* functions as an adverb because it modifies the verb *stood*. The infinitive phrase explains **why** the boy stood by the window.

1. ____________ Jasmine hopes to earn the top spot in her culinary class.
2. ____________ My sister's goal this summer is to organize her shoe closet.
3. ____________ His desire to achieve stardom is becoming an obsession.
4. ____________ Professor Cruz wants his research published to solidify his reputation.
5. ____________ The last step in the writing process is to proofread carefully each sentence.

EXERCISE 13.2: Infinitive Phrases

Add an infinitive phrase to each of these main clauses.

1. Susan wants her packages ______________________________.
2. The young man went to the dentist ______________________________.

3. The couple decided ________________________________ for their picnic.
4. Jim's goal is ____.
5. After opening the door, she was able _____________________________.
6. The new employee walked into the manager's office ________________.
7. Stephanie's mother asked her three times __________________________.
8. James stood in the doorway ____________________________________.
9. Clyde reached out his hand ____________________________________.
10. Bonnie turns slowly ____.

EXERCISE 13.3: Writing Infinitive Phrases

In the spaces below, compose five sentences that include different infinitive phrases. Underline the infinitive phrases in your sentences.

1. ____
____
2. ____
____
3. ____
____
4. ____
____
5. ____
____

PARTICIPIAL PHRASES

Participial phrases consist of present participles (verbals ending in *–ing*) or past participles (verbals ending in *–ed*) and modifiers or complements for those verbals.

USAGE NOTE While the present participle of any verb, regular or irregular, will end in *-ing*, the past participle of an irregular verb may end in *-en*, *-ed*, *-d*, *-t*, and even *-e* and *-g*. It is important to learn the four principal verb forms so that you are able to use and recognize past participles correctly. Review the list of irregular verbs and their four principal parts found in Chapter 7.

Participial phrases **always** function as adjectives. As adjectives, the participial phrase should be placed as close as possible to the noun it is modifying. If you place participial phrases too far from the noun they modify, you can end up miscommunicating your idea. For more on the problems associated with misplaced participial phrases, see "Common Writing Errors" on the student companion site available at CengageBrain.com.

Read the examples below and pay attention to the use of commas.

> The petulant teenager, having been grounded for a week, shut herself in her room.
>
> The participial phrase *having been grounded for a week* contains a present participle *having* and is functioning as an adjective as it describes the noun *teenager*. Notice the use of commas around the phrase. Chapter 9 discussed the use of commas with nonrestrictive clauses. Here the same principle applies. Because the participial phrase is coming between the subject *teenager* and the verb *shut* and because the phrase is interrupting the flow of the sentence, you insert commas around the phrase.

When a participial phrase is not necessary to the sentence, when the phrase does not add to our understanding of the subject, the phrase is called *nonrestrictive*. Many textbooks and instructors also use the term *nonessential* when discussing nonrestrictive material.

However, not all participial phrases need commas placed around them when they appear in the middle of a sentence. Just as there are restrictive clauses, there are restrictive phrases. Look at the example below.

> The monkeys swinging from the trees entertained the visitors at the zoo.
>
> The participial phrase *swinging from the trees* does not have commas around it because the phrase contains restrictive (necessary or essential) information. There are many monkeys in the zoo, and the phrase *swinging from the trees* tells us **which**

> monkeys are the ones entertaining the visitors. The phrase *swinging from the trees* is essential to our understanding of the subject *monkeys*.

Compare the two sentences below.

> Mr. Smith, encouraged by his doctor to exercise more, goes to the gym four times a week.
>
> In this first sentence, there are commas around the participial phrase *encouraged by his doctor to exercise more* because the subject *Mr. Smith* is specific. Since the participial phrase does not clarify the subject in any way, the phrase is not necessary for you to understand who the subject is. Therefore, commas are used to set off the phrase from the rest of the sentence. When you do not need the participial phrase to clarify the noun, think of the commas as hooks that you can use to remove the information from the sentence.
>
> The little girl selling cookies was a previous student of mine.
>
> In this second sentence, however, the participial phrase *selling cookies* is essential to our understanding of the subject, *girl*. Think of it this way: if you and I walk into a mall and if we see several little girls standing outside the mall entrance selling cookies, and I say, "The little girl was a previous student of mine," your first question would probably be "Which little girl?" Because you do not know to which girl I am referring, the participial phrase is necessary to understand which little girl was a previous student of mine.

For more discussion on comma usage with restrictive and nonrestrictive material, reread Chapter 9, pages 134-136.

Now, take a look at comma placement when you begin a sentence with a participial phrase:

> Mumbling and grumbling under his breath, the man searched for his car keys in the couch cushions.
>
> The participial phrase *mumbling and grumbling under his breath* is functioning as an adjective as it describes the noun *man*. Since the present participial phrase introduces the sentence, you place a comma after it to set it off from the main clause.

> Injured and confused, the accident victim stumbled to the side of the road.

The History 101 essays, corrected and recorded in the grade book, were ready to return to the students.

Both sentences above contain past participial phrases. The first participial phrase, *injured and confused*, is describing the noun *victim*, and the second participial phrase, *corrected and recorded in the grade book*, describes the noun *essays*. In both sentences, the phrases are nonessential to our understanding of the sentence; the subject is already clearly identified.

EXERCISE 13.4: Participial Phrases

Draw a line through each participial phrase in the sentences below. Then, place commas where necessary. There is one sentence in which the participial phrase is restrictive (or essential), so it does not need commas. Circle the number next to that sentence and be ready to explain why you believe that sentence does not need commas.

Example: ~~Working rapidly to help~~, the volunteers passed out water bottles to the earthquake victims.

1. Singing at the top of his lungs the contestant definitely got the attention of the judges.
2. The daughter and son escorted the widow crying loudly from the funeral.
3. The little girl knocking on my door sells Girl Scout cookies.
4. The tenth place runner frustrated and defeated fell to the ground in exhaustion.
5. Exasperated from all her daughter's whining and pleading the mother finally gave in and bought the doll.

EXERCISE 13.5: Participial Phrases

Add either a present or past participial phrase to each of the main clauses below. Try to use five present participial phrases and five past participial phrases. Remember to add necessary commas if you add an introductory participial phrase or a nonrestrictive participial phrase. Also, be sure the participial phrase you compose modifies the noun that precedes or follows the phrase.

1. ______________________________ Susan wanted her packages.
2. The young man went to the dentist ______________________.

3. ______________________________ the couple decided on cucumber sandwiches for their picnic.

4. ______________________________ the chemist poured the smoking liquid into the beaker.

5. She opened the door ______________________________.

6. The new employee ______________________________ walked into the manager's office.

7. Stephanie's mother ______________________________ asked her three times to take out the trash.

8. James ______________________________ stood in the doorway.

9. ______________________________ Clyde reached out his hand.

10. Bonnie turns slowly ______________________________.

EXERCISE 13.6: Writing Participial Phrases

In the spaces below, compose five sentences: three sentences that include present participial phrases and two sentences that include past participial phrases. Underline and label the participial phrases in your sentences. Be sure to insert commas wherever necessary.

1. ______________________________

____

2. ______________________________

____

3. ______________________________

____

4. ______________________________

____

5. ______________________________

____

SENTENCE COMBINING AND SENTENCE VARIETY

Using infinitive phrases and participial phrases in your sentences enables you to create more concise prose as well as add more variety and energy to your writing. Instead of writing sentences that follow the same pattern—for example subject, verb, object—convert some sentences to phrases and attach them to the main clause to vary your writing. Read the following sentences.

> Zach plays the guitar. He writes songs for his girlfriend. He wants to impress her.
>
> Zach plays the guitar and writes songs to impress his girlfriend.
>
> Combining the first two sentences and then converting the last sentence to an infinitive phrase creates a smoother piece of writing. Rather than the stilted choppiness of three sentences that each follow the same grammatical pattern (subject first, followed by a verb), the second sentence flows more smoothly and is more succinct.

Present participles also give sentences a feeling of action and movement.

> The sushi chef displays his knife skills. He chops and slices the fish.
>
> Chopping and slicing the fish, the sushi chef displays his knife skills.
>
> The use of present participles helps the reader to visualize the actions of chopping and slicing more than if the writer had simply used the present tense. And again, changing one sentence to a participial phrase and combining that phrase with a main clause creates a smoother sentence that communicates the information more effectively.

EXERCISE 13.7: Sentence Combining and Infinitive and Participial Phrases

Combine the following sentences following the directions.

1. Combine the following sentences to create a single sentence that includes an infinitive phrase.
   A. At seven years of age, Cantrell was happy.
   B. Cantrell was going to school.

   ____

   ____

2. Combine the following sentences to create a single sentence that includes an infinitive phrase.
   A. Cindy asked for some scissors.
   B. Cindy wanted to cut out dolls.

___

___

3. Combine the following sentences to create a single sentence that includes a present participial phrase.
   A. Sabine was standing in the rain.
   B. Sabine wished she had not forgotten her umbrella.

___

___

4. Combine the following sentences to create a single sentence that includes a present participial phrase.
   A. Mike did not hear the train conductor announce the next stop.
   B. Mike was reading his favorite Harry Potter novel.

___

___

5. Combine the following sentences to create a single sentence that includes a past participial phrase.
   A. Chad needed to tear down and rebuild the shed.
   B. The shed had been badly damaged in the storm.

___

___

6. Combine the following sentences to create a single sentence that includes a past participial phrase.
   A. The cat was hidden in the bushes.
   B. The cat watched the birds splash in the bird bath.

___

___

Chapter SUMMARY

- Infinitive phrases are word groups that consist of an ________________ and its ________________.
- A participial phrase is a word group that consists of ________________ or ________________ and ________________ or ________________ of those verbals.
- If a participial phrase is in the middle of a sentence, you insert commas around the phrase if the phrase is ________________, but no commas are placed around the phrase if the phrase is ________________.
- If a phrase is at the beginning of the sentence, you insert a comma after the phrase to set it off from the ________________.

COMPONENTS AT WORK

Using Your Skills in Sentences I

Underline the phrase in each sentence. Then, on the line below the sentence, write *INF* if it is an infinitive phrase or *PAR* if it is a participial phrase. On the second line, write *ADJ* if the phrase is functioning as an adjective, *ADV* if it is functioning as an adverb, or *N* if it is functioning as a noun.

> Example: Bragging about his straight-A average, the young man alienated his friends.
>
> PAR ADJ

1. To become the world's youngest chess champion was Adam's dream.

   _______ _______

2. The puppy, running around in circles, was truly excited to see his master.

   _______ _______ _______ _______

3. The kindergarten students attempted to sing "The Star Spangled Banner."

   _______ _______

4. Ashamed of himself, the shoplifter hung his head as he was led away in handcuffs.

   _______ _______

5. Cheyenne went back to school to earn her degree in nursing.

   _______ _______

Using Your Skills in Sentences II

Complete five sentence with an infinitive phrase and five sentences with either a present or past participial phrase. Make sure to add commas if necessary.

1. ______________________________ the children misbehaved during the church service.

2. Deep in the forest, a groggy grizzly bear wandered off ______________

   ____.

3. ______________________________ the snake slithered under a rock.

4. The main objective of the city council meeting was ______________________________.

5. Mr. Cardini flew to Europe ______________________________.

6. The tornado ______________________________ headed toward the small town.

7. ______________________________ the graduate student aced his exam.

8. The culinary student's dream was ______________________________.

9. Each team needed ______________________________.

10. The protagonist in the horror film ______________________________ ran down the deserted alley.

Using Your Skills in Sentences III

Combine the following pairs of sentences so that the finished sentences include either a participial phrase or an infinitive phrase.

1. Sarah felt ill. She asked her boss if she could leave early.

____

______________________________.

2. Carlos needed help on his essay. He went to the writing center.

____

______________________________.

3. Ruby felt excited and giddy. She walked on stage for her solo.

____

____.

4. Alec was leaving in a week for the Philippines. He was eager to begin his missionary work.

____

____.

The exercises for “Using Your Skills in Reading” and “Using Your Skills in Composition” for this chapter appear in a combination “Using Your Skills in Reading” and “Using Your Skills in Composition” exercise at the end of Chapter 14.

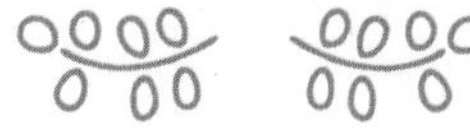

NOUN PHRASES

Prepositional, Absolute, and Appositive Phrases

Chapter PREVIEW

This chapter focuses on a second group of phrases—prepositional phrases, absolutes, and appositives—phrases created around nouns and pronouns.

In Chapter 13, you learned that you can use phrases to explain, to describe, and to elaborate on the main thought. In this chapter, you will learn three more types of phrases whose functions are to show relationships and to modify other parts of the sentence.

PREPOSITIONAL PHRASES

A **prepositional phrase** consists of a preposition, a noun or pronoun, and any words that may modify the noun or pronoun. Each prepositional phrase begins with a preposition and ends with a noun or pronoun (the object of the preposition). Remember, also, that if you end a prepositional phrase with a pronoun, the pronoun **must** be an object pronoun: *me, you, him, her, it, us, them, whom.*

Some prepositional phrases have the preposition and the object of the preposition only.

from shelves   at him   with kindness   in time   against them

However, you may also place an article or possessive pronoun between the preposition and the object of the preposition.

on	the	floor	through	the	clouds
(preposition)	(article)	(object)	(preposition)	(article)	(object)

in spite of	my	objections	beside	his	trailer
(preposition)	(poss. pro.)	(object)	(preposition)	(poss. pro.)	(object)

Additionally, you may place adjectives within the prepositional phrase.

over the large, shaggy buffalo
behind a contrite smile
toward the angry pedestrian

And prepositional phrases may also have multiple objects.

because of the wind and rain
after the boy and girl
to the dry cleaners and Laundromat

Finally, prepositional phrases may include adjectives and multiple objects.

within the lavish hotel and dining room
around the pruned bushes and trees

EXERCISE 14.1: Prepositional Phrases

Draw a line through each prepositional phrase in the sentences below.

Example: ~~During the violent storm,~~ the two dogs cowered ~~in their dog houses~~.

1. The newly married couple traveled to Jamaica for their honeymoon.
2. The kittens played rambunctiously in their cardboard box.
3. Like her Uncle Barney, Melissa preferred fruit pies to custard pies.
4. Carlos has been afraid of the dark since his first experience with an electrical blackout.
5. Ash from the volcanic eruption caused many delays at the airport.

EXERCISE 14.2: Prepositional Phrases

Add prepositional phrases to each subject and verb word group to create a more descriptive sentence. Once you finish, trade with a classmate and draw lines through the prepositional phrases in each other's sentences.

Example: 1. the baby cried

The baby cried ~~for three hours at the babysitter's house.~~

2. a siren blared

~~In the gritty neighborhood~~ a siren blared ~~like a wailing dog~~.

1. my professor lecture

____.

2. the rain poured

____.

3. an old man snored

____.

4. the surgeon operated

____.

5. the toddler pouted

____.

6. a motorcycle crashed

____.

7. the boss yelled

____.

8. a light flickered

____.

9. two bear cubs frolicked

____.

10. the president spoke

____.

ABSOLUTE PHRASES

An **absolute phrase** is a group of words consisting of a noun or pronoun and the *-ing* or *-ed* form of a verb (in other words, a present or past participle) and any modifiers. An absolute (from the Latin word meaning *loose*) phrase modifies the entire sentence and adds nonessential information. Study the following sentences.

> Their flight was booked. The family looked forward to their vacation.
>
> The artist's paintings are typically dark and depressing. The pictures hang in galleries around the world.
>
> The family hired a local contractor. Their neighbors highly recommended her.

Notice that the above sentences are largely short and choppy. When you combine the sentences by changing one of the sentences into an absolute phrase, you create a sentence that is more fluid and more clearly communicates the relationship between the ideas in the two individual sentences.

Now, look at how the original sentences have been combined using absolute phrases, which are highlighted in green. The noun and participle for each absolute phrase is indicated also.

> (noun) (part.)
> Their flight booked, the family looked forward to their vacation.
>
> Dropping the verb *was*, a form of the verb *to be*, from the first sentence creates the absolute phrase, *Their flight booked.*

(noun) (part.)
The artist's paintings, pictures hanging in galleries around the world, are typically dark and depressing.

Changing the main verb *hang* in what was originally the second sentence to *hanging* creates the absolute phrase, *pictures hanging in galleries around the world.*

(noun) (part.)
The family hired a local contractor, their neighbors highly recommending her.

By changing *recommended* in the second sentence to *recommending*, you create an absolute phrase that ends the sentence, *their neighbors highly recommending her.*

Since an absolute phrase modifies the entire sentence, you can insert the phrase most anywhere in your sentence, as illustrated in the above sentences. In addition to creating more fluid sentences, absolute phrases also add to your sentence variety. All in all, using an absolute phrase is an effective way to improve your writing.

At first glance, an absolute phrase may appear to be a sentence. But a form of the verb *to be* is missing or the main verb in the clause has been changed into its *-ing* form. So an absolute phrase cannot stand alone as a complete sentence.

EXERCISE 14.3: Absolute Phrases

Underline the absolute phrases in the following sentences.

Example: The phone ringing, Jessup looked at the caller ID.

1. Autumn stared at her bookcase, the shelves sagging under the weight of too many books.
2. The test completed, Tyler closed his eyes and smiled.
3. Kerry, her room cleaned and dusted, ran outside to join her friends.
4. Snow gently falling outside, Colleen sipped hot chocolate in her kitchen.
5. The professor lectured on the Civil War, his students furiously taking notes.

EXERCISE 14.4: Absolute Phrases

Combine the following sentences to create a single sentence modified by an absolute phrase. Remember to place a comma after an introductory absolute phrase, to surround the absolute phrase with commas if you insert it in the middle of your sentence, and to precede the absolute phrase with a comma if you place the absolute phrase at the end of your sentence.

Example: 1. The woman sits impatiently in the waiting room.

2. The cup of ice is shaking in her hand.

The cup of ice shaking in her hand, the woman sits impatiently in the waiting room.

1. A parrot landed in the tree.
2. The sun was shining brightly.

____

____

1. The empty serving tray was standing in the corner of the room.
2. The dinner guests waited eagerly for their first course.

____

____

1. A backpack was slung over his right shoulder.
2. The young man walked happily down the trail.

____

____

1. All the preliminary races were finished.
2. The finalists prepared for the last race.

____

____

COMPONENTS AT WORK

Using Your Skills in Sentences I

Compose sentences that include the phrases indicated. Circle the phrase. If necessary, review the various phrases and their functions from this chapter.

> Example: Prepositional phrase that ends the sentence
>
> The lawyers argued (in front of the judge.)

1. Prepositional phrase that begins the sentence

   ____

2. Prepositional phrase in the middle of a sentence

   ____

3. Absolute phrase

   ____

4. Restrictive appositive

   ____

5. Nonrestrictive appositive

   ____

Using Your Skills in Sentences II

Combine the following sets of sentences into a single main clause that includes the phrase indicated. If necessary, do not hesitate to review the various phrases from this chapter and Chapter 13.

> Example: A present participial phrase
>
> a. The interviewee asked for a glass of water.
> b. The man continually cleared his throat.
>
> Asking for a glass of water, the interviewee continually cleared his throat.

1. A present participial phrase
   a. The car passed a small herd of elk.
   b. The elk were standing by the side of the road.

____

____

2. A past participial phrase
   a. The shed needed to be repaired.
   b. The shed had been damaged in the recent storm.

____

____

3. A prepositional phrase
   a. The ducks swam lazily.
   b. The ducks were on the lake.

____

____

4. An absolute phrase
   a. The queen smiled and nodded.
   b. The crowd was jostling to see her majesty.

____

____

5. An appositive
   a. Dr. Jones teaches seismology.
   b. Seismology is the study of earthquake activity.

____

____

Using Your Skills in Reading

Read the following paragraph. Be sure you understand each word in its context. If you need to, look up words, so make sure to have a dictionary or your smart phone nearby. After reading through the paragraph for understanding, read it again and underline the phrases or phrases in each sentence.

Then, above each phrase write PREP if the phrase is a prepositional phrase, INF if the phrase is an infinitive phrase, PART if the phrase is a participial phrase, ABS if the phrase is an absolute phrase, and APP if the phrase is an appositive.

An Important Invention

What is the most important invention in the world in the last 500 years? People have suggested a number of items including the printing press, electricity, the wheel, the transistor, the automobile, the sewing machine, and antibiotics. All of these inventions and discoveries have, without a doubt, contributed to world progress. But an overlooked, yet good, candidate for the most important invention would have to be indoor plumbing, a relatively new home addition. The consequences of indoor plumbing are invaluable. Allowing towns and cities to bring clean water to large populated areas and rural families, indoor plumbing revolutionized America. Before indoor plumbing, people threw their bodily wastes into the streets and gutters or used the great outdoors and eventually outhouses, small, enclosed buildings situated over an open pit or latrine, similar to modern-day portable toilets or Porta Potties. In these situations, disease and illness were common, cholera, typhoid, and childhood diarrhea wiping out entire families. Indoor plumbing provided greater sanitation and reduced diseases and illnesses. In addition, before indoor plumbing, families often bathed only once a week, frequently members of the family using the same bath water, since water needed to be carried from a well and heated on

the stove. Indoor plumbing made bathing, previously suspected of contributing to illnesses, a more common activity because not only was water itself more accessible, but both cold and hot water was now available. Washing dishes and clothing also became easier. Also, with indoor plumbing, cities could build up rather than merely out. Imagine high rise buildings, apartments, and offices without indoor plumbing. Whether or not you believe indoor plumbing is the most important invention in the world, without a doubt indoor plumbing has profoundly impacted the way we live our lives.

Using Your Skills in Composition

Compose a paragraph about an object that you believe is important or essential in your life. Include at least one each of the following types of phrases in your paragraph: infinitive phrase (INF), participial phrase (PAR), prepositional phrase (PRE), absolute phrase (ABS), and an appositive (APP). Underline each one and identify it by the abbreviations indicated.

15 SIMPLE AND COMPOUND SENTENCES

Chapter PREVIEW

In this chapter you will learn about two of the four sentence types in English: simple and compound. Once you master simple and compound sentences, you will learn about complex and compound-complex sentences in Chapter 16. Understanding the four types of sentences will allow you to vary your sentence structures to create interesting prose and clear ideas.

Read the following paragraph:

> Tammy walks to the store. The store is down the street from her house. Tammy goes to the store to buy popsicles. Her throat is sore. She thinks the popsicles will help. She hopes the popsicles will make her throat feel better. Tammy forgets her wallet. She forgets her wallet because her throat hurts. She has to walk back home. She has to walk back home to get her wallet. Tammy has to walk back to the store to buy popsicles.

Because each sentence in the above paragraph follows the same structure (subject—verb—object) and because the writer repeats much of the information (*Tammy, popsicles, throat,* etc.), most readers would find the above paragraph monotonous and repetitious, even boring.

Now, compare the following paragraph to the one above:

> Tammy walks to the store down the street from her house. Because her throat is sore, she wants to buy popsicles, for she believes the popsicles will make her throat feel better. However, because her throat hurts so much, Tammy forgets her wallet, and she has to walk back home to get it before she can finally walk back to the store to buy some popsicles.

The second paragraph has more variety in sentence structure and, therefore, flows more easily and is more interesting for the reader.

To avoid writing lackluster, dreary, repetitive sentences, you should know how to use and compose four types of sentences:

- the simple sentence
- the compound sentence
- the complex sentence (Chapter 16)
- the compound-complex sentence (Chapter 16).

Knowing a variety of sentence types allows you not only the ability to vary your sentence structures to keep your prose fresh and appealing, but also the ability to communicate more effectively with your readers.

SIMPLE SENTENCES

A **simple sentence** consists of one main clause (for a review of both main and subordinate clauses see Chapter 9).

> A wooden figure of Shakespeare sits on my desk.
>
> This single main clause contains a single subject *figure* and a single verb *sits* and is a complete thought.

However, simple sentences can also have

- compound subjects and single verbs

> Barbara, Elena, and Sozan enjoy surfing California's beaches.
>
> The above sentence contains the compound subject *Barbara, Elena,* and *Sozan* and a single verb *enjoy*.

- single subjects and compound verbs

> Justin attends school during the day and works at night.
>
> The above sentence contains the single subject *Justin* and the compound verb *attends* and *works*.

- compound subjects and compound verbs

> Hector, Emily, and Victor rode motorcycles, fished several trout streams, and hiked part of the Pacific Crest Trail during their last vacation.
>
> The above sentence contains the compound subject *Hector, Emily,* and *Victor* and the compound verb *rode, fished,* and *hiked*.

USAGE NOTE When a sentence contains compound subjects and/or compound verbs, remember that the coordinating conjunction that links the subjects and/or the verbs is not part of the complete subject or the complete verb. So in the last example, the subject is *Hector, Emily, Victor*, **not** *Hector, Emily, and Victor*. And the verb is *rode, fished, hiked*, **not** *rode, fished, and hiked*.

Because a simple sentence is one main clause, a simple sentence contains a single idea or thought. However, even if a simple sentence contains compound subjects or compound verbs, since the word group is a single simple sentence, you still have only one idea or thought. Think of it this way: even though a compound subject may have two or more nouns or pronouns—such as Hector, Emily, and Victor—the nouns are working together as one unit, one subject.

EXERCISE 15.1: Subjects and Verbs in Simple Sentences

Identify the following simple sentences as single subject, single verb (SS), compound subject, single verb (CS), single subject, compound verb (SC), or compound subject, compound verb (CC).

Example: __SC__ Analise scratched her head and furrowed her brows during the difficult exam.

1. _____ Dan and Jan danced and sang throughout the evening.
2. _____ Stewart nicknamed his brother "Cricket."
3. _____ Diana polished her shoes and ironed her dress to prepare for the interview.
4. _____ With all the boxes and papers, Larry's office looks like a storage shed.
5. _____ Glen, Alvin, Stephanie, and Mary sing in the church choir.
6. _____ Coca Cola and Pepsi are two top selling soft drinks.
7. _____ Pictures and papers littered and overflowed the desk.
8. _____ Lizards and hummingbirds are territorial creatures.
9. _____ The birds splashed in the bird bath and then fluttered in the dust.
10. _____ Paper plates and plastic cups littered the park and filled the trash cans.

EXERCISE 15.2: Subjects and Verbs in Simple Sentences

Compose sentences according to the directions.

1. Compose a simple sentence with a single subject and a single verb.

   ____

   ____

2. Compose a simple sentence with a compound subject and a compound verb.

   ____

   ____

3. Compose a simple sentence with a single subject and a compound verb.

   ____

   ____

4. Compose a simple sentence with a compound subject and a single verb.

   ____

   ____

5. Compose a simple sentence of your choosing and underline your subject once and your verb twice.

____

____

COMPOUND SENTENCES

A **compound sentence** is composed of two or more main clauses. When you connect the main clauses, it is important that you do not create a run-on sentence, so pay attention to the correct ways to join main clauses together. There are three ways to correctly join main clauses:

- a comma and a coordinating conjunction

> I opened the refrigerator, but somebody had already eaten the last piece of apple pie.

- a semicolon

> I opened the refrigerator; somebody had already eaten the last piece of apple pie.

- a semicolon and an adverbial conjunction, which is followed by a comma.

> I opened the refrigerator; however, somebody had already eaten the last piece of apple pie.

Compound Sentences and Coordinating Conjunctions

To create a compound sentence using a comma and a coordinating conjunction, you must choose from among the seven coordinating conjunctions *for, and, nor, but, or, yet, so*, which you learned in Chapter 3.

The seven coordinating conjunctions convey distinct relationships between the two main clauses they connect.

> For = cause
> Jenny enjoyed camping, for it got her away from the office.
>
> And = addition
> At the store, I bought bagels, and I bought cream cheese.
>
> Nor = alternative or a negation of both main clauses
> alternative: I neither wish your help, nor do I want your pity.

Nor can be used with *neither* as a correlative conjunction; correlative conjunctions are discussed in Chapter 3.

negation: He does not smoke, nor does he drink.

But = contrast

I type well, but I do not type fast.

Or = alternative

I can drive, or I can navigate.

Yet = contrast

Rebecca seems well, yet I am worried.

So = purpose

I want to be the first in line for the concert, so I am camping out this week.

USAGE NOTE You can also use coordinating conjunctions to join not only main clauses but also words and phrases, for example,

Ted and Amisha enjoy eating Chile Verde.

Over by the fence but under the shed lives a ferret.

When a coordinating conjunction separates words or phrases, you do not place a comma before the coordinating conjunction. You place a comma before the coordinating conjunction only when the coordinating conjunction separates two or more main clauses.

Compound Sentences and Semicolons

When you join main clauses with a semicolon, you are telling your reader the two ideas in the two clauses have something in common; they reflect a logical relationship. You should not place a semicolon between main clauses if no obvious relationship between the clauses exists.

For example, the following compound sentence would **not** be a good use of the semicolon.

Sammy is well over six feet tall; he loves eating pizza.

What does Sammy's height have to do with his love of eating pizza? These two main clauses would be better presented as two simple sentences or joined by the coordinating conjunction *and*.

However, the following sentence shows correct usage of the semicolon.

> Sammy is well over six feet tall; he plays forward on his high school's basketball team.
>
> This sentence warrants the use of the semicolon since a logical relationship exists between a person's height and playing basketball.

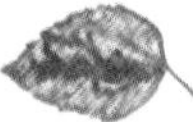

EXERCISE 15.3: Compound Sentences and Semicolons

Identify the compound sentences that use the semicolon correctly by marking an X on the line provided. Be prepared to explain your choices.

Example: _X_ Padme stared intently at the cell phone in her hand; she eagerly anticipated her agent's call.

(Explanation: The semicolon is used correctly here because the second main clause explains why Padme is staring at her phone. The two clauses show a cause/effect relationship)

1. _____ Coltrane is a designer; he usually goes to bed at 10:30 p.m.
2. _____ The bull stood contentedly under the cork tree; the tree's shade provided relief from the heat.
3. _____ The spider sat patiently in the middle of its web; it waited for its next meal.
4. _____ My calculator figures numbers to eight digits; I have five fingers on each hand.
5. _____ The silent movie starred Mr. John Barrymore; he performed in the 1920s.

EXERCISE 15.4: Semicolons and Compound Sentences

In the space following each main clause, insert a second main clause that logically follows from the first.

Example: <u>A sundial is useless on a cloudy day; a solar powered watch isn't much better</u>.

1. Texting while driving is increasing; ______________________________.
2. Timothy was hungry for pizza; ______________________________.
3. The bookshelf stood against the wall; ______________________________.

4. The rain fell heavily throughout the night; ________________________.

5. His room was a complete mess; ______________________________.

Compound Sentences and Adverbial Conjunctions

You may join main clauses with not only a comma and a coordinating conjunction or a semicolon, but also a semicolon, an adverbial conjunction (also known as an conjunctive adverb or a transition word), and a comma.

> Sally had the book opened on her lap; however, her eyes were closed.

Common adverbial conjunctions include the following (**Table 15.1**), which are categorized according to use:

TABLE 15.1 Common adverbial conjunctions

Time and Chronology	Cause and Effect	Comparison and Contrast	Additional Information	Emphasis
finally	therefore	on the other hand	additionally	certainly
then	as a result	however	for example	in fact
next	thus	likewise	for instance	still
meanwhile	accordingly	in contrast	furthermore	
	hence	nonetheless	also	
	consequently	instead	besides	
		nevertheless	in addition	
			moreover	

Like coordinating conjunctions, adverbial conjunctions also indicate the relationship between the two main clauses.

For example, if you want to show contrast, you might use the adverbial conjunctions *however* or *instead.*

> Bryan wanted to attend the AC/DC concert**;** however**,** he had to grade student papers.

Or if you want to show addition, you might use the adverbial conjunctions *in addition* or *likewise* or *moreover.*

> Christine ordered a large latte**;** in addition**,** she considered a bagel.

And if you wish to show cause or effect, you could use *consequently* or *subsequently* or *therefore.*

> The flashlight bulb went out**;** consequently**,** Gene tripped over the tree root.

6. _____ Silvia preened in front of the mirror for she wanted to impress her date.
7. _____ Myron could not remember the young boy or the young girl by name.
8. _____ Twelve pencils lay on the desk yet not one was sharpened.
9. _____ The old, faded blue jeans and the torn AC/DC t-shirt were the perfect outfit for the concert.
10. _____ Stan did not want to study nor did he want to go out so he went to bed.

EXERCISE 15.7: Compound Sentences and Coordinating Conjunctions

Follow the directions below.

1. Compose a compound sentence that uses the conjunction *and.*

   ____

   ____

2. Compose a compound sentence that uses the conjunctions *but* and *so.*

   ____

   ____

3. Compose a compound sentence that uses the conjunction *for.*

   ____

   ____

4. Compose a compound sentence that uses the conjunction *yet.*

   ____

   ____

5. Compose a compound sentence that uses the conjunction *nor.*

   ____

   ____

The illustration below will help you remember the type and number of clauses in simple and compound sentences. MC = Main Clause; cc = Coordinating Conjunction; ac = Adverbial Conjunction

Simple Sentence = **1 MC**
Compound Sentence = **2 MC or more (the clauses can be joined as illustrated below)**
MC, cc MC
MC; MC
MC; ac, MC

SIMPLE AND COMPOUND SENTENCES AND SENTENCE COMBINING

As noted at the beginning of this chapter, knowing the different sentence patterns will allow you to vary your sentence structure and make your writing more engaging and interesting.

A good exercise for learning to compose different sentence patterns is sentence combining. As you learned in Chapter 9, with sentence combining, you can make your writing more concise by

- joining the subjects of two simple sentences to create a compound subject for one simple sentence,
- joining the verbs of two simple sentences to create a compound verb for one simple sentence,
- or joining two simple sentences to create a compound sentence.

Look at the two simple sentences below:

> Bella went to the Laundromat. She also stopped at the grocery store.

You can combine these two simple sentences to create a simple sentence with a compound verb, or you can join the two simple sentences together to create a compound sentence.

> Bella went to the Laundromat and stopped at the grocery store.
>
> Bella went to the Laundromat, and she stopped at the grocery store.
>
> The first revision is a simple sentence with a single subject and a compound verb. The second revision is a compound sentence that joins together both simple sentences with a comma and the coordinating conjunction *and.* The coordinating conjunction between the clauses tells readers both activities were equally important.

EXERCISE 15.8: Sentence Combining and Simple and Compound Sentences

Combine the following sentences according to the directions for each exercise.

Example: Combine the following simple sentences to create a simple sentence with a compound verb.

A. Professor Singh shares personal stories in class.

B. Professor Singh laughs at his own jokes in class.

<u>Professor Singh shares personal stories and laughs at his own jokes in class</u>.

1. Combine the following simple sentences to create a simple sentence with a compound subject.
   A. Taylor drove to the park for a picnic.
   B. Nisa drove to the park for a picnic.

   ____

   ____

2. Combine the following simple sentences to create a simple sentence with a compound verb.
   A. Ms. Baker always mowed her lawn on Fridays.
   B. Ms. Baker always edged her lawn on Fridays.

   ____

   ____

3. Combine the following simple sentences to create a simple sentence with compound subjects and compound verbs.
   A. Dr. Kazinsky rode his bike to work each day and parked it in the bike lot.
   B. Dr. Kim rode his bike to work each day and parked it in the bike lot.

   ____

   ____

4. Combine the following simple sentences to create a compound sentence that uses an appropriate coordinating conjunction.
   A. Hilda swam ten miles each day.
   B. Her coach wanted her to swim twelve miles a day.

   ____

   ____

5. Combine the following simple sentences to create a compound sentence that uses a semicolon.
   A. Aimee enjoyed texting her friends.
   B. Aimee's last phone bill listed 9,000 texts.

   ____

   ____

6. Combine the following simple sentences to create a compound sentence that uses a semicolon and an appropriate adverbial conjunction.
   A. Nick was apprehensive about driving on the icy roads.
   B. Nick needs to attend the scheduled meeting.

   ____

   ____

Chapter SUMMARY

- The four types of sentences in English are (1) ____________________, (2) ____________________, (3) ____________________, and (4) ____________________.
- A simple sentence contains ____________________.
- A compound sentence contains ____________________.
- When you compose a compound sentence, you are telling your readers that the ideas in each clause are equally important. This concept is called ____________________.

COMPONENTS AT WORK

Using Your Skills in Sentences I

Using the components you have studied in Chapters 4, 9, 13, and 14, in the spaces below, compose five simple sentences as directed. Although the types of phrases you are instructed to use appear last in the directions, you may place them anywhere in the sentences.

1. Compose a simple sentence with a single subject and a single verb that includes an infinitive phrase.

   ____

   ____

2. Compose a simple sentence with a compound subject and a single verb that includes a present participial phrase.

   ____

   ____

3. Compose a simple sentence with a compound subject and a compound verb that includes a past participial phrase.

   ____

   ____

4. Compose a simple sentence with a single subject and a compound verb that includes a prepositional phrase.

   ____

   ____

5. Compose a simple sentence with a single subject and a single verb that includes an appositive.

   ____

   ____

Using Your Skills in Sentences II

Using the components you have studied in Chapters 9, 13, and 14, in the spaces below, compose five compound sentences as directed. Although the types of phrases you are instructed to use appear last in the directions, you may place them anywhere in the sentences.

1. Compose a compound sentence that uses a semicolon and a prepositional phrase.

   ____

   ____

2. Compose a compound sentence that uses the coordinating conjunction *but* and a present participial phrase.

   ____

   ____

3. Compose a compound sentence that uses the coordinating conjunction *so* and an infinitive phrase.

   ____

   ____

4. Compose a compound sentence that uses the coordinating conjunction *and* and an appositive.

   ____

   ____

5. Compose a compound sentence that includes an absolute phrase.

   ____

   ____

Using Your Skills in Reading

After reading the following paragraph once for understanding, read it again, paying attention to the sentence structures. Next to each number underneath the paragraph, identify that sentence as either simple or compound.

The Name Means What?

[1]The origin of a name, whether the name of a place or person, can be as interesting as the name itself. [2]For example, in Southern California just north of San Diego is the town of Escondido. [3]The word *escondido* is actually the past participle of the Spanish verb *esconder*, meaning *to hide,* so the word Escondido means *hidden.* [4]But today with a six-lane freeway coursing by, Escondido, California, is no longer hard to find. [5]The story about the naming of Plainview, Texas, goes like this: one day a young woman and her beau went out for a buggy ride, and after a few minutes, the young man asked the young woman for a kiss, but she looked back and could still see town and said, "No, we're still in plain view." [6]The land is flat in the northern part of Texas, Plainview's location, so the young man probably had to go quite a way before getting that kiss. [7]State names can also have curious origins. [8]Wyoming is an Algonquin Indian word meaning "large prairie place." [9]Georgia was named for King George II of England, reigning from 1727 until his death in 1760. [10]And *Idaho* seems to be an invented word. [11]Supposedly a mining lobbyist by the name of George M. Willing presented the name *Idaho,* allegedly a Shoshone Indian term meaning "Gem of the Mountains," to congress for a new territory. [12]Willing's lie was eventually exposed, but by that time, the name *Idaho* was commonly used; the name remained. [13]People's names can also be unusual. [14]Sarah Ann Hogg and her husband James Stephen Hogg must not have considered their daughter's feelings when naming her Ima; nevertheless,

James Hogg named his daughter after a character from the Civil War poem *The Fate of Marvin.* [15]One can only wonder: why didn't he name his daughter after the only other woman in the poem, Leila? [16]And the choice of the name Cassandra for a girl is curious. [17]In Greek mythology, Cassandra was granted the gift of prophecy; she foresaw the fall of Troy, and, in fact, warned the Trojans about trickery involved with the Trojan Horse. [18]Her foresight was true and accurate, but because of her curse, no one would believe her prophecies. [19]Many more interesting stories about the names of familiar places and people abound. [20]Learning the name origins of both the places and people in our lives broadens our appreciation of their uniqueness.

1. ______________________ 2. ______________________

3. ______________________ 4. ______________________

5. ______________________ 6. ______________________

7. ______________________ 8. ______________________

9. ______________________ 10. ______________________

11. ______________________ 12. ______________________

13. ______________________ 14. ______________________

15. ______________________ 16. ______________________

17. ______________________ 18. ______________________

19. ______________________ 20. ______________________

Using Your Skills in Composition

Write a paragraph composed of simple and compound sentences that examines the origins of your name as well as the names of your family members and/or friends. You could also investigate the name of the town in which you live and surrounding towns as well as local landmarks.

16 COMPLEX AND COMPOUND-COMPLEX SENTENCES

Chapter PREVIEW

In this chapter you will learn about the remaining two types of sentences in English: complex and compound-complex. Like simple and compound sentences, complex and compound-complex sentences allow you to add greater variety and convey importance.

COMPLEX SENTENCES

A **complex sentence** is a group of words that contains one main clause and one or more subordinate clauses. Study the several examples below.

> As Tabitha stood in the rain, she could feel the water dripping into her boots.
>
> In this complex sentence, an introductory subordinate adverb clause, in green, precedes the main clause.
>
> When Juan arrived at his home, which was in complete disarray, he immediately began cleaning.
>
> Two introductory subordinate clauses, one adverb and one adjective, precede the main clause in this complex sentence.
>
> Ruth was angry because the train [that she rode each day] was late once again.
>
> The main clause is followed by two subordinate clauses, an adjective clause, in square brackets, placed inside the adverb clause.

As you learned in Chapter 9, subordinate clauses can be identified as either adjective or adverb subordinate clauses.

As you will remember, adjective subordinate clauses begin with the relative pronouns:

That	Who	Whoever	Where
Which	Whose	Whomever	
	Whom		

Common adverb subordinate conjunctions are included in **Table 16.1**.

TABLE 16.1 Common adverb subordinate conjunctions

Cause and Effect	Concession	Condition	Comparison and Contrast	Manner	Opposition	Place	Time
as	although	even if	as	as if	although	where	after
because	as if	if	as if	as though	though	wherever	before
in order that	even though	in case (that)	although		even though		since
now that	though	only if	even though		whereas		when
since	while	provided that	whereas		while		whenever
so		unless	while				while
so that		until					until
		whether or not					as
							as . . . as
							once

EXERCISE 16.1: Complex Sentences with Adjective and Adverb Clauses

In the spaces provided, compose complex sentences following the directions.

Example: Compose a complex sentence that uses an adjective subordinate clause beginning with the relative pronoun *that*. Underline your adjective subordinate clause.

Example: Professor Collins asked his students to write an essay <u>that explained the process of photosynthesis</u>.

1. Compose a complex sentence that uses an adjective subordinate clause beginning with the relative pronoun *which*. Underline your adjective subordinate clause.

   ____

   ____

2. Compose a complex sentence that uses an adjective subordinate clause beginning with the relative pronoun *who*. Underline your adjective subordinate clause.

   ____

   ____

3. Compose a complex sentence that uses an adverb subordinate clause beginning with the subordinating conjunction *because*. Underline your adverb subordinate clause.

   ____

   ____

4. Compose a complex sentence that uses an adverb subordinate clause beginning with the subordinating conjunction *although*. Underline your adverb subordinate clause.

   ____

   ____

5. Compose a complex sentence that uses an adverb subordinate clause beginning with the subordinating conjunction *before*. Underline your adverb subordinate clause.

____

____

Complex Sentences and Subordination

Since a complex sentence contains one main clause and one or more subordinate clauses, a complex sentence contains two or more ideas or thoughts.

But unlike a compound sentence in which the clauses are equal in importance, the ideas in a complex sentence are arranged into a hierarchy of importance with the main clause presenting the most important idea and the subordinate clause or clauses presenting the lesser idea. Look at the following sentence:

> David jogs three miles each day, and he works out in the gym for another hour.
>
> In this sentence, since the two main clauses compose a compound sentence, both ideas are of equal importance.

Now, look at this next sentence:

> Even though David jogs three miles each day, he works out in the gym for another hour.
>
> In this second sentence, since the first clause is a subordinate adverb clause, the idea is secondary (subordinate) to the idea in the main clause. So in the second sentence, David's working out in the gym for an additional hour is a more important idea than the idea he runs three miles each day.

Can you change which clause is primary by changing the clause you subordinate? Of course, you can.

Instead of "Even though David jogs three miles each day, he works out in the gym for another hour," you could write, "David jogs three miles each day, although he works out in the gym for another hour." Now the primary idea is David runs three miles each day, and the secondary idea is David works out in the gym for an extra hour.

So depending upon how you want to arrange the ideas in your sentences, you can either coordinate or subordinate your thoughts to let your readers know which ideas are of primary importance and which ideas are of secondary importance.

Complex Sentences and Commas

When a subordinate clause introduces a sentence, put a comma after the introductory clause:

> When the sun rose over the mountain tops, the temperature slowly began to rise.
>
> As the dog ran along the shore, he splashed in the waves.
>
> Because his computer crashed, Tim couldn't finish his online game.

But when a subordinate clause ends a sentence, you generally do not place a comma before the concluding subordinate clause.

> The driver of the red car slammed on her brakes when a ball rolled into her path.

You do insert a comma before the subordinate clause, however, when the clause is a nonrestrictive adjective clause (for a review of both restrictive and nonrestrictive clauses see Chapter 9, pages 134-138).

> The horse leaned against the wooden fence, which bowed with the horse's weight.

You also add a comma when the subordinate clause following the main clause contradicts or opposes the idea in the main clause (for a review of comma usage with adverb subordinate clauses, see Chapter 9, pages 132-134).

> The quail ran across the front yard, although a cat lounged on the front porch.
>
> The cacti were all blooming, whereas the succulents were barren.

EXERCISE 16.2: Commas and Complex Sentences

Insert commas after introductory subordinate clauses or before nonrestrictive adjective clauses that end the sentence. If the sentence does not require a comma, mark the sentence with the letter *C* for correct.

1. After the game ended the team celebrated its victory over its cross-town rival.
2. The wallet lay on the desk which was cluttered with papers.
3. When Stanley opened the card he smiled after reading the verse inside.

4. Maria studied the pictures that she found in the old family album.
5. Because Serena's watch had stopped she had to check her cell phone for the time.
6. Gloria received an exquisite pair of driving gloves which were made from imported leather.
7. The couple continued their ice skating performance although the male skater had fallen early in the routine.
8. Even though some of the math problems required advanced computations the instructor did not allow his students to use calculators.
9. The garden included many cacti that were imported from deserts from around the world.
10. Since the sun had set the couple built a fire in the fireplace.

EXERCISE 16.3: Commas and Complex Sentences

Now that you have reviewed comma usage with complex sentences and practiced inserting commas where necessary in Exercise 16.2, go back to your sentences in Exercise 16.1. Check each sentence for correct comma placement, looking for both unnecessary commas as well as missing commas. Use a different colored pen, so you and your instructor can see where corrections were needed. Cross out any unneeded commas and add any missing commas.

COMPOUND-COMPLEX SENTENCES

You compose a **compound-complex** sentence when you join two main clauses and one or more subordinate clauses. The following sentence contains an introductory subordinate clause followed by two main clauses joined by the coordinating conjunction *and.*

> Before he went to bed, Gregory turned on the alarm, and he double-checked all the locks.
>
> In a compound-complex sentence, the subordinate clause or clauses can **begin** the sentence, as in the sentence above, come **between** the compound sentences, or **end** the compound-complex sentence.

Jocelyn asked for the most up-to-date phone for her birthday since she wanted all the new applications, but no one in her family could afford the phone.

The subordinate clause, in green, comes between the two main clauses.

Jocelyn asked for the most up-to-date phone for her birthday, but no one in her family could afford the phone since the phone cost several hundred dollars.

The two main clauses come before the subordinate clause, which ends the sentence.

Compound-Complex Sentences and Coordination and Subordination

Since compound-complex sentences contain at least three clauses, a compound-complex sentence contains at least three ideas. Writers punctuate compound-complex sentences in the same way they would compound sentences and complex sentences. Below are examples of various combinations of compound-complex sentences and their punctuation.

Unless Cinderella was home by midnight, her carriage would turn into a pumpkin, but she ran through the door with a few seconds to spare.

The example above shows an introductory subordinate clause, followed by two main clauses joined by the coordinating conjunction *but.*

Unless Cinderella was home by midnight, her carriage would turn into a pumpkin; she ran through the door with a few seconds to spare.

This example shows an introductory subordinate clause, followed by two main clauses joined by a semicolon.

Unless Cinderella was home by midnight, her carriage would turn into a pumpkin; however, she ran through the door with a few seconds to spare.

Here you see an introductory subordinate clause, followed by two main clauses joined by a semicolon, and an appropriate adverbial conjunction.

The prince followed Cinderella to her father's house, which was only a few blocks from the castle, and he tried to discover her hiding place.

In the example above, the two main clauses are separated by a nonrestrictive subordinate clause, which modifies *house.*

The prince followed Cinderella to her father's house, but he could not find her since she was hiding.

The two main clauses, joined by *but*, precede the subordinate adverb clause.

The prince followed Cinderella to her father's house; however, he could not find her since she was hiding.

The two main clauses, joined by the adverbial conjunction *however*, precede the subordinate adverb clause.

The prince followed Cinderella to her father's house, yet since he could not find her, he looked for her until the next day.

Here, the subordinate adverb clause is after the coordinating conjunction *yet* and before the remainder of the second main clause.

As the seven sentences above illustrate, you can arrange compound-complex sentences in many ways.

EXERCISE 16.4: Punctuation and Compound-Complex Sentences

Following the rules for punctuating compound and complex sentences, punctuate the following compound-complex sentences.

1. If we don't prune the apple trees we will not receive a good harvest of fruit however we could always buy apples at the grocery store.

2. Glen's car skidded and it slid into a curb when he slammed on the brakes to miss the cat running across the street.

3. Gary's illness which lasted more than a week kept him from going to work so he telecommuted when he could.

4. Jody enjoyed visiting museums that exhibited Freda Kahlo paintings and she also sought out the paintings of Georgia O'Keefe.

5. The grass needed mowing but the day was far too hot so Ashley stayed in the house which was air conditioned.

Below is a visual to help you remember the type and number of clauses in complex and compound-complex sentences. MC = Main Clause; SC = Subordinate Clause.

Complex Sentence = **1 MC + 1 (or more) SC**
Compound-Complex = **2 MC* + 1 (or more) SC**

*See Chapter 15 pages 250-254 for the three ways to join compound sentences.

COMPLEX AND COMPOUND-COMPLEX SENTENCES AND SENTENCE COMBINING

As noted in Chapter 15, using different sentence patterns will allow you to write more compelling and interesting sentences. Review Chapter 15 pages 257-259 on sentence combining before beginning the following exercises.

EXERCISE 16.5: Complex Sentences and Sentence Combining

Combine the following sentences according to the directions for each exercise. Be sure to insert commas when necessary and appropriate.

1. Combine the following simple sentences to create a complex sentence that uses the subordinate conjunction *when* to begin the subordinate clause.
   A. Wilbert bought a new XKE Jaguar for his birthday.
   B. All his neighbors stopped by to look at the new car.

   ____

   ____

2. Combine the following simple sentences to create a complex sentence that uses an appropriate subordinate conjunction to begin the subordinate clause.
   A. Andrew used a level to hang the two pictures.
   B. The pictures were still crooked.

   ____

   ____

3. Combine the following simple sentences to create a compound-complex sentence that uses the subordinate conjunction *when* with the first simple sentence. Join sentences B and C with the coordinating conjunction *and*. Be sure you punctuate correctly.
   A. Mario went to the store for snacks.
   B. He locked his keys in his truck.
   C. He missed most of Monday Night Football.

   ____

   ____

4. Combine the following simple sentences to create a compound-complex sentence. Be sure you punctuate correctly.
   A. Kerry arrived to class at the normal time.
   B. The test had begun a half-hour earlier.
   C. He did not receive as much time to take the test as the rest of the class.

   ____

   ____

5. Combine the following simple sentences to create a compound-complex sentence. Be sure you punctuate correctly.
   A. Lindsey received a $100 reward.
   B. Lindsey received a free dinner at a local restaurant.
   C. Lindsey returned the purse.
   D. The purse was lying in the street.

   ____

   ____

Chapter SUMMARY

- The four types of sentences in English are (1) ________________________, (2) ________________________, (3) ________________________, and (4) ________________________.
- A complex sentence contains ________________________ ________________________.
- A compound-complex sentence contains ________________________ ________________________.
- When you compose a complex sentence, you are telling your readers that the idea in the subordinate clause is less important than the idea in the main clause. This concept is called ________________________.

COMPONENTS AT WORK

USING YOUR SKILLS IN SENTENCES I

Compose sentences according to the directions. Be sure to add commas when necessary and appropriate to your sentences.

1. Compose a complex sentence beginning with a subordinate clause that starts with the subordinate conjunction *because.*

   ____

   ____

2. Compose a complex sentence in which the subordinate clause begins with the subordinate conjunction *after.*

   ____

   ____

3. Compose a complex sentence in which the subordinate clause begins with the relative pronoun *that.* If necessary, do not hesitate to review restrictive and nonrestrictive clauses in Chapter 9, pages 134-138.

   ____

   ____

4. Compose a complex sentence in which the subordinate clause begins with the relative pronoun *which.* If necessary, review restrictive and nonrestrictive clauses in Chapter 9, pages 134-138.

   ____

   ____

5. Compose a complex sentence of your own design.

   ____

   ____

6. Compose a compound-complex sentence in which the two main clauses are joined by the coordinating conjunction *so*, and the subordinate clause begins with the subordinating conjunction *when*.

____

____

7. Compose a compound-complex sentence in which the two main clauses are joined by a semicolon and the subordinate clause begins with the subordinating conjunction *until*.

____

____

8. Compose a compound-complex sentence in which the two main clauses are joined by an adverbial conjunction.

____

____

USING YOUR SKILLS IN SENTENCES II

Combine sentences following the directions.

1. Combine the following sentences to create a simple sentence with a compound verb.
   A. Vicki works hard at her job as a construction foreman.
   B. Vicki likes to participate in paintball war games.

____

____

2. Combine the following sentences to compose a simple sentence with a compound subject.
   A. Terry enjoys vacationing at Padre Island, Texas.
   B. Heather also enjoys vacationing at Padre Island, Texas.

____

____

3. Combine the following sentences to compose a compound sentence. Be sure to use an appropriate and logical coordinating conjunction.
   A. Dawn needed to prune the rose bushes in the backyard.
   B. Dawn had lent the pruning shears to her neighbor.

____

____

4. Combine the following sentences to compose a compound sentence that is connected by a semicolon.
   A. The temperature in August is almost always over 100 degrees.
   B. The Udalls rarely go outside during the afternoon in the summer.

____

____

5. Combine the following sentences to compose a compound sentence. Use a logical adverbial conjunction to join the main clauses.
   A. Jamal needed to wash the dinner dishes.
   B. Jamal also needed to do his laundry.

____

____

6. Combine the following sentences to compose a complex sentence. Subordinate sentence A using the subordinate conjunction *Although*.
   A. Nick wants to join his friends in playing online games.
   B. Nick's Internet connection is not fast enough.

____

____

7. Combine the following sentences to create a complex sentence that makes sentence B a nonrestrictive subordinate adjective clause.
   A. Sister Celeste teaches biology at Temple High School.
   B. Sister Celeste speaks four languages fluently.

____

____

8. Combine the following sentences to create a complex sentence.
   A. The person walked quickly out the front doors of the shop.
   B. An alarm bell began to ring.

   ____

   ____

9. Combine the following sentences to create a compound-complex sentence.
   A. The lake's water level was low.
   B. The recreational area was closed.
   C. People weren't allowed to use their boats or fish from the shore.

   ____

   ____

   ____

10. Combine the following sentences to create a compound-complex sentence.
    A. The alarm sounded at 6 a.m.
    B. Sable climbed out of bed.
    C. Sable shuffled toward the bathroom for a shower.

    ____

    ____

    ____

USING YOUR SKILLS IN READING

Read the following paragraph. Be sure you understand each word in its context. If you need to, look up words, so make sure to have a dictionary or your smart phone nearby. After reading through the paragraph for understanding, reread it and identify all simple sentences (S), compound sentences (CMP), complex sentences (CMX), and compound-complex sentences (CC) by writing the abbreviation next to the number that corresponds with the sentence.

Money

[1]We earn it; we save it; we spend it; we give it away. [2]Some people care little or nothing about it. [3]Others do all they can to acquire it. [4]"It," of course, is money. [5]Yet for something that is so prevalent in our society, what do we know about the item that "burns a hole in our pockets," "makes the world go round," or "is the root of all evil"? [6]Facts about money are noteworthy. [7]The first paper money was issued in the United States in 1862 to help finance the Civil War and to make up for the shortage of gold and silver coins people were hoarding. [8]Present day paper money measures 2.61 inches wide by 6.14 inches long and is 0.0043 inches thick. [9]A single bill weighs 1 gram; there are 454 grams in a pound. [10]The content of paper money is 25 percent linen and 75 percent cotton. [11]The Bureau of Engraving and Printing prints approximately 37 million bills of different denominations each day with a face value of about $696 million, and the vast majority of this money, 95 percent, goes to replace money already in circulation. [12]Even more surprising is that nearly 45 percent of those 37 million bills are $1 bills. [13]The largest bill ever printed by the Bureau of Engraving and Printing was the $100,000 bill, but this denomination was never in public circulation. [14]The largest denominations in circulation were the $500, $1,000, $5,000, and $10,000 bills, but they were discontinued during World War II, and while a few are still in public circulation, they are destroyed when a Federal Reserve Bank receives one. [15]While fewer denominations are

available to collectors, many people still collect paper money; people who collect money are called "numismatics." [16]So the next time you pull a piece of paper money from your wallet or pocket, take a long look at the piece of paper that led the American poet Ralph Waldo Emerson to say, "A man is usually more careful of his money than he is of his principles."

1. ________ 2. ________ 3. ________ 4. ________ 5. ________

6. ________ 7. ________ 8. ________ 9. ________ 10. ________

11. ________ 12. ________ 13. ________ 14. ________ 15. ________

16. ________

USING YOUR SKILLS IN COMPOSITION

Compose a 12- to 16-sentence paragraph about a common but essential object in our culture. Include at least one each of the following types of sentences in your paragraph. Underneath your paragraph, number from 1 to 12 (or to the number of sentences you have) and identify each sentence as a simple sentence (S), compound sentence (CMP), complex sentence (CMX), or compound-complex sentence (CC).

VERB TENSES AND MOOD

Chapter PREVIEW

In this chapter you will learn the twelve active voice verb tenses and their formation and meaning. You will also learn about mood, your attitude about what you are saying or writing.

TWELVE ACTIVE VERB TENSES

When you talk about verb tenses, you are talking about time. Verb tenses indicate the time when an event occurred, occurs, or will occur. In other words, a verb tense indicates a moment in time or the span of time an action takes place.

Twelve active verb tenses exist in English. In order to write effectively, you must learn the meaning and formation of each verb tense.

Verb tenses are arranged in four groups with three tenses in each group (**Table 17.1**):

TABLE 17.1
Verb tenses

Simple Tenses	Perfect Tenses	Progressive Tenses	Perfect Progressive Tenses
Simple present	Present perfect	Present progressive	Present perfect progressive
Simple past	Past perfect	Past progressive	Past perfect progressive
Simple future	Future perfect	Future progressive	Future perfect progressive

As you can see, each group has a present, past, and future form. So you can talk about the *simple past tense* or the *future perfect tense* or the *present perfect progressive tense.* And, as illustrated above, each verb tense expresses a different period of time.

You can better understand the twelve verb tenses when considering USE (when they are used), FORMATION (how they are formed), and ILLUSTRATION (how the tense can be visualized).

You will need to study the following definitions and illustrations to learn how to use each tense and to understand the time interval each tense communicates.

Simple Tenses: Present, Past, Future

Present Tense

USE: Use the **present tense** to express an action that recurs, meaning an action that occurs on a regular basis (**Figure 17.1**).

> They race motorcycles every weekend.
> She talks to my mother every day.
> I always eat pizza on Friday nights.
> He walks to school each day.

FORMATION: Form the present tense by using either the base form or the *-s* form of the verb.

I dance	We dance
You dance	You dance
He/She/It dances	They dance

USAGE NOTE While most regular verbs look the same, the third person singular present tense of regular verbs ends in *s*. No exception to this rule exists.

ILLUSTRATION:

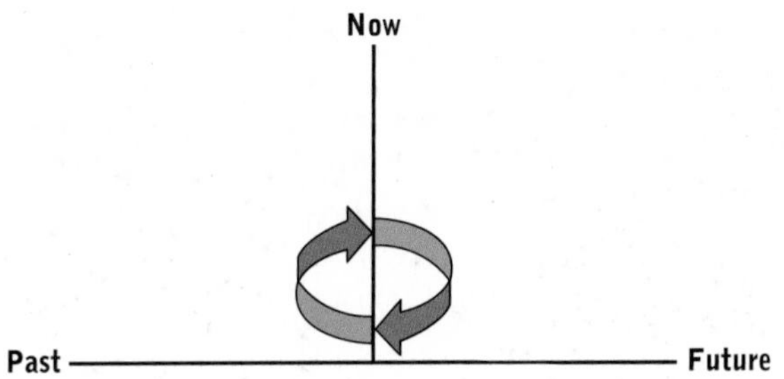

FIGURE 17.1
Present tense

Past Tense

USE: Use the **past tense** to express an action that occurred at a specific past time or place, which may or may not be mentioned in the sentence (**Figure 17.2**).

> He studied all weekend.
> They danced at the Electric Daisy Carnival.
> She skated in the last Winter Olympics.
> Two years ago, we visited China.
> They camped in Yosemite for their fifth grade field trip.

FORMATION: Form the past tense of regular verbs by adding *-d* or *-ed* to the base form of the verb.

I smiled	We smiled
You smiled	You smiled
He/She/It smiled	They smiled

ILLUSTRATION:

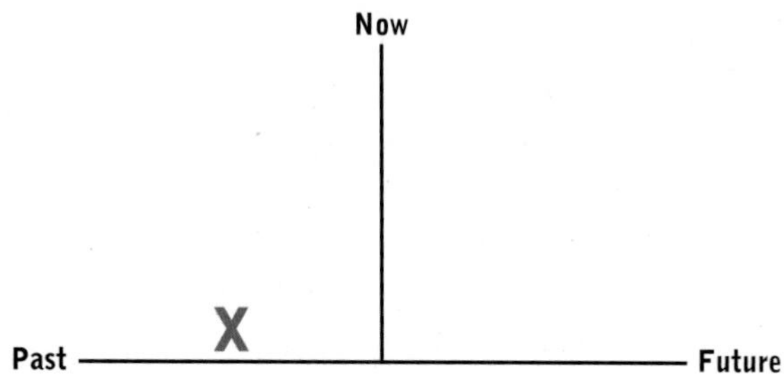

FIGURE 17.2
Past tense

Future Tense

USE: Use the **future tense** to express a future action that is expected to happen (**Figure 17.3**).

> We will clean the yard tomorrow after breakfast.
> I will study for the quiz before class tomorrow.
> I will type my letter of reference next week.

FORMATION: Form the future tense by adding the helping verb *will* to the base form of the verb.

I will walk	We will walk
You will walk	You will walk
He/She/It will walk	They will walk

ILLUSTRATION:

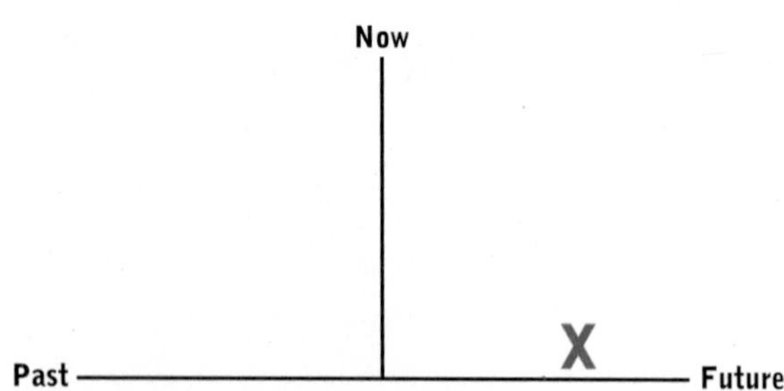

FIGURE 17.3
Future tense

Perfect Tenses: Present, Past, Future

Present Perfect Tense

USE: Use the **present perfect tense** to express

- an action that started in the past and continues in the present.

> She has run track since she was five years old.

- an action that started in the past and has just recently ended (**Figure 17.4**).

> At nineteen years of age, the cat has become too old to chase mice.

FORMATION: Form the present perfect tense by using *have* or *has* with the past participle.

I have driven	We have driven
You have driven	You have driven
He/She/It has driven	They have driven

ILLUSTRATION:

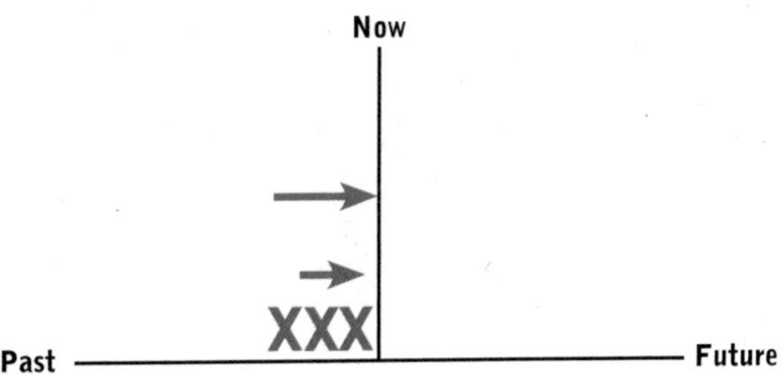

FIGURE 17.4
Present perfect tense

Past Perfect Tense

USE: Use the **past perfect tense** to express a past action (A) that ended before another past action (B) (**Figure 17.5**).

> The jewel thief had fled the scene (A) before the police arrived (B).
>
> I had eaten breakfast (A) before my wife awoke (B).

USAGE NOTE Remember that while the main clause uses the past perfect tense, the subordinate clause uses the simple past tense. Using the different tenses makes clear to your reader which action occurred first (past perfect) and which action occurred next (simple past).

FORMATION: Form the past perfect tense by using the helping verb *had* with the past participle.

I had skated	We had skated
You had skated	You had skated
He/She/It had skated	They had skated

ILLUSTRATION:

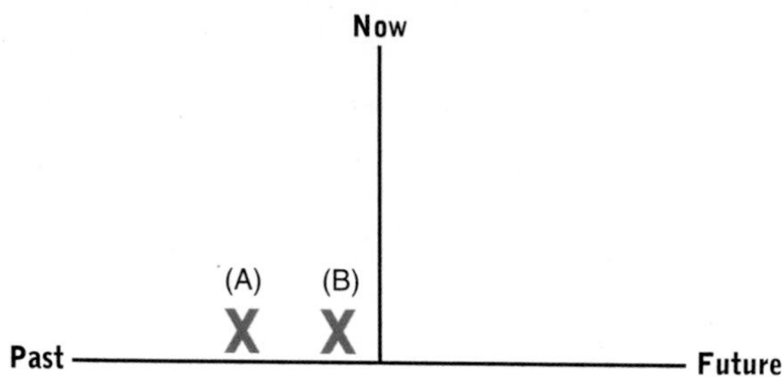

FIGURE 17.5
Past perfect tense

Future Perfect Tense

USE: Use the future perfect tense of the verb to express a future action (A) that will be completed before another future event (B). The second or (B) event is most often conveyed in either a prepositional phrase or a present tense subordinate clause (**Figure 17.6**).

> They will have eaten all of the fruit (A) before next weekend (B).
> He will have studied French for six years (A) as of next month (B).
> He will have finished college (A) before he turns twenty-one (B).

FORMATION: Form the future perfect tense by using *will* plus *have* and the past participle.

I will have eaten	We will have eaten
You will have eaten	You will have eaten
He/She/It will have eaten	They will have eaten

ILLUSTRATION:

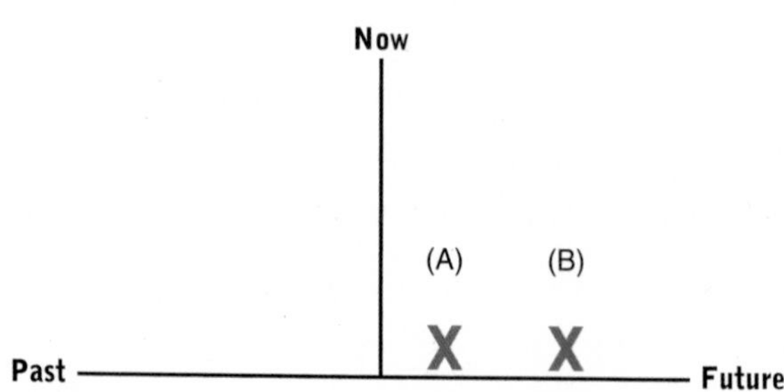

FIGURE 17.6
Future perfect tense

Progressive Tenses: Present, Past, Future

Present Progressive Tense

USE: Use the **present progressive tense** to express an action in progress (**Figure 17.7**).

> The students are meeting to discuss the new school mascot.
> Please don't bother me now; I am talking on the phone.
> I would like to go, but I am painting the living room right now.

USAGE NOTE Students frequently confuse the present tense and the present progressive tense. Just remember that the present tense describes events that occur on a regular basis. The present progressive tense describes events that are occurring right now.

> I call my mother every Sunday afternoon. (present tense)
> I am calling my mother. (present progressive tense)

FORMATION: Form the present progressive tense by using *am*, *is*, or *are* and the present participle.

I am singing	We are singing
You are singing	You are singing
He/She/It is singing	They are singing

ILLUSTRATION:

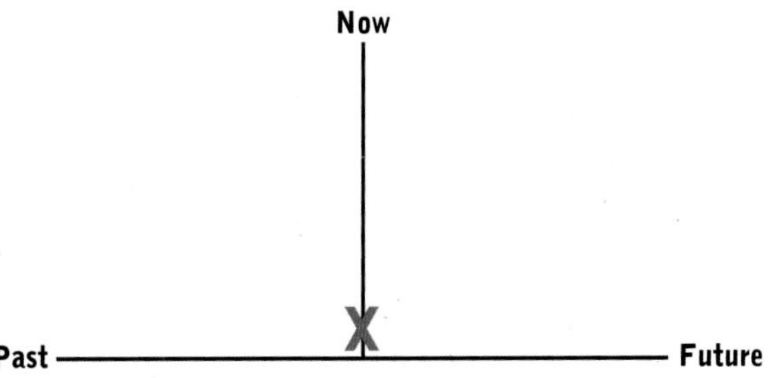

FIGURE 17.7 Present progressive tense

Past Progressive Tense

USE: Use the **past progressive tense** to express an ongoing action that occurred in the past (**Figure 17.8**).

> They were painting the house last weekend.

FORMATION: Form the past progressive tense by using *was* or *were* and the present participle.

I was riding	We were riding
You were riding	You were riding
He/She/It was riding	They were riding

ILLUSTRATION:

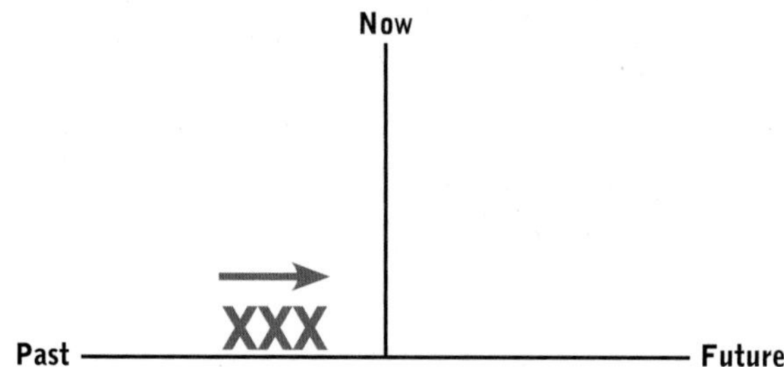

FIGURE 17.8
Past progressive tense

Future Progressive Tense

USE: Use the **future progressive tense** to express an ongoing future action (**Figure 17.9**).

> He will be writing his essay this weekend.

FORMATION: Form the future progressive tense by using *will* plus *be* and the present participle.

I will be seeing	We will be seeing
You will be seeing	You will be seeing
He/She/It will be seeing	They will be seeing

ILLUSTRATION:

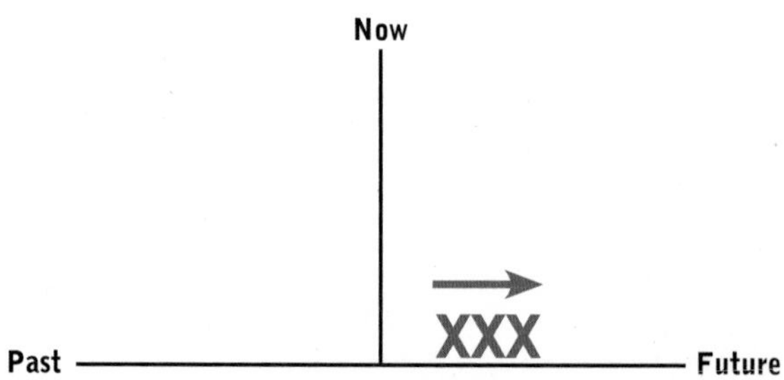

FIGURE 17.9
Future progressive tense

Perfect Progressive Tenses: Present, Past, Future

Present Perfect Progressive Tense

USE: Use the **present perfect progressive tense** to express an ongoing action that began in the past and is continuing in the present.

> The group has been reading the complete works of Douglas Adams.
> He has been studying Spanish for six years.
> She has been driving the same car for the last decade.

FORMATION: Form the present perfect progressive tense by using *have* or *has* plus *been* and the present participle.

I have been flying	We have been flying
You have been flying	You have been flying
He/She/It has been flying	They have been flying

ILLUSTRATION:

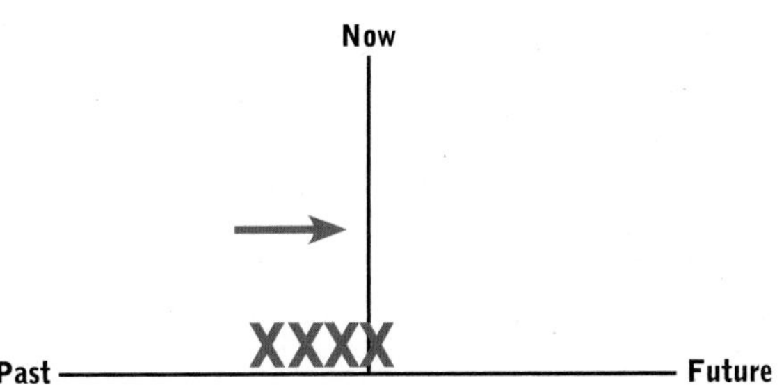

FIGURE 17.10 Present perfect progressive tense

Past Perfect Progressive Tense

USE: Use the **past perfect progressive tense** to express a continuing action that began in the past (A) before another past event started (B) (**Figure 17.11**).

> I had been singing for several years (A) before I got my first gig (B).
> She had been running for six months (A) before she entered her first race (B).
> They had begun painting the house (A) when the rain started (B).

USAGE NOTE In the past perfect progressive tense, only the main clause uses the past perfect progressive tense, but, similar to the past perfect tense, the subordinate clause uses the simple past tense. Using the different tenses makes clear to your reader which action occurred first (past perfect progressive) and which action occurred next (simple past).

FORMATION: Form the past perfect progressive tense by using *had* plus *been* and the present participle.

I had been digging	We had been digging
You had been digging	You had been digging
He/She/It had been digging	They had been digging

ILLUSTRATION:

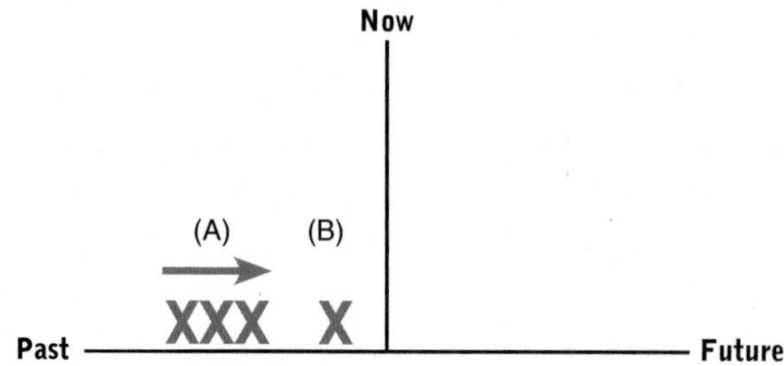

FIGURE 17.11 Past perfect progressive tense

Future Perfect Progressive Tense

USE: Use the **future perfect progressive tense** to express a continuous action (A) that will end at a specific time in the future (B). The (B) event is most often conveyed in either a prepositional phrase or present tense subordinate clause (**Figure 17.12**).

> I will have been keeping a journal for ten years (A) at the end of 2013 (B).
> They will have been dancing for six hours (A) when the club closes tonight at 2 a.m. (B).
> You will have been hula hooping for 55 minutes (A) at the end of the hour (B).

FORMATION: Form the future perfect progressive tense by using *will* plus *have* plus *been* plus the present participle.

I will have been hearing	We will have been hearing
You will have been hearing	You will have been hearing
He/She/It will have been hearing	They will have been hearing

ILLUSTRATION:

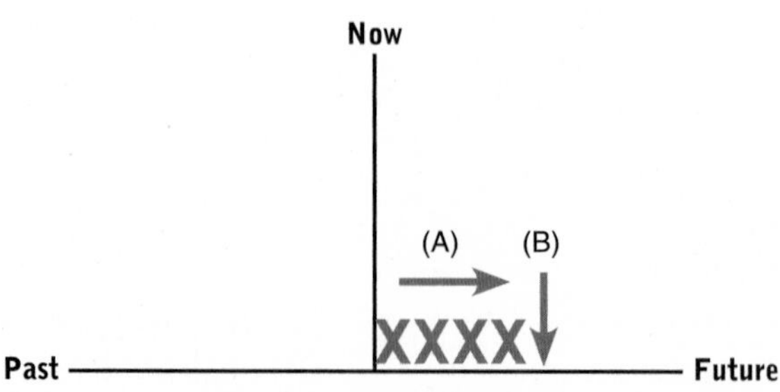

FIGURE 17.12 Future perfect progressive tense

Below is a chart (**Table 17.2**) that summarizes the formation of the twelve active verb tenses. Across the top are the four categories of tenses, and down the left side are the three time elements.

TABLE 17.2
Active verb tenses

	Simple	**Perfect**	**Progressive**	**Progressive Perfect**
Present	base form of verb or -s form of verb	has or have + past participle	am/is/are + present participle	have or has been + present participle
Past	-ed or -d	had + past participle	was/were + present participle	had been + present participle
Future	will + base form of verb	will have + past participle	will be + present participle	will have been + present participle

EXERCISE 17.1: Verb Tenses

Fill in the missing subject pronouns or missing verbs for the tenses below.

1. To Scratch—Simple Present Tense

I scratch	We ________________
You scratch	You scratch
________________ scratches	They scratch

2. To Lift—Simple Past Tense

I ________________	We lifted
You lifted	You lifted
He/She/It lifted	________________ lifted

3. To Type—Simple Future Tense

I will type	We ________________ type
You ________________	You will type
He/She/It will type	They will type

4. To Calculate—Present Perfect Tense

I ________________	We have calculated
You have calculated	You ________________
He/She/It ________________	They have calculated

5. To Write—Past Perfect Tense

I had written	We ________________
You ________________	You had written
He/She/It had written	They had written

6. To Draw—Future Perfect Tense

I ____________________	We will have drawn
You will have drawn	You will have drawn
He/She/It will have drawn	They ____________________

7. To Shine—Present Progressive Tense

I am shining	We are shining
You are shining	You ____________________
He/She/It ____________________	They are shining

8. To Wander—Past Progressive Tense

I was wandering	We ____________________
You were wandering	You were wandering
He/She/It was wandering	They ____________________

9. To Cut—Future Progressive Tense

I will be cutting	We will be cutting
You ____________________	You ____________________
He/She/It will be cutting	They will be cutting

10. To Drive—Present Perfect Progressive Tense

I have been driving	We ____________________
You have been driving	You have been driving
He/She/It ____________________	They have been driving

11. To Pitch—Past Perfect Progressive Tense

I ____________________	We had been pitching
You had been pitching	You had been pitching
He/She/It had been pitching	They ____________________

12. To Consider—Future Perfect Progressive Tense

I will have been considering	We will have been considering
You will have been considering	You ____________________
He/She/It will have been considering	They ____________________

 EXERCISE 17.2: Verb Tenses

Underline the complete verb in each sentence below. Then, in the spaces provided, identify the verb tense of each sentence. In order to identify the complete verb, it may be helpful to cross out any prepositional phrases.

1. I have seen many beautiful sunrises from the top of Haleakala on the Hawaiian island of Maui.

   ____

2. Mr. Jenkins' dog goes to obedience school every Wednesday evening.

   ____

3. Julie and Stan married in Las Vegas last weekend.

   ____

4. Deyonte was hoping to earn an A on his next chemistry test.

   ____

5. Gophers have been burrowing in our yard.

   ____

6. Sophia had never had the Chinese dish Peking Duck before.

   ____

7. Doctor Flannigan is researching a new treatment for the common cold.

   ____

8. My nephew will graduate with a Masters degree from Princeton next year.

   ____

9. By the last game this season, Marcus will have batted more than anyone else on his team.

   ____

10. I will be attending our company's wellness seminar this month.

    ____

11. Thieves had been stealing precious gems from Tony's grandfather's jewelry store.

    ___

12. This Friday, Mr. McGill, a farmer, will have been harvesting for two weeks.

    ___

EXERCISE 17.3: Verb Tenses

Compose sentences following the directions below.

1. Compose a sentence that uses the present tense of the verb *grow*.

   ___

   ___

2. Compose a sentence that uses the future tense of the verb *paint*.

   ___

   ___

3. Compose a sentence that uses the past perfect tense of the verb *carve*.

   ___

   ___

4. Compose a sentence that uses the future perfect tense of the verb *take*.

   ___

   ___

5. Compose a sentence that uses the future perfect progressive tense of the verb *write*.

   ___

   ___

VERBS AND MOOD

In grammar, mood is a verb form that indicates your attitude toward what you are saying or writing. You need to be familiar with three moods: indicative, imperative, and subjunctive.

You use the **indicative mood**

- to state a fact,
- to state an opinion, and
- to ask a question.

The indicative mood accounts for the majority of sentences you compose or speak.

> Jeremy slammed the car door.
>
> Fact
>
> The actors in the play were not professional.
>
> Opinion
>
> When do you want to leave?
>
> Question

The **imperative mood**, which you learned about in Chapter 5, expresses commands or gives directions. With these types of sentences, the subject is the understood *you.*

> Feed the dog.
>
> Command
>
> Turn right.
>
> Direction

In both of the above sentences, the subject *you,* while not stated, is understood in the command or the direction.

> (You) feed the dog.
>
> (You) turn right.

You can also express the imperative mood in single word sentences. The following examples use a *you understood* subject.

> Eat.
>
> Command
>
> Stop!
>
> Command
>
> Turn!
>
> Direction

You use the **subjunctive mood** to communicate

- suggestions or recommendations
- requirements
- desires or wishes
- conditions contrary to fact (something imaginary or hypothetical).

Unlike the verbs in the indicative and imperative moods, verbs in the subjunctive mood use unique forms. For conditions contrary to fact and desires, you use only the past tense form of the verb, and for the verb *be*, we use only the past tense form *were*.

The family wishes the seafood restaurant were not so far from home.
Desire or wish

I wish it were true that I understood physics.
Desire or wish

If she were to win the lottery, she would travel around the world.
Condition contrary to fact

If I were to leave, I would certainly take the cat.
Condition contrary to fact

With suggestions, recommendations, and requirements, use the base form of the verb.

I highly recommend that she park under that tree.
Suggestion or recommendation

Their recommendation that he leave the party upset him.
Suggestion or recommendation

The Department of Motor Vehicles requires every driver have auto insurance.
Requirement

Contest rules require every application be emailed.
Requirement

EXERCISE 17.4: Mood

Compose sentences according to the following directions.

1. Compose a sentence in the indicative mood that expresses a fact about your classroom.

   ____

   ____

2. Compose a sentence in the indicative mood that expresses an opinion about your classroom.

   ____

   ____

3. Compose a sentence in the indicative mood that asks a question about your classroom.

   ____

   ____

4. Compose a sentence in the imperative mood that expresses a command.

   ____

   ____

5. Compose a sentence in the imperative mood that gives a direction.

   ____

   ____

6. Compose a sentence in the subjunctive mood that expresses a wish or desire.

   ____

   ____

7. Compose a sentence in the subjunctive mood that expresses a condition contrary to fact.

____

____

8. Compose a sentence in the subjunctive mood that expresses a suggestion or recommendation.

____

____

9. Compose a sentence in the subjunctive mood that expresses a requirement.

____

____

10. Compose a sentence that uses either the indicative, imperative, or subjunctive mood and underline the word group that illustrates the mood you used.

____

____

- When we talk about verb tense, we are talking about ________________

  ____.

- Mood is a verb form that indicates the writer's ____________________

  ____.

- Writers use the indicative mood to ______________________________,

  ___________________________, and ______________________________.

- Writers use the imperative mood to ___________________________ and

  ____.

- Writers use the subjunctive mood to communicate

  ________________________________ or ____________________________,

  ________________________________, ___________________________ or

  ______________, and _______________________________________.

COMPONENTS AT WORK

USING YOUR SKILLS IN SENTENCES

Compose sentences as directed in the spaces provided. If necessary, review sentence types in Chapters 15 and 16 and/or review the formation of tenses in this chapter.

1. Compose a simple sentence in the simple present tense.

____

____

2. Compose a simple sentence in simple future tense.

____

____

3. Compose a simple sentence in the future perfect tense.

____

____

4. Compose a compound sentence in the simple past tense.

____

____

5. Compose a compound sentence in the present perfect tense.

____

____

6. Compose a compound sentence in the present progressive tense.

____

____

7. Compose a complex sentence in the future perfect tense. Remember that the (B) event will be a subordinate clause. See page 286 for review.

____

____

8. Compose a complex sentence in the simple past tense.

____

____

9. Compose a complex sentence in the present perfect tense.

____

____

10. Compose a complex sentence in the past progressive tense.

____

____

> The car door was dented in the parking lot.
>
> Since you do not know who built the house or who took the picture or who plowed the streets or who dented the car door, passive voice is preferable to sentences that read "Somebody built the house in 1998" or "Somebody dented the car door in the parking lot."

Second, you can also use the passive voice when the object or performer of the verb is less important than the subject.

> A cure for cancer was discovered by a team of scientists.
>
> In this case, what was discovered—a cure for cancer—is more important than who discovered the cure—a team of scientists.

Rewriting passive voice to active voice involves three steps:

1. Delete the form of the *to be* verb.
2. Use an active verb form rather than the past participial verb form.
3. Make the object of the preposition and any words associated with the object of the preposition (but do **not** include the preposition) the subject of the sentence.

> The pink cotton candy was eagerly eaten by the little boy. (Passive)
>
> The little boy eagerly ate the pink cotton candy. (Active)
>
> The picture was hung on the wall by the museum's curator. (Passive)
>
> The museum's curator hung the picture on the wall. (Active)
>
> The mountain was climbed by a thirteen-year-old boy. (Passive)
>
> A thirteen-year-old boy climbed the mountain. (Active)

EXERCISE 18.1: Passive Voice to Active Voice

Change the following passive voice sentences to active voice.

1. *The Cat in the Hat* was written by Dr. Seuss.

   ____

2. The jigsaw puzzle was completed in thirty minutes by the family.

   ____

3. The ticket was written by a police officer wearing sunglasses.

   ____

4. The zip line was ridden by a smiling, screaming young girl.

 ____

5. The car was backed over the curb by the new driver.

 ____

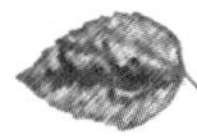

EXERCISE 18.2: Passive Voice to Active Voice

In the blank spaces below, first write a sentence in passive voice (P) and then rewrite the sentence in active voice (A).

1. (P) ______________________________.
1. (A) ______________________________.
2. (P) ______________________________.
2. (A) ______________________________.
3. (P) ______________________________.
3. (A) ______________________________.

PARALLEL STRUCTURE

You create **parallel structure**, sometimes called *parallelism*, when you compose words, phrases, clauses, or sentences that are the same grammatical forms. Study the following sentences and the explanations that follow each one.

> The large, muddy dairy cow stood in the rain.
>
> In the preceding sentence, the adjectives *large*, *muddy*, and *dairy* are used to modify the subject *cow*. Modifiers should be similar grammatical forms.
>
> On the porch beside the swing slept one of the family's three cats.
>
> In this sentence, two prepositional phrases are used to introduce the main clause.
>
> The road trip ended when the travelers decided to return home because the radiator had developed a leak.
>
> In this third sentence, two subordinate adverb clauses follow the main clause.

> My pen ran out of ink; my pencil lead broke; my calculator's batteries died.
>
> In the last group of words, you have three independent clauses that all follow the same pattern—possessive pronoun—subject—verb: *my pen ran*, *my lead broke*, and *my batteries died.*

Communication problems occur when the grammatical forms do not match. The majority of parallel structure errors occur with either single words in a series or phrases in a series. Again, study the following sentences and their explanations.

> Jenna enjoys singing, dancing, and the ability to play a guitar.
>
> In this sentence, *singing* is a gerund, *dancing* is a gerund, and *the ability to play a guitar* is a noun phrase.
>
> Chris wanted nothing more than the time to update his website, to play video games, and he truly wanted to sleep.
>
> In this sentence, *to update his website* is an infinitive phrase, *to play video games* is also an infinitive phrase, and *he truly wanted to sleep* is a main clause.
>
> Pictures adorned the library walls; tapestries hung on the dining room wall; sculptures stand in each corner of the living room.
>
> And in this sentence, the verb in the first main clause is past tense; the verb in the second main clause is past tense; the verb in the third main clause is present tense.

In all of the examples, one of the grammatical elements is not the same as the remaining two elements, so you have to change the one that doesn't match.

> Jenna enjoys singing, dancing, and playing guitar.
>
> Chris wanted nothing more than the time to update his website, to play video games, and to sleep.
>
> Pictures adorned the library walls; tapestries hung on the dining room wall; sculptures stood in each corner of the living room.

Now all the elements in the sentence are the same grammatical forms, and you have parallel structure.

Many parallel structure errors occur as well with correlative conjunctions, those conjunctions that work in pairs. See the following list.

not only . . . but also

both . . . and

neither . . . nor

either . . . or

whether . . . or

When using correlative conjunctions, you must make sure that the word or phrase that follows the first conjunction is the same type of word or phrase that follows the second conjunction. Look at the following examples.

> The physician's assistant told his patient not only to lose weight but also she needed to stop smoking.
>
> In the example above, an infinitive phrase follows *not only*, but an independent clause follows *but also*. See the following correction.
>
> The doctor told his patient not only to lose weight but also to stop smoking.
>
> Now both *not only* and *but also* are followed by infinitive phrases, so you have parallel structure.

Look at the following example with other correlative conjunctions.

> My brother, who wants to be financial advisor, needs either an MBA or needs to get his CFP certificate.
>
> *Either* is followed by a noun, whereas *or* is followed by a verb.
>
> My brother, who wants to be a financial advisor, needs either an MBA or a CFP certificate.
>
> Now, both correlative conjunctions are followed by nouns, so the sentence has parallel structure.

When you have two or more grammatical elements—whether words, phrases, subordinate clauses, or main clauses—you must be sure the elements are written in the same grammatical form.

EXERCISE 18.3: Faulty Parallel Structure

Correct the parallel structure errors in each of the sentences below.

1. Jeff couldn't help but laugh loudly, dance wildly, and he was extremely happy.

   ____

   ____

2. Amber turned on the kitchen light, opened the refrigerator door, and takes a soda off the shelf.

   ____

   ____

3. Standing on the porch, sipping iced tea, and to daydream about the upcoming dance, Mindy didn't hear her mother calling her.

   ____

   ____

4. The recipe required four odd ingredients: a cup of vinegar, three teaspoons baking powder were required, six drops of Worcestershire sauce, and a dash of cayenne pepper was also needed.

   ____

   ____

5. Having put his iPod in his shirt pocket, stuck his earbuds in his ears, and picking music to listen to, Jamie was ready to leave.

   ____

   ____

6. Wanting to eat but she did not want to cook, Gem couldn't decide what to do.

   ____

   ____

7. Teaching preschool children takes both patience and teachers also need to be creative.

____

____

8. The couple in the picture was standing in front of a curtain, smiling happily, and they were hugging.

____

____

9. Because they often stand on thin planks atop tall structures, construction workers should be neither clumsy nor should they be afraid of heights.

____

____

10. Clothed in black leather and her make up was gold glitter, she drove off to the Halloween party.

____

____

Chapter SUMMARY

- Voice is the relationship between ______________________________

  ____.
- Using passive voice is acceptable when (1) ______________________

  and (2)______________________________________.
- Revising passive voice to active voice requires you to

  (1) ______________________________________,

  (2) ______________________________________,

  and (3) ___________________________________.
- Parallel structure occurs when items in a series have the same ________

  ____.

COMPONENTS AT WORK

USING YOUR SKILLS IN SENTENCES I

Follow the direction for each set of sentences.

1. Combine the following sentences to create a simple sentence in passive voice.
   a. The family hung the holiday decorations.
   b. The decorations were hung on a pine tree in the front yard.

   ____

   ____

2. Rewrite the sentence you created in number 1 in active voice.

3. Combine the following sentences to create a simple sentence in active voice.

   a. The pencils were in a glass jar.
   b. The pencils were put there by Ethan.

4. Rewrite the sentence you created in number 3 in passive voice.

USING YOUR SKILLS IN SENTENCES II

Follow the directions for each sentence.

1. Compose a sentence that illustrates parallel structure using three adjectives.

2. Compose a sentence that illustrates parallel structure using three present participial phrases.

3. Compose a sentence that illustrates parallel structure using two subordinate adverb clauses.

4. Compose a sentence that illustrates parallel structure using a pair of correlative conjunctions.

____

____

5. Compose a sentence that illustrates parallel structure using three infinitive phrases.

____

____

USING YOUR SKILLS IN SENTENCES III

Follow the directions for each exercise below. Do not hesitate to look at the principal parts of the irregular verbs listed in Chapter 7.

1. Using the past participle of the irregular verb *to freeze*, compose a sentence in passive voice.

____

____

2. Rewrite the sentence you composed in number 1 in active voice.

____

____

3. Using the past participle of the irregular verb *to teach,* compose a sentence in passive voice.

____

____

4. Rewrite the sentence you composed in number 3 in active voice.

____

____

5. Using the past participle of the irregular verb *to overthrow*, compose a sentence in passive voice.

____

____

6. In the space below, rewrite the sentence you composed in number 5 in active voice.

7. Using the past participle of the irregular verb *to shake*, compose a sentence in passive voice.

8. In the space below, rewrite the sentence you composed in number 7 in active voice.

9. Using the past participle of the irregular verb *to forgive*, compose a sentence in passive voice.

10. In the space below, rewrite the sentence you composed in number 9 in active voice.

USING YOUR SKILLS IN READING

Read the following short essay. Be sure you understand each word in its context. If you need to, look up words, so make sure to have a dictionary or your smart phone nearby. After reading the essay for understanding, in the spaces between each line, revise passive voice into active voice and correct all faulty parallel structure errors. Not all sentences will need to be rewritten.

Yellowstone National Park

Yellowstone National Park, the first national park in the United States and the world, was established by Congress. The bill establishing the park was

signed into law by Congress on March 1, 1872. The park was also designated a World Heritage Site on September 8, 1978, by the United Nations.

The park spreads into three states: 96 percent in Wyoming, 3 percent in Montana, Idaho has 1 percent. Currently, the park covers 3,472 square miles or 2,221,766 acres, which is larger than the states of Delaware and Rhode Island combined. While the park is 80 percent forest, 15 percent of the park is grassland, and water covers the final 5 percent.

For thousands of years, Native Americans and mountain men visited and sometimes were living in Yellowstone. But not until September 1869 when three men—Charles Cook, David Folsom, and William Peterson—visited Yellowstone and began to tell others of the area's breathtaking wonders did people take an interest in the area. In August 1870, Henry Washburn, the surveyor general of Montana, and a detachment of US cavalry spent six weeks exploring the Yellowstone area. Washburn's enthusiasm and the belief that he embraced that the area should never be exploited by the public or by private institutions, led to further exploration. The next summer, in 1871, F. V. Hayden, a geologist, was sent by the US Congress to thoroughly explore the Yellowstone area. Hayden included in the expedition photographer William Henry Jackson and Thomas Moran, who was a painter. Hayden's report to Congress, along with Jackson's photographs and the sketches by Moran resulted in the Yellowstone Park Act, which became law on March 1, 1872.

While there are more than 300 geysers in Yellowstone Park, the most famous is Old Faithful Geyser. Old Faithful was given its name by the Washburn Expedition of 1870. One of the misconceptions about Old Faithful is that it erupts every hour on the hour. The frequency of Old Faithful's eruptions ranges between 45 and 125 minutes, the duration of an eruption lasts from 1.5 to 5 minutes, and the height of the eruption ranges from approximately 100 to 185 feet.

Another popular geological attraction in Yellowstone Park is the Grand Canyon of the Yellowstone. While not as deep or wide as the Grand Canyon located in Arizona, the Grand Canyon of the Yellowstone is 800 to 1,200 feet deep, 1,500 to 4,000 feet wide, and its length is approximately 20 miles. The canyon was carved out by the Yellowstone River over a period of 10,000 to 14,000 years. Two waterfalls on the river, Upper Yellowstone Falls and Lower Yellowstone Falls, are frequently photographed by visitors to the park. The Upper Falls is 109 feet tall; the Lower Falls reaches a height of 308 feet. Both are easily viewed by visitors from several viewpoints in the park.

In addition to the popular geological formations that attract people, Yellowstone National Park has a wide variety of fauna. Among the larger animals that are found in the park by visitors are bison, elk, moose, grizzly bear, black bear, bighorn sheep, antelope, and mule deer roam the park also. Smaller animals include otters, foxes, badgers, shrews, beavers, squirrels,

gophers, rabbits, mice, and porcupines. In the evening or during the night, a visitor may hear coyotes or the Yellowstone wolves howling. In all, sixty-seven different types of mammals live in Yellowstone National Park.

Birds, too, populate the park. The "Yellowstone National Park Checklist of Birds" lists 121 different types of birds. Among the birds found in Yellowstone are swans, ducks, geese, hawks, eagles, vultures, herons, cranes, caracaras, and falcons, and loons and coots also inhabit the area. Six species of birds are of special concern in Yellowstone as their population fluctuates from year to year; the six species include Common Loon, Harlequin Duck, Peregrine Falcon, Trumpter Swan, Bald Eagle, and Osprey. People who are interested in bird watching will have an enjoyable time during their stay at Yellowstone National Park.

Today Yellowstone National Park is a favorite year round destination: in the summer of 2009, 3,295,187 people visited the park, and 86,784 people vacationed in the park during the 2008-2009 winter. Whether visitors are interested in the park's geology or animals, Yellowstone National Park provides people the opportunity to see nature at its best.

PUNCTUATION MARKS

Chapter PREVIEW

In this chapter you will, first, learn additional uses for the comma. You will also learn how to use the semicolon, the colon, the dash, the hyphen, and the exclamation mark. Last, you will learn the various uses for quotation marks.

In the same way choosing the wrong words can confuse your reader, so can choosing the wrong punctuation or leaving it out altogether. Incorrect or missing punctuation can create meaning that you did not intend to create. Read the following examples.

> Let's eat, Grandma!
>
> Let's eat Grandma!

In the first sentence, the comma indicates that a grandchild is suggesting to Grandma that they eat. The comma shows that the grandchild is *addressing* the grandmother. However, in the second sentence, a completely different scenario is suggested, one that involves cannibalism. Without that comma, the grandchild is suggesting to someone else that they eat Grandma for dinner.

While the above example is a bit fanciful, it illustrates how correct punctuation is as important as correct grammar, sentence structure, and word choice. Look at the next two examples.

> A woman, without her man, is nothing.
>
> A woman: without her, man is nothing.

The two sentences above make opposite points. The first sentence makes the claim that without a man, a woman is nothing. The second sentence makes the claim that man is nothing without a woman. The words are exactly the same, but the different punctuation creates different meanings.

This chapter will help you navigate the rules and uses of different punctuation marks, so you can present your intended meaning and avoid any embarrassing confusion.

COMMA (,)

You have already learned many uses for the comma. In Chapter 9 you learned to insert commas around nonrestrictive clauses, and in Chapter 14 you learned how to use commas with appositives and absolute phrases. Then in Chapter 15 you learned how to use a comma in compound sentences (between two main clauses with a coordinating conjunction), and in Chapters 9 and 13 you learned to insert a comma after a dependent clause or phrase if it precedes a main clause (many instructors and textbooks call this rule the "introductory material" rule). Now, you will learn a few other important uses for this versatile punctuation mark.

Commas and Items in a Series

Whenever you list three or more items in a series, a comma must be placed after each item except the last ("items" can refer to words, phrases, and clauses). Study the examples below and pay careful attention to where the commas have been placed.

> Anthony wants to study astronomy**,** physics**,** and chemistry.
>
> The little girl leaped**,** jumped**,** and skipped in the rain puddles all the way home.
>
> After school I need to wash the dog**,** feed the cats**,** and fold the laundry.
>
> Jessie is president of the school's Green Club**,** Harold is the secretary**,** and Keisha is the treasurer.

In the first sentence, there is a series of nouns. In the second sentence, there is a series of verbs. In the third sentence, there is a series of infinitive phrases, and in the fourth sentence there is a series of clauses.

USAGE NOTE Because editors and printers at Oxford University Press have traditionally inserted the last comma before the word ***and*** when editing items in a series, the last comma is known as the Oxford comma. However, you may notice when you read the newspaper that the comma before the word ***and*** is absent when items are listed in a series. This deletion of the last comma is common in journalism but not in academics. Some grammar texts have referred to the Oxford comma as *optional*, but most style guides still call for its use. Most academic institutions and professors still expect to see the Oxford comma, so for the purposes of this chapter, the last comma before ***and*** will be required because omitting the final comma may cause a lack of clarity, but including the final comma never will. Look at the following two sentences.

> I invited my parents, Paul and Betty.
>
> I invited my parents, Paul, and Betty.

Omitting the Oxford comma implies that my parents' names are Paul and Betty. Inserting the Oxford Comma shows that I invited my parents along with Paul and Betty.

Commas between Coordinate Adjectives

Coordinate adjectives are adjectives that are equal in importance in describing the noun, meaning you could switch the order of their placement and the sentence would still make sense. Read the examples below.

> Sheryl's little girl has light brown hair.
>
> Sheryl's little girl has brown light hair.
>
> You can see in these sentences that *light* and *brown* are **not** coordinate adjectives because when you switch their order, the sentence does not make sense. The word *light* is subordinate to *brown*. Therefore, *light* must be placed before *brown* and you do not place a comma between the two adjectives.
>
> The beautiful, tall model strutted down the runway.
>
> The tall, beautiful model strutted down the runway.
>
> Here, you see that *tall* and *beautiful* are coordinate adjectives because their order can be reversed in the sentence, and the sentence still makes sense. The model is **both** tall and beautiful; one adjective does not take precedence over the other. Therefore, you place a comma between the adjectives.

When you are trying to figure out if you have coordinate adjectives that need a comma between them, ask yourself these questions:

1. Can I reverse the order of the adjectives in the sentence and still have the sentence make sense?

> The elderly man lived in an old, decrepit house.
>
> The elderly man lived in a decrepit, old house.
>
> Because the adjectives *old* and *decrepit* can each describe the house individually, and because they can be in any order and still make sense, a comma is placed between them.
>
> The oppressive summer sun burned the boy's skin as he mowed the lawn.
>
> The summer oppressive sun burned the boy's skin as he mowed the lawn.
>
> The second sentence sounds odd; you cannot reverse the order of the adjectives. The word *oppressive* is subordinate to the word *summer* and so must be placed before *summer*. Therefore, no comma is needed.

2. Does the word *and* sound natural between the two adjectives?

> The elderly man lived in an old and decrepit house.
>
> Because the word *and* sounds natural between the adjectives *old* and *decrepit*, you place a comma between them if you are not using the word *and*.
>
> The oppressive and summer sun burned the boy's skin as he mowed the lawn.
>
> You can hear the awkwardness of placing the word *and* between the adjectives. Therefore, no comma is needed.

EXERCISE 19.1: Commas

Insert commas where they are needed.

1. The packing list for the camping trip called for a sleeping bag a mess kit and a flashlight.
2. The Copper Age the Bronze Age and the Iron Age are all considered prehistoric periods.
3. My best friend has an easy-going carefree disposition.
4. The toddler in the department store clenched her teeth thrashed her head and stomped her feet as she threw her temper tantrum.
5. Our wedding planner still needs to hire the photographer research musicians and order flowers.
6. Turning off all technology for an hour offers the opportunity for reflection relaxation and inspiration.
7. The distinguished intelligent professor ended his lecture with a quote from Abraham Lincoln's Gettysburg Address.
8. Before we can begin the meeting, Fran needs to take roll Jackson needs to hand out the agenda and Julio needs to set up the projector.
9. The television the computer and the telephone all stopped working at once.
10. A torn dirty pair of jeans hung over the hood of the car.

EXERCISE 19.2: Composing with Commas

Write sentences following the directions below.

Write two sentences that use commas with a series of nouns.

1. ______________________________

____

2. ______________________________

____

Write two sentences that use commas with a series of verbs.

1. ______________________________

____

2. ______________________________

____

Write two sentences that use commas with a series of phrases.

1. ______________________________

____

2. ______________________________

____

Write two sentences that use commas with a series of clauses.

1. ______________________________

____

2. ______________________________

____

Write two sentences that use commas between coordinate adjectives.

1. ______________________________

____

2. ______________________________

____

Commas and Direct Quotations

Commas are used to set off direct quotations, words that someone said or wrote. Study the following examples.

The gamer yelled, "I am not a newbie."

In this first sentence, notice that the comma comes after a verb; the comma follows a clause that *introduces* the direct quotation

"I am not a newbie," the gamer yelled.

In this second sentence, the direct quotation is first; therefore, the comma is placed **inside** the quotation marks before the clause that tells you who was speaking.

"I am not a newbie," the gamer yelled, "nor am I a nerd."

In this last sentence, there are two commas; one comma follows the direct quotation within the quotation marks, and the second comma sets off the second part of the direct quotation. Because the second part of the direct quotation begins with a coordinating conjunction, using the comma is appropriate. If the second part of the direct quotation were not connected to the first with a coordinating or subordinating conjunction, instead of a comma, you would need to use a period.

Again, study the following examples.

"I abhor the taste of frogs' legs," stated Lily, "and I also detest the flavor of escargot."

In this first example, the second part of the direct quotation begins with a coordinating conjunction, so you use a comma before the coordinating conjunction.

"I have begun to appreciate Asian food," said Lily, "since my vacation in China last year."

In this second example, the second part of the quotation begins with a subordinating conjunction, so you use a second comma in this sentence as well.

"I adore eating caviar," swooned Lily. "In addition, I could eat linguini with clams every day of my life."

However, in this third example, the continuation of the direct quotation begins with an adverbial conjunction. Placing a comma before the adverbial conjunction would create a specific type of run-on sentence called a comma splice. Therefore, use a period.

The strategy to figuring out if you need a second comma or a period is to read whatever is within quotation marks and mentally delete what comes in the middle. Is the material in the quotation marks one sentence joined by a coordinating or subordinating conjunction? Do you have one sentence composed of a subordinate clause and a main clause? Or does the material make up two sentences? Once you know the answer, you can punctuate accordingly.

Another point to remember is that if the word *that* precedes a direct quotation, no comma is necessary. Notice the difference in the two sentences below.

> Aunt Martha wrote in my wedding book that "love is the key to happiness."
>
> Aunt Martha wrote in my wedding book, "Love is the key to happiness."
>
> Because the material within the quotation marks in the first sentence follows the word *that*, no comma is necessary since the word *that* is what introduces the direct quotation.

One mistake you may make is adding a comma anytime you see quotation marks. However, just because you see quotation marks, don't assume you need a comma before them. Quotation marks are used for titles of poems, articles, and songs, for instance, and you do not place commas before quotation marks when they are used for titles. Study the following examples.

> Mr. Washington's favorite poem is T.S. Eliot's "The Waste Land."
>
> Eric Clapton's "Tears in Heaven" always makes my mother cry.
>
> In both sentences above, no comma is necessary. The quotation marks are used to show the reader titles of a poem and a song. The quotation marks are not used to show the exact words someone said or wrote, so commas are not necessary to introduce the material within the quotation marks.

EXERCISE 19.3: Commas

Punctuate the following sentences correctly, adding commas or periods where necessary. Do not delete any existing commas. Some sentences may not need any commas or periods added. Simply write *C* next to those sentences.

1. "I don't want to go to Disneyland" exclaimed the little boy "because I am afraid of Mickey Mouse!"

2. The defendant told the judge "I do not understand the charges against me."

3. In my favorite play by William Shakespeare, Beatrice says "I cannot be a man with wishing; therefore, I will die a woman with grieving."
4. The high school's poetry reading will include Taylor Mali's poem "Speak with Conviction."
5. "My dermatologist told me to stop using tanning beds" said Terry "He says they can cause skin cancer just like too much sun can."
6. At tonight's talent show, my sister will be singing "Defying Gravity" from the musical *Wicked.*
7. "Please hand me the sea urchin" the executive chef told his sous-chef.
8. "Loan me a pencil" the boy whispered to his friend.
9. "You must turn in your essays" the professor announced "In addition, you need to pass up your journals."
10. The professor announced "You must turn in your essays. In addition, you need to pass up your journals."

Commas with Dates, Addresses, and Other Material

Commas are also used for dates and addresses. With dates, you place a comma between the day and the year, and if the complete date is in the middle of a sentence, you also place a comma after the year. Study the following examples.

> My parents were married on July 29**,** 1989.
>
> July 29**,** 1989**,** was one of the happiest days of their lives.

However, if you write just the month and year, no comma is necessary:

> July 1989 was one of the happiest months of my parents' lives.

You place commas between cities and states. If the city and the state come in the middle of a sentence, you place a comma after the state as well. Study the examples below.

> Her brother moved to Portland**,** Maine.
>
> Portland**,** Maine**,** is known for their lobster rolls.

However, you do **not** place a comma between a state and zip code.

> My brother's new address is 1456 Washington Avenue, Portland, Maine 04101.

With street addresses, you place commas between the street name and the city.

> My brother's new address is 1456 Washington Avenue, Portland, Maine.

You use commas to show that someone is being addressed (spoken to):

> Sir, do you know what the time is?
>
> Madame, have you decided on your order?
>
> Excuse me, young man, can you please remove your hat at the table?

EXERCISE 19.4: Commas

Add commas where necessary in the following sentences.

1. Most historians have concluded that the Declaration of Independence was signed nearly a month after its adoption, on August 2 1776 and not on July 4 as is commonly believed.
2. Excuse me Lisa can you please hand me my glasses?
3. The Empire State Building is located at 350 5th Avenue New York 10118.
4. Matthew will you teach me how to dance?
5. Stacey plans to move to Seattle Washington as soon as her youngest child graduates from high school.

Commas and Parenthetical Expressions

In writing, a parenthetical expression is a word or group of words that interrupts the main idea of the sentence. Parenthetical expressions are not required for the sentence to be complete; you can remove them without changing the meaning of the rest of the sentence. You can place parenthetical expressions at the beginning of a sentence, in the middle of a sentence, or at the end of a sentence. Study the following sentences.

> In fact, the impact of the meteor will create a crater the size of several football fields.
>
> Consequently, the child was grounded for his actions.
>
> The square root of 144 is, I believe, twelve.

> His joining the ski club, however, did not adversely affect his schoolwork.
>
> Students can use a phone book as a research source, for example.
>
> Our biology class field trip to the zoo is on a Saturday, naturally.

Since parenthetical expressions are not necessary to the meaning of the sentence, you use commas to set them off from the rest of the sentence. Think of parenthetical expressions as nonrestrictive elements.

As the examples above illustrate, if the parenthetical expression introduces the sentence, you place a comma after the word or phrase. If the parenthetical expression comes in the middle of the sentence, you surround the expression with commas. If the parenthetical expression concludes the sentence, you precede the expression with a comma.

Following is a partial list of words and phrases that need to be set off with a comma or commas when you use them as parenthetical expressions.

after all	for example	I believe (hope, think, etc.)
as a matter of fact	for instance	
by the way	furthermore	incidentally
consequently	however	in fact
in the first place	nevertheless	otherwise
moreover	of course	therefore
naturally	on the other hand	well

USAGE NOTE Many of the words and phrases in the above list can be used as adverbial conjunctions: words or phrases that link main clauses to form a compound sentence. You must remember that when you use a word or a phrase as an adverbial conjunction, as opposed to a parenthetical expression, main clauses must appear before and after the word or phrase. In addition, when you use an adverbial conjunction between clauses, you must place a semicolon or a period before the adverbial conjunction and a comma after. Study the sentences below, paying particular attention to the punctuation.

> He went home early; however, he could not sleep.
> He went home early. However, he could not sleep.
> He went home early; he could not sleep, however.

 EXERCISE 19.5: Commas and Parenthetical Expressions

Add commas and semicolons to the following sentences where appropriate and necessary. If the sentence is correct as it is, write *C* for correct. Be prepared to explain your choices.

1. The brochure explained for example the cost and amenities of the trip to Greece.
2. Papers littered the desk moreover several half-empty Styrofoam coffee cups sat on the floor.
3. Incidentally the distance from the school to the freeway entrance is about one mile.
4. A solar calculator does not function well at night as a matter of fact.
5. Exercise can help you not only lose weight but also reduce stress.
6. The icy roads made driving hazardous however few people stayed home.
7. Well the time to apply for the grant has passed.
8. A "Baby Boomer" is someone born I believe between 1946 and 1964.
9. Rubber bands seem to be naturally resilient.
10. The students studied their flash cards consequently they earned high grades on their quiz.

 EXERCISE 19.6: Commas and Parenthetical Expressions

Create sentences following the directions. Be attentive to punctuating the parenthetical expressions correctly.

1. Compose a sentence that uses the parenthetical expression *in the first place* at the beginning of the sentence.

   ____

   ____

2. Compose a sentence that uses the parenthetical expression *of course* at the end of the sentence.

   ____

   ____

3. Compose a sentence that uses the parenthetical expression *I think* in the middle of the sentence.

____

____

4. Compose a sentence that uses the parenthetical expression *for example.*

____

____

5. Compose a sentence that uses the parenthetical expression *therefore.*

____

____

SEMICOLON (;)

Semicolons and Independent Clauses

In Chapter 15, you learned how to use a semicolon between two independent clauses. Remember, when you join main clauses with a semicolon, you are telling your reader the two ideas in the two clauses have something in common; they reflect a logical relationship. You should not place a semicolon between main clauses if no obvious relationship between the clauses exists. Also, remember you may use a semicolon between two independent clauses with or without an adverbial conjunction. Read the examples below.

> Please return your response by August 29**;** I will be out of town after that date and unable to access the internet.
>
> I will be out of town after August 29**;** therefore, you must send in your response before then.

For more review of semicolons between independent clauses, see pages 251-253 in Chapter 15. Remember, semicolons **do not** go between an independent and a dependent clause.

Semicolons and Items in a Series

You also use the semicolon when you have a series of items and those items have commas within them. If you were to use commas in this case, your reader could become confused. Study the examples below.

> The most important days in Mary's life are July 13, 1975, her birth, March 31, 1999, her wedding day, and April 10, 2005, the birth of her son.
>
> The most important days in Mary's life are July 13, 1975, her birth**;** March 31, 1999, her wedding day**;** and April 10, 2005, the birth of her son.
>
> The semicolons in the second example eliminate the confusion caused by all of the commas in the first example. The semicolons make it clear that the specific events go with specific dates.

Read the next two examples below.

> The groups for the chemistry assignment are Jeff, Lemont, Lily, Stewart, Maria, Xochitl, and Alec, Laquisha, Zaima.
>
> The groups for the chemistry assignment are Jeff, Lemont, Lily**;** Stewart, Maria, Xochitl**;** and Alec, Laquisha, Zaima.
>
> The semicolons in the second sentence make clear exactly who is in what group.

EXERCISE 19.7: Semicolons

Create sentences using the semicolon according to the instructions.

1. Write a sentence that uses a semicolon, but no adverbial conjunction, to join two independent clauses. Do not hesitate to review the information on using semicolons to join main clauses found in Chapter 15, pages 251-253.

   ____

   ____

2. Write a sentence using a semicolon between two independent clauses with an adverbial conjunction. Underline the subject and verb in each clause. If needed, review pages 253-254.

   ____

   ____

3. Write a sentence using semicolons between items in a list that have commas within each item listed. Refer to the examples above.

   ____

   ____

COLON (:)

You can use the colon several different ways. First, you can insert a colon between two independent clauses when you want to directly introduce and emphasize the information in the second clause. You will never place a colon after a subordinate (dependent) clause. The word group after the colon may comprise a complete sentence or may not. Study the following example.

> Police Chief Assouli has two main objectives**:** he wants to form better community relations between his officers and the neighborhood residents, and he also wants to improve new officer training methods.
>
> You can see that the colon comes after an independent clause, a complete thought that could stand on its own. Following the colon are two other independent clauses.

However, sometimes colons are followed by words or phrases. Study the next examples.

> The textbook committee has added two new members**:** Shirley Hernandez and Joseph Hale.
>
> Two city officials still need to be alerted to the crisis**:** the Public Works Director and the City Manager.
>
> Christine checked the gear in her backpack**:** a stove, a sleeping bag, a tent, and extra socks.

As you can see in the three examples above, you may place a colon wherever you directly introduce information. A colon gives special emphasis to whatever you are introducing because readers must come to a stop at the end of the main clause, and so they pay more attention to what follows. The material that follows the clause (whether words, phrases, or clauses) explains, exemplifies, or illustrates the main clause.

USAGE NOTE In formal academic prose, you never place a colon after a verb. The verb itself is introducing the next element, so the use of the colon is unnecessary and redundant. Look at the difference between the following two sentences.

Kelly's favorite ethnic cuisines are Italian, Japanese, and Indian.

Kelly has three favorite ethnic cuisines: Italian, Japanese, and Indian.

Second, you also use colons to separate a main clause from a direct quotation that is also a main clause. Earlier you learned to introduce a direct quote with a comma, for example, "The author states, 'All Americans should pay a 10 percent flat tax.'" However, when the introduction to the direct quotation is more than just a subject and verb, use a colon instead. Look at the following example.

> The author exhibits his dissatisfaction with the current tax system by offering another method of taxation: "All Americans should pay a 10 percent flat tax."

Not only is the introductory statement a main clause, the introductory information is also a statement that explains or describes what is coming in the direct quotation.

EXERCISE 19.8: Colons

Place colons where necessary in the sentences below. Not all sentences require a colon. If the sentence does not need a colon, simply mark a *C* by the sentence.

1. Three things my mother told me are (1) never lie, (2) help when you can, and (3) never turn down a free meal.
2. Certain materials are necessary for success in geometry class a protractor, graph paper, and the textbook.
3. The instructor had one major objective to raise the pass rate to at least 80 percent.
4. Before the wedding, the best man checked his pocket he reconfirmed he had the wedding band.
5. Jeremy screamed after noticing my smoldering hair "You're on fire!"

APOSTROPHE (')

You can use apostrophes in two ways: (1) to combine words into contractions and (2) to make words possessive.

Contractions

The apostrophe in a contraction stands in for the letter or letters that are missing once two words have been combined. See the examples below.

cannot = can't
does not = doesn't
it is = it's
will not = won't

You will not use contractions much in your academic writing. In fact, some instructors will not accept a paper if it contains even just one contraction.

Possessives

When you make a word possessive, you show ownership. So if you write *The teacher's apple*, you mean *the apple of the teacher* or *the apple belonging to the teacher*.

EXERCISE 19.9: Apostrophes

Rewrite the following phrases to illustrate apostrophe use for possession.

Example: The water bottle belonging to the gymnast.

The gymnast's water bottle

1. The notebook of the student

   ____

   ____

2. The birthmark of the baby

   ____

   ____

3. The battery of the cell phone

   ____

   ____

4. The souvenir belonging to the tourist

   ____

   ____

5. The lid of the trash can

   ____

   ____

Possessives with Singular Nouns

When making a singular noun possessive, place the apostrophe at the end of the noun and then add an *s,* for example, *computer* becomes *computer's* and *sandwich* becomes *sandwich's.*

Possessives with Singular Nouns That End in *S*

When a singular noun ends in *s*—for example, *James* or *glass*—two ways exist to create the possessive. First, place the apostrophe after the *s* just as you would place the apostrophe after any final letter of a singular noun, but do not add another *s,* or second, add *'s* at the end of the word. Look at the several examples below.

James' or James's

glass' or glass's

Fritos' or Fritos's

Boss' or boss's

Possessives with Plural Nouns

When creating a possessive with a plural noun that ends in *s,* simply add an apostrophe after the *s* that ends the word. See the examples below.

clocks' dogs'

books' kiwis'

When creating a possessive with a plural noun that does not end in *s,* place an *'s* at the end of the word. Study the following examples.

children's

women's

men's

USAGE NOTE Do not make the mistake of adding an apostrophe to every word ending with an *s.* For example, singular verbs end in *s,* but you would never add an apostrophe to a singular verb. Also, plural nouns end in *s,* but do not always show possession. Remember, you use apostrophes to create contractions and to show ownership.

 EXERCISE 19.10: Apostrophes and Possession

In the following sentences, insert apostrophes where necessary and appropriate. Read carefully to determine if the apostrophe goes before or after the *s.* If the sentence does not need an apostrophe, simply mark a *C* by the sentence.

1. The little girl took the dogs water bowl and filled it with cola.
2. The purses clasp broke suddenly and unexpectedly.
3. The sesame seeds from the muffin stuck between my teeth.
4. All dresses were on sale in the womens department.
5. Chris car was a shiny 2010 Jaguar.
6. All of the parents *oohed* and *aahed* over the three girls dance routine.
7. The school books that belonged to Harold all had covers.
8. Carole swims ten laps every morning before going to work.
9. James needed to replace the alarm clocks batteries.
10. Many of the childrens toys were donated to charity.

 EXERCISE 19.11: Apostrophes and Possessives

Take each word below and (a) use the word in a sentence as a plural noun, (b) use the word in a sentence as a singular possessive, and (c) use the word in a sentence as a plural possessive.

Example: Baby

a. All three babies laughed hysterically________________.

b. The baby's diaper needed changing________________.

c. The parents washed the babies' bottles________________.

1. Mouse

a. ________________________________.

b. ________________________________.

c. ________________________________.

2. Table

   a. ______________________________________.

   b. ______________________________________.

   c. ______________________________________.

3. Leaf

   a. ______________________________________.

   b. ______________________________________.

   c. ______________________________________.

4. Boss

   a. ______________________________________.

   b. ______________________________________.

   c. ______________________________________.

5. Raspberry

   a. ______________________________________.

   b. ______________________________________.

   c. ______________________________________.

DASH (—)

When using a computer keyboard, you create a dash by typing two hyphens with no space in between them. The dash is not used much in academic writing, so it is important to know exactly when and under what circumstances you should use this punctuation mark.

1. You may use the dash to show an abrupt break in thought or change in tone. Study the following examples.

> Our professor would not change her mind—even for a Super Caramel Latté!—and we still had the test on punctuation.
>
> This sentence exhibits an abrupt change in thought and tone. The sentence goes from a controlled statement of fact to a more intense statement of incredulousness and then back to a controlled statement of fact.

> I gave the flowers to my best friend, my father.
>
> I gave the flowers to my best friend: my father.
>
> I gave the flowers to my best friend—my father.
>
> The use of the dash in the last sentence creates a change in tone; the tone becomes more dramatic. The colon is more dramatic than the comma, and the dash is more dramatic than the colon. The dash forces the reader to stop, if even for just a moment longer, and therefore creates suspense and magnitude.

2. You may use a dash before and after a list separated by commas. Study the following examples.

> Three girls on the swim team—Tracy, Lily, and Samantha—won gold in their individual events.
>
> Science professors from Mt. San Jacinto Community College—Dr. Jensen, Dr. Singh, and Dr. Kimoto—formed a panel at the Annual Community College Science and Technology Convention.

EXERCISE 19.12: Dashes

Write two sentences that illustrate the use of a dash to show a change in tone. Then write two more sentences that show a list set off by dashes.

1. ____

____

2. ____

____

3. ____

____

4. ____

____

QUOTATION MARKS (" ")

Use quotation marks to show exact spoken or written words. Quotation marks are also used around titles of short works such as stories, poems, songs, titles of single episodes of television shows, and newspaper and magazine articles.

When you place quotation marks around words to show exact language that has been spoken or written, the material quoted must remain exactly as found or heard in the source.

If the words are changed in any way, then you do not have a direct quotation; you have a paraphrase, and quotation marks are not necessary. Also, if you are presenting the quotation in third person, then you have an indirect quotation, and, again, quotation marks are not necessary. Read the examples below to see the difference between a direct quotation, an indirect quotation, and a paraphrase of spoken words.

Direct Quotation of Spoken Words

> James told me, "Algebra is my favorite subject."
>
> The words within quotation marks are exactly what James said; therefore, quotation marks are needed.

Indirect Quotation of Spoken Words

> James told me that algebra is his favorite subject.
>
> Notice the use of *that* and also notice the possessive pronoun has been changed from *my* to *his*. You are now hearing what James said through a third person. The quotation is now indirect rather than direct.

Paraphrase of Spoken Words

> James told me that he likes algebra more than all of his other subjects.
>
> Here, you are hearing about what James said indirectly, and also his words have been changed around a little bit. The words are not exactly as they came out of his mouth. No quotation marks are needed.

Now, following is an example of a direct quotation and paraphrase from a written work.

Direct Quotation of a Written Work

In Mary Shelley's *Frankenstein*, Victor Frankenstein tells the reader, "I thought that if I could bestow animation upon lifeless matter, I might in the process of time (although I now found it impossible) renew life where death had apparently devoted the body to corruption."

Paraphrase of a Written Work

In Mary Shelley's *Frankenstein*, Victor Frankenstein tells the reader that he once believed he could figure out how to bring the dead back to life.

In the first example, quotation marks are used because the words within the marks are exactly as they appear in the novel. In the second example, no quotation marks are used because the language has been changed.

Titles of Short Works

Quotation marks are also used around titles of short works such as songs, poems, short stories, newspaper and magazine articles, and television episodes. Titles of larger works such as novels, television shows, magazines, newspapers, textbooks, and movies are italicized. Study the following examples.

One of my favorite episodes of *Seinfeld* was "The Cigar Store Indian."

Did you read "Anthem Chief Is Stepping Down" in the *Los Angeles Times* today?

The Doors recorded "Light My Fire" in August 1966.

For tomorrow's class, read "Ode on Solitude" from the *Norton Anthology of English Literature*.

Other Uses for Quotation Marks

You also use quotation marks around words when you are referring to the words themselves and not the words in context. Read the following examples.

Imagination is the key to production.

"Imagination" comes from the Latin *imaginari* and refers to the bringing to life of the images in one's mind.

In the second example, quotation marks are placed around *imagination* because you are referring to the word itself and not to the idea or concept.

In writing, when you want to suggest irony, you place quotation marks around words that actually mean the opposite of what they are supposed to mean. Read the following.

> The cashier at the Mexican restaurant offered me some "homemade" salsa.
>
> The quotation marks around the word *homemade* indicate that, in fact, the salsa was not homemade at all, but rather salsa out of a jar that anyone could get from a market.
>
> Alice's dysfunctional family members often offer her their "guidance."
>
> The quotation marks around the word *guidance* indicate that the family's advice is ill-founded nonsense rather than sound recommendations.

EXERCISE 19.13: Quotation Marks

Add quotation marks where necessary in the sentences below. Not all sentences need quotation marks. If the sentence does not need the quotation marks, place a *C* in front of the sentence.

1. Daniel's father told him that dinner would be pizza and salad.
2. We will study Chapter 2: Adjectives and Adverbs: Strengthening the Core I in week 3 of the semester.
3. After I finished my sister's delicious dinner, I felt queasy all night.
4. The word prehistoric refers to time prior to written history.
5. The pilot announced, We will be landing in twenty minutes, so please fasten your seat belts.

HYPHEN (-)

There are four basic rules when using the hyphen.

1. Use a hyphen to join two or more words serving as a single adjective before a noun. However, if the adjective comes after the noun, they are not hyphenated.

> Angela loves chocolate-covered raisins.
>
> These raisins are chocolate covered.
>
> Stephen King is a well-known author.
>
> Stephen King is well known.

2. Use a hyphen with compound numbers.

Forty-two students entered the speech competition.

Grauman's Chinese Theater in Hollywood turned eighty-three this year.

3. Use a hyphen with the prefixes *ex-* (meaning former), *self-*, *all-*; with the suffix *-elect* ; between a prefix and a capitalized word; and with figures or letters.

Harold's ex-wife is remarrying.

The Jamaican resort vacation was all-inclusive.

The cousins will be arriving from Germany in mid-September.

The little boy's T-shirt was muddy and torn.

4. Use a hyphen to divide words at the end of a line. Here are the rules for dividing words:

- Make the break between syllables

in-sin-u-ate   pa-per

peo-ple   bi-o-gra-phy

- For line breaks in words ending in *-ing*, if a single final consonant in the root word is doubled before the suffix, hyphenate between the consonants; otherwise, hyphenate at the suffix itself:

run-ning   driv-ing

plan-ning   sell-ing

EXERCISE 19.14: Hyphens

For each rule listed below, write one sentence.

1. Use a hyphen to join two or more words serving as a single adjective before a noun. Remember, if the adjective comes after the noun, they are not hyphenated.

____

2. Use a hyphen with compound numbers.

____

3. Use a hyphen with the prefixes *ex-* (meaning former), *self-*, *all-*; with the suffix *-elect*; between a prefix and a capitalized word; or with figures or letters.

   ____

4. Use a hyphen to divide words at the end of a line.

   ____

EXCLAMATION MARK (!)

The exclamation mark, or the exclamation point, is not a punctuation mark that you will be using much, if at all, in your academic writing. Exclamation points are used at the end of emphatic statements or commands, and they add a sense of drama and urgency to the prose. You may use this punctuation mark judiciously when needed, for instance, in a personal narrative or piece of fiction for a creative writing class, but in your basic composition classes, leave out this punctuation mark. Following are a few examples of exclamation point use for personal, creative, or casual writing.

> "Get out of here now**!**" the firefighter shouted to the mother as he ran to save the baby.
>
> "I will never love again**!**" the teenager sobbed into the pillow.
>
> Harold stared at his lottery ticket: he couldn't believe his luck**!**

You will learn that the words you choose will add the drama and the urgency and the emphasis you desire, and strong words are better than exclamation points.

Chapter SUMMARY

- Commas are used with items in a ______________________, before ______________________, and with ______________________, ______________________, and ______________________.
- You may place a semicolon between two ______________________ ______________________ with or without an ______________________ conjunction. You can also use a semicolon with items in a series when the items in the series have ______________________ within the items.
- An ______________________ must always precede a colon.
- You use quotation marks around titles of short works such as ______________________, ______________________, ______________________ ______________________, and ______________________ ______________________.
- The difference between a direct quotation and an indirect quotation is ______________________.

COMPONENTS AT WORK

 USING YOUR SKILLS IN READING

Carefully read the story below and add any necessary punctuation. You will need to add commas (for all of the reasons discussed in this book, not just the reasons discussed in this chapter), semicolons, colons, quotation marks, apostrophes, dashes, hyphens, and exclamation marks. Read each sentence to its completion before you decide how to punctuate it.

Keisha Johnson was excited about her first shift at her new job. She was hired as a hostess at the recently opened McGraws Café. Keisha enjoyed meeting new people and she also enjoyed new challenges and responsibilities. Keisha thought this would be the perfect job for her however she found out it wasnt going to be as easy as she thought it would be.

As soon as she clocked in her manager Mr. Adani told her she had three responsibilities greeting the guests seating the guests and setting the tables. How easy Keisha exclaimed to herself. However, she had never anticipated how difficult her coworkers would be. The wait people on staff that afternoon Riley Thomas and Nina always enjoyed making the new employees suffer.

As Keisha was folding napkins to place on the newly cleaned tables Riley came up to introduce himself. Hello he said to Keisha. My names Riley. I am the head wait person and I demand the most tables.

Surprised by Rileys rudeness Keisha said But Mr. Adani told me to rotate tables within the sections. I'm not supposed to give anyone more tables than anyone else. Its supposed to be fair.

Riley smiled condescendingly and answered Let me tell you this Keisha Mr. Adani may sign your paycheck but I am the one that controls whether or not you have a good day at work. Riley then turned around and walked away.

While Keisha was trying to calm her pounding heart after that unpleasant encounter Thomas approached. Without even introducing himself he announced There are only three types of groups I want seated at my tables I want attractive rich middle aged couples hip stylish young couples and distinguished educated retired couples. They all leave the best tips. And as abruptly as he approached he turned and walked away.

As Keishas head was reeling from this last run in Nina walked up. Why are you just standing there looking dazed? Nina asked. Get to work she commanded.

Keisha began folding napkins again but then she snapped out of her stupor. Right as Mr. Adani walked by she declared I dont have to take this abuse Then Keisha stormed out of the restaurant.

What happened Mr. Adani asked.

The three wait people walked over to their manager. I have no idea said Riley.

Me either said Thomas.

We were all so nice to her said Nina.

Mr. Adani Riley Thomas and Nina looked at one another and shook their heads. It is so hard to find good employees these days said Mr. Adani. It is such a shame they cant all be like you he said as he patted Riley Thomas and Nina on the backs as he walked back to his office.

1 APPENDICES FOR GRAMMAR AND USAGE, NATURALLY

Grammar and Usage, Naturally is designed to teach you the composition skills you need to successfully begin the journey through not only your English courses but also any college course that requires writing. Beginning with the important foundational concepts and guiding you through increasingly more complex concepts, each chapter takes you through topics of grammar and sentence structure so that by the end of the book you are writing grammatically correct, coherent, and varied sentences.

However, even with all the instruction and practice, there may be times you face particularly challenging issues. Perhaps you struggle with a problem that other students in your class do not. Maybe your instructor thinks you need extra practice in a particular area of grammar or usage. Maybe you need to correct a problem that continually appears in your writing. Regardless, the two appendices here, as well as the three—"Fundamental Spelling Rules," "Common Writing Errors," and "Confusing and Misused Word Pairs"—located on the student companion website at cengagebrain.com, are meant to help you resolve those grammatical problems you may encounter in this class. Once you have, you will be the person in the image below: you will be walking contentedly out of the woods and into the clear.

CAPITALIZATION

Since people have begun emailing, texting, Twittering, and using other electronic communication methods, the use of proper capitalization and spelling has eroded. While not using proper capitalization during informal communication may be socially acceptable, in formal academic writing, you must follow correct capitalization rules.

Capitalization is the practice of writing a word with the first letter of the word an upper case letter and the remainder of the word lower case letters.

> Jerry
> Standing
> Lightning

Upper case letters in English are

> A B C D E F G H I J K L M N O P Q R S T U V W X Y Z.

Lower case letter in English are

> a b c d e f g h i j k l m n o p q r s t u v w x y z.

While the above information may seem elementary or obvious, you need to remember three points:

1. The practice of capitalization varies among languages, so what may be true for the rules of capitalization in English may not be true in Spanish, Italian, German, Russian, Latvian, etc. For example, in English we capitalize the days of the week: Sunday, Monday, Tuesday, Wednesday, Thursday, Friday, and Saturday. But in Spanish, the days of the week are not capitalized: *domingo, lunes, martes, miércoles, jueves, viernes, sábado.* Also, English is the only language to capitalize the pronoun *I.*
2. Capitalization rules vary depending upon the context. For example, what may be a capitalized word in one instance may not be capitalized in another:

> The President of the United States is speaking this afternoon.
>
> The president is speaking this afternoon.

Also, capitalization rules may vary between different fields of study: humanities, social sciences, natural sciences, etc.

3. Remember, too, that spell checkers may not identify words that need to be capitalized. For example, if you typed the following sentence, your spell-checker would identify only the three-word group *new york city* that needs to be capitalized.

> The board of trustees agreed to send student and faculty representatives to new york city for the 23rd annual community college convention and to visit the statue of liberty.
>
> The remaining words in the sentence that need to be capitalized are *Board, Trustees, Statue,* and *Liberty*. If the title of the convention was *The 23rd Annual Community College Convention,* each word in the phrase would need to be capitalized also.

Since the rules for capitalization can vary greatly, the rules discussed in this appendix are general and should apply to all formal writing situations in English. But, ultimately, if you are unsure whether a word should be capitalized, you should always check a standard college dictionary.

1. Capitalize the first word in each sentence.

> Even though the forecast calls for rain, the parade will continue.
>
> Birds are truly remarkable creatures.

2. Capitalize the first-person singular pronoun *I,* regardless of its position in a sentence.

> I have decided that I want to paint my room purple.

3. Capitalize the first letter of all parts of a person's name.

> Oscar Zoroaster Phadrig Isaac Norman Henkel Emmannuel Ambroise Diggs
>
> The full name for the Wonderful Wizard of OZ
>
> Sherman J. Alexie, Jr.
>
> Pablo Ruiz Picasso

4. Capitalize a personal or professional title when it precedes a person's name, for example, Uncle Dan, Grandmother Jones, Assistant Professor Garcia, and Doctor Kennedy. You would also capitalize titles that substitute for a proper name, such as Mother or Father.

I am enrolled with Dr. Jones, who is an associate professor.

I sent notes to Uncle Joseph, Aunt Maria, Grandpa Stephen, and crazy Cousin Kris.

But when possessive pronouns precede the titles, we do **not** capitalize the titles.

I sent notes to my uncle, my aunt, my grandpa, and my crazy cousin.

5. Capitalize the days of the week and the months of the year. Do **not** capitalize the seasons.

For the fall semester, school begins Monday, August 16, 2013.

The official beginning of spring is March 20, which in 2010 is a Saturday.

6. Capitalize the names of holidays, for example, New Year's Day, Labor Day, Martin Luther King Day, Memorial Day, Thanksgiving Day, Valentine's Day, and Veterans Day.

Both Veterans Day and Thanksgiving Day are in November.

February is a busy month for holidays: Groundhog Day, National Wear Red Day, Valentine's Day, Chinese New Year, Fat Tuesday, and Ash Wednesday.

7. Capitalize the name of countries, languages, and ethnicities, for example, Latvia, Mexico, and Laos; Spanish, Swahili, and Tagalog; Italians, Swedes, and Lapps.

I lived in Spain for six months and not only learned to speak Spanish well, but also traveled extensively in northwest Spain where the Basque live.

Many Europeans know three or four languages, such as French, German, Italian, Spanish, and English.

8. Capitalize the names of streets, cities, and states, such as First Avenue, Banner Street, Sommerville, Cleveland, Nevada, and Arkansas.

Please send the package to 1234 Sedgwick Avenue, Comanche, Texas.

Belle lived her entire life at 8765 Second Street, Prosperity, Indiana.

9. Capitalize the names of historical events, historical documents, historical eras, and historical movements, for example, the Korean War, the US Constitution, the English Renaissance, and the Progressive Movement.

> During the Spanish-American War, African-American troops participated in much of the fighting during the Battles of San Juan Hill and Kettle Hill.
>
> The first ten amendments to the United States Constitution are known as the Bill of Rights.
>
> The Age of Reason in the seventeenth century preceded the Age of Enlightenment in the eighteenth century.

10. Capitalize the names of religions and their followers, for example: Catholicism—Catholics; Christianity—Christians; Islam—Muslims. We also capitalize religious terms that are sacred within the religion: Buddha, Yahweh, God, Mohammad, Christ, the Bible, the Torah, and the Koran or Qur'an.

> Wicca and its followers, the Wica, do not advocate black magic as many believe.
>
> Catholics, Jews, and Muslims all lived peacefully and tolerantly together in Spain until King Ferdinand and Queen Isabella, who were Catholics, expelled the Jews and Muslims in 1492.

11. Capitalize the names of specific places and geographical areas, such as San Francisco, Telegraph Hill, the Empire State Building, the Grand Canyon, Niagara Falls, and the Mariana Trench.

> In New York City, the Statue of Liberty and Ellis Island attract many tourists.
>
> Astronauts can see the Great Salt Lake in Salt Lake City, Utah, from outer space.

12. Capitalize the brand name of products but not the product itself.

> I enjoy drinking Twinning's English breakfast tea with a teaspoon of Trader Joe's mesquite honey.
>
> An In-N-Out hamburger with fries and a Coca Cola is one of my favorite meals.

Some trademark names have become so common that they have lost their trademark status and are no longer associated with their original brand, for example, aspirin, band-aid, escalator, yo-yo, and zipper. If you are unsure whether to capitalize a product, look in a standard college dictionary.

13. Capitalize directions of a compass, as illustrated below, when the directions refer to specific geographical areas only, for example, the Southwest, the Midwest, the East coast. But do **not** capitalize the direction when they are general references.

> My wife and I are looking forward to retiring in the Southwest.
>
> Several of my friends live in the Pacific Northwest, which includes the states of Washington and Oregon, and the Canadian province of British Columbia.
>
> We were driving southwest trying to outrun a storm blowing in from the east.

14. Capitalize the titles of academic subjects only if they are proper nouns, for example, English or Spanish, or if the class is followed by a course number, for example, Sociology 101.

> For the spring semester, Geraldo enrolled in an English class, a math class, and Anthropology 102.
>
> Last semester, he took theater, dance, history, and an introductory Spanish class.

15. Capitalize the first word and all the important words in a title. Do not, however, capitalize articles, coordinating conjunctions, and prepositions (for example, *with, by, at, from*) unless they begin the title.

Book titles:

The Fairy Tale: The Magic Mirror of Imagination
It's All in the Frijoles
Their Eyes Were Watching God
The Hero with a Thousand Faces

Book chapter titles:

Chapter 1: "The Holy Priestess of Heaven"
Chapter 5: "Storytelling in a Weblog: Performing Narrative in a Digital Age"

Short story titles:

"Beauty and the Beast"
"The Yellow Wallpaper"

Poem titles:

"Ode to a Grecian Urn"
"The Love Song of J. Alfred Prufrock"
"The Windhover"

Song titles:

"It's a Long Way to the Top"
"Lovely Rita"

Appendix B

PRONOUNS

You have already learned four of the eight groups of pronouns. In Chapter 1, you learned the subject and object pronouns. In Chapter 5, you learned the indefinite pronouns. And in Chapter 9, you learned the relative pronouns.

1. POSSESSIVE PRONOUNS

The possessive pronouns include the following (**Table A.1**).

TABLE A.1
Possessive pronouns

	Singular	Plural
1st Person	My/Mine	Our/Ours
2nd Person	Your/Yours	Your/Yours
3rd Person	His/Her/Hers/Its	Their/Theirs

The function of possessive pronouns is to replace possessive nouns, which function as adjectives, and to let readers know who owns an object.

Look at the sentences below.

> Jill let Jill's brother Jack borrow Jill's CD player, but Jack lost Jill's CD player's ear buds, so Jill took Jill's brother's favorite comic book, and Jill soaked the comic book in a bucket of water.

If possessive pronouns did not exist, the above sentence imitates the way you would probably speak. But, thank goodness, possessive pronouns do exist.

> Jill let her brother Jack borrow her CD player, but he lost its earbuds, so she took his favorite comic book, and she soaked it in a bucket of water.

Remember these two important points. First, when you are using possessive pronouns, you want to make sure the noun to which the pronoun refers is clear so that you don't create confusion in your writing.

Look at the following sentence.

> Jill was telling her mother about what Jack did, but before she decided what to do, she wanted to hear more from her.

The pronoun *she* in the second clause is vague because *she* could refer to either Jill or her mother. And the pronouns *she* and *her* in the third clause are also unclear since either one could refer to Jill or her mother. You, as the writer, may know to whom or to what the pronoun refers, but your readers probably do not, so always make sure your pronouns have clear references.

> Jill was telling her mother about what Jack did, but before Jill's mother decided what to do, she wanted to hear more from Jill.

Second, since possessive pronouns are already in their possessive form, we never add an *'s*. So you should never use such forms as *your's* or *his's, her's* or *their's.*

REFLEXIVE AND INTENSIVE PRONOUNS

The reflexive and intensive pronouns include the following (**Table A.2**):

TABLE A.2 Reflexive and intensive pronouns

	Singular	Plural
1st Person	Myself	Ourselves
2nd Person	Yourself	Yourselves
3rd Person	Himself, Herself, Itself	Themselves

With intensive and reflexive pronouns, note that the singular pronouns end in *self,* while the plural pronouns end in *selves.* Constructions like *hisself* or *theirselves* or *yourselfs* are nonstandard forms that should never be used in formal academic prose.

Even though the reflexive and the intensive pronouns are the same, you use them differently:

- Use reflexive pronouns to show subjects performing actions on themselves.
- Use intensive pronouns to add emphasis to nouns.

Study the following sentences.

> Mandy painted herself blue for the sporting event. (Reflexive)
>
> Mandy herself painted the house. (Intensive)
>
> Stephen ordered himself to study more. (Reflexive)
>
> Stephen himself ordered a book. (Intensive)
>
> Thad and Clair bought themselves a fountain for their newly landscaped front yard. (Reflexive)

> Thad and Clair themselves landscaped their front yard. (Intensive)

A reflexive pronoun generally appears after the verb in the sentence and shows the subject performing the action of the verb on itself. An intensive pronoun follows immediately the subject and modifies and emphasizes the subject.

One last observation about reflexive and intensive pronouns: while using *myself* and other intensive and reflexive pronouns may sound more formal, you should not use them in place of subject and object pronouns.

Look at the following sentences.

> Jean and myself are planning on attending the graduation party.
>
> Katy was delighted with the present from myself.

In the first sentence, the pronoun *myself* is functioning as a subject pronoun. In the second sentence, the pronoun *myself* is functioning as an object pronoun. Since subject and object pronouns already exist, you should use them when appropriate.

> Jean and I are planning on attending the graduation party.
>
> Katy was delighted with the present from me.

INTERROGATIVE PRONOUNS

The interrogative pronouns are

who, whom, whose, what, which, when, where, why, and how.

Unlike the other pronoun groups you have studied so far, the interrogative pronouns have only one form each. With interrogative pronouns, you do not separate the interrogative pronouns into singular and plural forms.

Interrogative pronouns take the place of unknown people and things, and you use the interrogative pronouns to form questions:

> Who is at the door?
>
> For whom are you looking?
>
> Whose shoes are these lying in the hallway?
>
> What time do you want to eat?
>
> Which direction should I take to the market?
>
> When will we get there?

> Where do I sign up for the class?
>
> Why are your dirty clothes lying on the floor?
>
> How do you plan to gather the information?

The pronoun *who* always functions as the subject of a clause. The pronoun *whom* always functions as an object. Look at the following paired sentences and questions to see how *who* and *whom* replace specific nouns.

> Sam is going to drive this week.
>
> Who is going to drive this week?
>
> She took her sister to the movies.
>
> She took whom to the movies?

In the first paired group, *who* replaces *Sam*, the subject of the sentence. In the second paired group, *whom* replaces *sister*, the object of the sentence.

DEMONSTRATIVE PRONOUNS

The demonstrative pronouns are *this*, *that*, *these*, and *those*. Demonstrative pronouns identify another noun or pronoun and function as adjectives.

> This piece of chicken is undercooked.
>
> That costume took several weeks to sew.
>
> These apricots are just about ripe.
>
> Those bushes need to be trimmed.

The pronouns *this* and *that* refer to singular objects.

> This tree is dying.
>
> This pen is out of ink.
>
> That song reminds me of my ex.
>
> That car is not expensive.

The pronouns *these* and *those* refer to plural objects.

> These trees are dying.
>
> These pens are out of ink.

> Those songs remind me of my ex.
>
> Those cars are not expensive.

This and *these* refer to objects close by in time and space.

> Looking at the calendar, Randy said, "I can't wait for this weekend." (Time)
>
> Standing in front of the display case, Samantha pointed to an MP3 player and told the clerk, "I want this one, please." (Space)
>
> "These last several days of final exams have been brutal," moaned Kayla. (Time)
>
> Swatting at the mosquitoes buzzing around his head, Jordy exclaimed, "These bugs are driving me crazy!" (Space)

That and *those* refer to objects at a distance in time and space.

> "I am truly looking forward to that day when I graduate," mused Jamal, a sophomore in college. (Time)
>
> "I was hoping I could afford that truck on the other side of the lot," observed Lynn. (Space)
>
> "I can't help but wonder what is going to happen to those flowers when summer gets here," pondered Wilbert. (Time)
>
> "I think we should move those pictures on the wall over there to this wall," suggested Sandy. (Space)

GLOSSARY OF GRAMMATICAL TERMS

Absolute Phrase—A group of related words consisting of a noun or pronoun and the *-ing* or *-ed* form of a verb, in other words, a present or past participle, and any modifiers. An absolute phrase modifies an independent clause. See Chapter 14.

Action Verb—See *Verbs.*

Active Voice—The relationship between the subject and the verb in which the subject performs the action of the verb. See Chapter 18.

Adjective—A part of speech that modifies (describes) a noun or a pronoun. See Chapter 2. Adjectives answer the questions *which one, what kind, how many,* and *whose.*

Adjective Subordinate Clause—A group of related words that begins with a relative pronoun and functions as an adjective to modify a noun or a pronoun (also called a relative clause). See Chapter 9.

Adverbs—A part of speech that modifies (describes) three different parts of speech: verbs, adjectives, and other adverbs. See Chapter 2.

Adverb Subordinate Clause—A group of related words that begins with a subordinating conjunction and has a subject and a verb. See Chapter 9.

Adverbial Conjunctions—Sometimes called conjunctive adverbs and referred to as transitions, adverbial conjunctions connect words, phrases, or clauses to convey various relationships, such as cause and effect, comparison and contrast, etc. See Chapter 3 and Chapter 15.

Appositives—Nouns or pronouns that rename or identify other nouns or pronouns. Appositives almost always come immediately after the nouns or pronouns they identify. See Chapter 14.

Cause and Effect—A paragraph pattern that explains why something occurred and the results of the occurrence. See Chapter 10.

Classification—A paragraph pattern in which a writer takes a number of elements and groups the elements according to similar criteria. See Chapter 10.

Clause—A group of related words that contains **both** a subject and a verb. See Chapter 9.

Climactic Paragraph—A paragraph in which the topic sentence is located near the end or at the end of the paragraph. See Chapter 10.

Coherence—A logical interconnection of parts. When used in composition, the word "coherence" refers to the connectivity and organization of ideas in a paragraph. See Chapter 10.

Common Noun—See *Noun.*

Comparison—A paragraph pattern that explains how objects or ideas are similar. See Chapter 10.

Comparative Adjective—An adjective used to show the difference between two things. See Chapter 2.

Complete Verb—The combination of the main verb and the helping verb. See Chapter 1 and Chapter 6.

Complex Sentence—A sentence consisting of one main clause and at least one subordinate clause. See Chapter 16.

Compound Sentence—A sentence consisting of two or more main clauses. See Chapter 15.

Compound-Complex Sentence—A sentence consisting of two or more main clauses and at least one subordinate clause. See Chapter 16.

Conjunctions—Parts of speech that connect words, phrases, or clauses. See Chapter 3. See also *Adverbial Conjunctions, Coordinating Conjunctions, Correlative Conjunctions*, and *Subordinating Conjunctions.*

Connotative Definition—A paragraph pattern in which the writer provides subjective, frequently personal and individual, meanings to the definition. See Chapter 10.

Contrast—A paragraph pattern that explains how objects or ideas are different. See Chapter 10.

Coordinating Conjunctions—Conjunctions that convey a relationship of equal importance between words, phrases, or clauses. This relationship is called *coordination* and is shown by the words *for, and, nor, but, or, yet,* or *so* (FANBOYS). See Chapter 3 and Chapter 15.

Coordination—A relationship of equal importance among words, phrases, and clauses conveyed through the use of coordinating conjunctions. See Chapter 15.

Correlative Conjunctions—Word pairs that join two like sentence elements. See Chapter 3 and Chapter 18.

Denotative Definition—A paragraph pattern in which a writer provides precise dictionary-type definitions, definitions that are objective in that they provide an unprejudiced and neutral meaning. See Chapter 10.

Direct Paragraph—A paragraph in which the topic sentence is located at the beginning or near the beginning of the paragraph. See Chapter 10.

Division—A paragraph pattern in which a writer divides an object or concept into its various components or parts. See Chapter 10.

Four Principal Parts of a Verb—The present, past, present participial, and past participial forms of the verb used to create the twelve active verb tenses. See Chapter 7 and Chapter 17.

Future Tense—The verb tense used to express a future action that is expected to happen. See Chapter 17.

Future Perfect Tense—The verb tense used to express a future action that will be completed before another future event. This tense is formed with the helping verbs *will have* + the past participial form of the verb. See Chapter 17.

Future Perfect Progressive Tense—The verb tense used to express a continuous action that will end at a specific time in the future. This tense is formed with the helping verbs *will have been* + the *-ing* form of the verb. See Chapter 17.

Future Progressive Tense—The verb tense used to express an ongoing future action. This tense is formed with the helping verbs *will be* + the *-ing* form of the verb. See Chapter 17.

Gerund—A verb form ending in *-ing* that functions as a noun, so a gerund can be either a subject or an object in a sentence. See Chapter 5.

Helping Verb—See *Verbs.*

Illustration—A paragraph pattern that provides examples and details that explain and clarify the writer's topic sentence. See Chapter 10.

Imperatives—Sentences that give commands or convey directions. The subject is an unwritten or unspoken *you*. See Chapter 5 and Chapter 17.

Imperative Mood—The mood used to express commands, directions, and instructions. See "The Understood *You* of Imperatives" in Chapter 5 and "Verbs and Mood" in Chapter 17.

Indefinite Pronouns—Pronouns that refer to someone or something that is not definite or specific. See Chapter 5.

Indicative Mood—The mood used to state a fact, to state an opinion, or to ask a question. See "Verbs and Mood" in Chapter 17.

Infinitive—A verb form created by placing *to* in front of the base form of the verb. Infinitives are **not** verbs. Infinitives function as nouns, adjectives, and adverbs. See Chapter 5 and Chapter 13.

Infinitive Phrase—Word groups that consist of *infinitives* and their modifiers. See Chapter 13.

Interjections—A part of speech that stands alone to express emotion and is usually followed by an exclamation mark. See Chapter 3.

Irregular Verb—Verbs that do not follow the consistent spelling pattern (adding *-d* or *-ed*) for past tense verbs and past participles. See Chapter 7.

Linking Verb—See *Verbs*.

Main Clause—A group of related words that contains a subject and a verb and expresses a complete thought or idea. A main clause is a sentence. See Chapter 9.

Mood—A verb form that indicates a writer's attitude toward what she or he is saying or writing. See Chapter 17.

Narration—A paragraph pattern in which a writer recounts a series of events or tells a story. See Chapter 10.

Nonrestrictive Appositive—A noun phrase that is not essential in order to understand the noun or pronoun it renames. See Chapter 14.

Nonrestrictive Adjective Subordinate Clause—A clause that provides information **not** essential, **not** necessary for understanding or clarifying the modified noun. See Chapter 9.

Noun—A part of speech that names a person, place, thing, living creature, or idea. Nouns are generally divided into **common nouns** and **proper nouns**. Common nouns name *general* people, places, things, living creatures, and ideas; common nouns do not take capitalization. Proper nouns name *specific* people, places, living creatures, and belief systems, and they require capitalization. See Chapter 1.

Object—A noun or pronoun that receives the action of the verb. See Chapter 1.

Object of the Preposition—The noun or pronoun that completes the prepositional phrase. See Chapter 3 and Chapter 14.

Object Pronouns—Pronouns that act only as objects. See Chapter 1.

Objective Description—A paragraph pattern in which a writer explains the topic using physical senses, focusing almost exclusively on the measurable or quantifiable characteristics of the topic. See Chapter 10.

Paragraph—A series of sentences that focus on a single topic or subject. See Chapter 10.

Parallel Structure—The sentence structure created when a writer composes words, phrases, or clauses that are the same grammatical forms. See Chapter 18.

Participial Phrase—A phrase consisting of a present or past participle and its modifiers or complements. A participial phrase always acts as an adjective. See Chapter 13.

Parts of Speech—The eight categories of words that refer to the way we use the words in language. The eight categories are nouns, pronouns, and verbs (see Chapter 1), adjectives and adverbs (see Chapter 2), and conjunctions, prepositions, and interjections (see Chapter 3).

Passive Voice—The relationship between the subject and the verb in which the subject of the sentence is acted upon by another noun or subject pronoun. See Chapter 18.

Past Perfect Tense—The verb tense used to express a past action that ended before another past action. This tense is formed with the helping verb *had* + the past participle form of the verb. See Chapter 17.

Past Perfect Progressive Tense—The verb tense used to express a continuing action that began in the past before another past event started. See Chapter 17.

Past Progressive Tense—The verb tense used to express an ongoing action that occurred in the past. See Chapter 17.

Past Tense—The verb tense used to express an action that occurred before now at a specific time and place, which may or may not be mentioned in the sentence. See Chapter 17.

Persuasion—A paragraph pattern in which the writer presents logical evidence that supports the position stated in the topic sentence. See Chapter 10.

Predicate Adjective—An adjective that follows a linking verb. See Chapter 6.

Prepositions—Parts of speech that relate a noun or pronoun to another word. Prepositions show a relationship of location, direction, time, or condition. See Chapter 3.

Prepositional Phrase—A phrase that consists of a preposition, a noun or pronoun, and any words that may modify the noun or pronoun. The noun or pronoun that ends the prepositional phrase is called the *object of the preposition*. See Chapter 3 and Chapter 14.

Present Perfect Tense—The verb tense used to express either an action that started in the past and continues in the present or an action that started in the past and has just recently ended. This tense is formed with the helping verbs *have* or *has* + the past participial form of the verb. See Chapter 17.

Present Perfect Progressive Tense—The verb tense used to express a continuous action that began in the past and is still continuing. This tense is formed with the helping verbs *have* or *has* + *been* and the *-ing* form of the verb. See Chapter 17.

Present Progressive Tense—The verb tense used to express an action that is currently in progress. See Chapter 17.

Past Participle—The form of the verb used in the perfect verb tenses. See Chapter 7 and Chapter 17. This verb form may also be used as an adjective in participial phrases. See Chapter 13.

Present Participle—The form of the verb used in the progressive verb tenses. See Chapter 7 and Chapter 17. This verb form may also be used as an adjective in participial phrases. See Chapter 13.

Present Tense—The verb tense used to express an action that recurs, meaning an action that occurs on a regular basis. See Chapter 17.

Process Analysis—A paragraph pattern in which the writer analyzes the steps of a process or procedure. See Chapter 10.

Pronoun—A part of speech that takes the place of, refers to, or modifies a noun. See Chapter 1 and "Appendix B: Pronouns."

Proper Noun—See *Noun.*

Restrictive Appositive—A noun phrase that is essential in understanding the noun or pronoun it renames. See Chapter 14.

Restrictive Adjective Subordinate Clause—A clause that provides information essential for understanding the noun it modifies and the sentence's meaning. The adjective clause begins with a relative pronoun. See Chapter 9.

Simple Sentence—A sentence consisting of one main clause. See Chapter 15.

Subject—The noun or pronoun that performs the action of the clause. See Chapter 4 and Chapter 5. Subjects may be either single or compound. See Chapter 4.

Subject Pronouns—Pronouns that act only as subjects. See Chapter 1 and Chapter 4.

Subject-Verb Agreement—The relationship in number between the subject and verb of the clause. If the subject of the sentence is singular, the verb must be singular. If the subject of the sentence is plural, the verb must be plural. See Chapter 8.

Subjective Description—A paragraph pattern in which a writer, using physical senses as well as emotional responses, explains the topic. See Chapter 10.

Subordinate Clause—A word group that contains a subject and verb **but** cannot stand by itself as a complete thought because it is preceded by a subordinating conjunction or relative pronoun. Therefore, a subordinate clause is **not** a sentence. See Chapter 9.

Subordination—A relationship of unequal importance between clauses conveyed through the use of subordinating conjunctions. See Chapter 16.

Subordinating Conjunctions—Conjunctions that convey a relationship of unequal importance between clauses. This relationship is called *subordination.* See Chapter 3 and Chapter 16.

Subjunctive Mood—The mood used to communicate suggestions or recommendations, requirements, desires or wishes, and conditions contrary to fact. See "Verbs and Mood" in Chapter 17.

Superlative Adjective—An adjective used to show the difference among three or more things. See Chapter 2.

Support—The information a writer includes to illustrate, to explain, and/or argue for the paragraph's topic sentence. See Chapter 10.

Topic Sentence—A sentence that makes an observation or comment on the topic of a paragraph. The topic sentence is referred to as the controlling idea or main point of the paragraph. See Chapter 10.

Transitions—Words or phrases that create logical connections among the ideas in a paragraph. See Chapter 10.

Unity—The condition in which a series of parts are combined into a whole. When used in composition, unity serves the purpose of supporting one main idea in the paragraph. See Chapter 10.

Verb—A part of speech that shows what the subject of the sentence is doing. Verbs are categorized into three groups: *Action verbs*, *Linking verbs*, and *Helping verbs.* See Chapter 1 and Chapter 6. Action verbs show action. Linking verbs link or connect the subject of the sentence (which is always a noun or a pronoun) to another word.

Linking verbs connect the subject to

- another noun that **renames** the subject
- a pronoun that **renames** the subject
- an adjective that **describes** the subject
- a prepositional phrase that **names the location of** the subject.

Helping verbs show

- when something happened or will happen
- if something should happen
- the circumstances needed for something to happen.

Verbals—Verb forms that can function as nouns and modifiers but can never stand alone as the complete verb of a sentence. See Chapter 5 and Chapter 13.

Voice—In grammar, the relationship between the subject and the verb of the sentence. See Chapter 18.

INDEX

Note: Page numbers followed by *f* and *t* indicate figures and tables respectively.